Business Ethics

Business Ethics

Decision Making for Personal Integrity and Social Responsibility

Fifth Edition

Laura P. Hartman

School of Choice/L'Ecole de Choix

Joseph DesJardins

*College of St. Benedict/
St. John's University*

Chris MacDonald

Ryerson University

McGraw Hill

BUSINESS ETHICS: DECISION MAKING FOR PERSONAL INTEGRITY AND
SOCIAL RESPONSIBILITY, FIFTH EDITION

Published by McGraw-Hill Education, 2 Penn Plaza, New York, NY 10121. Copyright © 2021 by McGraw-Hill
Education. All rights reserved. Printed in the United States of America. Previous editions © 2018, 2014, and
2011. No part of this publication may be reproduced or distributed in any form or by any means, or stored in a
database or retrieval system, without the prior written consent of McGraw-Hill Education, including, but not
limited to, in any network or other electronic storage or transmission, or broadcast for distance learning.

Some ancillaries, including electronic and print components, may not be available to customers outside the
United States.

This book is printed on acid-free paper.

1 2 3 4 5 6 7 8 9 LCR 24 23 22 21 20

ISBN 978-1-260-26049-6 (bound edition)
MHID 1-260-26049-6 (bound edition)
ISBN 978-1-260-51293-9 (loose-leaf edition)
MHID 1-260-51293-2 (loose-leaf edition)

Director: *Michael Ablassmeir*
Associate Portfolio Manager: *Laura Hurst Spell*
Marketing Manager: *Lisa Granger*
Content Project Managers: *Melissa M. Leick; Emily Windelborn; Karen Jozefowicz*
Buyer: *Susan K. Culbertson*
Design: *Beth Blech*
Content Licensing Specialist: *Brianna Kirschbaum*
Cover Image: *Arrows: Pixel-Shot/Shutterstock; arrow sign: ©RTimages/Shutterstock; landscape:*
©imagedepotpro/E+/Getty Images; compass: ©Design Pics/Kristy-Anne Glubish
Compositor: *SPi Global*

All credits appearing on page or at the end of the book are considered to be an extension of the copyright page.

Library of Congress Control Number: 2019953715

mheducation.com/highered

To Rachel and Emma.

—Laura Hartman

To Michael and Matthew.

—Joseph DesJardins

To Georgia.

—Chris MacDonald

About the Authors

Laura P. Hartman   *The School of Choice/L'Ecole de Choix (Haiti)*

Laura Pincus Hartman is Executive Director of the School of Choice Education Organization, a U.S.-based nonprofit that she cofounded, which oversees the School of Choice/L'Ecole de Choix, a unique leadership development education program in Haiti that serves children and families living in extreme conditions of poverty.

Hartman also is professor emerita at DePaul University. She held a number of roles during her almost three-decade career there, including Associate Vice President for Academic Affairs, Vincent de Paul Professor of Business Ethics at DePaul University's Driehaus College of Business, and Director of its Institute for Business and Professional Ethics. From 2015–2017, Hartman also served as the inaugural Director of the Susilo Institute for Ethics in the Global Economy at Boston University and Clinical Professor of Business Ethics in BU's Department of Organizational Behavior. She has been privileged to serve as an Associated Professor at the Kedge Business School (Marseille, France) and has taught as a visiting professor at INSEAD (France), HEC (France), the Université Paul Cezanne Aix Marseille III, the University of Toulouse, and the Grenoble Graduate School of Business, and served as the Gourley Professor of Ethics at the Melbourne Business School.

Hartman is past president of the Society for Business Ethics and established its Professional Mentorship Program. She is the coauthor of *Employment Law for Business* (McGraw-Hill). Hartman graduated *magna cum laude* from Tufts University and received her law degree from the University of Chicago Law School. She divides her time between Haiti and Sint Maarten, and has been a mother to two daughters.

Joseph DesJardins   *College of St. Benedict/St. John's University*

Joseph DesJardins holds the Ralph Gross Chair in Business and the Liberal Arts and is professor of philosophy at the College of St. Benedict and St. John's University in Minnesota. His other books include *An Introduction to Business Ethics; Environmental Ethics: An Introduction to Environmental Philosophy; Environmental Ethics: Concepts, Policy & Theory; Contemporary Issues in Business Ethics* (coeditor with John McCall); and *Business, Ethics, and the Environment: Imagining a Sustainable Future.* He has served as president and executive director of the Society for Business Ethics and has published and lectured extensively in the areas of business ethics, environmental ethics, and sustainability. He received his BA from Southern Connecticut State University and his MA and PhD from the University of Notre Dame.

Chris MacDonald   *Ryerson University*

Chris MacDonald is an associate professor and director of the Ted Rogers Leadership Centre at Ryerson University's Ted Rogers School of Management in Toronto, Canada, and a senior nonresident fellow at Duke University's Kenan Institute for Ethics. His peer-reviewed publications range across business ethics, professional ethics, bioethics, the ethics of technology, and moral philosophy, and he is coauthor of a best-selling textbook called *The Power of Critical Thinking* (4th Canadian Edition, 2016). He is cofounder and coeditor of both the *Business Ethics Journal Review* and the news and commentary aggregator site *Business Ethics Highlights.* He is perhaps best known for his highly respected blog, *The Business Ethics Blog,* which is carried by *Canadian Business* magazine.

Preface

We began writing the first edition of this textbook in 2006, soon after a wave of major corporate scandals had shaken the financial world. Headlines made the companies involved in these ethical scandals household names: Enron, WorldCom, Arthur Andersen, KPMG, J.P. Morgan, Merrill Lynch, Morgan Stanley, Citigroup, Salomon Smith Barney. At that time, we suggested that, in light of such significant cases of financial fraud, mismanagement, criminality, and deceit, the relevance of business ethics could no longer be questioned.

Sadly, as we enter the fifth edition of this book, these same issues are as much alive today as they were a decade ago. While our second edition was preceded by the unprecedented financial meltdown in 2008–2009 and the ethical problems faced by such companies as AIG, Countrywide, Lehman Brothers, Merrill Lynch, and Bear Stearns, this current edition continues to witness financial and ethical malfeasance of historic proportions and the inability of market mechanisms, internal governance structures, or government regulation to prevent it.

But the story is not all bad news. While cases of corporate fraud continue to make headlines (think of the recent Volkswagen, Wells Fargo, and Facebook scandals), countless small and large firms provide examples of highly ethical—and profitable—business enterprises. The emergence of benefit corporations (see Chapter 5 for examples) is only one instance of corporations dedicated to the common good. In this edition, we aim to tell the stories of both the good and the bad in business.

As we reflect on both the ethical corruption and the ethical success stories of the past decade, the importance of ethics is all too apparent. The questions today are less about whether ethics should be a part of business strategy and, by necessity, the business school curriculum, than about which values and principles should guide business decisions and how ethics should be integrated within business and business education.

This textbook provides a comprehensive, yet accessible introduction to the ethical issues arising in business. Students who are unfamiliar with ethics will find that they are as unprepared for careers in business as students who are unfamiliar with accounting and finance. It is fair to say that students will not be fully prepared, even within traditional disciplines such as accounting, finance, human resource management, marketing, and management, unless they are sufficiently knowledgeable about the ethical issues that arise specifically within and across those fields.

Whereas other solid introductory textbooks are available, several significant features make this book distinctive. We emphasize a decision-making approach to ethics, and we provide strong pedagogical support for both teachers and students throughout the entire book. This decision-making approach balances the goals of helping student reach conclusions without imposing someone else's answers on them. Our goal is to help students make responsible decisions for themselves.

But ethical decision making is no small feat, especially in an area that is necessarily multidisciplinary. Numerous small cases and examples aim to help teachers and students integrate concepts and material from philosophy, law, economics, management, finance, and marketing with the very practical goal of making real-life decisions. We aim to bring students into these discussions by regularly grounding our discussions in issues with which they are already familiar, thus approaching them through subjects that have already generated their interest.

New to the Fifth Edition

While our goal for the fifth edition remains the same as for the first—to provide "a comprehensive yet accessible introduction to the ethical issues arising in business"—readers will notice a few changes. As always, the primary incentive of a new edition is to update the text with new and timely cases and topics. Readers will find new discussions of such companies as Facebook and Wells Fargo, as well as such topics as the #MeToo movement and digital privacy. Perhaps the most noticeable change, however, is the elimination of end-of-chapter readings, and this deserves some explanation.

When the first edition was published, our goal was to be as current and timely as possible, not only by including up-to-date examples throughout each chapter, but also through the end-of-chapter readings. Our thinking was that these readings would allow students and teachers to dive more deeply into the subject matter and access perspectives to broaden the scope of the conversation. They also could serve as convenient topics for written assignments or in-class discussions. However, at this point, accessing these perspectives has become so easy through the internet and other means that including them is no longer necessary to achieve our original goals. In fact, our choices instead can limit rather than broaden the range of ideas available.

Further, the increasing costs of textbooks are a serious concern for everyone in education. Students should know that while they are most directly affected by rising costs, teachers, authors, and, yes, even publishers are also troubled by this and regularly look for ways to reduce the costs of education. As we (the authors and our publisher, McGraw-Hill) looked for ways to control costs, the end-of-chapter readings stood out. Permission fees for reprinting readings have increased significantly in recent years, especially in this era of electronic and custom publishing, and the additional length added by the readings contributes to increasing production costs. We decided that these added costs were no longer justified by the benefits, especially considering that the readings are often readily available online, typically at no costs to students under the "fair use" copyright guidelines. The readings were always included only as a means to supplement the core text, and we have now concluded that students would be better served by eliminating the readings and focusing this edition more on the core text itself. In several cases, we have been able to integrate the content of the reading within the text as a Reality Check or Decision Point.

We have retained the same logical structure and chapter organization of previous editions because we have heard from many colleagues and reviewers that this structure works well for a semester-long course in business ethics. But every chapter has been revised to include new and updated material, cases, topics, and readings. Importantly, we continue to provide increased international perspectives, with particular references to Canadian and UK legislation and institutions.

Among the changes to this edition are the following:

New or revised Opening Decision Points for every chapter, including new cases or in-depth discussions on:

▸ Wells Fargo

▸ Job security and confidentiality

▸ Executive compensation

▸ Free expression in the workplace

▸ Facebook

▸ Digital marketing

▸ The business of food

New cases, Reality Checks, or Decision Points within the text on such companies and topics as:

▸ Mylan Epi-Pen

▸ Greed

▸ #MeToo movement

▸ Tesla

▸ Uber

▸ Marijuana in the workplace

▸ Digital privacy

▸ Gender and sexual identity

As always, we reviewed and revised the entire text for accessibility, consistency, and clarity.

Acknowledgments

A textbook should introduce students to the cutting edge of the scholarly research that is occurring within a field. As in any text that is based in part on the work of others, we are deeply indebted to the work of our colleagues who are doing this research. Our book is a more effective tool for both students and faculty because of their generosity.

In particular, thanks to Ryerson students **Stefania Venneri, Tanya Walia,** and **Daniel Marotta** for their useful suggestions, and to **Katrina Myers** at the University of Chicago and to **Summer Brown** at DePaul University for their exceptional research and editing assistance. In addition, we wish to express our deepest gratitude to the reviewers and others whose efforts served to make this manuscript infinitely more effective:

Cheryl Adkins
Longwood University

Lynda Fuller
Wilmington University

Daniel F. Nehring
Morehead State University

Richard Stillman
The Graduate Center, CUNY

Jeffrey Yoder
Fairfield University

Our thanks also go out to the team at McGraw-Hill Education who helped this book come into existence:

Michael Ablassmeir
Director

Laura Hurst Spell
Associate Portfolio Manager

Lisa Granger
Marketing Manager

Melissa M. Leick
Senior Content Project Manager

Brief Contents

Table of Contents

Ethics and Business

It takes 20 years to build a reputation and five minutes to ruin it. If you think about that you'll do things differently.

Warren Buffet

Ethics is the new competitive environment.

Peter Robinson, CEO, Mountain Equipment Co-op (2000-2007)

No snowflake in an avalanche ever feels responsible.

Voltaire, 1694-1778

Wells Fargo and Consumer Fraud[1]

In December 2013, the *Los Angeles Times* published the results of an ongoing investigation into Wells Fargo. The *Times* report described high-pressure sales practices that were aimed at marketing additional financial products to present customers, a practice known as cross-selling. The report told of Wells Fargo employees establishing new accounts in customers' names without their consent or knowledge. The *Times* story included interviews with numerous branch managers from across the United States who described unreasonably high sales targets and quotas that encouraged such unethical practices. In response to this story, Wells Fargo claimed that it took all legal or ethical lapses seriously but denied any systemic wrongdoing. A spokesperson cited a new corporate Ethics Program Office that would oversee compliance with corporate ethical standards.

Following this report, the City of Los Angeles, the State of California, and the U.S. Consumer Financial Protection Bureau (CFPB) began a series of investigations into Wells Fargo. Exactly how aggressive Wells Fargo had been in cross-selling became clear in September 2016 when the CFPB announced that Wells Fargo employees had fraudulently opened millions of unauthorized credit card and deposit accounts in the name of present customers. Wells Fargo admitted to the wrongdoing and agreed to pay fines of $185 million to state and federal authorities.

The investigations uncovered a wide range of fraudulent practices that included ordering credit cards, opening new accounts, establishing new lines of credit, or purchasing insurance and overdraft protection. All of this was done without the consent or knowledge of customers. In some cases, employees forged customers' signatures or used their own address so information about these accounts would be sent to their homes rather than to the defrauded customers. The process involved was reasonably easy. Employees, often in the type of entry-level positions that recent college graduates might fill, had ready access to the information needed to open new accounts: names, addresses, social security numbers, credit reports, and so forth. Applying for and confirming the sale of a new product for an existing customer could be done with a few clicks of a mouse. Investigations revealed that thousands of employees had taken part in the scheme.

Much of the activity described by the *Los Angeles Times* occurred at local branch offices and included every level of employee from tellers to personal bankers to the branch managers themselves. Of course, such widespread fraud could not have gone unnoticed by managers who had oversight of these branch offices. It soon became clear that mid-level management had actively participated in these activities, including providing instructions on how to do it and how to avoid detection by customers. Branch managers who failed to meet sales targets were publicly berated and threatened by their superiors. Employees who missed targets for cross-selling were required to work nights and weekends and were denied promotions and salary increases. It also appears that employees who were reluctant to participate, or who attempted to blow the whistle, not only lost their jobs but also received negative evaluations that effectively prevented them from finding future employment in the banking industry. Less directly, but perhaps much more effectively, management participated in the practice by creating and enforcing demanding sales quotas and wage and salary structures that rewarded those who met these targets.

Wells Fargo had a reputation as a leader in the business strategy of cross-selling, the practice of marketing additional products to existing customers. Traditionally, banks and financial services companies had seen themselves as professionals who provided advisory services to clients in much the same way that an attorney or an accountant provides professional services to his or her clients. In this model, success would be measured in terms of achieving the clients' interests in managing risks, return on investment, and so forth. This fiduciary model of business aims to align the interests of the firm with the interests of the client so that when the client succeeds, the firm succeeds. But many banks and financial institutions have moved away from this fiduciary model in recent decades to adopt a more transactional, consumerist model in which clients are viewed simply as customers to whom the company sells products. Here, the firm's success is measured in terms of how many products are sold and how much profit is earned from those sales. Of course, one trade-off of this shift is that client and business interests may not always align in that the business can profit whether or not the customer does. Wells Fargo was among the first banks to move aggressively in this direction.

At the time of the 2016 announcement, Wells Fargo admitted that since 2011 employees had opened more than 1.5 million fraudulent accounts and more than 500,000 unauthorized credit card applications in the names of present customers. Further investigations of activities prior to 2011 discovered that more than half a million additional fraudulent online bill-paying accounts also had been opened and hundreds of thousands of fraudulent insurance policies were sold to unsuspecting customers. By early 2018, Wells Fargo had admitted to selling more than 3.5 million unauthorized financial products to customers.

In April 2018, the CFPB and the U.S. Comptroller of the Currency announced additional fines to punish Wells Fargo for deceptively adding unneeded insurance to consumer auto loans and manipulating interest rates on mortgages. As many as 600,000 automobile loans might have been subjected to such unneeded additional insurance.

Initially, senior Wells Fargo executives, including CEO and Board Chair John Stumpf, claimed that the fault rested with "dishonest" individuals who had been fired for this behavior. In total, 5,300 employees were fired as a result of these frauds. Testifying to the U.S. Senate Banking Committee, Stumpf claimed: "I do want to make it clear that there was no orchestrated effort, or scheme as some have called it, by the company. We never directed or wanted our employees, whom we refer to as team members, to provide products and services to customers they did not want or need."[2] Stumpf explained the widespread nature of the fraud as likely resulting from employees talking to each other.

But closer analysis showed a pattern of decisions, behavior, and tone at the highest executive levels that contributed to a culture in which such widespread fraud flourished. Stumpf himself was known for his mantra, "eight is great," to promote a target of eight products for each customer in an industry where the average was less than half that. During every quarterly earnings call that took place while the fraud was occurring, Stumpf had boasted to investors of the ever-increasing levels of record cross-selling. Partially as a result, the value of Stumpf's own stock ownership increased by more than $200 million during the five years that the fraud was prevalent.

(continued)

There was also evidence that senior executives knew of the fraudulent sales well before the practice became public. After all, the *Los Angeles Times* article was published three years previously. Further, Wells Fargo's own training manual contained a reminder not to sell products without the explicit consent of customers—a reminder that the manual highlighted and emphasized in such a way to suggest that the practice was known to occur. Wells Fargo executives also had internal reports showing that the steady increase in cross-selling was directly correlated with a steady increase in accounts that were never used by customers.

The entire culture of Wells Fargo seemed designed to encourage cheating and discourage honest sales practices. For example, the incentive system, ranging from sales targets for hourly workers to executive bonuses, made it clear to everyone that aggressive cross-selling was the expectation for all. The senior executive who had direct oversight of the sales division received over $125 million when she retired just before the scandal was revealed. (Wells Fargo eventually recovered half that amount in a claw-back process.) Employees stated that reports to an internal ethics hotline and to the corporate ethics program were ignored. In response to claims that they failed to exercise their oversight function as required by U.S. federal law, board members later claimed they were left in the dark, learning about the scandal from the media. Like many corporations, the Wells Fargo CEO also served as the chair of the board.

It is worth noting that various government agencies were involved in this case. City of Los Angeles and California state investigators played a major role is uncovering the fraud. The federal CFPB and the Comptroller of the Currency also worked on the investigations and instituted the large fines against Wells Fargo. The U.S. Senate Banking Committee held several hearings in which members very publicly criticized Wells Fargo executives and its board. The U.S. Federal Reserve Bank, the primary regulator of U.S. banks, imposed strong penalties on the bank and its board. In an unprecedented punishment, the Fed restricted Wells Fargo's future growth and required the replacement of several board members for failing their oversight duty. But other government actions, including laws that prohibited fraud, protecting whistle-blowers, and laws that required ethical compliance and oversight by the board, proved ineffective in preventing widespread fraud that went on for many years.[3]

1. A helpful first step in ethical analysis is to look for harms and benefits. What harms were done by this fraud? Can you explain exactly what the ethical wrong was? Other than consumers, who else was harmed? Who benefited? Did the parties who benefited deserve the benefit? Were any benefits unfair or unethical?

2. Where would you place primary responsibility for this scandal: individual employees who forged customers' accounts, managers who oversaw those employees, senior executives, board members, or the corporation itself?

3. Sometimes when we assign responsibility, we are looking for someone to blame, someone who is at fault. Who do you blame in this case?

4. Sometimes the question of responsibility is asked so that we can identify the cause and, in turn, prevent it from happening again. What recommendations would you make to prevent this from happening again?

5. How do you understand the difference between a fiduciary model and a transactional, consumerist model of the business–customer relationship? What reasons exist for the fiduciary model? Why would a financial or banking firm (or law firm, accounting firm, or hospital) not seek to make as much money as possible from its customers? Is there an ethical difference between the fiduciary and transactional models?

 ## Chapter Objectives

After reading this chapter, you will be able to:

1. Explain three levels at which ethical decisions get made in business.
2. Explain the nature of business ethics as an academic discipline.
3. Explain why ethics is important in the business environment.
4. Explain why ethical responsibilities go beyond legal compliance.
5. Distinguish the ethics of personal integrity from the ethics of social responsibility.
6. Distinguish ethical norms and values from other business-related norms and values.
7. Describe ethical decision making as a form of practical reasoning.

Introduction: Getting Comfortable with the Topic

When we began work on the first edition of this book in the early 2000s, the legal, financial, and ethical implications of the Enron scandal were still front-page news. Almost twenty years later, Enron has faded from public consciousness. One reason for this, of course, is that as a direct consequence of these scandals neither Enron nor its accounting firm Arthur Andersen exists today. In 2000, they were both well-known and highly respected global firms.

Some years later, as we prepared another edition, the entire global economy was in the middle of the deepest economic recession since the Great Depression of the 1930s. That recession resulted from the collapse of a housing bubble that was brought about because of ethically questionable subprime mortgage lending practices, widespread trading of fraudulent financial instruments based on these risky mortgage-backed securities, and a failure of oversight on corporate, professional, and governmental levels. As a direct result of these ethical lapses, hundreds of banks failed and dozens of globally active financial institutions, including such major well-known firms as Lehman Brothers, Bear Stearns, Countrywide Financial, and Washington Mutual, ceased to exist, either through bankruptcy or by being acquired by other companies at greatly reduced prices.

The list of major business firms involved in significant ethical scandals during just the first two decades of the 21st century is depressingly long. Besides the corporations already mentioned, the list would include such major global firms as Walmart, Nike, Apple, Merrill Lynch, JP Morgan Chase, KPMG, Credit Suisse, Takata, Halliburton, AIG, WorldCom, Tyco, Global Crossing, Rite Aid, Sunbeam, Waste Management, HealthSouth, Ernst and Young, Citigroup, Salomon Smith Barney, Goldman Sachs, Bank of America, Deep Water Horizon, Exxon, Johnson & Johnson, Pfizer, Firestone, BP Global, Fannie Mae, and even the New York Stock Exchange itself.

Sadly, the list of corporate scandals continues to expand. Beside the Wells Fargo case that opens this chapter, in just the past few years, recent and ongoing ethical scandals have involved such major companies as Facebook, Google, Volkswagen, Purdue Pharma, Deutsche Bank, Cambridge Analytica, Nissan, Tesla, Equifax, and Uber.

But the news is not all bad. There are also countless examples of exemplary corporations and business practices. A relatively new business phenomena called "Benefit Corporations" (discussed in Chapter 5) allows for-profit businesses to adopt an explicit corporate mission of serving the common good. Such well-known firms as Ben and Jerry's, King Arthur Flour, Seventh Generation, and Patagonia have adopted the Benefit Corporation model. Further, the growing field of social entrepreneurship seeks to leverage the skills and creativity of entrepreneurs to address social challenges. Corporate philanthropy exists everywhere, from the large scale of corporate foundations that give away millions of dollars annually, to small businesses in every local community that support schools, arts programming, and community organizations such as Boys and Girls Clubs, the United Way, Red Cross, and Habitat for Humanity with hundreds of millions of dollars in charitable giving.

No doubt we can find good and bad behavior in contemporary business. We can find some firms that are deeply corrupt, and we can find some that are models of social responsibility. Most often, we can find both good and bad behavior, good and bad people, in every individual firm. Our hope is that this book can help you navigate your way through these challenges and avoid the pitfalls of unethical situations.

This opening chapter will introduce business ethics as a process of decision making. Simply put, the harms caused by the scandals associated with all the organizations just mentioned were brought about by ethical failures and unethical decisions. This text provides a decision-making model that we believe can help both analyzing these past ethical failures and avoiding future ones.

OBJECTIVE

As the Wells Fargo case demonstrates, business decision making occurs at several levels. Every day at Wells Fargo, individual human beings, from tellers and personal bankers at local branch offices to senior executives and board members, had to decide for themselves what they were going to do. Am I going to open this fraudulent account? How am I going to treat the people who work for me? Should I speak up and push back against these demands, or should I just go along and get along? Should I continue to work for a firm that asks me to do these unethical things? As a board member, should I ask questions and challenge the CEO, or should I judge his work solely on the basis of quarterly earnings?

Decisions at Wells Fargo also occurred at an organizational level. Individual decisions were made within the context of organizational policies, practices, expectations, and norms. The organization, through its management, created incentive policies, disciplinary policies, dismissal practices, sales targets, handbooks, ethics programs, executive bonuses, and even specific directions on how to create fraudulent accounts and how to prevent customers from learning about them. The organization had a culture that allowed, if not encouraged, such unethical behavior.

But this Wells Fargo case also raises questions that go beyond the decisions made within the organization. Beyond the personal and organizational level, there is a broader social and political level of decision making that is also relevant for business ethics. Given the many corporate scandals we've mentioned, and given all the people who have been harmed by them, citizens must ask questions about the role of government, the law, and regulations. For example, what type of laws and regulations should govern business? What expectations do we have for regulatory bodies such as the Consumer Financial Protection Bureau? How much of business decision making should be left to market mechanisms such as competition and consumer demand, and how much should be subject to legal and regulatory standards?

The field of business ethics helps us analyze and evaluate decision making at all three of these levels. Business ethics involves decisions at the individual, at the organizational, and at a broader social and governmental level. As individuals, each of us interacts with businesses as customers, as employees, and as citizens of the countries in which they operate. A business ethics class can help us think about what we would do if we were the customers defrauded by Wells Fargo, what we might have done had we been the individual employees who were expected to open fraudulent accounts, and what we should do as individual citizens in a country in which these frauds were possible.

But individuals do not exist in a vacuum. Again, as the Wells Fargo case suggests, it can be difficult for good people to live up to their standards within a corrupt organization. Likewise, it can be difficult for bad people to act unethically within an organization that promotes and lives up to high ethical standards. As we will see later in this book, organizational culture and corporate leadership have important roles to play in decision making. Yet, business organizations themselves do not exist in a vacuum. Every business is situated within one or more social, economic, and political structures. Just as individual decisions and behaviors are influenced by the surrounding organization, so too are the decisions of individual businesses and entire industries influenced by social, economic, and political environments. A business operating in Quebec, Canada, will face a different social and cultural environment than one operating in Dallas, Texas.

Obviously, the law itself is the major means by which a society imposes standards and expectations upon business. But, as we describe in a later section, obeying the law is not enough to fulfill ethical responsibilities. It is also true that the social, economic, and political environments in which businesses operate are heavily value-laden, and a class on business ethics should help us think through these social, economic, and political values as well as those individual values that each of us use in making decisions.

Given this description, it is clear that business ethics is a multidisciplinary field. First, the field of business ethics is rooted in the more general discipline of philosophical ethics. The role of philosophical ethics is to provide the fundamental language and categories of ethics. For thousands of years philosophers have thought and theorized about such things as rights and duties, virtues and values, social justice, responsibilities, liberty, equality, and the common good. How these various concepts fit together, how they might be justified, what their strengths and weaknesses are, and how and where they apply in life are questions that philosophers have examined for millennia. Learning about philosophical ethics provides a knowledge base for our own study of business ethics so that we won't have to start from scratch.

Business ethics also includes resources from such fields as psychology, business management, organizational behavior, leadership studies, and sociology. How and why people behave as they do, how the organizational environment encourages and discourages behaviors, how organizations and individuals within them can create a culture in which ethical behavior flourishes are questions that arise from this diverse group of social sciences.

Finally, broader social disciplines such as law, economics, and political science contribute to business ethics as we think about how business organizations fit into a broader social and political context.

OBJECTIVE

To summarize, as a field, business ethics investigates ethical questions that arise at the individual, organizational, and social/political level. As ethically responsible people, each of us should consider how we interact with business as individual consumers, individual employees, managers, executives, and citizens. This text is a contribution to the academic field of business ethics. Its aim is to describe, examine, and evaluate ethical issues that arise within business settings and to help each of us become more ethical individuals and help us create more ethical institutions. A business ethics class therefore has many goals, including helping us to:

1. Develop the knowledge base and skills needed to identify ethical issues.
2. Understand how and why people behave unethically.
3. Decide how we should act, what we should do, and the type of person we should be as individuals.
4. Create ethical organizations.
5. Think through the social, economic, and political policies that we should support as citizens.

Making the Case for Business Ethics

OBJECTIVE

For business students, the need to study ethics should be as clear as the need to study the other sub-fields of business education. As discussed earlier, without this background, students simply will be unprepared for a career in contemporary business. Businesses themselves must take ethics into account and integrate ethics into their organizational structure, for both ethical and business reasons. But even for individuals who do not anticipate a career in business management or business administration, familiarity with business ethics is crucial. Our lives as employees, as consumers, and as citizens are affected by decisions made within business institutions; therefore, everyone has good reasons for being concerned with the ethics of those decision makers.

As recently as the mid-1990s, articles in such major publications as *The Wall Street Journal* and the *Harvard Business Review* questioned the value of teaching business ethics. Even today, it is not uncommon to encounter skepticism among students about the need and value of a class in business ethics. Part of this skepticism may come from a general skepticism about ethics itself. Many people view ethics as a mixture of sentimentality and personal opinion that would interfere with the efficient operation of business. From this perspective, ethics is a subjective matter of feelings and opinions that can safely and reasonably be ignored. (See the Decision Point "Who Is To Say What Is Right or Wrong?" in Chapter 3)

separation thesis
The separation thesis asserts that ordinary ethical standards should be kept separate from, and not be used to judge, business decisions because business has its own standards of good and bad.

A more influential version of this skepticism involves what some have called the "separation thesis."[4] This perspective holds that ordinary ethical considerations should be kept separate from business decisions because business has its own standards of right and wrong. A version of this was most famously expressed by the Nobel Prize–winning economist Milton Friedman. In a 1970 article that has become a classic in business ethics, "The Social Responsibility of Business Is to Increase Its Profits," Friedman claimed that "there is one and only one social responsibility of business—to use its resources and engage in activities designed *to increase its profits so long as it stays within the rules of the game, which is to say, engages in open and free competition without deception or fraud."*[5] Elsewhere in that essay, Friedman explained that the "rules of the game" included both law and "ethical custom."

It is fair to say that this separation thesis remains common in business circles. According to this view, business practice should be kept separate and independent of ordinary ethical concerns. Business fulfills its social and ethical responsibilities by pursuing profits within the law and within the rules of the economic game. Those economic rules are the conditions necessary to ensure the efficient operation of economic markets. In a marketplace free from fraud and deception, competitive pressures and market demand will direct the self-interested pursuit of profit to ethically appropriate goals. Thus, there is no reason to complicate the matter with outside ethical considerations.

Questions about the relationship between ethics and economics are as old as the field of economics itself. Adam Smith, often considered the founder of modern market economics, suggested in *The Wealth of Nations* that, under the conditions of a competitive market, self-interest alone would lead, "as if by an invisible hand," to ethically appropriate ends.[6] Yet in his other major book, *The Theory of Moral Sentiments,* Smith argued that sympathy and benevolence were among the most fundamental of all human motivations. The relationship between these two books has long puzzled scholars. How does one reconcile an economic model that seems to treat self-interest as sufficient for securing socially good ends with a moral psychology that treats benevolence and sympathy as fundamental?

The truth of the matter, and what was likely Smith's own view, is that human beings are capable of a wide diversity of motivations and behaviors, ranging from narrow self-interest to wide empathy and altruism. In this, business is no different from any other aspect of human life. Some motivations like selfishness, greed, and the pursuit of money, power, fame, or prestige can lead people to make decisions that can cause harm, that violate basic principles, and that can corrupt what the American president Abraham Lincoln once called the "better angels of our nature." Smith's market conditions were intended as a means to channel self-interested motives to greater social ends, but Smith himself did not think that humans are always and necessarily self-interested. (To consider a view that does consider humans as always self-interested, see the Reality Check "Psychological Egoism: Are Humans Naturally Selfish?")

While questioning the relevance of ethics to business was at one time an open question, today the more pressing question is not *whether to,* but *how to* effectively integrate ethics into business practice. After all, even the separation thesis holds that business ought to be governed by some ethics and some values. We should not lose sight of the fact that obedience to the law, avoiding fraud and deception, and engaging in free and open competition are themselves ethical considerations. The separation thesis claims that this narrow range of ethical considerations is enough for business to fulfill its responsibilities. Especially in light of the many cases of corporate scandal and corruption already mentioned, many would disagree with that judgment.

Consider the Wells Fargo case. Thousands of people lost their jobs, tens of thousands of consumers faced increased costs and lower credit ratings, some consumers even had their cars repossessed when they were unable to pay fraudulently increased loan costs. Or consider the Enron case, in which thousands of innocent people lost their jobs and investors, including countless pension funds and retirement funds, lost billions of dollars.

Most dramatically, consider the harms caused by the global economic collapse of 2008, a collapse largely brought about by ethical failures in the financial and real estate industries. In the United States alone, investigators found that more than 26 million people lost jobs and more than $11 trillion in household wealth was lost as a result of the 2008 economic meltdown. Within the first year of that recession, Canadian unemployment rose from 6.3% to 8.6%, with more than 400,000 Canadians losing their jobs. Within the U.S. and Canada, hundreds of thousands of families lost their homes, hundreds of banks failed, and countless other businesses went bankrupt. This crisis had cascading consequences, as the economic meltdown quickly spread across the globe.

psychological egoism
An alleged theory of human motivation that claims that all human actions are selfish and motivated by self-interest.

The official U.S. government investigation of this recession concluded that the financial crisis was avoidable because it resulted from failures of business management, regulatory oversight, and corporate governance, as well as a "systemic breakdown in accountability and ethics."[7] Within a year of this report, the U.S. government established the Consumer Financial Protection Bureau, the very governmental regulatory body that investigated the Wells Fargo fraud.

Reality Check *Psychological Egoism: Are Humans Naturally Selfish?*

In the background to some skepticism about the relevance of ethics to business, and often part of the reasoning behind the separation thesis, lies a theory called **psychological egoism.** This theory purports to be an account of human motivation, asserting that humans are fundamentally and unavoidably motivated by self-interest. In other words, everything that we do is one for our own, egoistic, benefit. Because this is thought a "fact" of human nature, so the argument goes, ethical considerations that expect us to act for the interests of others is unrealistic. Thus, it is only realistic to keep business rules separate from ordinary ethics.

Psychological egoists conclude that because humans are incapable of acting out of altruistic motivation, our only reasonable option is to arrange institutions in ways that channel individual egoism to the social good. The social contract tradition in political philosophy associated with Thomas Hobbes, for example, acknowledges the reality of self-interested individuals but argues that cooperative social behavior is in the self-interest of individuals. Adam Smith's theory provides another variation of this approach. Smith argues that rationally self-interested egoists acting within an open and competitive market and constrained by prohibitions against fraud and coercion would, as if led "by an invisible hand," promote the greater social good.

But is psychological egoism an accurate theory of human motivation? Does psychological egoism pose a serious challenge to doing business ethics? The first thing to note is that if this is to be a challenge to ethics, defenders must claim that egoism is something more than merely a tendency of humans. If humans acted selfishly only some of the time but were capable of altruistic behavior at other times (as Adam Smith himself seems to have concluded), then we have no reason to give up on ethics and no reason to adopt the separation thesis. In fact, this may well be the major point of ethics: People *tend* to act selfishly; therefore, ethics exists to establish constraints upon this selfish behavior.

In order for psychological egoism to threaten the relevance of ethics, defenders must claim that humans not only have a general tendency to act selfishly, but must always and only act out of self-interest. But, on the face of it, such a claim is obviously false. Parents and friends are two

everyday examples of humans who regularly act for the well-being of others. More generally, if psychological egoism were true, we would either need to radically revise or totally abandon such concepts as friendship, love, charity, volunteering, sacrifice, generosity, loyalty, and countless others acts that assume altruistic motivation.

Egoists have two ways to answer these facts. First, they might claim that when people act in such ways, they are still doing what they want and, therefore, are still acting selfishly. But this option is deeply misguided. On one hand, if this is intended as an empirical claim about human behavior, it is obviously false. People do things that they don't "want" to do all the time (consider going to the dentist and doing philosophy homework as examples!). On the other hand, if this is not intended as an empirical claim—if it is an attempt to define self-interest as doing *whatever* an individual wants—then the egoist has abandoned the attack on ethics. That is, if the egoist admits that people are capable of two types of self-interested acts—those in which they want to benefit the self and those in which they want to benefit others—then the door is still open for ethics to sometimes require the latter rather than the former.

A second response commonly made by egoists is to claim that even in cases of sacrifice and charity, people derive satisfaction out of ethical acts, and this suggests that selfishness underlies even the most beneficent act. So, even the mother who sacrifices for her baby is self-interested because she gets the satisfaction of lovingly caring for her baby from the act. But this response also fails because it confuses the intention or motivation for acting (one of the things with which ethics is concerned) with the feelings or reactions that follow from the act. I am selfish egoist only if the reason (or intent or motivation) that I have for helping my children is *in order to* feel good about myself. I am selfish if my intent for helping my friends is only to derive some personal benefit from this act. But that is not what motivates parents, or friends, or many of us much of the time. Our reason and motivation are to help others, and feeling good about it after the fact does not diminish the ethical nature of the act.

Familiarity with psychological egoism will be helpful for the study of business ethics. Ethics will sometimes require business managers to sacrifice their own

(continued)

self-interest, often in the form of profits, in order to fulfill their ethical responsibilities. It is not uncommon for people to think that such a requirement is unrealistic and unreasonable. This may be particularly true for those people who have been taught by certain economic theories that humans are naturally selfish. But psychological egoism provides no support for such conclusions.

Note: You will see Reality Checks throughout each chapter. Slightly different from Decision Points, these boxes offer practical applications of the concepts discussed during that chapter segment or examples of the ways in which the concepts are implemented in "real" business decision making.

By now, the case for business ethics should be clear. Decisions made in business can have a significant impact on the well-being of countless individuals both within and outside of the business itself. Business decisions can no more escape ethical judgment than any other aspect of living a human life. As some of the examples already discussed demonstrate, both the very existence of a firm and the conditions under which it operates require that decision makers move beyond the narrow view of responsibilities that are captured by the separation thesis to consider the impact of those decisions on a wide range of **stakeholders.** In a general sense, a business *stakeholder* will be anyone who affects or is affected by decisions made within the firm, for better or worse. Failure to consider these additional stakeholders will have a detrimental impact on those stakeholders, on stockholders and on the firm's long-term sustainability as a whole. This perspective is articulated effectively by Whole Foods Market's "Declaration of Interdependence."

stakeholder

In a general sense, a stakeholder is anyone who can be affected by decisions made within a business. More specifically, stakeholders are considered to be those people who are necessary for the functioning of a business.

> Satisfying all of our stakeholders and achieving our standards is our goal. One of the most important responsibilities of Whole Foods Market's leadership *is to make sure the interests, desires and needs of our various stakeholders are kept in balance.* We recognize that this is a dynamic process. It requires participation and communication by all of our stakeholders. It requires listening compassionately, thinking carefully and acting with integrity. Any conflicts must be mediated and win-win solutions found. Creating and nurturing this community of stakeholders is critical to the long-term success of our company. [Emphasis added.][8]

The Reality Check "How Does the Law Support Ethical Behavior?" describes some legal requirements that have been created in the United States since the Enron scandal. Beyond these specific legal obligations, organizational survival relies upon ethical decisions in a great many ways. Unethical behavior not only creates legal risks for a business, it creates financial and marketing risks as well. Managing these risks requires managers and executives to remain vigilant about their company's ethics. It is now more clear than ever that a company can lose in the marketplace and go out of business, and its employees go to jail, if no one is paying attention to the ethical standards of the firm.

As a final point, we should acknowledge that there are good business and financial reasons for practicing good ethics. First, a good reputation is itself good for business. Major firms such as Patagonia and Ben and Jerry's explicitly market themselves as pursuing ethically beneficial goals. More generally, look to retail marketing advertisements to see how often firms use such words as "trust," "honest,"

As we will explain in the following section, ethics and the law are not the same. But law and ethics overlap in many ways. Good laws become law precisely because they promote important ethical values. But in some cases, laws are passed to help support ethical behavior in another way, namely by focusing the attention of corporate leaders on the need to work hard to ensure ethical behavior in their organizations. In 2002, for example, the U.S. Congress passed the Sarbanes-Oxley Act to address the wave of corporate and accounting scandals. Section 406 of that law, "Code of Ethics for Senior Financial Officers," requires that corporations have a code of ethics "applicable to its principal financial officer and comptroller or principal accounting officer, or persons performing similar functions." The code must include standards that promote:

1. Honest and ethical conduct, including the ethical handling of actual or apparent conflicts of interest between personal and professional relationships.
2. Full, fair, accurate, timely, and understandable disclosure in the periodic reports required to be filed by the issuer.
3. Compliance with applicable governmental rules and regulations.

"reliable," "dependable," and "caring" to promote business in the marketplace. Second, as some of the most dramatic corruption cases have demonstrated, unethical behavior can cause serious harm to the firm itself, up to and including bankruptcy. Third, attracting and retaining employees is easier for firms with good ethics than those with bad reputations. Finally, as such firms as Nike, McDonald's, Facebook, Walmart, Chick-fil-A, Nestlé, and Target have learned, consumer boycotts of unethical business practices can have significant financial costs.

Ethics and the Law

OBJECTIVE

Before turning to a discussion of ethical decision making, it is worth reflecting on the role played by the law. Any discussion of norms and standards of proper business behavior would be incomplete without considering the law. In fact, some defenders of the separation thesis would argue that the law provides the only social norms and standards needed for business ethics.

It is certainly true that deciding what one *should do* in business does require consideration of what the law requires, expects, or permits. The law does provide an important guide to ethical decision making, and this text will integrate legal considerations throughout. But legal norms and ethical norms are not identical, nor do they always agree. For example, some ethical requirements, such as treating one's employees with respect, are not legally required, though they are ethically justified. On the other hand, some actions that may be legally permitted, such as firing an employee for no reason, would fail ordinary ethical standards.

As reflected in the separation thesis, some people continue to believe, perhaps more commonly prior to the scandals of recent years than after, that a business fulfills its social responsibility simply by obeying the law. From this perspective, an ethically responsible business is merely one that complies with the law; there is no responsibility to do anything further. Individual businesses may choose to go beyond this legal minimum, such as when a business supports the local arts, but these choices are voluntary. A good deal of management literature on corporate social responsibility centers on this approach. Business ethics requires obedience to the law; anything beyond that is a matter of corporate philanthropy and charity, something praiseworthy and allowed, but not ethically required.

Over the last two decades, many corporations have established ethics programs and have hired ethics officers who are responsible for managing corporate ethics programs. Ethics officers do a great deal of good and effective work, but it is fair to say that much of their work focuses on legal compliance issues. Of course, the environment varies considerably from company to company and industry to industry. The Sarbanes-Oxley Act, the U.S. law established after the Enron scandal, created a dramatic and vast new layer of legal compliance issues for companies doing business in the United States. But is compliance with the law all that is required to behave ethically? In order to move forward to our discussion of ethics as a more effective guidepost for decision making, let us briefly explore at this point several persuasive reasons that legal compliance alone is insufficient.

1. Believing that obedience to the law is sufficient to fulfill one's ethical duties raises questions of whether the law, itself, is ethical. Dramatic examples from history, including Nazi Germany and apartheid in South Africa, demonstrate that one's ethical responsibility may run counter to the law. On a more practical level, this question can have significant implications in a global economy in which businesses operate in countries with legal systems different from those of their home country. For instance, some countries permit discrimination on the basis of gender and some strictly censure internet content. A firm that does business in such a country must decide whether to obey the local law or remain true to ethical principles. From the perspective of ethics, a business does not avoid its need to consider ethical responsibilities just by obeying the law because sometimes it may have to decide if the law itself deserves to be obeyed.

2. Societies that value individual freedom will be reluctant to legally require more than just an ethical minimum. Such liberal societies will seek legally to prohibit the most serious ethical harms, although they will not legally require acts of charity, common decency, and personal integrity that may otherwise constitute the social fabric of a developed culture. The law can be an efficient mechanism to prevent serious harms, but it is not very effective at promoting "goods." Even if it were, the cost in human freedom of legally requiring such things as personal integrity would be extremely high. What would a society be like if it legally required parents to love their children, or even had a law that prohibited lying under all circumstances?

3. On a more practical level, a business acting as if its ethical responsibilities end with obedience to the law is just inviting more legal regulation. Consider the difficulty of trying to create laws to cover each and every possible business challenge; the task would require such specificity that the number of regulated areas would become unmanageable. Additionally, it was the failure of personal ethics among such companies as Enron, after all, that led to the creation of

Reality Check *Are Business Executives Perceived as Corrupt?*

Transparency International: Perceived Corruption in Business		
Transparency International asked people worldwide to respond to this statement: **"How many business executives in your country do you think are involved in corruption?"** Responses saying "most" or "all" from selected countries are displayed below.		
Country	Most	All
Australia	16%	5%
Brazil	25%	10%
Chile	31%	25%
China	9%	2%
Egypt	28%	11%
France	14%	3%
Ghana	29%	10%
Japan	15%	2%
Russia	18%	9%
United Kingdom	15%	6%
United States	25%	10%

Source: Data extracted from Transparency International; Putting Corruption out of Business: Business' Responsibility; www.transparency.org/research/bps2011.

the Sarbanes-Oxley Act and the corruption of subprime mortgage lending that led to the creation of the Consumer Financial Protection Bureau. If business restricts its ethical responsibilities to obedience to the law, it should not be surprised to find a new wave of government regulations and legal restrictions. Public perception of business can play a major role in what laws are created to regulate business. See the two Reality Checks "Are Business Executives Perceived as Corrupt?" and "Ethics in the Corporate World."

4. The law cannot anticipate every new ethical issue that businesses might face, so often there may not be a regulation for the particular dilemma that confronts a business leader. For example, when workplace email was in its infancy, laws regarding who actually owned the email transmissions (the employee or the employer) were not yet in place. As a result, one had no choice but to rely on the ethical decision-making processes of those in power to respect the appropriate boundaries of employee privacy while also adequately managing the workplace (see Chapter 7 for a more complete discussion of the legal implications of workplace monitoring). When new quandaries arise, one must be able to rely on ethics because the law might not yet—or might never—provide a solution.

Reality Check   *Ethics in the Corporate World*

It's no secret that a substantial portion of the public has trouble trusting corporate CEOs. Every time another corporate scandal makes headlines, chatter increases about the fundamental untrustworthiness of business in general, and of business leaders in particular. But just how little does the public trust CEOs? And how does the public's trust in CEOs differ from their trust in members of other occupations and professions? In 2014, the Ted Rogers Leadership Centre at Ryerson University (in Toronto, Canada) conducted a national survey to ask Canadians their perceptions of the ethics of political leadership. One question they asked is: "In general, how much do you trust members of the following professions to behave ethically in their roles—that is, to live up to both public and professional standards in fulfilling their duties?"

Here are the percentages of respondents who indicated that they trust members of the following professions to behave ethically:

Doctors: 78 percent

Judges: 65 percent

Police officers: 60 percent

Public servants: 36 percent

Journalists: 33 percent

Business CEOs: 22 percent

Union leaders: 20 percent

Political staff: 16 percent

Politicians: 13 percent

Lobbyists: 9 percent

Of course, there are important questions about just how to interpret such data. It is worth noting that these numbers suggest a correlation between how much we *trust* various professions and how familiar we are with what they do. Most people know and rely on their family physician, and most people have a pretty good idea of what a judge does. On the other hand, fewer people understand what a CEO does. So what is expressed as a lack of trust *may* just reflect a lack of understanding. Or it might not! But we should always consider a range of explanations in the face of data such as these.

Source: "Public Perceptions of the Ethics of Political Leadership," Ted Rogers Leadership Centre (November 5, 2014), www.ethicssurvey.ca (accessed June 6, 2016). The survey was conducted among a nationally representative sample of $n = 1,039$ Canadians between October 17 and 22, 2014, using an online panel.

5. Finally, the perspective that compliance is enough relies on a misleading understanding of law. To say that all a business needs to do is obey the law suggests that laws are clear-cut, unambiguous rules that can be easily applied. This rule model of law is very common, but it is not quite accurate. Some laws—speed limits on highways, for example—are clear and unambiguous. But many other laws, especially in the area of civil law that governs most commercial transactions, are not. Of course, if the law was clear and unambiguous, there would not be much of a role for lawyers and courts.

These considerations demonstrate that business cannot avoid making ethical judgments, even if it is fully committed to obeying the law. Consider, for example, what would be required of a business committed to obeying the legal requirements established by a law such as the Americans with Disabilities Act (ADA). Like similar laws in many countries, this law requires American employers to make reasonable accommodations for employees with disabilities. (In the United Kingdom, the comparable law is called the Equality Act, 2010. In Canada, where employment law is a provincial matter, there are laws such as the Ontarians with Disabilities Act, 2002, and the Accessibility for Manitobans Act, 2013.) All of these laws use such ambiguous terms as "reasonable" or "barriers" or even the word "disability" itself. But what counts as a disability and what would be considered a "reasonable" accommodation? What creates a barrier to employment? Over the years, claims have been made that relevant disabilities include obesity, depression, dyslexia, arthritis, hearing loss, high blood pressure, facial scars, and the fear of heights. Whether such conditions are covered under the law depends on a number of factors, including the severity of the illness and the effect it has on the employee's ability to work, among others. Imagine that you are a corporate human resource manager and an employee asks you to reasonably accommodate his allergy. How would you decide whether allergies constitute a disability under the ADA?

In general, most of the laws that concern business are based on the common law of past cases that establish legal precedents. Each precedent applies general rules to the specific circumstances of an individual case. The law provides general guidance to make "reasonable accommodations" for a "disability." But courts decide, on a case-by-case basis, whether some action was or was not reasonable or whether this condition is or is not a disability. In most business situations, asking, "Is this legal?" is really asking, "Are these circumstances similar enough to past cases that the conclusions reached in those cases will also apply here?" Because there will always be some differences among cases, the question will always remain somewhat open. Thus, there is no unambiguous answer for the conscientious business manager who wishes only to obey the law. There are few situations where a decision maker can simply find the applicable rule, apply it to the situation, and deduce an answer from it. The decision maker cannot avoid responsibility for her own judgment of what should be done.

Without aiming to criticize the legal profession (especially because one of the authors of this text has a legal background!) but merely to demonstrate the preceding ambiguity, it is worth remembering that many of the people involved in the wave of recent corporate scandals were themselves lawyers. In the Enron case, for example, corporate attorneys and accountants were famously encouraged to "push the envelope" of what was legal. Especially in civil law (as opposed to criminal law), where much of the law is established by past precedent, as described earlier, there is always room for ambiguity in applying the law. Further, in civil law there is a real sense that one has not done anything illegal unless and until a court decides that one has violated a law. This means that if no one files a lawsuit to challenge an action, it is *perceived as* legal.

As some theories of corporate social responsibility suggest, if a corporate manager is told that she has a responsibility to maximize profits within the law, a competent manager will go to her corporate attorneys and tax accountants and ask what the law allows. Or ask those professionals to "push the envelope" to see what they can legally get away with, and that typically means what they would be willing to defend in court. A responsible attorney or accountant will advise how far the manager can reasonably go before it would obviously be illegal. In this situation, the question is whether a manager has a *responsibility* to "push the envelope" of legality in pursuit of profits.

Most of the cases of corporate scandal mentioned at the start of this chapter involved attorneys and accountants who advised their clients or bosses that what they were doing could be defended in court. The off-book partnerships that were at the heart of the collapse of Enron and Arthur Andersen were designed with the advice of attorneys who thought that, if challenged, they had at least a reasonable chance of winning in court. In the business environment, this strategy falls within the domain of organizational **risk assessment,** defined as "a process . . . to identify potential events that may affect the entity, and manage risk to be within its risk appetite, to provide reasonable assurance regarding the achievement of entity objectives."[9] Accordingly, the decision to "push the envelope" becomes a balance of risk assessment, cost–benefit analysis, and ethics—what is the corporation willing to do, *willing to risk?* Using this model, decision makers might include in their assessment before taking action:

risk assessment
A process to identify potential events that may affect the entity, and manage risk to be within its risk appetite, to provide reasonable assurance regarding the achievement of entity objectives.

- The likelihood of being challenged in court.
- The likelihood of losing the case.
- The likelihood of settling for financial damages.
- A comparison of those costs.
- The financial benefits of taking the action.
- The ethical implication of the options available.

It is important to recognize that risk assessment is not simply a value-neutral process of professional judgment. While determining the *likelihood* of one particular outcome versus another can be a professional judgment for attorneys and accountants, deciding whether the risk is worth taking is not. That, ultimately, is a value judgment, and when the risks involve potential harms and benefits to a variety of stakeholders, it is a judgment that involves ethics as well.

Because the law is often ambiguous—because in many cases it simply is not clear what the law requires—there is seldom certainty with regard to these decisions. Therefore, business managers will often face decisions that will require their ethical judgments. To suggest otherwise simply presents a false picture of corporate reality. Thus, even those businesspeople who are committed to strictly obeying the law will be confronted on a regular basis by the fundamental ethical questions: What should I do? How should I live?

As suggested earlier, whether we step back and explicitly ask these questions, each of us implicitly answers them every time we make a decision about how to act. Responsible decision making requires that we *do* step back and reflect on them, and then consciously choose the values by which we make decisions. No doubt this is a daunting task, even for experienced, seasoned leaders. Fortunately, we are not alone in meeting this challenge. There can be better and worse ways to think about ethical issues and make decisions on how to act.

Business Ethics as Ethical Decision Making

As the title of this book suggests, our approach to business ethics will emphasize **ethical decision making.** No book can magically create ethically responsible people or change behavior in any direct way, and that's certainly not our goal here. But students can learn and practice responsible and accountable ways of thinking and deliberating. We believe that decisions that follow from a process of thoughtful and conscientious reasoning will be more responsible and ethical. In other words, *responsible decision making and deliberation will result in more responsible behavior.*

So what, exactly, is the goal of a business ethics course? On one hand, *ethics* refers to an academic discipline with a centuries-old history; we might expect knowledge about this history to be among the primary goals of a class in ethics. Thus, in an ethics course, students might be expected to learn about the great ethicists of history such as Aristotle, John Stuart Mill, and Immanuel Kant. As in many other courses on other subjects, this approach to ethics would focus on the *informational content* of the class.

Yet, ethical theories and the history of ethics can seem beside the point. Many observers, including some businesses looking to hire college graduates, business schools, and business students, expect an ethics class to address, if not produce, ethical *behavior,* not just information and knowledge about ethics. After all, what good is an ethics class if it does not help prevent future scandals such as Wells Fargo or Enron? Knowledge *about* ethics is one thing, but ethical *behavior* is another, and many believe that it is the behavior not the knowledge that should be the goal of a business ethics class.

For our purposes, ethics refers not only to an academic discipline, but also to that arena of human life studied by this academic discipline, namely, *how human beings should properly live their lives.* We believe that business ethics should aim for both knowledge about ethics and more responsible behavior. And we believe the tools provided in this book will better equip students to think clearly about such questions. At very least, after taking a course based on this book, you should be better equipped than the average person to think clearly about ethical issues in business, and to offer a reasoned point of view about those issues.

A caution about influencing behavior within a classroom is appropriate here. Part of the hesitation about teaching ethics involves the potential for abuse; should teachers be promoting particular ethical views in the classroom? Many believe that teachers should remain value-neutral in the classroom and not try to impose their own views on students. Part of this concern is that the line between motivating students and manipulating students is a narrow one. There are many ways to influence someone's behavior, including threats, guilt, pressure, bullying, and intimidation. Some of the executives involved in the worst of the recent corporate scandals were very good at using some of these methods to motivate the people who worked for them. Presumably, none of these approaches belong in a university classroom, and certainly not in an ethical classroom.

But the alternative is not to abandon any hopes of contributing to a more ethical business climate. Not all forms of influencing behavior raise concerns about manipulating or coercing behavior. There is a big difference between manipulating someone and persuading someone, between threatening (unethical) and reasoning (more likely ethical). This textbook resolves the tension between influencing behavior and manipulation by emphasizing ethical judgment and ethical decision making. We agree with those who believe that an ethics class should attempt to produce more ethical *behavior* among the students who enroll. But we believe that the only academically and ethically legitimate way to achieve this objective

ethics
Derived from the Greek word *ethos,* which refers to those values, norms, beliefs, and expectations that determine how people within a culture live and act. Ethics steps back from such standards for how people *do* act, and reflects on the standards by which people *should* live and act. At its most basic level, ethics is concerned with how we act and how we live our lives. Ethics involves what is perhaps the most monumental question any human being can ask: How *should* we live? Following from this original Greek usage, ethics can refer to both the standards by which an individual chooses to live her or his own personal life and the standards by which individuals live in community with others (see also *morality*). As a branch of philosophy, ethics is the discipline that systematically studies questions of how we ought to live our lives.

is through careful and reasoned decision making. Our fundamental assumption is that a process of rational decision making, a process that involves careful thought and deliberation, can and will result in behavior that is more reasonable, accountable, and ethical.

Perhaps this is not surprising after all. Consider any course within a business school curriculum. Most people would agree that a management course aims to create better managers. And any finance or accounting course that denied a connection between the course material and financial or accounting practice would likely be counted as a failure. Every course in a business school assumes a connection between what is taught in the classroom and appropriate business behavior. Classes in management, accounting, finance, and marketing all aim to influence students' behavior. We assume that the knowledge and reasoning skills learned in the classroom will lead to better decision making and, therefore, better behavior within a business context. A business ethics class follows this same approach.

While few teachers think that it is our role to *tell* students the right answers and to *proclaim* what students ought to think and how they ought to live, still fewer think that there should be no connection between knowledge and behavior. Our role should not be to preach our own ethical beliefs to a passive audience, but instead to treat students as active learners and to engage them in an active process of thinking, questioning, and deliberating. Taking Socrates as our model, philosophical ethics rejects the view that passive obedience to authority or the simple acceptance of customary norms is an adequate ethical perspective. Teaching ethics must, in this view, challenge students to *think for themselves*.

normative ethics

As a *normative* discipline, ethics deals with norms and standards of appropriate and proper (normal) behavior. Norms establish the guidelines or standards for determining what we should do, how we should act, what type of person we should be. Contrast with *descriptive ethics*.

Business Ethics as Personal Integrity and Social Responsibility

descriptive ethics

As practiced by many social scientists, provides a descriptive and empirical account of those standards that actually guide behavior, as opposed to those standards that should guide behavior. Contrast with *normative ethics*.

At its most basic level, ethics is concerned with deciding how we act and how we live our lives. Ethics involves what is perhaps the most monumental question any human being can ask: *How should we live?* Ethics is, in this sense, *practical,* having to do with how we act, choose, behave, and do things. Philosophers often emphasize that ethics is **normative,** which means that it deals with our reasoning about how we *should* act. Social sciences, such as psychology and sociology, also examine human decision making and actions; but these sciences are **descriptive** rather than normative. When we say that they are descriptive, we refer to the fact that they provide an account of how and why people *do* act the way they do—they describe; as a normative discipline, ethics seeks an account of how and why people *should* act a certain way, rather than how they *do* act. (For an exploration of some of the relevant factors in such a decision, see the Decision Point "Management and Ethics.")

OBJECTIVE

How should we live? This fundamental question of ethics can be interpreted in two ways. "We" can mean each one of us individually, or it might mean all of us collectively. In the first sense, this is a question about how I should live my life, how I should act, what I should do, and what kind of person I should be. This meaning of ethics is based on our value structures, defined by our moral systems;

Imagine that you are examining this chapter's Opening Decision Point in one of your classes on marketing or organizational behavior. What conclusions would you reach about who or what is responsible? What advice would you offer to Wells Fargo or government regulators to prevent a repetition of what happened? After offering your analysis and recommendations, reflect on your own thinking and describe what values underlie those recommendations.

1. What facts would help you make your decision?
2. What aspects of this case raise values that are particular to managers?
3. What stakeholders should be involved in your advice?
4. What values do you rely on in offering your advice?

morality
Sometimes used to denote the phenomena studied by the field of ethics. This text uses *morality* to refer to those aspects of ethics involving personal, individual decision making. "How should I live my life?" or "What type of person ought I be?" are taken to be the basic questions of morality. Morality can be distinguished from questions of *social justice,* which address issues of how communities and social organizations ought to be structured.

personal integrity
The term *integrity* connotes completeness of a being or thing. Personal integrity, therefore, refers to individuals' completeness within themselves, often derived from the consistency or alignment of actions with deeply held beliefs.

and, therefore, it is sometimes referred to as **morality.** It is the aspect of ethics that we refer to by the phrase "**personal integrity.**" There will be many times within a business setting where an individual will need to step back and ask: What should I do? How should I act? Imagine that you were a personal banker working at Wells Fargo and your supervisor directed you to open up a new account for an existing customer without that customer's knowledge. What would you do? If morals refer to the underlying values on which our decisions are based, ethics refers to the applications of those morals to the decisions themselves. So, an individual could have a moral value of honesty, which, when applied to her or his decisions, results in a refusal to process a fraudulent account.

In the second sense, "How should we live?" refers to how we live *together* in a *community.* This is a question about how a society and social institutions, such as corporations, ought to be structured and about how we ought to live together. This area is sometimes referred to as **social ethics,** and it raises questions of justice, public policy, law, civic virtues, organizational structure, and political philosophy. In this sense, business ethics is concerned with how business institutions ought to be structured, about whether they have a responsibility to the greater society (corporate social responsibility, or CSR), and about making decisions that will have an impact on many people other than the individual decision maker. This aspect of business ethics asks us to examine business institutions from a social rather than from an individual perspective. Thus, we might conclude that Wells Fargo's cross-selling practices were unethical. We refer to this broader social aspect of ethics as decision making for *social responsibility.*

In essence, managerial decision making will always involve both of these aspects of ethics. Each decision that a business manager makes involves not only a personal decision but also a decision on behalf of, and in the name of, an organization that exists within a particular social, legal, and political environment. Thus, our book's title makes reference to both aspects of business ethics. Within a business setting, individuals will constantly be asked to make decisions affecting both their own personal integrity and their social responsibilities.

social ethics
The area of ethics that is concerned with how we should live together with others and how social organizations ought to be structured. Social ethics involves questions of political, economic, civic, and cultural norms aimed at promoting human well-being.

Expressed in terms of how we should live, the major reason to study ethics becomes clear. Whether we explicitly *examine* these questions, each and every one of us *answers* them every day through our behaviors in the course of living our lives. Whatever decisions business managers make, they will have taken a stand on ethical issues, at least implicitly. The actions each one of us takes and the lives we lead give very practical and unavoidable answers to fundamental ethical questions. We therefore make a very real choice as to whether we answer them deliberately or unconsciously. Philosophical ethics merely asks us to step back from these implicit everyday decisions to examine and evaluate them. More than 2,000 years ago Socrates gave the philosophical answer to why you should study ethics: "The unexamined life is not worth living."

To distinguish ethics from other practical decisions faced within business, consider two approaches to the Enbridge oil spill scenario in the Decision Point "Ethics after an Oil Spill." This case could just as well be examined in a management, human resource, business law, or organizational behavior class as in an ethics class. The more social-scientific approach common in management or business administration classes would examine the situation and the decision by exploring the factors that led to one decision rather than another or by asking why the manager acted in the way that he did.

norms
Those standards or guidelines that establish appropriate and proper behavior. Norms can be established by such diverse perspectives as economics, etiquette, or ethics.

A second approach to the Enbridge case, from the perspective of ethics, steps back from the facts of the situation to ask what *should* the manager do? What *rights and responsibilities* are involved? What *good* will come from this situation? Is Enbridge being *fair, just, virtuous, kind, loyal, trustworthy?* This normative approach to business is at the center of business ethics. Ethical decision making involves the basic categories, concepts, and language of ethics: *shoulds, oughts, rights* and *responsibilities, goodness, fairness, justice, virtue, kindness, loyalty, trustworthiness,* and *honesty.*

6

OBJECTIVE

To say that ethics is a *normative* discipline is to say that it deals with **norms:** those standards of appropriate and proper (or "normal") behavior. Norms establish the guidelines or standards for determining what we should do, how we should act, and what type of person we should be. Another way of expressing this point is to say that norms appeal to certain values that would be promoted or attained by acting in a certain way. Normative disciplines presuppose some underlying values.

values
Those beliefs that incline us to act or to choose in one way rather than another. We can recognize many different types of values: financial, religious, legal, historical, nutritional, political, scientific, and aesthetic. Ethical values serve the ends of human well-being in impartial, rather than personal or selfish, ways.

But to say that ethics is a normative discipline is not to say that all normative disciplines involve the study or discipline of ethics. After all, business management and business administration are also normative, are they not? Are there not norms for business managers that presuppose a set of business values? One could add accounting and auditing to this list, as well as economics, finance, politics, and the law. Each of these disciplines appeals to a set of values to establish the norms of appropriate behavior within each field.

These examples suggest that there are many different types of norms and values. Returning to our distinction between values and ethics, we can think of **values** as the underlying beliefs that cause us to act or to decide one way rather than another. Thus, the value that I place on an education *leads me to make the decision* to study this evening, rather than to play video games. I believe that education is more

In August 2011, it was reported that an oil pipeline, owned by the energy company Enbridge, had sprung a leak near the tiny, remote town of Wrigley in Canada's Northwest Territories. Not surprisingly, residents were unhappy about the spill, confronting Enbridge with the twin dilemmas of how to clean it up and what to do about the people of Wrigley. More generally, managers at Enbridge had to figure out, in the wake of the leak, what their obligations would be and to whom those obligations were owed.

Wrigley—slightly farther north than Anchorage, Alaska, but much farther inland—in 2011 had a population of about 165. Most community residents are members of the Canadian aboriginal group known as the Dené. Citizens of the town of Wrigley have very low levels of education—most of the population has received no formal education whatsoever. More than half of the community is unemployed. Poverty and access to the basic amenities of modern life are a serious challenge. At present, there isn't even a year-round road into the town. They maintain a traditional lifestyle based on hunting, fishing, and trapping, one that leaves them almost entirely dependent on the health of local forests and waterways. Environmental protection isn't just a question of principle for the people of Wrigley; it's a matter of survival.

After the spill was discovered, it was estimated that 1,500 barrels of oil had leaked, but company officials said luckily none of the oil had reached the nearby Willowlake River. Locals were skeptical, with some claiming that the water now tasted odd. Immediately after the spill was discovered, the company devised a detailed cleanup plan—a document more than 600 pages long. But locals were not impressed and said the complex technical document was too difficult to understand. When the company offered $5,000 so that the community could hire its own experts to evaluate the plan, locals were offended. How could a rich oil company insult them that way, first polluting their land and then offering such a tiny payment?

For Enbridge, the spill was a significant blow to its ongoing effort to maintain a positive image. Just a year earlier, in the summer of 2010, the company had made headlines when one of its pipelines ruptured in Michigan, spilling more than 20,000 barrels of oil into local rivers. At the time, Enbridge was in the midst of trying to win approval for its proposed Northern Gateway Pipeline project and faced serious opposition from environmental groups and aboriginal communities.

The company faced a number of difficult issues in the wake of the Wrigley spill. The first concern, clearly, would be to clean up the spilled oil. Then there was the issue of remediation—the process of attempting to restore the polluted land back to something like its original state. Further, there was the question of whether and how to compensate the local community for the pollution and loss of use of some of their traditional hunting grounds. All of this was set against a backdrop of controversy surrounding the impact that oil pipelines have on the lands and communities through which they run.

1. What do you think motivated the company's decision to offer the community $5,000 to hire its own expert? Why do you think the community was insulted? If you were the company's local manager, what would you have done?

2. What facts would be helpful to you, as an outsider, in evaluating the company's behavior after the spill?

(continued)

(concluded)

3. What values are involved in this situation? How would Enbridge answer that question internally? How would the people of Wrigley answer that question, if asked?

4. Did Enbridge have obligations that went beyond cleaning up the area directly affected by the spill from the company's pipeline? Was it obligated to offer the $5,000? Consider the suggestion made by a member of the community that Enbridge should donate money to build a swimming pool or hockey arena for local kids. Would a donation of this kind help satisfy the company's obligations to the community?

worthy, or valuable, than playing games. I make the decision to spend my money on groceries rather than on a vacation because I value food more than relaxation. A company's core values, for example, are those beliefs that provide the ultimate guide to its decision making.

Understood in this way, many different types of values can be recognized: financial, religious, legal, historical, nutritional, political, scientific, and aesthetic. Individuals can have their own personal values and, importantly, institutions also have values. Talk of a corporation's culture is a way of saying that a corporation has a set of identifiable values that establish the expectations for what is normal within that firm. These norms guide employees, implicitly more often than not, to behave in ways that the firm values and finds worthy. One important implication of this guidance, of course, is that an individual's or a corporation's set of values may lead to either *ethical* or *unethical* results. The corporate culture at Wells Fargo, for example, seems to have been committed to pushing cross-selling as far as possible in pursuit of profit. Values? Yes. Ethical values? No.

One way to distinguish these various types of values is in terms of the ends or goals they serve. Financial values serve monetary ends; religious values serve spiritual ends; aesthetic values serve the ends of beauty; legal values serve law, order, and justice; and so forth. Different types of values are distinguished by the various ends served by those acts and choices. How are ethical values to be distinguished from these other types of values? What ends do ethics serve?

Values, in general, were earlier described as those beliefs that incline us to act or choose in one way rather than another. Consider again the harms attributed to the ethical failures of Wells Fargo. Thousands of innocent people were hurt by the decisions made by some individuals seeking to boost corporate income or their own salaries. This example reveals two important elements of **ethical values.** First, ethical values serve the ends of human well-being. Acts and decisions that seek to promote human welfare are acts and decisions based on ethical values. Controversy may arise when we try to define human well-being, but we can start with some general observations. Happiness certainly is a part of it, as are respect, dignity, integrity, and meaning. Freedom and autonomy surely seem to be necessary elements of human well-being, as are companionship and health.

ethical values
Those properties of life that contribute to human well-being and a life well lived. Ethical values would include such things as happiness, respect, dignity, integrity, freedom, companionship, and health.

Second, the well-being promoted by ethical values is not a personal and selfish well-being. After all, Wells Fargo and all the other corporate scandals we've mentioned resulted from many individuals seeking to promote their own well-being. Ethics requires that the promotion of human well-being be done impartially. From the perspective of ethics, no one person's welfare is more worthy than any other's. Ethical acts and choices should be acceptable and reasonable from all relevant points of view. Thus, we can offer an initial characterization of ethics and ethical values: *Ethical values are those values—those decision-guiding beliefs—that impartially promote human well-being.*

OBJECTIVE

practical reasoning
Involves reasoning about what one ought to do, contrasted with *theoretical reasoning,* which is concerned with what one ought to believe. Ethics is a part of practical reason.

theoretical reasoning
Involves reasoning that is aimed at establishing truth and therefore at what we ought to believe. Contrast with *practical reasoning,* which aims at determining what is reasonable for us to do.

We described ethics as *practical* and *normative,* having to do with our actions, choices, decisions, and *reasoning* about how we should act. Ethics is therefore a vital element of practical reasoning—reasoning about what we should do—and is distinguished from theoretical reasoning, which is reasoning about what we should *believe.* This book's perspective on ethical decision making is squarely within this understanding of ethics' role as a part of practical reason.

Thinking of ethics as a type of practical reason helps us be clear about what we an expect of ethics. Many think that ethics should be able to prove its conclusions, and it can be tempting to believe that if you cannot do that, then there can be no way to establish or justify ethical judgments. If one cannot "prove" what is right or wrong, then why bother doing ethics? Aristotle used the distinction between practical reasoning and theoretical reasoning to show the mistake in this way of thinking.

Theoretical reason is the pursuit of truth, which is the highest standard for what we should believe. According to this tradition, science is the great arbiter of truth. Science provides the methods and procedures for determining what is true, and it does that by establishing what counts as a "proof" in science. Thus, the scientific method can be thought of as the answer to the fundamental questions of theoretical reason: What should we believe? So the question arises, is there a comparable methodology or procedure for deciding what we should do and how we should act?

The simple answer is that there is no single methodology that can in every situation provide one clear and unequivocal answer to that question. But there are guidelines that can provide direction and criteria for decisions that are more or less reasonable and responsible. The goal of practical reason is not to establish what is true and what you should believe, but what is reasonable to do. We suggest that the traditions and theories of philosophical ethics can be thought of as contributing to reasonable decision making in just this way. Over thousands of years of thinking about the fundamental questions of how human beings should live, philosophers have developed and refined a variety of approaches to ethical questions. These traditions, or what are often referred to as ethical theories, explain and defend various norms, standards, values, and principles that contribute to responsible ethical decision making. Ethical theories are patterns of thinking, or methodologies, to help us decide what is reasonable to do.

The following chapter will introduce a model for making ethically responsible decisions. This can be considered as a model of practical reasoning in the sense that, if you walk through these steps in making a decision about what to do, you

As of April 2019, Wells Fargo had been penalized more than $1.5 billion for its actions during this scandal by state and federal governments. In addition, the company had paid more than $600 million to settle various lawsuits resulting from the scandal. As further punishment, the U.S. Federal Reserve Bank prohibited Wells Fargo from expanding its banking business in the United States until such time that it could demonstrate that it had significantly changed the culture in ways that would prevent these frauds from happening again. As of April 2019, that prohibition had still not been lifted.

In March 2019, *The New York Times* published a follow-up story to the Wells Fargo case that suggested that challenges remain. This article pointed out that while senior executives were claiming that abuses have been addressed and the Wells Fargo culture had changed, interviews with employees across the United States described a corporate culture in which many of the high-pressure sales practices that led to the scandal continued.

Employees described a gap between corporate words and deeds of actual practice. While senior executives claimed that safeguards were in place to prevent a reoccurrence of past practices, employees at local branch offices described a culture where aggressive sales targets continued in place. Employees were quoted as describing corporate claims of improvement as "superficial" and "doublespeak," aimed at creating good public relations but not actually changing much in the local offices.

As an example, corporate executives pointed out that Wells Fargo had greatly reduced the use of bonuses tied to sales targets to compensate employees. This change in the incentive system was aimed at reducing the pressure on employees to sell more products. Yet, employees claimed that one result of this was a loss of income for employees, while corresponding sales targets were kept steady, or in some cases even increased. It was not lost on employees that during this same period, Wells Fargo CEO Timothy Sloan received $17 million in compensation, an increase of 36% over the previous year.

This apparent disconnect between corporate statements and the perceived reality at branch offices has been an ongoing challenge for Wells Fargo. Reflect back to the explanation offered by former CEO John Stumpf when the scandal first became public. Stumpf attributed responsibility to dishonest individuals while denying any corporate or systemic problems. Stumpf's explanation for how the fraud became so widespread was to suggest that employees were simply learning from each other by word of mouth.

This Wells Fargo case provides a good opportunity to reflect on the various levels at which ethical analysis must take place. There are decisions being made by individuals in various roles, from entry-level tellers, to mid-level personal bankers, loan officers, and branch managers, to senior executives. Yet, there is also a corporate and organizational reality that significantly affects the decisions that individuals make. While often subtle, this corporate culture plays a powerful role in decision making, and figuring out the interaction between individual decisions and corporate culture is an important element of business ethics. (Chapter 4 will examine the topic of corporate culture in detail.)

Reflect on two extreme interpretations of what happened at Wells Fargo. On one hand, as Stumpf's initial response seemed to suggest, we had a situation in which thousands of "dishonest" individuals, relying on word of mouth, chose to make unethical decisions and defraud thousands of customers. Somehow the organization was unable to prevent this from happening and, as a result, the organization itself became corrupted by the actions of its individual members. Thus, the organization's remaining responsibility is to create structures and policies to prevent dishonest people from acting on their unethical motivations.

On the other hand, as the employees interviewed by *The New York Times* seemed to suggest, individuals who are basically decent and honest found themselves in an organization that rewarded malfeasance and discouraged honesty. It established policies and practices that created an environment in which corruption flourished. Otherwise good people ended up committing unethical acts because this is what the organization expected and rewarded.

Return to the discussion questions at the end of the opening case and consider where you would assign responsibility in the Wells Fargo case. Who or what is most at fault? What most needs to change in order to prevent a reoccurrence?

would certainly be making a decision grounded in sound reasoning. You will not be able to "prove" that your judgment is true in the way that science can establish truth, but a judgment that results from a careful step-by-step process will be more reasonable than one that does not. The decision-making model outlined in the following chapter offers one such process. The ethical traditions and theories that we describe in Chapter 3 will help flesh out and elaborate on this decision procedure. Other approaches are possible, and this approach will not guarantee one single and absolute answer to every decision. But this is a helpful beginning in the development of responsible, reasonable, and ethical decision making.

Questions, Projects, and Exercises

1. Questions of ethics and values also arise frequently in a variety of university courses—particularly in business and professional schools. Are there other courses in your school's curriculum that talk about "the right thing to do," without necessarily using words such as *ethics* or *social responsibility?* How do courses in economics and finance involved value dimensions?

2. Why might legal rules be insufficient for fulfilling one's ethical responsibilities? Can you think of cases in which a businessperson has done something that is legally permitted but ethically wrong? What about the opposite—are there situations in which a businessperson might have acted in a way that was legally wrong but ethically right?

3. What might be some benefits and costs of acting unethically in business? Distinguish between benefits and harms to the individual and benefits and harms to the firm.

4. Review the distinction between personal morality and matters of social ethics. Can you think of cases in which some decisions would be valuable as a matter of social policy but bad as a matter of personal ethics? Something good as a matter of personal ethics and bad as a matter of social policy?

5. As described in this chapter, the Americans with Disabilities Act requires firms to make reasonable accommodations for employees with disabilities. Consider such conditions as obesity, depression, dyslexia, arthritis, hearing loss, high blood pressure, facial scars, mood disorders, allergies, attention deficit disorders, post-traumatic stress syndrome, and the fear of heights. Imagine that you are a human resource manager and an employee asks that accommodations be made for these conditions. Under what circumstances might these conditions be serious enough impairments to deserve legal protection? What factors would you consider in answering this question? After making these decisions, reflect on whether your decision was more a legal or ethical decision.

6. Do an internet search for recent news stories about oil spills. Do any of those stories report behaviors that seem especially wise or unwise on the part of the oil companies involved? Do you think that controversies over big pipeline projects like the Keystone pipeline alter how people evaluate the ethics of oil-spill cleanups?

7. Construct a list of all the people who were adversely affected by the Wells Fargo case. Who, among these people, would you say had their rights violated? What responsibilities, if any, did Wells Fargo have to each of these constituencies?

8. Do "ethical" behaviors need to be grounded in ethical values in order to be considered ethically *good?* If a business performs a socially beneficial act in order to receive good publicity, or if it creates an ethical culture as a business strategy, has the business acted in a less-than-ethically praiseworthy way? Is thinking of ethics as "good for business" misleading or just practical?

9. During the recession of 2008–2009, many reputable companies suffered bankruptcies while others struggled to survive. Of those that did remain, some chose to reduce the size of their workforces significantly. Imagine yourself helping run a company during such a recession. Imagine the company that has been doing fairly well, posting profits every quarter and showing a sustainable growth expectation for the future; however, the general uneasiness in the market has caused the company's stock price to fall. In response to this problem, the CEO decides to lay off some of her employees, hoping to cut costs and to improve the bottom line. This action raises investor confidence and, consequently, the stock price goes up. What is your impression of the CEO's decision? Was there any kind of ethical lapse in laying off the employees, or was it a practical decision necessary for the survival of the company?

10. Every year, *Ethisphere Magazine* publishes a list of the world's most ethical companies. Go to its website and find and evaluate its rating methodology and criteria. Then engage in an assessment (that is, provide suggestions for any modifications you might make for a more or less comprehensive list, and so on).

Key Terms

After reading this chapter, you should have a clear understanding of the following key terms. For a complete definition, please see the Glossary.

descriptive ethics, *p. 20*	norms, *p. 22*	separation thesis, *p. 9*
ethical values, *p. 24*	personal integrity, *p. 21*	social ethics, *p. 21*
ethics, *p. 19*	practical reasoning, *p. 25*	stakeholder, *p. 12*
morality, *p. 21*	psychological egoism, *p. 11*	theoretical reasoning, *p. 25*
normative ethics, *p. 20*	risk assessment, *p. 18*	values, *p. 22*

Endnotes

1. Decision points appear throughout each chapter in the text. These challenges are designed to introduce the concepts discussed in each chapter by raising the ethical issues in real-life cases. Discussion of these cases should introduce the ethical issues and various perspectives that might be taken on each.

2. Source: Testimony of Wells Fargo John Stumpf in front of the Senate Banking Committee, September 20, 2016.

3. This case was developed from E. Scott Reckard, "Wells Fargo's Pressure-Cooker Sales Culture Comes at a Cost," *Los Angeles Times* (December 21, 2013), www.latimes.com/business/la-fi-wells-fargo-sale-pressure-20131222-story.html; Emily Flitter and Stacy Cowley, "Wells Fargo Says Its Culture Has Changed. Some Employees Disagree" (March 9, 2019), www.nytimes.com/2019/03/09/business/wells-fargo-sales-culture.html?action=click&module=Top%20Stories&pgtype=Homepage.

4. A critique of the separation thesis can be found in R. Edward Freeman and Jared D. Harris, "The Impossibility of the Separation Thesis, "*Business Ethics Quarterly* 18, no. 4 (October 2008), pp. 541–48. A thorough analysis of the nuances involved in the separation thesis can be found in J. Sandberg, "Understanding the Separation Thesis," *Business Ethics Quarterly* 18, no. 2 (2008), pp. 213–32.

5. Source: Milton Friedman, "The Social Responsibility of Business Is to Increase Its Profits," *The New York Times Magazine* (September 13, 1970)

6. The full quote from Smith is: *Every individual . . . neither intends to promote the public interest, nor knows how much he is promoting it . . . he intends only his own security; and by directing that industry in such a manner as its produce may be of the greatest value, he intends only his own gain, and he is in this, as in many other cases, led by an invisible hand to promote an end which was no part of his intention.* Adam Smith, *An Inquiry into the Nature and Causes of The Wealth Of Nations,* Book 4, ch. 2, p. 456, para. 9 (1776).

7. Financial Crisis Inquiry Commission, *The Financial Crisis Inquiry Report: Final Report of the National Commission on the Causes of the Financial and Economic Crisis in the United States* (Washington, D.C.: Government Printing Office, January 25, 2011). Canadian data are taken fromhttps://www150.statcan.gc.ca/n1/pub/75-001-x/2009112/article/11048-eng.htm.

8. Source: Whole Foods Market IP, LLP, "Declaration of Independence," www.wholefoodsmarket.com/company/declaration.php (accessed January 15, 2012). See also Knowledge @ Wharton, "Building Companies That Leave the World a Better Place," February 28, 2007, p. 2, excerpting R. Sisodia, J. Sheth, and D. Wolfe, *Firms of Endearment: How World-Class Companies Profit from Passion and Purpose* (Philadelphia, PA: Wharton Business School Publishing, 2007), ch. 6.

9. Committee of Sponsoring Organizations (COSO) of the Treadway Commission, "Executive Summary," *Enterprise Risk Management–Integrated Framework,* September 2004, p. 2.

10. See "Wrigley Residents Voice Pipeline Spill Concerns," *CBC News* (August 12, 2011), www.cbc.ca/news/canada/north/story/2011/08/11/nwt-wrigley-enbridgemeeting.html (accessed July 19, 2012).

Chapter

2

Ethical Decision Making: Personal and Professional Contexts

It is very important to know who you are. To make decisions. To show who you are.

Malala Yousafzai

On an important decision one rarely has 100% of the information needed for a good decision no matter how much one spends or how long one waits. And, if one waits too long, he has a different problem and has to start all over. This is the terrible dilemma of the hesitant decision maker.

Robert Greenleaf

There are two kinds of people, those who do the work and those who take the credit. Try to be in the first group; there is less competition there.

Indira Gandhi

You work for a company that is one of the major health care providers in the region. The company operates a large hospital and numerous medical offices and clinics throughout the area. Your own background is in accounting and you have worked on the business side of health care for fifteen years.[1]

Like many other industries, health care is going through a period of significant consolidation, driven largely by increasing specialization within medicine and ever-increasing costs, especially of diagnostic and treatment technologies. Given your background in accounting, you fully appreciate the economic argument for consolidation in this field. You have firsthand experience with major cost savings created by efficiencies in patient record keeping, scheduling, and, especially, insurance administration and reimbursement. However, you also believe that consolidation is in the patient's best interests as well. Once integrated into a regional medical system, patients will have greater access to specialized care and treatment, while economic efficiencies help keep costs low as well.

Two years ago, as part of its strategic plan, your company acquired another smaller health care company that operated a number of clinics in rural towns across the region. In most cases, these clinics are the only health care provider in town. A typical clinic is staffed full time by several clerical and administrative workers and several nurses with advanced diagnostic training and a license to prescribe medication. A physician is on-site several days each week. Much of the day-to-day work at the clinics involves routine medical procedures: diagnosing and treating minor illnesses, advising on wellness care, and providing routine checkups and examinations. More serious or complicated cases are scheduled when the physician is on-site, or referred to specialists at larger health care facilities.

Your own work during most of this period has been to help these individual clinics integrate their own accounting procedures and administrative operations into your company's system. You have spent time working and getting to know the employees at each of these clinics. At first, you sensed that they perceived you as an outsider who posed some threat to local operations. Employees understood that, as often occurs in many acquisitions, there was a chance that some people might lose their jobs and even some clinics might close. Nevertheless, they soon realized that your work was aimed to help them integrate their operations into your company's system, and over time you succeeded in creating relationships of trust and mutual respect with many of the employees.

More recently, however, you have been asked to assist senior management in analyzing the longer-term financial viability of each individual clinic. Based on previous acquisitions and the company's strategic plan, you believe that the least profitable of these smaller clinics will be closed and the more profitable ones will expand. In all cases, much of the administrative side of the clinics—record-keeping, scheduling, and insurance processing—will be consolidated with the central office. All of the reasons that explain the move towards consolidation in general make equal sense on the local level. Economic and operational efficiencies make a strong case for following this strategy. You know that if this consolidation happens, the health care professionals—all of the nurses, physician assistants, and the physicians—will be offered positions at other clinics, but most of the other employees will lose their jobs.

As a result of this change in assignment, you have noticed that the nature of your relationship with the employees at the clinics has begun to change as well. Part of this, no doubt, stems from your own hesitance. Knowing that some people will lose their jobs as a result of your recommendations, you have tried to remain somewhat aloof, have been reluctant to join in conversations, and have declined invitations to lunch. The information that you are requesting and the questions you are asking are also beginning to raise suspicions among employees.

After a recent visit to one clinic, you receive an email from the office receptionist. She begins by telling you that based on your previous work relationship, she thinks that she can trust and confide in you. She then reminds you how important the clinic is for the local town. She points out that the majority of the cases they treat involve children and the elderly, and that they know most of their patients on a first-name basis. The clinic provides the type of personalized health care that is increasingly unusual in a large system. Finally, she tells you that the office is full of rumors that the clinic is about to be closed. She explains that there are few jobs in this small rural community and that she is worried about losing her job. She then tells you that she knows of another job, but with lower pay and fewer benefits than her present job. She asks you directly if the clinic is likely to be closed. She concludes by asking: "Am I about to lose my job?" "Should I pursue this other job?"

1. How would you answer?

Chapter Objectives

After reading this chapter, you will be able to:

1. Describe a process for ethically responsible decision making.
2. Apply this model to ethical decision points.
3. Explain the reasons why "good" people might engage in unethical behavior.
4. Explore the impact of managerial roles on the nature of our decision making.

Introduction

Chapter 1 introduced our approach to business ethics as a form of practical reasoning, a process for decision making in business. Putting ethics into practice requires not simply decision making, but *accountable* decision making. Chapter 1 also suggested that, even if a person does not consciously think about a decision, her or his own actions will involve making a choice and taking a stand. Like the accountant in the opening decision point, you will not be able to avoid making a decision, whether by act or omission. Whatever you do—or do not do—in answering the employee's question, you will have made a choice that will be evaluated in ethical terms and have ethical implications.

The previous chapter provided a general context for thinking about business ethics; in the current chapter, we begin to bring this topic to a more practical level by examining ethical decision making as it might occur in everyday business situations. We will examine various elements involved in individual decision making and apply those concepts to the decisions individuals make every day in business. This chapter also examines various ways in which ethical decision making can go wrong, as well as the ways in which business leaders can model the most effective ethical decision making.

A Decision-Making Process for Ethics

OBJECTIVE

ethical decision-making process
Requires a persuasive and rational justification for a decision. Rational justifications are developed through a logical process of decision making that gives proper attention to such things as facts, alternative perspectives, consequences to all stakeholders, and ethical principles.

Let us begin to develop an initial sketch of an **ethical decision-making process** by considering some possible responses to the email described at the end of the opening discussion case. You might first reflect on the fact that you honestly do not know what will happen to this particular clinic. While your analysis will heavily influence the decision, you are not the decision maker and your analysis is not yet complete. Your initial thought is to reply that you don't know and perhaps explain further that it is not your decision. You also do not know this woman very well and you are uncomfortable giving anyone, much less just an acquaintance, advice about leaving a job.

But you hesitate and put off making any reply. Your immediate reaction was to feel uncomfortable being in this position, and you begin to explore that feeling. What makes you uncomfortable? Partially, it is because you are being asked to reveal information that is not your responsibility to disclose. You also are sensitive to the obvious fear and worry being expressed by this woman. But you are also uncomfortable because, in fact, you know that your analysis likely will recommend closing the clinic and that this will result in exactly the harms that the person fears. And you recognize that these harms will result from your own decisions and recommendations.

As you hesitate, you also reflect on what the employee has said. The clinic does serve an important function in a small town, and you wonder if your financial analysis has given full weight to those facts. While you have been asked to provide a financial analysis, you wonder if your role should include asking wider social questions. But how could you account for that in your analysis? Should you account for those facts in what was intended to be only a standard financial analysis?

Stepping back from this case, we should recognize that an important **first step** in making any responsible decision is to *determine the facts* of the situation. Making an honest effort to understand the situation, to distinguish facts from mere opinion, is essential. Sometimes, what appears to be a disagreement of ethics might turn out to be a disagreement about the facts. For example, one person might believe that losing the clinic is unethical because it will deprive people of health care. Another person will believe that the same act is ethically justified because, in fact, he or she knows about alternative health care arrangements that will provide improved care.

But determining the facts is not as simple as it might seem. Is it a fact that your report will recommend closure? In one sense, your answer is *no* because the report is yet to be written so right now it is not a fact. Yet, it would be a little disingenuous to say that you do not know. You know that your company is planning on closing several clinics and that senior executives have always followed your recommendations and at this point you think that you will recommend closure.

You also believe that what the employee has said about job prospects in that town is not fully correct. While there may not be many jobs with comparable salary and benefits, you do know that the labor market is not as bleak as the employee believes. But this might be easy for you to believe because of your own job skills and employability. You wonder how a woman working in a small town with few transferable skills might perceive the situation. This recognition suggests that beyond the facts, **perceptual differences** surrounding how individuals experience and understand situations can explain many ethical disagreements. A woman supporting a family on her salary will perceive the loss of a job very differently than a corporate executive with many other job prospects. Knowing the facts and carefully reviewing the circumstances can go a long way toward resolving disagreements and setting the foundation for a responsible decision.

What facts would be useful to know before making a decision? Would you be more inclined to answer the email if you knew that this clinic will remain open? Suppose you had been explicitly told not to disclose any information to employees? Suppose you had been told to use your own judgment? Imagine that you know that your company has plans to introduce a new telemedicine system in areas where clinics are closed to allow patients to access diagnostic help and treatments online using their computers or smart phones?

An ethical judgment made in light of a diligent determination of the facts is a more reasonable ethical judgment than one made without regard for the facts. A person who acts in a way that is based on a careful consideration of the facts has acted in a more ethically responsible way than a person who acts without deliberation. Given the general importance of determining the facts, there is a role for science (and critical thinking) in any study of ethics. The sciences, and perhaps especially the social sciences, can help us determine the facts surrounding our decisions. Determining the facts will often involve making predictions about the future. For example, what will happen to health care costs for patients in rural communities after a clinic closes? Answering this question about likely future outcomes—determining the facts—will involve applying some basic principles of economics.

For another business example, consider what facts might be relevant for making a decision regarding child labor. Consider how the social sciences of anthropology and economics, for example, might help us understand the facts surrounding employing children in the workplace within a foreign country. Applying this strategy to a business operation would encourage business decision makers to seek out perhaps alternative or somewhat less-traditional methods of gathering facts to ensure that she or he has compiled all of the necessary data in processing the most ethical decision.

A **second step** in responsible ethical decision making requires the ability to recognize a decision or issue as an ethical decision or ethical issue. *Identifying the*

perceptual differences
Psychologists and philosophers have long recognized that individuals cannot perceive the world independently of their own conceptual framework. Experiences are mediated by and interpreted through our own understanding and concepts. Thus, ethical disagreements can depend as much on a person's conceptual framework as on the facts of the situation. Unpacking our own and others' conceptual schema plays an important role in making ethically responsible decisions.

ethical issues involved is the next step in making responsible decisions. It is easy to be led astray by a failure to recognize that there is an ethical component to some decisions. (Certainly, the first and second steps might arise in reverse order, depending on the circumstances. At times, you have a selection of facts that give rise to a particular ethical dilemma or issue. However, just as likely, there may also be times when you are presented with an issue from the start, say, when a colleague asks you for guidance with a challenging ethical predicament. The issue identification, therefore, becomes the first step, while fact gathering is a necessary second step.)

In this case, a number of ethical issues are immediately apparent. First, you do have a responsibility to your employer to keep confidential information private. Your feelings of empathy and compassion for the employees are also ethical issues that should be acknowledged. The harms of losing one's job, or the social harms to a small community in losing a health care clinic, are other ethical issues. Being truthful and avoiding deception are ethical values that also come into play in deciding how to reply to the email.

Perhaps nowhere in business will the challenge of identifying ethical issues be more important than in situations where there is a temptation to describe a decision simply as a "business" or "financial" decision. In many situations, what appears to be an ethical issue for one person will be perceived as simply a financial decision by others. In a move that is connected to the separation thesis discussed in Chapter 1, there is a common tendency to think that business decisions are immune from ethical criticism if they are made on economic or financial grounds. This can be especially prevalent when we are justifying our decisions to ourselves.

Consider how easy it was to dismiss accounting for the social impact of closing the clinic by claiming that you are conducting "only" a standard financial analysis. If you can categorize a decision as an accounting or economic decision, then it is easy to think that you no longer need to worry about the ethics involved. There is another misleading tendency, also sometimes associated with the separation thesis, that ethical concerns can be discounted because that are only "feelings" or "emotions." So, for example, it would not be uncommon for someone to react to the clinic case by assuming that the decision should be based on the "hard facts" of accounting and economics, rather than the "soft feelings" of empathy and compassion.

But how does one determine that a question raises an ethical issue? When does a *business* decision become an *ethical* decision? First, of course, we need to recognize that "business" or "economic" decisions and ethical decisions are not mutually exclusive. Just because a decision is made on economic grounds does not mean that it does not involve ethical considerations as well. One is not excused from ethical responsibility just because a decision is made to further profit or economic efficiency. Beyond financial considerations, we also need to ask how our decisions will impact the well-being of the people involved—what are the implications for stakeholders? Ultimately, how our decisions impact the well-being of others is what brings a decision into the realm of ethics. Being sensitive to ethical issues is a vital characteristic that needs to be cultivated in ethically responsible people.

Consider how ethics and economics intersect in the decision, announced in 2016 by Adidas AG, to resume manufacturing in Germany. Adidas is a German company that makes shoes and sportswear, and for decades it had conducted its manufacturing activities primarily in developing countries. The decision by Adidas to "return" to Germany might have been cause for celebration among Germans looking for jobs, but there was a catch: The shoes Adidas would be making in Germany would be made by robots. On one hand, a decision regarding what technology to use in manufacturing seems like a purely technical question. And the question of *where* to manufacture seems like a simple question of operational efficiency. But both questions have clear ethical implications. Having shoes made by robots means fewer jobs for people. Having them made in Germany (rather than, say, in Indonesia) means at least some jobs for Germans. But it means no (new) jobs for Indonesians, who, on average, are much poorer—and hence need jobs much more desperately—than Germans. Whether this decision is better, or worse, than a different decision is not obvious, but what *should* be obvious is that it is a decision with a significant ethical dimension.

A fundamental commitment of ethics lies with the *impartial* promotion of human well-being. An ethically responsible person is concerned not only with her own well-being, or the well-being of only her friends or family, but with the well-being of everyone involved. The reaction of empathy and compassion is not some random emotion or feeling, but a recognition that, just like oneself, other individuals can be hurt and harmed. To the degree that a decision affects the well-being—the happiness, health, dignity, integrity, freedom, respect—of all the people involved, it is an ethically responsible decision. To the degree that it ignores or disregards the well-being of others, it is an ethically irresponsible decision. In the end, it is almost impossible to conceive of any major business decision that does not have some impact on the well-being of others. Accordingly, one could argue that practically all of our business decisions have ethical implications.

In many business contexts, one can easily become so involved in the technical aspects of decisions that one loses sight of the ethical aspects. Perhaps the Adidas board did not contemplate the differential impact its decision would have on various employees and potential employees. Consider again the situation where the social costs of closing a clinic are ignored when conducting a financial analysis. Some writers have called this inability to recognize ethical issues **normative myopia,** or shortsightedness about values.[2] Normative myopia is a problem not only in business, of course, but in a business context people may be especially likely to focus on the technical aspects of the task at hand, and thus fail to recognize the ethical aspect. (See the Reality Check "Is There an Ethics of Writing Papers?")

Business scholars Chugh and Bazerman similarly warn of **inattentional blindness,** which they suggest results from focusing on too narrow a range of questions.[3] If we happen to focus on—or if we are told specifically to pay attention to—only one particular element of a decision or event, we are likely to miss many of the surrounding details, no matter how obvious. These focusing failures then result in a moment when we ask ourselves, "How could I have missed that?" You may recall having a conversation with someone while driving and perhaps missing a highway turn-off because your "mind was elsewhere."

normative myopia
The tendency to ignore, or the lack of the ability to recognize, ethical issues in decision making.

inattentional blindness
If we happen to focus on or are told specifically to pay attention to a particular element of a decision or event, we are likely to miss all of the surrounding details, no matter how obvious.

Reality Check *Is There an Ethics of Writing Papers?*

Perhaps the most common ethical issue that students and teachers confront involves plagiarism. In fact, a 2010 survey of 43,000 high school students showed that one student in three admitted to using the Internet to plagiarize an assignment.* From the academic perspective, there is no more serious offense than plagiarizing the work of others. Yet, many students seem honestly surprised to learn that what they believed was research is interpreted as unethical behavior by their teachers.[†]

Many students rely on internet sources while writing their school papers. It is all too easy to cut and paste sections of an online source into one's own writing assignment and to neglect to put it inside quotation marks and cite a source. On one particular website, users can post a question that they are struggling with and identify the amount they are willing to pay for an answer. "Tutors" then write a custom lesson that answers the questions posted in order to receive payment. The website claims it does not help the student cheat; instead, it is simply offering an online tutoring service. It contends that all users, both students and tutors, must agree to the website's academic honesty policy in order to use the website's services.

No doubt, some of this is intentional cheating, such as when a student downloads or purchases an entire paper or answer from a "tutor" or other internet source. But, in many cases, students seem honestly confused that their teacher treats an unattributed cut-and-pasted passage as cheating. Most teachers can recall situations in which they have had to explain to a student why this practice is unethical.

Such cases are not rare. People often make bad ethical decisions because they fail to understand that there is an ethical issue involved. Typically, they have not thought through the implications of their decision and have not stepped back from their situation to reflect on their choice and to consider their decision from other points of view. Often, they are simply too involved in the immediate situation to think about such things. This is a good example of normative myopia and inattentional blindness.

*"Installment 2: The Ethics of American Youth: 2010," Josephson Institute: Center for Youth Studies (February 10, 2011), http://charactercounts.org/programs/reportcard/2010/installment02_report-card_honesty-integrity.html (accessed July 17, 2012).

†For just one website of many that compiles definitions of violations of academic integrity, as well as strategies to maintain academic integrity, see http://academicintegrity.depaul.edu.

The problem is that when we focus on the wrong thing, or fail to focus, we may fail to see key information that will lead us to success or prevent unethical behavior; we may fail to use the information because we do not know it is relevant; or we may be aware, but we might fail to contribute it to the group. Any of these breakdowns can have disastrous or dangerous consequences. (For more about failures to see relevant information, see the Reality Check "Fooling Ourselves.")

Chugh and Bazerman identify a third means by which ethical issues might go unnoticed: **change blindness.** This omission occurs when decision makers fail to notice gradual changes over time. They offer the example of the Arthur Andersen auditors who did not notice how low Enron had fallen in terms of its unethical decisions. One of the means by which to protect against these decision risks is to ensure that decision makers seek input from others in their decision processes. The researchers report that group input—*any* other input—is almost always a positive factor because individuals collectively can possess and utilize more information than any single person.

The **third step** involved in ethical decision making involves one of its more important elements. Responsible decision making expects us to *identify and to consider all of the people affected by a decision, the people often called stakeholders.*

change blindness
A decision-making omission that occurs when decision makers fail to notice gradual changes over time.

Reality Check *Fooling Ourselves*

"People view themselves as more ethical, fair, and objective than others, yet often act against their moral compass."

Sezer, Gino, and Bazerman, "Ethical Blind Spots"*

The key factors that these authors say contribute to ethical blind spots include:

- Implicit biases. ("Individuals typically fail to recognize the harm that implicit favoritism of in-group members causes to members of social out-groups.")

- Temporal distance. (We tend to believe that we will follow our moral compasses "when the time comes," but when the time actually comes, we become more likely to go with our immediate wants.)

- Failure to notice others' unethical behavior. (We are less likely to condemn other people's ethical behavior when we benefit from it, or when we have encouraged it.)

*O. Sezer, F. Gino, and M. H. Bazerman, "Ethical Blind Spots: Explaining Unintentional Unethical Behavior," *Current Opinion in Psychology* 6 (2015), pp. 77–81.

"Stakeholders," in this general sense, include all of the groups and/or individuals affected by a decision, policy, or operation of a firm or individual (see Figure 2.1). Examining issues from a variety of perspectives other than one's own helps make one's decisions more reasonable, accountable, and responsible. And, to the contrary, thinking and reasoning from a narrow and personal point of view virtually guarantees that we will not fully understand the situation. Making decisions from a narrow and personal point of view likewise ensures that we are liable to make a decision that does not give due consideration to other persons and perspectives.

One helpful exercise for considering the effects of a decision on others is to shift one's role. Rather than being in the position of the person who recommends a clinic closing, what would you think of this case if you were the person who

FIGURE 2.1
Stakeholder Map

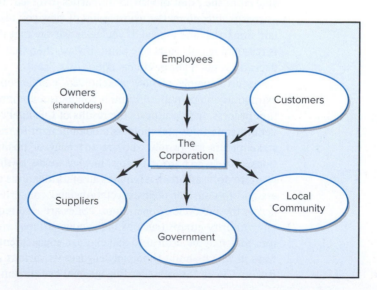

Reality Check *Stakeholder Engagement at Johnson Matthey*

The website for British chemicals company Johnson Matthey gives a detailed analysis of who its stakeholders are and the methods the company uses to engage them.

In other words, the company recognizes that it is not enough, ethically, to know who your stakeholders are; you need to engage them in discussion. The company also recognizes that different stakeholders need to be engaged in different ways.

The following table shows the ways in which Johnson Matthey engages just a few of its key stakeholders:

Stakeholder Engagement at Johnson Matthey

Stakeholder*	Ongoing Dialogue	Surveys/ Questionnaires	Regular Meetings	Reviews	Audits	Integrated Annual Report
Employees	Yes	Yes	Yes	Yes		Yes
Shareholders	Yes	Yes	Yes			Yes
Customers	Yes	Yes	Yes		Yes	Yes
Regulatory Bodies	Yes					Yes

*Johnson Matthey also lists, among its stakeholders, institutional investors/analysts, suppliers, NGOs, trade associations, ethical investment markets, and voluntary schemes.

Source: Johnson Matthey, "Our Stakeholders," www.matthey.com/sustainability/sustainability-governance/stakeholders.

stands to lose her job or of the person likely to lose access to a local health care provider? How does that affect your thinking? What would your judgment be if you were the person who was asked for advice? A long tradition in philosophical ethics argues that a key test of ethical legitimacy is whether a decision would be acceptable from the point of view of all parties involved. If you could accept a decision as reasonable, no matter whose point of view you take, that decision is likely to be fair, impartial, and ethical. If you acknowledge that the decision to close the clinic is reasonable only from one point of view, then that is a strong indication that the decision is not a fair or ethical one.

As an example of how stakeholders can be considered, global mining and extraction company BHP Billiton conducts a comprehensive stakeholder exploration process and then posts the results of this analysis on the internet in order to demonstrate to its stakeholders a commitment to transparency.[4] It defines its key stakeholders as "people who are adversely or positively impacted by our operations, those who have an interest in what we do, or those who have an influence on what we do"[5]; and then it requires all of its locations to identify their key stakeholders and to consider their expectations and concerns for all operational activities across the life cycle of operations. "Sites are also required to specifically consider any minority groups (such as indigenous groups) and any social and cultural factors that may be critical to stakeholder engagement."[6] You can see the range of ways in which another company engages its various stakeholders by looking at the Reality Check "Stakeholder Engagement at Johnson Matthey."

Think back to the Opening Decision Point in Chapter 1. It seems unlikely that the employees involved in the fraud ever seriously considered how their actions would impact their customers.

Consider the decisions made at every level of Wells Fargo, from the board of directors, to the CEO and other senior executives, to mid-level managers and branch managers, to front-line employees. At each level, consider the range of stakeholders that likely were considered, and then imagine the entire range of stakeholders that should have been considered. Who were the stakeholders who were affected by the shift from a fiduciary business model to a transaction model? Which stakeholders were affected by the compensation model that rewarded high rates of cross-selling? Which stakeholders have been affected by the resultant scandal?

Consider also Enbridge's decisions after the oil spill in Wrigley as described in the Decision Point in Chapter 1. As a publicly traded company, Enbridge has a financial obligation to its shareholders. Considering only this obligation might lead to a decision to satisfy only the minimum legal requirements for cleaning up the spill site to avoid additional costs that would negatively affect profits. However, a decision that considers only the shareholders' point of view would not be a responsible decision. The spill also affected the residents of Wrigley, who are heavily dependent on the forests and waterways in the area for their livelihood and ways of life. The Reality Check "Stakeholder Engagement at Johnson Matthey" further explores stakeholder implications.

The fact that many decisions will involve the interests of multiple stakeholders also helps us understand a major challenge to ethical decision making. The very fact that there are many perspectives and interests at stake means that ethical decisions often involve conflicts and dilemmas. Each alternative will impose costs on some stakeholders and offer benefits to others. Making a decision that benefits one group often means that other stakeholders will be denied benefits. Economists define costs in terms of opportunities forgone, and in this way every decision we make imposes costs in that every decision closes out some opportunities while opening others. Ethics demands that we consider who bears the costs, who gets the benefits, and how the costs are distributed.

Once we have examined the facts, identified the ethical issues involved, and identified the stakeholders, we turn to a **fourth step** and *consider the available alternatives*. What options exist? Sometimes we fall into a decision by failing to consider a range of alternatives, and this can be a failure of imagination. Creativity in identifying ethical options—also called moral imagination—is one element that distinguishes good people who make ethically responsible decisions from good people who do not.[7] It is important not only to consider the obvious options with regard to a particular dilemma, but also the much subtler ones that might not be evident at first glance.

Consider again the opening discussion case. One person might believe that the only options are a truthful answer (that the clinic is very likely to be closed and

moral imagination
When one is facing an ethical decision, the ability to envision various alternative choices, consequences, resolutions, benefits, and harms.

Reality Check *Recognizing the Value of Stakeholders' Trust*

Statement of Prof. Dr. Martin Winterkorn, CEO of Volkswagen AG (September 20, 2015):

The U.S. Environmental Protection Agency and the California Air Resources Board (EPA and CARB) revealed their findings that while testing diesel cars of the Volkswagen Group they have detected manipulations that violate American environmental standards.

The Board of Management at Volkswagen AG takes these findings very seriously. I personally am deeply sorry that we have broken the trust of our customers and the public. We will cooperate fully with the responsible agencies, with transparency and urgency, to clearly, openly, and completely establish all of the facts of this case. Volkswagen has ordered an external investigation of this matter.

We do not and will not tolerate violations of any kind of our internal rules or of the law.

The trust of our customers and the public is and continues to be our most important asset. We at Volkswagen will do everything that must be done in order to re-establish the trust that so many people have placed in us, and we will do everything necessary in order to reverse the damage this has caused. This matter has first priority for me, personally, and for our entire Board of Management.

Source: "Statement of Prof. Dr. Martin Winterkorn, CEO of Volkswagen AG" (September 20, 2015), www.volkswagenag.com/content/vwcorp/info_center/en/news/2015/09/statement_ceo_of_volkswagen_ag.html (accessed June 17, 2016).

that the employee is likely to lose her job) or a deceptive one (claiming that you do not know). Another person might offer a more nuanced reply. A more creative person might have anticipated these problems and developed a strategy before the process began, seeking to proactively calm fears and explain options.

A **fifth step** in the decision-making process is to *compare and weigh the alternatives.* Create a mental spreadsheet (or, if you have time and the situation is complex, create a real one!) that evaluates the impact of each alternative you have devised on each stakeholder you defined. Perhaps the most helpful way to accomplish this task is to try to place oneself in the other person's position, as discussed earlier. Understanding a situation from another's point of view, making an effort to "walk a mile in their shoes," contributes significantly to responsible ethical decision making. Weighing the alternatives will involve predicting the likely, the foreseeable, and the possible consequences to all the relevant stakeholders. A critical element of this evaluation will be the consideration of ways to mitigate, minimize, or compensate for any possible harmful consequences or to increase and promote beneficial consequences.

Ethics experts sometimes ask the decision maker to consider whether he would feel proud or ashamed if *The Wall Street Journal* (or the *Globe and Mail,* or whatever is your relevant daily newspaper) printed this decision as a front-page article. Or, as might happen in this case, imagine if your emailed response was widely forwarded. Would your behavior change if other people knew about it? Full transparency, or the lack of transparency, is a very good test of the ethical nature of a decision. The point of this exercise is to recognize that a fully responsible and ethical decision should be explainable, defensible, and justifiable to the entire range of stakeholders involved. Typically, it is the irresponsible decisions that we wish to keep hidden. (See the Reality Check "Recognizing the Value of Stakeholders' Trust.")

Reality Check *Seeking Guidance?*

It's better to hang out with people better than you. Pick out associates whose behavior is better than yours and you'll drift in that direction.

Warren Buffett

I believe that every right implies a responsibility; every opportunity, an obligation; every possession, a duty.

John D. Rockefeller Jr.

Men of integrity, by their existence, rekindle the belief that as a people we can live above the level of moral squalor. We need that belief; a cynical community is a corrupt community.

John W. Gardner

There is nothing noble about being superior to some other people. The true nobility is in being superior to your previous self.

Hindu Proverb

I hope that my achievements in life shall be these— that I will have fought for what was right and fair, that I will have risked for that which mattered, and that I will have given help to those who were in need, that I will have left the earth a better place for what I've done and who I've been.

C. Hoppe

Laws and principles are not for the times when there is no temptation: they are for such moments as this, when body and soul rise in mutiny against their rigour. . . . If at my convenience I might break them, what would be their worth?

Charlotte Bronte, in Jane Eyre

But consequences to all stakeholders are not the only means for comparing alternatives. Some alternatives might concern matters of principles, rights, or duties that override consequences. Within business settings, individuals may often have specific duties associated with their position. A purchasing manager for a large retail store has a duty associated with her role that directs her to avoid conflicts of interest in dealing with suppliers. Are duties associated with company rules, professional codes of conduct, business roles, or legal duties involved? This might be among the first things you reflect on in responding to the employee's email. You have a duty of confidentiality to your employer and that would seem to prohibit offering any advice. Perhaps guidance is available in specific circumstances from these sources or others (see the Reality Check "Seeking Guidance?").

One additional factor in comparing and weighing alternatives requires consideration of the effects of a decision on one's own integrity, virtue, and character. Understanding one's own character and values should play a role in decision making. People often make decisions based on an understanding of who they are and what kind of person they want to be. A responsible person will ask: "What type of person would make this decision? What kind of habits would I be developing by deciding in one way rather than another? What type of corporate culture am I creating and encouraging? How would I, or my family, describe a person who decides in this way? Is this a decision that I am willing to defend in public?" Such questions truly go to the heart of ethical business leadership. An honest person might not even think about misleading the clinic employee.

Once you have explored these variables, the **final step** is to *make a decision*. However, the process is not yet complete. Decisions in business are not typically simple

Let's give it a try: Should a burger chain—say, McDonald's or Burger King—voluntarily decide to pay its workers the $15 per hour that advocates suggest should be the new, legal minimum wage?

For years, advocates have argued that government should raise the minimum wage substantially—perhaps to as high as $15 per hour. How would *you* make this decision, using the ethical decision-making process provided in this chapter? Let's think through the first few steps.

What facts might be relevant? You would need to consider first what you are currently paying per hour and how many hours per week a typical worker works. You might also consider how the resulting total pay compares to the cost of living. Also relevant would be the pay received in other workplaces, by workers with similar levels of skill. Consider: Who *are* your employees? Are they parents trying to support a family or young people working their first job for a bit of spending cash? Would paying more enable you to attract better workers? If you raise the pay per hour, what will you need to do to offset the additional cost?

What ethical issues does this case raise? To most people, the most significant ethical issue is one of fairness. But fairness can mean many things. One kind of fairness has to do with what counts as fair compensation for a day's work. Another has to do with a fair distribution of benefits among various stakeholders such as employees, customers, and shareholders.

Who are the stakeholders? The most obvious stakeholders are your workers and their families. Also relevant would be more senior frontline workers, who might resent the fact that junior workers now make as much as *they* do after several years of experience. Your customers may also have a stake here, particularly if increased labor costs imply a need to raise your prices. And finally, if your company is a publicly traded one, your shareholders are another obvious stakeholder group.

What alternatives are available? Many options are available. Keeping things just as they are is one option, as is raising pay to the level demanded by activists. Of course, a smaller raise is also an option. A further option would be to reduce the significance of the issue (as some burger joints have done) by hiring fewer minimum-wage employees and installing self-serve kiosks. But don't forget to use your imagination, to go beyond the obvious options. There may be other options that employees would value nearly as much as a raise in pay—things like additional perks, health care benefits, assistance with university or college tuition, and so on.

Complete the process yourself! How would you weigh the alternatives available to a restaurant chain? What decision do you think the restaurant should make, based on this weighing of alternatives? How should the company monitor the outcomes to make sure the appropriate lessons are learned?

Note: As of 2019, the U.S. federal minimum wage is $7.25 per hour. Some states have established higher minimums. Many U.S. states have established minimums above the federal level, and in 2014, several U.S. cities (San Francisco, Seattle, and Los Angeles) approved a $15 minimum, to be phased in over time. For comparison, in Canada, where minimum wage is strictly a provincial matter, minimum wage varies from province to province but is generally in the $9 to $12 range.

FIGURE 2.2

An Ethical
Decision-Making
Process

- Determine the facts.
- Identify the ethical issues involved.
- Identify stakeholders and consider the situation from their point of view.
- Consider the available alternatives—also called using moral imagination.
- Compare and weigh the alternatives, based on:
  - Consequences (for all stakeholders).
  - Duties, rights, principles.
  - Implications for personal integrity and character.
- Make a decision.
- Monitor and learn from the outcomes.

"yes" or "no" decisions; in most cases, making a decision means formulating a plan and carrying it out. Further, to be accountable in our decision making, it is not sufficient to deliberate over this process, only to later throw up our hands once the decision is made: "It's out of my hands now!" Instead, we have the ability as humans to learn from our experiences. That ability implies a responsibility to complete the process by proceeding to the final step: evaluate the implications of our decisions, *monitor and learn from the outcomes,* and modify our actions accordingly when faced with similar challenges in the future. In institutional terms, this can mean using what is learned to develop a plan for preventing future crises, to institute new practices, and to develop new policies and procedures. The Decision Point "Applying the Decision-Making Model" gives us a chance to put this decision-making process into practice.

OBJECTIVE

The ethical traditions and theories that we describe in the next chapter will help us flesh out and elaborate on this decision process. Other approaches to ethically responsible decision making are possible, and this approach will not guarantee one single and absolute answer to every decision. But it is a helpful beginning in the development of responsible and ethical decision making (see Figure 2.2).

When Ethical Decision Making Fails: Why Do "Good" People Engage in "Bad" Acts?

To say that each individual has the ability to follow a similar decision-making process or that each of us has the capacity to make autonomous decisions is not to say that every individual always *does* so. There are many ways in which responsible decision making can go wrong and many ways in which people fail to act in accordance with the ethical judgments they make. Sometimes, of course, people can simply choose to do something unethical. We should not underestimate the real possibility of immoral choices and unethical behavior.

But at other times, even well-intentioned people fail to make ethical choices. What factors determine which companies or individuals engage in ethical behavior and which do not? Why do people we consider to be "good" sometimes do "bad" things? To say that the person who did the bad thing is really a good person does not mean that these unethical decisions or acts are excusable, but that the individuals who engage in the unethical behavior may have done so for a variety of reasons that may not immediately be clear to us. As it turns out, there are many stumbling blocks to responsible decision making and behavior.

OBJECTIVE

Some stumbling blocks standing in the way of responsible action are cognitive or intellectual. As the model of ethical decision making outlined in this chapter suggests, a certain type of ignorance can account for bad ethical choices. Sometimes that *ignorance* can be almost willful and intentional. Returning to the opening discussion case, you might rationalize to yourself that closing a clinic is not your decision to make, and therefore reply with a curt, "I cannot say." You might try to justify the decision by convincing yourself that you are only doing what anyone else would do in this circumstance. You might not really believe that, but it's a comforting story to tell yourself. You might even choose not to think about it and try to put any guilty feelings out of your mind.

Another cognitive barrier is that we sometimes *consider only limited alternatives.* When faced with a situation that suggests two clear alternative ways forward, we often consider only those two clear paths, missing the fact that other alternatives might be possible. Responsible decision making would require that we discipline ourselves to explore additional methods of resolution. If you think carefully about the clinic case, you will likely see that there are quite a few different ways forward. In our ethical decision-making process, we refer to this as the use of moral imagination.

We human beings also often feel most comfortable with *simplified decision rules.* Having a simple rule to follow can be reassuring to many decision makers. For example, you avoid responsibility by saying that company rules prevent you from commenting. Or you might appeal to simplistic economic rules: "Of course, if the clinic is not profitable enough, it should be closed." Using a simple decision rule might appear to relieve us of responsibility for the decision even if it may not be the best possible decision. You did not "make" the decision, you might think; the rule *required* that decision to be made. It's a comforting thought, but it can lead us astray.

We also often select the alternative that satisfies *minimum decision criteria,* otherwise known as satisficing. We select the option that suffices, that is, "good enough," even if it might not be the best. But sometimes, perhaps especially in ethics, "good enough" may be neither good, nor enough. Imagine a work team that needs to make a decision. They may spend hours arriving at a result and finally reach agreement. At that point, it is unlikely that someone will stand up and say, "Whoa, wait a minute; let's spend another couple of hours and figure out an even *better* answer!" The very fact that a decision was reached by consensus (or exhaustion, or frustration) can convince everyone involved that it must be the most reasonable decision, even though it clearly isn't.

Other stumbling blocks are less intellectual or cognitive than they are a question of motivation and willpower. The Greek philosopher Aristotle referred to this as

Reality Check *The Ethics of Cheating*

A 2010 survey of 43,000 American high school students found that a third of boys and a quarter of girls admitted to having stolen from a store within the last year. Almost 60 percent admitted to having cheated on a test in the last year. But almost 90 percent said that it is more important to be a good person than it is to be rich.*

As appalling—or disturbing—as those statistics might be, students fare worse when they are categorized by academic discipline. Research has demonstrated that *business* undergraduate students are *the most likely* to have cheated on a test, when compared with prelaw students and the general population.[†] In response to a statement claiming that *not* cheating is the best way to get ahead in the long run, business students claimed, "You snooze, you lose."[‡] Does this mean that, perhaps, there is a failure in ethics in the business arena because the people who go into business already cheat? Or is it that business students are aware that the business arena demands this type of unethical conduct so they prepare themselves for it from the start? Competitiveness might blur the border

between ethical and unethical. Either way, as our parents have told us, simply because an environment is replete with a certain type of behavior does not mean that we must follow suit, nor does it relieve us of our responsibility for actions in that environment (thus, the common parental question, "If Janie jumps off a bridge, are you going to follow?").

*"Installment 2: The Ethics of American Youth: 2010," Josephson Institute: Center for Youth Studies (February 10, 2011), http://charactercounts.org/programs/reportcard/2010/installment02_report-card_honesty-integrity.html (accessed July 17, 2012).

[†]Rick Tetzeli, "Business Students Cheat Most," *Fortune*, July 1, 1991, p. 14. See also James Stearns and Shaheen Borna, "A Comparison of the Ethics of Convicted Felons and Graduate Business Students: Implications for Business Practice and Business Ethics Education," Teaching Business Ethics 2 (1998), pp. 175–95. This research found that MBA students were more likely to cheat than convicted felons.

[‡]James Stearns and Shaheen Borna, "A Comparison of the Ethics of Convicted Felons and Graduate Business Students: Implications for Business Practice and Business Ethics Education," *Teaching Business Ethics* 2 (1998), p. 18.

"weakness of will" in explaining why some people act unethically even when they know what is right. As contemporary author John Grisham explained in his novel *Rainmaker,* "Every (lawyer), at least once in every case, feels himself crossing a line he doesn't really mean to cross. It just happens."[8] Sometimes it is simply *easier* to do the wrong thing. Consider how you would answer the questions asked in the Reality Check "The Ethics of Cheating."

Unfortunately, we do not always draw the lines for appropriate behavior in advance, and even when we do, they are not always crystal clear. As Grisham suggests, it is often easy to do a little thing that crosses the line, and the next time it is easier, and the next easier still. And then, one day, you find yourself much further over your ethical line than you thought you would ever be.

People also sometimes make decisions they later regret because they *lack the courage* to do otherwise at the time. It is not always easy to make the right decision; you might lose income, your job, or other valuable components of your life. Sherron Watkins, a senior executive at Enron who eventually testified against others, explained that her reluctance to stand up against dishonesty was due to the culture of intimidation and fear that characterized upper management at Enron. Many branch managers at Wells Fargo expressed similar fears when asked about their participation in the fraud.

Courage is also necessary when responding to significant *peer pressure*. Though we might have believed that we could leave this behind in high school or college, unfortunately, we are subject to it throughout our lives. We tend to give in to peer pressure in our professional environments, both because we want to "fit in" and to achieve success in our organizations, and also because our *actual* thinking is influenced by our peers. We worry that our disagreement means that we might be wrong. Accordingly, we either change our minds to fit our environments, or we simply listen only for the evidence that supports this new way of thinking until our minds slowly change on their own. No doubt, something very much like this occurred in the Wells Fargo, Enron, Volkswagen, and many other corporate scandals.

Of course, the usual suspects for explaining unethical conduct are still very much apparent in the scandals that make the front pages every day. The shockingly high levels of corporate executive compensation, lack of oversight of corporate executive decisions, significant distance between decision makers and those whose lives they affect, financial challenges, and a set of ethical values that has not yet caught up to technological advances—all of these factors can create an environment rife with ethical challenges and unethical decisions. The truth is that we can often benefit from unethical acts, from gaining something as simple as a positive work review to something as significant as a salary package of $180 million. Greed and temptation are often all around us and any person can succumb to it. The questions that are most difficult to answer are often those that are most important to answer in defining who we are. Give it a try in the Decision Point "Ethical Oil: Choose Your Poison."

Making ethically responsible decisions throughout one's life is perhaps the most serious challenge we all face. The easiest thing to do would be to remain passive and simply conform to social and cultural expectations, to "go with the flow." But such passivity is exactly the sort of unexamined life that Socrates claimed was not worth living. To live a meaningful human life, we must step back and reflect on our decisions, taking responsibility as autonomous beings.

Before leaving this discussion, it is worth reflecting on the fact that not every decision we make results from a conscious deliberation and choice. In many, perhaps most, of our own day-to-day actions, we do not stop to deliberate and consciously choose to act. We just do it. Imagine that the questions posed in the opening discussion case occurred not in an email but in a face-to-face meeting. In that situation, you would not have time to determine facts, identify the ethical issues, consider alternatives, and so forth.

In the following chapter, we will describe an ethical tradition that emphasizes ethical character and virtues. For many people, ethically difficult situations do not raise much of a dilemma at all. Many people would not have to *deliberate* about what to do or go through a decision-making process before acting. Many people have developed a certain type of character, a set of ethical habits, that will encourage them, without deliberation, to act ethically. A kind and gentle person would respond to the in-person question differently than a brusque and insensitive person. In many situations, we do not act as a result of a deliberate decision as much as we act from our character or because this is the type of the person we are.

Consider, for example, the issue of executive compensation. In 1980, a senior U.S. corporate executive was paid an average of 40 times more than the typical

In the fall of 2011, a Canadian organization called EthicalOil.org started a public relations campaign aimed at countering criticism of commercial development of Canada's oil sands, a set of oil-extraction sites that require the use of hot water and steam to extract very heavy crude oil from sands buried deep beneath the earth's surface. Critics have aimed harsh criticism at the oil sands development, claiming that this method of extracting oil does immense environmental damage along with posing risks to human health. EthicalOil.org seeks to counter such criticism by pointing out the alternative: Anyone choosing not to buy oil harvested from Canada's oil sands, they argue, is effectively choosing oil produced by certain nondemocratic Middle Eastern countries with very bad records of human rights abuses. Who could be in favor of supporting countries engaged in human rights abuses? Thus, the claim is that Canadian oil, far from being worthy of criticism, is indeed "ethical oil."

Of course, the fact that EthicalOil.org says oil from Canada's oil sands is "ethical oil" does not make it true.

Remember, the gas you put in your car is refined from oil. Imagine you have the choice, as a consumer, between (1) buying gas for your car that comes from a country where oil extraction does vast environmental damage and (2) buying gas from a country where the profits from that oil help support a dictatorship with a history of human rights abuses. Which gas will you buy? Why? Are you willing to pay a bit extra to get oil that is more ethical, whatever that means to you?

Next, imagine that you are responsible for securing a contract to provide gas for your company's fleet of vehicles. If the choice is available to you, will you choose the most environmentally friendly gas? Or the gas least associated with human rights abuses? Or will you just go with the cheapest gas available?

Finally, consider whether the choice between buying gas that harms the environment and gas that contributes to human rights abuses exhausts the alternatives in these scenarios. Are there other courses of action available to the individual car-owning consumer? To the manager responsible for procuring gas for the company fleet?

Source: Adapted from Chris MacDonald, "Ethical Oil: Choose Your Poison," *Canadian Business* [Blog] (September 21, 2011), www.canadianbusiness.com/blog/business_ethics/46555 (accessed July 19, 2012).

worker in his or her company; today, the average ratio of highest-to-lowest pay has catapulted to more than 300 to 1 for publicly traded corporations. Such numbers have raised considerable concern, with critics accusing many CEOs of inexcusable greed. In the context of this dramatic rise in executive compensation, Whole Foods CEO John Mackey's decades-long adherence to a publicized pay ratio cap stands out as a remarkable exception to the norm. In 2010, the Whole Foods pay ratio was set at 19 to 1, while Mackey himself has voluntarily set his own salary at $1 per year and receives no stock awards or bonuses.[9] Similarly, the steelmaker Nucor Corp. has not laid off an employee in its forty-year history. Under the stewardship of then-CEO Daniel DiMicco, the company maintained fidelity to its "no layoffs" philosophy through the economic hardship of the late-2000s recessionary period by tightly linking the compensation of all employees—including senior executives—to performance.[10] Developing such habits, inclinations, and character is an important aspect of living an ethical life, and developing a corporate culture that reinforces these habits is an important strategy for creating an ethical organization. (See the Reality Check "Fooling Ourselves" earlier in the chapter.)

In both the following chapter's discussion of virtues and in Chapter 4's discussion of corporate culture, we will examine situations in which the decision-making model provides an incomplete account of ethical actions. However, in most business contexts in which decisions are being made in an organizational setting, conscious, deliberative decision making will be the norm, and, we believe, ethically responsible decision making can be achieved.

Ethical Decision Making in Managerial Roles

In this text, we have already emphasized that individual decision making can be influenced by the social context in which it occurs. Social circumstances can make it easier or more difficult to act in accordance with one's own best judgment. In the world of business, an organization's context sometimes makes it difficult for people to act ethically, even when they really want to. Likewise, the right organizational culture and structure can make it difficult for a dishonest person to act out his or her impulse to behave unethically. Responsibility for the social context that can encourage ethical behavior and can discourage unethical behavior falls predominantly to the business management and executive team. Chapter 4 will examine this issue in more detail as we introduce the concepts of corporate culture and ethical leadership, but it is helpful to begin to explore this topic here within the context of decision making.

The decision-making model introduced in this chapter starts from the point of view of an individual who finds herself in a particular situation. Personal integrity lies at the heart of such individual decision making: What kind of person am I or do I want to be? What are my values? What do I stand for? Every individual also fills a variety of social roles, and these roles carry with them a range of expectations, responsibilities, and duties. Within a business setting, individuals must consider the ethical implications of both **personal and professional decision making.** Some of our roles are social: friend, son or daughter, spouse, citizen, neighbor. Some roles are institutional: manager, employee, parent, child, professor, president of a student club. Among the major roles and responsibilities that we will examine in this text are those associated with specific professions, including lawyers, accountants, auditors, financial analysts, and others. Decision making in these contexts raises broader questions of social responsibilities and social justice.

Consider how different roles might impact your judgment about how you would respond to the email from the clinic employee. Your judgment about this will surely be influenced by your own position as an employee who has responsibilities to keep work-related information confidential. As an employee, you also have

personal and professional decision making
Individuals within a business setting are often in situations in which they must make decisions both from their own personal point of view and from the perspective of the specific role they fill within an institution. Ethically responsible decisions require an individual to recognize that these perspectives can conflict and that a life of moral integrity must balance the personal values with the professional role-based values and responsibilities.

OBJECTIVE

Opening Decision Point Revisited   *Am I About to Lose My Job? What Would You Do?*

Applying our decision-making model to this case, we should first try to determine the facts. We discussed some of this earlier in this chapter. Perhaps the first set of facts that you would consider involves anticipating what will happen in the future. On one hand, it is true that you do not know with certainty what will happen. On the other hand, knowing what you do about this particular clinic and knowing what you do about your own firm's practices, you have good reason to believe that the most likely outcome will be closure. You might also want to explore the facts about employment prospects in the community as well as alternative health care options for people in this community.

Identifying the ethical issues would surely include such concerns as confidentiality, truthfulness and deception, and participating in causing harm to other people. The most obvious interpretation of this scenario is that you find yourself in an ethical dilemma in which you must choose between honoring an employment duty of confidentiality and answering a question truthfully.

Interpreting the case in this way provides a clear way to identify at least three stakeholders: you, the clinic employee who sent the email, and your own employer. Upon reflection, you might also want to consider other staff members, both the professionals who will be offered other employment and those who will not. You might also consider the clinic's clients, who will lose ready access to their health care provider but perhaps gain access to a wider range of health care options. You might also consider the broader community that will lose its only clinic and several good jobs.

An ethical dilemma is often characterized as a situation where you have only two options, each of which are problematic. The decision-making model's rule to consider alternatives aims to undercut the reality of any dilemma by challenging us to look for other options that are less problematic. Use your moral imagination to look for alternatives. Could you speak with your managers to seek guidance, or permission to respond? Can you think of a way to answer the email that neither divulges confidential information nor misleads the employee? Might you even look to develop company policies in anticipation of this happening again?

Once you identify alternatives, the next obvious step is to calculate the consequences, good and bad, of these various alternatives. You know that employees will learn their fate eventually, but will a delay now cause unnecessary harm by preventing the employee from pursuing another job? Will you jeopardize your own position by disclosing information, or is this something that likely will be excused by your managers? No doubt, part of this will also involve comparing alternative consequences and considering possible trade-offs to minimize harm and maximize beneficial results.

But you will also want to consider any principles or rules that are at stake. Does the principle of telling the truth override the risks to your own employment? Does the duty to hold information confidential override the possible harms suffered by the employee?

Next, you might think about your own integrity. Can you live with being the type of person who will knowingly mislead and deceive people? Are you the type of

(continued)

(*concluded*)

person who will work to find ways to mitigate harms and resolve conflicts? Is it most important to you that you avoid conflict and conform to the expectations set by your employer?

Ultimately, of course, you need to decide. (Recognize that even if you try to avoid the situation by ignoring the email and not responding, you have still made a decision. Making a decision is unavoidable!)

So, what would you decide to do? Why?

Finally, imagine that it is some time later and your team has come together to review what happened. The team begins by asking you to review your decision and the thinking that led up to it. What lessons have been learned? What recommendations do you have for the next time?

Reality Check *So What's the Right Answer?*

After reasoning through the Opening Discussion Case with guidance from the decision-making model, there is a very normal tendency to expect a clear answer. What should you do? What is the right answer? Should you answer truthfully or not? In our own experiences teaching business ethics, students have often expected to get answers and understandably get frustrated when no clear and unambiguous answer is forthcoming. Why go through the trouble of a decision-making procedure, indeed why even take a business ethics course, unless you can get answers?

Because ethics deals with issues that are important to human life, it is understandable that we want certain and unambiguous answers. But ethics is not like science, mathematics, or accounting where the correct answer can be calculated with precision. The decision-making procedure that we introduce in this book is not intended to offer *proof* of any conclusions, but it can help you become more and more *reasonable*. As we discussed in the previous chapter, ethics is a branch of practical reason and it aims at establishing reasonable decisions, not absolute or certain ones.

Compare the person who responds to the email in this case without thinking to someone who systematically thinks through the case by applying some version of a decision-making process. Perhaps the first person is someone who simply reacts to a situation or who appeals to a simplistic rule. The second person first gets clear on the facts, understands the issues and all the perspectives at stake, considers alternatives, weighs the consequences to all stakeholders, and reflects on relevant principles and rules. It is, of course, possible that they end up acting in the same way, but certainly we would describe the second person as being more reasonable, more thoughtful, and more considerate than the first. Ultimately, that is the goal of a business ethics class: helping you reach more reasonable, thoughtful, and considerate decisions.

In the following chapter, we will examine a philosophical position called ethical relativism that reaches more skeptical conclusions about ethics because of its inability to offer provable conclusions. We hope that this chapter has provided you with the resources for rejecting that skepticism.

a role to play in creating and shaping your own firm's culture. Your decision will also be influenced by your professional responsibilities as an accountant. But your personal relationship to the person asking for information will also play a role; you are more inclined to provide more information to a close friend than you would be to an occasional acquaintance.

In a business context, individuals fill roles of employees (including both new hires and "old hands"), managers, senior executives, and board members.

Managers, executives, and board members have the ability to create and shape the organizational context in which all employees make decisions. They therefore have a responsibility to promote organizational arrangements that encourage ethical behavior and discourage unethical behavior.

The following three chapters develop these topics. Chapter 3 provides an overview of how some major ethical traditions might offer guidance both to individual decision makers and to those who create and shape social organizations. Chapter 4 examines topics of corporate culture, ethical organizations, and ethical leadership. Chapter 5 looks at corporate social responsibility, the goals toward which ethical organizations and ethical leaders should aim.

Questions, Projects, and Exercises

1. Think about a situation in which you have witnessed someone engaging in unethical behavior but in which you failed to do anything about it. (If you can't think of an example from your own experience, imagine yourself in the position of someone you know about who has witnessed such a situation.) Do you wish you had done something? What would it have taken for you to speak up, either to stop the bad behavior or to report it? How could a person in a position of authority have made it easier for you to take action?

2. Consider your own personal values and explain where they originated. Can you pinpoint their origins? To what degree have you chosen your own values? To what degree are your own values products of your family, your religious or cultural background, or your generation? Does it matter where values come from?

3. What one small *change* do you think would have the biggest impact on the world today? Share it in a brief essay, then convince your reader why it is so important that she or he should also care about that issue to the same extent. It may be effective to use the theories discussed in prior chapters to persuade your reader of the value of your argument.

4. Your CEO recognizes you as having unusually strong skills in decision making and communications, and so she asks for guidance on how to best communicate her plans for an imminent reduction in your company's workforce. What are some of the key strategies you will suggest she employ in reaching such a decision and making the announcement?

5. Describe the qualities you believe are necessary in an "ethical leader." Provide support for your point of view and explain why a leader should display these qualities in order to be considered "ethical." Then identify someone you believe embodies these qualities in her or his leadership and provide examples of relevant behavior. Finally, provide an example of someone whom you believe *does not* possess these qualities and describe that person's leadership.

6. How can a global firm best ensure that it is taking into account the perceptual differences that may exist as a result of diverse cultures, religions, ethnicities, and other factors when creating a worldwide marketing plan?

7. Many people have blamed the global financial crisis of 2008–2009 on a single value or motive, namely, greed. How would you define greed? How common do you think true greed is in the general population? Do you think it is more common on, say, Wall Street than in the general population?

8. As a class exercise, write a brief account of any unethical or ethically questionable experience you have witnessed in a work context. Read and discuss the examples in class, keeping the authors anonymous. Consider how the organization involved allowed or encouraged such behavior and what might have been done to prevent it.

9. Linda is trying to raise funds to support the creation of a free clinic in a poor neighborhood in her hometown. She has been trying very hard, but she has not been able to raise enough money to get the clinic up and running. One day, she gets a huge check from a high-profile business executive whom she met at a fund-raiser. She is ecstatic and finally sees her dream taking shape. However, after a few days, the person who gave Linda the money is arrested for fraud, money laundering, and tax evasion. What should she do? Should she still keep the money and look the other way? Does the source of the money matter, or does the end justify the means?

10. What values do you think motivated the engineers at Volkswagen who devised the method for falsifying emissions tests? How do you think their motivation may have evolved over the years that the scheme was in play? What do you think they would have said if asked, five years before being caught, to reflect on the values that inspired them in their work?

Key Terms

After reading this chapter, you should have a clear understanding of the following key terms. For a more complete definition, please see the Glossary.

change blindness, *p. 38*
ethical decision-making process, *p. 34*

inattentional blindness, *p. 37*
moral imagination, *p. 41*
normative myopia, *p. 37*

perceptual differences, *p. 35*
personal and professional decision making, *p. 50*

Endnotes

1. This fictional case is an amalgam of the experiences of several former students, working in separate industries, who described examples of ethical dilemmas they have faced in their own work. Details have been combined and changed in ways that prevent identifying either the students or their employers, but which maintain the essential details of their real-life work experiences.

2. The concept of normative myopia as applied to business executives can be found in Diane Swanson, "Toward an Integrative Theory of Business and Society," *Academy of Management Review* 24, no. 3 (July 1999), pp. 506–21.

3. D. Chugh and M. Bazerman, "Bounded Awareness: What You Fail to See Can Hurt You," *Mind & Society* 6 (2007), p. 1.

4. See, for example, BHP Billiton, "Our Future: Sustainability Report 2011," pp. 36–37, www.bhpbilliton.com/home/aboutus/sustainability/Pages/default.aspx (accessed January 20, 2012).

5. Source: BHP Billiton, "Our Future: Sustainability Report 2011," www.bhpbilliton.com/home/aboutus/sustainability/Pages/default.aspx (accessed January 20, 2012), pp. 36–37.

6. Source: BHP Billiton, "Our Future: Sustainability Report 2011," www.bhpbilliton.com/home/aboutus/sustainability/Pages/default.aspx (accessed January 20, 2012), pp. 36–37.

7. For a far more in-depth analysis of moral imagination, please see P. H. Werhane, *Moral Imagination and Management Decision-Making* (New York: Oxford University Press, 1999).

8. Source: John Grisham, *Rainmaker* (New York: Doubleday, 1995).

9. Kristin Lin, "Companies Disclose Pay Ratio Before SEC's Final Rule," *The Wall Street Journal* (July 20, 2015), http://blogs.wsj.com/cfo/2015/07/20/companies-disclose-pay-ratio-before-secs-final-rule/ (accessed June 20, 2016).

10. "National Magazine Inducts 10 Manufacturing Leaders into the IW Manufacturing Hall of Fame," press release, *Market Watch* (December 14, 2011), www.marketwatch.com/story/national-magazine-inducts-10-manufacturing-leaders-into-the-iw-manufacturing-hall-of-fame-2011-12-14 (accessed January 21, 2012); C. Helman, "Test of Mettle," *Forbes* (May 11, 2009), www.forbes.com/forbes/2009/0511/081-executives-companies-business-test-of-mettle.html (accessed January 21, 2012).

3

Philosophical Ethics and Business

The unexamined life is not worth living.

Socrates, Apology, Plato's Account of the Trial of Socrates *(Translated by Benjamin Jowett)*

It's better to hang out with people better than you. Pick out associates whose behavior is better than yours and you'll drift in that direction.

Warren Buffett

A business that makes nothing but money, is a poor type of business.

Henry Ford

In April 2019, the CEOs of seven of the largest U.S. banks were called to testify before the U.S. House Financial Services Committee. (Missing was the CEO of Wells Fargo, Timothy Sloan, who had resigned weeks earlier as a result of the scandal described in Chapter 1.) Following the economic recession in 2008–2009, U.S. government action, including financial bailouts, helped many of these banks avoid serious financial difficulties, including bankruptcy. The government's reasoning at this time was that many of these banks were "too big to fail." Now, ten years after that crisis, the congressional committee was examining how the banks were performing.

One topic that received significant attention during these hearings was excessive CEO pay. Congresswoman Nydia M. Velázquez of New York questioned Michael Corbat, CEO of Citigroup, about his $24 million salary in 2018. The congresswoman pointed out that Corbat's salary was 486 times higher than the average salary of a Citigroup employee. Congresswoman Katie Porter of California challenged Jamie Dimon, CEO of J.P. Morgan, to explain how a J.P. Morgan employee in Irvine, California, Porter's home town, could survive on the bank's starting salary of $16.50 per hour. Porter calculated that at this wage, an employee would fall over $500 short each month with normal living expenses in Irvine. Dimon was paid $31 million in 2018, or more than 900 times the pay of the $16.50 hourly wage employee. The very day that Dimon testified before Congress, J.P. Morgan reported record revenues and profits for the first quarter of 2019.

The gap between executive pay and the lowest- or average-wage employee is a common measure for determining when executive salaries are excessive. That gap, particularly within the United States, has grown to levels that would have been unimaginable just a few decades ago. Research by the Economic Policy Institute, a nonpartisan think tank focused on issues of economic equality, concludes that in 1960 the after-tax average for CEOs was 12 times the average pay earned by a factory worker; by 1965 it had risen to a factor of 20 and by 1989 to 59. In 1998, in an article titled "The Great CEO Pay Heist," *Fortune* magazine estimated that the gap had reached 182 times and by 2007 that the gap had reached 275 times the average worker salary. In 2018, Corbat's differential was 486 and Dimon's was 949.

Shortly after these bank CEOs appeared before Congress, another example of excessive CEO pay was in the news. The 2018 pay of Disney CEO Bob Iger was criticized from an unlikely source. Abigail Disney, granddaughter of the Disney company co-founder Roy Disney, publicly condemned Iger's $65 million salary as "insane." In her public criticism, she pointed out that this amounted to 1,424 times the pay for the lowest-paid Disney employee. In her public remarks, she explained that Iger's one-year compensation could have given every Disney employee a 15% raise, and still have provided Iger with a $10 million salary.

There are, of course, two approaches for lowering such pay differentials. First, the wages of lower-paid employees could be raised. Second, CEO pay could be lowered. There are some recent examples of both approaches. A number of major corporations have announced plans to increase wages beyond what is required by law. In his April 2019 letter to shareholders, Amazon CEO Jeff Bezos wrote:

"Today I challenge our top retail competitors (you know who you are!) to match our employee benefits and our $15 minimum wage. Do it! Better yet, go to $16 and throw the gauntlet back at us. It's a kind of competition that will benefit everyone."[1] Target Corporation had previously announced plans to increase its minimum wage to $15 hourly by 2020, but as of 2019 its hourly minimum was still only $13. Walmart's minimum hourly wage was $11, but Walmart responded to Bezos's comments by pointing out that when benefits are included, its average worker earned $17.55 hourly.

A second approach would be to limit CEO pay. One example of this occurred in April 2015, when CEO Dan Price of Gravity Payments made a shocking announcement. Price, who is also founder and co-owner of Gravity, decided to cut his own salary by 93 percent, and then to use that money—along with a big chunk of corporate profits—to ensure that every single one of his employees makes a minimum of $70,000.[2] (Over a 2,000-hour work-year, this would be equivalent to $35 hourly.)

The news was certainly welcomed by Gravity's employees. (For the lowest-paid employees, the raise to $70k meant a doubling of their salaries.) And Price was widely applauded by commentators and on social media.

Price's move was especially noteworthy against the background in which many CEOs have been criticized for accepting astronomically high levels of pay. Beyond the bank CEOs mentioned above, a 2015 article on executive compensation from *Bloomberg.com* reported,[3] for example, that Elon Musk, the entrepreneurial CEO of Tesla Motors Inc., earned just over $100 million in 2014. But even that was far from the high end of executive compensation: The same article noted that Nicholas Woodman, CEO of GoPro Inc., had earned a whopping $285 million that year. Criticism of CEO pay has not focused solely on the absolute amount earned, but also on the ratio of CEO pay to what those CEOs' employees are paid. According to the *Bloomberg* article, "The CEOs of 350 Standard & Poor's 500 companies made 331 times more than their employees in 2013."[4]

Some people defend high levels of pay for CEOs, pointing out that the highest levels of compensation are achieved through stock options, which means that CEOs do well only when the value of the company's stock goes up, a sign that the CEO is actually doing a good job. Others, however, are skeptical. As the *Bloomberg* article points out, "Stock options, once believed to align executives with shareholders because they appreciate when the stock price rises, are now derided for encouraging short-term financial engineering at the expense of long-term planning."* In other words, stock options encourage CEOs to find short-term ways to boost stock prices (such as reducing costs by cutting employees), even if those moves aren't in the long-term interests of the company and its shareholders. The Wells Fargo case described at the beginning of Chapter 1 provides an example of how a CEO can benefit from stock prices that are manipulated by unethical means.

Let's turn back to Price's decision. Different people had different reactions to the decision. Some applauded it as a move toward justice or fairness in compensation. Others thought it was a savvy business move, aimed at producing better outcomes for Gravity Payments by motivating employees and gaining free publicity for the company. Still others thought it spoke well of Price's character; to them, Price looked like what a good CEO ought to look like, in comparison to the greedy CEOs of so many other companies.

(continued)

(concluded)

1. Do you think Dan Price is a hero? Why or why not? Are there any further facts that you would want to know before making a judgment about this case?
2. Gravity Payments is privately owned by Dan Price and his brother. If Gravity were a publicly traded company with thousands of shareholders, would that change your view about the ethics of his decision? If so, in what way?
3. If you were an employee at Gravity Payments, already making $70,000, how would you feel about employees who made half what you make suddenly making the same amount as you?
4. Minimum wage laws are common in the U.S., Canada, and many other countries. Should there be a maximum wage law (perhaps by creating an upper limit on wages that can be deducted from tax bills)?

*Source: Caleb Melby, "Executive Pay: Valuing CEOs (March 15, 2015)," *Bloomberg.com* www.bloomberg.com/quicktake/executive-pay (accessed June 26, 2016).

 # Chapter Objectives

After reading this chapter, you will be able to:

1. Explain the ethical framework of utilitarianism.
2. Describe how utilitarian thinking underlies economic and business decision making.
3. Explain how the free market is thought to serve the utilitarian goal of maximizing the overall good.
4. Explain some challenges to utilitarian decision making.
5. Explain the principle-based, or rights-based, framework of ethics.
6. Explain the concept of human rights and how they are relevant to business.
7. Distinguish moral rights from legal rights.
8. Explain several challenges to principle-based ethics.
9. Describe and explain virtue-based framework for thinking about ethical character.

Introduction: Ethical Frameworks—Consequences, Principles, Character

Consider the reasons that might be offered to defend or criticize either Dan Price's decision to equalize his own salary with that of his employees or the decision to pay CEOs tens of millions of dollars in an annual salary. Upon reflection, we believe that you will discover that these reasons fall into three general categories. Some reasons appeal to the *consequences* of this move: They either will or will not provide incentives for producing good work and beneficial future consequences. Other reasons appeal to certain principles: "No one's work is worth 14 times what someone else's work is worth," or "everyone deserves to be paid a living wage." Other reasons cite matters of *personal character:* Accepting millions in compensation while others can barely pay the rent is greedy, or distasteful. Giving employees a raise when you've got the ability to do that is just what a good and decent boss would do.

As it turns out, the three major traditions of ethical framework that we will rely on in this text are represented by these three categories. This should be no surprise because ethical traditions in philosophy reflect common ways to think and reason about how we should live, what we should do. Ethics of consequences, ethics of principles, and ethics of personal character are the three traditions that will be introduced in this chapter.

Chapters 1 and 2 introduced ethics as a form of practical reasoning in support of decision making about how we should live our lives. Ethics involves what is perhaps the most significant question any human being can ask: How *should* we live our lives? But, of course, this question is not new; every major philosophical, cultural, political, and religious tradition in human history has grappled with it. In light of this, it would be unwise to ignore these traditions as we begin to examine ethical issues in business.

Nevertheless, many students think that discussions of philosophical ethics are too abstract to be of much help in business. Discussion of ethical "frameworks" often seems to be too *theoretical* to be of much relevance to business. Throughout this chapter, we hope to suggest a more accessible and pragmatic understanding of ethics, one that will shed some light on the practical and pragmatic application of these frameworks to actual problems faced by businesspeople.

An ethical framework is nothing more than an attempt to provide a systematic answer to the fundamental ethical question: How should human beings live their lives? In many ways, this is a simple question that we ask, at least implicitly, every day. What am I going to do today, and why? Ethics can be understood as the practice of examining these decisions and thinking about answers to the question: Why?

Ethics attempts to answer the question of how we should live, but it also gives *reasons* to support the answers. Ethics seeks to provide a rational justification for why *we* should act and decide in a particular prescribed way. Anyone can offer prescriptions for what you should do and how you should act, but a *philosophical* and reasoned ethics must answer the "why?" question as well.

Why does the question "why?" matter so much? At least two reasons can be offered. First, "why" matters because without offering reasons, all we are doing is giving an opinion. An opinion, on its own, is not terribly useful. You may think your company should fire a particular employee, but if you're to convince the *boss,* your mere opinion won't do much. In order to convince the boss, you'll need to offer opinions. In business, there is just about *always* someone you need to convince, whether it's your boss or your employees or your teammates.

utilitarianism
An ethical theory that tells us that we can determine the ethical significance of any action by looking to the consequences of that act. Utilitarianism is typically identified with the policy of "maximizing the overall good" or, in a slightly different version, of producing "the greatest good for the greatest number."

principle-based framework
A framework for ethics that grounds decision making in fundamental principles such as justice, liberty, autonomy, and fairness. Principle-based ethics typically assert that individual rights and duties are fundamental and thus can also be referred to as a rights-based or duty-based (deontological) approach to ethics. Often distinguished from consequentialist frameworks, which determine ethical decisions based on the consequences of our acts.

virtue ethics
An approach to ethics that studies the character traits or habits that constitute a good human life, a life worth living. The virtues provide answers to the basic ethical question "What kind of person should I be?"

Second, the question "why?" matters because superficial agreement can mask underlying *dis*agreement. Imagine that a three-person management team agrees on the need to fire a particular employee named Tahmina. Should you be comforted by the fact that you all agree? What if, unbeknownst to all of you, one of you thinks Tahmina should be fired because he (wrongly) believes that Tahmina has not performed well as an employee; another thinks she should be fired because you need to cut costs; and the third thinks Tahmina should be fired because of her sexual orientation? What looks like agreement, here, actually masks deep and important *dis*agreements, ones that need to be sorted out before any action is taken.

Many people and cultures across the world would answer this "why" question in religious terms and base their normative judgments on religious foundations. "You ought to live your life in a certain way because God commands it." Or: "You ought to behave as commanded in our holy book!" The biggest practical problem with this approach, of course, is that people differ widely about their religious beliefs, and are dedicated to different holy books or to none at all. If ethics is based on religion, and if different cultures have widely divergent religious beliefs, then it would seem that ethics cannot escape the predicament of relativism. (See the Decision Point "Who Is to Say What Is Right or Wrong" for more on ethical relativism.)

Unlike religious ethics that explains human well-being in religious terms, philosophical ethics provides justifications that must be applicable to all people regardless of their religious starting points. The justifications of philosophical ethics tend to connect the "oughts" and "shoulds" of ethics to some underlying account of human well-being. Thus, for example, "you should contribute to disaster relief because it will reduce human suffering" is a philosophical justification for an ethical judgment, whereas "you should contribute to disaster relief because God commands it, or because it will bring you heavenly rewards" are religious rather than philosophical justifications.

Ethics is not comprised of a single principle or framework. Different ethical frameworks have evolved over time and have been refined and developed by many different thinkers. The insights of an ethical framework prove to be lasting if they truly do pick out some important elements of human experience. To emphasize this fact, this chapter will refer to these theories more commonly as ethical "traditions." These traditions have their origins in the works of specific philosophers, but they are ways of thinking that have been widely influential in our culture, in our literature, and in our legal thinking.

This chapter will introduce three ethical frameworks that have proven influential in the development of business ethics and that have a very practical relevance in evaluating ethical issues in modern business. **Utilitarianism** is an ethical tradition that directs us to decide based on overall consequences of our acts. The **principle-based framework** directs us to act on the basis of moral principles such as respecting human rights. **Virtue ethics** tells us to consider the *moral character* of individuals and how various character traits can contribute to, or obstruct, a happy and meaningful human life.

ethical relativism
An important perspective within the philosophical study of ethics that holds that ethical values and judgments are ultimately dependent on, or relative to, one's culture, society, or personal feelings. Relativism denies that we can make rational or objective ethical judgments.

Are you an ethical relativist? Ethical relativism holds that ethical values are relative to particular people, cultures, or times. Relativism denies that there can be any rationally justified or objective ethical judgments. When there are ethical disagreements between people or cultures, the ethical relativist concludes that there is no way to resolve that dispute and prove one side is right or more reasonable than the other.

Often, people describe behavior they don't approve of as "distasteful." Ordinarily, we think of matters of taste as personal, subjective things. You enjoy spicy Indian food, while I prefer a simple burger and fries. It is all a matter of personal taste. You might think sky-high executive salaries are distasteful, but others find them well deserved. Ethical relativists believe that ethical values are much like tastes in food; it all depends on, or it is all relative to, one's own background, culture, and personal opinions.

Most ethicists believe that ethical relativism is not a credible point of view, but many people still find it tempting.

Do *you* believe that there is no way to decide what is ethically right or wrong? Imagine a teacher returns an assignment to you with a grade of F. When you ask for an explanation, you are told that, frankly, the teacher does not believe that people "like you" (e.g., men, Christians, African Americans) are capable of doing good work in this field (e.g., science, engineering, math, finance). When you object that this is unfair and wrong, the teacher offers a relativist explanation. "Fairness is a matter of personal opinion," the professor explains. "Who determines what is fair or unfair?" you ask. Your teacher claims that his view of what is fair is as valid as any other. Because everyone is entitled to his or her own personal opinion, the professor is entitled to fail you because, in his personal opinion, you do not deserve to succeed.

1. Would you accept this explanation and be content with your failing grade? If not, how would you defend your own opposing view?
2. Are there any relevant facts on which you would rely to support your claim?
3. What values are involved in this dispute?
4. What alternatives are available to you?
5. Besides you and your teacher, are there any other stakeholders—people who are or should be involved in this situation?
6. What reasons would you offer to the dean in an appeal to have the grade changed?
7. What consequences would this professor's practice have on education?
8. If reasoning and logical persuasion do not work, how else could this dispute be resolved?

Utilitarianism: Making Decisions Based on Ethical Consequences

OBJECTIVE

consequentialist theories
Ethical theories, such as utilitarianism, that determine right and wrong by calculating the consequences of actions.

The first ethical tradition that we shall examine, utilitarianism, has its roots in 18th- and 19th-century social and political philosophy, but its core idea is just as relevant in the 21st century. Utilitarianism's fundamental insight is that outcomes matter, and so we should decide what to do by considering the overall *consequences* of our actions. In this sense, utilitarianism has been called a **consequentialist** approach to ethics and social policy: We should act in ways that produce better consequences than the alternatives we are considering. Much more needs to be said to turn this simple insight into an adequate approach to ethics. The first, and most obvious, question is: What is meant by "better consequences"?

Consider how consequentialist thinking plays out in some common responses to the topic of executive pay. One typical defense of such exorbitant salaries appeals to the incentives provided by high salaries. The claim is that the promise of high rewards will provide an incentive for executives to better serve the business. Especially when CEO pay is tied to stock performance, the CEO benefits only when the overall company benefits. CEOs receive high pay only if the company benefits. This is a consequentialist argument: CEO pay is justified by the beneficial consequences that it produces.

In a business context, a temptation is to answer in terms of financial consequences: The right decision is one that produces the best financial returns. But this answer would reduce ethics to economics by identifying ethically best as economically best. A more useful and reasonable answer to this question can be given in terms of the ethical values described in the previous chapters. "Better consequences" are those that promote human well-being: the happiness, health, dignity, integrity, freedom, and respect of all the people affected. If these elements are basic human values, then an action that promotes more of them than the alternative action does is more reasonable from an ethical point of view. A decision that promotes the greatest amount of these values for the greatest number of people is the most reasonable decision from an ethical point of view.

Utilitarianism is commonly identified with the rule of producing "the greatest good for the greatest number." The ultimate ethical goal, according to utilitarians, is to attempt to produce the best consequences overall, taking into account all parties affected by the decisions. Decisions that accomplish this goal are the right decisions to make ethically; those that produce bad consequences are ethically wrong.

The emphasis on producing the greatest good for the greatest number makes utilitarianism a social philosophy that opposes policies that aim to benefit only a small social, economic, or political minority. Historically, utilitarianism has provided strong support for democratic institutions and policies. Government and all social institutions exist for the well-being of all, not to further the interests of the monarch, the nobility, or some small group of the elite. Likewise, the economy and economic institutions exist to provide the highest standard of living for the greatest number of people, not to create wealth for a few. Thus, a different consequentialist argument could be offered to critique high executive pay. Some would argue that while the incentive of high salary might lead to beneficial short-term consequences for the stockholders, it does not maximize benefits for a wider range of stakeholders, including long-term investors.

As another business-related example, consider the case of child labor, discussed in further detail in Chapter 6. Utilitarian thinking would advise us to consider all the likely consequences of a practice of employing young children in factories. Obviously, there are some harmful consequences: Children suffer physical and psychological harms, they are denied opportunities for education, their low pay is not enough to escape a life of poverty, and so forth. Many of the human values previously described are diminished by child labor. But these consequences must be compared to the consequences of alternative decisions. What are the consequences if children in poor regions are denied factory jobs? These children would still be denied opportunities for education; they would be in worse poverty; and they would have less money for food and family support. In many cases, the only alternatives for obtaining any income available to young children who are prohibited from joining the workforce might include crime, drugs, or prostitution. Further, we should consider not only the consequences to the children themselves, but to the entire society. Child labor can have beneficial results for bringing foreign investment and money into a poor country. In the opinion of some observers, allowing children to work for pennies a day under sweatshop conditions produces better overall consequences than the available alternatives. Thus, one might argue on utilitarian grounds that such labor practices are ethically permissible because they produce better overall consequences than the alternatives.

This example highlights several important aspects of utilitarian reasoning. Because utilitarians decide strictly on the basis of consequences, and because the consequences of our actions will depend on the specific facts of each situation, utilitarians tend to be very pragmatic thinkers. No type of act is ever absolutely right or wrong in all cases in every situation; it will always depend on the consequences. For example, lying is neither right nor wrong in itself, according to utilitarians. There might be situations in which lying will produce greater overall good than telling the truth. In such a situation, it would be ethically justified to tell a lie. In the case of CEO pay, the utilitarian judgment would depend on whether or not, in fact, high pay provides an effective incentive that does produce overall benefits. In one case it might, but in other cases it might not. (Reflect back on the Wells Fargo case as an example.)

The example of child labor also highlights the fact that utilitarian reasoning usually acknowledges some support for competing available alternatives—that is, ban child labor as harmful to the overall good or allow child labor as contributing to the overall good. Utilitarianism realistically admits that there may be conflicting evidence in favor of different options. Deciding on the ethical legitimacy of alternative decisions requires that we make judgments about the likely consequences of our actions. How do we do this? Within the utilitarian tradition, there is a strong inclination to turn to social science for help in making such predictions. After all, social science studies the causes and consequences of individual and social

Reality Check   *Everyone Matters*

While the obligation to maximize pleasure or happiness sounds selfish and egoistic, utilitarianism differs from egoism in important ways. Egoism is also a consequentialist theory, but it focuses exclusively on the happiness of the individual making the decision. In other words, instead of determining the "greatest good for the greatest number," egoism seeks "the greatest good for me!"

Utilitarianism judges actions by their consequences for the general and overall good. Consistent with the utilitarian commitment to democratic equality, however, the general good must take into consideration the well-being of each and every individual affected by the action. In this way, utilitarianism serves the ultimate goal of ethics: the impartial promotion of human well-being. It is impartial in that it considers the consequences for everyone, not just for the individual. People who act in ways to maximize only their own happiness or the happiness of their company are not utilitarians; they are egoists.

egoism

As a psychological theory, egoism holds that all people act only from self-interest. Empirical evidence strongly suggests that this is a mistaken account of human motivation. As an ethical theory, egoism holds that humans ought to act for their own self-interest. Ethical egoists typically distinguish between one's perceived best interests and one's true best interests.

OBJECTIVE

actions. Who is better situated than a social scientist to help us predict the social consequences of our decisions? Consider the fields to which one might turn in order to determine the likely consequences of child labor. Economics, anthropology, political science, sociology, public policy, psychology, and medical and health sciences are some of the fields that could help determine the likely consequences of such practices in a particular culture.

In general, the utilitarian position is that happiness is the ultimate good, the only thing that is and can be valued for its own sake. Happiness is the best and most reasonable interpretation of human well-being. (After all, does it sound plausible to you to claim that *un*happiness is good and happiness is bad?) The goal of ethics, both individually and as a matter of public policy, should be to maximize the overall happiness. (See the Reality Check "Everyone Matters.")

Utilitarianism and Business

We previously claimed that studying ethical theories had a practical relevance for business ethics. In fact, perhaps utilitarianism's greatest contribution to philosophical thought has come through its influence in economics. With roots in Adam Smith, the ethical view that underlies much of 20th-century economics—essentially what we think of as the free market—is decidedly utilitarian. In this way, utilitarianism continues to have a very strong impact on business and business ethics.

Utilitarianism answers the fundamental questions of ethics—for example, What should we do?—by reference to a very simple rule: maximize the overall good. This rule might remind you of the financial practice of conducting a cost–benefit analysis and making a decision based on maximizing net benefits over costs. But even if we agree that maximizing the overall good is the right goal, another question remains to be answered: *How* do we achieve this goal? Utilitarian social policy can be understood in terms of means and ends. What is the best *means* for attaining the utilitarian *end* of maximizing the overall good? Two answers prove especially relevant in business and business ethics.

OBJECTIVE

One movement within utilitarian thought points to the line of thinking that originated with Adam Smith, and claims that free and competitive markets are the best means for attaining utilitarian ends. The argument here is that voluntary transactions make people better off, and so a *system* of such transactions—a free market—is going to maximize benefit overall. This version of utilitarianism would promote policies that deregulate private industry, protect property rights, allow for free exchanges, and encourage competition. In such situations, decisions of rationally self-interested individuals will result, as if led by an "invisible hand," in Adam Smith's terms, to the maximum satisfaction of individual happiness.

In classic free-market economics, economic activity aims to satisfy consumer demand. People are made happy—human welfare or well-being increases—when they get what they desire. Overall human happiness is increased, therefore, when the overall satisfaction of consumer demand increases. The law of supply and demand tells us that economies should, and healthy economies do, produce (supply) those goods and services that consumers most want (demand). Because scarcity and competition prevent everyone from getting all that they want, the goal of free-market economics is to optimally satisfy wants and thus maximize happiness. Free markets accomplish this goal most efficiently, according to defenders, by allowing individuals to decide for themselves what they most want and then bargain for these goods in a free and competitive marketplace. This process will, over time and under the right conditions, guarantee the optimal satisfaction of wants, which this tradition equates with maximizing overall happiness.

Given this utilitarian goal, current free-market economics advises us that the most efficient means to attain that goal is to structure our economy according to the principles of free-market capitalism. This requires that business managers, in turn, seek to maximize profits. This idea is central to one common perspective on corporate social responsibility. By pursuing profits, business ensures that scarce resources are going to those who most value them and thereby ensures that resources will provide optimal satisfaction. Thus, competitive markets are seen as the most efficient means to the utilitarian end of maximizing happiness.

A second influential version of utilitarian thought turns to policy experts who have insight into the outcome of various policies and design and implement policies that will attain utilitarian ends. Because utilitarian reasoning determines what to do on the basis of consequences, reasonable judgments must take into account the likely consequences of our actions. But predicting consequences of human action can be studied and improved by careful observation. Experts in predicting such consequences, usually trained in the social sciences such as economics, political science, and public policy, are familiar with the specifics of how society works and they therefore are in a position to determine which policy will maximize the overall good. (See the Reality Check "Utilitarian Experts in Practice.")

This approach to public policy underlies one theory of the entire administrative and bureaucratic side of government and organizations. Consider, for example, the American political system. From this view, the legislative body (from Congress to local city councils) establishes the public goals that they believe will maximize overall happiness. The administrative side (presidents, governors, mayors) executes (administers) policies to fulfill these goals. The people working within the administration know how the social and political system works and use this knowledge to

Consider how central banks (such as the U.S. Federal Reserve Board or the Bank of England) set interest rates. There is an established goal, a public policy "good," that the central bank takes to be the greatest good for the country. (This goal is something like the highest sustainable rate of economic growth compatible with minimal inflation.) The central bank examines the relevant economic data and makes a judgment about the present and future state of the economy. If economic activity seems to be slowing down, the central bank might decide to lower interest rates as a means for stimulating economic growth. If the economy seems to be growing too fast and the inflation rate is increasing, it might choose to raise interest rates. Lowering or raising interest rates, in and of itself, is neither good nor bad; the rightness of the act depends on the consequences. The role of public servants is to use their expertise to judge the likely consequences and make the decision that is most likely to produce the best result for the public as a whole.

carry out the mandate of the legislature. Governments are filled with such people, typically trained in fields such as economics, law, social science, public policy, and political science. This utilitarian approach, for example, would be sympathetic to government regulation of business on the grounds that such regulation will ensure that business activities do contribute to the overall good.

It is important to see that these two approaches to policy are both grounded in utilitarianism. They both seek to implement policies that will tend to maximize good outcomes overall; but they differ strongly in the approach that they believe will achieve that outcome.

The dispute between these two versions of utilitarian policy, what we might call the "market" and the "administrative" versions of utilitarianism, characterize many disputes in business ethics. One clear example concerns regulation of workplace health and safety. (Similar disputes might arise over product safety, environmental protection, regulation of advertising, and almost every other example of government regulation of business.) One side argues that questions of safety and appropriate levels of risk should be determined by experts who then establish standards that business is required to meet. Government regulators are then expected to enforce safety standards. (See the Decision Point "Is Regulation Making Cars Too Safe?")

The other side argues that the best judges of acceptable risk and safety are workers themselves. A free and competitive labor market will ensure that workers get the level of safety that they want. Individuals calculate for themselves what risks they wish to take and what trade-offs they are willing to make in order to attain safety. Workers willing to take risks likely will be paid more for their labor than workers who demand safer and less risky employment. The very basic economic concept of efficiency can be understood as a placeholder for the utilitarian goal of maximum overall happiness. Thus, according to this view, market-based solutions will be best at optimally satisfying these various and competing interests and will thereby serve the overall good.

Decision Point

The North American auto industry is heavily regulated. Fuel efficiency is, of course, regulated (by the Environmental Protection Agency in the United States and by Transport Canada in Canada), as are tailpipe emissions. But even more significant are the safety regulations to which the modern North American vehicle is subject. Safety standards cover everything from the design of seat belts to the performance of braking systems, the presence and functioning of air bags, and the ability of front and rear bumpers to survive low-speed collisions. All of these things have made the cars driven by North Americans (and Europeans) vastly safer—both under "normal" driving conditions and during emergencies—than they were, say, fifty years ago.

Economist and blogger Alex Tabarrok points out that in order to fully evaluate the outcomes of safety regulations, we need to look at how those regulations affect people's decisions.* One way they affect consumer decision making is through their impact on prices. Safety features have inevitably driven up the price of cars. This has made cars unaffordable to some consumers, with some consumers instead opting to drive motorcycles. Motorcycles, after all, are much less expensive. As just one example, in North America a basic Honda motorcycle costs less than one-third as much as Honda's cheapest model of car, the Honda Fit.

But motorcycles are not only less expensive than cars—they are *less safe*, too. (The U.S. National Highway Traffic Safety Administration says that per mile traveled, motorcycles are twenty-six times more deadly than cars.†) As we all know, air bags have made cars safer, but also more expensive. And as Tabarrok points out, motorcycles don't have air bags. So what is the net effect of regulations that increase the safety of car drivers, but that also push some drivers to buy motorcycles instead? It's not clear that anyone knows the answer to that.

1. If careful study showed that more people were being killed by automotive safety requirements than saved, would you be in favor of regulations that allowed manufacturers to make at least some cars that are less safe?

2. If a single potential car buyer opts to buy a motorcycle because cars are now too expensive for her, and if she dies or is injured in a motorcycle accident, should we blame regulators?

3. If regulators didn't force car makers to install safety equipment, would consumer demand be enough to get car makers to do so anyway? Or would car makers abuse the fact that most consumers don't know which safety features are really most worth paying for?

*Alex Tabarrok, "Unsafe Cars Can Save Lives," *Marginal Revolution* (May 23, 2016), http://marginalrevolution.com/marginalrevolution/2016/05/safety-is-relative.html (accessed June 28, 2016).

†Insurance Institute for Highway Safety, Highway Loss Data Institute, "Motorcycles," www.iihs.org/iihs/topics/t/motorcycles/fatalityfacts/motorcycles (accessed June 28, 2016).

Source: Inspired by "When Are Safer Cars a Bad Idea?" *Business Ethics Highlights* (May 23, 2016), https://businessethicshighlights.com/2016/05/23/when-are-safer-cars-a-bad-idea/ (accessed June 26, 2016).

Challenges to Utilitarian Ethics

OBJECTIVE

While the utilitarian tradition contributes much to responsible ethical decision making, it is not without problems. A review of some general challenges to utilitarianism can guide us in evaluating later applications of utilitarian decision making.

A first set of problems concerns the need for utilitarian reasoning to count, measure, compare, and quantify consequences. If utilitarianism advises that we make decisions by comparing the consequences of alternative actions, then we must have a method for making such comparisons. In practice, however, some comparisons and measurements are very difficult.

For example, in principle, utilitarianism tells us that the interests of all stakeholders who will be affected by a decision ought to be included in calculating the consequences of a decision. But there simply is no consensus among utilitarians on how to measure and determine the overall good. Many business ethics issues highlight how difficult this could be. Consider the consequences of using nonrenewable energy sources and burning fossil fuels for energy. Imagine trying to calculate the consequences of a decision to invest in construction of a nuclear power plant whose wastes remain toxic for tens of thousands of years. Or consider how difficult it would be to calculate all the consequences of the decision faced by members of Congress to provide hundreds of billions of dollars to bail out companies that are "too big to fail."

A second challenge goes directly to the core of utilitarianism. The essence of utilitarianism is its reliance on consequences. Ethical and unethical acts are determined by their consequences. In short, for utilitarians the end justifies the means. But this seems to deny one of the earliest ethical principles that many have learned: The end does *not* always justify the means.

This challenge can be explained in terms of ethical principles. When we say that "the ends do not justify the means," what we are saying is that there are certain things we must do, certain rules we should follow, no matter what the consequences. The ends (or goals) of our actions are not all that matters; it also matters how we *achieve* those ends (i.e., the means we use). Put another way, we have certain duties or responsibilities that we ought to obey even when doing so does not produce a net increase in overall happiness. Examples of such duties are those required by such principles as truth-telling, justice, loyalty, and respect, as well as the responsibilities that flow from our roles as a parent, spouse, friend, citizen, or professional.

Several examples can be used to explain why this is a serious criticism of utilitarian reasoning. Because utilitarianism focuses on the overall consequences, utilitarianism seems willing to sacrifice the good of some individuals for the greater overall good. So, for example, it might turn out that the overall happiness would be increased if children were held as slave labor. Utilitarians would object to child labor, not as a matter of principle, but only if and to the degree that it detracts from the overall good. If it turns out that slavery and child labor increase the net overall happiness, utilitarianism would have to support these practices. In the judgment of many people, such a decision would violate fundamental ethical principles of justice, equality, and respect.

The ethical tradition that we will turn to in the next section argues that individuals possess certain basic rights that should not be violated even if doing so would increase the overall social happiness. Rights function to protect individuals from being sacrificed for the greater overall happiness. Thus, for example, it is often argued that child labor is ethically wrong in principle even if it contributes to the overall social good because it violates the rights of young children.

A similar example cites those principles that arise from commitments that we all make in our daily lives and the duties that flow from them. For example, as parents we love our children and have certain duties to them. Violating such commitments and duties in order to maximize utility for some larger group would require individuals to sacrifice their own integrity for the common good.

Such commitments and duties play a large role in business life. Contracts and promises are commitments that one ought to honor, even if the consequences turn out to be unfavorable. The duties that one takes on as part of a professional role function in a similar way. Looking back on the Enron case, Arthur Andersen's auditors should not have violated their professional duties simply to produce what they saw as greater overall beneficial consequences. Similarly, the engineers who designed the deceptive emissions device for Volkswagen should not have violated their professional duties in falsifying test results. Lawyers have a duty not to help their clients find ways to violate the law, even if they are offered a high salary to do so. Teachers should not violate their professional duties by failing students whom they do not like. Similarly, a person might argue against a decision to close a medical clinic by pointing out that although this risks bad overall consequences, she must remain loyal to employees as a matter of principle. We will consider similar themes, concerning professional commitments, and duties when later chapters examine the role of professional responsibilities within business institutions.

Despite these challenges, utilitarian reasoning does contribute to an ethically responsible decision in important ways. First, and most obviously, we are reminded that responsible decision making requires that we consider the consequences that our actions have on a wide range of people. But it is equally important to remember that utilitarian reasoning does not exhaust the range of ethical concerns. Consequences are only part of the ethical landscape. Responsible ethical decision making also involves matters of duties, principles, and personal integrity. We turn to such factors in the following sections.

An Ethics of Principles and Rights

OBJECTIVE

Consideration of the likely consequences of the available options certainly should be part of responsible ethical decision making. But this approach must be enriched with the recognition that some decisions should be a matter of principle, not consequences. As noted earlier, the ends do not always justify the means. But how do we know what principles we should follow, and how do we decide when a principle should outweigh our desire to produce beneficial consequences? Principle-based ethical frameworks work out the details of such questions.

Consider as an example the relationship between the legislative and judicial branches of government found in constitutional democracies. The legislative role in a democracy can be thought of as pursuing the utilitarian goal of creating policies to produce the greatest good for the greatest number, while the judiciary's role is to enforce basic principles of justice and fairness. The essential insight of constitutional democracies is that majority-rule decisions that seek the greatest happiness for the most people should be restricted by constitutional limits that reflect fundamental principles of human rights. This political example reflects the idea that a utilitarian framework should be supplemented by a framework that also accounts for fundamental ethical principles. In other words, utilitarian ends do not justify any and all means to those ends.

The second ethical framework that will prove crucial for business ethics begins with the insight that we should make some ethical decisions as a matter of principle rather than consequences. Ethical principles can be thought of as a type of rule, and this approach to ethics tells us that there are some rules that we ought to follow even if doing so prevents good overall consequences from happening or even if it results in some bad consequences. Principles are ethical rules that put values into action. We may *value* honesty but disagree as to how to put that into action. It is only once we have stated a principle—"never lie," or "never lie except to prevent great harm," for example—that we know what valuing honesty means in practical terms.

principles
Ethical rules that put values into action.

It is also worth noting that principles (e.g., "obey the law," "keep your promises," "uphold your contracts") create ethical duties that bind us to act or decide in certain ways. For example, there is an ethical rule prohibiting slave labor, even if this practice would have beneficial economic consequences for society.

duties
Those obligations that one is bound to perform, regardless of consequences. Duties might be derived from basic ethical principles, from the law, or from one's institutional or professional role.

What principles or rules should guide our decisions? Legal rules, obviously, are one major set of rules that we ought to follow. We have a duty to pay our taxes, even if we think the money might be more efficiently spent on our children's college education. I ought to stop at a red light, even if no cars are coming and I could get to my destination a little sooner by going straight through the light. I ought not to steal my neighbor's property, even if he will never miss it and I will gain many benefits from it. Decision making within a business context will involve many situations in which one ought to obey legal rules even when the consequences, economic and otherwise, seem to be undesirable.

Other rules are derived from various institutions in which we participate, or from various social roles that we fill. As a teacher, I ought to read each student's assignment carefully and diligently, even if they will never know the difference and their final grade will not be affected. In my role as teacher and university faculty member, I have taken on certain responsibilities that cannot be abandoned whenever it is convenient for me to do so. As the referee in a sporting event, I have the duty to enforce the rules fairly, even when it would be easier not to do so. Similar rule-based duties follow from our roles as friends ("do not gossip about your friends"), family members ("do your chores at home"), students ("do not plagiarize"), church members ("contribute to the church's upkeep"), citizens ("inform yourself about the issues"), and good neighbors ("do not operate your lawn mower before 8 A.M.").

Reality Check *Ethical Principles and the United Nations Global Compact*

Ethical principles and duties can often be found in corporate and professional codes of conduct. One example of such a code that has had worldwide impact is the UN Global Compact's Ten Principles. The United Nations launched the UN Global Compact in 2000 as a means to encourage businesses throughout the world to commit to ethical business practices. Businesses joining the Global Compact commit to following ten universal principles in the areas of human rights, labor, the environment, and anticorruption. The UN Global Compact Ten Principles are as follows:

Human Rights

Principle 1: Businesses should support and respect the protection of internationally proclaimed human rights; and

Principle 2: make sure that they are not complicit in human rights abuses.

Labour Standards

Principle 3: Businesses should uphold the freedom of association and the effective recognition of the right to collective bargaining;

Principle 4: the elimination of all forms of forced and compulsory labour;

Principle 5: the effective abolition of child labour; and

Principle 6: the elimination of discrimination in respect of employment and occupation.

Environment

Principle 7: Businesses should support a precautionary approach to environmental challenges;

Principle 8: undertake initiatives to promote greater environmental responsibility; and

Principle 9: encourage the development and diffusion of environmentally friendly technologies.

Anti-Corruption

Principle 10: Businesses should work against corruption in all its forms, including extortion and bribery.

Source: United Nations Global Compact, *The Ten Principles,* www.unglobalcompact.org/what-is-gc/mission/principles. Reprinted with permission of United Nations Global Compact.

There will be many occasions in which such role-based duties arise in business. As an employee, one takes on a certain role that creates duties. Every business will have a set of rules that employees are expected to follow. Sometimes these rules are explicitly stated in a code of conduct, other times in employee handbooks, whereas still others are simply stated by managers. (See the Reality Check "Ethical Principles and the United Nations Global Compact.") Likewise, as a business manager, there are many rules one ought to follow in respect to stockholders, employees, suppliers, and other stakeholders.

Perhaps the most dramatic example of role-based duties concerns the work of professionals within business. Lawyers, accountants, auditors, financial analysts, and bankers have important roles to play within political and economic institutions. Many of these roles, often described as "gatekeeper functions," ensure the integrity and proper functioning of the economic, legal, or financial system. Chapter 2 introduced the idea of professional responsibilities within the workplace, and this theme will be developed further in Chapter 10.

The Enron and Arthur Andersen case provides a helpful example for understanding professional duties. While examining Enron's financial reports, the auditors at Arthur Andersen knew that diligent application of strict auditing standards

Reality Check *Alternative Medicine and the Risks of Consequence-Based Reasoning*

Homeopathy and other "alternative" therapies (such as Reiki and Traditional Chinese Medicine) continue to be controversial. Scientists tell us, with a high degree of confidence, that homeopathy in particular absolutely cannot have any therapeutic value; homeopathic remedies contain no active ingredients, and the principles according to which they are supposed to work conflict with all kinds of well-established science. Other alternative therapies (including some herbal remedies) may have some physical effects, but often such effects are poorly established, and in some cases manufacturing standards are quite low, leading to products of highly variable quality. But many pharmacies continue to sell homeopathy and other alternative treatments nonetheless. The U.S. National Center for Complementary and Integrative Health estimates that Americans spend over $33 billion on such treatments every year.* But this presents a puzzle. Pharmacies are generally overseen by pharmacists, who are health professionals with scientific training that enables them to understand the damning evidence against the effectiveness of alternative medicines. How can scientifically trained professionals sell scientifically doubtful or even disproven products?

One hypothesis, of course, is greed. Such products are *profitable*. But other, less cynical reasons are available. Some pharmacists are comfortable with selling homeopathy, for example, because they see little harm. There are, after all, absolutely no side effects (recall that homeopathy

has no active ingredients!), and for minor ailments, a "placebo" may bring patients psychological comfort. But on the other hand, if a very sick patient makes use of a homeopathic remedy instead of seeking an effective medicine prescribed by a physician, the outcome could be very bad indeed. Then again, if the patient really *wants and believes in* homeopathy, the pharmacist might well alienate the patient entirely if she refuses to discuss or sell a homeopathic remedy. This might lead to mistrust, and lead the patient even farther from scientifically proven medicines. So the full consequences of selling (or refusing to sell) homeopathic remedies may be hard to see,[†] and a pharmacist (or pharmacy owner) may naturally tend to see only the positive consequences of selling such a profitable product, and to downplay the negative ones.

The risks of consequence-based reasoning in such contexts is why many pharmacists promote a simpler, principle-based form of ethical reasoning, which includes this central principle: *Pharmacists should never sell a product that they do not believe to be supported by sound scientific evidence.*

*National Center for Complementary and Integrative Health, "The Use of Complementary and Alternative Medicine in the United States: Cost Data," https://nccih.nih.gov/news/camstats/costs/costdatafs.htm (accessed July 2, 2016).

[†]For more on the ethics of selling alternative medicines, see Chris MacDonald and Scott Gavura, "Alternative Medicine and the Ethics of Commerce," *Bioethics* 30, no. 2 (2016), pp. 77–84.

required one particular decision—to disclose the fraudulent financial practices of Enron. But they also knew that the consequences of this diligent application would be harmful to Arthur Andersen's business interests because Enron was one of its largest customers. A fair analysis of this aspect of the Enron–Arthur Andersen scandal would point out that Andersen's auditors failed their ethical duties precisely because they did not follow the rules governing their professional responsibilities and allowed beneficial consequences to override their professional principles.

Similarly, Volkswagen's engineers were caught between their professional duties and the business interests of their employer. As engineers, they had a responsibility to certify that the software program in the VW's emissions devices accurately reported output. As employees, they knew that doing so would mean that VW's diesel automobiles would fail to meet both environmental and financial targets, resulting in harmful business consequences. (For another case of professional duties and consequences, see the Reality Check "Alternative Medicine and the Risks of Consequence-Based Reasoning.")

So far we have mentioned legal rules, organizational rules, role-based rules, and professional rules. We can think of these rules as part of a very broad social agreement, or social "contract," that functions to organize and ease relations between individuals. No group could function if members were free at all times to decide for themselves what to do and how to act. By definition, any cooperative activity requires cooperation, that is, requires rules that each member follows.

In the view of many philosophers, there are ethical duties that are more fundamental and that bind us in a stricter way than the way we are bound by contracts or by professional duties. You should not be able to "quit" ethical duties and walk away from them in quite the way that one can dissolve a contract or walk away from professional duties by quitting the profession. In the language of many philosophers, ethical duties should be categorical imperatives rather than hypothetical. Hypothetical duties would be like a professional code of conduct that binds you *only if* you are a member of the profession. For example, I have a duty to accurately report on my employer's financial situation only if I am an auditor hired to do so. Categorical duties do not contain this "if" clause. I *should* or *must* (an imperative) obey a fundamental ethical rule *no matter what* (a categorical). I have, for example, a duty not to exploit children in the workplace, no matter what.

Human Rights and Duties

OBJECTIVE

Are there *any* such fundamental or "categorical" duties? Are there any rules we should follow, decisions we should make, no matter what the consequences and no matter who we are or what we desire? Many ethical traditions have answered these questions in terms of a fundamental respect owed to each human being. These traditions agree that each and every human being possesses an intrinsic value, or essential dignity, that should never be violated. Some religious traditions, for example, see this inherent dignity as something "endowed by the creator" or that stems from being created in the image and likeness of God.

A common way of expressing this insight is to say that each and every human being possesses a fundamental human right to be treated with respect and that this right creates duties on the part of every human to respect the rights of others. Eighteenth-century philosopher Immanuel Kant expressed this as the fundamental duty we all have to treat each person as an end in themselves and never only as means to our own ends. In other words, our fundamental duty is to treat people as subjects capable of living their own lives and not as mere objects that exist for our own purposes. To use the familiar subject/object categories from grammar, humans are subjects because they make decisions and perform actions rather than being objects that are acted upon. Humans have their own ends and purposes and therefore should not be treated simply as a means to the ends of others. Persons, in other words, must never be treated as mere tools. (One can understand why ethicists in this tradition cringe at the phrase "human resource management," rejecting the assumption that humans can be "resources" to be managed.)

categorical imperative
An imperative is a command or duty; "categorical" means that it is without exception. Thus, a categorical imperative is an overriding principle of ethics. Philosopher Immanual Kant offered several formulations of the categorical imperative: act so as the maxim implicit in your acts could be willed to be a universal law; treat persons as ends and never as means only; treat others as subjects, not objects.

Such human rights, or moral rights, have played a central role in the development of modern democratic political systems. The U.S. Declaration of Independence speaks of "inalienable rights" that cannot be taken away by government. Other democracies have similar rights embedded in their constitutions, such as in the Canadian Charter of Rights and Freedoms or France's Declaration of the Rights of Man and of the Citizen. Following World War II, the United Nations created the UN's Declaration of Human Rights as a means for holding all governments to fundamental standards of ethics.

To return to an earlier example, this rights-based framework of ethics would object to child labor because such practices violate our duty to treat children with respect. We violate the rights of children when we treat them as mere means to the ends of production and economic growth. We are treating them merely as means because, as children, they have not rationally and freely chosen their own ends. We are simply using them as tools, objects, or resources. Thus, even if child labor produced beneficial consequences, it would be ethically wrong because it violates a fundamental human right.

In this way, the concept of a human or moral right is central to the principle-based ethical tradition. The inherent dignity of each individual means that we cannot do whatever we choose to another person. Human rights protect individuals from being treated in ways that would violate their dignity and that would treat them as mere objects or means. Rights imply that some acts and some decisions are "off-limits." Accordingly, our fundamental moral duty (the categorical imperative) is to respect the fundamental human rights of others. Our rights establish limits on the decisions and authority of others.

Consider how rights function relative to the utilitarian goal of maximizing the overall good. Suppose that you owned a local business and your local government decided that your property would make a great location for a city park. Imagine that you are the only person who disagrees. On utilitarian grounds, it might seem that your land would best serve the overall good by being used for a park. However, your property *rights* prevent the community from taking your land (at least without fair compensation) to serve the public.

A similar point could be made by considering the case of the hackers who in 2014 hacked the iCloud file-storage accounts of a number of celebrities.[5] The hackers then stole and posted online a number of private photos, many of them containing nudity. Some might be tempted to argue, on utilitarian grounds, that this was a good thing to do. After all, while posting the photos caused embarrassment to the celebrities who were targeted, a very large number of people enjoyed having access to the photos. It is possible, then, that the hackers had caused more happiness overall by posting the photos than had they left the celebrities' iCloud accounts alone. But such an analysis ignores the celebrities' right to privacy. The photos may have been enjoyed by a large number of people, but those people didn't own them. They were the private property of the celebrities involved. And surely the celebrities involved would argue that their rights should not have been violated simply to produce happiness for other people.

In summary, we can say that human rights are meant to offer protection of certain central human interests, prohibiting the sacrifice of these interests merely to provide a net increase in the overall happiness. The standard account of human rights offered through the Western ethical tradition connects basic human rights to some theory of a basic human nature. The Kantian tradition claims that our fundamental human rights, and the duties that follow from them, are derived from our nature as free and rational beings. Humans do not act only out of instinct and conditioning; they make free choices about how they live their lives, about their own goals. In this sense, humans are said to have a fundamental human right of **autonomy,** or "self-rule."

Human Rights and Social Justice

autonomy
From the Greek for "self-ruled," autonomy is the capacity to make free and deliberate choices. The capacity for autonomous action is what explains the inherent dignity and intrinsic value of individual human beings.

From these origins, we can see how two related rights have emerged as fundamental components of social justice. If autonomy, or self-rule, is a fundamental characteristic of human nature, then the liberty to make our own choices deserves special protection as a basic right. But because all humans possess this fundamental characteristic, equal treatment and equal consideration must also be fundamental rights. Liberty and equality are, according to much of this tradition, "natural rights" that are more fundamental and persistent than the legal rights created by governments and communities. (See the Reality Check "Are Fundamental Human Rights Universally Accepted?")

Liberty and equality are also the core elements of most modern conceptions of social justice. They are in particular fundamental to theories of social justice upon which democratic societies and capitalist economies have been built and, thus, are crucial to an understanding of business ethics.

Libertarian understandings of social justice argue that individual liberty—freedom from coercion by others—is the most central element of social justice. This means that a just society is one in which individuals are free from governmental intrusion as long as they are not harming others. Political perspectives that seek to reduce the size of government and limit government regulation of the market typically cite individual liberty as their primary ethical justification.

If we acknowledge liberty as the most basic human right, it would be easy to generate an argument for a more laissez-faire, free-market economic system. As long as individuals are not harming others, they should be free to engage in any voluntary economic exchange. Government's only role, in such a system, is to ensure that there is free and open competition and that economic transactions are free from coercion, fraud, and deception.

From this libertarian perspective, businesses should be free to pursue profit in any voluntary and nondeceptive manner. An ethical business is one that pursues profit within the law. Unethical business practices would include fraud, deception, and anticompetitive behavior. Government regulation aimed at preventing such behaviors, as well as government activity to enforce contracts and compensate for harms, would be just. All other government regulation would be seen as unjust interference in the market.

Reality Check *Are Fundamental Human Rights Universally Accepted?*

In 1948—just three years after the end of the Second World War—the United Nations adopted a Universal Declaration of Human Rights. Since that time, this Declaration has been translated into more than 300 languages and dialects. The Declaration contains 30 articles outlining basic human rights. In part, the Declaration includes the following:

PREAMBLE

Recognition of the inherent dignity and of the equal and inalienable rights of all members of the human family is the foundation of freedom, justice and peace in the world.

Article 1.

All human beings are born free and equal in dignity and rights. They are endowed with reason and conscience and should act towards one another in a spirit of brotherhood.

Article 2.

Everyone is entitled to all the rights and freedoms set forth in this Declaration, without distinction of any kind, such as race, colour, sex, language, religion, political or other opinion, national or social origin, property, birth or other status.

Article 3.

Everyone has the right to life, liberty and security of person.

Article 4.

No one shall be held in slavery or servitude; slavery and the slave trade shall be prohibited in all their forms.

Article 5.

No one shall be subjected to torture or to cruel, inhuman or degrading treatment or punishment.

Article 9.

No one shall be subjected to arbitrary arrest, detention or exile.

Article 10.

Everyone is entitled in full equality to a fair and public hearing by an independent and impartial tribunal, in the determination of his rights and obligations and of any criminal charge against him.

Article 18.

Everyone has the right to freedom of thought, conscience and religion; this right includes freedom to change his religion or belief, and freedom, either alone or in community with others and in public or private, to manifest his religion or belief in teaching practice, worship and observance.

Article 19.

Everyone has the right to freedom of opinion and expression; this right includes freedom to hold opinions without interference and to seek, receive and impart information and ideas through any media and regardless of frontiers.

Article 23.

(1) Everyone has the right to work, to free choice of employment, to just and favourable conditions of work and to protection against unemployment.

(2) Everyone, without any discrimination, has the right to equal pay for equal work.

(3) Everyone who works has the right to just and favourable remuneration ensuring for himself and his family an existence worthy of human dignity, and supplemented, if necessary, by other means of social protection.

(4) Everyone has the right to form and to join trade unions for the protection of his interests.

Article 25.

(1) Everyone has the right to a standard of living adequate for the health and well-being of himself and of his family, including food, clothing, housing and medical care and necessary social services, and the right to security in the event of unemployment, sickness, disability, widowhood, old age or other lack of livelihood in circumstances beyond his control.

Article 26.

(1) Everyone has the right to education.

Source: United Nations, Declaration of Human Rights.

Egalitarian versions of justice, on the other hand, argue that equality is the most central element of social justice. *Socialist* egalitarian theories argue that equal distribution of basic economic goods and services is at the heart of social justice. Other egalitarian theories argue that equal opportunity, more than equality of outcome, is crucial. Egalitarian theories of social justice typically support greater governmental responsibility in the economy as a necessary means to guarantee equality of opportunity outcomes.

Human Rights and Legal Rights

OBJECTIVE

human rights
Those moral rights that individuals have simply in virtue of being a human being. Also called *natural rights* or *moral rights.*

It will be helpful at this point to distinguish between human rights and legal rights. To illustrate this distinction, let us take employee rights as an example. Three kinds of employee rights are common in business. First, there are those *legal* rights granted to employees on the basis of legislation or judicial rulings. For example, employees have a right to receive a minimum wage, to have equal opportunity, to bargain collectively as part of a union, to be free from sexual harassment, and so forth. Second, employees have rights to those goods that they are entitled to on the basis of contractual agreements with employers. In this sense, a particular employee might have a right to a specific health care package, a certain number of paid holidays, pension funds, and the like. Finally, employees have rights grounded in moral entitlements to which employees have a claim independently of any particular legal or contractual factors. Examples of such rights include the right not to be bullied, the right not to be lied to, and the right not to be sexually harassed. Such rights would originate with the respect owed to them as human beings.

It is worth considering how legal and contractual rights interact. In general, both parties to an employment agreement bargain over the conditions of work. Employers offer certain wages, benefits, and working conditions and in return seek worker productivity. Employees offer skills and abilities and seek wages and benefits in return. Thus, employment rights emerge from contractual promises. However, certain goods are legally exempt from such negotiation. An employer cannot make a willingness to submit to sexual harassment or acceptance of a wage below the minimum established by law a part of the employment agreement. In effect, legal rights place certain issues outside the realm of the employment contract. Such legal rights set the basic legal framework within which business operates. They are established by the legal system and, in this sense, are part of the price of doing business.

So, too, human rights lie outside of the bargaining that occurs between employers and employees. Unlike the minimum wage, moral rights are established and justified by moral, rather than legal, considerations. Moral rights establish the basic moral framework for the legal environment itself, and more specifically for any contracts that are negotiated within business. Thus, as described in the U.S. Declaration of Independence and in the Canadian Charter of Rights and Freedoms, governments and laws are created in order to secure more fundamental natural moral rights. The rights outlined earlier in the excerpt from the United Nations fit this conception of fundamental moral rights. (See Decision Point "Should All Human Rights Become Legal Rights?")

Decision Point

Should All Human Rights Become Legal Rights?

Employees have both human rights (as persons) and legal rights (as employees). Some rights—such as the right to be treated equally regardless of sexual identity—have only quite recently been recognized as legal rights. For example, in 2015 the U.S. Equal Employment Opportunity Commission ruled that workplace discrimination based on sexual orientation is a form of sex discrimination, and is hence illegal under the the 1964 Civil Rights Act.* And yet many would argue that freedom from such discrimination is a human right. That is, they would argue that all employees had a right not to be discriminated against all along. From an ethical point of view, that right didn't just appear with the recent *legal* recognition of it—the right was there all along. This raises an interesting question: Should all human rights be entrenched in law, such that they become legal rights? Why or why not? Why might some rights be recognized as human rights and yet not turned into legal rights?

*Dale Carpenter, "Anti-gay Discrimination Is Sex Discrimination, Says the EEOC," *Washington Post* (July 16, 2015), www.washingtonpost.com/news/volokh-conspiracy/wp/2015/07/16/anti-gay-discrimination-is-sex-discrimination-says-the-eeoc/ (accessed July 3, 2016).

Challenges to an Ethics of Rights and Duties

OBJECTIVE

So what rights do we have, and what does that mean for the duties of others? In the U.S. Declaration of Independence, Thomas Jefferson claimed that we have "inalienable rights" to life, liberty, and the pursuit of happiness. Jefferson was influenced by the British philosopher John Locke, who spoke of "natural rights" to life, health, liberty, and possessions. The UN Universal Declaration of Human Rights (see again the Reality Check "Are Fundamental Human Rights Universally Accepted?") lists more than 26 human rights that it says are universal.

Acknowledging this diversity of rights makes it easy to understand the two biggest challenges to this ethical tradition. There appears to be much disagreement about what rights truly are basic human rights and, given the multiplicity of views about this, it is unclear how to apply this approach to practical situations, especially in cases where rights appear to conflict.

Take, for example, a possible right to health care. Many societies have concluded that health care is a human right, and many countries have instituted national health plans to provide citizens with at least minimal health care. The UN Declaration would seem to agree, claiming that humans have a right "to a standard of living adequate for the health and well-being" and that this right includes medical care. But many disagree and point out that such a right would carry significant costs for others. During debates over health care reform in the U.S. Congress in 2017, for example, many disputed the claim that humans have a right to health care. If every human has a right to health care, who has the duty to provide it and at what costs? Does this mean that doctors and nurses can be required to provide free medical care? Does it mean that the government has a duty to provide and pay for heath insurance? Does this right entail a right to the best treatment possible? To elective surgeries? To wellness care or nursing homes? To cosmetic surgery?

Critics charge that unless there is a specific person or institution that has a duty to provide the goods identified as "rights," talk of rights amounts to little more than a wish list of things that people want. What are identified as "rights" often are nothing more than good things that most people desire. But, if every human truly does have a right to a standard of living adequate for all the goods mentioned in Article 25 of the UN Declaration, who has the duty to provide them?

More relevant to business is the Declaration's Article 23 that everyone has a "right to work, to free choice of employment." What would this mean to a business? Is it helpful to say that an employee's human rights are violated if he or she is laid off during a recession? Who has the duty to provide jobs to every unemployed person? This same article refers to a "right to just and favourable remuneration." But what is a just wage, and who gets to decide?

The first major challenge to an ethics based on rights is that there is no agreement about the scope and range of such rights. Which good things qualify as rights, and which are merely things that people want? Critics charge that there is no uncontroversial way to answer this. Yet, unless there is some clear way to distinguish the two, the list of rights will only grow to unreasonable lengths and the corresponding duties will unreasonably burden everyone.

A second challenge also points to practical problems in applying a theory of rights to real-life situations. With a long list of human rights, all of which are claimed to be basic and fundamental, how would we decide between one individual's right to medical care and the physician's right to just remuneration of her work? Suppose the person needing medical care could not afford to pay a just fee for the care?

Perhaps the most important rights-related conflict in a business setting would occur when an employer's rights to property come into conflict with an employee's alleged rights to work, just wages, and health care. While the UN Declaration does not mention a right to property as a basic human right, many philosophers in the Western tradition agree with John Locke and include it among our natural rights. Granting economic rights to employees would seem to create numerous conflicts with the property rights of employers. Critics point out that the ethical tradition of rights and duties has been unable to provide a persuasive and systematic account for how such conflicts are to be resolved.

Virtue Ethics: Making Decisions Based on Integrity and Character

OBJECTIVE

For the most part, utilitarian and principle-based frameworks focus on rules that we might follow in deciding what we should do, both as individuals and as citizens. These approaches conceive of a practical reason in terms of deciding how to act and what to do. Chapter 1 pointed out, however, that ethics also involves questions about the type of person one should become. Virtue ethics is a tradition within philosophical ethics that seeks a full and detailed description of those character traits, or virtues, that would constitute a good and full human life.

Reality Check *Virtues in Everyday Language*

The language of "virtues" and "vices" may seem old-fashioned or quaint for modern readers, but this was a dominant perspective on ethics in the Western world for centuries. Go ahead and develop a short list of adjectives that describe a good person's character, and you will find that the language of virtues and vices is not as outdated as it may seem.

The ancient Greeks identified four primary virtues: courage, moderation, wisdom, and justice. Early Christians described the three cardinal virtues of faith, hope, and charity. Boy Scouts pledge to be trustworthy, loyal, helpful, friendly, courteous, kind, obedient, cheerful, thrifty, brave, clean, and reverent.

According to ancient and medieval philosophers, the virtues represented a balanced midpoint, the "golden mean," between two extremes, both of which would be considered vices. Thus, for example, a brave person finds the balance between too little courage, which is cowardice, and too much courage, which is reckless and foolhardy.

The virtues are those character traits or habits that would produce a good, happy, and meaningful life. To practice such virtues and habits and act in accord with one's own character is to live a life of integrity.

When you stop to think about it, you'll find that talking about ethics in terms of character traits comes quite naturally. Can you think of examples of how we express appreciation of someone's character in everyday conversation with friends? Or how such appreciation is expressed in military contexts? Or in action movies? Or even in rap music?

Virtues can be understood as those character traits that would constitute parts of a good and meaningful human life. Being friendly and cheerful; having integrity; being honest, forthright, and truthful; having modest wants; and being tolerant are some of the characteristics that are typically thought of as making for a good and meaningful human life. (For additional qualities, see the Reality Check "Virtues in Everyday Language.") One can see virtue ethics at play in everyday situations: We all know people we look up to because we respect them for their character, and we all know people whom we describe as being people of integrity.

Perhaps the best place to see the ethics of virtue is in the goal of every good parent who hopes to raise happy and decent children. Parents confront the question of virtues and vices every day. I know my children will lead happier and more meaningful lives if they are honest, respectful, cheerful, moderate, and not greedy, envious, gloomy, arrogant, and selfish. Yet, simply *telling* my children to be honest and to avoid greed is insufficient. I cannot remain passive and assume that these traits will develop naturally. Instilling these character traits and habits is a long-term process that develops over time.

We'll find the language of virtue ethics at several points in this book, most notably in discussions of leadership and corporate culture. Consider how you would answer the question: What makes a good leader? Words like *decisive, transparent, honest, integrity, visionary, fair, empowering, respectful, inspirational,* and *courageous* come to mind. Each of the words describes a human virtue, traits that others can rely on because they are deeply ingrained within the person's character. Virtues are not characteristics that a person adopts one day, but forgets about and drops the next. They are enduring because they describe who that person truly is. Bad leaders not only lack such characteristics, they might also be described by such vices as self-centered, egoistic, mean-spirited, timid, unreliable, and undisciplined.

Similarly, consider how you might describe a good, ethical employee. Again, virtue words come to mind, characteristics such as trustworthy, loyal, creative, hard-working, motivated, reliable, and honest. Virtues for an employee in the retail sector might especially include cheerfulness, patience, and helpfulness. Bad employees might be characterized as lazy, dishonest, unreliable, or easily distracted.

To understand how virtue ethics differs from utilitarian and principle-based frameworks, consider the problem of egoism. As mentioned previously, egoism is a view that holds that people act only out of self-interest. Many economists, for example, seem to assume that all individuals always act out of self-interest; indeed, many seem to assume that rationality itself should be defined in terms of acting out of self-interest. The biggest challenge posed by egoism, and, according to some, the biggest challenge to ethics, is the apparent gap between self-interest and altruism, or between motivation that is "self-regarding" and motivation that is "other-regarding." Ethics requires us, at least at times, to act for the well-being of others. Yet, those who believe in egoism would claim that this is not possible.

An ethics of virtue shifts the focus from questions about what a person should *do,* to a focus on who that person *is.* This shift requires not only a different view of ethics but, at least as important, a different view of ourselves. Implicit in this distinction is the recognition that our identity as individuals is constituted in part by our wants, beliefs, values, and attitudes. A person's **character**—those dispositions, relationships, attitudes, values, and beliefs that popularly might be called a "personality"—is not some feature that remains independent of that person's identity. Character is not like a suit of clothes that you step into and out of at will. Rather, the self is identical to a person's most fundamental and enduring dispositions, attitudes, values, and beliefs.

character
The sum of relatively set traits, dispositions, and habits of an individual. Along with rational deliberation and choice, a person's character accounts for how she or he makes decisions and acts. Training and developing character so that it is disposed to act ethically is the goal of virtue ethics.

Note how this shift changes the nature of justification in ethics. If, as seems true for many people, justification of some act requires that it be tied to self-interest, we should not be surprised to find that this justification often fails. Ethical controversies often involve a conflict between self-interest and ethical values. Why should I do the ethical thing if it would require me to give up a lot of money? To a person whose personality does not already include a disposition to be modest, the only avenue open for justification would involve showing how such a disposition serves some other interest that person has, such as her own profit. Why should an executive turn down a multimillion-dollar bonus? The only way to answer this question appears to be to show how it would be in her self-interest to do so. But this is at times unlikely.

On the other hand, for the person already characterized by modest, down-to-earth desires, the question of justifying smaller salaries is less relevant. If I am the type of person who has moderate and restrained desires for money, then there is no temptation to be unethical for the sake of a large bonus. For many people, the "self" of self-interest is a caring, modest, authentic, altruistic self. For these people, there simply is no conflict between *self*-interest and altruism.

The degree to which we are capable of acting for the well-being of others therefore seems to depend on a variety of factors such as our desires, our beliefs, our dispositions, and our values; in short, it depends on our character or the type of person we are. If people are caring, empathetic, charitable, and sympathetic, then the challenge of selfishness and egoism is simply not a factor in their decision making.

Virtue ethics recognizes that our motivations—our interests, wants, desires—are not the sorts of things that each of us chooses anew each morning. Instead, human beings act according to who they are, according to their character. By adulthood, these character traits typically are deeply ingrained and conditioned within us. Given that our character plays such a key role in our behavior, and given the realization that our character can be shaped by factors that are controllable (by conscious individual decisions, by how we are raised, by the social institutions in which we live, work, and learn), virtue ethics seeks to understand how those traits are formed and which traits are conducive to and which ones undermine a meaningful, worthwhile, and satisfying human life.

Virtue ethics can offer us a more fully textured understanding of life within business. Rather than simply describing people's behavior as good or bad, and decisions as right or wrong, an ethics of virtue encourages a fuller description of persons as a whole. For example, we might describe a whistle-blower as heroic and courageous. We might describe a boss like Dan Price as a man of integrity, who sympathizes with employees and cares about their well-being. Other executives might be described as greedy or ruthless, proud or competitive. (See Reality Check "The Greed Is Astounding.") Faced with a difficult dilemma, we might ask not, What should I do? but, What would a person with *integrity* do? What would an *honest* person say? Do I have the *courage* of my convictions? In other words, you might think of (or imagine) someone you believe to be especially virtuous and ask yourself what that person would do in this situation. What would a virtuous person do?

Besides connecting the virtues to a conception of a fuller human life, virtue ethics also reminds us to examine how character traits are formed and conditioned. By the time we are adults, much of our character is formed by such factors as our parents, schools, church, friends, and society. But powerful social institutions such as business and especially our own places of employment and our particular roles within them (e.g., manager, professional, and trainee) have a profound influence on shaping our character. Consider an accounting firm that hires a group of trainees fully expecting that fewer than half will be retained after one year and where only a very small group will make partner. That corporate environment encourages motivations and behavior very different from a firm that hires fewer people but gives them all a greater chance at long-term success. A company that sets unrealistic sales goals will find it creates a different sales force than one that understands sales more as customer service. Virtue ethics reminds us to look to the actual practices we find in the business world and to ask what types of people are being created by these practices. Many individual moral dilemmas that arise within business ethics can best be understood as arising from a tension between the type of person we seek to be and the type of person business expects us to be. (See the Reality Check "Where Do Virtues Come From?")

Reality Check *The Greed Is Astounding*

Mylan Inc. is a U.S. pharmaceutical company that manufactures the EpiPen, an easy-to-use auto-injection medical device. EpiPen delivers the proper dosage of epinephrine, a drug that safely and effectively counteracts anaphylaxis, a severe allergic reaction that can close a person's breathing passages and cause death. EpiPen is especially effective because the proper dosage can be quickly delivered by anyone—the person him- or herself, co-workers, teachers, bystanders—by simply placing the device against the skin and pushing a button. Because of the ease of use, EpiPens are especially popular for treating severe allergies in children, and as a result they have saved countless lives.

The device itself is simple and inexpensive, costing at most a few dollars to manufacture. The drug epinephrine is also inexpensive, costing less than one dollar per dose. But epinephrine degrades over time, so medical professionals recommend that unused devices be replaced at least once a year. It is not uncommon for someone susceptible to anaphylaxis to keep several on hand at work, school, or home. Because the EpiPen has been in use and proven its effectiveness for over forty years, the initial investment required to develop the product has long since been recovered.

Mylan purchased rights to the EpiPen in 2007. At the time, EpiPens sold for under $60 each, and annual sales approached $200 million. By 2016, when few competitors remained and Mylan had a 90% share of the market, the company had raised the price for a two-pack of EpiPens to over $600. It was estimated that in 2016, sales of EpiPen produced close to $1.5 billion in revenues. During this same period, Mylan's CEO's pay rose from $2.3 to $19 million annually. In 2016, former CEO Robert Coury was reported to have received over $90 million in compensation from Mylan.

In 2016, Mylan came under serious public criticism for increasing the price of EpiPen. Some critics pointed out that Mylan's CEO, Heather Bresch, was the daughter of former West Virginia governor and present U.S. Senator Joe Manchin. These critics claimed that her political connections helped paved the way for governmental regulations, including increased risk warnings for anaphylaxis; encouragement to schools to stock EpiPens; and regulations to make EpiPens as publicly available as defibrillators.

In October 2016, Bresch was called to testify before the U.S. Congress to defend Mylan's actions. During Bresch's testimony to the U.S. House Oversight and Government Reform Committee, Congressman John Duncan told her, "The greed is astounding, it's sickening and disgusting. I'm a very conservative, pro-business Republican, but I am really sickened by what I heard today and by what I've read before about this situation. In my opinion, no one can really earn or deserve $19 million a year."*

1. Is it accurate to describe a CEO who is paid $19 million annually as "greedy"? How about a $90 million payment upon retirement?

2. In the 1987 movie *Wall Street*, the character Gordon Gekko, played by actor Michael Douglas, famously claimed that "greed is good." Is greed a virtue or a vice? Do greedy people tend to live a better or worse human life?

*__Source:__ Congressman John Duncan, October 2016, *Response to Heather Bresch, Mylan CEO during testimony in front of U.S. House Oversight and Government Reform Committee.*

Consider an example described by someone (whom the authors of this textbook know) who has conducted empirical studies of the values found within marketing firms and advertising agencies. This person reported that, on several occasions, advertising agents told her that they would never allow their own children to watch the very television shows and advertisements that their own firms were producing. By their own admission, the ads for such shows aim to manipulate children into buying, or getting their parents to buy, products that had little or no real value. In some cases, the ads promoted beer drinking and the advertisers themselves admitted, as their "dirty little secret," that they were intended to target the teenage

Reality Check   *Where Do Virtues Come From?*

Where do virtues come from? How do we become good people?

Plato's famous dialogue the *Meno* opens with the title character asking Socrates this basic question: Can virtue be taught? If ethics involves developing the right sort of character traits and habits, as the virtue theorist holds, then the acquisition of those traits becomes a fundamental question for ethics. Can we teach people to be honest, trustworthy, loyal, courteous, moderate, respectful, and compassionate?

Meno (the title character of the dialogue) initially cast the question in terms of two alternatives: either virtue is taught or it is acquired naturally. In modern terms, this is the question of nurture or nature, environment or genetics. Socrates's answer is more complicated. Virtue cannot simply be taught by others, nor is it acquired automatically through nature. Each individual has the natural potential to become virtuous, and learning from one's surroundings is a part of this process. But, ultimately, virtues must be developed by each individual through a complex process of personal reflection, reasoning, practice, and observation as well as social reinforcement and conditioning. Virtues are habits, and acquiring any habit is a subtle and complex process.

Parents confront this question every day. I know my children will lead happier and more meaningful lives if they are honest, respectful, cheerful, moderate, and not greedy, envious, gloomy, arrogant, or selfish. Yet simply telling my children to be honest and to avoid greed is insufficient; nor can I remain passive and assume that these traits will develop naturally. Instilling these character traits and habits is a long-term process that develops over time.

Business institutions also have come to recognize that character formation is both difficult and unavoidable. Employees come to business with certain character traits and habits, and these can get shaped and reinforced in the workplace. Hire a person with the wrong character traits, and there will be trouble ahead. Designing a workplace or creating a corporate culture to reinforce good character traits and discourage bad ones is one of the greatest challenges for an ethical manager.

market. Further, their own research evidenced the success of their ads in increasing sales.

Independent of the ethical questions we might ask about advertising aimed at children, a virtue ethics approach would look at the type of individuals who are so able to disassociate themselves and their own values from their work and the social institutions and practices that encourage it. What kind of people are willing to subject others' children to marketing practices that they are unwilling to accept for their own children? Such individuals seem to lack even the most elementary form of personal integrity. What kind of organization encourages people to treat children in ways that they willingly admit are indecent? What kind of people do they become working in such an organization?

Finally, the virtue ethics focus on character formation should lead us to ask questions about the choices we make and how those choices affect our character. This can happen in two ways. First, note that each decision you make has a subtle but meaningful impact on subsequent decisions. Each lie, as the saying goes, makes it easier to tell the next lie. Indeed, each small lie makes it easier for you to tell bigger and bigger lies. This suggests that there is a reciprocal relationship between character and action: Our character affects how we act, but how we act ends up affecting our character. (For more about the way our choices affect the person we eventually become, see the Reality Check "What Will They Say When You Retire?")

Reality Check *What Will They Say When You Retire?*

One useful way to think about character is to ask yourself this question: When you retire, likely many years from now, what will people say about you at your retirement party? Certainly they will congratulate you, and point to your various achievements, and to the important milestones of your career. But they will likely also talk about who you *are*. What will they say about the kind of person you are—about your character?

More to the point, what do *you* *want* them to say about you? Do you want them to say that throughout your career you were "a tough-minded businessperson" or "a

kind and generous co-worker"? Do you aspire to being remembered as a "watchful boss" or as a "supportive mentor"? Do you hope they will describe you as "dedicated to your job" or as "devoted to friends and family"? What other character traits do you hope, looking forward, they will use to describe you and your career?

Finally, ask yourself: What can I do between now and then to make that wish come true? How should I behave over the coming decades to make myself into the kind of person who will earn the kinds of words I hope they'll use to describe me when I retire?

The second way in which our choices affect our character is through the people we choose to associate with and the organizations we choose to become part of. If you spend time with patient, gentle people, you are liable to become more like them. If you spend time with mean, belligerent people, you are likely to become more like *them*. This has important implications for the companies we choose to work for. As we will discuss further in Chapter 4, the organizational cultures that we become part of will inevitably change who we are as persons. So it is best to choose carefully.

A Decision-Making Model for Business Ethics Revisited

This chapter provided an introduction to three historically and philosophically important ethical frameworks. While some of the material covered in this chapter might appear esoteric and too abstract for a business ethics class, all of it has a very practical aim. Understanding the philosophical basis of ethics will enable you to become more aware of ethical issues, better able to recognize the significance of your decisions, and more likely to make better-informed and more reasonable decisions. In addition, the theories allow us to better and more articulately explain ourselves when we are asked why we have made or intend to make a particular decision. Whereas a statement such as "we should do this because it is the right thing to do" will often be seen as vague or unpersuasive, an alternative explanation such as "we should do this because more people will be better off than will be harmed if we do so" could be much more effective and convincing. When a key stakeholder asks you why you support or oppose a specific proposal, your response now has comprehensive substance behind it and will therefore be more sophisticated, credible, and convincing.

These ethical theories and traditions also provide important ways in which to develop the decision-making model introduced in Chapter 2. These ethical

Over the course of the year following Dan Price's April 2015 announcement, he was embroiled in a legal battle with his brother Lucas, co-owner of Gravity Payments.* Lucas Price sued Dan, claiming that his brother had violated the 2008 agreement governing the ownership and management of the company. Under the terms of that agreement, Dan owned 67.5 percent of the company, and Lucas stepped away from what had previously been his day-to-day involvement in the company. Lucas sued, in part, because he says his brother had failed to involve him even in very major decisions—including the decision to change how much Gravity workers were paid. The lawsuit also claimed that Dan was paying himself too much. Court documents showed that Dan had tried to get his own total compensation raised to $5.5 million, which amounted to more than half of the company's total revenue. At the time of writing, the judge in the case had agreed to the two brothers' request to be allowed to attempt to resolve their problems out of court, through mediation.

1. Dan Price's decision to pay Gravity employees more required spending some of the company's profits. Did this violate the rights of his brother, Lucas, given that Lucas wasn't consulted first?

2. Dan Price's announcement that he would himself be taking a substantial cut in pay (to pay for *part* of the raise his employees would be getting) came just two weeks after he learned that his brother was suing him. Does that change your assessment of the ethics of his decision to shift most of his own compensation to his employees?

3. Using the vocabulary of virtue ethics, how would you describe your original impression of Dan Price? How would you describe him in light of the information on this page?

*Rachel Lerman, "Gravity Payments Brothers Square Off in Court," *Seattle Times* (May 31, 2016), www.seattletimes.com/business/technology/brothers-square-off-in-court-over-company-paying-employees-70k-a-year/.

theories, after all, provide systematic and sophisticated ways to think and reason about ethical questions. We now can offer a more detailed version of our decision-making model, one in which ethical theories are integrated into an explicit decision procedure. The decision-making process introduced here aims, above all else, to help you make ethically responsible business decisions. To summarize, we now review that decision-making process in more detail.

1. **Determine the facts.** Gather all of the relevant facts. It is critical at this stage that we do not unintentionally bias our later decision by gathering only those facts in support of one particular outcome.

2. **Identify the ethical issues involved.** What is the ethical dimension? What is the ethical issue? Often we do not even notice the ethical dilemma. Avoid normative myopia.

3. **Identify stakeholders.** Who will be affected by this decision? What are their relationships, to me, and what is their power over my decision or results? Who has

a stake in the outcome? Do not limit your inquiry only to those stakeholders to whom you believe you owe a duty; sometimes a duty becomes clear only once the impact on a stakeholder is assessed. For instance, you might not necessarily first consider your competitors as stakeholders; however, once you understand the impact of your decision on those competitors, an ethical duty may arise.

4. **Consider the available alternatives.** Exercise "moral imagination." Are there creative ways to resolve conflicts? Explore not only the obvious choices, but also those that are less obvious and that require some creative thinking or thinking "outside the box."

5. **Compare and weigh the alternatives.** Take the point of view of other people involved. How is each stakeholder affected by my decision? Compare and weigh the alternatives: Ethical theories and traditions can help here.

   a. Consequences
      i. Beneficial and harmful consequences to all parties affected.
   b. Duties, rights, principles
      i. What does the law say?
      ii. Are there professional duties involved?
      iii. Which principles are most obligatory?
      iv. Are people being treated fairly, with respect for their autonomy and equality?
   c. Implications for personal integrity and character
      i. What type of person am I becoming through this decision?
      ii. What are my own principles and purposes?
      iii. Can I live with public disclosure of this decision?
      iv. Is this a decision of which I can be proud? Is this a decision that will prove embarrassing?

6. **Make a Decision.** Is this a point-in-time decision, or something that will be carried out over time? What is your plan, and how are you going to implement it? What will you do if something unexpected happens as a result?

7. **Monitor and Learn.** Have you built in mechanisms for assessment of your decision and possible modifications? Make sure that you learn from each decision and move forward with that increased knowledge; you may face similar decisions in the future or find it necessary to make changes to your current situation. Do policies or procedures need to be revised as a result of this situation or its resolution?

Questions, Projects, and Exercises

1. Not all ethical norms get entrenched in law. In which philosophical tradition—consequences, rights, or virtue—are we most likely to find norms that have ended up becoming laws?

2. What makes a decision or issue an *ethical* one? How would you explain the differences between ethical/nonethical, on one hand, and ethical/unethical, on the other?

3. What ethical disputes or dilemmas have you experienced in your own workplace? What about in a club or student group you belong to? How were these disputes or dilemmas resolved?

4. Do an internet search on international human rights and/or fundamental moral rights. Can you find any moral rights that seem to be universally acknowledged across all cultures?

5. Why might economic growth be considered a utilitarian goal?

6. Some political philosophers understand the ethical foundations of legislatures to be utilitarian, while the ethical foundation of the judiciary is deontological. How would you explain this distinction?

7. If the right to *autonomy* is the right to make your own free and deliberate choices, what limits do you think there must be on that right? Does the right to autonomy literally allow us to do anything we want?

8. The right of private property is often described as a "bundle" of rights. What rights are involved in ownership of property? Given this understanding, should shareholders be considered owners of corporations?

9. Can such character traits as honesty, loyalty, trustworthiness, compassion, and humility be taught? Do people learn to be selfish, greedy, or aggressive, or do these traits come naturally?

10. Do professionals such as physicians, accountants, and lawyers have duties and obligations that other people do not? Where would such duties come from?

Key Terms

After reading this chapter, you should have a clear understanding of the following key terms. For a complete definition, please see the Glossary.

autonomy, *p. 77*	duties, *p. 72*	principles, *p. 72*
categorical imperative, *p. 75*	egoism, *p. 66*	utilitarianism, *p. 62*
	ethical relativism, *p. 63*	virtue ethics, *p. 62*
character, *p. 83*	human rights, *p. 79*	
consequentialist theories, *p. 64*	principle-based framework, *p. 62*	

Endnotes

1. Source: Jeff Bezos, April 2019. *Letter to Amazon Shareholders.*

2. Patricia Cohen, "One Company's New Minimum Wage: $70,000 a Year," *The New York Times* (April 13, 2015), www.nytimes.com/2015/04/14/business/owner-of-gravity-payments-a-credit-card-processor-is-setting-a-new-minimum-wage-70000-a-year.html (accessed June 26, 2016).

3. Caleb Melby, "Executive Pay: Valuing CEOs," *Bloomberg.com* (March 15, 2015), www.bloomberg.com/quicktake/executive-pay (accessed June 26, 2016).

4. Caleb Melby, "Executive Pay: Valuing CEOs," *Bloomberg.com* (March 15, 2015), www.bloomberg.com/quicktake/executive-pay (accessed June 26, 2016).

5. See "iCloud Leaks of Celebrity Photos," *Wikipedia,* https://en.wikipedia.org/wiki/ICloud_leaks_of_celebrity_photos (accessed July 3, 2016).

Chapter

The Corporate Culture—Impact and Implications

Culture eats strategy for breakfast.

Peter Drucker

If you are lucky enough to be someone's employer, then you have a moral obligation to make sure people do look forward to coming to work in the morning.

John Mackey, CEO and co-founder, Whole Foods Market

I came to see, in my time at IBM, that culture isn't just one aspect of the game, it is the game. In the end, an organization is nothing more than the collective capacity of its people to create value.

Louis Gerstner, past chairman and CEO, IBM

Imagine that you work in the Human Resources department of your company. Your CEO has asked your department to develop an ethics program for the firm, and you have been assigned responsibility for creating it. You have been asked to report back to your CEO in two weeks with a draft version of a code of ethics for the company, a summary of other elements that the ethics program will include, and a proposal for how you will be able to assess whether the program is working. Your CEO also asks that you come prepared to explain what role she can play in promoting ethics and how she can help to ensure the success of the overall ethics program.

You begin your research and quickly find that there are a number of desirable and potentially overlapping outcomes of ethics programs. Successful programs can be effective in:

1. Uncovering unethical/illegal behavior and reducing meltdowns, helping your firm to either avoid or reduce fines and/or criminal charges.
2. Raising awareness of ethical and legal issues.
3. Serving as a resource for guidance and advice.
4. Ensuring more accurate reports of wrongdoing.
5. Encouraging greater customer loyalty, resulting in increased sales and better reputation.
6. Encouraging staff to incorporate firm values in decision processes.
7. Enhancing employee commitment and loyalty to the organization, resulting in higher productivity.
8. Raising satisfaction of external and internal stakeholder needs (all resulting in more effective financial performance).

Play the role of this HR person in several different types of businesses: a fast-food restaurant, an automobile dealership, a retail store selling consumer electronics, a government agency, and a large international corporation.[1]

1. List the issues you think should be addressed in a code of ethics.
2. Other than a code of ethics, what other elements would you include in an ethics program?
3. How will you define "success"? Are there any facts that you will need to gather to make this judgment?
4. How would you measure success along the way? How will you measure whether your ethics program is "working" before you reach any end objective?
5. Whom will you define as your primary stakeholders?
6. What are the interests of your stakeholders in your program and what are the impacts of your program on each stakeholder? How might the measurement of the program's success influence the type of people attracted to the firm or people who are most motivated within your organization?
7. How will you answer the CEO's questions about her own role in promoting ethics?

Chapter Objectives

After reading this chapter, you will be able to:

1. Define corporate culture.
2. Explain how corporate culture impacts ethical decision making.
3. Discuss the differences between a compliance-based culture and a values-based culture.
4. Discuss the role of corporate leadership in establishing the culture.
5. Explain the difference between effective leaders and ethical leaders.
6. Discuss the role of mission statements and codes in creating an ethical corporate culture.
7. Explain how various reporting mechanisms such as ethics hotlines and ombudspersons can help integrate ethics within a firm.
8. Discuss the role of assessing, monitoring, and auditing the culture and ethics program.
9. Explain how culture can be enforced via governmental regulation.

What Is Corporate Culture?

This chapter examines the ways in which corporations develop ethical cultures. Cultures in organizations encourage and support individuals in making ethically responsible decisions—or they do not! The ethical decision-making model emphasizes individual responsibility for the decisions we make. These decisions impact your personal integrity and also have consequences for many stakeholders with whom business organizations interact.

But personal decision making does not exist in a vacuum. Decision making within a firm is influenced, limited, shaped, and, in some cases, virtually determined by the corporate culture of the firm. Individuals can be helped—or hindered—in making the "right" or "wrong" decision (according to their own values) by the expectations, values, and structure of the organization in which they live and work. We will explore in this chapter some of the major issues surrounding the development, influence, and management of a corporate culture, as well as the role of business leaders in creating, enhancing, and preserving cultures that support ethical behavior.

Even in this age of decentralized corporations and other institutions, there remains a sense of culture in organizations. This is especially true in small local firms, but it is just as true of major global corporations such as BMW or Google. Despite the fact that corporations have many locations, with diverse employee groups and management styles, an individual working for a large global firm in one country will share various aspects of her or his working culture with someone working for the same firm halfway around the world. This is not to say that their working environments cannot be wholly different in many regards; the corporate culture, however, survives the distance and differences.

FIGURE 4.1

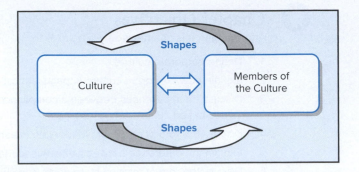

OBJECTIVE

culture
A shared pattern of
beliefs, expectations,
and meanings that influ-
ences and guides the
thinking and behaviors
of the members of a par-
ticular group.

What do we mean by *corporate culture?* Every organization has a **culture** fashioned by a shared pattern of beliefs, expectations, and meanings that influences and guides the thinking and behaviors of the members of that organization. While culture shapes the people who are members of the organization, it is also shaped by the people who make up that organization. (See Figure 4.1.)

Consider how your own company or organization or school, dormitory, or fraternity/sorority differs from a similar one. Is there a "type" of person who is stereotypical of your organization, dormitory, or fraternity/sorority? Are there unspoken but still persuasive standards and expectations that shape students at your school or workplace? How would you be different if you had chosen a different university, joined a different fraternity or sorority, or participated in a different organization? (See the Reality Check "Built to Last.") As you think about stereotypes, consider also how gender roles and expectations might impact corporate culture. We will unpack that question, and the impact of the #MeToo movement on the workplace environment, in Chapter 6, where we discuss "Rights and Responsibilities in Conflict," and also offer some background in the Reality Check included in that section, "#MeToo in the Work Place."

If culture involves a shared pattern of beliefs, expectations, and meanings, then we will find it at different levels including:

- Religious, ethnic, and linguistic affiliation.
- Generation.
- Gender.
- Social class.
- Organization/corporate.
- Family.

The cultural elements might then be illustrated by various characteristics such as language, the use of space, perceptions of time, the interpretation of nonverbal behaviors, the importance of hierarchy, the definition of gender roles, and criteria for success, among many others. The most well-known scholar in national culture research is Geert Hofstede. Though somewhat controversial, he organized national cultures into six "dimensions," or categories of predispositions.

Reality Check *Built to Last*

Does a corporate culture matter? James Collins and Jerry Porras, authors of the perennially best-selling book *Built to Last: Successful Habits of Visionary Companies,* researched successful companies looking for common practices that might explain their success. These companies not only outperformed their competitors in financial terms; they outperformed their competition financially *over the long term.* On average, the companies Collins and Porras studied were more than 100 years old. Among their key findings was the fact that the truly exceptional and sustainable companies all placed great emphasis on a set of core values. They defined core values as the "essential and enduring tenets" that help define the company and are "not to be compromised for financial gain or short-term expediency."*

Collins and Porras cite numerous examples of core values that were articulated and promoted by the founders and CEOs of such companies as IBM, Johnson & Johnson, Hewlett-Packard, Procter & Gamble, Walmart, Merck, Motorola, Sony, Walt Disney, General Electric, and Philip Morris (now called Altria). Some companies made "a commitment to customers" their core value, while others focused on employees, their products, innovation, or even risk-taking. The common theme was that core values and a clear corporate purpose, which together are described as the organization's core ideology, were essential elements of sustainable and financially successful companies.

In his follow-up book, *How the Mighty Fall: And Why Some Companies Never Give In,* Collins emphasized the importance of core values in staving off corporate decline. His later research reveals that key clues to corporate decline include when people cannot easily articulate what the organization stands for, where core values have eroded to the point of irrelevance, and when the organization has become "just another place to work." It is at this point when employees lose faith in their ability to triumph and prevail. Instead of passionately believing in the organization's core values and purpose, employees become distrustful, regarding visions and values as little more than PR and rhetoric.†

Harvard professors Jim Heskett and Earl Sasser, along with coauthor Joe Wheeler, strongly support the conclusions reached by Collins and Porras. In their book *The Ownership Quotient,* they connect strong, adaptive cultures to the valuable corporate outcomes of innovation, productivity, and a sense of ownership among employees and customers. By analyzing traits that the authors found common to these organizations, we can learn much about what sustains them.

1. Leadership is critical in codifying and maintaining an organizational purpose, values, and vision. Leaders must set the example by living the elements of culture.
2. Like anything worthwhile, culture is something in which you invest.
3. Employees at all levels in an organization notice and validate the elements of culture.
4. Organizations with clearly codified cultures enjoy labor cost advantages.
5. Organizations with clearly codified and enforced cultures enjoy great employee and customer loyalty.
6. An operating strategy based on a strong, effective culture is selective of prospective customers.
7. The result of these cultural elements is "the best serving the best."
8. This operating strategy becomes a self-reinforcing source of operating leverage, which must be managed carefully to make sure that it does not result in the development of dogmatic cults with little capacity for change.
9. Organizations with strong and adaptive cultures foster effective succession in the leadership ranks.
10. Cultures can sour.‡

Not only does a strong corporate culture create a sense of ownership among employees, but it also results in measurable financial returns. Haskett argues in his book *The Culture Cycle: How to Shape the Unseen Force That Transforms Performance* that an effective culture can account for a 20 to 30% differential in financial performance over companies without strong cultures! Haskett used what he calls a **"Four R Economic Model"** to measure a culture's impact on the bottom line. The Four Rs include Referrals, Retention, Returns to labor, and Relationships with customers. These variables prove how important a strong corporate culture can be

(continued)

to the ultimate financial performance of a successful organization.§

*James Collins and Jerry Porras, *Built to Last: Successful Habits of Visionary Companies* (New York: HarperCollins, 1994), p. 73.

†James C. Collins, *How the Mighty Fall: And Why Some Companies Never Give In* (New York: HarperCollins, 2009).

‡Adapted from Jim Heskett, Earl Sasser, and Joe Wheeler, *The Ownership Quotient: Putting the Service Profit Chain to Work for Unbeatable Competitive Advantage* (Boston: Harvard Business Publishing, 2008).

§James L. Heskett, *The Culture Cycle: How to Shape the Unseen Force That Transforms Performance* (Upper Saddle River, NJ: FT Press, 2012).

1. *Power distance index:* The distance between individuals at different levels of a hierarchy (more equal = low power distance).

2. *Individualism vs. collectivism:* The degree to which people prefer to act individually or in groups.

3. *Uncertainty avoidance index:* The extent to which people are comfortable with uncertainty, ambiguity, change, and risks.

4. *Long-term orientation (LTO) vs. short-term orientation:* A high LTO suggests a comfort with long-term commitments, traditions, and rewards linked to hard work, strong relationships, and status. A low LTO indicates that change may occur more rapidly.

5. *Masculinity vs. femininity:* A low masculinity score indicates greater equality, stronger maintenance of warm personal relationships, service, care for the weak, and solidarity. A high masculinity score suggests a strong culture of assertiveness, success, and competition. [Note that issues relating to gender, and its specific impact on corporate culture, will be explored in greater detail in Chapter 6.]

6. *Indulgent vs. restrained:* The extent to which people try to control their desires and impulses.

Hofstede validated his country scores across over 400 measures from other sources.[2] However, as mentioned above, his conclusions remain controversial. Critics contend that his resulting culture divisions remain based on generalizations, if not outright stereotypes. Further, while our national cultures certainly are important to our understanding of international business and each other, it does not explain everything that is different from one place and people to another. Hofstede focused his work during a single period of time, they argue, and a particular global firm (IBM). However, to be fair, his results have been replicated many times since. Critics continue their challenges, explaining that his perspective is biased by his Western views and limited number of countries included.

Just as there are national cultures, businesses also have unspoken, yet influential standards and expectations. If you are an investment banker, you might think it is appropriate to wear a dark suit to work, but it might not be considered okay to wear flip flops. At some offices, the dress code might be white shirts and grey suits, while dark shirts are out. To the contrary, one of Google's 10 principle philosophies is "you can be serious without a suit." Steve Jobs reportedly walked around Apple's office barefoot. Some companies have a straight nine-to-five work schedule; others expect employees to work long hours and on weekends. A person who joins the second type of firm with a "nine-to-five attitude," intending to leave as the clock strikes five, might not "fit" and is likely not to last long. The same might hold true for a firm's values. If you join a firm with a culture that supports values other than those with which you are comfortable, there will be values conflicts—for better or worse.

No culture, in business or elsewhere, is static. Cultures change; but modifying culture—indeed, having any impact on it at all—is a bit like moving an iceberg. The iceberg is always moving, and if you ignore it, the iceberg will continue to float with whatever currents hold sway at the moment. One person cannot alter its course alone, but strong leaders—sometimes from within, but often at the top—can have a significant impact on a culture. A strong business leader can certainly have a significant impact on a corporate culture.

A firm's culture can be its sustaining value, offering it direction and stability during challenging times, or it can prevent a firm from responding to challenges in creative and timely ways. For example, some point to Trader Joe's culture—embodied in its 7 Core Values—as the basis for its high quality and customer satisfaction,[3] while others question Trader Joe's model. (See Reality Check "It's Just Groceries.")

The stability that a corporate culture provides can be a benefit at one time and a barrier to success at another time. Review Trader Joe's 7 Core Values in the Reality Check "It's Just Groceries" and reflect on which values might contribute to a culture of high-quality products and which might contribute to a culture of defensiveness and secrecy.

While some corporate cultures are defined from the top down, others are developed by the employees themselves. At Zappos, the employees persuaded CEO Tony Hsieh to establish a code of ethics. He did so by emailing all employees in the company to ask them what they thought were the core values of Zappos. His email resulted in 10 "Core Values," which represent a strong emphasis on employee and customer satisfaction.[4] Take a look at the Reality Check "Living Our Core Values" and consider how those values may have been influenced by employee input.

While Zappos employees drove culture development at that firm, it was Tesla Motors CEO Elon Musk who set the values shift in action at his organization. Musk conveys his expectations via regular emails. For example, in response to a report relating to injury rates in 2017, Musk asked that every injury be reported directly to him, and he committed to replicating the same action as every injured driver so that he could understand their experience with the vehicle.

Other communications directed employees to "forget the chain of command" or to leave meetings once your input is no longer relevant or valuable. Unlike other companies such as Zappos, Tesla does not have formal culture-related documents to guide employees. Instead, Musk creates Tesla's culture organically through active and communicative leadership.[5] Through a tweet in 2018, Musk shared this message, "There are way easier places to work, but nobody ever changed the world

Reality Check *It's Just Groceries*

Trader Joe's operates a chain of grocery stores throughout the United States and had 474 stores as of 2018. While a normal grocery store carries somewhere around 50,000 items, Trader Joe's chooses to carry about one-tenth that amount, has a smaller footprint, does not carry options made in China, and has discontinued most unsustainable fish. Its stores are, on average, a third of the size of an the average supermarket in the United States, and the stores do not offer nearly everything that a customer can find in a regular grocery store.

A 2018 study by Market Force found that Trader Joe's did not even make the top seventeen in convenient location or good sales and promotions.* Regardless of location, Trader Joe's ranks high for consistency and dependability of its customer experience. High customer satisfaction may be correlated with high employee satisfaction. Trader Joe's employees receive extensive training about the company's culture surrounding customer service. They are also taught the company's core values and expectations.

One former employee describes how she felt a part of a "family" while working at Trader Joe's. The hierarchy of each store—with its "captain," eight to twelve "mates" (middle managers), and the crew—allows for a more equal distribution of the work. The large number of mates allows oversight of opening and closing shifts to be distributed evenly and tasks to be rotated throughout the week. This ensures that no single person is stuck overseeing the 4 A.M. food truck delivery every day. Even for the crew, work schedules are flexible and the pay and benefits are good. Employees are not given a script and are encouraged to be friendly and engage with customers, even on often-forbidden topics in retail such as politics, religion, philosophy, and movies.

Even as it remains one of America's best-loved grocery chains, it does not take itself too seriously. On a stressful day, you might hear a captain or mate remind its crew, "it's just groceries." This may be why Trader Joe's remains ranked one of the best places to work in the United States.[†]

Trader Joe's is privately held corporation. To keep prices low, 80 to 90% of the products sold in Trader Joe's are store-brand, bought from manufacturers or growers, rather than from distributors or middlemen, making it unique in this high proportion.[‡] It also contracts with existing brands, such as Stacy's Pita Chips, which packages its product under Trader Joe's private label. Trader Joe's gets the product at a reduced price, and the contractor is able to sell more product without losing brand loyalty by letting loyal customers know that they could get the product cheaper elsewhere. These contracts are guarded with the utmost secrecy. This lack of transparency poses a few concerns, however. Customers are unable to know where their food comes from, whether it was ethically sourced, or if the supplier is a brand the customer wants to support.

Review Trader Joe's 7 Core Values below, and reflect on which might have contributed to the high levels of customer and employee satisfaction. How might its emphasis on middle management and the freedom and flexibility it gives its employees support loyalty? Consider which of its core values might be compromised by its business model centered around the secrets of the Trader Joe's brand.

TRADER JOE'S 7 CORE VALUES

1. *Integrity.* In the way we operate stores and the way we deal with people. Act as if the customer was looking over your shoulder all the time.

2. *Product-driven.* Our strategy emphasizes price, product, access, service, and experience. We want to excel at one, be very good at another, and meet customer expectations on the others.

3. *Produce customer wow experiences.* We celebrate the special way we treat and relate to our customers. We think retailing is all about customer experience, and that is what really differentiates us.

4. *We hate bureaucracy.* We give everyone a license to kill bureaucracy. All officers are in cubicles. The CEO is in a conference room. We have very few layers—a very simple organization.

5. *Kaizen.* Each one of us every day is trying to do a little better. This is infused into our training programs. We really stress teamwork and working together, while we do not do elaborate budgeting at the store level.

6. *Treat the store as the brand.* Individual products are not the brand. The store is. Brand is really the covenant between the company and the customer, and

the real key is day-to-day consistency in meeting and satisfying needs.

7. *We are a "national/neighborhood" company.* Our customers benefit from our national buying ability, but we want each store to be close to the customer and really a part of their neighborhood.[§]

*Market Force Information, "New Market Force Information Study: Online Delivery and Click-to-Collect Use Is Up, Although Printed Circulars Maintain Strong Following" (June 26, 2018), www.marketforce.com/industry/grocery-drug (accessed February 26, 2019).

[†]H. Benham-Archdeacon-Lattice, "What Trader Joe's Figured Out about Work Culture That My Other Past Employers Haven't," *Fast Company* (September 18, 2017), www.fastcompany.com/40468445/what-trader-joes-figured-out-about-work-culture-that-my-other-past-employers-havent (accessed February 26, 2019); A. Cain, "Trader Joe's Is One of the Best Places to Work in the US—Employees Share the 7 Best Parts of the Job," *Business Insider* (July 11, 2018), www.businessinsider.com/trader-joes-jobs-best-parts-2018-7 (accessed February 26, 2019).

[‡]Bloomberg, "Company Overview of Trader Joe's Company," www.bloomberg.com/research/stocks/private/snapshot.asp?privcapId=4204435 (accessed February 26, 2019); Dan Myers, "10 Things You Didn't Know about Trader Joe's Products," *Insider* (May 10, 2017), www.thisisinsider.com/10-things-you-didnt-know-about-trader-joes-products-2017-5 (accessed February 26, 2019).

Source: A. Molaro, "The Trader Joe's Way for Libraries," *The Information Activist Librarian* (November 27, 2013), https://informationactivist.com/2013/11/27/the-trader-joes-way-for-libraries-a-manifesto-part-iii/ (accessed February 26, 2019).

on 40 hours a week," inspiring responses that were both supportive and less so, including this reply: "If you can't organize your factory in a way that people aren't overworked, then something is wrong."[6] Musk has issued additional directives encouraging staff to "talk to your manager's manager without his permission, you can talk directly to a VP in another dept, you can talk to me."[7] Imagine how all of these communications combined might be viewed as both positive and challenging elements to a culture!

When a culture is not clear, sometimes neither are resulting decisions or the public-facing reputation of the firm. In 2013, United Airlines experienced an online pricing glitch. Though the airline would not say how many tickets were sold for only $5 to $10 in taxes, rather than their original full price, it agreed to honor the tickets sold. Two years later, however, when an exchange rate error caused transatlantic first and business class tickets to be sold for only $50, United handled the situation in the opposite manner and refused to honor the sale price.[8] Two years later, in April 2017, the airline again faced backlash after it dragged a bloodied customer off an overbooked flight after he refused to give up his seat. One year later, a puppy died after a United flight attendant forced the dog's owner to put the dog in its TSA-approved carrier in an overhead bin, and that same week the airline flew a Kansas-bound dog to Japan.[9]

United employees' actions appear to be quite disconnected from the company's slogan "Fly the Friendly Skies." Though it is arguable that United employees may be inappropriate, United's critics attribute actions to the company's lack of cultural leadership.[10] CEO Oscar Munoz and the executive team have failed to cultivate the culture of the company. Critics contend that the unhealthy and poor-performing culture can be attributed to vapid promises and vague values, prioritization of operational performance over employees, and failure to respect and listen to employees.

Reality Check *Living Our Core Values*

ZAPPOS' CORE VALUES

Zappos' Core Values emphasize its commitment to its customers and also to its employees through integrity and honesty, based on input received from its employees.

1. Deliver WOW Through Service.
2. Embrace and Drive Change.
3. Create Fun and a Little Weirdness.
4. Be Adventurous, Creative, and Open-Minded.
5. Pursue Growth and Learning.
6. Build Open and Honest Relationships With Communication.
7. Build a Positive Team and Family Spirit.
8. Do More With Less.
9. Be Passionate and Determined.
10. Be Humble.

Source: Zappos.com Inc., Code of Business Conduct and Ethics (May 1, 2010)

UNITED AIRLINES' CORE VALUES

In a letter to "the world we serve," CEO Oscar Munoz writes:

First, **our Shared Purpose: "Connecting people. Uniting the world."**

Every day, we help unite the world by connecting people to the moments that matter most. This shared purpose drives us to be the best airline for our employees, customers and everyone we serve.

That's our destination. Our Shared Values are what will get us there:

We Fly Right: On the ground and in the air, we hold ourselves to the highest standards in safety and reliability. We earn trust by doing things the right way and delivering on our commitments every day.

We Fly Friendly: Warm and welcoming is who we are.

We Fly Together: As a united United, we respect every voice, communicate openly and honestly, make decisions with facts and empathy, and celebrate our journey together.

We Fly Above and Beyond: With an ambition to win, a commitment to excellence, and a passion for staying a step ahead, we are unmatched in our drive to be the best.

As you fly with us, I hope you see and feel these values being put into action with everything we do to serve you.

Source: Oscar Munoz, "Connecting People. Uniting the World," *United* (February 8, 2017), https://hub.united.com/connecting-people-uniting-world-2247890534.html (accessed March 6, 2019).

Take a look at the Reality Check "Living Our Core Values" and consider how United's values differ from those of Zappos. What values do you think you might have emphasized as an employee responding to your CEO in each of these companies? What do these core values suggest about the companies' respective cultures?

Defining the specific culture within an organization is not an easy task because it is partially based on each participant's perception of the culture. In fact, perception may actually impact the culture in a circular way—a culture exists, we perceive it to be a certain type of culture, we respond to the culture on the basis of our perception, and we thereby impact others' experience of the culture. Several of the elements that are easiest to perceive, such as attitudes and behaviors, are only a small fraction of the elements that comprise the culture. In addition, culture is present in and can be determined by exploring any of the following, among others:

- Tempo of work.
- The organization's approach to humor.
- Methods of problem solving.

FIGURE 4.2

Used by permission of Nancy Margulies

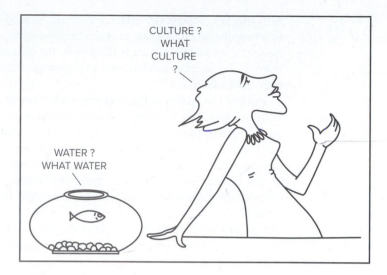

- The competitive environment.
- Incentives.
- Individual autonomy.
- Hierarchical structure.

Even with this list of cultural elements, it can be difficult for individuals in a firm to identify the specific characteristics of the culture within which they work. That phenomenon is best illustrated by the cartoon in Figure 4.2. Culture becomes so much a part of the environment that participants do not even notice its existence. Consider the culture you experience within your family. Often, it is only when you first move away from your family (when you go off to college, for example) that you can recognize that your family has its own culture. As you delve into the quirky particularities of your family's relationships, choices, preferences, communication styles, even gift-giving practices, you will notice that each family has a culture that is distinct and self-perpetuating. It is the same with business.

Culture and Ethics

How, exactly, does the notion of culture connect with ethics? More specifically, what role does corporate culture play in business ethics? We can answer these questions by reflecting on several topics introduced previously in this chapter and our text.

OBJECTIVE

In Chapter 1, we considered the law's limitations in ensuring ethical compliance. For example, U.S. law requires a business to make reasonable accommodations for employees with disabilities. But the law can be ambiguous in determining whether a business should make a reasonable accommodation for an employee with allergies, depression, dyslexia, arthritis, hearing loss, or high blood pressure. In situations where the law provides an incomplete answer for ethical decision making, the business culture is likely to be the determining factor in the decision. Ethical businesses must find ways to encourage, to shape, and to allow ethically responsible decisions.

Each of the factors in the decision-making model we introduced in Chapter 2, from fact gathering through moral imagination to assessment, can be supported or discouraged by the environment in which the decision is made. An ethical environment, or culture, would be one in which employees are empowered and expected to act in ethically responsible ways, even when the law does not require it. Later in this chapter, we will examine types of cultures and various ways in which a corporation can create or maintain a culture that encourages ethical action. But to understand that cultures can influence some types of behaviors and discourage others, let's have a look at the role of culture in the ethical dilemmas that Wells Fargo Bank has encountered over the past few years, and which we first examined in Chapter 1.

Wells Fargo long enjoyed a reputation for sound management. The bank was able to avoid many of the pitfalls and risky investments that led to the U.S. recession that began in 2008 and emerged from it relatively unscathed. *Fortune* magazine praised Wells Fargo for "a history of avoiding the rest of the industry's dumbest mistakes." *American Banker* described Wells Fargo as "the big bank least tarnished by the scandals and reputational crises."[11]

Wells Fargo's original success came from deep customer relations paired with an actively engaged sales culture. The Wells Fargo vision is to "satisfy our customers' needs, and help them succeed financially." In 2015, Wells Fargo held the number 7 spot on *Barron's* list of the most respected U.S. companies. By 2017, however, Wells Fargo fell to dead last, below two Big Tobacco companies (Altria Group and Phillip Morris).[12]

So what happened? The decline was the result of a number of poor decisions, including the cross-selling scandal uncovered in 2016. The bank set daily sales targets, including quotas assigned to branch managers for the number and types of products sold. If a bank failed to meet its goals on one day, the shortfall was added to the quota for the next day, and employees received significant financial incentives to meet these goals. The goals created incentives for "cross-selling," which meant that a salesperson would sell a customer more than one type of service.

In 2013, rumors began circulating that Wells Fargo employees in California were engaging in aggressive tactics to meet their quotas, including opening new accounts and issuing debit or credit cards *without customer knowledge.* At times, employees would even forge customer signatures.

When the scandal became public in September 2016, a Wells Fargo spokesman explained, "Our team members do have goals. And sometimes they can be blinded by a goal." Wells Fargo's chief financial officer at the time, Tim Sloan, refuted criticism of the company's quota system, explaining, "I'm not aware of any overbearing sales culture." Protections that were in place—including an ethics program, a reporting help line, and a senior management incentive system to promote best practices—were insufficient to curb the systemic problem. In the weeks that followed, the senior management and the board of directors wrestled with how to adequately condemn the situation and take responsibility for the bank's infractions, while also convincing the public that the problem was contained. The bank insisted that the actions of a few employees were not indicative of the wider bank culture.

In November 2016, a public filing from the bank disclosed that the Securities and Exchange Commission was investigating the bank for the creation of as many as 2 million fake accounts. Later, the number of known fake accounts grew to nearly 3.5 million, suggesting that the cross-selling scandal was not an isolated event. Despite protections in place, the Wells Fargo executive team failed to listen to whistle-blowers who attempted to expose the scheme, as nearly a half a dozen former employees reported experiencing retaliation after they tried to blow the whistle on the illegal sales tactics.

You might think that a fine of more than $185 million would be enough of a lesson, but, in 2017, Wells Fargo admitted to additional (and subsequent) wrong-doing! It was engaged in illegally repossessing over 860 cars without court order in violation of federal law; it also admitted to charging at least 570,000 customers for auto insurance that they did not need; and the bank acknowledged that 110,000 mortgage holders were fined for missing a deadline, despite the fact that the delay was the bank's fault.[13]

The saga continued in 2018, when the bank uncovered 870 customers who had been incorrectly denied mortgage changes, resulting in 545 customers losing their homes. Finally, in August 2018, Wells Fargo agreed to pay a $2.09 billion fine for issuing mortgage loans that it knew contained faulty income information and that were found to have contributed to the 2008 Great Recession. Later that year, Wells Fargo's private bank head, Jay Welker, announced he would retire following a gender bias investigation in Wells Fargo's wealth and investment management unit, and two of its CEOs left after appearing before the U.S. Congress. The series of scandals has severely damaged the bank's reputation and hurt Wells Fargo's bottom line.

How could a bank with what sounded like a good start fall so dramatically? Analyzed according to the theories from Chapter 3, the Wells Fargo culture lacked ethical grounding. Explored from a utilitarian perspective, it certainly was not a culture that revolved around the consequences of its decision-making process. The culture did not place weight on the long-term impact of its process or decisions on its stakeholders. One might be able to argue that, in some cases, the decision makers in fact were placing human well-being, including the fundamental needs and dignity of its stakeholders (such as shelter), as a high priority. These loans, in some instances, allowed individuals who otherwise did not qualify now to access funds for a home loan. On the other hand, there is a reason they did not qualify, and, as history demonstrated, they were unable to repay the loans or the property was not worth the amount of the loans.

The decisions made over the course of years at Wells Fargo reflects the attitudes, expectations, habits, and culture of the organization. The notion of expectations and habits is linked closely to a topic raised in our discussion of the philosophical foundations of ethics. Chapter 3 introduced the ethics of virtue and described the virtues as character traits and habits. The cultivation of habits, including the cultivation of ethical virtue, is greatly shaped by the culture in which one lives. When we talk about decision making, it is easy to think in terms of a rational, deliberative process in which a person consciously deliberates about and weighs each alternative before acting. But the virtue ethics tradition reminds us that our decisions and our actions are very often less deliberate than that. We are as likely to act out of habit and based on character as we are to act after careful deliberations. So the question of where we get our habits and character is all-important.

Part of the answer surely is that we can choose to develop some habits rather than others. But it is also clear that our habits are shaped and formed by education and training—by culture. This education takes place in every social environment, ranging from our families and religions, to entire societies and cultures. It also takes place in the workplace, where individuals quickly learn behaviors that are appropriate and expected and through which they get rewarded and promoted. Intentionally or not, business institutions provide an environment in which habits are formed and virtues, or vices, are created.

The effect of this workplace culture on decision making cannot be overemphasized. The Ethics Resource Center reports that "by every measure, strong ethics programs and strong ethics cultures produce substantially better outcomes—less pressure, less misconduct, higher reporting, and less retaliation—than in weaker ethical environments."[14] It is not difficult to see, therefore, that an ethical culture can have a direct and practical impact on the bottom line. Research supports this impact; when indexed together, the publicly traded businesses on the Ethisphere Institute's World's Most Ethical Companies list regularly outperform other major indices, including the U.S. Large Cap Index.[15] If attended to and supported, a strong ethical culture can serve as a deterrent to stakeholder damage and improve bottom-line sustainability. Timothy Erblich, CEO of the Ethisphere Institute, also states that "the World's Most Ethical Companies in particular continued to show exemplary leadership. And that is no surprise to us, as not only is it the right thing to do, it is the best long-term strategy. . . . Research from McKinsey tells us companies with more diverse work forces outperform their peers. Edelman's Trust barometer shows employees increasingly look to their companies for societal leadership."[16] If ignored, the culture could instead reinforce a perception that "anything goes" and "any way to a better bottom line is acceptable," destroying long-term sustainability in both financial performance and employee retention/recruitment. See, also, how the devastating impact is not limited to a single industry or type of business, as is demonstrated by the Reality Check "Ignore at Your Peril!"

Responsibility for creating and sustaining such ethical corporate cultures rests on business leaders. In fact, former Johnson & Johnson CEO and chair Ralph Larsen sets the leadership example by affirming that at J&J its "credo is all about personal responsibility."

Collins and Porras' authoritative and historic text, book *Built to Last: Successful Habits of Visionary Companies* explains the power of a corporate culture to shape

Reality Check *Ignore at Your Peril!*

Consider the costs involved in the following examples of unethical behavior:

- **General Motors:** In 2014, General Motors recalled 3 million cars for ignition problems. Employees within the company sent an email warning executives that the ignition parts were faulty, but the executives did not take action until the issue was noticed by consumers!*

- **Samsung:** Within a few days of its release, Samsung's Galaxy Note 7 phone started exploding and burning, resulting in massive recalls. Employees had tried to warn executives that the structure, which included too many pieces crammed into the aggressive design, was risky. The company ignored the warnings and released the product anyway.*

- **Uber:** The year 2017 was not a good year for Uber from an ethics perspective. Susan Fowler came forward in February, alleging a culture of sexual harassment at Uber. In May, the Justice Department revealed a criminal probe into Uber's alleged use of software that would help it avoid regulators in geographic regions where the company was operating illegally. In November, it was revealed that Uber had been hacked and that at least some of its 57 million users' data was compromised. By the end of 2017,

Uber lost a significant percent of its market share, reporting control of 74 percent of the U.S. market, down from 84 percent the year before.[†]

- **Fox News Channel:** In 2016, news anchor Gretchen Carlson filed a lawsuit alleging sexual harassment against Fox's news chief Roger Ailes. In 2017, it was reported that Bill O'Reilly had paid five women millions of dollars to keep silent about their accusations of sexual harassment. Fox reportedly knew about the allegations against O'Reilly when it had renewed O'Reilly's contract the previous January. Shareholders considered the multiple allegations as a sign that the company culture allowed for sexual harassment, and Fox had agreed to pay $90 million to settle shareholder claims relating to the O'Reilly and Ailes scandals.[†]

*B. Morgan, "10 Major Corporate Blunders That Wouldn't Have Happened if Companies Listened to Their Employees," *Forbes* (January 3, 2018), www.forbes.com/sites/blakemorgan/2018/01/03/10-major-corporate-blunders-that-wouldnt-have-happened-if-companies-listened-to-their-employees/#710104d843fa (accessed February 26, 2019).

[†]L. Shen, "The 10 Biggest Business Scandals of 2017," *Fortune* (December 31, 2017), http://fortune.com/2017/12/31/biggest-corporate-scandals-misconduct-2017-pr/ (accessed February 26, 2019).

the individuals who work within it. While it may be true that individuals can shape an organization, and perhaps charismatic leaders can do this especially well, it is equally true, if not more so, that organizations shape individuals. Imagine spending a twenty-, thirty-, or even forty-year career in the same organization. The person you become, your attitudes, values, expectations, mindset, and habits, will be significantly determined by the culture of the organization in which you work. (See also the earlier Reality Check "Built to Last.")

Compliance and Values-Based Cultures

OBJECTIVE

In the 1990s, a distinction emerged between different types of corporate cultures: Some firms were classified as **compliance-based cultures** (the "traditional" approach), while others were considered to be integrity-based or **values-based cultures** (a more "progressive" approach). These latter cultures are perceived to be more flexible and far-sighted corporate environments. The distinction between

Traditional	Progressive (Effective Practices)
Audit focus	Business focus
Transaction-based	Process-based
Financial account focus	Customer focus
Compliance objective	Risk identification, process improvement objective
Policies and procedures focus	Risk management focus
Multiyear audit coverage	Continual risk-reassessment coverage
Policy adherence	Change facilitator
Budgeted cost center	Accountability for performance improvement results
Career auditors	Opportunities for other management positions
Methodology: Focus on policies, transactions, and compliance	Methodology: Focus on goals, strategies, and risk management processes

compliance-based culture

A corporate culture in which obedience to laws and regulations is the prevailing model for ethical behavior.

values-based culture

A corporate culture in which conformity to a statement of values and principles rather than simple obedience to laws and regulations is the prevailing model for ethical behavior.

compliance-based and values-based cultures perhaps is most evident in accounting and auditing situations, but it can also be used more generally to understand wider corporate cultures. See Table 4.1 for an analysis of the differences between the traditional, compliance-based culture and the more progressive-style cultures that have evolved.

As the name suggests, a compliance-based culture emphasizes adherence to the rules as the primary responsibility of ethics. A compliance-based culture will empower legal counsel and audit offices to mandate and monitor compliance with the law and with internal codes.

A values-based culture is one that reinforces a particular set of *values* rather than a particular set of *rules.* Certainly, these firms may have codes of conduct, but those codes usually are based on a statement of values, and it is presumed that the code includes mere examples of how to apply the values. Integrating these values into the firm's culture is based on a decision-making process that uses the values as underlying principles to guide employee decisions rather than as hard-and-fast rules.

The argument in favor of a values-based culture is that a compliance culture is only as strong and as precise as the rules with which workers are expected to comply. A firm can have only a certain number of rules, and the rules can never unambiguously apply to every conceivable situation. A values-based culture recognizes that where a rule does not apply, the firm must rely on the personal integrity of its workforce when decisions need to be made. (See the Reality Check "Compliance versus Values.")

This is not to say that values-based organizations do not include a compliance structure. The relationship between ethical culture and strong ethics and compliance programs is often symbiotic. In 2018, the Ethics & Compliance Initiative (ECI) found that high-quality ethics and compliance programs "are linked with stronger ethics cultures. Stronger cultures lay the groundwork for better ethics

Reality Check *Compliance versus Values*

The master said, govern the people by regulations, keep order among them by chastisements, and they will flee from you, and lose all self-respect. Govern them by moral force, keep order among them by ritual, and they will keep their self-respect and come to you of their own accord.

The Analects of Confucius

outcomes such as employees seeking guidance and being prepared to handle situations that could be unethical."[17] Businesses recognize this strong relationship, as the ECI study points out: "Corporations have historically organized their ethics and compliance (E&C) programs around a priority to align with legal and regulatory expectations. Yet increasingly, organizations are going above and beyond historic regulatory risk mitigation." Moreover, "[t]he data shows that improving the quality of certain factors of an E&C program at any stage of the program implementation process, has a positive impact on the organization."[18] Have a look at one perspective on that positive impact in the Reality Check "Going Deep on Values."

The goals of a traditional compliance-oriented program may include meeting legal and regulatory requirements, minimizing risks of litigation and indictment, and improving accountability mechanisms. The goals of a more evolved and inclusive ethics program may entail a broader and more expansive application to the firm, including maintaining brand and reputation, recruiting and retaining desirable employees, helping unify a firm's global operations, creating a better working environment for employees, and doing the right thing in addition to doing things right. You should notice the more comprehensive implications of the latter list for the firm, its sustainability, and its long-term bottom line.

If a firm were to decide that it prefers the benefits and structure of a values-based orientation to its ethics program, the next question is how to integrate ethics into the compliance environment to most effectively prevent these common dilemmas and to create a "culture" of ethics. That question is addressed in the next section.

Ethical Leadership and Corporate Culture

If the goal of corporate culture is to cultivate values, expectations, beliefs, and patterns of behavior that best and most effectively support ethical decision making, it becomes the primary responsibility of corporate leadership to steward this effort. Leaders are charged with this duty in part because stakeholders throughout the organization are guided to a large extent by the "tone at the top." This is not at all to relieve leaders throughout an organization from their responsibilities as role models, but instead to suggest the pinnacle position that the executive leader plays in setting the direction of the culture. In fact, neither can be successful independent of the other; there must be a consistent *tone* throughout the firm.

Reality Check   *Going Deep on Values*

"We will never ever let our culture not permeate through the deepest depths of our organization. Our company culture and values is [sic] truly the most sacred thing we have in our company. We hold it on such high ground and tend to it every day, and it is truly the backbone of our success. I couldn't imagine operating in an environment without a great culture and great values, you'd be finished. To build a successful company, you better be a values-driven organization and have a great company culture."*

Cameron Mitchell, president and founder, Cameron Mitchell Restaurants

While CMR gained attention when it sold two of its concepts to Ruth's Chris Hospitality Group for $92 million in 2008, CMR currently brings in over $300 million in revenue through its more than 60 restaurants located predominantly in Ohio.

Source: G. Perna, "Restaurant Company CEO Cooks Up Company Culture," *Chief Executive* (November 20, 2018), https://chiefexecutive.net/restaurant-company-ceo-cooks-culture/ (accessed March 8, 2019).

Unfortunately, according to one study published in 2013, senior leaders are more likely than lower-level employees to break rules, and 60 percent of misconduct reported is attributed to managers.[19] This is an alarming trend that should be considered by businesses as they develop their ethics and compliance training programs. Ralph Larsen, past chair and CEO of Johnson & Johnson, explains: "Being bound together around the values . . . around our credo . . . being bound together around values is like the trim tab for leadership at Johnson & Johnson."[20] Seventy-five years after the credo was introduced, company leadership still has regular "credo sessions," where current CEO Alex Gorsky will guide top executives through a review of the credo and facilitate a discussion on what is working and what is not.[21]

If a leader is perceived to be shirking her or his duties, misusing corporate assets, misrepresenting the firm's capabilities, or engaging in other inappropriate behavior, stakeholders receive the message that this type of behavior is not only acceptable, but perhaps expected and certainly the way to get ahead in that organization! Consider the responsibilities of leaders, both for their own actions and also for the decisions and actions of the leaders that precede them. Mary Barra, CEO of General Motors, had to answer for the prior wrongs of her predecessor (see the Decision Point "A Leader Takes Responsibility").

Instead, if a leader is clearly placing her or his own ethical behavior above any other consideration, stakeholders are guided to follow that role model and to emulate that priority scheme. Ethical leaders say no to conduct that would be inconsistent with their organization's and their own personal values. If they demonstrate this courage, they are sending the message that this is the way to succeed in this culture. They also expect others to say no to them. Clearly, one of a leader's primary responsibilities, therefore, is to be a role model by setting a good example, by keeping promises and commitments, by maintaining his or her own standards, and by supporting others in doing so. Employees are often looking to leaders/supervisors

Today's GM will do the right thing. That begins with my sincere apologies to everyone who has been affected by this recall, especially the families and friends [of those] who lost their lives or were injured. I am deeply sorry.*

> *Mary Barra, CEO and chair of General Motors, apologizing for a botched recall of 2.6 million GM vehicles that contained dangerous and deadly ignition switch defects*

The above quote is the public apology of Mary Barra, CEO and chair of General Motors, when she appeared before the U.S. Congress in April 2014. She was there to answer for thirteen deaths that GM says were caused by a faulty ignition switch, as well as for GM's ten-year delay in issuing a recall for the vehicles containing this dangerous defect.

Barra faced serious questions from the U.S. House of Representatives about why GM waited almost ten years when internal documents demonstrated that the company knew about the defect as early as 2005 but decided that the $0.57 modification was too costly. The House of Representatives asked Barra what had changed at GM to ensure this same process of decision making does not occur in the future.

Barra had stepped into the CEO and chair role at GM only three months prior to her U.S. Congress appearance, in January 2014. The defect was made known to the public in February 2014. Therefore, much of Barra's testimony reiterated that the decisions—and culture—that caused this ethical lapse in judgment came before her time and knowledge. However, she emphasized that her primary focus was to change GM from a "cost culture" to a "customer culture." She explained to Congress that she had recently established a new position specifically responsible for global vehicle safety in order to encourage interdepartment communication, and she assured the congressional members that GM was doing a full investigation of the issue. She also hired a high-profile compensation consultant to consider appropriate compensation for victims' families. However, House members did report that no engineer or manager was fired for his or her culpability in the incident.

In June 2015, Barra fired fifteen employees deemed responsible for not tracking the problem attentively enough. By August 2015, 124 deaths and an additional 275 injuries were linked to faulty ignition switches.† In 2018, a federal judge in New York dismissed the Department of Justice's (DOJ's) criminal case brought against GM at the request of federal prosecutors after a plea agreement had been made. At the time of the dismissal, GM had paid more than $2.6 billion in penalties and settlements, including fines to the DOJ. GM also recalled 2.6 million vehicles.

In 2018, during the days between Thanksgiving and the December holidays, Barra announced job cuts of more than 14,800, explaining, "I accept no excuses for why we can't be the best." Perhaps Barra is moving back to a "cost culture," but only time will tell if the earlier culture of mistakes also will follow.

1. Do you think it is fair for Barra to be held responsible for mistakes made under prior CEOs? If not, then how do we hold organizations responsible once a leader departs? Was it sufficient merely to fire the fifteen lower-level employees?

2. Barra was criticized for spending a significant portion of her congressional testimony responding that she just "didn't know." From what you read here, do you think that she made effective decisions on her arrival at GM to address the problem?

(*continued*)

(concluded)

3. What additional facts might you need to uncover, if any, to respond to this particular issue?

4. Do you see any additional ways to respond to the issue(s) facing Barra? If you were Barra, what else might you do at GM to (1) respond to this particular issue and (2) modify the culture?

5. Who are Barra's primary stakeholders in her most pressing decisions right now?

6. What would you suggest might be Barra's most effective ethical strategy for decision making at present?

Sources: C. Isidore and K. Lobosco, "GM CEO Barra: 'I Am Deeply Sorry,'" *CNN Money.com* (April 1, 2014), https://money.cnn.com/2014/04/01/news/companies/barra-congress-testimony/index .html (accessed February 26, 2019).

K. Korosec, "Ten Times More Deaths Linked to Faulty Switch Than GM First Reported," *Fortune* (August 24, 2015), http://fortune.com/2015/08/24/feinberg-gm-faulty-ignition-switch/ (accessed February 26, 2019).

for guidance on how to act. (For more insights on ethics and compliance training, see the Reality Check "Perceptions on Ethics Training.")

OBJECTIVE

ethics officers
Individuals within an organization charged with managerial oversight of ethical compliance and enforcement within the organization.

Beyond personal behavior, leadership sets the tone through other mechanisms such as the dedication of resources. Ethical business leaders not only talk about ethics and act ethically on a personal level, but they also allocate corporate resources to support and to promote ethical behavior. There is a long-standing credo of management: "budgeting is all about values." More common versions are "put your money where your mouth is" and "walk the talk."

For example, when **ethics officers** were first introduced to the corporate structure in the early 1990s, the extent to which they were supported financially indicated their relevance and influence within the organization. Ethics was not a priority if the general counsel served as the ethics officer in her "spare time" and no additional resources were allocated to that activity. Ethics holds a different position in the firm if a highly skilled individual is hired into an exclusive position as ethics officer and is given a staff and a budget to support the work required. Similarly, if a firm mandates ethical decision making from its workers through the implementation of a code of conduct, extending the same standard for its vendors, suppliers, and other contractors, then trains all of these stakeholders with regard to these expectations and refers to the code and this process on a regular basis, these efforts demonstrate how seriously the firm takes the code.

When firms are effective in enacting ethics programs, employees are more likely to see themselves as participants in an ethical workplace culture. In a global survey completed in 2018, over two-thirds of employees responded that they reported misconduct when they observed it in their workplaces (23 percent higher than when the survey was first conducted in 2000). The report indicates that wrongdoing

Reality Check *Perceptions on Ethics Training*

Even when companies offer ethics and compliance training programs, employees continue to share concerns surrounding ethics, culture, and ethical leadership within their workplaces.

In its global survey in 2018, NAVEX Global evaluated ethics and compliance programs and found that 73 percent of organizations train their board of directors on ethics and compliance. While it might seem disconcerting that over one-quarter are **not** training their boards on ethics and compliance, it is heartening to hear that the top-ranked objective of their training programs is to evolve a culture of integrity, ethics, and respect (68% report).

That is compared to 8% who report that establishing strong legal defenses is the top priority.

The quality that most could agree upon that epitomizes this culture is one that encourages "speaking up," asking questions, and raising concerns.

It might seem tremendously difficult to measure compliance program effectiveness (see later section of this chapter for some additional ideas), but the survey respondents suggest that one look to adherence to the code of conduct, internal audit reports, exit interviews, employee surveys, internal help line reports, reports from training programs, comparisons with benchmarks, incident reports, external monitoring (such as Glass Door or on social media), and measurement against prior fines or regulations.

Source: I. Fredeen, "2018 Ethics & Compliance Training Benchmark Report," *NAVEX Global* (2018), http://trust
.navexglobal.com/rs/852-MYR-807/images/NAVEX%20
Global%202018%20Training%20Benchmark%20
Report.PDF?_ga=2.15313717.248971748.1542084026-
976355436.1542084026 (accessed February 16, 2019).

is significantly reduced and reporting is far more likely (36 percent more likely) where there is a strong workplace culture.[22]

Creating a shared company culture is a key responsibility of leaders, if they wish to prioritize ethics in their respective companies. One way in which leaders create that shared culture was explored in a study of the nature of ethical leadership that emphasized the importance of being *perceived* as a people-oriented leader, as well as the importance of leaders engaging in *visible ethical action.* Beyond people orientation, traits that were important also included receptivity, listening, and openness in addition to the more traditionally considered traits of integrity, honesty, and trustworthiness. Finally, being perceived as having a broad ethical awareness, showing concern for multiple stakeholders (a responsibility *to* stakeholders, rather than *for* them), and using ethical decision processes are also important.[23] Those perceived as ethical leaders do many of the things "traditional leaders" do (e.g., reinforce the conduct they are looking for, create standards for behavior, and so on), but they do that within the context of an ethics agenda. People perceive that the ethical leader's goal is not simply job performance, but performance that is consistent with a set of ethical values and principles. Finally, ethical leaders demonstrate caring for people (employees and external stakeholders) in the process.

However, as mentioned earlier, all of these traits and behaviors must be visible. If an executive is "quietly ethical" within the confines of the top management team, but more distant employees do not know about her or his ethical stance, the executive is not likely to be perceived as an ethical leader. Traits and behaviors must be socially visible and understood in order to be noticed and influence perceptions.[24]

Reality Check *Perception of Leadership Qualities*

A 2014 study conducted by Zenger and Folkman evaluated the effectiveness of women as business leaders. The scholars collected data from 16,000 business leaders comprised of two-thirds men and one-third women.

Overall, 54.5% of participants perceived women to be *more effective leaders* than men. Women ranked higher than men in 12 of the 16 listed leadership competencies, including:

- Takes initiative.
- Displays high integrity and honesty.
- Drives for results.
- Practices self-development.
- Develops others.
- Inspires and motivates others.
- Builds relationships.
- Utilizes collaboration and teamwork.
- Champions change.
- Establishes stretch goals.

Men ranked higher than women on the following four qualities:

- Solves problems and analyzes issues.
- Communicates powerfully and prolifically.
- Connects the group to the outside world.
- Innovates.

The researchers asked the woman participants why they thought that women came out ahead as effective leaders. The most common response was "in order to get the same recognition and rewards, I need to do twice as much, never make a mistake and constantly demonstrate my competence."

Source: Adapted from K. Sherwin, "Why Women Are More Effective Leaders Than Men," *Business Insider* (January 24, 2014), www.businessinsider.com/study-women-are-better-leaders-2014-1 (accessed February 26, 2019).

Take a look at the importance of that visibility in the Reality Check "Perception of Leadership Qualities." People notice when an executive walks the talk and acts on concerns for the common good and society as a whole, and long-term business prospers. Executives are expected to be focused on the financial bottom line and the short-term demands of stock analysts, but it is noteworthy when they focus on these broader and longer-term concerns.

The impact of ethical leadership is significant, which is why in this chapter we have focused on the issue of ethical leadership. We have discussed how leaders have the opportunity to influence the tone of a culture because research shows how a culture can influence employees' level of commitment to their work and also whether they intend to leave.[25] Average annual employee turnover has hovered in the mid-teens throughout this decade (18 percent in 2017),[26] and the cost of turnover can surpass 250 percent of the employee's annual salary for management and sales positions.[27] Therefore, maintaining employee satisfaction with the culture is a high priority!

Effective Leadership and Ethical, Effective Leadership

As we have discussed, being perceived as a leader plays an important role in a leader's ability to create and transform an ethical corporate culture. Key executives have the capability of transforming a business culture, for better or for worse. If the corporate culture has a significant impact on ethical decision making within the firm, leaders have the responsibility for shaping that environment so that ethical decision making can flourish. But what is the difference between the effective leader and the *ethical,* effective leader?

OBJECTIVE

This distinction is clearly critical because there are many effective leaders; are they all ethical? What do we mean by an "ethical" leader? Because leaders guide, direct, and escort others toward a destination, an effective leader is someone who does this successfully and, presumably, efficiently. Effective leaders are able to get followers to their common destination. Not every effective leader is an ethical leader, however.

One key difference lies with the means used to motivate others and achieve one's goals. Effective leaders might be able to achieve their goals through threats, intimidation, harassment, and coercion. They can also lead using more amenable interpersonal means such as modeling ethical behavior, persuading, or using the impact of their institutional role.

Some of the discussions in the literature on leadership suggest that ethical leadership is determined solely by the *methods* used in leading. Promoters of certain styles of leadership suggest that their style is a superior style of leadership. Consequently, they tend to identify a method of leading with "true" leadership in an ethical sense. Along this line of thinking, for example, Robert Greenleaf's "Servant Leadership" suggests that the best leaders are individuals who lead by the example of serving others, in a nonhierarchical style. Other discussions similarly suggest that "transformative" or "transactional" leaders employ methods that empower subordinates to take the initiative and to solve problems for themselves, and that this constitutes the best in ethical leadership.

Certainly, ethically appropriate methods of leadership are central to becoming an ethical leader. Creating a corporate culture in which employees are empowered and expected to make ethically responsible decisions is a necessary part of being an ethical business leader. But, while some means may be ethically more appropriate than others (e.g., persuasion rather than coercion), it is not the method alone that establishes a leader as ethical. The other element of ethical leadership involves the *end* or *objective* toward which the leader leads.

Recalling our discussion of ethical theory from Chapter 3, this focus on both means and ends should sound reminiscent of the emphasis on means in the deontological theory of universalism and the focus on ends or results in utilitarianism. Ethical leadership embodies both elements. If we judge a leader solely by the results produced—the utilitarian greatest good for the greatest number—we might ignore the mistreatment of workers that was necessary to achieve that end. Alternatively, if we look only to the working conditions protected by universalism, we may not consider a failure to produce a marketable product or one that brings in a profit necessary to sustain adequate working conditions.

Similarly, in the business context, productivity, efficiency, and profitability are minimal goals in order to be sustainable. A business executive who leads a firm into bankruptcy is unlikely to qualify as an effective or successful leader. On the flip side, an executive who transforms a business into a productive, efficient, and profitable business likely will be judged as a successful business leader. One who succeeds in a manner that respects subordinates and/or empowers them to become creative and successful in themselves is, at least at first glance, both an effective and an ethical leader. But are profitability and efficiency accomplished through ethical means alone enough to make a business leader an ethical leader?

Imagine a business leader who empowers her or his subordinates, respects their autonomy by consulting and listening, but who leads a business that publishes child pornography or pollutes the environment or sells weapons to radical organizations. Would the *method* of leading alone determine the ethical standing of such a leader? Beyond the goal of profitability, other socially responsible goals might be necessary before we conclude that the leader is fully ethical. Chapter 5 will pick up on this theme as we examine corporate social responsibility.

Building a Values-Based Corporate Culture

Recall the iceberg example we discussed in our introduction to this chapter: We explained that modifying culture alone seems about as tough as moving an iceberg. Each individual in an organization has an impact on the corporate culture, although no one individual can build or change the culture alone. Culture is built and maintained through leadership, integration, assessment, and monitoring. But what does that look like?

Mission Statements, Credos, Codes of Conduct, and Statements of Values

One of the key elements of ethical leadership is the communication of values throughout the organization. Of course, this communication may evolve after a process of values identification that includes voices throughout the entire organization; it does not have to simply mimic the particular values of one executive (such as the CEO). However, it is that leader's responsibility to ensure that the firm is guided by *some* set of organizing principles that can guide employees in their decision-making processes.

But do these codes and other documents make any difference at all? Consider the Reality Check "Do Codes Make a Difference?" which seeks to answer that question by exploring Johnson & Johnson's experience as one of the first firms to have a code.[28]

OBJECTIVE

code of conduct
A set of behavioral guidelines and expectations that govern all members of a business firm.

Before impacting the culture through a **code of conduct** or statement of values, a firm must first *determine its mission* so that decision makers have direction when faced with dilemmas. In the absence of other values, the only value is profit—at any cost. Consequently, without additional guidance from the top, a firm is sending a clear message that a worker should do whatever it takes to reap profits. A code of conduct, therefore, may more specifically delineate this foundation both for internal stakeholders, such as employees, and for external stakeholders, such as customers. In so doing, the code has the potential to both enhance corporate reputation and to provide concrete guidance for internal decision making, thus creating a built-in risk management system.

The mission can be inspiring—indeed it *should be* inspiring. For instance, the corporate mission of Southwest Airlines emphasizes the importance of treating

Reality Check *Do Codes Make a Difference?*

Do codes actually mean anything at all, or do people just ignore them and go about their work?

Let's consider the culture of Johnson & Johnson, which is often mentioned in positive terms for its quick and effective management of the Tylenol crisis in 1982. At that time, seven people died after ingesting the cyanide-laced capsules that happened to be J&J's best-selling product. J&J responded immediately, pulling it from shelves and replacing it with market-leading, tamper-proof packaging and a broad media campaign. Its market share jumped from a low of 7% back up to 30%.

J&J said that its decisions at the time were clear and simple as a result of its credo,* which specifically directs it to "put the needs and well-being of the people we serve first." Former CEO Ralph Larsen explains that the credo is "the glue that holds our decentralized company together. . . . For us, the credo is our expression of managing the multiple bottom lines of products, people, planet and profits. It's the way we conceptualize our total impact on society."†

By following that credo, not only did J&J emerge as a company that consumers could trust during a frightening time, but J&J could boast over thirty consecutive years of earnings increases and fifty-one consecutive years of dividend increases. J&J has been held up as evidence that a firm that lives according to its strong values and a culture that supports those values can not only survive but sustain a profit over the long term.‡

Of course, no credo or code on its own can preclude all problems. J&J has not been immune from ethical blindspots—or worse. In 2013, J&J agreed to pay $2.2 billion to settle claims against it for allegedly bribing doctors and pharmacies to prescribe its products to elderly people, children, and individuals with disabilities, despite health risks or a lack of scientific evidence showing any benefits to patients.§ In 2018, it was ordered to pay almost $5 billion to claimants based on allegations that asbestos in its talcum powder products caused them to develop ovarian cancer. The award triggered a 10% drop in stock price.

While J&J's credo is widely regarded as a leading example of how an ethics statement can guide corporate decisions effectively during a crisis—or otherwise—perhaps the more important lesson is that it must guide it *consistently.*

Choosing to act in an ethical manner (whether in our personal or professional lives) is not like deciding where to eat tonight, or which music you prefer. Instead, it is **the choice to act according to your values in a consistent way.** The failure to make the right choice often can be breathtakingly costly, in so many ways.

*Johnson & Johnson, "Our Credo," www.jnj.com/about-jnj/jnj-credo (accessed March 6, 2019).

†Source: R. Larsen, "Leadership in a Values-Based Organization," Sears Lectureship in Business Ethics, Bentley College, Waltham, MA (February 7, 2002)

‡Johnson & Johnson, "Investor Fact Sheet" (2011), http://files.shareholder.com/downloads/JNJ/0x0x567750/0E7DB88A-558D-454B-9DBB-FC425B2391D8/2011_Fact_Sheet.pdf (accessed March 6, 2019); "Johnson & Johnson at a Glance," *Forbes* (n.d.), http://finapps.forbes.com/finapps/jsp/finance/compinfo/CIAtAGlance.jsp?tkr=JNJ (accessed March 6, 2019).

§ D. Ingram and R. Krasny, "Johnson & Johnson to Pay $2.2 Billion to End U.S. Drug Probes," *Reuters.com* (November 4, 2013), www.reuters.com/article/2013/11/04/us-jnj-settlement-idUSBRE9A30MM20131104 (accessed March 6, 2019).

Source: Johnson & Johnson, "Our Credo," www.jnj.com/about-jnj/jnj-credo (accessed March 6, 2019); Erika Johnson, "8 Fun Facts about Our Credo—Johnson & Johnson's Mission Statement" (February 6, 2018), www.jnj.com/our-heritage/8-fun-facts-about-the-johnson-johnson-credo (accessed March 6, 2019).

employees, as well as customers, with respect and dignity. Founder and former CEO Herb Kelleher explains, "It began by us thinking about what is the right thing to do in a business context. We said we want to really take care of these people, we want to honor them and we love them as individuals. Now that induces the kind of reciprocal trust and diligence that made us successful."[29] By establishing (especially through a participatory process) the core tenets on which a company is built, corporate leadership is effectively laying down the law with regard to the

mission statement
A formal summary statement that describes the goals, values, and institutional aim of an organization.

basis and objectives for all future decisions. In fact, the **mission statement** or corporate credo serves as an articulation of the fundamental principles at the heart of the organization and those that should guide all decisions, without abridgment.[30] From a universalist perspective, while many decisions might be made with the end in mind (utilitarian), none should ever breach the underlying mission as an *ultimate dictate.*

Developing the Mission and Code

Since the beginning of this century, we have seen a proliferation of corporate codes of conduct and mission statements as part of the corporate response to the Federal Sentencing Guidelines for Organizations and the Sarbanes-Oxley Act (see later in this chapter). The success of these codes depends in large part on how they are conceived and written, as well as their implementation. As with the construction of a personal code or mission, it is critical to first ask yourself what you stand for or what the company stands for. Why does the firm exist? What are its purposes? How will it implement these objectives? Once you make these determinations, how will you share them and encourage a commitment to them among your colleagues and subordinates? (See Table 4.2.)

The second step in the development of guiding principles for the firm is the articulation of a *clear vision* regarding the firm's direction. Why have a code? After allegations of sexual harassment arose during the #MeToo movement, Hayma Washington, chair and CEO of the Television Academy, explained the value of the Academy's Guidelines when she clarified expectations of Academy leadership: "Our revised Academy guidelines make clear that we expect nothing less from Academy leadership, members and staff than respectful conduct and behaviors that foster and maintain environments free of disruption, abuse, discrimination and harassment of others—during and outside of Academy events." If guidelines and codes are effective, they help stakeholders to understand exactly what an

TABLE 4.2
Ethics Code Guidelines

Ethics Resource Center, "Code Construction and Content," https://www.ethics.org/resources/free-toolkit/code-construction/ (accessed March 6, 2019). Reprinted with permission of Ethics Resource Center.

The Ethics Resource Center provides the following guidelines for writing an ethics code:

1. Be clear about the objectives the code is intended to accomplish.

2. Get support and ideas for the code from all levels of the organization.

3. Be aware of the latest developments in the laws and regulations that affect your industry.

4. Write as simply and clearly as possible. Avoid legal jargon and empty generalities.

5. Respond to real-life questions and situations.

6. Provide resources for further information and guidance.

7. In all its forms, make it user-friendly because ultimately a code fails if it is not used.

organization stands for and how the stakeholders are expected to act in their daily business practices.[31]

The third step in this process is to identify *clear steps* as to how this cultural shift will occur. You have a code, but you cannot simply "print, post and pray," as Ethics Resource Center past president Stuart Gilman has referred to Enron's experience. Do you just post a sign on the wall that says, "Let's make more money!" Of course not. You need to have processes and procedures in place that support and then sustain that vision. Put in a different way, "a world-class code is no guarantee of world-class conduct," caution four other scholars in a *Harvard Business Review* article on benchmarking codes. "A code is only a tool, and like any tool, it can be used well or poorly—or left on the shelf to be admired or to rust."[32]

Finally, to have an effective code that will successfully impact culture there must be a belief throughout the organization that this culture is actually possible and achievable. If conflicts remain that will prevent certain components from being realized, or if key leadership is not on board, no one will have faith in the changes articulated. See Table 4.2 for Ethics Resource Center guidelines on writing an effective ethics code.

It should be noted that, although many organizations have individual codes of conduct, industries and/or professions might also publish codes of conduct that apply to firms or people who do business in those arenas. While adherence to some codes is prerequisite to participation in a profession, such as the legal community's Code of Professional Responsibility, many codes are produced by professional associations and are voluntary in nature. For example, certified public accountants, the defense industry, the direct marketing industry, and some faculty associations all have codes.[33] One might presume that implementation would be effective in all areas based on the industrywide approach; however, research shows that the key elements of success are specific goals; performance measures oriented to outcomes; monitoring by independent, external groups to verify compliance; and fully transparent disclosure to the public.[34]

Culture Integration: Ethics Hotlines, Ombudspersons, and Reporting

OBJECTIVE

Recalling Gilman's warning not to "print, post and pray," many business firms must have mechanisms in place that allow employees to come forward with questions, concerns, and information about unethical behavior. Integrating an ethical culture throughout a firm and providing means for enforcement is vitally critical both to the success of any cultural shift and to the impact on all stakeholders. Integration can take a number of different forms, depending both on the organizational culture and the ultimate goals of the process.

One of the most decisive elements of integration is communication because without it there is no clarity of purpose, priorities, or process. Communication of culture must be incorporated into the firm's vocabulary, habits, and attitudes to become an essential element in the corporate life, decision making, and determination of success. In the end, the Ethics & Policy Integration Centre contends

You are a corporate vice president of one of the largest units in your organization. Unfortunately, you have noticed over the past few years that your unit has developed a singular focus on profits, since employees' performance appraisals and resulting compensation increases are based in significant part on "making the numbers." Though the unit has done well in this regard, you have noticed that people have been known to cut corners, to treat others less respectfully than you would like, and to generally disregard other values in favor of the bottom line. While this might be beneficial to the firm in the short run, you have grave concerns about the long-term sustainability of this approach.

1. What are the ethical issues involved in striving to define or impact the culture of a unit?
2. How might you go about defining the culture of your unit so that employees might be able to understand your concerns?
3. What will be the most effective means by which to alter this culture?
4. What stakeholders would be involved in your suggestion in response to the previous question? How might the different stakeholder groups be impacted by your decision on this process?
5. How can you act in order to ensure the most positive results? How will you measure those results or determine your success? Will you measure inputs or outcomes, responsibilities, and rights?

that communication patterns describe the organization far better than organization charts! The Decision Point "Short Term versus Long Term" challenges you to create some of those integrative mechanisms, while the Reality Check "Examples of Culture Integration" demonstrates how two firms have imaginatively responded to this very challenge.

To explore the effectiveness of a corporation's integration process, consider whether incentives are in the right place to encourage ethical decision making and whether ethical behavior is evaluated during a worker's performance review. It is difficult to reward people for doing the right thing, such as correctly filing an expense report, but as the Lockheed Martin Chairman's Award shows (see the Reality Check "Examples of Culture Integration"), incentives such as appropriate honors and positive appraisals are possible.

There is no question that incentives can have an impact. They indicate to employees the priorities of an organization and the path to success. But it is important also to consider the other messages they send. Think about this example. If a parent tells a child that she or he will be rewarded for mowing the law—maybe with a few extra bucks or additional screen time that week—the child may perceive that activity as optional. If the child wants the reward, he or she mows the lawn. Similarly, if acting ethically reaps a bonus (or whatever is defined as the incentive), the firm might be sending a message that unethical behavior is okay; you just do not get a bonus.

Reality Check *Examples of Culture Integration*

- **Walmart's Integrity in Action Award** recognizes associates who demonstrate integrity through consistent actions and words, and who inspire other associates always to do the right thing. The award is based on voluntary nominations received from associates, and global votes determine an award recipient from each country for the most inspiring associate.[*]

- **Lockheed Martin offers an Ethics Awareness Training** for its employees, based on Dr. Mary Gentile's book *Giving Voice to Values*. The annual training equips employees with the knowledge and skills to recognize and react to situations that may require ethical decision making. The training engages every member across the company's organizational structure, starting from its chair, president, and CEO, by empowering managers to train their respective teams.[†]

- **PepsiCo's Global Compliance & Ethics Department,** led by the Global Chief Compliance & Ethics officer, promotes, monitors, and enforces the Global Code of Conduct, which is available in twenty-eight languages. Every year, PepsiCo requires all associates, regardless of level in the company, to participate in its Code of Conduct training. In 2017, over a quarter of a million employees participated in in-person or online training. Many of the in-person workshops were led by managers. In addition to annual training, employees received local and global communications, including internal articles, digital signage, portal updates, tone-at-the-top messaging, and ethics and values campaigns. Also, in 2017, 72,000 employees completed the online Anti-Bribery training, and over 4,200 employees participated in an online Human Rights Modern Slavery course.[‡]

- **Dell uses a game developed by LRN called the Honesty Project** to reinforce the important lessons of ethics and compliance by allowing employees to describe the damage corruption and bribery causes, recognize red flags that may indicate corruption or bribery, and identify the appropriate contact when confronted with a solicitation to pay a bribe or when witnessing a bribe being paid.[§]

- **At Lilly, employees receive The Red Book,** their code of business conduct, which includes key requirements from their corporate policies and sets expectations for how they conduct business. Lilly employees receive training on The Red Book. The ethics and compliance program is periodically reviewed and updated to meet changing business needs.[**]

[*]Walmart, "Promoting Good Goverance," https://corporate.walmart.com/2016grr/promoting-good-governance (accessed March 6, 2019).

[†]Lockheed Martin, "Ethics Awareness Training" (2016), www.lockheedmartin.com/us/who-we-are/ethics/training.html (accessed March 6, 2019).

[‡]PepsiCo, "Ethics & Integrity," www.pepsico.com/docs/album/policies-doc/ethics-and-integrity-a-z-topics.pdf (accessed March 6, 2019).

[§]Ben DiPietro, "Turning Employees into Ethics Believers," *The Wall Street Journal* [Blog] (September 26, 2014), http://blogs.wsj.com/riskandcompliance/2014/09/26/turning-employees-into-ethics-and-compliance-believers/ (accessed March 6, 2019).

[**]Lilly, "Ethics and Compliance Program," www.lilly.com/caring/operating-responsibly/ethics-and-compliance-program (accessed March 6, 2019).

Acting according to company values—or fundamental values, depending on the decision in question—is arguably a basic job expectation and, therefore, should not be rewarded beyond basic compensation. However, the counterargument to this proposition is that incentives are in place not to honor expected behavior but instead to acknowledge those actions that go above and beyond job expectations. A mediocre evaluation in this area would indicate that someone is merely doing the bare minimum, rather than exceeding those expectations.

Are employees comfortable raising questions relating to unethical behavior? Are multiple and varied reporting mechanisms in place? Do employees believe their reports will be free from retaliation? What can be done to ensure that employees who violate the company code are disciplined appropriately, even if they are good performers?

How does communication about ethical matters occur? The fact of the matter is that reporting ethically suspect behavior is a difficult thing to do. Childhood memories of "tattletales" or "snitches," along with a general social prohibition against informing on others, create barriers to reporting unethical behavior. More ominously, individuals often pay a real cost when they report on unethical behavior (such as retaliation), especially if workplace superiors are involved in the report of wrongdoing.

whistle-blowing
A practice in which an individual within an organization reports organizational wrong doing to the public or to others in position of authority.

Whistle-blowing is one of the classic issues in business ethics. Whistle-blowing refers to situations where an employee discloses unethical or illegal activities to someone who is in a position to take action to prevent or punish the wrongdoing. Whistle-blowing can expose and end unethical activities. But it can also seem disloyal; it can harm the business, and sometimes it can exact significant costs on the whistle-blower. Therefore, whistle-blowing can have extremely negative connotations, depending on the culture and environment where it occurs. In some cultures, blowing the whistle is akin to "ratting someone out," and one's decision can follow that individual for the rest of his or her career.

To encourage a different, more positive image for the concept of whistle-blowing, some firms call their reporting systems "help lines" instead of "hotlines," or "speakup" programs. At a minimum, the individual is considered to be a reporter rather than a whistle-blower. Vocabulary has an impact, and a change of language could inspire workers to feel a sense of empowerment from their contribution to the corporate culture in contrast to a sense that one is *blowing the whistle* on a peer.

Reporting can occur both internally and externally. One of the most highly visible cases of internal reporting cases occurred when Sherron Watkins shared her concerns about Enron's accounting practices to Enron CEO Ken Lay. External reporting happens when someone shares her or his concerns with a regulatory agency, other authorities, or the public, such as when Susan Fowler Rigetti, a former engineer at Uber, posted her blog exposing Uber's culture of sexual harassment, which eventually went viral. In February 2017, Fowler Rigetti published a blog post titled "Reflecting on one very, very strange year at Uber," where she accused Uber's Office of Human Resources of ignoring rampant sexual harassment at the company. More broadly, she also described a culture of general sexism across the company. The blog post was immediately quickly shared broadly and prompted an investigation into Uber's culture. More than twenty people were terminated, and investor response forced CEO Travis Kalanick to resign.[35]

Reporting to external stakeholders, such as the press and the legal authorities, carries risks—both to the reporter and to the firm itself—so there are arguments in favor of trying to report internally first. However, internal reporting is preferable only if those internal mechanisms are effective: They must allow for confidentiality, if not anonymity, and must strive to protect the rights of all parties. In addition to or as part of ethics and compliance officers' responsibilities, many firms have created ethics ombudspersons and internal or external ethics reporting help lines. These mechanisms allow employees to report wrongdoing and to create mechanisms for follow-up and enforcement.

Company norms and culture also can encourage internal reporting. A study by Harvard found that, where the firm culture encourages workers to detect potential threats or problems, employees are more likely to report issues such as safety violations or breaches of work practices, even when the worker is less likely to speak up in other social environments.[36]

A global survey in 2018 found that effective internal report systems do far more than simply protect firms from the court house. Certainly, litigation costs go way down—not only is there a 20 percent reduction in settlement costs but also almost a 7 percent decline in lawsuits. In addition, there is a significant financial return on investment! There is evidence of greater profitability and productivity and, in the end, fewer reports to external stakeholders.[37]

It is a benefit to firms, therefore, to encourage internal reporting. The same survey mentioned above found that internal reporting was at its all-time high at 1.4 reports per 100 employees, and a low rate of retaliation reports (0.66%, a drop since 2016).[38]

While these reporting systems might seem evident, reasonable, and commonplace, many organizations do not have them in place for a variety of reasons. In addition, even when they are in place, people who observe threats to the organization might choose not to report the threat or possible wrongdoing.

Consider NASA's *Columbia* space shuttle disaster. While it occurred decades ago, its lessons remain critically relevant today. On February 1, 2003, the *Columbia* space shuttle lost a piece of its insulating foam while the shuttle reentered Earth's atmosphere, resulting in the death of seven astronauts, one of NASA's most serious tragedies. The foam had dislodged during the original launch, damaging one of the shuttle's wings, and ultimately causing the accident a few weeks later on reentry. When the foam dislodged, no one could assess the true extent of the damage. No one could "see around the corner," so to speak. The engineers saw the foam strike the wing but, because of a poor angle of sight and the fact that foam strikes had not caused major accidents in the past, senior managers minimized the threat.

Was this an operations failure or a failure in judgment? Did the tragedy result from pressure from above to complete the shuttle mission or from the cavalier, cowboy culture of NASA to keep moving forward *at any cost? Columbia*'s engineers worked in a data-driven culture, one in which decisions were made only where there were data to support conclusions. Therefore, unless there were data to prove that the shuttle was unsafe with the current "proven" technology, there remained insufficient justification for the extra cost of scheduling a moonwalk to investigate.

Is this a crisis of culture or a failure in a whistle-blowing system? Some analysts consider it instead a "natural, albeit unfortunate, pattern of behavior . . . a prime example of an ambiguous threat—a signal that may or may not portend future harm."[39]

One of the challenges with reporting systems is that they do not make the values of the organization clear, nor what is or is not accepted within a particular culture. Therefore, while massive threats might give rise to quite clear responses, "the most dangerous situations arise when a warning sign is ambiguous and the event's potential for causing a company harm is unclear. In these cases, managers tend to actively ignore or discount the risk and take a wait-and-see attitude."[40] However, there are methods by which firms might actively curtail these negative influences:

- Leaders should *model* the act of reporting wrongdoing, in an obvious manner, so that everyone throughout the organization can see that reporting is the highest priority—not covering up malfeasance.

- Leaders can explain the process of decision making that led to their conclusion.

- While "crisis management" teams or plans are often unsuccessful (because they are so seldom used, there is no habit formed at all), *practicing* reports is a valuable exercise. Running drills or rehearsals of challenging events will allow for much greater comfort and generate a level of expectation among workers that might not otherwise exist.

- In addition, a culture that allows sufficient time for reflection in order to reach responsible decisions is most likely to encourage consideration of appropriate implications.

- Finally, the most effective way to ensure clarity and thereby ensure a successful reporting scheme is to consistently and continuously communicate the organization's values and expectations to all stakeholders, and to reinforce these values through the firm's compensation and reward structure.

There also are questions of cultural differences in reporting sensitivities and processes, as well as basic logistical questions in global implementation of its code of conduct and ethics and compliance program.

- How will the code and accompanying program align with local standards of practice, laws, and customs?

- Will there be just one version of the code for world operations, or multiple versions for each local base of operations, and not simply in the local language but modified in order to be sensitive to these local standards and customs?

- How "deep" will your code reach into your supply chain? The codes of some firms apply only to their employee base, while others apply to all vendors, suppliers, and other contracting parties.

- Must you consult with (or even seek approval from) labor representatives, unions, and/or works councils prior to implementing the code or program in any of the countries in which you operate?

- Finally, be aware that the standard acknowledgment form that many employees are asked to sign upon receipt of a code of conduct in the United States may be presumed to be coerced in other environments, given the unequal bargaining positions of the parties. While you might opt to dispense with that requirement, how will you serve the purpose of demonstrating acceptance and understanding?

Assessing and Monitoring the Corporate Culture: Audits

Unfortunately, if you do not measure something, people often perceive that you do not value it ("what you do not measure, you do not treasure"). The same result occurs with regard to culture. If we cannot or do not measure, assess, or monitor culture, it is difficult to encourage others throughout the organization to pay any attention to it. Alternatively, monitoring and an ongoing ethics audit allow organizations to uncover silent vulnerabilities that could pose challenges later to the firm, thus serving as a vital element in risk assessment and prevention. By engaging in an ongoing assessment, organizations are better able to spot these areas before other stakeholders (both internal and external) spot them.

Beyond uncovering vulnerabilities, an effective monitoring system also may include other significantly positive objectives. You can figure out how to better allocate resources, determine whether a program is keeping pace with organizational growth, whether all of the program's positive results are being accurately measured and reported, whether your firm's compensation structure is adequately rewarding ethical behavior, and whether the "tone at the top" is being shared effectively.

Identifying positive results might be a familiar process. But how do you detect a potentially damaging or ethically challenged corporate culture—sometimes referred to as a "toxic" culture?

- **Values:** The first clear sign would be a lack of any generally accepted fundamental values for the organization, as discussed earlier.
- **Relationships:** In addition, warning signs can occur in the various component areas of the organization. How does the firm treat its customers, suppliers, clients, and workers? The management of its internal and external relationships is critical evidence of its values.
- **Finances:** How does the firm manage its finances? Of course, a firm can be in a state of financial disaster without engaging in even one unethical act (and vice versa), but the manner in which it manages and communicates its financial environment is telling.

Consulting firm LRN suggests myriad options by which to measure the impact of efforts to change a culture. The first is to determine whether employee perception of the culture or working conditions has changed. Surveys of employee job satisfaction in general or about specific elements of the culture may return interesting data, though sometimes employees will tell the firm what they believe the organization wishes to hear. Alternatively, leaders may opt for an audit by an independent organization in order to determine the employee perception or to assess the firm's vulnerabilities or risks. The external auditor will also be able to provide information relating to benchmarking data in connection with the firm's code, training program, or other education or integration components, as well as the evaluation of those programs if they are offered. Data surrounding the help line or hotline are also noteworthy in terms of both the quantity and quality of the calls and responses. As with any element of the working environment, any feedback or other communication from employees, whether at the beginning of employment, throughout, or subsequent to employment, should be gathered and analyzed for valuable input regarding the culture.[41]

Mandating and Enforcing Culture: The Federal Sentencing Guidelines for Organizations

OBJECTIVE

United States Sentencing Commission (USSC)

An independent agency in the United States judiciary created in 1984 to regulate sentencing policy in the federal court system.

Federal Sentencing Guidelines for Organizations (FSGO)

Developed by the United States Sentencing Commission and implemented in 1991, originally as mandatory parameters for judges to use during organizational sentencing cases. By connecting punishment to prior business practices, the guidelines establish legal norms for ethical business behavior. However, since a 2005 Supreme Court decision, the FSG are now considered to be discretionary in nature and offer some specifics for organizations about ways to mitigate eventual fines and sentences by integrating bona fide ethics and compliance programs throughout their organizations.

While it is not the case in every economy around the world, when internal mechanisms for creating ethical corporate cultures prove inadequate, there is a possibility that the federal government may step in to fill the void. In the United States, the **United States Sentencing Commission (USSC)** was created in 1984 to create more consistency in sentences in the federal court system. Before the USSC, the U.S. Congress had been struggling to resolve issues relating to differences in sentencing, arbitrary punishments, and crime control.

Beginning in 1987, the USSC prescribed mandatory **Federal Sentencing Guidelines for Organizations (FSGO)** for individual and organizational defendants in the federal system, bringing some amount of uniformity and fairness to the system. These directions, based on the severity of the offense, assign most federal crimes to one of forty-three "offense levels."

In its 2005 decision in *United States v. Booker,*[42] however, the U.S. Supreme Court separated the "mandatory" element of the guidelines from their advisory role, holding that their mandatory nature violated the Sixth Amendment right to a jury trial. Accordingly, though no longer mandatory, a sentencing court is still required to consider guideline ranges. The court is also permitted to individually tailor a sentence in light of other statutory concerns. You can imagine that this modification from mandatory to "required to consider" has created a bit of confusion.

The relevance of these guidelines to our exploration of ethics and, in particular, to our discussion of the proactive corporate efforts to create an ethical workplace is that the USSC strived to use the guidelines to create both a legal *and an ethical* corporate environment. (See Figure 4.3.) In fact, as explained further below, if firms can show that they have established effective ethics program, their **fines can be reduced by up to 95 percent**!

In recognition of the significant impact of corporate culture on ethical decision making, the USSC updated the guidelines in 2004 to include references not only to compliance programs but also to "ethics and compliance" programs and also required that organizations promote "an organizational culture that encourages ethical conduct and commitment to compliance with the law." The revision also includes a requirement that organizations assess areas of risk for ethics and compliance, and periodically measure the effectiveness of their programs. In addition, the criteria for an effective program, which used to be outlined only in the guidelines's commentary, are now found in a separate specific guideline.

As mentioned above, companies that find themselves in court as a result of a "bad apple" or two, but that also can demonstrate that they have effective ethics and compliance programs, may find that the recommended penalty will be reduced (called a "mitigated" penalty). On the other hand, firms that do not have effective ethics and compliance systems will be sentenced to an additional term of probation and ordered to develop a program during that time (called an "aggravated" penalty).

FIGURE 4.3

Sources of Culture

> **Review: Culture Derives from Leadership, Integration, and Assessment/Monitoring**
>
> 1. **Leadership** (and maintenance) of the control environment
>   - Through high-level commitment and management responsibility, leaders set the standard and the tone
> 2. **Control activities, information, and communication**
>   - Statements, policies, operating procedures, communications and training
>   - Constant/consistent integration into business practices
> 3. **Review, assessment, ongoing monitoring**
>   - Monitoring, evaluation, historical accountability

The critical question, then, is *how do you know if you have an effective ethics and compliance program?* The USSC says that organizations shall "exercise due diligence to prevent and detect criminal conduct; and otherwise promote an organizational culture that encourages ethical conduct and a commitment to compliance with the law." The guidelines identify those specific acts of an organization that can serve as due diligence in preventing crime and the *minimal* requirements for an effective compliance and ethics program. These include the following actions:[43]

1. **Standards and Procedures.** The organization shall establish standards and procedures to prevent and detect criminal conduct.

2. **Responsibility of Board and Other Executives; Adequate Resources and Authority.**
   (A) The organization's board shall be knowledgeable about the compliance and ethics program and shall exercise reasonable oversight with respect to its implementation and effectiveness.
   (B) High-level personnel must be assigned to have responsibility for the program and must then ensure its effectiveness.
   (C) Specific individual(s) within the organization shall be delegated day-to-day operational responsibility for the program and shall report periodically to these high-level personnel and, as appropriate, to the governing authority, or an appropriate subgroup of the governing authority, on the effectiveness of the compliance and ethics program. They shall also be given adequate resources, appropriate authority, and direct access to the governing authority.

3. **Preclusion from Authority: Prior Misconduct.** The organization shall avoid placing people in charge of the program who have previously engaged in illegal activities or other conduct inconsistent with an effective compliance and ethics program.

4. **Communication and Training.** The organization shall communicate its standards and procedures to all members of the organization through training or other means appropriate to such individuals' respective roles and responsibilities.

5. **Monitoring, Evaluation, Reporting Processes.** The organization shall take reasonable steps:

   (A) to ensure that the organization's compliance and ethics program is followed, including monitoring and auditing to detect criminal conduct;

   (B) to evaluate periodically the effectiveness of the organization's compliance and ethics program; and

   (C) to have and publicize a system, which may include mechanisms that allow for anonymity or confidentiality, whereby the organization's employees and agents may report or seek guidance regarding potential or actual criminal conduct without fear of retaliation.

6. **Incentive and Disciplinary Structures.** The organization's compliance and ethics program shall be promoted and enforced consistently throughout the organization through:

   (A) appropriate incentives to perform in accordance with the compliance and ethics program; and

   (B) appropriate disciplinary measures for engaging in criminal conduct and for failing to take reasonable steps to prevent or detect criminal conduct.

7. **Response and Modification Mechanisms.** After criminal conduct has been detected, the organization shall take reasonable steps to respond appropriately to the criminal conduct and to prevent further similar criminal conduct, including making any necessary modifications to the organization's compliance and ethics program.

In connection with item number one on the list, imagine the challenges faced by companies seeking to ensure compliance in a variety of distinct cultures throughout the world. The Reality Check "The Global Culture for Corporations" explores some of those obstacles with regard to Turkey. Turkey was chosen simply to provide a window into the array of issues for which companies need to be prepared today.

Item number two on the FSGO list above requires that the organization's governing body (usually, a board of directors) has the duty to act prudently, to be knowledgeable about the content and operation of the compliance and ethics program, and must undergo ongoing and consistent training. The content could include instruction surrounding the nature of board fiduciary duties, personal liability, stock exchange regulations, insider trading, confidentiality, intellectual property, and business secrets. For additional guidance on the elements of an effective ethics and compliance program, see the Reality Check "A Measurement Framework for Effective Ethics and Compliance Programs."

There is not great news to report about training efforts at the board level. While ethics-related training at the employee level has intensified, a 2018 survey by LRN found that only about half of current or former chief ethics and compliance officers (CECOs) at large companies had received any training on ethics or compliance at all. Further, fewer than half of the CECOs said that their boards had metrics in place for measuring E&C effectiveness or were willing to hold

Reality Check *The Global Culture for Corporations: The Case Study of Turkey*

TURKEY CORRUPTION REPORT

Snapshot

Corruption is widespread in Turkey's public and private sectors. Public procurement and construction projects are particularly prone to corruption, and bribes are often demanded. Turkey's Criminal Code criminalizes various forms of corrupt activity, including active and passive bribery, attempted corruption, extortion, bribing a foreign official, money laundering and abuse of office. Anti-corruption laws are inconsistently enforced, and anti-corruption authorities are ineffective. Punishment for bribery may include imprisonment of up to twelve years and companies may face seizure of assets and revocation of state-issued operating licenses. Companies should note that despite facilitation payments and gifts being illegal, they are frequently encountered.

Judicial System

There is a high risk of corruption when dealing with Turkey's judiciary. Companies report very low confidence in the independence of the judiciary and the ability of the legal framework to settle disputes or challenge regulations. Bribes and irregular payments in return for favorable judicial decisions are perceived by companies to be fairly common. About a third of Turks perceive judges and judicial officers as being corrupt. Political interference, slow procedures, and an overburdened court system create a high risk for corruption in Turkey's judiciary. The dismissal of more than 3000 members of the judiciary following the attempted coup in 2016 has further exacerbated concerns over political interference. The prosecutors who initiated an anti-corruption investigation into several senior government officials and their families were accused by the government of abusing their authority and were subsequently suspended. The government's response raised concerns of impunity and executive influence negatively impacting the independence, along with impartiality and efficiency of the judiciary. Enforcing a contract in Turkey is more time-consuming than the regional average.

Despite the Turkish courts having accepted international agreements on arbitration of investment disputes between foreign investors and the state, they have on occasion failed to uphold an international arbitration ruling involving private companies, and are reportedly biased against foreigners. Turkey is a signatory to the 1958 New York Convention on the Recognition and Enforcement of Foreign Arbitral Awards, and a member state to the International Centre for the Settlement of Investment Disputes.

Police

Corruption in the Turkish police is a moderately high risk. Companies indicate that they perceive the police force as not adequately reliable. More than half of Turks believe most or all police officers are corrupt, and one in twenty Turks indicate[s] they have been asked for a bribe by a police officer in the preceding year. Police impunity is a problem due to inadequate mechanisms to investigate and punish alleged corruption.

Public Services

There is a moderate risk of corruption when dealing with Turkey's public services. Bribes and irregular payments when dealing with public services are fairly uncommon. About one in twenty companies expect[s] to give gifts to officials to get things done. Nearly two out of five Turks believe local government officials are corrupt. One in twenty Turks report[s] having been asked for a bribe by a municipal official in 2016, which is a reduction of fifty percent compared to 2014. Impunity of corrupt officials is reported. Corruption in the public administration remains widespread, particularly at the local level. Municipalities controlled by the governing AKP party are generally shielded from close scrutiny by law-enforcement authorities and inspectors, while municipalities controlled by other political parties face close scrutiny.

Starting a business takes less time but requires more procedural steps and capital than the regional average. Dealing with construction permits takes more steps than the regional average, but the time required is significantly shorter.

* * *

Customs Administration

There is a moderately high risk of corruption at the Turkish border. Businesses report that bribes and irregular payments during customs procedures are common. Three out of five Turks perceive customs officers as corrupt.

Companies are not satisfied with the time-predictability of import procedures in Turkey and complain about burdensome customs procedures. The time required to comply with import procedures is generally lower than the regional average, but costs are significantly higher.

More than twenty customs officers were arrested in September 2017 on corruption charges; they are being accused of, among other things, forging documents and engaging in bribery.

* * *

Legislation

The Turkish Criminal Code criminalizes various forms of corrupt activity, including active and passive bribery, facilitation payments, attempted corruption, extortion, bribing a foreign official, money laundering and abuse of office. Facilitation payments are prohibited. Law on Asset Disclosure, Struggle against Bribery and Corruption, (in Turkish) and the law on Public Servants, provide regulations for gifts and hospitality. There is no formal distinction between gifts and bribes, and there is no minimum threshold for a gift to potentially be considered a bribe. Private bribery is also prohibited. Enforcement of legislation varies and the government has been criticized for its lack of willingness to tackle corruption. Individuals may be incarcerated for up to twelve years for bribery offenses. Companies may face seizure of assets or income as a penalty. Other relevant legislation includes the Law on the Right to Information, the Law on the Prevention of Money Laundering, the Prevention of Laundering Proceeds of Crime Law, the Law on Public Procurement Contracts, the Public Procurement Law, the Public Financial Management and Control Law and the Act on Declaration of Property and Fight with Bribe and Corruption. The legislative protection of whistleblowers is weak and insufficient. The OECD Working Group on corruption continues to express concerns about Turkey's low levels of enforcement of foreign bribery legislation and failure to follow up on the working group's recommendations.

Turkey has ratified the United Nations Convention against Corruption (UNCAC), the OECD Anti-Bribery Convention (declining an exception for facilitation payments), the Council of Europe Criminal Law Convention on Corruption and the Council of Europe Civil Law Convention on Corruption. Turkey is a member of the Council of Europe Group of States against Corruption (GRECO) but has not responded to GRECO's most recent recommendations.

Civil Society

Media freedom has steadily declined in the past decade of rule by Erdogan and declined more dramatically after the attempted coup in 2016, after which over 150 media outlets were forced to close. It is estimated that between 81 and 145 journalists are jailed for their reporting as of December 2016. The government has made aggressive use of the penal code and anti-terrorism legislation to punish and jail journalists for critical reporting. The state has also actively engaged in ownership change at many outlets, resulting in more consistent positive coverage for the government in mainstream media outlets. The judiciary has also been used by the state to intimidate media outlets through judicial investigations. Self-censorship among journalists is common. Social media platforms Twitter and YouTube were repeatedly blocked by Erdogan's administration in an attempt to quell corruption allegations against the government. Turkey's media environment is considered 'not free'.

Civil society organizations (CSOs) have a limited influence on decision-making processes; when the government does consult with CSOs, it tends to be with pro-government actors. CSOs working in the field of human rights, LGBT rights and women's groups regularly face harassment by the government in the form of frequent detailed audits and threats of large fines.

Source: GAN Business Anti-Corruption Portal, "Turkey Corruption Report" (June 2018), https://www.business-anti-corruption.com/country-profiles/turkey/. Used with permission.

senior executives accountable for misconduct.[44] What is really disconcerting is that these results basically replicate results from a 2009 survey of 1,600 in-house corporate attorneys, which found that only half of the respondents had provided their boards with compliance or ethics training.[45] In other words, there has been basically zero progress in this particular area in almost ten years, notwithstanding the FSGOs.

Reality Check   *A Measurement Framework for Effective Ethics and Compliance Programs*

The Ethics & Compliance Initiative (ECI) offers the following framework for organizations to use in measuring performance as high-quality ethics and compliance programs. The ECI offers far more detailed information to firms in order to assess achievement of these principles based on five levels of maturity, along with an earlier report on the nature of "high quality programs" (HQP). These additional details can be found in materials on ECI's website at www.ethics.org.

HIGH-QUALITY ETHICS & COMPLIANCE PROGRAM PRINCIPLES

PRINCIPLE 1
STRATEGY: Ethics & Compliance is central to business strategy

PRINCIPLE 2
RISK MANAGEMENT: Ethics & Compliance risks are identified, owned, managed and mitigated

PRINCIPLE 3
CULTURE: Leaders at all levels across the organization build and sustain a culture of integrity

PRINCIPLE 4
SPEAKING UP: The organization encourages, protects and values the reporting of concerns and suspected wrongdoing

PRINCIPLE 5
ACCOUNTABILITY: The organization takes action and holds itself accountable when wrongdoing occurs

Source: K. Capsaddle, and S. Scarpino, "High Quality Ethics; Compliance Program Measurement Framework," *Compliance Initiative.* https://www.ethics.org/wp-content/uploads/2018/09/ECI-Framework-Final.pdf (accessed February 21, 2019).

In 2010, the USSC adopted amendments to the Federal Sentencing Guidelines for Organizations (FSGO) to lower the penalties for compliance violations if the organization meets the following four conditions:

1. The individual or individuals with operational responsibility for the compliance and ethics program have direct reporting obligations to the governing authority or an appropriate subgroup thereof (e.g., an audit committee of the board of directors).
2. The compliance and ethics program detected the offense before discovery outside the organization or before such discovery was reasonably likely.
3. The organization promptly reported the offense to appropriate governmental authorities.
4. No individual with operational responsibility for the compliance and ethics program participated in, condoned, or was willfully ignorant of the offense.[46]

The first condition is designed to reward companies that ensure that personnel who implement an organization's compliance and ethics programs have reporting access to boards of directors. In order to qualify for eased penalties under the first condition, compliance and ethics personnel must be authorized explicitly to *communicate to the board of directors "promptly on any matter involving criminal conduct or potential criminal conduct," and "no less than annually on the implementation and effectiveness of the compliance and ethics program."*[47] The other three conditions also seek to encourage reporting by providing incentives to detect and

Protecting confidentiality is one of the most effective tools in creating a corporate culture in which illegal and unethical behavior can be uncovered. Corporate ethics officers, ombudspersons, and ethics hotlines typically guarantee that any reports of illegal or unethical behavior will be held in strictest confidence. Ethics officers promise anonymity to whistle-blowers, and those who report wrongdoing trust that this promise of confidentiality will be upheld.

However, Federal Sentencing Guidelines can create real ethical dilemmas for corporations that promise anonymity and confidentiality. The guidelines call for significantly reduced punishment for firms that immediately report potential wrongdoing to government authorities. Failure to report evidence of wrongdoing can mean the difference between a significant penalty and exoneration. Of course, failure to promise confidentiality can also be evidence of an ineffective ethics and compliance system, itself a potential risk for receiving stiffer legal penalties.

1. Should ethics officers guarantee confidentiality to those who report wrongdoing, and should they violate that confidence to protect the firm from prosecution?
2. What facts would you want to know before making this decision?
3. Can you imagine any creative way out of this dilemma?
4. To whom does the ethics officer owe duties? Who are the stakeholders?
5. What are the likely consequences of either decision? What fundamental rights or principles are involved?

report misconduct and to discourage weak, ineffectual, or corrupt compliance and ethics programs.

Though these steps are likely to lead to an effective program, a report by the Ethics Resource Center on the occasion of the twentieth anniversary of the enactment of the FSGO highlights the challenge posed to business managers by the lack of clarity in some portions of the guidelines. "On the one hand," the ERC report points out, "FSGO criteria are principles-based, which provides organizations with valuable flexibility in tailoring an approach that best fits their circumstances and avoids a 'one-size-fits-all' standard for compliance."[48]

On the other hand, "the benefits of flexibility and innovation notwithstanding, the principles-based nature of the FSGO criteria means that reasonable minds can disagree on what certain high-level principles mean."[49] For instance, the guidelines require an investigation in response to a report of wrongdoing, but they also seem to require more than that. A firm must learn from its mistakes and take steps to prevent recurrences such as follow-up investigation and program enhancements. The USSC also mandates consideration of the size of the organization, the number and nature of its business risks, and the prior history of the organization; mitigating factors such as self-reporting of violations, cooperation with authorities, and acceptance of responsibility; and aggravating factors such as its involvement in or tolerance of criminal activity, a violation of a prior order, or its obstruction

You have developed and implemented an ethics program. But how do you know whether the ethics program is "working"? How will you define "success"? Whom do you define as your primary stakeholders? What are their interests in your program and what are the impacts of your program on each stakeholder? How could you modify your program to ensure even greater success?

This Decision Point asks you to define the "success" of an ethics program, an extraordinary challenge even for those in this business for many years. One way to look at the inquiry would be to consider the measures by which you might be willing to be evaluated because this is your project. Overall, you will need to explore whether there are pressures in your environment that encourage worker misconduct. You will need to consider whether there are systematic problems that encourage bad decisions. Have you identified all the major legal, ethical, and reputational risks that your organization faces, and have you determined the means by which to remediate those risks?

Because you will encourage the performance that you plan to measure, it is important to determine whether you will be most concerned with the end results or consequences or with the protection of particular values articulated by your program or codes. If you measure outcomes alone, you will have a singular focus on the achievement of those outcomes by decision makers. If you measure the protection of rights alone, you may be failing to consider the long-range implications of decisions in terms of their costs and benefits to the firm.

According to the Ethics Resource Center, the Federal Sentencing Guidelines are rarely applied to large corporations today. Those guidelines apply only to decisions by courts, and it is more common for cases against large corporations to be settled by means of Deferred Prosecution Agreements or Non-Prosecution Agreements.[*] On the other hand, ethics programs seem to be having an effect internally. A 2018 study found that rates of observed misconduct are on the decline, coming close to historic lows. Reporting of suspected wrongdoing has also reached record highs. However, employees' reporting of suspected wrongdoing has reached highs, and employees feel that retaliation for reporting wrongdoing has reached record highs.[†]

To provide some context to this exploration, consider which offenses are most likely to lead to a fine for an organization. In 2017, the USSC received information on 131 organizations sentenced. Of those, 29% had been charged with fraud; 16.8% were charged with environmental offenses related specifically to water; 6.1% were charged with import/export offenses. Approximately 74.8% were required to pay a fine (or a fine plus restitution), and another 12.2% were required to pay restitution only. The average restitution payment imposed was over $27 million, and the average fine imposed was more than $67.2 million. The average fine for cases involving fraud was more than $129.3 million, while the average fine in environmental offenses related to air was $352.3 million, and in antitrust cases, the average was $18.1 million.[‡]

[*]Ethics Resource Center, "Federal Sentencing Guidelines for Corporations" (2012), www.theagc.org/docs/f12.10.pdf (accessed March 6, 2019).

[†]Ethics & Compliance Initiative, "The State of Ethics & Compliance in the Workplace" (March 2018), www.boeingsuppliers.com/GBES2018-Final.pdf (accessed November 17, 2018); Ethics Resource Center, "2018 National Business Ethics Survey" (2018), www.ethics.org/knowledge-center/2018-gbes/ (accessed February 21, 2019).

[‡]U.S. Sentencing Commission, *2017 Sourcebook of Federal Sentencing Statistics* (2017), www.ussc.gov/sites/default/files/pdf/research-and-publications/annual-reports-and-sourcebooks/2017/2017SB_Full.pdf (accessed February 21, 2019).

of justice. These standards are to be judged against applicable industry standards; however, this requires that each firm benchmark against comparable companies. Consider the challenges involved in developing an airtight system and process in the Decision Point "Legal Pressure to Violate Confidentiality."

Questions, Projects, and Exercises

1. To help understand an organizational culture, think about some organization to which you belong. Does your company, school, or fraternity/sorority have its own culture? How would you describe it? How does it influence individual decision making and action? Would you be a different person had you attended a different school or joined a different fraternity/sorority? How would you go about changing your organization's culture?

2. Consider how you evaluate whether a firm is "one of the good guys" or not. What are some of the factors you use to make this determination? Do you actually know the facts behind each of those elements, or has your judgment been shaped by the firm's reputation? Identify one firm you believe to be decent or ethical and make a note of the basis for that conclusion. Next, identify a second firm that you do not believe to be ethical or that you think has questionable values and write down the basis for that alternate conclusion. Now, using the Internet and other relevant sources, explore the firms' cultures and decisions, checking the results of your research against your original impressions of the firms. Try to evaluate the cultures and decisions of each firm as if you had no idea whether they were ethical. Were your impressions accurate or do they need to be modified slightly?

3. You will need to draft a memorandum to your chief executive identifying the value of a triple-bottom-line approach, which would represent an enormous shift from the firm's current orientation. What are three key points that you could make, and how would you best support this argument?

4. Now that you have an understanding of corporate culture and the variables that impact it, how would you characterize an ethically effective culture, one that would effectively lead to profitable and valuable long-term sustainability for the firm?

5. One element that surely impacts a firm's culture is its employee population. While a corporate culture can shape an employee's attitudes and habits, it will do so more easily if people who have already developed those attitudes and habits are hired in the first place. How would you develop a recruitment and selection process that would most successfully allow you to hire the best workers for your particular culture? Should you get rid of employees who do not share the corporate culture? If so, how would you do that?

6. What are some of the greatest benefits and hazardous costs of compliance-based cultures?

7. Assume you have a number of suppliers for your global apparel business. You have in place a code of conduct both for your workplace and for your suppliers. Each time you visit a particular supplier, even on unannounced visits, it seems as if that supplier is in compliance with your code. However, you have received communications from that supplier's employees that there are violations. What should you do?

8. You are aware of inappropriate behavior and violations of your firm's code of conduct throughout your operation. In an effort to support a collegial and supportive atmosphere, however, you do not encourage co-workers to report on their peers. Unfortunately, you believe that you must make a shift in that policy and institute a mandatory reporting

structure. How would you design the structure, and how would you implement the new program in such a way that the collegiality that exists is not destroyed?

9. *Wasta* is the term used in the United Arab Emirates (UAE) for favoritism. In the UAE it is a highly valued element of the culture. In fact, while nepotism might be kept under wraps or discussed in hushed tones in an American firm, *wasta* is more likely to be worn on one's sleeve among UAE professionals. It is precisely who you know that often dictates the position you might get in many companies or how fast you might get approved for certain processes. If you were assigned to build and then lead a team based in the UAE that would be comprised of both UAE nationals (called "Emiratis") as well as U.S. expatriates (expats), how might you most effectively respond to this culture of historical and embedded preferential treatment, reflecting the local realities, while at the same time respecting your own or your home country's value structure, *if different?*

10. A large U.S.-based corporation has decided to develop a mission statement and then conduct training on a new ethics program. It engages you to assist in these endeavors. What activities would you need to conduct in order to complete this project? What are some of the concerns you should be sure to consider?

11. Put yourself in the position of someone who is establishing an organization from the ground up. What type of leader would you want to be? How would you create that image or perception? Do you create a mission statement for the firm and/or a code of conduct? What process would you use to do so? Would you create an ethics and/or compliance program, and how would you then integrate the mission statement and program throughout your organization? What do you anticipate might be your successes and challenges?

12. With regard to employee recognition in the workplace, what effects would a program like "employee of the month" have on the corporate culture, and what factors might lead you to recommend it as a motivational program for your company?

13. Identify an industry in which you would like to work and choose a company for whom you would like to work, ideally. Use the company's website to learn about its core values and culture in order to find your best fit and then explain your choice. Next, identify a company at which you would *not* like to work based on its core values and culture. Explain your reasons.

Key Terms

After reading this chapter, you should have a clear understanding of the following key terms. For a complete definition, please see the Glossary.

code of conduct, *p. 114*
compliance-based culture, *p. 105*
culture, *p. 94*
ethics officers, *p. 110*

Federal Sentencing Guidelines for Organizations (FSGO), *p. 124*
mission statement, *p. 116*

United States Sentencing Commission (USSC), *p. 124*
values-based culture, *p. 105*
whistle-blowing, *p. 120*

Endnotes

1. Adapted from EPIC, "Measuring Organizational Integrity and the Bottom Line Results One Can Expect," www.ethicaledge.com/quest_7.html (accessed February 26, 2019).

2. Geert Hofstede, *Culture's Consequences: Comparing Values, Behaviors, Institutions and Organizations Across Nations* (Thousand Oaks, CA: Sage Publications, 2001).

3. See, e.g., R. Turcsik, "Publix, Trader Joe's Lead in Customer Satisfaction, Survey Reports," *Supermarket News* (February 27, 2018), www.supermarketnews.com/consumer-trends/publix-trader-joe-s-lead-customer-satisfaction-survey-reports (accessed February 26, 2019).

4. Max Chafkin, "The Zappos Way of Managing," *Inc.* (May 1, 2009), www.inc.com/magazine/20090501/the-zappos-way-of-managing.html#ixzz39pzykw7s (accessed December 13, 2018); Tony Hsieh, *Delivering Happiness: A Path to Profits, Passion and Purpose* (New York: Business Plus, 2010).

5. F. Lambert, "Elon Musk Says He Will Perform Same Tasks as Tesla Workers Getting Injured in the Factory," *Elektrek* (June 2, 2017), https://electrek.co/2017/06/02/elon-musk-tesla-injury-factory/ (accessed December 13, 2018); J. Haden, "This Elon Musk Email to Tesla Employees Is a Powerful Lesson in Authentic, Heartfelt Leadership," *Inc.* (December 7, 2017), www.inc.com/jeff-haden/this-elon-musk-email-to-tesla-employees-is-a-powerful-lesson-in-authentic-heartfelt-leadership.html (accessed December 13, 2018).

6. E. Musk, tweet from November 26, 2018, https://twitter.com/elonmusk/status/1067173497909141504 (accessed March 6, 2019).

7. Source: Musk, E., Tweet from November 26, 2018. Accessed March 6, 2019. https://twitter.com/elonmusk/status/1067173497909141504.

8. Q. Fottrell, "Why United Honored Accidental Free Flights," *Market Watch* (September 19, 2013), www.marketwatch.com/story/the-real-reason-united-honored-those-free-flights-2013-09-18 (accessed February 26, 2019); A. Hern, "United Airlines Cancels Thousands of Bargain Tickets Sold in Pricing Glitch," *The Guardian* (February 12, 2015), www.theguardian.com/technology/2015/feb/12/united-airlines-cancels-bargain-tickets-pricing-glitch (accessed February 26, 2019).

9. L. Zumbach, "A Year after Passenger Was Dragged off a United Flight, Everyday Indignities Remain," *Chicago Tribune* (April 9, 2018), www.chicagotribune.com/business/ct-biz-united-passenger-dragging-anniversary-20180405-story.html (accessed February 26, 2019); A. Lutz and B. Zhang, "United Airlines Is Being Slammed after a Puppy Died in an Overhead Bin—and It Reveals a Glaring Flaw with the Business," *Business Insider* (May 13, 2018), www.businessinsider.com/dog-dies-united-flight-2018-3 (accessed February 26, 2019); Associated Press, "United Mistakenly Flies Kansas-Bound Dog to Japan," *Business Insider* (March 14, 2018), www.businessinsider.com/ap-united-mistakenly-flies-kansas-bound-dog-to-japan-2018-3 (accessed February 26, 2019).

10. D. Yohn, "How to Fix United Airlines' Culture Problem," *Forbes* (March 28, 2018), www.forbes.com/sites/deniselyohn/2018/03/28/how-to-fix-united-airlines-culture-problem/#7539d2a0fd3d (accessed February 26, 2019).

11. B. Tayan, "The Wells Fargo Cross-Selling Scandal," Harvard Law School Forum on Corporate Governance and Financial Regulation (December 16, 2016), https://corpgov.law.harvard.edu/2016/12/19/the-wells-fargo-cross-selling-scandal/ (accessed February 26, 2019).

12. R. McDermid, "The Least-Respected Company in America Is Headquartered in San Francisco, According to a Barron's Pool of Money Managers," *San Francisco Business Times* (June 6, 2017), www.bizjournals.com/sanfrancisco/news/2017/06/06/wells-fargo-wfc-respect-barrons-survey.html (accessed February 26, 2019).

13. M. Egan, "Wells Fargo Illegally Repossessed Another 450 Service Members' Cars," *CNN* (November 17, 2017), https://money.cnn.com/2017/11/14/investing/wells-fargo-repossess-cars-military/index.html?iid=EL (accessed February 26, 2019); J. Wattles et al., "Wells Fargo's 20-Month Nightmare," *CNN* (April 24, 2108), https://money.cnn.com/2018/04/24/news/companies/wells-fargo-timeline-shareholders/index.html?iid=EL (accessed February 26, 2019).

14. Source: Ethics Resource Center, National Business Ethics Survey (2011).

15. T. Erblich, "A Letter from Ethisphere's CEO," *Ethisphere,* www.worldsmostethical companies.com/letter-from-our-ceo/ (accessed February 26, 2019).

16. Source: T. Erblich, "A Letter from Ethisphere's CEO," *Ethisphere,* http://www.worldsmostethicalcompanies.com/letter-from-our-ceo/ (accessed February 26, 2019).

17. Source: Ethics & Compliance Initiative, "Global Benchmark on Workplace Ethics Report" (2018). https://www.ethics.org/knowledge-center/2019-gbes/ (accessed November 6, 2018).

18. Source: Ethics & Compliance Initiative, "Measuring the Impact of Ethics & Compliance Programs" (June 2018), https://customer.acua.org/app_themes/acua_custom/documents/webinars/Measuring%20the%20Impact%20of%20Ethics%20and%20Compliance%20Programs-June%202018.pdf (accessed March 6, 2019).

19. Ethics Resource Center, "National Business Ethics Survey of the U.S. Workforce" (2013), www.ibe.org.uk/userassets/surveys/nbes2013.pdf (accessed March 6, 2019).

20. Source: R. Larsen, "Leadership in a Values-Based Organization," Sears Lectureship in Business Ethics, Bentley College, Waltham, MA (February 7, 2002).

21. R. Feloni, "All Executives at Johnson & Johnson Are Annually Measured against a 75-Year-Old Essay," *Business Insider* (March 12, 2018), www.businessinsider.com/johnson-and-johnson-alex-gorsky-credo-measures-performance-2018-3 (accessed February 26, 2019).

22. Ethics and Compliance Initiative, "The State of Ethics and Compliance in the Workplace" (2018), www.ethics.org/knowledge-center/2018-gbes-2/ (accessed February 26, 2019).

23. L. Trevino, M. Brown, and L. Hartman, "A Qualitative Investigation of Perceived Executive Ethical Leadership: Perceptions from Inside and Outside the Executive Suite," *Human Relations* 56, no. 1 (January 2003), pp. 5–37.

24. L. Trevino, M. Brown, and L. Hartman, "A Qualitative Investigation of Perceived Executive Ethical Leadership: Perceptions from Inside and Outside the Executive Suite," *Human Relations* 56, no. 1 (January 2003), pp. 5–37.

25. O. Demirtas and A. A. Akdogan, "The Effect of Ethical Leadership Behavior on Ethical Climate, Turnover Intention, and Affective Commitment," *Journal of Business Ethics* (May 11, 2014).

26. Society for Human Resource Managment (SHRM), *2017 Human Capital Benchmarking Report* (December 2017), www.shrm.org/hr-today/trends-and-forecasting/research-and-surveys/Documents/2017-Human-Capital-Benchmarking.pdf (accessed November 12, 2018).

27. W. G. Bliss, "Cost of Employee Turnover," *The Advisor* (June 17, 2014), www.alexanderporter.com.au/wp-content/uploads/2015/07/The-Cost-of-Employee-Turnover.pdf (accessed December 13, 2018).

28. Erika Johnson, "8 Fun Facts about Our Credo—Johnson & Johnson's Mission Statement" (February 5, 2018), www.jnj.com/our-heritage/8-fun-facts-about-the-johnson-johnson-credo(accessed March 6, 2019).

29. Quoted in E. G. Flamholtz and Y. Randle, *Corporate Culture: The Ultimate Strategic Asset* (Stanford, CA: Stanford University Press, 2011), p. 101.

30. For an exceptional analysis of the distinction between four types of ethics statements (values statements, corporate credos, codes of ethics, and internet privacy policies), see P. E. Murphy, "Developing, Communicating and Promoting Corporate Ethics Statements: A Longitudinal Analysis," *Journal of Business Ethics* 62 (2005), pp. 183–89.

31. D. Birnbaum, "Television Academy Sets New Standards of Professional Conduct," *Variety* (February 22, 2018), https://variety.com/2018/tv/news/television-academy-standards-of-professional-conduct-1202708624/ (accessed March 6, 2019).

32. Source: L. S. Paine, R. Deshpande, J. D. Margolis, and K. E. Bettcher, "Up to Code: Does Your Company's Conduct Meet World-Class Standards?" *Harvard Business Review* (December 2005).

33. American Institute of Certified Public Accountants, www.aicpa.org/RESEARCH/STANDARDS/CODEOFCONDUCT/Pages/default.aspx (accessed March 6, 2019); Defense Industry Initiative on Business Ethics and Conduct, www.dii.org/home (accessed March 6, 2019); Academy of Management, http://aom.org/ (accessed March 6, 2019).

34. S. Prakash Sethi, *Globalization and Self-Regulation: The Crucial Role That Corporate Codes of Conduct Play in Global Business* (New York: Macmillan, 2011), pp. 11–12.

35. A. Hartmans, "The Engineer Who Blew the Whistle on Uber's Culture of Sexual Harassment Was Just Hired by The New York Times," *Business Insider* (July 23, 2018), www.businessinsider.com/uber-whistleblower-susan-fowler-rigetti-hired-new-york-times-tech-opinion-editor-2018-7 (accessed February 21, 2019).

36. H. Kakkar and S. Tangirala, "If Your Employees Aren't Speaking Up, Blame Company Culture," *Harvard Business Review* (November 6, 2018), https://hbr.org/2018/11/if-your-employees-arent-speaking-up-blame-company-culture (accessed February 21, 2019).

37. NAVEX Global, "Strength in Numbers: The ROI of Compliance Program Hotline Reporting" (2018), www.navexglobal.com/en-us/campaigns/roi-of-compliance-white-paper (accessed February 21, 2019).

38. C. Penman, "2018 Ethics & Compliance Hotline and Incident Management Benchmark Report," NAVEX Global (2018), https://assets.toolbox.com/research/2018-ethics-compliance-hotline-and-incident-management-benchmark-report-81781 (accessed February 22, 2019).

39. Source: M. Roberto, R. Bohmer, and A. Edmondson, "Facing Ambiguous Threats," *Harvard Business Review* (November 2006), pp. 106–13. http://hbr.org/2006/11/facing-ambiguos-threats/ar/1 (accessed March 6, 2019).

40. Source: M. Roberto, R. Bohmer, and A. Edmondson, "Facing Ambiguous Threats," *Harvard Business Review* (November 2006), pp. 106–13. http://hbr.org/2006/11/facing-ambiguos-threats/ar/1 (accessed March 6, 2019).

41. LRN, *The Impact of Codes of Conduct on Corporate Culture* (Los Angeles, CA: LRN, 2006).

42. 543 U.S. 220 (2005).

43. USSC, *Guidelines Manual,* sec. 8B2.1, "Effective Compliance and Ethics Program" (2011), www.ussc.gov/Guidelines/2011_Guidelines/Manual_HTML/8b2_1.htm (accessed March 6, 2019).

44. S. Reisinger, "Focusing on the Board on the Heart of Ethics and Compliance Issues" (June 11, 2018), www.law.com/corpcounsel/2018/06/11/focusing-the-board-on-the-heart-of-ethics-and-compliance-issues/?slreturn=20181017144920 (accessed February 21, 2019).

45. S. Reisinger, "Focusing on the Board on the Heart of Ethics and Compliance Issues" (June 11, 2018), p. 8, www.law.com/corpcounsel/2018/06/11/focusing-the-board-on-the-heart-of-ethics-and-compliance-issues/?slreturn=20181017144920 (accessed February 21, 2019). See also Michael D. Greenberg, "Directors as Guardians of Compliance and Ethics within the Corporate Citadel: What the Policy Community Should Know," *Conference Proceedings, RAND Center for Corporate Ethics and Governance* (2010), p. 8, www.rand.org/pubs/conf_proceedings/CF277.html (accessed February 21, 2019).

46. USSC § 8C2.5(3).

47. Source: USSC, § 8C2.5(3).

48. Source: Ethics Resource Center.

49. Source: Ethics Resource Center, *The Federal Sentencing Guidelines for Organizations at Twenty Years: A Call to Action for More Effective Promotion and Recognition of Effective Compliance and Ethics Programs* (2012), https://www.theagc.org/docs/f12.10.pdf (accessed March 6, 2019).

Chapter

Corporate Social Responsibility

Business has to take account of its responsibilities to society in coming to its decisions, but society has to accept its responsibilities for setting the standards against which those decisions are made.[1]

Sir Adrian Cadbury

We are not in business to make maximum profit for our shareholders. We are in business . . . to serve society. Profit is our reward for doing it well. If business does not serve society, society will not long tolerate our profits or even our existence.[2]

Kenneth Dayton, former chair of the Dayton-Hudson Corporation

Make the World a Better Place

Ben and Jerry's

Corporations are people.

Mitt Romney

In October 2017, one year after the 2016 U.S. presidential election, executives from Twitter, Google, and Facebook testified before both the U.S. House and U.S. Senate Intelligence Committees investigating Russian interference in the U.S. elections. The committees were presented with thousands of ads, tweets, and posts that were placed by Russian agents. Facebook alone presented the committees with over 3,000 such ads. Some of the ads aimed to aggravate social tensions within the U.S. on such topics as immigration, Black Lives Matter, the confederacy, Muslims, and gun rights. One ad promoted a rally to oppose the "Islamization" of America, while another ad promoted an opposing rally to defend Islam scheduled at the same time and place. Other ads took specific positions supporting or opposing candidates, most of which were critical of Hilary Clinton and supported Donald Trump. For example, one ad depicted the devil promising that if Hilary Clinton wins, the devil wins, while Jesus promises that he will help defeat both the devil and Clinton.

Paid advertising was only one way that the Russians used Facebook to promote their agenda. They created false accounts and fictional groups where they could simply post information like any other Facebook user. Similarly, Russians not only bought ads on Twitter and Google, but they created false accounts on all these platforms, used bots to post false tweets, and posted videos on Google's YouTube and photos on Facebook's Instagram.

The Russians promoted their ads, posts, and agenda the same way any digital marketer operates on Facebook. They relied on Facebook data to target individuals and groups who would be predisposed to "buy" what they were selling. They created ads that would appeal to these people, and then paid Facebook to place the ads on the targeted audience's page. They created accounts and groups that attracted thousands of other users and then stepped back as Facebook users did much of the rest of the work to increase circulation by "liking" and forwarding ads and posts to "friends."

Facebook initially told Congress that some 3,000 ads reached as many as 10 million Americans. In later testimony, those numbers changed to 80,000 items (ads and posts) that were viewed by 29 million people, who then forwarded them to more than 10 million more people. By 2018, Facebook revised their estimate to as many as 126 million people who were exposed to a Russian-linked ad or post between 2015 and 2017.

Many observers thought that Facebook, and in particular its founder and CEO Mark Zuckerberg and COO Sheryl Sandberg, were slow to respond to the issues raised by this. Zuckerberg's first public statement described the idea that fake information on Facebook could have influenced the election "a pretty crazy idea." Initially, Facebook denied any responsibility, claiming that it was more a victim of Russian meddling than an accomplice. It claimed that it did not know about Russian interference and could not have done much about it without becoming a censor of content, a step that it was unwilling or unable to take.

Critics argued that Facebook had many options available that would have prevented such widespread Russian meddling. Most traditional media companies such as television stations, newspapers, and radio stations, have a marketing department that works directly with advertisers and reviews each advertisement individually. Given the nature of the business and the medium, it would be unimaginable for a television station or newspaper to run an ad if it didn't know its content or who was paying for it. As demonstrated by the Russian political ads, within Facebook's business model it was easy for someone to buy ads, post political content, and pay for it without Facebook's review or approval.

Facebook's critics pointed out that if the company in fact did not know that Russians were behind these ads, it was negligent for not knowing. During hearings before the U.S. Senate Intelligence Committee, Senator Al Franken challenged Facebook's general counsel, Colin Stretch.

"Mr. Stretch, how did Facebook, which prides itself on being able to process billions of data points and instantly transform them into personal connections for its users, somehow not make the connection that election ads, paid for in rubles, were coming from Russia? Those are two data points: American political ads and Russian money, rubles. How could you not connect those two dots?"[3] Senator Franken also reminded Mr. Stretch that it is illegal for foreign individuals and organizations to contribute to or participate in U.S. elections.

Underlying Facebook's initial response was its view that it was not a media company comparable to cable providers or newspapers, but was simply a company that provided a platform that people could use to communicate. It claimed that its priority at the time was to guarantee the reliability and security of that communication platform. In reply to Franken, Facebook's attorney admitted that during 2016 Facebook was more focused on protecting the security of accounts and preventing theft of content than on deceptive or compromised content.

On that view, Facebook saw itself more like a telephone company than a newspaper. It provided the means for people to communicate but could not be held responsible for what was communicated through the use of its platform. Its primary responsibility was to ensure the quality, reliability, and security of the communication that took place, but not its content. But, of course, in one important way, Facebook is very different from a telephone company. Unlike a phone company, Facebook makes its money not by charging users but by collecting huge amounts of data about its users and selling access to its users and its users' data to paying customers.

However, there are obvious tensions built into the Facebook business model. There is the tension between the goals of profiting from selling access to data and Facebook's stated goal of protecting the security and privacy of users' accounts. In response to this challenge, Facebook has created policies to limit access to its platform and restrict what developers can do with the information provided about users. However, it is in Facebook's financial interests to ensure that its policies do not overly discourage developers and advertisers. Apps and ads developed by outside vendors that are more successful in drawing and keeping users active in the platform are more valuable to Facebook because users are thereby spending more time viewing ads and providing information. The more Facebook provides open access to its platform, the more it increases the market it can provide to those willing to pay for access to that audience.

Facebook's failure to navigate the inherent tensions between providing security and privacy for users' data and gaining financially from those data underlies most of Facebook's ongoing social and political scandals. In 2011, Facebook settled a series of complaints issued by the U.S. Federal Trade Commission (FTC) by agreeing to better protect consumer privacy and by keeping users better informed of how their information was used. The FTC had charged Facebook with deceptive

(continued)

(*concluded*)

and unfair business practices associated with its failure to keep user information private. In 2018, Facebook suffered a massive data breach in which software flaws allowed the private data of more than 50 million users to be taken by hackers.

The 2018 data breach followed the 2016 unauthorized use of consumer data by the political consulting firm Cambridge Analytica. In that scandal, Cambridge Analytica gained legitimate access to Facebook (unlike the 2018 unauthorized data breach) by paying Facebook to place an app that asked users to participate in a survey. Users were asked for their informed consent for what was described as academic research purposes. Cambridge Analytica then violated Facebook's policies by using those data as part of its political agenda supporting campaigns of Texas Senator Ted Cruz, President Donald Trump, and the 2016 Brexit vote. Facebook ultimately admitted that data from as many as 87 million users were involved in this breach of privacy.

Facebook's troubles increased in late 2018 when *The New York Times* reported that beyond these unauthorized releases of user data, Facebook has long provided authorized access to user information to more than 100 partners, including Microsoft, Amazon, Netflix, and Spotify. Facebook defended these practices by pointing out that it did not sell the data to other companies but merely shared them so that users would be provided with better service from all the companies involved. For example, by knowing your Facebook friends and "likes," Microsoft's Bing search engine could provide more specific search results, or Amazon could provide more detailed shopping suggestions, or Netflix and Spotify could provide better suggestions for movies to watch or songs to listen to.

1. Does Facebook have particular responsibilities regarding political ads and apps? Should it be responsible for ensuring that political ads and their sponsors are identified?

2. It is often said that business has a responsibility to its customers. Who are Facebook's customers and what responsibilities does Facebook have to them?

3. Facebook has also been criticized for allowing hate speech and postings from neo-Nazis, white supremacists, and racists on its platform. What responsibility does Facebook have for policing the content of what is posted?

4. The legal right of freedom of speech is a right against government censorship. Do private companies like Facebook have a duty to respect free speech, or should they have a right to limit what is said on their platform?

5. Like all other social media platforms and software companies, Facebook has a "terms of usage" agreement that users acknowledge when they sign up for a Facebook account. To what degree does this mean that users have consented to Facebook's policies and practices?

6. Use the decision procedure described in Chapters 1 and 2 to analyze this case. What further facts would you need to know? What are the ethical issues involved? Who are the stakeholders involved in this case?

7. Should Facebook censor hate speech? What criteria should Facebook use to censor posts, ads, or apps?

Chapter Objectives

After reading this chapter, you will be able to:

1. Define corporate social responsibility.
2. Distinguish key components of the term *responsibility*.
3. Describe and evaluate the economic model of corporate social responsibility.
4. Describe and evaluate the stakeholder model of corporate social responsibility.
5. Describe and evaluate the integrative model of corporate social responsibility.
6. Explain the role of reputation management as motivation behind CSR.
7. Evaluate the claims that CSR is "good" for business.

Introduction

The quotation from Mitt Romney used on the first page of this chapter occurred during the 2012 U.S. presidential campaign. During that campaign, Republican nominee Mitt Romney responded to a heckler who criticized him for supporting tax breaks for corporations that "Corporations are people, too." While the response was ill-advised politically, it was accurate as a matter of U.S. law. It would be just as accurate as a matter of law in Canada, the United Kingdom, the European Union, and many other countries.

The idea that corporations are legal persons has roots that go back well into medieval Europe when towns and churches were allowed to enter into contracts. This idea was later expanded to cover banks and trading companies that received government charters, essentially contracts between the government and the organization for exclusive access to some markets. When a mayor, minister, or corporate official signed a contract, they were signing not as individuals but on behalf of the organization. The rights and responsibilities established by the contract belonged to the organization itself, not to the individual who signed the contract. In this sense, organizations were considered legal "persons" because they could enter into legally enforceable contracts and had the same rights to seek judicial remedies as natural human persons.

Within the United States, the concept of legal personhood has expanded notably in recent years. The U.S. Supreme Court has recognized other corporate legal rights beyond those of the legal rights to contract, including the free speech right to contribute to political elections (*Citizens United*[4]) and the religious freedom right to be exempt from government mandates on religious grounds (*Hobby Lobby*[5]).

Treating corporations as persons by granting them rights raises an interesting ethical question: If corporations have rights, do they also have responsibilities to the societies in which they operate and, if so, what are they? The Facebook case provides an opportunity to examine many of the ways in which a business can be said to have social responsibilities.

This chapter addresses the nature of corporate social responsibility (CSR) and how firms opt to meet this perceived responsibility. No one denies that business has *some* social responsibilities. At a minimum, it is indisputable that business has a social responsibility to obey the law. A large part of this legal responsibility includes the responsibility to fulfill the terms of contract with employees, customers, suppliers, lenders, accounting firms, and so forth. Legal responsibilities also include responsibilities to avoid negligence and other liabilities under tort law. Economists might also say that business has a social responsibility to produce the goods and services that society demands. If a firm fails to meet society's interests and demands, it will fail. But beyond these legal and economic responsibilities, controversies abound.

As Chris MacDonald explains in Reality Check "BP and Corporate Social Responsibility," there are ambiguities involved in each of the three terms *corporate, social,* and *responsibilities.* In general terms, we can say that the primary question of corporate social responsibility (CSR) is the extent to which business organizations and the managers who run them have ethical responsibilities that go *beyond* producing needed goods and services within the law. There are a range of answers to this question, and it will be helpful to clarify some initial concepts before turning to competing models of CSR.

Ethics and Social Responsibility

OBJECTIVE

As a first step toward a better understanding of corporate social responsibility, we should recognize that the words *responsible* and *responsibility* can be used in several different ways. One meaning involves attributing something as a cause for an event or action. For example, poor lending practices were *responsible* for (i.e., the cause of) the collapse of many banks during the 2008 economic crisis; and faulty airbags have been *responsible* for injuries and deaths in many car accidents.

Being responsible in this causal sense does not carry any ethical attribution; it merely describes events. So, for example, we might say that the wind was *responsible* for the damage to a house or a particular gene is *responsible* for blue eyes.

In a second sense, to be responsible does carry an ethical connotation. When we say that business is responsible *to* someone or *for* something, we are referring to what a business ethically ought or should do. Ethical responsibilities establish limits to our decisions and actions. To say, for example, that a business has a responsibility to its employees is to say that there are ethical limits to how a business should treat its employees.

Both meanings of being responsible will be at play in business ethics. Issues regarding product safety and employee health and safety, for example, involve these various meanings of being responsible. When a consumer is injured by a product, for instance, a first question to ask is whether the product was responsible for the injury. For example, in May 2019 a jury in Oakland, California, concluded that Monsanto's Roundup weed killer was responsible for the cancer suffered by a long-time user. Once this causal question was settled, the jury then had to

Reality Check   *BP and Corporate Social Responsibility*

I've long been critical of the term "CSR," or Corporate Social Responsibility. In particular, I've argued that all three parts of the term—"corporate" and "social" and "responsibility"—are misleading, at least if the term CSR is thought of, as it often is, as referring to the full range of ethical issues in business. After all, many businesses, including some very large and important ones, are not corporations. So the word "corporate" is out of place there. And many important ethical issues are not "social" issues. An employee's right to a safe workplace, for example, results in his or her employer having an obligation to him or her as an individual; it is not in any clear way a "social" obligation. And the word "responsibility" does not come close to summing up all the ethical questions that apply to individuals and organizations in the world of business: we are interested in questions not just about responsibilities, but also about rights, duties, entitlements, permissions, and actions that are ethically good but not required. If we think about how business should behave purely in terms of "responsibility," we are leaving a lot out.

But for a lot of people, the word "CSR" is virtually a synonym for the much broader term, "Business Ethics." And that's a mistake. Of course, social responsibility is still an important topic. It is good for corporations to think about what their social responsibilities are, and to try hard to live up to them. But the term "CSR" often leads such thinking astray.

The BP *Deepwater Horizon* explosion and oil spill of 2010 serves as a good example to illustrate this problem. The ethical problems associated with that catastrophic event demonstrate nicely the distinction between those ethical issues that do fit nicely under the heading of "CSR," and those that clearly do not. In particular, that oil spill illustrates the terrain carved out by the "S," or "Social," aspect of CSR. Too many people use the term "CSR" when they actually want to talk about basic business ethics issues like honesty or product safety or workplace health and safety—things that are not, in any clear way at least, matters of a company's *social* responsibilities. But the BP oil spill raises genuine CSR questions—it's very much a question of corporate, *social*, responsibility.

Let's take a look at the range of ethical obligations that fall to a company like BP. BP—the company formerly known as British Petroleum—is in the business of finding crude oil, refining it, and selling the refined gasoline and various by-products that result. In the course of doing business, BP interacts with a huge range of individuals and organizations, and those interactions bring with them an enormous range of ethical obligations. A short list of the very *basic* ethical obligations that fall to such a business would include things like:

a. the obligation to provide customers with the product they're expecting—rather than one adulterated with water, for example;

b. the obligation to deal honestly with suppliers;

c. the obligation to ensure reasonable levels of workplace health and safety;

d. the obligation to make an honest effort to build long-term share value;

e. the obligation to comply with environmental laws and industry best practices;

. . . and so on.

It is important to recognize that most of those obligations are obligations to identifiable individuals—to individual customers, employees, shareholders, and so on. There's nothing really "social" about any of those obligations, if we take the word "social" seriously as implying something to do with society as a whole. The possible exception is the obligation to comply with the law, which probably is best thought of as a social obligation.

And it is entirely possible that BP, in the weeks leading up to the spill, met most of ethical obligations on that list. In other words, the company may well have lived up to its ethical obligations to most of the individuals and groups it dealt with. The exception, of course, involves the company's obligations regarding workplace health and safety—eleven workers were killed in the *Deepwater Horizon* blowout, likely indicating failures within the company to give safety the level of attention it deserves. But even had no one been killed or hurt during the blowout, and if we could thus conclude that the company had met literally all of its ethical obligations to all the individuals it dealt with, that would certainly not mean that BP had acted ethically. A question of social responsibility would remain. That is why the *Deepwater Horizon* spill makes it especially appropriate to talk about CSR.

(continued)

So, what makes the oil spill a matter of social responsibility? Precisely the fact that the risks of BP's deepwater drilling operations, and the eventual devastating consequences of those operations, were borne by society at large, rather than just by specific individuals. The spill resulted in enormous negative externalities—negative effects on people who weren't involved economically with BP, and who didn't consent (at least not directly) to bear the risks of the company's operations. The fishing industry up and down the gulf coast was brought to a standstill. The tourism industry in affected regions ground to a virtual halt. The resulting unemployment meant huge costs for various elements of the tax-supported social safety net. And the massive cleanup effort undertaken in the wake of the spill required very substantial participation by a range of government agencies, all of which implied significant costs. In other words, BP imposed risks, and eventually costs, on American society as a whole. The company seems to have failed in its social responsibilities.

Sources: This Reality Check is based in part on Chris MacDonald, "BP and CSR," *Business Ethics Blog* (September 1, 2010), http://businessethicsblog.com/2010/09/01/bp-and-csr/; Chris MacDonald, "CSR Is Not C-S-R," *Business Ethics Blog* (August 10, 2009), http://businessethicsblog.com/2009/08/10/csr-is-not-c-s-r/.

decide if the manufacturer was responsible in the sense of doing what was required ethically. That jury concluded that Monsanto failed to live up to its ethical and legal responsibilities, found it at fault for the harm, and awarded the family $2 billion in punitive damages.

When we speak of corporate social responsibility, we are referring to the ethical expectations that society has for business. Ethical responsibilities are those things that we ought, or should, do, even if sometimes we would rather not. We are ethically expected to fulfill our responsibilities, and we will be held accountable if we do not. Thus, to talk about corporate social responsibility is to be concerned with society's interests that should restrict or limit business's behavior. Social responsibility is what a business should or ought to do for the sake of society, even if this comes with an economic cost.

OBJECTIVE

Philosophers often distinguish among three different levels of responsibility on a scale that goes from less to more obligatory. First, there are ethical responsibilities to do good. Volunteering and charitable work are typical examples of responsibilities in this sense. For example, we often say that everyone has a responsibility to give back to one's community. While doing a good thing is ethically responsible and something that ethics encourages, we normally do not fault someone for choosing not to contribute to charity. To call an act volunteer work is precisely to suggest that it is optional; one does not have a duty to do it, but it is still a good thing to do. Examples of corporate philanthropy, as when a business sponsors a charity event or contributes to a school project, fit this sense of social responsibility. Ethical considerations would encourage business to support charities or the arts, but it is not something ethically mandatory or required.

A second, more obligatory sense of ethical responsibility is the responsibility to prevent harm. What are often referred to as Good Samaritan cases are examples of people acting to prevent harm, even though they have no strict duty or obligation to do so. Thus, for example, we might say that a company has a responsibility to use renewable energy, even though its actions alone are not causing harm and fossil fuels are legal to use. In the Facebook case, the failure to police political ads aimed at disrupting the U.S. election or its failure to protect user information from unauthorized hacks might be seen as failures to prevent harm and therefore a failure of Facebook's social responsibilities.

The most demanding sense of responsibility is the responsibility not to cause harm to others. Often called a duty or an obligation to indicate that they oblige us in the strictest sense, responsibilities in this sense bind, or compel, or require us to act in certain ways. Society expects fulfillment of these responsibilities and uses the full force of social sanctioning, including the law and legal punishment, to enforce them. Thus, a business ought not to sell a product that causes harm to consumers, even if there would be a profit in doing so. Again in the Facebook case, the decision to share user data with business partners might be seen as causing harm to users and, thus, another failure of social responsibility.

Is there a duty for business not to cause harm? Let us consider how each of these three types of responsibilities might be seen in business. The strongest sense of responsibility is the duty not to cause harm. Even when not explicitly prohibited by law, ethics would demand that we not cause avoidable harm. If a business causes harm to someone and if that harm could have been avoided by exercising due care or proper planning, then both the law and ethics would say that business should be held liable for violating its responsibilities. By all accounts, this ethical duty not to cause harm overrides business's pursuit of profit.

In practice, this ethical requirement is the type of responsibility established by the precedents of tort law. When it is discovered that a product causes harm, then business can appropriately be prevented from marketing that product and can be held liable for harms caused by it. So, in the classic case of cigarettes, tobacco companies can be restricted in marketing products that have been proven to cause cancer even if this prevents them from maximizing profits for shareholders.

Is there a responsibility for business to prevent harm? There are also cases in which business is not causing harm but could easily prevent harm from occurring. A more inclusive understanding of corporate social responsibility would hold that business has a responsibility to prevent harm. Consider the actions taken by the pharmaceutical firm Merck & Co. with its drug Mectizan. Mectizan is a Merck drug that prevents river blindness, a disease prevalent in tropical nations. River blindness infects between 40 and 100 million people annually, causing severe rashes, itching, and loss of sight. A single tablet of Mectizan administered once a year can relieve the symptoms and prevent the disease from progressing—quite an easy and effective means to prevent a horrendous consequence.

On the surface, Mectizan would not be a very profitable drug to bring to market. The once-a-year dosage limits the demand for the drug among those people who require it. Further, the individuals most at risk for this disease are among the poorest people living in the poorest regions of Africa, Asia, Central America, and South America. However, in 1987 Merck began a program that provides Mectizan free of charge to people at risk for river blindness and pledged to "give it away free, forever." Cooperating with the World Health Organization, UNICEF, and the World Bank, Merck's program has donated billions of doses of Mectizan to tens of millions of people since 1987. The program has also resulted in the development

---

Reality Check *Corporate Philanthropy: How Much Do Corporations Give?*

In 2018, total charitable giving in the United States was estimated to be over $425 billion. Individual contributions totaled more than $290 billion. Corporate giving totaled $20 billion.

Source: "Giving USA 2019: The Annual Report on Philanthropy for the Year 2018/Executive Summary" (June 18, 2019), https://givingusa.org/giving-usa-2019-americans-gave-427-71-billion-to-charity-in-2018-amid-complex-year-for-charitable-giving/.

---

of a health care system, necessary to support and administer the program, in some of the poorest regions of the world. Merck's actions were explained by reference to part of its corporate identity statement: "We are in the business of preserving and improving human life."[6]

Clearly Merck was not at all responsible for causing river blindness and, therefore, Merck had no social responsibility in a narrow legal sense. The drug was not profitable and Merck had no legal obligation to provide it. In fact, a narrow economic model of corporate social responsibility might well fault Merck's management for failing to maximize shareholder value. But Merck's management saw the issue differently. Given the company's core business purpose and values, its managers concluded that they did have a social responsibility to prevent a disease easily controlled by their patented drug. George W. Merck, Merck's founder, explains, "We try never to forget that medicine is for the people. It is not for the profits. The profits follow and, if we have remembered that, they have never failed to appear. The better we have remembered it, the larger they have been."[7]

Is there a responsibility to do good? The third, and perhaps the most wide-ranging, standard of CSR would hold that business has a social responsibility to do good things and to make society a better place. Corporate philanthropy would be the most obvious case in which business takes on a responsibility to do good. Corporate giving programs to support community projects in the arts, education, and culture are clear examples. Some corporations have a charitable foundation or office that deals with such philanthropic programs. (See the Reality Check "Corporate Philanthropy: How Much Do Corporations Give?") Small-business owners in every town across America can tell stories of how often they are approached to give donations to support local charitable and cultural activities.

Some people argue that, like all cases of charity, philanthropy is something that deserves praise and admiration, but it is not something that every business *ought* to do. Philosophers sometimes distinguish between obligations and responsibilities precisely in order to make this point. A responsible person is charitable, but donating to charity is not an obligation. Others argue that business does have an obligation to support good causes and to "give back" to the community. This sense of responsibility is more akin to a debt of gratitude and thankfulness—something less binding than a legal or contractual obligation perhaps, but more than a simple act of charity. Perhaps a clear way to understand the distinction is to compare it to your obligation to write a thank-you note for a birthday gift. You might not have a legal requirement to send the note, but nevertheless you have a responsibility to do so.

These considerations suggest that there are competing understandings of corporate social responsibility and management's role in fulfilling these responsibilities. What we will call the narrow *economic model* of CSR holds that managers have an obligation to maximize profit and shareholder wealth and recognizes only legal limitations on the pursuit of profit. A variation of this model acknowledges that philanthropy is an ethically good thing that can indirectly contribute to profit by improving reputation and brand recognition.

Another model recognizes that there is a wide range of ethical duties that are owed to others and that management must balance these responsibilities against the responsibility to shareholders. What we will call the *stakeholder model* asserts that neither a business nor the individuals who work for it are exempt from the ordinary ethical responsibilities that everyone has to cause no harm, to prevent harm, and to sometimes do good.

Finally, some businesses might choose to make social responsibility part of its very purpose and mission. In what we will call the *integrative* model of CSR, part of the managerial responsibility to shareholders is to serve the social good. These three models are summarized in Figure 5.1.

FIGURE 5.1

Models of Corporate Social Responsibility

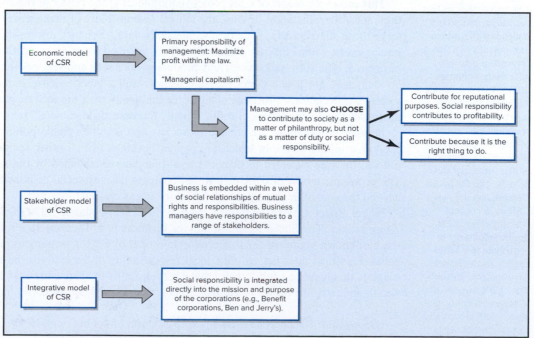

Economic Model of CSR

OBJECTIVE 2

managerial capitalism
The theory that the primary obligation of business managers is to serve the interests of stockholders by maximizing profits.

OBJECTIVE 3

corporate social responsibility (CSR)
The responsibilities that businesses have to the societies within which they operate. In various contexts, it may also refer to the voluntary actions that companies undertake to address economic, social, and environmental impacts of their business operations and the concerns of their principal stakeholders. The European Commission defines CSR as "a concept whereby companies decide voluntarily to contribute to a better society and a cleaner environment." Specifically, CSR suggests that a business identify its stakeholder groups and incorporate its needs and values within its strategic and operational decision-making process.

Most involved in the business would accept the general definition of the term **corporate social responsibility (CSR)** as referring to the ethical responsibilities that a business has to the society in which it operates. From a narrow economic perspective, a business is an institution that exists to benefit society by producing goods and services and, by doing this, creates jobs and wealth that provide further social benefits.

The law has created a form of business called a *corporation,* which promotes these economic ends by limiting the liability of individuals for the risks involved in these activities. Legislatures thought that businesses could be more efficient in raising the capital necessary for producing goods, services, jobs, and wealth if investors were protected from undue personal risks. This fact reminds us that business organizations in general, and corporations specifically, are social institutions created by society to serve social ends.

What we shall refer to as the **economic model of CSR** holds that businesses' sole social responsibility is to fulfill the economic functions they were designed to serve. This general model has direct implications for the proper role of business management. Corporations are understood to be a particular legal form of property that the owners get to use for their own ends. Managers are employees, or agents, of those owners and must work to further the owners' interests, primarily by maximizing profits. Many observers identify this perspective as the dominant model of CSR and refer to it as "**managerial capitalism.**"

This economic model of CSR places shareholders at the center of the corporation, and, from this point of view, the ethical responsibility of management is to serve those shareholders. Specifically, managers have a primary responsibility to pursue profit within the law. Because profit is assumed to be an indication that business is efficiently and successfully producing the goods and services that society demands, profit is a direct measure of how well a business firm is meeting society's expectations. (To understand some ambiguity with the idea of pursuing profit, see the Reality Check "Profits: Pursue, Increase, or Maximize?")

Because corporations are created by society and require a stable political and economic infrastructure in which to conduct business, like all other social institutions, they are expected to obey the legal mandates established by the society. The economic model of CSR denies that business has any social responsibilities beyond the economic and legal ends for which it was created.

Nobel Prize–winning economist Milton Friedman's classic 1970 *New York Times* article "The Social Responsibility of Business Is to Increase Its Profits" is the best-known argument for this economic model of CSR. Contrary to popular belief, Friedman does not ignore ethical responsibility in his analysis; he simply suggests that managers fulfill their ethical responsibility by increasing shareholder wealth and pursuing profit. Friedman explains that a corporate executive has a

> responsibility to conduct business in accordance with [his or her employer's] desires, which generally will be to make as much money as possible while conforming to the basic rules of society, *both those embodied in law and those embodied in ethical custom.* [Emphasis added.][8]

Reality Check *Profits: Pursue, Increase, or Maximize?*

Two important assumptions underlie much of the controversy surrounding corporate social responsibility. First, many people assume that the competition between profit and other social goals is a zero-sum game and that if a business manager pursues one, she must sacrifice the other. The second assumption is that stockholders always desire the highest possible rate of return on their investment. But once again, this is an area where careful thinking can go a long way toward resolving some of the controversies.

The tension between social responsibility and profit will vary significantly whether we are focused on *pursuing profit*, *increasing profit*, or *maximizing profit*. The goal of *pursuing profit* simply recognizes that to keep a business operating, management must maintain profitability. But there is nothing inherently contradictory about pursuing profit and social goals at the same time. The Reality Check "Benefit Corporations" in this chapter provides examples of businesses that do just that. For example, Ben and Jerry's has been profitable for many years while also vigorously pursuing, and attaining, social goals.

To *increase profits* suggests that business should be looking for ways to grow and improve profitability. Consistent with a utilitarian justification of market economics, this prescription advises managers to continue to increase profits because, in an ideal market, this would ensure increasing efficiency in the allocation of resources. This approach is reflected in the title of the Milton Friedman article quoted earlier: "The Social Responsibility of Business Is to Increase Its Profits." But once again, there is no inherent contradiction between increasing profit and pursuing some social agenda. Ben and Jerry's increased its profits annually while pursuing its social agenda.

The only time that the pursuit of social goals does cause conflicts is when one assumes that the business goal should be to *maximize*, or *optimize, profit* and assumes that a social agenda cannot be a means to that goal. The dominant economic model makes both of these

assumptions. In this case, any corporate resource that is used for a social goal instead of being retained for profit violates managerial responsibility to "make as much money as possible" (in Friedman's words) for shareholders. But why should we assume that business always ought to aim to *maximize* profit?

The most common answer is that this is what shareholders (or "owners" as Friedman describes them) desire. But is this answer true? In one sense, it seems to be. Every investor presumably prefers more rather than less return on his or her investment. However, two important and related variables should cause us to be cautious in assuming that every investor wants to maximize profits.

First, as we learn in finance and economics, increasing profits typically come with increasing risks. Many investors, particularly institutional investors such as mutual funds, pension plans, and insurance companies, much prefer less risk and steady profit than higher risk for the possibility of higher profit. Second, the desire for maximum profits also depends on the time frame involved. Short-term investors, perhaps better described as traders rather than as owners, may well prefer that managers use all the corporate resources to maximize profits. But short-term profit poses greater risks, especially to those investors seeking stable long-term returns on their investments. Managing quarterly earnings reports to demonstrate maximum profit over the short term can greatly increase the risk to long-term profitability.

Thus, we should be careful when using general terms like *shareholders* or *stockholders*. Corporate shares are owned by individuals and institutions who have a variety of purposes. Asserting that the primary responsibility of management is to maximize profit can give those who seek short-term maximum profit a priority over other shareholders that is unjustified. Whenever one hears the claim that business should maximize profit, one should immediately ask: "Over what time period?" and "For whom?"

economic model of CSR

Limits a firm's social responsibility to the minimal economic responsibility of producing goods and services and maximizing profits within the law.

This common view of corporate social responsibility has its roots in the utilitarian tradition and in neoclassical economics (as discussed in the section on utilitarianism in Chapter 3). As agents of business owners, the contention is that managers do have social responsibilities, but their primary responsibility is to serve shareholders. By maximizing profits, a business manager will allocate resources to their most efficient uses. Consumers who most value a resource will be willing to pay

Reality Check *Putting Your Money Where Your Mouth Is?*

Do you make purchases based on a company's social contributions? Are you more or less likely to buy something if you know that a company supports causes that are (or are not) important to you? Philanthropic CSR suggests that businesses contribute to society in the hopes that this will have beneficial reputational payoffs.

According to a 2011 global survey conducted by Cone Communications, consumers in general do care about corporate responsibility. For instance, 94% of respondents worldwide indicated that where price and quality are the same, they would be likely to switch brands to one associated with a worthwhile cause. And 93% of consumers indicated that they would boycott a company that they felt had conducted itself irresponsibly. In addition, 65% said that they had, within the last 12 months, bought a product associated with a cause.

Interestingly, consumers were less focused on expressing their opinions to companies directly: Only a third of consumers indicated that they had actually given feedback about social responsibility to a company within the last 12 months.

The same survey suggested interesting international differences: 95% of Chinese respondents said they were likely to believe a company's statements about its social and environmental impact, whereas only 39% of French respondents and 42% of Russian respondents said the same.

Source: Cone Communications, *2011 Cone/Echo Global CR Opportunity Study* (Boston, MA: Cone), www.conecomm.com/research-blog/2011-cone-echo-global-cr-opportunity-study.

the most for it; so profit is the measure of optimal allocation of resources. Over time, the pursuit of maximum profit will continuously work toward the optimal satisfaction of consumer demand, which, in one interpretation of utilitarianism, is equivalent to maximizing the overall good.

But even within this dominant economic model, there is room to pursue social responsibilities. What we might identify as a philanthropic offshoot of the economic model holds that, like individuals, business is free to contribute to social causes as a matter of philanthropy. From this perspective, business has no strict obligation to contribute to social causes, but it can be a good thing when it does so. Just as individuals have no ethical *obligation* to contribute to charity or to do volunteer work in their community, business has no strict ethical responsibility to serve wider social goods. But, just as charity is a good thing and something that we all want to encourage, business should be encouraged to contribute to society in ways that go beyond the narrow obligations of law and economics. This approach is especially common with small, privately owned businesses where the owners also often play a prominent leadership role within their local community.

Within the philanthropy offshoot, there are occasions in which charity work is done because it brings the firm good public relations, provides a helpful tax deduction, and builds goodwill and/or a good reputation within the community. (See the Reality Check "Putting Your Money Where Your Mouth Is?") Many corporate sponsorships in sports or the arts, or contributions to community events, benefit businesses in this way. Peruse the program you receive when entering a local art gallery, museum, theater, or school event and you will likely see a list of local businesses that serve as donors or sponsors that have contributed to the event. In these cases, businesses have engaged in supporting these activities, and they have received some benefit in return.

You might notice that cases where a business supports a social cause for the purpose of receiving good public relations, or other business benefits, are not much different from the economic view of CSR. In these situations, a business manager exercises managerial discretion in judging that the social contribution will have economic benefits. In these cases, the social contribution is as much an investment as it is a contribution. Certainly, proponents of the economic model of CSR would support social responsibility from this perspective. Thus, there is a great deal of overlap between decision makers who engage in the economic model for reputational reasons and those who follow the economic view of business's social responsibilities.

But there are also those cases in which a business might contribute to a social cause or event without seeking any reputational benefit. Some firms contribute to charity anonymously. Some support causes that have little or no business or financial payoff as a matter of giving back to their communities. In such cases, one might contend that corporate support for these social causes is not done for potential business benefits, but instead because the business manager or owner decides that it is simply a good and right thing to do. Others could suggest that the contributor has concluded that the society in which the firm does business is a stronger or better one if this particular activity exists.

stakeholder model of CSR

The view that business exists within a web of social relationships. The stakeholder model views business as a citizen of the society in which it operates and, like all members of a society, business must conform to the normal range of ethical duties and obligations that all citizens face.

The economic model in which business support for a social cause is done simply because it is the right thing to do differs from the reputational version only in terms of the underlying motivation. To some, this seems a trivial difference. In one case, the social good is done as a means to economic ends; in the other, it is done as an end in itself. Yet, this different motivation is, in the opinion of others, precisely what makes one action ethically responsible and the other not. From the perspective of the economic model of CSR, only philanthropy done for reputational reasons and financial ends is ethically responsible. Because business managers are the agents of owners, they have no right to use corporate resources except to earn owners greater returns on their investment. (Milton Friedman called such acts a "tax" on owners being levied by managers.)

Stakeholder Model of CSR

OBJECTIVE

A second perspective on CSR is called the **stakeholder model of CSR.** The stakeholder model understands that business exists within a web of social and ethical relationships. The stakeholder model holds that businesses exist to create value for a range of stakeholders, including employees, customers, suppliers, and local communities as well as investors and stockholders. Business managers have responsibilities to all those who have a stake in the success or failure of the company, not only to those who have invested financially.

Philosopher Norman Bowie has defended one version of CSR that expands the economic model in this direction.[9] Bowie argues that, beyond the economic model's duty to obey the law, business has an equally important ethical duty to respect human rights. Respecting human rights is the "moral minimum" that we expect of every person, whether they are acting as individuals or within corporate institutions. To explain this notion of a "moral minimum," Bowie appeals to the framework for distinguishing responsibilities that was described earlier and that is derived from the principle-based traditional ethics described in Chapter 3.

Bowie identifies his approach as a "Kantian" theory of business ethics. In simple terms, he begins with the distinction described previously between the ethical imperatives to cause no harm, to prevent harm, and to do good. People have a strong ethical duty to cause no harm, and only a *prima facie* duty to prevent harm or to do good. The obligation to cause no harm, in Bowie's view, overrides other ethical considerations. The pursuit of profit legitimately can be constrained by this ethical duty. On the other hand, Bowie accepts the economic view that managers are the agents of stockholder-owners and, thus, they also have responsibilities derived from the contract between them to further the interests of stockholders. Thus, while it is ethically good for managers to *prevent harm* or *to do good,* their duty to stockholders overrides these concerns. As long as managers comply with the moral minimum and cause no harm, they have a responsibility to maximize profits.

Thus, Bowie would argue that business has a social responsibility to respect the rights of its employees, even when not specified or required by law. Such rights might include the right to safe and healthy workplaces, right to privacy, and right to due process. Bowie would also argue that business has an ethical duty to respect the rights of consumers to such things as safe products and truthful advertising, even when not specified in law. But the contractual duty that managers have to stockholder-owners overrides the responsibility to prevent harm or to do (philanthropic) good.

Perhaps the most influential version of **stakeholder theory** was introduced by R. Edward Freeman.[10] Stakeholder theory begins with the recognition that every business decision affects a wide variety of people, benefiting some and imposing costs on others. Think of the best-known business ethics cases—Facebook, Wells Fargo, Volkswagen, Walmart, Enron, and Arthur Andersen; AIDS drugs in Africa; executive compensation; Merck and river blindness—and recognize that decisions made by business managers produce far-ranging consequences to a wide variety of people. Remember, as well, the economic lesson about opportunity costs. Every decision involves the imposition of costs, in the sense that every decision also involves opportunities forgone, choices given up.

Stakeholder theory recognizes that every business decision imposes costs on someone and mandates that those costs be acknowledged. A manager who seeks to maximize profit is imposing costs on employees, consumers, and suppliers. The dominant economic model argues that these costs are justified because managers owe an ethical duty to shareholders. The stakeholder model simply acknowledges this principle and points out that other ethical duties have an equal claim on managerial decision making. Any theory of corporate social responsibility must explain and defend answers to the questions: For whose benefit and at whose costs should the business be managed?

The economic model argues that the firm should be managed for the sole benefit of stockholders. This view is justified by appeal to the rights of owners, the fiduciary duty of managers, and the social benefits that follow from this arrangement. The stakeholder theory argues, on factual, legal, economic, and ethical grounds, that this

stakeholder theory
A model of corporate social responsibility that holds that business managers have ethical responsibilities to a range of stakeholders that go beyond a narrow view that the primary or only responsibility of managers is to stockholders.

is an inadequate understanding of business. Let us examine who the stakeholders are, what reasons can be offered to justify the legitimacy of their claims on management, and what the practical implications of this view for business managers are.

Stakeholder theory argues that the narrow economic model fails both as an accurate descriptive and as a reasonable normative account of business management. As a descriptive account of business, the classical model ignores over a century of legal precedent arising from both case law and legislative enactments. While it might have been true over a century ago that management had an overriding obligation to stockholders, the law now recognizes a wide range of managerial obligations to such stakeholders as consumers, employees, competitors, the environment, and individuals with disabilities. Thus, as a matter of law it is false to claim that management can ignore duties to everyone but stockholders.

We also need to recognize that these legal precedents did not simply fall from the sky. It is the considered judgment of the most fundamental institutions of a democratic society, the courts, and legislatures that corporate management must limit their fiduciary duty to stockholders in the name of the rights and interests of various constituencies affected by corporate decisions.

Factual, economic considerations also diminish the plausibility of the economic model. The wide variety of market failures recognized by economists show that, even when managers pursue profits, there are no guarantees that they will serve the interests of either stockholders or the public. When markets fail to attain their goals, society has no reason to sanction the primacy of the fiduciary obligation to stockholders.

But perhaps the most important argument in favor of the stakeholder theory rests in ethical considerations. The economic model appeals to two fundamental ethical norms for its justification: utilitarian considerations of social well-being and individual rights. On each of these normative accounts, however, due consideration must be given to all affected parties. Essential to any utilitarian theory is the commitment to balance the interests of all concerned and to give to each (arguably, equal) consideration. The stakeholder theory simply acknowledges this fact by requiring management to balance the ethical interests of all affected parties. Sometimes, as the classical model would hold, balancing will require management to maximize stockholder interests, but sometimes not. Utilitarianism requires management to consider the consequences of its decisions for the well-being of all affected groups. Stakeholder theory requires the same.

Likewise, any theory of moral rights is committed to equal rights for all. According to the rights-based ethical framework, the overriding moral imperative is to treat all people as ends and never as means only. Corporate managers who fail to give due consideration to the rights of employees and other concerned groups in the pursuit of profit are treating these groups as means to the ends of stockholders. This, in the rights-based ethical framework, is unjust. (Of course, ignoring the interests of stockholders is equally unjust.)

Thus, the stakeholder theory argues that on the very same grounds that are used to justify the classical model, a wider "stakeholder" theory of corporate social responsibility is proven ethically superior. Freeman argues that "the stakeholder

Reality Check   *What Is the Purpose of a Corporation According to Leading Corporate CEOs?*

In August 2019, the Business Roundtable, an organization comprised of CEOs of many of the world's largest corporations, issued a statement on the purpose of a corporation. For over 20 years, the Business Roundtable had endorsed the principle of shareholder primacy as the fundamental corporate purpose. Shareholder primacy, of course, is another way of expressing the perspective that this chapter identifies as the economic model of CSR, or managerial capitalism. As captured in the quotation from Milton Friedman, this perspective argues that the primary purpose of a corporation is to serve shareholders by maximizing profit.

The revised statement on corporate purpose represents a dramatic change away from that perspective. The new statement replaces shareholder primacy with a "fundamental commitment" to serve all stakeholders. The new statement affirms the principle that the purpose of a corporation is to create value for all stakeholders, including customers, employees, suppliers, and communities. Shareholders are included among all stakeholders, of course, but no longer function as the primary focus of corporate responsibility. The statement recognizes that all stakeholders are essential for a corporation to exist and that, therefore, corporate managers have equal responsibilities to all stakeholders.

The statement commits corporate leaders to serve customers by "meeting and exceeding their expectations"; to serve employees by providing fair pay and benefits, adequate training, and a diverse and respectful workplace; to serve suppliers by treating them "fairly and ethically"; to serve their communities by protecting the environment and engaging in sustainable practices; and to serve shareholders by providing long-term value and transparent communication.

The statement reaffirmed the commitment for the "free market system" but acknowledged that business must play a central role in guaranteeing that the free market system serves the entire society. In releasing the statement, Jamie Dimon, the Business Roundtable chair and CEO of JPMorgan Chase, stated: "These modernized principles reflect the business community's unwavering commitment to continue to push for an economy that serves all Americans."

The statement was signed by the CEOs of 181 of the largest corporations in the world, including Jeffrey Bezos of Amazon, Tim Cook of Apple, and such prominent corporations as GM, Ford, Best Buy, Target, Walmart, 3M, Xerox, Visa, Mastercard, UPS, and IBM.

Source: Business Roundtable, "Business Roundtable Redefines the Purpose of a Corporation to Promote 'An Economy That Serves All Americans,'" press release (August 19, 2019), https://www.businessroundtable.org/business-roundtable-redefines-the-purpose-of-a-corporation-to-promote-an-economy-that-serves-all-americans.

theory does not give primacy to one stakeholder group over another, though there will be times when one group will benefit at the expense of others. In general, however, management must keep the relationships among stakeholders in balance."[11]

Firms exist in a web of relationships with many stakeholders, and these relationships can create a variety of responsibilities. As we have seen in several of the cases and examples mentioned previously, it may not be possible to satisfy the needs of each and every stakeholder in a situation. But stakeholder theory also recognizes that some stakeholders have different power and impact on decisions than others—that organizations have distinct missions, priorities, and values affecting the final decisions. Therefore, social responsibility would require decisions to prioritize competing and conflicting responsibilities. To consider what corporate executives themselves think of the debate between the economic model and the stakeholder model, see the Reality Check "What Is the Purpose of a Corporation According to Leading Corporate CEOs?"

Integrative Model of CSR

OBJECTIVE

Most discussions about CSR are framed in terms of a debate: Should business be expected to sacrifice profits for social ends? Much of the CSR literature assumes a tension between the pursuit of profit and social responsibility. But, of course, there have always been organizations that turn this tension around, organizations that pursue social ends as the very core of their mission. Nonprofits—such as hospitals, nongovernmental organizations (NGOs), foundations, professional organizations, schools, colleges, and government agencies—have social goals at the center of their operations. The knowledge and skills taught in business schools, from management and marketing to human resources and accounting, are just as relevant in nonprofits as they are in for-profit organizations. For this reason alone, students in these various subdisciplines of a business school curriculum should be familiar with nonprofit business models.

But there is a growing recognition that some for-profit organizations also have social goals as a central part of the strategic mission of the organization. Within the growing benefit corporation movement, many for-profit businesses are placing social responsibility at the core of their strategic mission and corporate purpose. (For more details of such a business model, see the Reality Check "Benefit Corporations.")

integrative model of CSR

For some business firms, social responsibility is fully integrated with the firm's mission or strategic plan.

Because these firms fully integrate economic and social goals by bringing social responsibilities into the core of their business model, we refer to this as the **integrative model of CSR.** At first glance, firms that adopt the integrative model raise no particular ethical issues. Even advocates of the narrow economic model of CSR such as Milton Friedman would agree that owners of a firm are free to make the pursuit of social goals a part of their business model. They would just disagree that these social goals should be part of *every* business's mission.

No one claims that every business should adopt the principles of benefit corporations and devote all their activities to service of social goals. There are clearly other needs that businesses are designed to address. At best, benefit corporations demonstrate that profit is not incompatible with doing good, and therefore that one can do good profitably. (See the Reality Check "Fairness in a Cup of Coffee: Example of the Integrative Model.") On the other hand, there are some who would argue that the ethical responsibilities associated with sustainability are relevant to every business concern. In some ways, sustainability offers a model of CSR that suggests that ethical goals should be at the heart of every corporate mission. There are reasons to think that sustainability promises to be a concept of growing importance in discussions of CSR.

The Implications of Sustainability in the Integrative Model of CSR

Sustainability, and specifically its definition, will be discussed in greater detail in Chapter 9; but as a topic within CSR, sustainability holds that a firm's financial goals must be balanced against, and perhaps even overridden by, environmental

Reality Check   *Benefit Corporations*

There appears to be an inherent tension between the legal responsibility of business managers and the call for greater corporate social responsibility. Pursuing general goals of social responsibility would appear to violate the primary legal responsibility of business managers to pursue profits. But what if the stockholders themselves choose socially responsible goals in addition to, and perhaps even superior to, profit maximization? Benefit corporations, a new legal model created by more than 20 states (including Delaware), aim to do just this.

Like any corporation, a benefit corporation is a legal entity with legal rights and duties created to achieve the general benefits of any corporation: limiting liability, protecting owner assets, achieving tax advantages, and so on. Importantly, benefit corporations are not nonprofits; they are for-profit businesses that create value for their stockholders as a by-product of creating values for a wide range of other stakeholders. Benefit corporations differ from traditional corporations in that their boards and managers are given the legal authority to pursue social and environmental goals in addition to the financial goals that corporations generally pursue. This means that benefit corporations are free to make social and environmental goals part of the very mission and identity of the corporation and therefore make the boards and managers accountable to wider social goals. The profit sought by stockholders thus becomes one among other equally legitimate goals sought by a range of corporate stakeholders. The tension that is thought to exist between social ends and profit disappears in the benefit corporation model.

One estimate is *that there were over 2,000 active benefit corporations in the United States in 2015.** Some of the best-known companies include King Arthur Flour, Patagonia, Kickstarter, Seventh Generation, and Plum Organics. These for-profit businesses recognize that without profitability they will neither remain in business nor attract the investment needed to grow. But profit is recognized as a means, not an end in itself. Profits serve socially responsible ends by making the business financially sustainable so that it can pursue social ends.

A number of advantages are claimed for benefit corporations besides the normal financial benefits of any incorporation. Perhaps the most important is that the benefit corporation model allows corporations with socially responsible missions to protect that mission by giving both managers and boards the legal ability to prioritize mission over profits. Especially at a time when corporations and their managers are judged by short-term, quarterly earnings reports, normal corporate charters can create pressures on managers to back away from social missions in order to increase short-term profit. Recognizing that there can be different paths to profitability, benefit corporations hold management accountable for finding a path that also achieves socially responsible mission goals.

Advocates also claim that benefit corporations have the advantage of attracting employees, especially among a younger generation that is concerned as much with workplace quality as with such traditional benefits as salary and status. One study reported that businesses with a clear social mission and a reputation for creating social benefits were more successful in attracting and retaining millennial employees.[†]

Benefit corporations are also better positioned to attract socially motivated customers and investors. There is a growing market among socially conscious consumers for businesses that serve the common good. There is also a growing capital market among institutional and individual investors seeking socially responsible investments. Pursuit of socially responsible ends is part of the legal charter of benefits corporations and not something done simply as a public relations ploy.

Ben and Jerry's was among the first and best-known corporations that adopted a strong socially responsible mission. From its earliest years in the 1980s, Ben and Jerry's made its social responsibility goals part of its corporate mission. Although legally not a benefit corporation (the legal designation did not exist when the company was incorporated in 1984), its founding owners Ben Cohen and Jerry Greenfield committed the company to a range of social and environmental causes.

Ben and Jerry's famously identified three fundamental goals as its corporate mission: to make the world's best ice cream, to run a financially successful company, and to "make the world a better place." It also started a foundation that was funded from 7.5% of the pretax earnings of the company. However, as a publicly traded corporation, the fiduciary responsibility of Ben and Jerry's management and board remained primarily a financial duty.

1. How do benefit corporations fit into the model of private property, free-market capitalism?

2. Suppose shareholders objected not to the mission to "make the world a better place," but to the mission to "make the world's best ice cream" and claimed that Ben and Jerry's could maximize profits by making mediocre ice cream. Should shareholder desire override that aspect of the corporate mission?

*Ellen Berrey, "How Many Benefit Corporations Are There?" (May 5, 2015), http://ssrn.com/abstract=2602781.

†Deloitte Millennial Survey (January 2014).

Reality Check *Fairness in a Cup of Coffee: Example of the Integrative Model*

The integrative model of CSR is evidenced in a company called Equal Exchange (www.equalexchange.com), which is a worker-owned and governed business committed to Fair Trade with small-scale coffee, tea, and cocoa farmers. Its "Vision of Fairness to Farmers" explains its model:

A Vision of Fairness to Farmers

Fairness to farmers. A closer connection between people and the farmers we all rely on. This was the essence of the vision that the three Equal Exchange founders—Rink Dickinson, Michael Rozyne, and Jonathan Rosenthal—held in their minds and hearts as they stood together on a metaphorical cliff back in 1986.

The three, who had met each other as managers at a New England food co-op, were part of a movement to transform the relationship between the public and food producers. At the time, however, these efforts didn't extend to farmers outside of the U.S.

The founders decided to meet once a week—and did so for three years—to discuss how best to change the way food is grown, bought, and sold around the world. At the end of this time they had a plan for a new organization called Equal Exchange that would be:

- *A social change organization that would help farmers and their families gain more control over their economic futures.*
- *A group that would educate consumers about trade issues affecting farmers.*
- *A provider of high-quality foods that would nourish the body and the soul.*
- *A company that would be controlled by the people who did the actual work.*
- *A community of dedicated individuals who believed that honesty, respect, and mutual benefit are integral to any worthwhile endeavor.*

No Turning Back

It was a grand vision—with a somewhat shaky grounding in reality. But Rink, Michael, and Jonathan understood that significant change only happens when you're open to taking big risks. So they cried "¡Adelante!" (rough translation from the Spanish: "No turning back!") and took a running leap off the cliff. They left their jobs. They invested their own money. And they turned to their families and friends for start-up funds and let them know there was a good chance they would never see that money again.

The core group of folks believed in their cause and decided to invest. Their checks provided the $100,000 needed to start the new company. With this modest financing in hand, Rink, Michael, and Jonathan headed into the great unknown. At best, the project, which coupled a for-profit business model with a nonprofit mission, was viewed as utopian; at worst it was regarded as foolish. For the first three years Equal Exchange struggled and, like many new ventures, lost money. But the founders hung on and persevered. By the third year they began to break even.

Source: From Equal Exchange Coop, www.equalexchange.coop/story. Reprinted with permission.

Reality Check   *Will Sustainability Reports Replace the Annual Financial Reports?*

Various laws and regulations require corporations to file an annual report that provides a comprehensive accounting of a business's activities in the preceding year. The report is intended to provide shareholders and the public with information about the financial performance of the company in which they have invested. While varied information is contained in an annual report, it is primarily a financial report and will include an auditor's report and summary of revenues and expenses.

As corporations move to more fully integrate social responsibilities into their corporate mission, a different type of reporting and assessment mechanism will be required. Within the last decade, thousands of companies have supplemented this financial annual report with a **corporate sustainability report,** which provides an overview of the firm's performance on environmental and social, as well as financial, grounds. In some cases, sustainability reports are replacing financial reports by integrating assessment of financial,

environmental, and social performance into one comprehensive report.

Global Reporting Initiative, a nonprofit organization that was instrumental in creating a widely accepted sustainability reporting framework, defined sustainability reporting as follows:

> Sustainability reporting is a process for publicly disclosing an organization's economic, environmental, and social performance. Many organizations find that financial reporting alone no longer satisfies the needs of shareholders, customers, communities, and other stakeholders for information about overall organizational performance. The term "sustainability reporting" is synonymous with citizenship reporting, social reporting, triple-bottom line reporting and other terms that encompass the economic, environmental, and social aspects of an organization's performance.

Source: Global Reporting Initiative, www.globalreporting.org.

---

corporate sustainability report
Provides all stakeholders with financial and other information regarding a firm's economic, environmental, and social performance.

considerations. Defenders of this approach point out that all economic activity exists within a biosphere that supports all life. They argue that the present model of economics, and especially the macroeconomic goal of economic growth, is already running up against the limits of the biosphere's capacity to sustain life. Fundamental human needs for goods such as clean air, water, nutritious food, and a moderate climate are threatened by the present dominant model of economic activity.

From this perspective, the success of a business must be judged not only against the financial bottom line of profitability, but also against the ecological and social bottom lines of sustainability. A business or industry that is financially profitable, but that uses resources (e.g., fossil fuels) at unsustainable rates and that creates wastes (e.g., carbon dioxide) at rates that exceed the earth's capacity to absorb them, is a business or industry that is failing its fundamental social responsibility. Importantly, a firm that is environmentally unsustainable is also a firm that is, in the long term, financially unsustainable. (To learn more about how firms are sharing the results of their sustainability efforts, see the Reality Check "Will Sustainability Reports Replace the Annual Financial Reports?")

The sustainability version of CSR suggests that the long-term financial well-being of every firm is directly tied to questions of how the firm both affects and is affected by the natural environment. A business model that ignores the biophysical and ecological context of its activities is a business model doomed to failure.

Exploring Enlightened Self-Interest: Does "Good Ethics" Mean "Good Business"?

OBJECTIVE

In one of the quotations that opened this chapter, the former chair of the Dayton–Hudson Corporation, Kenneth Dayton, explained that "If business does not serve society, society will no long tolerate our profits or even our existence." This logic suggests that CSR not only provides benefits to society, but it can also benefit an organization by securing its place within a society. Are there other reasons besides self-interest and economics for a business to engage in socially responsible activities? Can we make a "business case" for CSR, such as the reputational value we discussed earlier?

Perhaps the most obvious answer is the one we touched on earlier with regard to the impact that CSR can have on a firm's reputation within a community. CSR-related activities can improve profitability by enhancing a company's standing among its stakeholders, including consumers and employees. For example, some evidence suggests that employees who are well treated in their work environments may prove more loyal, more effective, and more productive in their work. Liz Bankowshi, director of social missions at Ben & Jerry's Homemade Ice Cream Company, claims that 80% to 90% of Ben & Jerry's employees work there because "they feel they are part of a greater good."[12] The positive impact on the bottom line, therefore, stems not only from customer preference but also from employee preference.

The problem with a focus on reputation, however, is that social responsibility then can become merely social marketing. That is, a firm may use the image of social responsibility to garner customer support or employee loyalty while the facts do not evidence a true commitment. Paul Hawken, cofounder of Smith & Hawken gardening stores and an advocate of business social responsibility, reminds us that

> you see tobacco companies subsidizing the arts, then later you find out that there are internal memos showing that they wanted to specifically target the minorities in the arts because they want to get minorities to smoke. That's not socially responsible. It's using social perception as a way to aggrandize or further one's own interests exclusively.[13]

Of course, the gap between perception and reality can work in the opposite direction as well. Consider Procter & Gamble Co., which was harshly criticized by respondents to a survey seeking to rank firms on the basis of their corporate philanthropy. Respondents contended that P&G did "absolutely nothing to help" after the September 11 tragedy in New York City.[14] However, in truth, P&G provided more than $2.5 million in cash and products, but it simply did not publicize that contribution. The same held true for Honda Motor Co., which donated cash, all-terrain vehicles, and generators for use at the World Trade Center site during the same time period. Perhaps unaware of these efforts, respondents instead believed these companies to lack compassion for their failure to (publicly) support America.

reputation management
The practice of caring for the "image" of a firm.

The practice of attending to the "image" of a firm is sometimes referred to as **reputation management.** There is nothing inherently wrong with managing a firm's reputation, and in fact the failure to do so might be a poor business decision. But some critics challenge firms for engaging in CSR activities solely for the purpose of affecting their reputations. The criticism suggests that if a firm engages in socially responsible activity only to improve its reputation, it somehow is not really being ethical or socially responsible. Of course, if a firm uses CSR only as window-dressing to conceal an unethical reality, that is a problem. But surely socially responsible behavior can be both good for business and good in itself. That is, reputation management often works!

There are many aspects of a firm's reputation. It can be well-respected for its products and services, for its financial performance, as a good place to work, and as a good corporate citizen. If a firm creates a good self-image, it builds a type of trust bank—consumers, employees, and other stakeholders seem to give it some slack if they then hear something negative about the firm that otherwise has a good reputation. Similarly, if a firm has a negative image, that image may stick, regardless of what good the corporation may do. Further, a good reputation can also serve to establish a set of expectations that shape a firm's culture. As discussed in Chapter Four, corporate culture can play a significant role in creating and reinforcing ethical behavior.

Likewise, if a firm develops a bad reputation—for its products, its financial performance, as a place to work, or as a citizen—it can create significant barriers to business success. On the issue of reputation management and the impact of a variety of stakeholders on a firm's reputation, see the Reality Check "Enron and BP as Most Admired?" and examine the perspectives of various consumer and advocacy groups in connection with well-known businesses at any of the following websites:

- www.ethicalconsumer.org/boycotts/boycottslist.aspx
- www.cokespotlight.org
- www.noamazon.com

In some ways, reputation may often be more forceful than reality, as with the P&G and Honda cases mentioned earlier. Shell Oil has publicized its efforts toward good citizenship in Nigeria, but it has an unfortunate record in terms of the timing of its responsiveness to spills, and its community development projects have created community rifts in areas around oilfields. Similarly, British American Tobacco heavily and consistently promotes its high health and safety standards, but it receives ongoing reports from contract farmers in Brazil and Kenya about ill health as a result of tobacco cultivation. Which image would you expect to be more publicized and, therefore, more likely to remain in stakeholders' consciousness?

A larger question involves the possible correlation between profits and ethics. Is good ethics also good business? One important justification offered for CSR, what is often called *enlightened self-interest,* presumes that it is, or at least it can be. A great deal of research has concentrated on examining this connection. In fact, theorists continue to dispute whether ethical decisions lead to more significant profits than unethical decisions. While we are all familiar with examples of

Reality Check *Enron and BP as Most Admired?*

Would you rather be an unethical firm with a good reputation or an ethical firm with a reputation for injustice? Some very-high-profile firms have reaped enormous praise, while at the same time conducting themselves in a manner that would soon lead to scandal. Enron and BP are good examples.

Enron included the following accomplishments in its 2000 Corporate Responsibility Annual Report. The list drives home the challenges incumbent in any awards mechanism that strives to reward a trait such as "most innovative" or "all-star, most admired" rather than an enduring, measurable element of the corporate environment. On the other hand, awards such as those listed here can serve as influential motivating factors in corporate financial decisions, so many executives in fields affected by these honors would prefer they remain.

AS REPORTED IN ENRON'S 2000 CORPORATE RESPONSIBILITY ANNUAL REPORT:

The Most Innovative Company in America

—*Fortune* magazine for six consecutive years

100 Best Companies to Work for in America

—*Fortune* magazine for three consecutive years, ranked number 22 in 2000

All-Star List of Global Most Admired Companies

—*Fortune* magazine, ranked number 25 in 2000

100 Fastest Growing Companies

—*Fortune* magazine, ranked number 29 in 2000

THE CALM BEFORE THE STORM

In April 2010, a tragic oil spill that polluted the Gulf Coast made BP into one of the most despised corporations in the world. The name *BP* became widely associated with unethical, irresponsible corporate behavior. But prior to that, BP had enjoyed a strong reputation. In 2005, for example, BP was named one of the 100 Most Sustainable Companies. BP was also among the top 10 companies listed on *Fortune* magazine's Accountability Rating for 2006, 2007, and 2008. In 2007, it was ranked number one on that list.

Sources: *2000 Enron Corporate Responsibility Annual Report* (2001), pp. 2–3; "2005 Global 100 List," www.global100.org/annual-lists/2005-global-100-list.html; The Accountability Rating, www.accountabilityrating.com/past_results.asp.

unethical decisions leading to high profits, there is general agreement that, in the long run, ethics pays off. However, measurement of that payoff can be a challenge. Often, the benefits of a good reputation derived from socially responsible action occurs over the long-term, and this can be a challenge in a world in which performance is measured in short-term, quarterly financial reports.

OBJECTIVE

Though there are many justifications for ethics in business, often the discussion returns to, well, *returns*—is there a business case for a return on investment from ethics? There is evidence that good ethics is good business; yet the dominant thinking is that, if it cannot be measured, it is not important. As a result, efforts have been made to measure the bottom-line impact of ethical decision making.

Measurement is critical because the business case is not without its detractors. David Vogel, a political science professor at Berkeley, contends that although there is a market for firms with strong CSR missions, it is a niche market and one that therefore caters to only a small group of consumers or investors.[15] He argues that, contrary to a global shift in the business environment, CSR instead should be perceived as just one option for a business strategy that might be appropriate for certain types of firms under certain conditions, such as those with well-known brand names and reputations that are subject to threats by activists. He warns of the exposure a firm might suffer if it then does not live up to its CSR promises. He also cautions against investing in CSR when consumers are not willing to pay higher prices to support that investment. Though this perspective is persuasive, a review of the scholarly research on the subject suggests the contrary on numerous counts, most predominantly the overall return on investment to the corporation.

Persuasive evidence of impact comes from a study titled "Developing Value: The Business Case for Sustainability in Emerging Markets," based on a study produced jointly by SustainAbility, the Ethos Institute, and the International Finance Corporation. The research found that in emerging markets, cost savings, productivity improvement, revenue growth, and access to markets were the most important business benefits of sustainability activities. Environmental process improvements and human resource management were the most significant areas of sustainability action. The report concludes that it does pay for businesses in emerging markets to pursue a wider role in environmental and social issues, citing cost reductions, productivity, revenue growth, and market access as areas of greatest return for multinational enterprises (MNEs).

In addition, studies have found that there are a number of expected—and measurable—outcomes to ethics programs in organizations. Some people look to the end results of firms that have placed ethics and social responsibility at the forefront of their activities, while others look to those firms that have been successful and determine the role that ethics might have played. (For additional areas of measurement, see the Reality Check "So They Say.") With regard to the former, consider Johnson & Johnson, known for its quick and effective handling of its experience with tainted Tylenol. As highlighted in the Reality Check "Do Codes Make a Difference" in Chapter 4, Johnson & Johnson has had more than seven decades of consecutive sales increases, two decades of double-digit earnings increases, and four decades of dividend increases. Each of these quantifiable measurements can perhaps serve as proxies for success, to some extent, or at least would be unlikely to occur in a company permeated by ethical lapses.

Moreover, a landmark study by Professors Stephen Erfle and Michael Frantantuono found that firms that were ranked highest in terms of their records on a variety of social issues (including charitable contributions, community outreach programs, environmental performance, advancement of women, and promotion of minorities) had greater financial performance as well. Financial performance was better in terms of operating income growth, sales-to-assets ratios, sales growth, return on equity, earnings-to-asset growth, return on investment, return on assets, and asset growth.[16] The Reality Check "So They Say" demonstrates that these perspectives are gaining traction worldwide.

In addition, the researchers found that these same firms had a significantly better reputation among corporate directors, security analysts, and senior executives. The same result was found in a 2001 *Fortune* survey of most admired companies. The UK-based Institute of Business Ethics did a follow-up study to validate these findings and found that, from the perspectives of economic value added, market value added, and the price/earnings ratio, those companies that had a code of conduct outperformed those that did not over a 5-year period.[17] The higher

Reality Check *So They Say*

Whether at the World Trade Organization, or at the OECD, or at the United Nations, an irrefutable case can be made that a universal acceptance of the rule of law, the outlawing of corrupt practices, respect for workers' rights, high health and safety standards, sensitivity to the environment, support for education and the protection and nurturing of children are not only justifiable against the criteria of morality and justice. The simple truth is that these are good for business and most business people recognize this.*

Thomas d'Aquino, CEO of Canada's Business Council on National Issues

We all pay for poverty and unemployment and illiteracy. If a large percentage of society falls into a disadvantaged class, investors will find it hard to source skilled and alert workers; manufacturers will have a limited market for their products; criminality will scare away foreign investments, and internal migrants to limited areas of opportunities will strain basic services and lead to urban blight. Under these conditions, no country can move forward economically and sustain development. . . . It therefore makes business sense for corporations to complement the efforts of government in contributing to social development.[†]

J. Ayala II

Our findings, both cross-sectional and longitudinal, indicate that there are indeed systematic linkages among community involvement, employee morale, and business performance in business enterprises. To the best of our knowledge, this is the first time that such linkages have been demonstrated empirically. Moreover, the weight of the evidence produced here indicates that community involvement is positively associated with business performance, employee morale is positively associated with business performance, and the interaction of community involvement—external involvement—with employee morale—internal involvement—is even more strongly associated with business performance than is either "involvement" measure alone.[‡]

Report of a study by UCLA graduate school of business professor David Lewin and J. M. Sabater (formerly IBM director of corporate community relations) in 1989 and 1991 involving in-depth, statistical research surveys of over 150 U.S.-based companies to determine whether there is a verifiable connection between a company's community involvement and its business performance

*Source: Quoted in C. Forcese, "Profiting from Misfortune? The Role of Business Corporations in Promoting and Protecting International Human Rights" (MA thesis, Norman Paterson School of International Affairs, Carleton University, Ottawa 1997), referred to in C. Forcese, "Putting Conscience into Commerce: Strategies for Making Human Rights Business as Usual" (Montréal International Centre for Human Rights and Democratic Development, 1997).

[†]Source: J. Ayala II, "Philanthropy Makes Business Sense," *Ayala Foundation Inc. Quarterly* 4, no. 2 (July–September, October, November 1995), p. 3.

[‡] Source: D. Lewin and J. M. Sabater, "Corporate Philanthropy and Business Performance," *Philanthropy at the Crossroads* (Bloomington: University of Indiana Press, 1996), pp. 105–126.

performance translated into significantly more economic value added, a less volatile price/earnings ratio (making the firm, perhaps, a more secure investment), and 18% higher profit/turnover ratios. The research concluded:

> This study gives credence to the assertion that "you do business ethically because it pays." However, the most effective driver for maintaining a high level of integrity throughout the business is because it is seen by the board, employees and other stakeholders to be a core value and therefore the right thing to do. . . . [A] sustainable business is one which is well managed and which takes business ethics seriously. Leaders of this type of business do not need any assurance that their approach to the way they do business will also enhance their profitability, because they know it to be true.[18]

By any account, 2018 was an ethically challenging year for Facebook. The year 2019 began no better. As a result of the failures to protect user privacy, Facebook met with significant social and governmental criticism. In early 2019, Facebook announced to investors that it expected to be fined as much as $5 billion by the FTC for failing to live up to the conditions of the 2011 settlement. At the same time, it was disclosed that the European Union was also considering major fines estimated in the range of $1.7 billion for violating the European General Data Protection Regulation (GDPR) laws.

In March 2019, a gunman attacked two mosques during prayer services in Christchurch, New Zealand, killing fifty-one people and wounding dozens more. For 17 minutes, he live-streamed this attack on Facebook, with copies uploaded to other social media sites, including YouTube, Twitter, and Facebook's own WhatsApp and Instagram. Facebook responded by promising to increase its efforts to detect such content but admitted that it has a limited ability to police such tragedies. This was not the first, or the last, violent crime to be live-streamed on Facebook. Reports of violent attacks, rapes, and suicides have been reported since Facebook introduced live streaming in 2016.* In April 2019, the shooting death of a 74-year-old man was live-streamed on Facebook by the murderer.

Social criticisms reached a peak in May 2019 when Chris Hughes, a co-founder of Facebook, wrote an op-ed in the *New York Times* calling for the breakup of Facebook. Hughes described Facebook as a dangerous monopoly and argued that his co-founder and present CEO Mark Zuckerberg is unable or unwilling to make the necessary changes to move Facebook towards greater socially responsible behavior.

*Zak Doffman, "Facebook Admits It Can't Control Facebook Live—Is This the End for Live Streaming?" *Forbes,* March 24, 2019.

This chapter sought to answer the question of whether there exists a social responsibility of business. Several sources of that responsibility were proposed. The responsibility may be based in a concept of good corporate citizenship, a social contract, or enlightened self-interest. Notwithstanding its origins, we then explored the challenge of how an inanimate entity like a corporation could actually have a responsibility to others and discussed the extent of that obligation, in both law and ethics.

No matter how one answers the several questions posed by this chapter, however, one thing is certain: It is impossible to engage in business today without encountering and addressing CSR. Despite substantial differences among companies, research demonstrates that almost all companies will confront CSR issues from stakeholders at some point in the near future.[19]

**Questions,
Projects,
and Exercises**

1. What is your overall perspective on CSR after reviewing this chapter? If market forces do not encourage responsibility for social causes, should a firm engage in this behavior? Does social responsibility apply only to firms, or do consumers have a responsibility as well to support firms that take socially responsible action and withhold our support from firms that fail to exhibit socially responsible behavior? If we stand by and allow irresponsible actions to take place using profits made on our purchases, do we bear any responsibility?

   • How did you reach your decision? What key facts do you need to know in order to judge a firm's actions or your complicity in them by supporting a firm with your purchases or other choices?

   • How do you determine responsibility? Do you pay attention to these issues in your purchases and other choices?

   • Would you be more likely to support a company by purchasing its products or services if the company (a) donated a portion of the proceeds to a cause that was important to you, (b) paid its workers a "fair" wage (however, you would define that concept), or (c) was a good investment for its stockholders? Which consequence is more influential to you? On the contrary, would you refrain from purchasing from a firm that failed in any of those areas?

   • How do the alternatives compare? Do you believe different purchasing decisions by consumers could really make a difference?

2. Which of the three models of CSR is most persuasive to you and why? Which do you believe is most prevalent among companies that engage in CSR efforts?

3. This chapter has asked in several ways whether the social responsibility of the companies you patronize has ever made any difference to your purchasing decisions. Will it make any difference in the future as a result of what you have learned? Consider your last three largest purchases. Go to the websites of the companies that manufacture the products you bought and explore those firms' social responsibility efforts. Are they more or less than what you expected? Do your findings make a difference to you in terms of how you feel about these firms, your purchases, and/or the amount of money you spent on these items?

4. Court decisions in the United States have recognized corporations as having legal rights beyond the narrow right of being able to enter into contracts. Do you agree that corporations should have rights to free political speech? Religious freedom? Should they have a right to vote?

5. Some years ago, Nestlé S.A. CEO Peter Braeck-Letmathe argued, "Companies shouldn't feel obligated to 'give back' to communities because they haven't taken anything away. Companies should only pursue charitable endeavors with the underlying intention of making money. It is not our money we're handing out but our investors'. A company's obligation is simply to create jobs and make products. What the hell have we taken away from society by being a successful company that employs people?"[20] Which model of CSR would the Nestlé CEO advocate, and do you agree with his assessment?

6. What kind of organization would you like to work for? What would be the best? What would be the most realistic? Think about its structure, physical environment, lines of communication, treatment of employees, recruitment and promotion practices, policies toward the community, and so on. Consider also, however, what you lose because of some of these benefits (e.g., if the company contributes in the community or offers more benefits for employees, there might be less money for raises).

7. Take another look at the quote by Paul Hawken in the section titled "Exploring Enlightened Self-Interest" in this chapter. He seems to be saying that it is not acceptable to use social perception as a way to further one's own interests (exclusively). Now find the Smith & Hawken site on the web and any additional information you can locate regarding Smith & Hawken or Paul Hawken and CSR. Would you identify Smith & Hawken as a firm interested in CSR? Would you identify Paul Hawken as an individual interested in CSR or personal social responsibility? Which model of CSR would you suggest that Paul Hawken supports?

8. Make a list of the five products on which you have spent the most money over the past 3 years. Using the internet, find corporate sustainability reports for the companies that produced those products or that had some responsibility in their production. Are you able to find a sustainability report for each company? What can you determine about the company's sustainability efforts by reviewing these reports? Can you determine anything about their sincerity? Do you perceive that the company is undergoing a fundamental transformation in its efforts to sustainability, or does it seem more a matter of window-dressing (or, in other words, for the *sole* purpose of reputation)?

9. Have you ever boycotted a product because you disagree with some action by the company that produces it? Would you boycott a product because the company advertises on a television program that promotes political views with which you disagree? Why or why not?

10. Is there any action that Facebook could do that would lead you to delete your Facebook, Instagram, or WhatsApp account? If so, what would lead you to do this? If not, why not?

Key Terms

After reading this chapter, you should have a clear understanding of the following key terms. For a complete definition, please see the Glossary.

corporate social responsibility (CSR), *p. 150*
corporate sustainability report, *p. 160*
economic model of CSR, *p. 150*

integrative model of CSR, *p. 157*
managerial capitalism, *p. 150*
reputation management, *p. 162*

stakeholder model of CSR, *p. 153*
stakeholder theory, *p. 154*

Endnotes

1. Source: Sir Adrian Cadbury. (September/October 1987). "Ethical Managers Make Their Own Rules." *Harvard Business Review*.
2. Source: Stakeholder Alliance, www.stakeholderalliance.org/Buzz.html (accessed April 11, 2010).
3. Source: Senator Al Franken.
4. *Citizens United v. Fed. Election Comm'n*, 558 U.S. 310 (2010).
5. *Burwell v. Hobby Lobby Stores*, 573 U.S. 682 (2014).
6. "Mission Statement: Our Values," www.merck.com/about/mission.html (accessed April 11, 2010).
7. Source: George Merck.
8. Source: Milton Friedman, "The Social Responsibility of Business Is to Increase Its Profits," *New York Times Magazine* (september 13, 1970).

9. Norman Bowie, *Business Ethics: A Kantian Perspective,* 2nd ed. (New York: Cambridge University Press, 2017).

10. R. Edward Freeman, *Strategic Management: A Stakeholder Approach* (Marshfield, MA: Pittman, 1984).

11. Source: William Evan and R. Edward Freeman, "A Stakeholder Theory of the Modern Corporation: Kantian Capitalism," in *Contemporary Issues in Business Ethics,* 4th ed., Joseph R. DesJardins and John McCall eds. (Belmont, CA: Wadsworth Publishing, 2000), p. 89.

12. Joel Makower, *Beyond the Bottom Line* (New York: Simon & Schuster, 1994), p. 68.

13. Source: Joel Makower, *Beyond the Bottom Line* (New York: Simon & Schuster, 1994), p. 15.

14. Ronald Alsop, "For a Company, Charitable Works Are Best Carried out Discreetly," *The Wall Street Journal,* January 16, 2002, Marketplace Section, p. 1.

15. David Vogel, *The Market for Virtue: The Potential and Limits of Corporate Social Responsibility* (Washington, DC: Brookings Institution, 2005).

16. Joel Makower, *Beyond the Bottom Line* (New York: Simon & Schuster, 1994), pp. 70–71.

17. Simon Webley and Elise More, *Does Business Ethics Pay?* (London: Institute of Business Ethics, 2003), p. 9.

18. Source: Simon Webley and Elise More, *Does Business Ethics Pay?* (London: Institute of Business Ethics, 2003), p. 9.

19. Margot Lobbezoo, "Social Responsibilities of Business" (unpublished manuscript) (available from the author).

20. Source: Jennifer Heldt Powell, "Nestlé Chief Rejects the Need to 'Give Back' to Communities," *Boston Herald,* (March 9, 2005), p. 33, www.bc.edu/schools/csom/cga/executives/events/brabeck/; www.babymilkaction.org/press/press22march05.html (accessed April 11, 2010).

Chapter

6

Ethical Decision Making: Employer Responsibilities and Employee Rights

Hire character. Train skill.

Peter Schutz

The employer generally gets the employees he deserves.

J. Paul Getty

If a man does not keep pace with his companions, perhaps it is because he hears a different drummer. Let him step to the music which he hears, however measured or far away.

Henry David Thoreau (American poet, essayist, and philosopher who also became known for his perspectives on abolition and civil disobedience)

You manage things, you lead people.

Rear Admiral Grace Murray Hopper

Article 19 of the Universal Declaration of Human Rights provides that "everyone shall have the right to hold opinions without interference" and "everyone shall have the right to freedom of expression; this right shall include freedom to seek, receive and impart information and ideas of all kinds, regardless of frontiers, either orally, in writing or in print. . . ." Later amendments restrict these broad rights when necessary "[f]or respect of the rights or reputation of others" or "[f]or the protection of national security or of public order (order public), or of public health or morals."[1]

While some societies respect this concept more than others, the concept of free speech in the United States is so ingrained that sometimes we focus on the right and omit to consider its limitations. To the contrary, however, our statements are not protected in every environment. Consider your perspective on the following examples of employees' choices to express themselves.

In Fall 2016, Juli Briskman posted a photo of herself giving the finger to the U.S. president's motorcade. Her firm terminated her at-will employment, claiming that she violated company policy that banned obscene content on social media. From a *legal* perspective, the termination was valid. The employer is a private entity and therefore the First Amendment protection of free speech does not apply. While Virginia does protect against terminations in direct violation of public policy, a court asked to review the case dismissed it because Briskman could not point to a particular statute that was violated.[2]

You may recall another case where someone stood up (or, in this situation, refused to stand) because of his values. In 2016, National Football League quarterback Colin Kaepernick chose to kneel during the National Anthem in protest against racial injustice. In fall 2017, he filed an NLRB grievance against the NFL, claiming that the owners colluded to keep him from receiving any offers of employment. While the NLRB permitted the case to go forward, in February 2019, he opted instead to withdraw the grievance after reaching a confidential settlement.[3]

In a third case that happened in Fall 2017, James Damore, an engineer at Google, wrote a lengthy memo that detailed his concerns about widespread bias at Google concerning diversity and inclusion, in favor of women. The memo outlined a number of "facts" to support Damore's conclusion that women are instead less equipped to handle the industry than men. Damore was fired from Google when his memo became public.[4]

According to Damore's memo, Google's culture was characterized by a political bias that attributed any disparity among men and women within the technology profession to oppression and that silenced anyone who dared to disagree. The result was an "echo chamber" in which only discussions deemed politically correct were allowed. This, according to Damore, created an authoritarian culture in which unfair and divisive discrimination against white males was the accepted means to address workplace disparity. Damore asserted, "Only facts and reason can shed light on these biases, but when it comes to diversity and inclusion, Google's left bias has created a politically correct monoculture that maintains its hold by shaming dissenters into silence."

Damore's memo then went on to cite the "facts and reason" that he believed explained the workplace disparity between men and women. Damore claimed that "men and women are biologically different in many ways." These biological differences, in turn, explain personality differences, which are the best explanations for workplace inequality, especially in such fields as software engineering.

According to the memo, women are more "directed towards feelings and aesthetics rather than ideas." They "have a stronger interest in people rather than things," and this explains why women "prefer jobs in social or artistic areas." On the other hand, "men may like coding because it requires systemizing and even within SWEs [software engineering], comparatively more women work on front end, which deals with both people and aesthetics."

Damore went on to claim that women are more gregarious than men, who tend to be more aggressive, and that this "leads to women generally having a harder time negotiating salary, asking for raises, speaking up, and leading." Finally, Damore claimed that women characteristically have higher levels of "neuroticism (higher anxiety, lower stress tolerance)" and that this "may contribute to the higher levels of anxiety" and "to the lower number of women in high stress jobs." In contrast, men have "a higher drive for status that makes them more tolerant of longer work hours and a high stress work environment."[5]

Sundar Pichai, Google's CEO, and Danielle Brown, Vice President for Diversity, defended their decision to fire Damore based on Google's commitment to equal opportunity in the workplace. They explained that, while Google was committed to the values of free speech and diverse perspectives, it had a stronger commitment to equal treatment of all employees and to a workplace free from discrimination. In their judgment, Damore's memo violated that commitment.

Damore filed a complaint with the National Labor Relations Board to protect his "concerted activity" to address workplace issues (rather than under a more general claim of free speech), which he subsequently withdrew. However, before that withdrawal, the NLRB found that his termination was legal based on the discriminatory nature of his statements.[6]

1. Using ethical analysis (rather than the legal analysis included above), evaluate whether it was ethical for Briskman to have been fired, for Kaepernick to have been blacklisted, and for Damore to have been terminated. Was each of these employees acting ethically in voicing or acting on their values, and, if so, were their employers acting ethically in their decisions as well?

2. What are the key facts relevant to your conclusion?

3. What are the ethical issues involved in your decision?

4. Who are the stakeholders in this scenario? Are any stakeholders' rights compromised or limited by the employers' decisions, other than the three employees mentioned? In what way?

5. Using ethical theories, how would you advocate on the employers' behalf in each circumstance?

6. Co-author Chris MacDonald suggests, "A good test of your moral intuitions is generally to put the shoe on the other foot. In particular, when you applaud the exercise of autonomous judgment or freedom by some individual, group, or company, ask whether you would still applaud it if the individual, group, or company had values different from your own." In your answers to the above questions, consider your own consistency and whether you would respond the same if the content were different.

Chapter Objectives

After reading this chapter, you will be able to:

1. Distinguish between the two distinct perspectives of the ethics of workplace relationships.
2. Explain the concept of due process in the workplace.
3. Define employment at will (EAW) and its ethical rationale.
4. Describe how to downsize in an ethical manner.
5. Explain the difference between intrinsic and instrumental value in terms of health and safety.
6. Illustrate an employer's responsibility with regard to employee health and safety and why the market is not effective at managing this responsibility.
7. Explain the basic arguments for and against regulation of the global labor environment.
8. Describe the argument for a market-based resolution to workplace discrimination.
9. Define diversity as it applies to the workplace, as well as its benefits and challenges.
10. Explain affirmative action and describe the three ways in which affirmative action may be legally permissible.

Introduction

Ethics in the employment context is perhaps the most universal topic in business ethics because nearly every reader will have the experience of being employed or employing someone else. While legislators and the courts have addressed many aspects of the working environment, countless ethical issues remain that these regulatory and judicial bodies have left unresolved. The law provides guidance for thinking about ethical issues in the workplace, but these issues go well beyond legal considerations! In fact, three-quarters of the reports to firms' internal help lines are related to human resource issues.[7]

This chapter explores those areas of ethical decision making in the workplace where the law remains relatively fluid and where answers are not easily found by simply calling the company lawyer. Issues may also arise where the law does seem clear, but, for one reason or another, it is insufficient to protect the interests of all stakeholders. We will examine various ethical challenges that face the nature of employer responsibilities and the employee, whether that employee is a worker on an assembly line, the manager of a restaurant, or the CEO of a large corporation. Although individual perspectives may change, similar conflicts and stakeholders present themselves across business settings.

As you examine each issue raised in this chapter, consider how you might use the ethical decision-making process we have discussed to reach the best possible conclusion for the stakeholders involved. Severe time constraints, limited information, and pressure usually accompany these challenging business decisions. Though using the ethical decision-making process may seem cumbersome at the outset, once the process becomes embedded in the professional landscape and culture, its effectiveness and efficiency in resolving these issues will become apparent. In fact, utilizing an ethical decision-making process will avoid later hurdles, thus removing barriers to progress and momentum. Let us consider the issues that exist in the current workplace environment to test the effectiveness of the ethical decision-making process.

Ethical Issues in the Workplace: The Current Environment

We all have decisions to make about how we will treat others in the workplace and how we will ask to be treated. Ethics at work and in human resource management is about our relationships with others and with our organizations. Research demonstrates that companies that place employees at the core of their strategies produce higher long-term returns to shareholders than their industry peers—practically double![8]

The same holds true for an employee's relationship with her or his employer. Fifty percent of U.S. workers feel a very strong sense of loyalty to their employer (and that number rises to 62% when considering only those born between 1965 and 1979, often called Gen Xers).[9] When asked about the greatest influence on their commitment, workers responded that the most important factor is to feel valued by elements such as benefits like health care coverage and also opportunities for professional growth—key components of an ethical working environment. Of course, these benefits will change from country to country, depending on what already is covered (such as universal health care in some environments).

These influences play out in practical ways for businesses because commitment and loyalty are impacted by the ethical culture of the workplace. Seventy-eight percent of employees who have experienced unethical or uncivil behavior at work report that their commitment to the organization declined, and 66% report that their performance declined.[10] When employees do not perceive a positive ethical culture in the workplace, they also tend not to report misconduct. A choice not to report misconduct is a big problem—the Ethics Resource Center's Global Business Ethics Survey for 2018 found a significant increase over the prior year in pressure on employees to engage in misconduct! More than one in every six employees has felt pressure to do something wrong, and that is an increase of almost 25% since 2013. In fact, almost two-thirds of employees report that they observe bad conduct *rewarded,* so these violations might be more likely to happen over and over again.[11]

OBJECTIVE

Whether you are reading this text from the perspective of an employee or employer (or both), these observations above should alert you to the fact that there are two very distinct, and sometimes competing, perspectives on the ethics of workplace relationships. One type of employer might create a culture where employees are treated well as a *means to produce greater workplace harmony and productivity* and, as several studies have demonstrated, higher levels of innovation.[12] This approach, focusing on end results, should be recognizable as an application of utilitarian analysis discussed in Chapter 3 if couched in terms of the creation of a better workplace for all.

On the other hand, this perspective might raise a question about moral motivation and the employer's instrumental, self-interested reasons for doing good, similar to our discussion of corporate social responsibility in Chapter 5). While no one is claiming that employees have some universal right to a "happy" workplace,[13] scholar Jeffrey Pfeffer suggests that effective firms are characterized by a set of common practices, all of which involve treating employees in humane and respectful ways.[14]

As an example of these concerns, consider the role of emotion in the workplace. Studies suggest that managers can have a significant impact on the emotions of their workers, and this impact can greatly affect productivity and loyalty, as well as perceptions of fairness, care, and concern. Scholar Neal Ashkanasy and colleagues suggest that managers should pay attention to the emotional impact of various jobs within their workplace and model a positive emotional environment.[15] The topic of interpersonal relationships and emotions in the workplace also brings to mind issues of what is appropriate (and inappropriate) behavior. We will explore that question, and the impact of the #MeToo movement on the workplace environment, later in this chapter in the section on "Rights and Responsibilities in Conflict," and the Decision Point in that section, "#MeToo in the Workplace?"

Rewards and compensation structures can clearly impact the emotions of workers, as can the composition of teams or the power relationships within a workplace. When employees see that a firm values their emotions, as well as exhibits values such as honesty, respect, and trust, they feel less pressure, more valued as employees, and more satisfied with their organizations. Because reporting to external stakeholders has become such a key issue in recent scandals, one might also want to consider whether a more satisfied employee is more or less likely to report misconduct to outside parties.

A second type of employer might create a culture where employees are treated well out of a sense of duty and rights, regardless of the utilitarian or self-interested consequences in productivity. This approach—which might remind you of Kant and Universalism—emphasizes the rights and duties of all employees. It suggests that employees should be treated well simply because "*it is the right thing to do.*" Defenders of employee rights argue that employees should be protected from being constantly subjected to utilitarian and financial calculations—they are not mere machines hired to generate a profit for their employers. A sense of duty to employees might stem from the law, professional codes of conduct, corporate codes of conduct, or such moral principles as fairness, justice, or human rights on the part of the organization's leadership. (See the Reality Check "Protecting Employee Rights through Unions.")

Reality Check   *Protecting Employee Rights through Unions*

In 1960, about one-third of the American workforce was represented by unions. In both 2016 and 2017, that figure was 10%. This compares to:

- 8% in Hungary,
- 12% in Mexico,
- 14% in Australia,
- 17% in Japan,
- 23% in the United Kingdom,
- 26% in Canada,
- 66% in Sweden, and
- 90% in Iceland.*

Not surprisingly, federal and state regulations governing work practices have exploded as union membership has declined. The variety of protections is prodigious: antidiscrimination laws, wage and hour laws, worker safety laws, unemployment compensation, workers' compensation, and social security, to name a few.

Five states—North Carolina, South Carolina, Virginia, Texas (excluding firefighters and police officers), and Georgia (excluding firefighters)—prohibit collective bargaining with public employees.[†] In the wake of the 2008 economic downturn, almost every state proposed legislation changes to public-sector unions.[‡] These legislative proposals have been met with strong resistance by public employees and their supporters.

In 2011, large protests flared up between public-sector unions and legislatures in several states, led by demonstrations of up to 100,000 marchers in Wisconsin. Much of the legislation that led to the protests made its way through the federal courts with various outcomes (most typically ended with a compromise position). Noteworthy is a 2014 U.S. Supreme Court decision that restricted the definition of *public employee* in order to uphold the First Amendment rights of certain workers (who did not wish to join or support a union) not to have public union dues automatically deducted from their paychecks.[§]

*Organization for Economic Cooperation and Development, "Trade Union Density," https://stats.oecd.org/Index.aspx?DataSetCode=TUD (accessed March 6, 2019).

[†]M. Greer and C. Wheatley, "Subcommittee Report: States Without Bargaining Legislation," American Bar Association (January 25, 2018), https://www.americanbar.org/content/dam/aba/events/labor_law/2018/papers/States%20Without%20Bargaining%20Legislation.pdf (accessed March 6, 2019).

[‡]Julia Edwards, "Union Protests Spread across the U.S.," *NationalJournal.com* (April 8, 2011), https://archive.li/LK8ht (accessed November 5, 2018).

[§]*Harris v. Quinn*, 573 U.S. 616 (2014); see also www.scotusblog.com/case-files/cases/harris-v-quinn/ (accessed March 6, 2019).

Defining the Parameters of the Employment Relationship

The following section explores the legal and ethical boundaries that will help us define the employment relationship based on some of the principles discussed earlier. Just imagine you are hired by someone—a relationship is now formed between you and your employer. Ethical issues are bound to arise. Your employment arrangement raises issues of power, obligation, responsibility, fair treatment, and expectations. In many circumstances, your very livelihood is at stake, but you also are contributing to the livelihood of your employer by your work, so you both rely on each other's contributions to the relationship.

Though legal requirements might serve to protect some of your and your employer's interests, these requirements only can go so far and cover so many bases. We will begin by looking at the ethics underlying the concepts of due process and fairness that help determine what is or is not acceptable behavior in the workplace. We will discover some of the ways in which employers might be able to remain true to these principles, even when specifically challenged by vexing circumstances such as a reduction in force. The relationship is further defined by the application of these principles to working conditions such as health and safety, both in domestic operations and abroad.

Note that the issues in the following sections are predominantly settled from an ethical perspective by their *justification.* In other words, as just one example, people of goodwill would be likely to agree that an employee has a right to a safe and healthy workplace. Disagreements remain regarding the implementation, interpretation, or extent of that right. In contrast, the second section of this chapter explores several issues that are not perceived as settled from either a legal or ethical point of view. Reasonable minds may differ not only as to whether the means to achieve the ends are justified but whether the ends themselves are just, fair, or ethical. An example of this latter issue would be affirmative action, a thorny matter for courts, managers, and philosophers alike.

Due Process and Just Cause

OBJECTIVE

Employment security—getting and keeping a job—is perhaps the most significant aspect of work from the employee's ethical perspective. Fundamental questions of justice arise because employees are subject to considerable harms from a lack of security in their jobs and do not have much power to create security. But should employers' rights and ability to hire, fire, or discipline employees therefore be restricted in order to prevent injustices? Are there any other means by which to protect against unethical behavior or unjust results?

due process

The right to be protected against the arbitrary use of authority. In legal contexts, due process refers to the procedures that police and courts must follow in exercising their authority over citizens. In the employment context, due process specifies the conditions for basic fairness within the scope of the employer's authority over its employees.

Philosophically, the right of **due process** is the right to be protected against the arbitrary use of authority. In legal contexts, *due process* refers to the procedures that police and courts must follow in exercising their authority over citizens. Few dispute that the state, through its police and courts, has the authority to punish citizens. This authority creates a safe and orderly society in which we all can live, work, and do business. But that authority is not unlimited; it can be exercised only in certain ways and under certain conditions. Due process rights specify these conditions.

Similarly, due process in the workplace acknowledges an employer's authority over employees. Employers can tell employees what to do, and when, and how to do it. They can exercise such control because they retain the ability to discipline or fire an employee who does not comply with their authority. Because of the immense value that work holds for most people, the threat of losing one's job is a powerful motivation to comply. However, basic fairness—implemented through due process—demands that this power be used *justly.* It is the definition of basic fairness that remains the challenge. Review, for instance, the conflicting versions of fair labor standards between Europe and the United States, discussed in the Reality Check "Protests in Support of Employment Security in Europe."

Unfortunately, there is evidence to suggest that this acknowledged authority of employers over employees, or simply managers over subordinates, is not always exercised in a just or fair manner—and it is not only the worker who suffers the

Reality Check   *Protests in Support of Employment Security in Europe*

As discussed elsewhere in this chapter, a number of states maintain employment "at will" for employees. The term *employment at will* means that, unless an agreement specifies otherwise, employers are free to fire an employee at any time and for any reason, except for a reason prohibited by case law or statute *(see the following text discussing Learning Objective 3)*. However, this is not the case in some other countries.

In Europe, for instance, there is no concept of at-will employment. If a European employer wishes to terminate an employee, it must go through very specific legal procedures. Varying from country to country, termination laws may require long periods of prior notification, government approval for dismissal, or legal recourse for unfair dismissal, or they may include other mechanisms that limit the capacity of companies to dismiss workers at will. Plus, even after following those procedures, the employer is required to pay severance pay or "notice pay," which is quite costly, unless it can demonstrate good cause.

In response to the global economic recession, which began in 2008, countries across Europe enacted austerity measures to encourage economic growth. While some countries, such as Spain, faced up to 20% to 25% unemployment rates, governments looked for ways to provide companies with greater flexibility in hiring and firing,

increased the retirement age, and generally reduced strong European labor laws. In response, protests immediately flared.

In the years that followed, while most of Europe experienced a modest recovery from the recession, many of the southern European countries such as Italy, Spain, and Greece continued to report high unemployment. In 2014, new protests of up to 65,000 people occurred in both Italy and Spain, challenging the continued labor reform.*

Since that time, many employers have responded by offering employees only temporary employment contracts in order to avoid regulations on full-time employees. For instance, in Spain, more than 90% of all employment contracts offered are now for temporary positions.†

*"Timeline: Tracking Europe's Debt Crisis," *CBC News* (October 2, 2013), www.cbc.ca/news2/interactives/europe-debt-crisis-timeline/ (accessed March 6, 2019); "Anti-austerity Protest in Italy Turns Violent," *Al Jazeera* (April 13, 2014), www.aljazeera.com/news/europe/2014/04/anti-austerity-protest-italy-turns-violent-20144122357869885.html (accessed March 6, 2019); "Anti-austerity Protesters March in Spain," *Al Jazeera* (March 23, 2014), www.aljazeera.com/news/europe/2014/03/anti-austerity-protesters-march-spain-2014322192956618925.html (accessed March 6, 2019).

†Bird & Bird, "A European View on Employment Law," https://www.twobirds.com/~/media/pdfs/european-view-on-employment-law.pdf (accessed March 6, 2019).

consequence. As of 2018, 37% of workers (54 million people) reported that they had experienced workplace "bullying" in their workplaces, and another 19% have witnessed it. Workplace bullying is defined as "the repeated, malicious, health-endangering mistreatment of one employee . . . by one or more employees."[16] The mistreatment need not be physically threatening, of course, but might simply involve a boss who is constantly yelling dictates at workers or a co-worker who spreads rumors about another in order to sabotage his or her position.

These behaviors lead not only to emotional abuse but also to a complete loss of personal dignity, intimidation, and fear. Moreover, others in the workplace suffer vicariously with these same sensations; evidence demonstrates that the employer has significant bottom-line expenses from workers' compensation claims based on stress and other emotional stimuli, and there are increased costs related to potential litigation arising from claims of abusive work situations. There is also the indirect impact on employee morale, and certainly the negative effects that occur when one would prefer not to be at the workplace: turnover, absenteeism, poor customer relationships, and acts of sabotage. (Please see Decision Point "Bullying in the Workplace?")

Should states enact anti-bullying laws that would enable victims of workplace bullying to sue their harassers and also to hold their employers accountable? Surveys show that at least 38% of U.S. workers have experienced bullying in their place of employment or have seen others experience bullying.* Advocates of anti-bullying laws argue that the extent of the problem—when considered alongside evidence that bullying causes significant physical, emotional, and economic harm to its victims—calls for a legislative response. On the other hand, critics worry that anti-bullying legislation would lead to a spike in employee lawsuits and point to the difficulty of determining whether abusive bullying has taken place, particularly in high-pressure work environments.[†]

Since 2003, thirty states and two territories have introduced workplace-bullying legislation that would allow workers to sue for harassment without requiring any evidence of discrimination.[‡] New Hampshire, for example, began considering a bill in 2013 that defines bullying broadly and would include "the repeated use of derogatory remarks, insults, and epithets, as well as conduct that a 'reasonable person' would find threatening, intimidating or humiliating."[§] The bill passed both the New Hampshire House and Senate, only to be vetoed by the governor. As of 2019, only one U.S. state—Tennessee—has passed an anti-bullying statute into law.[**]

Other countries have progressed beyond the United States in their protection of employees in this area. Queensland, Australia, prohibits workplace bullying under its Workplace Health and Safety Act, while Quebec, Canada, protects employees through the psychological harassment section of its labor standards. Ireland includes a prevention and resolution of bullying in its Code of Practice in the workplace, while Sweden contains specific provisions against bullying in its Provisions on Measures against Victimization at Work.

1. How would you define "bullying" if you were to design an anti-bullying law? What stakeholder groups should be considered in crafting your definition?

2. As a manager, what steps might you take to prevent bullying behavior in your company?

3. Do you believe that legislation is needed to respond to the problem of workplace bullying? Why or why not?

4. A 2017 study revealed that the majority of workplace bullying is against women (two-thirds), with basically the same level of bullying coming from men as from women (65% from men and 67% from women).[††] How do these data points affect your views about anti-bullying legislation? Why or why not?

*G. Namie, "2017 Workplace Bullying Institute U.S. Workplace Bullying Survey," Workplace Bullying Institute (2017), http://workplacebullying.org/multi/pdf/2017/2017-WBI-US-Survey.pdf (accessed March 6, 2019).

[†]Roy Maurer, "Workplace-Bullying Laws on the Horizon?" Society for Human Resource Management (July 16, 2013), www.shrm.org/hrdisciplines/safetysecurity/articles/pages/workplace-bullying-laws. aspx (accessed March 6, 2019).

[‡]The Healthy Workplace Bill (April 3, 2017), http://healthyworkplacebill.org/ (accessed March 6, 2019).

[§]Kathleen Ronayne, "NH Gov. Veto of Partial Workplace Bullying Bill Holds," *The Boston Globe* (September 18, 2014), www.bostonglobe.com/metro/2014/09/17/lawmakers-uphold-veto-work-place-bullying-bill/9HZdQ8Lu7iAlzF6NfqWR6H/story.html (accessed March 6, 2019).

[**]L. Nagele-Piazza, "Workplace Bullying and Harassment: What's the Difference?" Society for Human Resource Management (March 28, 2018), https://www.shrm.org/resourcesandtools/legal-and-compliance/state-and-local-updates/pages/workplace-bullying.aspx (accessed March 6, 2019).

[††]Namie, "2017 Workplace Bullying Institute U.S. Workplace Bullying Survey."

The issue of workplace bullying is one that we hear about more and more, especially in economies based on strong service sectors. There have been countless newspaper articles, business journals, academic journals, conferences, and even television news programs devoted to the subject in recent years. It is more predominant in the service sector because that work relies significantly on interpersonal relationships and interaction. "Frequent, ongoing personal interaction between workers often becomes a basic element of a job, especially in work arrangements between supervisors and subordinates. The more people interact, the more likely it is that personalities will clash," says scholar and bullying expert David Yamada.[17] Add to those interactions the personal threats that people sense from pressures during a downturn in the economy, and one can only imagine the boiling points that might ensue.

Ironically, while basic fairness may demand that employer power be used justly, the law has not always clearly supported this mandate of justice. Much employment law within the United States instead evolved in a context of a legal doctrine known as **employment at will (EAW).** Employment at will holds that, in the absence of a particular contractual or other legal obligation that specifies the length or conditions of employment, all employees are employed "at will." (See the Reality Check "Employing 'Employees.'") This means that, unless an agreement specifies otherwise, employers are free to fire an employee at any time and for any reason. In the words of an early court decision, "all may dismiss their employee at will, be they many or few, for good cause, for no cause, or even for cause morally wrong."[18] In the same manner, an EAW worker may opt to leave a job at any time for any reason, without offering any notice at all; so the freedom is *theoretically* mutual.

The ethical rationale for EAW, both historically and among contemporary defenders, has both utilitarian and deontological elements. EAW was thought to be an important management tool. Total discretion over employment gives managers the ability to make efficient decisions that should contribute to the greater overall good. It was thought that the manager would be in the best position to know what was best for the firm and that the law should not interfere with those decisions. Another basis for EAW was the rights of private property owners to control their property more effectively by also controlling those who work on their property.

Both legal and ethical analyses of these claims, however, demonstrate that there are good reasons to limit EAW. Even if EAW proved to be an effective management tool, justice demands that such tools not be used to harm other people. Further, even if private property rights grant managers authority over employees, the right of private property itself is limited by other rights and duties. Also, though the freedom to terminate the relationship is theoretically mutual, the employer is often responsible for the employee's livelihood, while the opposite is unlikely to be true; the differential creates an unbalanced power relationship between the two parties.

Considerations such as these have led many courts and legislatures to create exceptions to the EAW rule (see Table 6.1). Civil rights laws, for example, prohibit firing someone on the basis of membership in certain prohibited classes such as race, sex, disability, age, national origin, religion, or ethnic background. Labor laws prevent employers from firing someone for union activities. When the employer is the government, constitutional limitations on government authority are extended into the workplace to protect employees.

OBJECTIVE

employment at will (EAW)

The legal doctrine that holds that, absent a particular contractual or other legal obligation that specifies the length or conditions of employment, all employees are employed "at will." Unless an agreement specifies otherwise, employers are free to fire an employee at any time and for any reason. In the same manner, an EAW worker may opt to leave a job at any time for any reason, without offering any notice at all; so the freedom is *theoretically* mutual.

Reality Check   *Employing "Employees"*

Because the status of employment at will depends on the determination of whether someone is employed at all, the definition of *employee* becomes critical. The employment relationship brings with it a variety of benefits and responsibilities, which means that either party might try to argue in its favor, or against. However, most often it is the worker who is arguing in favor of employee status.

There are several tests that courts use in order to determine whether a worker is an employee or, to the contrary, an "independent contractor." Usually, the common (layperson's) understanding of an independent contractor is someone who works for another, according to her or his own methods, and who is not under the other's control regarding the physical details of the work. The tests used by the courts include the "common-law agency test," which focuses on the right of control; the U.S. Internal Revenue Service (IRS) "20-factor analysis"; and the "economic realities analysis." Some courts also use a hybrid approach, reaching a decision by combining factors from several of the tests.

Under the **common-law agency test,** a persuasive indicator of independent contractor status is the ability to control the manner in which the work is performed. Under this analysis, the employer need not actually control the work but must merely *have the right or ability* to control the work for a worker to be classified an employee.

In two landmark 2014 cases heard by the Ninth Circuit Court of Appeals, the federal court evaluated whether Federal Express ground package drivers in California and Oregon (a total of over twenty-five hundred drivers) were employees entitled to reimbursement for work-related expenses (for uniforms, specific trucks, and so on), overtime pay, and other federal benefits. The court applied the common-law test and found that they were, in fact, employees. The court explained that FedEx had a broad right to "control the manner in which the drivers perform their work" because "the drivers must wear FedEx uniforms, drive FedEx-approved vehicles, and groom themselves according to FedEx's appearance standards. . . . FedEx tells its drivers what packages to deliver, on what days, and at what times."[*]

Not all courts or circuits agree with the Ninth Circuit on this issue, however. The same issue has been litigated in other states, and those courts have found in favor of

FedEx, holding that the workers' ability to hire their own employees, manage multiple routes, and sell those routes without FedEx's permission "as well as the parties' intent expressed in the contract, argues strongly in favor of independent contractor statutes." It is not a black-and-white issue![†]

The second test is the **IRS 20-factor analysis,** a list of twenty factors to which the IRS looks to determine whether someone is an employee or an independent contractor. The IRS compiled this list from the results of judgments of the courts relating to this issue.

Finally, under the **economic realities test,** courts consider whether the worker is economically dependent on the business; what the expectations of the parties were; or, as a matter of economic fact, if the worker is in business for herself or himself rather than working for someone else. In one case, church volunteers sued a pastor for failing to pay minimum wage for their work at the church's "Lord's buffet." The court held that, because the churchgoers had no expectation of compensation, the economic realities test did not apply.[‡]

Some employers hire individuals as employees rather than independent contractors as a matter of principle. Phyllis Apelbaum, CEO of Arrow Messenger Service in Chicago, explains that her guiding philosophy in terms of her workers is to "hire hard working, friendly messengers; compensate them fairly including benefits and treat them as your greatest asset!" Her employees make a strong contribution to the culture and values of the firm. When Apelbaum considered using independent contractors instead of employees about 15 years ago, she explained, "I wouldn't be able to sleep at night and thought, it'll never work. Well, it has worked for 15 years for other companies. Because of that ethical decision, we have not grown to be the biggest in the city. We've grown nicely, no question about it. But we battle everyday that company that has independent contractors. Because, if you have employees, you've got about a 28 percent bottom number there. So, if the two of us walk in the door, and he charges you a dollar, I'm going to have to charge you $1.28. I'm always fighting that. The ethical decision to go in that direction meant that we had to work harder at our vision to provide better service. Otherwise, why should you be willing to pay 28 cents more? Why? There would be no reason for it."[§]

We should note that state courts can impact the above general precedents and applications—and do, in significant ways. As just one example, through one 2018 decision, some have said that the California Supreme Court "transformed millions of independent contractors into full-time employees with the stroke of a pen." Whether this is a gain of deserved employment protections for those millions of workers or the demise of their freedoms and loss of work because of increased costs remains a hotly debated contest. It does not help either side that the court limited its ruling to the purpose of extending California's wage order rules—lawyers since have sought to apply the new standard in other environments.

In any case, the court adopted a new test in *Dynamex v. Superior Court*** (named the ABC test) that presumes a worker is an employee unless the firm can prove she or he is an independent contractor by showing that:

1. The firm does not direct or control the worker in the performance of her or his job,

2. The worker performs work outside the scope of the company's typical business (such as a musician who performs at a special event for a real estate company), and

3. The worker is normally engaged in an independently established business or occupation of her or his own (can be shown by incorporating on her or his own or filing own taxes).

All three criteria must be satisfied.

***Source:** *Slayman v. FedEx*, Nos. 12-35525 and 12-35559, http://cdn.ca9.uscourts.gov/datastore/opinions/2014/08/27/12-35525.pdf; *Alexander v. FedEx*, Nos. 12-17458 and 12-17509, 9th Cir; 2014 U.S App. LEXIS 16585, http://cdn.ca9.uscourts.gov/datastore/opinions/2014/08/27/12-17458.pdf

[†]*FedEx Home Delivery v. NLRB*, 563 F.3d 492 (D.C. Cir. 2009).

[‡]*Acosta v. Cathedral Buffet, Inc.*, No. 17-3427, 2018 U.S. App. LEXIS 13925 (6th Cir. May 24, 2018).

[§]**Source:** P. H. Werhane, et al., *Women in Business: The Changing Face of Leadership* (New York: Greenwood Publishing, 2007).

***Dynamex Operations W., Inc. v. Super. Ct.*, 4 Cal. 5th 903 (2018).

common-law agency test

A persuasive indicator of independent contractor status that provides the employer the ability to control the manner in which the work is performed. Under the common-law agency approach, the employer need not actually control the work, but must merely have the right or ability to control the work for a worker to be classified an employee.

IRS 20-factor analysis

A list of 20 factors to which the IRS looks to determine whether someone is an employee or an independent contractor.

TABLE 6.1

Exceptions to the Doctrine of Employment at Will

States vary in terms of their recognition of the following exceptions to the doctrine of employment at will. Some states recognize one or more exceptions, while others might recognize none at all. In addition, the definition of these exceptions may vary from state to state.

- Bad faith, malicious, or retaliatory termination in violation of *public policy.*

- Termination in breach of the *implied covenant of good faith and fair dealing.*

- Termination in breach of some other *implied contract term,* such as those that might be created by employee handbook provisions (in certain jurisdictions).

- Termination in violation of the doctrine of *promissory estoppel* (where the employee reasonably relied on an employer's promise, to the employee's detriment).

- Other exceptions as determined by *statutes* (such as the Worker Adjustment and Retraining Notification Act [WARN] or the Family and Medical Leave Act [FMLA]).

economic realities test

A test by which courts consider whether the worker is economically dependent on the business or, as a matter of economic fact, is in business for himself or herself.

just cause

A standard for terminations or discipline that requires the employer to have sufficient and fair cause before reaching a decision against an employee.

A crucial element to recognize with these exceptions, however, is the fact that EAW has priority unless the employee can prove that her or his case falls under one of the exceptions. That is, EAW is the default position on which courts will rely until and unless an exception can be demonstrated. The burden of proof lies with the dismissed employee to show that she or he was unjustly or illegally fired. Due process and **just cause,** whether instituted as part of internal corporate policy or through legislation, would reverse this burden of proof and require employers to show cause to justify the dismissal of an employee.

Where else do due process issues arise in the workplace? Employees are constantly supervised and evaluated, and benefits such as salary, working conditions, and promotions also can be used to motivate or sanction employees. So, being treated fairly in the workplace also involves fairness in areas such as promotions, salary, and benefits. Because these decisions are typically made on the basis of performance appraisals, due process rights should also extend to this aspect of the workplace.

Now that you have learned about the EAW environment, consider the ethical questions that remain: Is the EAW atmosphere the fairest and most just for all stakeholders? Does it lead to the most effective employment outcomes, compared to the European environment, for example? Does an EAW workplace satisfactorily protect the rights and interests of both employers and employees? Asking these questions helps us to reach ethical conclusions. Consider the key facts relevant to issues of due process and fairness. What are the ethical issues involved in your decision and implementation? Who are the stakeholders involved in your decision? What alternatives are available to you? Might there be a way to safeguard the rights of the stakeholders involved while also protecting the interests of the decision makers? If, for instance, you are striving to serve the autonomy of the employer, could you perhaps serve the due process interests of the employee by offering additional notice of termination or more information about alternatives?

Recall that due process is the right to be protected against the *arbitrary* use of authority. It is your role as decision maker to ensure protection against those arbitrary decisions. Employers should be fair in their implementation of judgments and just in their implementation of process in order to serve the preceding principles. The overarching obligation here is to make sure that decisions are made in light of reasons that can be defended from an ethical perspective.

Consider the three examples offered in the Opening Decision Point. Is there an argument that could be made that any of those three scenarios involved the arbitrary use of authority by the decision maker? Often it helps to consider the same circumstances with slightly different facts to see if the same result would have been reached. In other words:

- Do you believe that Briskman would have been fired by her firm if the politics would have been reversed (if she had posted the same photo against a president from the other political party), or was the termination politically motivated?

- Is the blacklisting of Kaepernick an arbitrary use of authority by the NFL owners, or is there an argument that it is fair, just, and according to due process?
- What was it about Damore's memo that led to his termination? Is there an argument that it was arbitrary?

Downsizing

downsize
The reduction of human resources at an organization through terminations, retirements, corporate divestments, or other means.

One of the most emotional issues for both employees and corporate decision makers arises not only when there is one single termination but where a firm makes a decision to fire many workers at once—to **downsize.** Terminating workers—whether 1 or 100—is not *necessarily* an unethical decision! However, the decision itself raises ethical questions because maybe there were alternatives available to an organization in financial difficulty. The ethical dilemma exists when the firm has a choice between firing someone (or a group of people) or cutting costs through some other method—which answer is closer to your values and those of your firm, and which will pose the greatest strategic benefit in the long run? In addition, because a number of negative consequences may result, it is important to consider the impact of each alternative from the perspective of all stakeholders involved.

These negative outcomes may include poor recommendations of the firm by former employees, a decline in customer service by surviving employees, an increase in errors or even dangerous behavior by employees, or merely a bad attitude by staff who fear that they might be the next to be cut. The impact may extend to perceptions related to your corporate social responsibility or strategy as well. The more responsibility given to leadership for the downsizing, the more likely that stakeholders also will have a negative perception of a firm's commitment to corporate social responsibility—everything is connected, whether you see a connection or not.[19]

OBJECTIVE

Accordingly, the question of whether to resort to widespread terminations based on financial challenges in place of other options that may be available does not always lead to a clear answer. Once the decision has been made, are there ways in which an organization can act more ethically in the process of downsizing? How might our earlier discussion of due process and fairness offer some guidance and/or define limitations in a downsizing environment?

Professor José Luis Illueca García-Labrado argues, "people affected by the restructuring process must be treated with the same respect and interest that was shown when hiring them. . . . When they were hired, they were important to the success of the company; now they are equally important to the company's survival as they leave."[20] Ethics, therefore, must be central to the design and management of layoff policies. In fact, our decision-making model offers significant guidance in a situation such as a downsizing.

First, the decision regarding downsizing should be made by a representative group so that all stakeholder interests can be considered and so as to earn the trust of those who will be impacted. The facts should be collected and issues should be determined. Because employees should be kept aware of business conditions, the need for a downsizing effort should not come as a great surprise. However, the question of notice is debatable.

It can be argued that a firm should give notice of an intent to downsize as soon as it decides the downsizing is going to happen, and let those who will be impacted know who will be let go as soon as that list is created. One large-scale survey involved more than four thousand workers who stayed after layoffs at more than three hundred companies. The survey found that productivity and quality were more than two-thirds less likely to plummet when managers exhibited visibility, approachability, and candor.[21] On the other hand, the uncertainty and rumors that are sure to develop between the time of the layoff announcement and the notice of who will be terminated might outweigh the benefits gained by early notification. In addition, letting a worker stay in a position for a period of time once she or he has been notified of an impending termination might not be the best option. Workers may interpret early notice as an effort to get the most out of them before departure rather than an effort to allow them time to come to grips with the loss of their jobs.

These costs and benefits must be weighed in any communication decision and certainly considered in managing and interacting with employees following a lay-off. "Managers need to be highly visible to their staff, approachable even when they don't have anything new to say, and candid about the state of things in order to build their trust and credibility. If your company has to conduct a layoff, it is imperative that you train your managers how to both manage that process and deal with the highly debilitating aftermath. Otherwise you will waste any potential cost savings from the layoff on lost productivity, quality problems and service break-downs," says Mark Murphy, chair of Leadership IQ.[22]

Once the stakeholders are identified, it will be vital to enumerate any and all possible options with regard to the downsizing efforts and to catalog the impact of each option on each group of stakeholders. (See the Reality Check "Is It Really 'Inevitable'?" for a discussion of options.) When a firm decides to downsize, as with any other termination, it is critical to lessen the impact as much as possible and to allow the terminated employees to depart with dignity (e.g., unless there is some other reason for the decision, having a security guard follow terminated employees until they leave the building might not be the best option). Above all, during a time when relationships might be strained, it is critical to be honest and forthright and to be sensitive to the experiences of those who will be affected.

From a legal perspective, the decision about whom to include in a downsizing effort must be carefully planned. If the firm's decision is based on some criterion that seems to be neutral on its face, such as seniority, but the plan results in a different impact on one group than another, the decision may be suspect. For example, assume the firm does make termination decisions based on longevity with the organization. Also assume that those workers who are most senior are almost entirely male because women entered this industry only in recent years. If the firm moves forward with this process, the majority of those fired will be women and the majority of those remaining will be men. In this case, the effort may violate Title VII's prohibition against discrimination based on gender because the termination policy has a more significant—and negative—impact on women.

To avoid this result, firms should review both the fairness of their decision-making process and the consequence of that process on those terminated and the

Reality Check   *Is It Really "Inevitable"?*

As inevitable as downsizing may seem during downturns in the economy, some firms have survived decade after decade without any layoffs. How do they do it? While many firms became quite creative during the economic crisis that began during the second half of 2008, other firms have maintained these innovations for years.

Some industries are less prone to layoffs than others, while, in other cases, it is a firm's culture. Southwest Airlines has never engaged in layoffs, according to its CEO, and, even though the energy industry has its ups and downs, somehow NuStar Energy has found a way to avoid layoffs. The Container Store has a policy against layoffs, which, as a consumer retail operation, seems difficult, but its CEO explains, "You can't go around calling yourself an employee-first company and then lay people off."*

Another company, Nucor Corporation, has not laid off a worker for over 30 years. However, it maintains a "pay for performance" policy. When the plant has large contracts and everyone is busy, workers earn up to $24 per hour. But when business is slow, the company reduces wages to $12 per hour.† Other firms have entered into agreements with their workers under which the firm promises not to terminate workers for reasons of the economy as long as the workers agree to lower wages or decreased hours during tough periods. For instance, Marvin Windows and Doors, a privately held Minnesota company employing more than four thousand workers, upheld its vow to avoid terminations by cutting pay, reducing benefits, and suspending profit-sharing payments to both employees and owners during the worst of the recession.

Company president Susan Marvin said that her no-layoff policy was "as much a business wager as an act of benevolence." Taking the long-term view, Marvin believed that maintaining the company's skilled workforce would benefit the company over time despite short-term losses. This view proved true, as the company began distributing profit-sharing checks again in December 2012.‡

Other options to stave off terminations can include the obvious decision to freeze hiring, to offer attractive voluntary retirement packages that provide an overall financial benefit to the firm, to reduce hours for all rather than fewer positions, to redeploy staff elsewhere in the firm, to lower salaries, to reduce or delay giving raises, or even to ask employees for a reduction in salary in exchange for an equity share in the company. Finally, some employers have chosen to cut benefits for which they would normally pay, such as bonuses, employer contributions to retirement plans, training, or education allocations.

*S. Becker, "Job Search? These 5 Companies Have Policies That Prevent Layoffs," *CheatSheet* (January 8, 2017), https://www.cheatsheet.com/money-career/job-search-these-companies-have-policies-that-prevent-layoffs.html/ (accessed March 5, 2019).
†R. Barrett, "No Lay Offs at Nucor, Despite Bad Economy," *Milwaukee Journal Sentinel* (May 22, 2010), www.jsonline.com/business/93960929.html (accessed November 5, 2018); see also Nucor Corporation, "Benefits," www.nucor.com/careers/why/ (accessed March 6, 2019).
‡Andrew Martin, "No Lay-Off Company Now Writes Profit Sharing Checks," *The New York Times* (December 21, 2012), www.nytimes.com/2012/12/22/business/marvin-windows-and-doors-offers-workers-profit-sharing-checks.html (accessed March 6, 2019); Andrew Martin, "Housing Slump Forces Cuts at Small Town Company," *The New York Times* (September 11, 2011), www.nytimes.com/2011/09/25/business/economy/housing-slump-forces-cuts-at-a-small-town-company.html (accessed March 6, 2019).

resulting composition of the workforce. One of the most effective philosophical theories to employ in downsizing decisions is John Rawls's theory of distributive justice. Under a formulation he developed called the "veil of ignorance," you would consider what decision you would make (such as whether to downsize or how to downsize) if you did not know what role you would be playing following the decision. In other words, you might be the corporate executive with the secure position; you might be a terminated employee with years of seniority who was close to retirement; or you might be a worker who survives the termination slips. If you do not know which role you would be playing, Rawls argues that you are more likely to reach a decision that is relatively fairest to all impacted. Consider what facts might shift your decision in one way or another based on this formulation.

Perhaps the most important consideration in the event of a downsizing or layoff is the fact that there are people who will be impacted by the decisions involved—countless stakeholders. Ralph Larsen, past chair and CEO of Johnson & Johnson, explains the angst he experienced when he made a decision to close approximately 50 small plants around the world.

> I was responsible to our employees in those plants, but I was also responsible to the patients who needed our products to keep them affordable. And I was responsible to all of our other employees around the world to keep the company healthy and growing. The harsh reality was that a great many more would be hurt down the road if I failed to act and we became less and less competitive.

> In addition to our employees, I was also responsible to the tens of thousands of stockholders (individuals, retired folks, pension plans, and mutual funds) who owned our stock. The facts were clear. . . . I knew what had to be done, and we did it as thoughtfully and sensitively as possible. But the decision was hard, because it was personal.[23]

Health and Safety

The previous sections addressed ethics in the creation or termination of the employment relationship. The following discussion explores one particular responsibility within that relationship—the employer's role in protecting the employees' health and safety while at work. Throughout the world, there is a broad consensus that employees have a fundamental right to a safe and healthy workplace. For purposes of this discussion, we will presume that the fact that protections might not exist or be enforced in a particular country or environment does not necessarily mean that people there do not believe that they have a right to those protections.

However, in some workplaces in our world, employees lack even the most basic health and safety protections. These work environments have been called *sweatshops.* That term and the concepts behind it will be discussed later in this chapter. Even within the United States, the question of employee health and safety becomes quite complicated upon closer examination. Not only is the very extent of an employer's responsibility for workplace health and safety in dispute, there is also significant disagreement concerning the best policies to protect worker health and safety.

Like work itself, health and safety are "goods" that are valued both as a means for attaining other valuable ends and also as ends in themselves. Whatever else we desire out of life, being healthy and safe makes it much more likely that we will be capable of attaining our goals. In this sense, health and safety have a very high instrumental value because part of their value derives from the fact that we use them to attain other things of value. Insurance therefore seeks to compensate workers for injuries they incur by paying the employees for the wages they lose as a result of being unable to work.

OBJECTIVE

Yet, health and safety also have intrinsic value—they are valuable not only based on how they help us to achieve our objectives. To understand this distinction, consider how you might respond if someone asks you how much your life is worth. The life of one who dies in a workplace accident has instrumental value that can be measured, in part, by the lost wages that would have been earned had that person lived. But these lost wages do not measure the *intrinsic* value of the life, something that financial compensation simply cannot replace.

What is the value of health, and what does it mean to be healthy? When is a workplace safe? When is it unsafe? If "healthy" is taken to mean a state of flawless physical and psychological well-being, arguably no one is perfectly healthy. If "safe" means completely free from risk, certainly no workplace is perfectly safe. If health and safety are interpreted as ideals that are impossible to realize, then it would be unreasonable to claim that employees have a right to a healthy and safe workplace.

Health and Safety as "Acceptable Risk"

Employers cannot be responsible for providing a completely safe and healthy workplace. Instead, discussions in ethics about employee health and safety will tend to focus on the *relative* risks workers face and the level of *acceptable risk* in the workplace. In this discussion, "risks" can be defined as the probability of harm, and we determine "relative risks" by comparing the probabilities of harm involved in various activities. Therefore, scientists who compile and measure data can determine both risks and relative risks (see Figure 6.1). It is an easy step from these calculations to certain conclusions about acceptable risks. If it can be determined that the probability of harm involved in a specific work activity is equal to or less than the probability of harm of some more common activity, then we can conclude that this activity faces an "acceptable level of risk." From this perspective, *a workplace is safe if the risks are acceptable.*

Imagine if we generalize this conclusion and determine all workplace health and safety standards in this manner. Such an approach would place the responsibility for workplace safety solely on management. A business would hire safety engineers and other experts to determine the risks within their workplace. These experts would know the risk levels that are otherwise accepted throughout the society. These might involve the risks involved in driving a car, eating high-fat food, smoking, jogging, and so forth. Comparing these to the risks faced in the

FIGURE 6.1
Calculating Acceptable Level of Risk

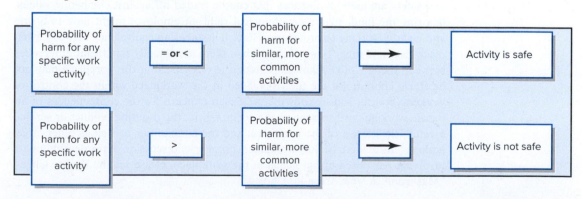

Reality Check   *Marijuana: A New Arena for Choice*

As of publication, the nonmedical possession (and presumed use) of marijuana has been decriminalized in thirteen states and legalized in ten additional states plus the District of Columbia and the Northern Mariana Islands. Decriminalization means that, if a person is found in possession of small amounts of marijuana, she or he will be subject only to minor civil penalties. Marijuana remains prohibited under federal law as a Schedule I illegal substance, but U.S. attorneys do not enforce it.*

Employers are never required to allow or accommodate marijuana use in the workplace. However, as you might imagine, even if a worker has a legal right to use marijuana (whether for medical or recreational purposes), there may be concerns about that person's off-work use of marijuana because it may have an effect on a person's response time, judgment, or other aspects of decision-making capacity. These impairments could have consequences on the health and safety environment of the workplace, workplace interactions (whether with co-workers or other stakeholders), or other areas of policy development.

In addition, where the substance is used for medical reasons, the interaction of an employer's decision with the Americans with Disabilities Act (ADA) must be considered. Without offering too deep a dive into the legal complexities of that statute here, the ADA requires, under certain circumstances, that the employer consider whether the employee is covered by the Act, whether the employee has requested the accommodation of marijuana use (outside of work), and whether that accommodation is reasonable within the scope of her or his employment. In some positions, an accommodation may not be possible; however, some states also prohibit employers from discriminating based on an employee's status as a qualified medical marijuana user.

*Associated Press, "Jeff Sessions Says Prosecutors Won't Pursue 'Small Marijuana Cases,'" *CBS News* (March 10, 2018), www.cbsnews.com/news/jeff-sessions-doj-prosecutors-will-not-pursue-small-marijuana-cases/ (accessed November 9, 2018).

workplace, safety experts could perform a risk assessment and determine the relative risks of work. If the workplace were less risky than other common activities, management could conclude that they have fulfilled their responsibility to provide a healthy and safe workplace.

However, such an approach to workplace health and safety issues has several problems. First, this approach treats employees disrespectfully by ignoring their input as stakeholders. Such paternalistic decision making effectively treats employees like children and makes crucial decisions for them, ignoring their role in the decision-making process. Second, in making this decision, we assume that health and safety are mere preferences that can be traded off against competing values, ignoring the fundamental deontological right an employee might have to a safe and healthy working environment. Third, it assumes an equivalency between workplace risks and other types of risks when there are actually significant differences between them. Unlike many daily risks, the risks faced in the workplace may not be freely chosen, nor are the risks faced in the workplace within the control of workers. Fourth, it disregards the utilitarian concern for the consequences of an unsafe working environment on the social fabric, the resulting product or service created, the morale of the workforce, and the community, as well as other large-scale results of an unhealthy workplace. For a brief discussion of the developments involving risk posed by marijuana in the workplace, please see the Reality Check "Marijuana: A New Arena for Choice."

TABLE 6.2
Challenges to the Acceptable Risk Approach to Health and Safety

- Treats employees disrespectfully by ignoring their input as stakeholders.
- Ignores the fundamental deontological right an employee might have to a safe and healthy working environment.
- Assumes an equivalency between workplace risks and other types of risks when there are significant differences between them.
- Improperly places incentives because the risks faced at work could be controlled by others who might stand to benefit by *not* reducing them.

Perhaps most important, unlike some daily risks each of us freely undertakes, the risks faced at work could be controlled by others, particularly by others who might stand to benefit by *not* reducing the risks. For instance, making the workplace safe may pose substantial costs to employers. Relative to the risks one might face by smoking, for example, working in a mill and inhaling cotton dust may not seem as risky. But, in the former case, the smoker chooses to take the risk and could take steps to minimize or eliminate the risk by herself or himself. In the latter case, the mill worker cannot avoid the risks as long as she or he wants to keep a job. Often, someone else can minimize or eliminate these risks, but this other party also has a financial incentive not to do so. In one case, smoking, the decision maker freely chooses to take the risk, knowing that she or he can control it. In the other case, the worker's choices and control are limited. The challenges involved in the acceptable risk approach to workplace health and safety are summarized in Table 6.2.

Health and Safety as Market Controlled

Perhaps we can leave health and safety standards to the market. Defenders of the free market and the classical model of corporate social responsibility would favor individual bargaining between employers and employees as the approach to workplace health and safety. On this account, employees would be free to choose the risks they are willing to face by bargaining with employers. Employees would balance their preferences for risk against their demand for wages and decide how much risk they are willing to take for various wages. Those who demand higher safety standards and healthier conditions presumably would have to settle for lower wages; those willing to take higher risks presumably would demand higher wages.

In a competitive and free labor market, such individual bargaining would result in the optimal distribution of safety and income. Of course, the market approach can also support compensation to injured workers when it can be shown that employers were responsible for causing the harms. So an employer who fails to install firefighting equipment in the workplace can be held liable for burns an employee suffers during a workplace fire. The threat of compensation also acts as an incentive for employers to maintain a reasonably safe and healthy workplace. The Decision Point "Should Clinical Trials for New Drugs Be Exported?" considers whether it is therefore ethical for a pharmaceutical company to outsource its medical trials to countries with fewer health and safety regulations than the United States and a population willing to accept lower pay for participation in trials.

If one follows the market-based recommendation to allocate workplace risks on the basis of an optimal distribution of risks and benefits, one would conclude that, from a business perspective, dangerous jobs ought to be exported to those areas where wages are low and where workers are more willing to accept risky working conditions. The harms done by dangerous jobs, in terms of forgone earnings, are lower in regions with low wages and lower life expectancies. The benefits of providing jobs in regions with high unemployment would also outweigh the benefits of sending those jobs to regions with low unemployment. (See also the discussion of global labor markets, later in this chapter.)

Following this market-based logic, many U.S.-based pharmaceutical companies seeking to test new medications conduct pharmaceutical trials abroad—and China and India are their fastest-growing locations. Clinical trials in developing economies tend to be subject to far fewer regulations than trials in the United States and, therefore, are significantly less costly.* For example, 90% of new pharmaceuticals approved in 2017 were tested outside of North America.

1. What facts would you want to know before deciding whether the practice of exporting clinical trials was fair and responsible?

2. What alternatives to exporting clinical trials exist for a pharmaceutical company?

3. Who are the stakeholders of your decision? What is the impact of each alternative mentioned here on each stakeholder you have identified?

4. Should local legal regulations govern the situation or the legal regulations in the pharmaceutical company's home country?

5. What are the consequences of such a decision? What rights and duties are involved? If the consequences are effective and valuable to the majority but fundamental rights are implicated, how will you decide what to do?

*R. Robbins, "Most Experimental Drugs Are Tested Offshore—Raising Concerns about Data," *Scientific American* (September 10, 2017), www.scientificamerican.com/article/most-experimental-drugs-are-tested-offshore-raising-concerns-about-data/ (accessed November 5, 2018); D. L. Barnett and J. B. Steele, "Deadly Medicine," *Vanity Fair* (January 2011), www.vanityfair.com/politics/features/2011/01/deadly-medicine-201101 (accessed November 5, 2018).

6

OBJECTIVE

This free-market approach has a number of serious problems. First, labor markets are not perfectly competitive and free. Employees do not have the kinds of free choices that the free-market theory would require in order to attain optimal satisfactions. Though enlightened self-interest would be a valuable theory to introduce and apply in this environment, it is unrealistic to presume employees always have the choices available to them that make it possible. For example, risky jobs are often also the lowest-paying jobs, and people with the fewest employment choices hold them. Individuals are forced to accept the jobs because they have no choice but to accept; they are not actually "balancing their preferences for risk against their demand for wages" because they do not have options. Second, employees seldom, if ever, possess the kind of complete information efficient markets require. If employees do not know the risks involved in a job, they will not be in a position to freely bargain for appropriate wages and therefore they will not be in a position to effectively protect their rights or ensure the most ethical consequences. This is a particular concern when we recognize that many workplace risks are in no sense obvious. An employee may understand the dangers of heavy machinery or a blast furnace, but few employees can know the toxicity or exposure levels of workplace chemicals or airborne contaminants.

Such market failures can have deadly consequences when they involve workplace health and safety issues. Of course, market defenders argue that over time, markets will compensate for such failures, employers will find it difficult to attract workers to dangerous jobs, and employees will learn about the risks of every workplace. But this raises what we call a "first-generation" problem. The market gathers information by observing the harms done to the first generation exposed to imperfect market transactions. Thus, workers learn that exposure to lead is dangerous when some female workers exposed to lead suffer miscarriages or when others have children who are born with serious birth defects. We learn that workplace exposure to asbestos or cotton dust is dangerous when workers subsequently die from lung disease. In effect, markets sacrifice the first generation in order to gain information about safety and health risks. These questions of public policy—questions that, after all, will affect human lives—would never even be asked by an individual facing the choice of working at a risky job. To the degree that these are important questions that ought to be asked, individual bargaining will fail as an ethical public policy approach to worker health and safety. Table 6.3 summarizes the challenges inherent in the free-market approach to health and safety.

Health and Safety as Government-Regulated Ethics

In response to such concerns, government regulation of workplace health and safety appears more appropriate from an ethical perspective. Mandatory government standards address most of the problems raised against market strategies. Standards can be set according to the best available scientific knowledge and thus overcome market failures that result from insufficient information. Standards prevent employees from having to face the fundamentally coercive choice between job and safety. Standards also address the first-generation problem by focusing on prevention rather than compensation after the fact. Finally, standards are fundamentally a social approach that can address public policy questions ignored by markets.

TABLE 6.3
Challenges with the Free-Market Approach to Health and Safety

- Labor markets are not perfectly competitive and free.
- Employees seldom, if ever, possess the kind of perfect information markets require.
- We ignore important questions of social justice and public policy if we approach questions solely from the point of view of an individual.

Occupational Safety and Health Administration (OSHA)
An agency of the federal government that publishes and enforces safety and health regulations for U.S. businesses.

In 1970, the U.S. Congress established the **Occupational Safety and Health Administration (OSHA)** and charged it with establishing workplace health and safety standards. Since that time, the major debates concerning workplace health and safety have focused on how such public standards ought to be set. The dominant question concerns the appropriateness of using cost–benefit analysis to set health and safety standards.

When OSHA was first established, regulations were aimed at achieving the safest *feasible* standards. This "feasibility" approach allows OSHA to make trade-offs between health and economics, but it is prejudiced in favor of health and safety by placing the burden of proof on industry to show that high standards are not economically feasible. Health and safety standards are not required, no matter the cost; however, an industry is required to meet the highest standards attainable within technological and economic reason.

Some critics charge that this approach does not go far enough and unjustly sacrifices employee health and safety. From that perspective, industries that cannot operate without harming the health and safety of its employees should be closed. But the more influential business criticism has argued that these standards go too far. Critics in both industry and government have argued that OSHA should be required to use cost–benefit analysis in establishing such standards. From this perspective, even if a standard is technologically and economically feasible, it would still be unreasonable and unfair if the benefits did not outweigh the costs. These critics argue that OSHA should aim to achieve the optimal, rather than highest feasible, level of safety.

Using a cost–benefit analysis to set standards in effect returns us to the goals of the market-based, individual bargaining approach. Like that market approach, this use of cost–benefit analysis faces serious ethical challenges. We should note, however, that rejecting cost–benefit analysis in setting standards is not the same as rejecting cost-effective strategies in implementing those standards. A commitment to cost-effectiveness would require that, once the standards are set, we adopt the least expensive and most efficient means available for achieving those standards. Cost–benefit analysis, in contrast, uses economic criteria in setting the standards in the first place. It is cost–benefit, not cost-effectiveness, analysis that is ethically problematic. (See the Reality Check "Do Health and Safety Programs Cost Too Much?" as well as the Decision Point "How Much Is Enough?" for an application of cost–benefit analysis.)

The use of cost–benefit analysis in setting workplace health and safety standards commits us to treating worker health and safety as just another commodity, another individual preference, to be traded off against competing commodities. It treats health and safety merely as an instrumental value and denies its intrinsic value. Cost–benefit analysis requires that an economic value be placed on one's life and bodily integrity. Typically, this would follow the model used by the insurance industry (where it is used in wrongful death settlements, for example) in which one's life is valued in terms of one's earning potential. Perhaps the most offensive aspect of this approach is the fact that because, in feasibility analysis, health and safety are already traded off against the economic viability of the industry, a shift to cost–benefit analysis entails trading off health and safety against profit margin.

Reality Check   *Do Health and Safety Programs Cost Too Much?*

Evidence collected by the Occupational Safety and Health Administration suggests just the opposite: Safety and health programs *add* value and *reduce* costs. Workplaces can reduce injuries 20 to 40% by establishing safety and health programs. Several studies have estimated that safety and health programs save $3 to $6 for every dollar invested. These savings result from a decrease in employee injuries and illnesses, lower workers' compensation costs, decreased medical costs, reduced absenteeism, lower turnover, higher productivity, and increased morale. Employers are finding that disease prevention and wellness programs are important tools in the battle to reduce rising medical costs.*

According to World Economic Forum statistics, companies that have implemented proactive wellness programs have saved an average $700 per year, per employee. Plus, employees are more attracted to and value a business that appreciates them; so companies with an employee wellness program have lower turnover. The Bureau of Labor Statistics reports that, as of 2017,

two-thirds of government workers and over one-third of workers in the private sector have access to workplace wellness programs. These plans include programs to quit smoking, exercise or physical fitness programs, weight-control programs, nutrition education, blood-pressure tests, physical examinations, stress management programs, back-care courses, and lifestyle assessment tests.

*"Safety and Health Add Value," OSHA Publication 3180 (n.d.), www.osha.gov/Publications/safety-health-add-value.html (accessed November 10, 2018).

Sources: "Safety and Health Add Value," OSHA Publication 3180 (n.d.), www.osha.gov/Publications/safety-health-add-value.html (accessed March 1, 2019); World Economic Forum, "The Workplace Wellness Alliance—Making the Right Investment: Employee Health and the Power of Metrics" (January 31, 2013), www3.weforum.org/docs/WEF_HE_WorkplaceWellness Alliance_Report_2013.pdf (accessed March 1, 2019); Bureau of Labor Statistics, "Employee Access to Wellness Programs in 2017" (January 3, 2018), www.bls.gov/opub/ted/2018/employee-access-to-wellness-programs-in-2017.htm (accessed March 1, 2019).

The policies that have emerged by consensus within the United States seem to be most defensible. Employees have a legitimate ethical claim on mandatory health and safety standards within the workplace. To say that employees have a right to workplace health and safety implies that they should not be expected to make trade-offs between health and safety standards and job security or wages. Further, recognizing that most mandatory standards reduce rather than eliminate risks, employees should also have the right to be informed about workplace risks. If the risks have been reduced to the lowest feasible level and employees are fully aware of them, then a society that respects its citizens as autonomous decision makers has done its duty.

Global Applications: The Global Workforce and Global Challenges

As you consider the issues of due process, fairness, and health and safety raised thus far in the chapter, note that the application of the law discussed here is limited predominantly to workers who are employed in the United States. Workers outside the United States may be subject to some U.S. laws if they work for an American-based organization, though enforcement is scattered. In some cases, workers in other countries are protected by laws that are even more stringent than those in the United States. Many countries in the European Union, for example, have strong

While there is a cost associated with workplace health and safety violations, some argue that this cost is not sufficiently high to deter violations. In other words, they advocate higher fines in order to deter violations or to encourage employers to provide safer conditions. In one 2009 case, OSHA imposed a fine of $87.5 million on British Petroleum (BP), the largest fine in OSHA's history. OSHA had found more than four hundred new safety violations at the company's Texas City refinery. The violations were considered egregious because they were discovered in 2009, 4 years after a deadly explosion at the refinery (fifteen deaths, 170 injured) had led BP to sign an OSHA agreement promising to improve safety conditions. The top penalty is four times the amount of the total issued penalty that earned the second spot, which, unfortunately, also is held by BP from a few years earlier.*

If you were on the OSHA Commission to review the amounts of fines imposed, how would you reach a decision as to how much is enough in BP's second (later) case? What factors would you consider?

1. Who are the stakeholders involved in your decision?
2. What do you foresee will be the impact of your decision on the stakeholders involved?
3. How might ethical theory assist you in reaching this particular decision?
4. Once you have reached your decision, which constituencies do you anticipate will be most supportive and which will be most against your decision, and why?

*U.S. Department of Labor, Occupational Safety and Health Administration, "Top Enforcement Cases Based on Total Issued Penalty" (n.d.), www.osha.gov/dep/enforcement/top_cases.html; B. Deavellar, "The Top 5 Largest OSHA Fines," *Spec on the Job* (May 18, 2018), http://speconthejob.com/largest-osha-fines/ (accessed November 5, 2018).

laws protecting workers' rights to due process, privacy, and union participation. However, in many other cases, especially in certain developing countries, workers find themselves subject to conditions that U.S.-based workers would find intolerable. For example, while U.S. workers may benefit from battles fought in years past for occupational safety and health, workers in certain Southeast Asian countries may be fighting for bathroom breaks. (See Reality Check "Self-Test: Where in the World . . . ?" for an additional example.)

OBJECTIVE

The response to this stark contrast is not a simple one. Though few people, if any, would argue for the continuation of the circumstances described earlier as sweatshops, some economists and others do not agree about a solution. One argument is that the use of cheap labor allows developing countries to expand export activities and thereby improve their economies. This economic growth brings more jobs, which will cause the labor market to tighten, which in turn will force companies to improve conditions in order to attract workers (see Figure 6.2). In fact, several commentators argue that encouraging greater global production will create additional opportunities for expansion domestically, providing a positive impact on more stakeholders.[24] Though it is an unpopular sentiment with

Reality Check *Self-Test: Where in the World . . . ?*

Can you name the six countries in the world where women's rights in the workplace are guaranteed by law to be equivalent to men's (as of 2019)?

.

.

According to the World Bank, only Belgium, Denmark, France, Latvia, Luxembourg, and Sweden protect men and women equally at work. France showed the largest improvement over the past 10 years, jumping 10% to a new score of 100 (equivalency), while the average score of all 187 economies is 74.7. You may be surprised to learn that, as recently as 2009, no country would have made this list.

Source: World Bank Group, *Women, Business and the Law 2019* (2019), https://openknowledge.worldbank.org/bitstream/handle/10986/31327/WBL2019.pdf (accessed March 3, 2019)

the general consuming public, many economists argue that the maintenance of **sweatshops** is therefore supported by economic theory. Indeed, even the term *sweatshop* remains open to debate.

Philosophers Benjamin Powell and Matthew Zwolinski explore the issue from a slightly different perspective in a seminal article titled "The Ethical and Economic Case against Sweatshop Labor: A Critical Assessment." They defend the moral legitimacy of sweatshops and respond to the question of whether a worker under these conditions can actually consent to them or be considered to be working "voluntarily" at all. They conclude that a worker actually *is able* to give consent. Therefore, the moral imperative of supporting sweatshops "is the welfare of the least advantaged—sweatshop workers, potential sweatshop workers, and future generations of workers and potential workers who deal with the economic aftermath of today's economic and political decisions."[25] They argue that workers see the extreme dangers sometimes associated with working in sweatshops, but the workers make the decision that working in a sweatshop will give them economic

FIGURE 6.2

How Low-Cost Labor May Contribute to Better Working Conditions, in Time

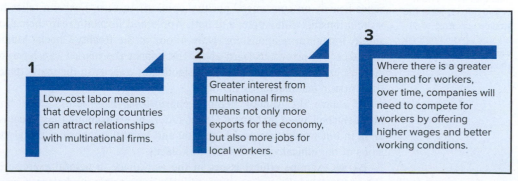

1 Low-cost labor means that developing countries can attract relationships with multinational firms.

2 Greater interest from multinational firms means not only more exports for the economy, but also more jobs for local workers.

3 Where there is a greater demand for workers, over time, companies will need to compete for workers by offering higher wages and better working conditions.

sweatshops
A term that remains subject to debate. Some might suggest that all workplaces with conditions that are below standards in more developed countries are sweatshops because all humans have a right to equally decent working conditions. (See the discussion in Chapter 6 and D. Arnold and L. Hartman, "Beyond Sweatshops: Positive Deviancy and Global Labor Practices," *Business Ethics: A European Review* 14, no. 3 [July 2005].) In this text we use the following definition: Any workplace in which workers are typically subject to two or more of the following conditions: systematic forced overtime, systematic health and safety risks that stem from negligence or the willful disregard of employee welfare, coercion, systematic deception that places workers at risk, underpayment of earnings, and income for a 48-hour workweek less than the overall poverty rate for that country (one who suffers from overall poverty lacks the income necessary to satisfy one's basic nonfood needs such as shelter and basic health care).

power that they have not accessed previously. Choice, within a severely limited set of options, is still a choice. Thus, they conclude, "genuine respect for workers' dignity requires recognizing their freedom to decide for themselves issues of central importance to their lives."[26]

On the other hand, opponents to this perspective argue that allowing sweatshops to continue will not necessarily lead to the anticipated result, just as voluntarily improving legal compliance, wages, and working conditions will not inevitably lead to the negative consequences the free market advocates threaten. During his experience as a sweatshop inspector, T. A. Frank saw a sign in large characters on a factory's wall: "If you don't work hard today, look hard for work tomorrow." One might presume that Frank would take issue with Zwolinski's claim of worker consent to conditions where few alternatives exist. (Frank's first-hand report, "Confessions of a Sweatshop Inspector," containing his pointed insights and experiences, is unmatched for its access and straightforward approach. It is accessible here: https://washingtonmonthly.com/2008/04/01/confessions-of-a-sweatshop-inspector/.)

An interesting and high-profile case involving working conditions unfolded in 2012 when the public realized—through the aid of the media—that their iPhones and other Apple devices were largely created in China by suppliers under conditions that might not be deemed ethically acceptable in the United States and that certainly violated internal standards issued by Apple and local Chinese labor laws.

Apple and its Chinese partner Foxconn responded immediately after the media attention, but some say the response was significantly tardy because some violations went back for several years. Apple continues to partner with Foxconn and, while iPhones (for instance) are designed in the United States, most continue to be produced outside of the U.S.

In 2017, then–Apple CEO Tim Cook explained that Apple did not actually manufacture its products in China to exploit low-cost labor opportunities. Instead, he said, "there's a confusion about China. The popular conception is that companies come to China because of low labor cost. I'm not sure what part of China they go to but the truth is China stopped being the low labor cost country many years ago. And that is not the reason to come to China from a supply point of view. The reason is because of the skill, and the quantity of skill in one location and the type of skill it is."[27]

Consider Aristotle's statement "we are what we do" as you orient your perspective on Apple's decision making. Is it relevant that Apple is a company that relies heavily on consumers' positive opinion? In turn, Foxconn relies heavily on its relationship with Apple; and both Apple and Foxconn reap their profits from stable, long-term relationships. Have a look at the Reality Check "Making Better Mistakes Tomorrow" to learn about the impact the market can have—both after Apple's experience and then after a significant tragedy in the marketplace, one of the worst in manufacturing history.

Of course, the Apple/Foxconn scenario took place across global boundaries, between the United States and China. Often, as we examine the ethical issues that arise in our workplaces, it is both vital and helpful to consider the global dimensions of our ethically responsible workplaces.

As we examine ethical issues in the workplace, a helpful exercise is to consider the global dimension of an ethically responsible workplace. Certainly, it is

Reality Check *Making Better Mistakes Tomorrow*

Those who cannot remember the past are condemned to repeat it.

Santayana, *The Life of Reason, 1905*

Just one year following the public attention to the Apple case discussed in the text, a large factory considered a sweatshop in Bangladesh called Raza Plaza collapsed in 2013 due to shoddy building materials and overused facilities. The tragedy killed over eleven hundred workers and injured over twenty-five hundred. It is considered the deadliest garment-factory accident in history, as well as the deadliest accidental structural failure in modern human history.

Major global retailers, including Benetton, the Children's Place, Joe Fresh, and Walmart, produced goods using this facility and faced an international outcry both to compensate the victims' families and also to make changes in their use of what was considered to be sweatshop labor.

Under pressure to avoid future tragedies, many of the companies that purchased apparel from (any) Bangladeshi factories formed organizations to improve safety and working conditions at those factories. A group of 17 major North American retailers, including Walmart, The Gap, Target, and Macy's (several of whom were not directly connected to the factory that collapsed, but to other locations), announced a plan to improve factory safety in Bangladesh. Unfortunately and unlike a separate accord joined mainly by European retailers (such as H&M), the North American plan lacked legally binding commitments to pay for those improvements.

One year later, an international watchdog group did find that many of the nation's garment factories were indeed being upgraded, monitoring of safety conditions improved, and new labor laws were making it easier for workers there to organize. Alliance signatories also have committed $42 million to victims' compensation. Of course, Bangladeshi working conditions remain a far cry from those in developed nations.

Since the time of the factory collapse, factory owners argue that they cannot win. They are subject to pressure from stakeholders to enhance safety, but also to keep their prices low. Prices they are willing to pay have decreased—not increased—since the Rana Plaza event by an average of 13%! And yet the owners are asked to invest in safety upgrades.

All parties remain at a standstill at press time since a plan for monitoring was stopped by the Bangladeshi high courts in mid-2018. For additional ethical perspectives on this situation, please consult sources below, beginning with co-author Chris MacDonald's blog.

Sources: C. MacDonald, "Rejecting the Bangladesh Safety Accord," *The Business Ethics Blog* (May 17, 2013), https://businessethicsblog.com/2013/05/17/rejecting-the-bangladesh-safety-accord/(accessed January 13, 2019); C. MacDonald, "Top Retailers Sign New Bangladesh Safety Initiative," *The Business Ethics Blog* (July 22, 2013), https://businessethicsblog.com/2013/07/22/top-retailers-sign-new-bangladesh-safety-initiative/ (accessed January 13, 2019); Clare O'Connor, "These Retailers Involved in Bangladesh Factory Disaster Have Yet to Compensate Victims," *Forbes* (April 26, 2014), www.forbes.com/sites/clareoconnor/2014/04/26/these-retailers-involved-in-bangladesh-factory-disaster-have-yet-to-compensate-victims/ (accessed January 13, 2019); Bruce Kennedy, "The Bangladesh Factory Collapse One Year Later," *CBS News* (April 23, 2014), www.cbsnews.com/news/the-bangladesh-factory-collapse-one-year-later/ (accessed January 13, 2019); M. Wadud, "Rana Plaza, Five Years on: Safety of Workers Hangs in Balance in Bangladesh," *The Guardian* (April 24, 2018), www.theguardian.com/global-development/2018/apr/24/bangladeshi-police-target-garment-workers-union-rana-plaza-five-years-on (accessed January 13, 2019); D. Styles, "Bangladesh Accord Dealt Major Blow by High Court," *Ecotextile News* (April 10, 2018), www.ecotextile.com/2018041023388/social-compliance-csr-news/bangladesh-accord-dealt-major-blow-by-high-court.html (accessed January 13, 2019).

arguable that some minimum standards might apply and multinationals may have some core ethical obligations to employees, just as Foxconn owes its employees a commitment both to local Chinese labor laws as well as to Apple's minimum core values. But, in the absence of some specific guidance, how do we determine what those might be? Should the best employment practices in the United States set the standard for the global economy? That would mean concluding that the standards of one particular country are appropriate for all countries and cultures of the world, not necessarily the optimal conclusion.

Instead, some scholars have argued that Kantian universal principles should govern the employment relationship and that the ethical obligation of respect for persons should guide the employment interactions. "To fully respect a person, one must actively treat his or her humanity as an end, and not merely as a means to an end. This means that it is impermissible to treat persons like disposable tools."[28] Though different ethical theories may yield conflicting responses, it is arguable that a fundamental moral minimum set of standards exists that should be guaranteed to workers in all countries notwithstanding culture, stage of economic development, or availability of resources. Philosophers Denis Arnold and Norman E. Bowie contend that multinationals "must ensure the physical well-being of employees and refrain from undermining the development of their rational and moral capacities. . . . [R]especting workers in global factories requires that factories of multinational corporations (MNCs), including contract factories, adhere to local labor laws, refrain from the use of coercion, provide decent working conditions, and provide wages above the overall poverty line for a 48-hour workweek."[29] Others contend the list should also include a minimum age for child labor, nondiscrimination requirements (including the right to equal pay for equal work), and free association including the right to organize and to bargain collectively in contract negotiations.[30]

Even defining a "living wage" is problematic. In a world that cannot seem to agree on the number of people living in poverty,[31] figuring out how much is sufficient to offer a subsistence quality of life represents hurdles. A number of companies have implemented living-wage policies in their global operations. For example, almost 100 companies (including Burberry, Gap Inc., and The Body Shop International) have joined the Ethical Trade Initiative (ETI), an alliance of corporations, trade unions, and voluntary organizations dedicated to improving the conditions of workers.[32] The ETI has established a "Base Code" of ethical standards that all signatories commit to uphold. The portion of the Base Code addressing living wages states the following:

- Wages and benefits paid for a standard working week meet, at a minimum, national legal standards or industry benchmark standards, whichever is higher. In any event, wages should always be enough to meet basic needs and to provide some discretionary income.

- All workers shall be provided with written and understandable information about their employment conditions in respect to wages before they enter employment and about the particulars of their wages for the pay period concerned each time that they are paid.

- Deductions from wages as a disciplinary measure shall not be permitted nor shall any deductions from wages not provided for by national law be permitted without the expressed permission of the worker concerned. All disciplinary measures should be recorded.[33]

Nonwage benefits are an important and neglected aspect of the debate over global sweatshops. In many instances, such benefits can provide an advantage to both the worker and the employer. For example, a multinational firm's factory that provides free health checkups and basic health care services to workers through a factory clinic will typically have a healthier and more productive workforce than factories that lack such benefits. Levi Strauss & Company provides medical services to employees, their families, and members of the surrounding communities. Since 1999, the company's factories have sponsored vaccination, nutrition, and mental health campaigns. Since 2007, Levi Strauss & Co. has participated in HER-project, a partnership of global corporations and local networks that uses peer education to improve existing factory clinic resources by providing low-wage women workers with access to critical health information and services.[34] Because public health care in the locations where the Levi Strauss factories are located is generally poor, particularly in smaller cities and remote rural areas, companies play a vital role in providing additional assistance. Levi Strauss is not the only company to provide a medical clinic but one of the few to see the business value of investing in women's health as a pathway to strengthening whole communities.

International nongovernmental organizations have also attempted to step into this fray to suggest voluntary standards to which possible signatory countries or organizations could commit. For instance, the International Labour Office has promulgated its Tripartite Declaration of Principles Concerning Multinational Enterprises and Social Policy, which offers guidelines for employment, training, conditions of work and life, and industrial relations. The "Tripartite" part of the title refers to the critical cooperation necessary from governments, employers' and workers' organizations, and the multinational enterprises involved.

As mentioned earlier, the discussion of legal and ethical expectations and boundaries in this chapter is based on the law in the United States. However, awareness of the limitations of this analysis and sensitivity to the challenges of global implementation are critical in today's multinational business operations. We will revisit the quandary of varying ethical standards as applied to diverse economic and social environments in the next section with regard to the issue of child labor.

The Case of Child Labor

One of the key issues facing business in today's globalized economy is the potential for cultural or legal conflicts in connection with worldwide labor management. Though the issues stir our consciences, their resolution is not so clear. Let us consider, for example, the case of **child labor.** As we begin to understand the circumstances facing children worldwide, we can see that a simple prohibition might not offer us the best possible solution. But what options exist? (For a general inquiry, see the Decision Point "What to Do About Child Labor.")

According to International Labour Office estimates, 152 million children between 5 and 17 years old currently work in developing countries. The ILO explains that they are classified as "child laborers" when they are either too young to work or working in hazardous conditions, and, in the least developed countries, approximately one in four children are subject to this classification.[35]

Because work takes children out of school, nation-specific studies show that high levels of child labor are associated with low literacy levels. In addition, regions with a high prevalence of child labor are also characterized by high levels of

child labor
Though the term literally signifies children who work, it has taken on the meaning of exploitative work that involves some harm to a child who is not of an age to justify his or her presence in the workplace. The elements of that definition—harm, age of the child, justification to be in the workplace relative to other options—remain open to social and economic debate. UNICEF's 1997 State of the World's Children Report explains, "Children's work needs to be seen as happening along a continuum, with destructive or exploitative work at one end and beneficial work—promoting or enhancing children's development without interfering with their schooling, recreation and rest—at the other. And between these two poles are vast areas of work that need not negatively affect a child's development."

As you explore the question of child labor in this section, consider the many stakeholders involved and the power each one holds (or lack thereof), the options available to the multinational corporations, and the options consumers have in determining from whom they will buy, what rights might be implicated and the consequences of protecting them, and how you would respond if you were a labor advocate seeking to determine the best next steps in the debate.

1. What are the key facts relevant to your decision regarding child labor?
2. What are the ethical issues involved in child labor? What incentives might be in place that would actively support or pose challenges to your response?
3. Who are the stakeholders in connection with child labor?
4. What alternative responses might you suggest?
5. How would each of your alternatives affect each of the stakeholders you have identified?
6. Is there any guidance available from global organizations to assist you in resolving this particular dilemma?

childhood morbidity associated with HIV/AIDS, non-HIV infectious diseases, and malaria. The harmful effects are not limited to child laborers themselves; because children who work are more likely to earn low wages as adults, the risk that poverty and child labor will be passed to the next generation increases.[36]

Of course, employers in many economically developed countries currently use children as laborers, albeit with restrictions (e.g., children are employed in roles on television and in movies, all of the time!); so one should carefully review the social and economic structure within which the labor exists. While the easy answer may be to rid all factories of all workers under 18 years of age, that is often not the best answer for the children or the families involved, depending on the economy in question. Prospects for working children in developing countries are often bleak. Children may begin work as young as 3 years old. They not only may work in unhealthy conditions; they also may live in unhealthy conditions. The labor opportunities that exist almost always require children to work full time, thereby precluding them from obtaining an education. However, if children are not working, their options are not as optimistic as those of children in developed economies. Sophisticated education systems or public schools are not always available. Often children who do not work in the manufacturing industry are forced to work in less-hospitable "underground" professions, such as drug dealing or prostitution, simply to earn their own food each day.[37]

Moreover, even if educational alternatives are available in some environments, recommending removal of the child from the workplace completely ignores the financial impact of the child leaving his or her job. The income the youth worker generates may, at the very least, assist in supporting his or her fundamental needs (food, clothing, and shelter); at the most, it may be critical in supporting the entire family.

Bolivia allows children to work legally from the youngest age of 10 years old, with Dominica permitting the next youngest workers at 12. While certain readers throughout the world may consider these allowances unconscionable, lawmakers argue that the laws are meant to protect children who are going to be in the work-place—whether it is legal or not. Further, research suggests that legalizing child labor actually may *lower* the number of children who work. Scholars explain that, in environments where child labor is illegal, employers who choose to hire children anyway pay them lower wages because they factor in the cost of the risk of fines for their illegal labor when determining wages. As a result, families often have to send more children to work to make up for that lower wage.

As one article on child labor in Bolivia states, "we would all like, of course, for there to be less child labour, greater safety at work and for all to have greater leisure. But it's necessary for there to be sufficient economic wealth to allow such things before the regulations and legislation happen."[38]

Rights and Responsibilities in Conflict: Discrimination, Diversity, and Affirmative Action

In preceding sections, we explored the ethical environment of several elements of the employment relationship. As explained in our introduction, the ethical issues discussed in the first section of this chapter are, for the most part, settled. Though our discussion addressed particular areas of outstanding contention, the underlying rights have been established.

In the following section, we consider several topics on which people still continue to debate. The focus is on those subtle areas where the law may not yet be completely settled, where it remains open to diverse cultural interpretations, strong minority opinions, and value judgments. Though the courts have issued judgments in these areas, their decisions might not be unanimous or might reverse a strong lower-court opinion representing a contrary perspective. Consider how you feel about these issues because these areas are the ones where advocacy could be most powerful in swaying public (and the court's) opinion!

From a Kantian, deontological perspective, agreement on fundamental rights impacted by the following issues and on their appropriate prioritization is not yet universal. From a utilitarian viewpoint, reasonable minds engaged in these ethical issues do not always agree on which resolution might lead toward the greatest common good, or even what that good should ultimately be. Distributive justice does not provide a clear-cut solution as each camp can often make an argument for fairness. Our purpose here is to articulate and apply the ethical decision-making process to the challenges presented, provide a cross section of the arguments advocates involved make, and explore the insights that ethical theory might supply.

Discrimination

The courts have carefully construed legal precedent in the decades since Title VII of the U.S. Civil Rights Act was passed in 1964 and created the prohibited classes of discrimination. Although several specific areas of delicate and subtle quandaries remain, many of the original legal and ethical debates have been fought and resolved, offering business decision makers arguably clear guidance on appropriate behavior in the workplace. Some debates though continue to reappear, even when we might have thought they were settled.

For instance, sexual harassment emerged as a new legal basis for a legal complaint during the last century, and both employers and employees had to sort out the boundaries of its legal definition. Today sexual harassment training in workplaces has become commonplace. The Equal Employment Opportunity Commission (EEOC),[39] as well as many other sources, offer guidance, legal direction and parameters for both employees and employers. However, as the #MeToo movement (which began in 2006 but went viral in October 2017) demonstrated, perceptions and definitions in this arena continue to fluctuate and vary significantly from culture to culture. See Decision Point "#MeToo in the Workplace?" to examine how this environmental shift has impacted workplace relationships.

As we have stated throughout this text, the law can only go so far. While it is not our purpose to explore in detail the law relating to workplace discrimination, suffice it to say that the law allows employers to make decisions on *any basis* other than those prohibited by the Constitution, precedent, and several statutes (such as age, religion, race, disability, gender, national origin, color, and, depending on the jurisdiction, sexual orientation). Some commentators would contend that this broad mandate allows employers enormous autonomy in their employment decisions while many employers still bemoan any regulation of their workplaces.

Widespread disagreement on a global basis persists about the rights of employees with regard to discrimination, the extent of protected classes, and the more specific subtopics such as diversity and affirmative action that we will examine shortly. Even in the United States, the concept of discrimination remains one of the most intensely debated issues today. Employers continue to advocate for their rights to manage the workplace and to be permitted to hire, retain, and terminate employees without external influence or control. Employees fear unfair treatment and a loss of power based on reasons completely outside their control. Judge (now retired) Richard Posner argues in the Decision Point "Who Needs Ethics? Can the Market 'Fix' Discrimination?" how the market might be able to relieve employees of some of these fears—*at least in theory.*

The numbers demonstrate that the individuals holding positions of leadership in business today do not reflect the racial or gender composition of the communities they represent. In 2018, a massive multiyear study by McKinsey that included data of more than 13 million employees found that the corporate suite in America was represented by 4% of women of color, 9% of men of color, 19% of white women, and 68% of white men.[40]

The same report concluded that the underrepresentation of women and people of color cannot be explained by attrition—instead it pointed to the pipeline. For example, it found that not only are women less likely to be hired directly to manager-level roles, but 25% more men are promoted into manager-level positions than women. In other words, for every one hundred men promoted, only seventy-nine women move forward.

The #MeToo movement was inspired and established by Tarana Burke in 2006 as a means to assist underrepresented women of color affected by sexual abuse, and the term went viral when tweeted by actress Alyssa Milano in October 2017 as a rallying cry for all women who have been sexually assaulted. The tweet was sent at the same time that allegations of rape and other forms of sexual assault were leveled against media mogul Harvey Weinstein. Those public allegations and the viral tweets opened the floodgates to claims by other women (and some men) of their own experiences of rape, sexual assault, and other forms of sexual-based misconduct, millions communicating using the hashtag #MeToo. These communications resulted in payouts well into the millions of dollars and a *New York Times* report that approximately two hundred prominent men had lost their positions after allegations had been filed against them.

The Equal Employment Opportunity Commission reported that it experienced a 12% increase in the number of sexual harassment charges filed in the year ending September 2018, and on that basis filed 50% more lawsuits against employers than it did the prior year. The EEOC believes that these numbers continue to represent underreported figures of the extent of misconduct in this area.

While most firms already have anti–sexual harassment policies in place, more than one in five companies do not offer training programs that cover sexual harassment. Those that do often discuss the topic as part of the new hire training and then do not mention it again. The #MeToo movement has showcased the need for ongoing attention to these issues throughout a firm's culture in order to be effective.

Not all companies are eager to change corporate culture. When Nike management refused to acknowledge the problem of sexual harassment in the workplace, female executives distributed a survey to Nike's female employees, asking respondents whether they had experienced sexual harassment or bias while at the company. Within a few weeks after the surveys were taken to the Nike CEO, six high-level male executives left the company.

A 2018 survey of over two thousand human resource professionals found that one-third of the organizations represented had made changes to their sexual harassment training over the prior year, including adding workplace civility to the training and tailoring the training to specific groups within their workforces.

Has the workplace changed since #MeToo? More attention to the nature of sexual harassment and a sexually charged workplace can bring valuable benefits, respect, and dignity for workers of all genders, and lead to greater productivity. Heightened awareness also can increase reporting. Yet, some claim that there also has been a backlash. There are reports of greater levels of discomfort in the workplace. For instance, a male executive might choose not to include a female junior executive on a business trip out of concern for "how it would look"; men might not invite female colleagues to social events with clients "in case something happens"; and others even have claimed to reduce their female hires because "just hiring a woman these days is 'an unknown risk.' What if she took something he said the wrong way?"

In these examples, the female businessperson is excluded from an opportunity, while the male sees it as risk management. The results of these choices, however, can be devastating to women's advancement. A 2018 study found that the above

(continued)

(*concluded*)

stories occurred with an alarming consistency—senior male executives were almost four times more likely to have dinner with a male colleague than a female one, and five times more likely to travel for work with a man from work than a woman. Perhaps most devastating to advancement, these experienced executives say they are three times more uncomfortable mentoring women.

In other cases, some argue that the issues arise as a result of perceived cultural differences. For example, one executive explains that he grew up around "Latinos who were expressive and dispensed hugs freely, and also among Southerners who often used terms like 'honey,' 'sweetheart' and 'sugar' with their acquaintances."* He wonders whether these subtle cultural differences might now be the source of a harassment report in a workplace.

Companies and municipalities have responded since #MeToo has brought greater attention to the subject of harassment, in order to create a more welcoming workplace for all involved. In 2018, both Google and Microsoft removed the requirement in its employment agreements that all sexual harassment and gender discrimination cases go to confidential arbitration. Google made that decision immediately following a massive global employee walkout that emerged in part as a protest against a workplace culture that they believed shielded perpetrators of sexual misconduct. Google also committed to make information about sexual misconduct cases available to employees, to enhance its misconduct prevention training, and to require the training every year rather that every other year.

Facebook also published its anti–sexual harassment policy for the first time in 2018. And California instituted a mandate that all publicly traded firms based in that state must have at least one female director by 2021. What other actions might have an impact on workplace culture in this regard?

1. Given the current environment, how do you define the issue facing companies today? As we know, defining the issue is vital in ethical decision making and the question is important. Is our dilemma a question of what policy to implement, how to mold a culture, what guidance to offer workers? Or is it a deeper issue involving changing mind-sets? Some might argue that it is not an employer's place to engage in the latter effort, nor even possible. If Harvey Weinstein had gone to a sexual harassment training, would he have acted any differently?

2. Notwithstanding your personal perspective on the #MeToo movement, there is no question that it has had an impact on the workplace, and practically all employers sense a need to respond in some manner. What do you believe are some effective actions an employer could take? For instance, should there be a no-fraternization (no dating) policy in the workplace, in order to reduce risk?

*Source: Jorge L. Ortiz, "Will #MeToo Turn into #NotHer?" *USA Today* (October 4, 2018).

Sources: A. Nova, "Office Sexual Harassment Policies Lag behind the #MeToo Movement," *CNBC.com* (April 19, 2018), www.cnbc.com/2018/04/19/office-sexual-harassment-policies-lag-behind-the-metoo-movement.html (accessed March 10, 2019); Society for Human Resource Management, "Harassment-Free Workplace Series: The Executive View" (October 4, 2018), www.shrm.org/hr-today/trends-and-forecasting/research-and-surveys/Pages/Workplace-Sexual-Harassment.aspx (accessed March 10, 2019); J. Ortiz, "Will #MeToo Turn into #NotHer? Movement May Come with Unintended Workplace Consequences," *USA Today* (October 4, 2018), www.usatoday.com/story/news/2018/10/04/metoo-movement-unintended-career-consequences-women/1503516002/(accessed March 10, 2019); J. Ortiz, "California's 'Giant Step Forward': Gender-Quotas Law Requires Women on Corporate Boards," *USA Today* (September 30, 2018), www.usatoday.com/story/news/2018/09/30/california-law-sets-gender-quotas-corporate-boardrooms/1482883002/(accessed March 10, 2019); J. Horowitz, "Workplace Sexual Harassment Claims Have Spiked in the #MeToo Era," *CNN Business* (October 5, 2018), www .cnn.com/2018/10/04/business/eeoc-sexual-harassment-reports/index.html (accessed March 10, 2019); M. Zetlin, "Women at Nike Fight Hostile Culture with a Simple but Effective Tool That You Can Use Too," *Inc.* (April 20, 2018), www.inc.com/minda-zetlin/nike-sexual-harassment-survey-gender-bias-executives-fired-trevor-edwards.html (accessed March 10, 2019); G. Tan and K. Porzecanski, "Wall Street Rule for the #MeToo Era: Avoid Women at All Cost," *Bloomberg* (December 3, 2018), www.bloomberg.com/news/articles/2018-12-03/a-wall-street-rule-for-the-metoo-era-avoid-women-at-all-cost (accessed March 10, 2019); V. Zarya, "Since #MeToo, the Number of Men Who Are Uncomfortable Mentoring Women Has Tripled," *Fortune* (February 6, 2018), http://fortune.com/2018/02/06/lean-in-sheryl-sandberg/ (accessed March 10, 2019).

It is hard to pinpoint any single cause for the disparity in these numbers. We can say "discrimination," but what does that really mean? The McKinsey report suggests that black women in particular face "everyday discrimination" that can amount to a significant impact over the course of a career. For example, 42% of black women reported being asked to provide more evidence of their competence than others are asked to provide (and often in front of others), compared to only 16% of men (almost three times as often). Black women are often presumed to hold a much lower professional rank—at more than twice the rate of men. Certainly, these examples are not limited to black women, and often the experiences are more intense when the woman is the only female in the work environment.

OBJECTIVE

Without diminishing the impact of overt acts of discrimination or their continuation in the workplace, covert forms of discrimination are also widely prevalent, though they often go unnoticed. For instance, discrimination persists simply on the basis of one's name. In one study involving almost 13,000 fake résumés, researchers found that people with Chinese-, Indian-, or Pakistani-sounding names were 28% less likely to get an interview than candidates with precisely the same qualifications but with English-sounding names.[41]

Discrimination around the world persists not only with regard to race and ethnicity, but also in connection with gender. Considering just pay, both on a global level and in the United States, men were paid almost 19% more than women as of 2018.[42] In the U.S., specifically, women often face challenges that are distinct from those faced by men. For instance, women and men are both subject to gender stereotyping but suffer from different expectations in that regard.

Marianne Cooper, sociologist and lead researcher for the *New York Times* best-selling book *Lean In: Women, Work and the Will to Lead* (written by Facebook COO Sheryl Sandburg), explains that success and likability do not go together for women. Often, women are "applauded for delivering results at work but then reprimanded for being 'too aggressive,' 'out for herself,' 'difficult,' and 'abrasive.'"[43]

Oddly, a similar catch-22 does not exist for men. Less-emotional men are viewed in positive terms—going after what they want, and not letting anything get in their way—and men who demonstrate a bit of emotion are praised for having a softer side and understanding the women's perspective. Cooper uses the example of a former executive editor of the *New York Times,* Jill Abramson. Abramson was described by certain staffers as "impossible to work with" and "not approachable";

Decision Point

Who Needs Ethics? Can the Market "Fix" Discrimination?

One approach toward discrimination in employment calls for no corporate or governmental intervention. Defenders of the market argue that if the market were left to its own devices, we could expect discrimination to fall by the wayside. That is, if a firm hires its employees on the basis of prejudices and discriminatory views (such as that women cannot do a certain job), then it is limiting its pool of possible employees. Another firm that does not discriminate can choose from the larger pool and is more likely to obtain the *most* qualified individual for the job. There is therefore an opportunity cost to discrimination. Labor is clearly a factor of production; when we leave productive resources unused, the entire economy suffers. The human capital of women and minorities is lost when we deny them opportunities in the economy. Retired Judge Richard Posner explains the economic impact of this theory in terms of race discrimination as follows:

> In a market of many sellers, the intensity of the prejudice against blacks will vary considerably. Some sellers will have only a mild prejudice against them. These sellers will not forgo as many advantageous transactions with blacks as their more prejudiced competitors (unless the law interferes). Their costs will therefore be lower, and this will enable them to increase their share of the market. The least prejudiced sellers will come to dominate the market in much the same way as people who are least afraid of heights come to dominate occupations that require working at heights: they demand a smaller premium.*

1. Should corporate policymakers and government leave such issues to the market? Should employees' fears or concerns about workplace discrimination be relieved on understanding Judge Posner's theory? Why or why not?

2. What key facts do you need to determine whether the market can solve this challenge? Under what circumstances would Posner's argument fail? What market failures might prevent economic forces from efficiently ending discrimination?

3. What are some of the other ethical issues that come to mind when you consider this proposed "solution"? What is the effect of regulation such as Title VII on Posner's argument? Even if the market could work against discrimination, is this matter sufficiently important from an ethical perspective that society should address it more actively through legislation?

4. Who are the stakeholders involved in this particular issue?

5. What alternative responses could you propose? Are you more comfortable with management through legislation or a free market? Consider the implications if the discriminating firm held a monopoly on its good or service.

6. How would each of your alternatives affect each of the stakeholders you have identified?

7. Where might you look for additional guidance to assist you in resolving this particular dilemma?

8. Finally, the United States has more significant antidiscrimination provisions than some other countries, such as those in the Middle East. Is this information in support of or contrary to the judge's proposition?

*Source: Richard A. Posner, *Economic Analysis of Law* (New York: Aspen, 2002), p. 616.

yet, the paper won four Pulitzer Prizes under her leadership—the third highest number ever received by the newspaper. There was also speculation that Abramson pushed for pay and pension benefits equal to those of her predecessor, a man, after discovering the discrepancy. While the pay gap was closed after she complained, the lingering tension with her management was speculated as a major reason for her ultimate termination—a suspect scenario for a company that was once sued by female employees for discriminatory practices.[44]

A study of the effects of gender stereotyping on communication styles adds support to the experiences reported by powerful women.[45] The study found that women who believed that they were being stereotyped on the basis of their gender tended to adopt a more masculine style of communication. However, other test subjects rated these women as less likable and were less likely to follow their leadership.

We can identify the results of gender (and other forms of) stereotyping. There are many textbooks written on discrimination, and the law offers one environment in which to respond. The question is whether ethical decision making offers employers alternatives in order to create a more positive working environment for all stakeholders. In the next two sections, we discuss diversity and affirmative action, both of which integrate legal and ethical responses to the dilemma of a workplace that some argue does not yet accurately represent or include all qualified workers in a just manner.

Diversity

The U.S. workforce today is significantly more diverse than ever before, and all data suggest that this will continue. Efforts toward eliminating discrimination in employment over the past 30 years are partially responsible for this change. But a changing population is also a major factor in the increasingly diverse workplace.

Diversity refers to the presence of differing cultures, languages, ethnicities, races, affinity orientations, genders, religious sects, abilities, social classes, ages, and national origins of the individuals in a firm. Sixty-six percent of executives in the United States consider diversity and inclusion as important or very important. This level of attention is about mid-level globally when compared to a high of 86% in Japan and a low of 56% in Belgium (of those countries included in the survey conducted by Deloitte).[46]

European countries have outpaced the United States in terms of diversity efforts and, in particular, in connection with board representation. While the average representation of women on European boards in 2018 was 33.6% (a significant increase from 15% in 2012), some countries have significantly higher numbers, in part because of legislation that requires it. For instance, Norway has a federal law that requires companies to have at least 40% of of its corporate board seats filled by women or face a complete shutdown of operations. As a result, 42% of corporate board seats are held by women. Norway is joined by Germany, France, Spain, Iceland, Italy, the UK, and Belgium.[47] Women hold over 44.2% of board seats in France and 32% of board seats in Finland. Almost 60% of firms in Europe have at least one female director.[48]

OBJECTIVE

diversity
Diversity refers to the presence of differing cultures, languages, ethnicities, races, affinity orientations, genders, religious sects, abilities, social classes, ages, and national origins of the individuals in a firm. When used in connection with the corporate environment, it often encompasses the values of respect, tolerance, inclusion, and acceptance.

Reality Check   *Diversity = Less Risk?*

As discussed in this section, research demonstrates that adding women to boards of directors can have a significant impact on end results. While the nearby bulleted list referred to the impact of three female board members, scholars who examined decisions and performance of more than two thousand companies between 1998 and 2011 found that firms that brought on even one sole woman to a previously all-male board of directors were more risk-averse; spent less on capital expenditures, research and development, and acquisitions; and demonstrated lower volatility in their stock returns. These changes resulted in greater financial stability and higher financial returns for shareholders.

This research suggests that the addition of a woman, therefore, is not simply a public relations move but, in addition, can mean a stronger and more sustainable future for the firm. One of the coauthors of the study, Ya-wen Yang, explains that diverse boards experience "greater challenges in communicating and accepting one shared decision," so they may not reach consensus as quickly as a homogeneous board. They are therefore more likely to shy away from risks. While these boards may miss a risky venture that could provide benefits in the end, they also could reduce severely unwarranted risks, thereby providing an effective balancing mechanism.

Source: Michael Casey, "Study Finds a Diverse Corporate Boards Rein in Risk, Good for Shareholders," *Fortune* (July 30, 2014), http://fortune.com/2014/07/30/study-finds-a-diverse-corporate-boards-rein-in-risk-good-for-shareholders (accessed March 10, 2019).

Other regions also have established quotas, including India where, as of 2017, 12.4% of corporate directors were women (an increase of 4.7% over the prior 2 years). The increase is the result of legislation that requires any public company with five or more directors to have at least one female board member.[49]

The United States does not have any similar requirement. The *Fortune* 500 for 2017 had 22% female representation on its boards (only a 1% increase over the prior year), and minorities represented 17%.[50] The business case for gender diversity is strong. Diversity has been found to lead to more enhanced innovation, employee engagement, and stronger financial performance. A 2018 study found that, where there is greater diversity in leadership teams and boards, they also reap these financial benefits:

- **53% increase in return on equity (ROE)** (where *Fortune* 500 companies have at least three female board members).
- **Increase of 6% in their net profit margin** (where companies have at least 30% of executive roles filled by women).
- **Increase of 9% in EBIT** (earnings before interest and taxes).
- **Increase of 19% in innovation.**[51]

The Reality Check "Diversity = Less Risk?" further details how gender diversity can contribute further to the bottom line and lead to long-term sustainability of an organization.

On the flip side, while diversity has brought benefits to the workplace, diversity efforts have also created new areas of conflict. Recall the definition of *diversity* given earlier: Diversity refers to the presence of differing cultures, languages, ethnicities, races, affinity orientations, genders, religious sects, abilities, social classes, ages, and national origins of the individuals in a firm. When a firm brings together individuals with these (or other) differences—often exposing these individuals to such differences for the first time—areas of tension and anxiety may emerge. In addition, the organization is likely to ask its employees to work together toward common goals, on teams, in supervisory or subordinate roles, and in power relationships, all requests that might lead to conflicts or tension even without additional stressors such as cultural challenges.

In a 2018 survey of board directors, more than half responded that they believed diversity efforts were motivated by political correctness, and 48% thought that shareholders were too preoccupied with diversity at the expense of other concerns.[52]

Diversity can potentially increase tension in several areas. Where differences are new or strong, *and* where negative stereotypes previously ruled interactions between particular groups, sensitivity to the potential for conflict is necessary.

Another concern involves integrating diverse viewpoints with a preexisting corporate culture. There seems nothing inappropriate about seeking to ensure that workers will support the particular values of a firm, but it might be difficult to do this while also encouraging diversity. Diversity, which might be the source of positive gains for the organization, might also be the source of fundamental differences in values that must be balanced. Some scholars suggest that job applicants be screened with regard to their values, but how can employers do so? Hiring is not an area to be taken lightly, but most firms go with a "gut" instinct about whether or not a job applicant will "fit in." In the same way that you might apply the "can you sleep at night" test to an ethical dilemma after considering all the implications of a decision, you might trust an employment choice to the same test.

It is not discriminatory to refuse to hire someone about whom you simply have a "bad feeling," unless that bad feeling is based on their difference in race or gender. On the other hand, it is vital to be wary of prejudgments based solely on differences in interpretations of culturally based standards. While variance in fundamental standards might justify a sense of a "bad fit" between a potential employer and employee, divergence in culturally based standards such as attire, hairstyles, or manner of speaking might instead be treated differently. Efforts at understanding **multiculturalism,** such as acknowledging and promoting diversity through celebration and appreciation of various cultures in the workplace, can serve both to educate and to encourage the benefits linked to diversity efforts.

Honoring diversity or promoting freedoms of expression can certainly be taken to an extreme and go too far. One might imagine the "bad fit," mentioned earlier, where a divergence of cultures between a potential employee and one's clientele means that a particular hire just will not work out. Though the law is slow to catch up to social mores, it does eventually. Even statutes and other codes are changed, though, of course, a few gray areas always seem to remain.

On the other hand, the cost of ignoring diversity is high, not only in terms of losses of productivity, creativity, and other performance-based measures, but also in terms of legal liability. Though seemingly an old tale, Texaco's experience with what insiders refer to simply as "the crisis" in 1996 offers an instructive lesson.

multiculturalism
Similar to diversity, refers to the principle of tolerance and inclusion that supports the co-existence of multiple cultures, while encouraging each to retain that which is unique or individual about that particular culture.

The company was required to pay $175 million to settle a racial discrimination lawsuit that was brought based on taped conversations of executives using racist language—referring to some of their workers as "black jelly beans"—as well as documented compensation below the minimum salary for minorities in a number of positions.

A firm often reaches its depths before it emerges anew, and Texaco's numbers subsequent to the lawsuit tell a much different story. Six years after the settlement, minority hires accounted for 46% of all new employees, including some key senior executives, and more than 20% of promotions and 34% of new hires were women. Texaco pledged to spend at least $1 million with minority and women contractors within 5 years of the settlement and, of course, diversity training is now mandated for all workers, with management compensation tied to the attainment of success in implementing new initiatives.

These types of cases cross industry lines as well. A group of black financial advisers filed a lawsuit in 2005 against Merrill Lynch alleging that their bosses systematically steered the most profitable business to white employees. They also were able to show that white workers made salaries averaging 43% more than black employees at the firm. Eight years later, in 2013, Merrill Lynch agreed to pay $160 million, to be distributed among all black investment brokers and trainees who worked at the firm from mid-2001 to that time (around 1,200 people).

At the time of the suit, black traders made up so few of the firm's staff that Merrill branches in more than half of U.S. states did not even have a single black broker. The suit claimed that Merrill Lynch sometimes relied on stereotypes, once allegedly suggesting that its managers encourage black brokers to "learn to play golf or other activities designed to learn how business gets done in manners (they) might not be familiar with." They also found that, beginning in the first month of the training program for new hires, the company gave more and larger accounts from new customers or retiring brokers to the white trainees. Merrill Lynch has a history of discrimination issues, settling gender discrimination suits in the 1970s and 1990s, plus an ongoing suit over a company training course recommending women employees read a book called *Seducing the Boys Club: Uncensored Tactics from a Woman at the Top.*[53]

There has been just one published report on the impact of the 2013 judgment on the Merrill culture, and it appears that Merrill is continuing its efforts beyond its commitment to a 3-year program designed to improve conditions for African American workers. The firm said that the program "will enhance opportunities for financial advisers in the future." The firm was not to distribute accounts to trainees in their first year and committed to placing extra emphasis on the clients trainees bring in on their own. The firm said it would hire two coaches to work with black brokers and two experts, one chosen by the plaintiffs and one by Merrill Lynch, to study the impact of team selection. Finally, all the settlement efforts would be overseen by a council of black brokers. The firm also created new minority recruitment incentives, added an Office of Diversity to the duties of the unit's operating chief, and went on a hiring spree that, for a period, more than doubled the number of black financial advisers.[54]

See the Decision Point "Women's Economic Development Programs" for a discussion of Walmart's efforts to respond to its own diversity challenges, and the Reality Check "Bias Interrupters" for other ideas on how to respond to these challenges.

Affirmative Action

Throughout this chapter, we have discussed the means by which to protect employer interests and employee rights. With regard to the latter, we have focused on employee rights to fair treatment and due process in the workplace. A question arises, however, when individual rights compete with each other, which might seem to happen in the case of **affirmative action.** The question regarding affirmative action is not necessarily whether an employee has a right to fair process in connection with employment but instead whether someone has a right to the job in the first place. Does one person deserve a position *more* than another person? For instance, efforts to encourage greater diversity may also be seen as a form of **reverse discrimination:** discrimination against those traditionally considered to be in power or the majority, such as white men. A business that intentionally seeks to hire a candidate from an underrepresented group might be seen as discriminating against white males, for example.

The arguments on both sides of this issue have a tendency toward emotional persuasion. Imagine you are hiring a social worker to serve an overwhelmingly African American community that is currently facing issues, among others, of teen pregnancy. Not only might you argue that you want to hire someone who is African American; you might also want a female social worker who you presume might be better able to speak with the teenage women in that community. On the other hand, imagine that you are interviewing a 40-year-old white male with a master's degree from an extraordinarily reputable program. He has years of experience in the field and in fact has an adopted African American daughter himself. He claims he can handle the job. In fact, he claims he *deserves* the job. Does he? Does it matter whether he deserves it? Does he have a *right* to the job? Assume that the next person on your list is a younger African American woman closer in age to the women in your community. What is the fairest decision? Fair to whom? Fairest to the young women of your community, to the applicants you are interviewing, or to other stakeholders? How should you decide? What will be the consequences of your decision?

The word *reverse* above presumes that discrimination only travels in one direction. If instead it travels in a different direction, it is "backing up" or heading in reverse. Yet, surely it does not feel that way to the subject of the discrimination. Perhaps discrimination against a member of a group that normally holds power or is well represented is atypical or not the norm, but discrimination on the basis of someone's membership in a protected class *is still wrongful discrimination.*

One brief example might offer a helpful illustration. The Mazzoni Center in Philadelphia is a nonprofit, LGBT-focused facility that offers health care and wellness services resources. In 2018, it hired a new CEO, who happened to be a straight woman. Mazzoni's community was not universally pleased with the choice. Some

affirmative action
A policy or a program that strives to redress past discrimination through the implementation of proactive measures to ensure equal opportunity. In other words, affirmative action is the intentional inclusion of previously excluded groups. Affirmative action efforts can take place in employment environments, education, or other arenas.

reverse discrimination
Decisions made or actions taken against those individuals who are traditionally considered to be in power or the majority, such as white men, or in favor of a historically nondominant group.

Decision Point

In September 2011, Walmart Stores Inc. announced its Global Women's Economic Power Initiative and planned to invest billions in new programs aimed at women, including a commitment to double its purchases from women-owned businesses by 2016, provide support for training women in factories and farms that supply its stores, and donate $100 million to organizations that foster women's economic development. "We're stepping up our efforts to help educate, source from and open markets for women around the world," said Walmart CEO Mike Duke.

As of 2018, Walmart has achieved and surpassed each of these objectives. It has sourced $20 billion from women-owned businesses; supported the training of 1 million women; and fostered diversity and inclusion among its major suppliers.

Three months prior to the creation of the initiative, the U.S. Supreme Court dismissed a class-action suit, first filed by six employees in 2001, that alleged systematic gender discrimination in pay and promotion decisions at Walmart, the nation's largest private employer. Representing 1.6 million female Walmart employees and a potential for losses in the billions for the corporation, the case was the biggest sex discrimination class action in history. Although Walmart was victorious in defeating the class-action suit, the Supreme Court decision allows individual employees to file civil actions. In addition, the company faced negative publicity from the high-profile case.

Corporate spokespersons denied any connection between the gender discrimination charges and the launch of the new women's programs. However, some charged that the initiative represents a public relations attempt by Walmart to improve its reputation and, as a Wall Street strategy analyst proposed, "get out in front of any potential future lawsuits."

1. What do you believe was Walmart's motivation for the initiative discussed here?
2. Who are its key stakeholders for this launch announcement—and for the programs themselves?
3. With the current level of giving and the collaborations established, do you think that Walmart is living up to its commitment? What do you believe would be the key components to make this program successful?
4. One of the key goals for Walmart's initiative is "creating the building blocks of success and self-sufficiency for women," and much of its funding goes to highly practical efforts to help women help themselves. Some argue that this objective is in line with Walmart's conservative stance on economic opportunity and demonstrates no acknowledgment or empathy for other economic forces that undermine earning power for low-skilled workers (e.g., race, poverty). Do you think this critique is justified?

Sources: Walmart, "Supplier Diversity," http://corporate.walmart.com/suppliers/supplier-diversity/ (accessed March 10, 2019); S. Clifford and S. Strom, "Wal-Mart to Announce Women-Friendly Plans," *The New York Times* (September 14, 2011), www.nytimes.com/2011/09/14/business/wal-mart-to-announce-women-friendly-plans.html (accessed March 10, 2019); J. Shipps, "Teach a Woman to Fish: The Walmart Foundation and Women's Empowerment," *Inside Philanthropy* (October 16, 2014), www.insidephilanthropy.com/home/2014/10/16/teach-a-woman-to-fish-the-walmart-foundation-and-womens-empo.html (accessed March 10, 2019); Walmart, "About the Initiative" (Spring 2017), https://corporate.walmart.com/womensempowerment/about (accessed March 10, 2019).

Reality Check *Bias Interrupters*

What do you think that companies can do to make workplaces fairer, more diverse, and more inclusive? Joan C. Williams, a professor of law at the University of California–Hastings, offers three "bias interrupters," basic interventions that can stop bias in its tracks in the workplace.

Williams suggests that companies examine areas of possible bias within their cultures, identify key metrics for tracking the results of interventions, and implement these interrupters on an ongoing basis.

EXAMPLES OF BIAS INTERRUPTERS

Interventions may be as simple as rewriting help-wanted advertisements to remove traditionally masculine words.

Williams offers the example of Google, which redesigned the process by which people receive promotions. Google found that men received promotions far more often than women. The company uncovered one of the reasons: Google had a system that required employees to nominate themselves for promotions, and, traditionally, this is

not something that women are socialized to do. In fact, Google found that men routinely nominated themselves at far higher rates than women did.

What did Google do? It changed the culture. Google asked every employee who met promotion requirements to nominate herself or himself and then also asked managers to follow the same model. Also, Google nurtured role models among female senior leaders. It asked these senior women to speak at meetings and also within the women's "employee resource group" to highlight the value and benefits of self-promotion. These efforts created a culture where self-promotion became expected and desirable for everyone. As a result, the difference between male and female promotions diminished.

Source: Katherine Reynolds Lewis, "How to Make Your Company Less Sexist and Racist," *The Atlantic* (March 31, 2015), www.theatlantic.com/business/archive/2015/03/how-to-make-your-company-less-sexist-and-racist/388931/ (accessed March 10, 2019).

critics questioned her qualifications, but others suggested that the Center should have hired a CEO who more appropriately represented the communities Mazzoni "is funded to serve."

The board responded to the community by saying,

> When it comes to matters of employment, Mazzoni Center does not discriminate on the basis of race, creed, religion, color, national origin, ancestry, age, sex, gender identification or gender expression, sexual orientation, disability, marital status or any other protected status covered by federal, state or local law. Thus, all employment-related decisions are made solely on the basis of a candidate's skills, ability, experience, education, training, and other legitimate factors related to the requirements of the job.[55]

Any decision by the Board that would have considered LGBT status would rise to the level of illegal discrimination.

OBJECTIVE

Let us take a closer look at affirmative action to explore the ethical issues it raises. The term *affirmative action* refers to a policy or a program that tries to respond to instances of past discrimination by implementing proactive measures to ensure equal opportunity today. It may take the form of intentional inclusion of previously excluded groups in employment, education, or other environments.

The use of affirmative action policies in both business and universities has been controversial for decades. In its first discussion of affirmative action in employment, the U.S. Supreme Court held that employers were permitted to include minorities intentionally (and thereby exclude others) in order to redress past wrongs. However, the holding had some restrictions, and those restrictions have caused confusion. Even today, the law is not clear, and we must turn to our ethical decision-making systems to provide direction, which we will discuss shortly.

Affirmative action arises in the workplace in three ways. The first way is through legal requirements. Executive Order 11246 requires affirmative action efforts in order to ensure equal opportunity. However, this Executive Order only applies to federal contractors with fifty or more employees, so it reaches only about 20% of the workforce.

Where Executive Order 11246 does not apply, courts may require "judicial affirmative action" in order to remedy a finding of past discrimination. A third form of affirmative action involves voluntary affirmative action plans. These plans involve employer-designed programs that are created to overcome barriers to equal opportunity. They might include training plans and programs, focused recruiting activity, or the elimination of particular hiring criteria that exclude a particular group. Affirmative action efforts under these latter two options (in other words, for the private sector) are only permitted after demonstrating underrepresentation of a particular group or a finding of past discrimination.

Through case law, courts have provided employers with basic guidelines for creating these programs and policies. Consider how the following *legal* constraints to an affirmative action program also are in line with deontological and teleological frameworks, and support your ethical decision-making process:

1. The affirmative action efforts or policy may not unnecessarily infringe upon other employees' rights or create an absolute bar to their advancement (e.g., it would be inappropriate to discharge or lay off others in order to achieve a racial balance).

2. The affirmative action effort or policy may not set aside any specific positions for women or minorities, and may not be construed as quotas to be met.

3. It may not change legitimate expectations of employees (in other words, it may not require the reduction of expectations or require the hiring of unqualified individuals).

4. It must be temporary, lasting only until it attains, rather than maintains, a balanced workforce.

Opponents to affirmative action contend that the efforts do more harm than good, that affirmative action creates ill will and poor morale among workforces. They argue that it translates into current punishment of past wrongs and therefore is inappropriate because those who "pay" for the wrongs are unfairly burdened and should not bear the responsibility for the acts of others.

Critics of affirmative action programs are not only the perceived "majority" voices; Supreme Court Justice (and African American) Clarence Thomas writes in his autobiography that the affirmative action program at Yale Law School was responsible for the difficulties he faced in finding a job after graduation. In his view, prospective employees doubted that he was as intelligent as his grades at the Ivy League law school indicated, due to their presumption that he had been favored as an African American student. His Yale law degree was basically worthless, Justice Thomas wrote, because it bore "the taint of racial preference."[56]

In its first ruling on this issue in more than a decade, the Supreme Court addressed affirmative action again through a case of "reverse discrimination" in 2003. While this particular case involved university admissions, American business was a stakeholder in the case as well. The University of Michigan Law School relied on an admissions policy that took into account the ability of each applicant to contribute to the school's social and intellectual life. As part of this criterion, the school considered the applicant's race on the assumption that a diverse student body would contribute to the goals of the law school and that a critical mass of minority students was required to accomplish that goal. Thus, although scores from LSAT tests, undergraduate college grades, letters of recommendation, and other traditional factors were primarily used to grant admission, an applicant's race was also a factor. Two white females who were denied admission brought the lawsuit, arguing that admission of minority students with lower grades and test scores violated their rights to equal treatment.

General Motors Corporation filed an *amicus curiae* ("friend of the court") brief in support of the law school's admission policy. By doing so, GM went out of its way at great expense to identify itself as a business stakeholder and argue publicly in support of affirmative action. In its brief, GM claimed that the need to ensure a racially and ethnically diverse student body was a compelling reason to support affirmative action policies. GM claimed that "the future of American business and, in some measure, of the American economy depends on it." In its own business experience, "only a well educated, diverse workforce, comprising people who have learned to work productively and creatively with individuals from a multitude of races and ethnic, religious, and cultural backgrounds, can maintain America's competitiveness in the increasingly diverse and interconnected world economy." Prohibiting affirmative action likely "would reduce racial and ethnic diversity in the pool of employment candidates from which the nation's businesses can draw their future leaders, impeding businesses' own efforts to achieve and obtain the manifold benefits of diversity in the managerial levels of their work forces."[57]

The Court seemed to agree.

> Diminishing the force of such stereotypes is both a crucial part of the Law School's mission, and one that it cannot accomplish with only token numbers of minority students. Just as growing up in a particular region or having particular professional experiences is likely to affect an individual's views, so too is one's own, unique experience of being a racial minority in a society, like our own, in which race unfortunately still matters. The Law School has determined, based on its experience and expertise, that a "critical mass" of underrepresented minorities is necessary to further its compelling interest in securing the educational benefits of a diverse student body.[58]

In a case challenging the admissions policies of the University of Texas in 2013, the U.S. Supreme Court upheld the idea that race-conscious selection can be constitutionally permissible in states that wish to use it. However, in 2014 the Supreme

In each of the cases discussed on our Opening Decision Point, consider how the employers involved might have handled the circumstances differently, perhaps leading to alternative results. In other words, whether you agree or disagree with the decisions surrounding the terminations, perhaps there might have been more ethical or effective ways to respond to the employees' actions that still could promote and protect the firm's cultures and missions.

In each case, a great deal of media attention resulted from the terminations (or, in Kaepernick's case, the failure to find a position). There are some who use the opportunities available through social media to enhance the attention and others who might prefer to have received no attention at all. In either case, the fact that the (ex)employee could gain respect and popularity—and the employer could receive negative publicity—through this attention remains a possibility.

If an employee violates a workplace expression policy, are there alternatives to termination? Perhaps Briskman's employer, Akima, could have asked her to remove the photo from social media that violated its policy. However, solutions that sound simple are often far more complicated in practice. We will discuss how far employers are permitted to regulate "off-work" acts in Chapter 7, and the ethical issues involved in those decisions.

Consider for now the question of whether Google had options other than firing Damore for his published memo. Damore was exceptionally clear about his perceptions about women and, in particular, their abilities. As one former engineer asked, "You have just created a textbook hostile workplace environment. Could you imagine having to work with someone who had just publicly questioned your basic competency to do your job?"* If Google allowed him to remain in his position, and if a woman later complained that she was subject to bias (or other improper conduct) as a result, its choice now would be equivalent to a conscious disregard of his earlier statement—intentional wrongdoing.

While Damore may have a right to express his views, he also has a responsibility for the consequences. He worked for a firm where those consequences included his termination.

On the other hand, there does not seem to be a clear answer in the Kaepernick case, and reasonable minds tend to reach diverse conclusions. The law will provide its answer here, but, from an ethical perspective, firms may reach varying decisions. While striving not to speculate too much, apparently the NFL owners responded in a way that they thought was either according to their values or best for their brand. Other brands, such as Nike, perceived Kaepernick's decision as laudable and held him up as a model of integrity. In both cases, these decisions may earn and lose support and might be better discussed in a conversation on marketing. But within the employment context, both a firm's underlying values and mission should be considered, as well as the decision's long-term consequences.

Source: Y. Zunger, "So, About This Googler's Manifesto," *Medium* (August 5, 2017), https://medium .com/@yonatanzunger/so-about-this-googlers-manifesto-1e3773ed1788 (accessed February 22, 2019).

Court upheld a Michigan constitutional amendment that bans affirmative action in admissions to the state's public universities (an amendment that passed as a result of its prior 2013 decision). This decision opened the door to similar amendments in seven other states. As a result, states that forbid affirmative action in higher education, such as Florida and California as well as Michigan, have seen a significant drop in the enrollment of black and Hispanic students in their most selective colleges and universities.[59]

Do you believe that a diverse student body contributes to the ability of a school to accomplish its educational mission? Should the law prohibit, allow, or require affirmative action programs? Would General Motors be ethically correct in adopting a similar affirmative action hiring policy? Can you think of cases in which an employee's race or ethnic background would be a qualification—or a disqualification—for employment? Given the most recent cases discussed, do you think the Court effectively has dismissed affirmative action as an option for college admissions committees?

Questions, Projects, and Exercises

1. Maya confides in her friend and colleague, Alicia, "My husband Gene is very sick. I haven't shared this with anyone else at work because I didn't want them to think I couldn't manage my responsibilities. He was diagnosed last year with progressive Parkinson's and I thought it would move slowly, and that I could handle everything. Believe me, I am trying to keep everything under control, but our home life is just overwhelming me already. You couldn't imagine how hard this is—physically and emotionally—plus there's the added pressure of keeping it under wraps at work. You know they'll start diminishing my role on those larger projects if they knew my attention might be diverted, and Gene and I just can't risk the financial instability that it might cause. I really appreciate being able to talk to you. I had to get this off my chest, and I knew I could trust you." Alicia offered her shoulder and told Maya that she could count on her to cover for her, if need be, or to support her in any way she needed. Three weeks later, Alicia and Maya are separately called into the president's office and told that they are both being considered for a more senior-level position. This new position would require a great commitment of both time and energy and would involve taking on a large number of subordinates for mentoring and development. Both women express a strong interest in the position and are told that they will learn of the president's decision within 2 weeks. What should Alicia do with the information Maya gave her, if anything? Notwithstanding your response to the previous question, if Alicia chooses to inform the president of Maya's current situation, would you consider that action to be wrong, unethical? If you were the president in this current scenario, what could you do to impact the corporate culture to ensure that your preferred result in this dilemma occurred in the future?

2. Review the discussion in the chapter regarding global labor challenges. Choose a specific issue, such as child labor or sweatshop labor. Go online and find a news story about a particular company accused of employing child labor or sweatshop labor. How did the company involved defend itself against the accusations? Did it deny involvement in those practices or, rather, defend the practices themselves? Do you find the company's defense convincing? Why or why not? Would a different defense be more plausible?

3. We can distinguish due process from just cause in the following way: Imagine a company wanted to abandon the arbitrary nature of employment at will and ensure that its employees were treated fairly in any termination decision. Can you imagine how the employment environment in that firm might be different than in other firms? One approach would be to specify the acceptable reasons for terminating an employee. Obvious candidates would include absenteeism, incompetent job performance, theft, fraud, and economic necessity. This approach might also identify unacceptable reasons for dismissal. Such a policy would be identified as a "just cause" practice because it defines the factors that would justify dismissing an employee for cause. But creating such a list could be a challenge in that one would have to know beforehand all possible reasons for firing someone. As the common law clearly shows, one cannot anticipate all future ways in which something unjust could occur. As a result, a due process policy might be created to complement, or substitute for, a just cause policy. A policy guaranteeing due process, for example, would outline procedures that must be followed before an employee can be dismissed. The process itself is what determines a just dismissal. If an employer followed the process, the decision would be considered just; if the process was violated, then dismissal would be considered unjust. Such procedures might include regular written performance appraisals, prior warnings, documentation, probationary periods, rights to appeal, or response to accusations. Can you imagine other ways in which this hypothetical firm might change standard processes to ensure fairness?

   - What are the key facts relevant to issues of due process and fairness?
   - What are the ethical issues involved in your decision and implementation?
   - Who are the stakeholders involved in your decision?
   - What alternatives are available to you?
   - How would each of your alternatives affect each of the stakeholders you have identified?
   - Where might you look for additional guidance to assist you in resolving this particular dilemma?

4. What is the difference in your mind, and in your common usage, between a perception, a generalization, and a stereotype? Can you give an example of each? After doing so, go to the web and find dictionary-equivalent definitions of the terms to determine whether your common understanding is the correct one. Is each or are all consistently unethical judgments or are they sometimes or always ethically justified in their use and implementation? Under what conditions?

5. A particular research study provides some evidence that those born between 1979 and 1994 are perceived as "impatient, self-serving, disloyal, unable to delay gratification and, in short, feeling that they are entitled to everything without working for it." The study dubs this group the "entitlement generation." Do you know people born during those years? Is this true generally or would you consider the perception instead a stereotype? From where do you think it stems?

6. As a result of rising health care costs and the challenge to contain them, companies are trying to encourage employees to take better care of themselves, and some are even penalizing employees if they do not. In 2012, Walmart Inc. started charging tobacco-using employees higher health care premiums, but also offered free smoking cessation programs to all employees. While the Patient Protection and Affordable Care Act (passed in 2012) prohibits health insurers from rejecting people with preexisting

conditions, it still allows insurers to charge higher premiums based on risk factors such as age, location, family composition, and tobacco use. Tobacco use carries the heaviest penalties, allowing insurers to charge premium rates as much as 50% higher for smokers than nonsmokers under the law. A survey conducted by a consulting firm and the National Business Group on Health reports that about 40% of American employers reward or penalize employees based on tobacco use (smoke and smokeless). In addition, a growing number of companies are refusing to hire smokers. What do you think of businesses' attempts to decrease health care costs by helping employees become healthier? What are the ethical issues associated with a firm's choice to cut health care costs by eliminating people who are unhealthy? What rights, duties, responsibilities, and consequences does this strategy imply? Do you think people who don't take care of themselves should be responsible for their increased health care costs? How would you feel personally if your past health conditions and current health practices were part of an employment application?

7. You run a small consulting business that serves a relatively diverse community and have twenty-four employees in professional positions. You are not subject to Executive Order 11246. You are concerned that, of the employees in professional positions, your workplace has only one African American, no other employees of color, and three women. At this time, your upper-level management—the top six executives and you—are all white males. On the other hand, you have fifteen support staff (secretaries and other clerical workers), of whom fourteen are women and eleven are either African American or Latino.

   You would very much like to better represent the community in which you do business, and you believe a diverse workforce has significant business benefits. You therefore decide to institute a program that will increase the numbers of minorities and women in professional positions as soon as possible. Is this permissible? Do you have all the relevant facts you will need to answer this question? What steps will you undertake in your plan to increase these proportions, and what pitfalls must you avoid?

8. You are a senior global human resource manager for a large apparel retailer that purchases goods from all over the world. The media have focused a great deal of attention on the conditions of your suppliers' workplaces and, for myriad reasons including a strong commitment to your values-based mission as well as a concern for your reputation, you are paying close attention to the wages paid to the workers who construct your clothing. Your suppliers in several locations have agreed to talk with you about developing a policy that would apply throughout your operations—now and in the future, wherever you plan to do business—and would impose a minimum wage requirement for all factory workers. You begin to explore some of the resources publicly available to you, such as www.globalexchange.org, www.workersrights.org, www.fairlabor.org, and www.ethicaltrade.org/, to find out what other firms are doing and what labor advocates recommend in terms of language for policies such as these. You explore Nike's website at www.nikeinc.com, Adida's website at www.adidas-group.com, and others. Now it is time to begin constructing your own policy. What will you include, how specific will you make this policy, how will you determine what will be the "living wage" in each region, and what elements will it contain? Please draft a policy for your company on implementing a living wage worldwide.

9. As a project manager, Kelly is leading a team on an international business trip where she is scheduled to do a presentation on its project and to negotiate a deal. Just a few days before the trip, Kelly gets a call asking whether she is willing to let a male member of her team do all the talking because the managers at the company with whom they were

planning to do business feel more comfortable dealing with men. Kelly is told that she would still be in charge and that this would never happen again. If this deal works out, it would prove very profitable for the company as well as for Kelly's career. Kelly thinks about the situation in which she finds herself; she has worked very hard on this project and, if the deal is successful, she is bound to get a promotion. On the other hand, she feels discriminated against based on the fact that she is a woman. She has the choice of acting on her principles and calling off the deal, or going ahead with this modification on a "one-time basis" and getting a promotion. After contemplating the issue for a while, she decides to go ahead with the deal and let someone else do all the talking. When they get back, she is promoted and everybody is happy. What do you think of Kelly's decision? Could this situation be prevented all together? If you were in a similar situation, what would you choose to do, and why?

10. *Fortune* magazine compiles a "Best Companies to Work For" list every year. Go to its website, http://fortune.com/best-companies/, and review the full list. See if you can spot trends or similarities, if any, among the listed companies and find policies or programs that you think may help attract employees.

Key Terms

After reading this chapter, you should have a clear understanding of the following key terms. For a complete definition, please see the Glossary.

affirmative action, *p. 213*

child labor, *p. 201*

common-law agency test, *p. 182*

diversity, *p. 209*

downsize, *p. 185*

due process, *p. 178*

economic realities test, *p. 182*

employment at will (EAW), *p. 181*

IRS 20-factor analysis, *p. 182*

just cause, *p. 184*

multiculturalism, *p. 211*

Occupational Safety and Health Administration (OSHA), *p. 194*

reverse discrimination, *p. 213*

sweatshops, *p. 197*

Endnotes

1. Source: United Nations, Universal Declaration of Human Rights.

2. D. C. Weiss, "Judge Tosses Wrongful Termination Claim by Woman Forced to Resign after Flipping off Trump Motorcade," *ABA Journal* (July 2, 2018), www.abajournal.com/news/article/wrongful_termination_claim_trump_motorcade/ (accessed February 22, 2019). See also C. MacDonald, "Was It Right to Fire an Employee for Giving President Trump the Finger?" *Canadian Business* (November 13, 2017), www.canadianbusiness.com/blogs-and-comment/trump-middle-finger-fired/ (accessed March 5, 2019).

3. K. Draper and K. Belson, "Colin Kaepernick and the N.F.L. Settle Collusion Case," *The New York Times* (February 15, 2019), www.nytimes.com/2019/02/15/sports/nfl-colin-kaepernick.html (accessed February 21, 2019).

4. M. Ehrenkranz, "Let's Be Very Clear About What Happened to James Damore," *Gizmodo* (January 17, 2018), https://gizmodo.com/lets-be-very-clear-about-what-happened-to-james-damore-1822160852 (accessed February 22, 2019).

5. Source: James Damore, Google's Ideological Echo Chamber (Memo) (Fall 2017).

6. J. Eidelson, "Google's Firing of Engineer James Damore Did Not Break Labor Law, NLRB Lawyer Concludes," *LA Times* (February 16, 2018), www.latimes.com/business/la-fi-tn-google-james-damore-20180216-story.html (accessed February 22, 2019).

7. NAVEX Global, *Top 10 Ethics & Compliance Trends for 2019* (2019), http://trust.navex-global.com/rs/852-MYR-807/images/top-ten-trends-2019-ebook.pdf.

8. A. Edmans, "28 Years of Stock Market Data Shows a Link Between Employee Satisfaction and Long-Term Value," *Harvard Business Review* (March 24, 2016), https://hbr.org/2016/03/28-years-of-stock-market-data-shows-a-link-between-employee-satisfaction-and-long-term-value (accessed March 6, 2019); D. Pontefract, "If Culture Comes First, Performance Will Follow," *Forbes* (May 25, 2017), www.forbes.com/sites/danpontefract/2017/05/25/if-culture-comes-first-performance-will-follow/#45db31586e62 (accessed March 6, 2019).

9. K. Higginbottom, "U.S. Employees Are Still Loyal to Their Employers," *Forbes* (September 30, 2018), www.forbes.com/sites/karenhigginbottom/2018/09/30/us-employees-still-loyal-to-their-employers/#e81990c7fc05 (accessed March 6, 2019).

10. Christine Porath and Christine Pearson, "The Price of Incivility," *Harvard Business Review* 91, no. 1/2 (2013), pp. 114–21.

11. Ethics Resource Center, "The State of Ethics and Compliance in the Workplace: Global Business Ethics Survey" (March 2018), www.ethics.org/knowledge-center/2018-gbes/ (accessed March 6, 2019).

12. W. Frick, "When Treating Workers Well Leads to More Innovation," *Harvard Business Review* (November 3, 2015), https://hbr.org/2015/11/when-treating-workers-well-leads-to-more-innovation (accessed March 6, 2019); N. Andriotis, "Want Better Business Results? Involve Your Employees," *eFrontLearning.com* (December 2017), www.efrontlearning.com/blog/2017/12/employee-involvement-great-business-results.html (accessed March 6, 2019); E. Ivanov, "Innovation 'Quid Pro Quo': Firms That Treat Workers Better Are More Innovative," *Innovation Observer* (March 22, 2018), https://innovationobserver.com/2018/03/22/innovation-quid-pro-quo-firms-that-treat-workers-better-are-more-innovative/ (accessed March 6, 2019).

13. For a curious legal case on this question, see *Sampath v. Concurrent Tech. Corp.*, No. 08-2370, 299 F. App'x (3d Cir. Nov. 14, 2008), www.ca3.uscourts.gov/opinarch/082370np.pdf (accessed August 11, 2012) ["Title VII does not 'mandate a happy workplace.'"]; and *Jensen v. Potter,* 435 F.3d 444, 451 (3d Cir. 2006), *overruled in part on other grounds by Burlington N. & Santa Fe Ry. Co. v. White,* 548 U.S. 53 (2006).

14. Jeffrey Pfeffer, "Shareholders First? Not So Fast . . .," *Harvard Business Review* 87 no. 7/8 (2009); see also Jeffrey Pfeffer, *The Human Equation: Building Profits by Putting People First* (Boston: Harvard University Press, 1998).

15. Neal M. Ashkanasy, W. J. Zerbe, and Charmine E. J. Härtel, *Emotions and the Organizational Fabric* (Bingley, UK: Emerald, 2014), www.emeraldinsight.com/1746-9791/10 (accessed February 21, 2019).

16. E. Fink-Samnick , "The Side Effects of Workplace Bullying in Healthcare," *ICD10 Monitor* (June 18, 2018), www.icd10monitor.com/the-side-effects-of-workplace-bullying-in-healthcare (accessed March 5, 2019); see also G. Namie, "2017 Workplace Bullying Institute U.S. Workplace Bullying Survey," Workplace Bullying Institute (2017), http://workplacebullying.org/multi/pdf/2017/2017-WBI-US-Survey.pdf (accessed March 6, 2019).

17. Source: D. Yamada, "Workplace Bullying and Ethical Leadership," *Legal Studies Research Paper Series,* 08-37 (November 14, 2008), http://ssrn.com/abstract=1301554 (accessed March 6, 2019).

18. Source: *Payne v. Western & A.A.R. Co.*, 81 Tenn. 507 (1884).

19. C. Lakshman et al., "Ethics Trumps Culture? A Cross-National Study of Business Leader Responsibility for Downsizing and CSR Perceptions," *Journal of Business Ethics Online*

(October 4, 2013), http://link.springer.com/article/10.1007%2Fs10551-013-1907-8 (accessed March 6, 2019).

20. Source: José Luis Illueca García-Labrado, "Ethics and Restructuring: Promising Match or Marriage of Convenience?" *IESE Business School: Business Ethics Blog* (January 24, 2014), http://blog.iese.edu/ethics/2014/01/24/ethics-and-restructuring-promisingmatch-or-marriage-of-convenience/ (accessed February 21, 2019).

21. Leadership IQ, "Don't Expect Layoff Survivors to Be Grateful," *PRWeb* (December 10, 2008), www.prweb.com/releases/Leadership_IQ/Layofs/prweb1754974.htm (accessed March 6, 2019).

22. Source: Leadership IQ, "Don't Expect Layoff Survivors to Be Grateful" (December 10, 2008), www.prweb.com/releases/Leadership_IQ/Layoffs/prweb1754974.htm (accessed March 6, 2019).

23. Source: R. S. Larsen, "Leadership in a Values-Based Organization," *The Sears Lectureship in Business Ethics at Bentley College* (February 7, 2002).

24. S. Khimm, "Offshoring Creates as Many U.S. Jobs as It Kills, Study Says," *Washington Post* (July 12, 2012), www.washingtonpost.com/news/wonk/wp/2012/07/12/study-offshoring-creates-as-many-u-s-jobs-as-it-kills/?utm_term=.7464c07945a0 (accessed March 1, 2019); K. Amadeo, "How Outsourcing Jobs Affects the U.S. Economy," *The Balance* (March 19, 2018), www.thebalance.com/how-outsourcing-jobs-affects-the-u-s-economy-3306279 (accessed March 1, 2019).

25. Source: Benjamin Powell and Matt Zwolinski, "The Ethical and Economic Case against Sweatshop Labor: A Critical Assessment," *Journal of Business Ethics* 107, no. 4 (2012), pp. 449–72.

26. Benjamin Powell and Matt Zwolinski, "The Ethical and Economic Case against Sweatshop Labor: A Critical Assessment," *Journal of Business Ethics* 107, no. 4 (2012), pp. 449–72.

27. Source: G. Leibowitz, "Apple CEO Tim Cook: This Is the Number 1 Reason We Make iPhones in China (It's Not What You Think)," *Inc.* (December 17, 2017), https://www.inc.com/glenn-leibowitz/apple-ceo-tim-cook-this-is-number-1-reason-we-make-iphones-in-china-its-not-what-you-think.html (accessed March 5, 2019).

28. Source: D. Arnold and L. Hartman, "Worker Rights and Low Wage Industrialization: How to Avoid Sweatshops," *Human Rights Quarterly* 28, no. 3 (August 2006), pp. 676–700.

29. Source: Denis G. Arnold and Norman E. Bowie, "Sweatshops and Respect for Persons," Business Ethics Quarterly 221 (2003), pp. 223–224.

30. L. Hartman, B. Shaw, and R. Stevenson, "Exploring the Ethics and Economics of Global Labor Standards: A Challenge to Integrated Social Contract Theory," *Business Ethics Quarterly* 13, no. 2 (2003), pp. 193–220.

31. P. Werhane, S. Kelley, L. Hartman, and D. Moberg, *Alleviating Poverty through Profitable Partnerships: Globalization, Markets and Economic Well-Being* (New York: Routledge/Taylor & Francis, 2009), chap. 1.

32. Ethical Trade Initiative, "Our Members," www.ethicaltrade.org/about-eti/our-members (accessed March 6, 2019).

33. Ethical Trading Initiative, "ETI Base Code," secs. 5.1–5.3, www.ethicaltrade.org/eti-base-code.

34. "HERProject: Investing in Women for a Better World" (2010), http://herproject.org/ (accessed March 6, 2019).

35. UNICEF, "Child Labour" (December 2017), https://data.unicef.org/topic/child-pro-tection/child-labour/ (accessed March 6, 2019); ECLT Foundation, "152 MILLION CHILDREN in Child Labour" (n.d.), www.eclt.org/en/152-million-children-in-child-labour (accessed March 6, 2019).

36. P. Roggero, V. Mangiaterra, F. Bustreo, and F. Rosati, "The Health Impact of Child Labor in Developing Countries: Evidence from Cross-Country Data," *American Journal of Public Health* 97, no. 2 (2007), pp. 271–75. doi: 10.2105/AJPH.2005.066829.

37. However, some advocacy groups fail to consider all perspectives. For example, the Global Reporting Initiative's discussion on its Child Labour Indicators fails to take into account the impact of the termination of children beyond their removal from the workplace.

38. Source: Tim Worstall, "Bolivia Legalises Child Labour and Child Labour Might Decline in Bolivia," *Forbes* (July 21, 2014), http://www.forbes.com/sites/timworstall/2014/07/21/bolivia-legalises-child-labour-and-child-labour-might-decline-in-bolivia/ (accessed March 6, 2019).

39. EEOC, "Sexual Harassment" (n.d.), www.eeoc.gov/laws/types/sexual_harassment.cfm (accessed March 6, 2019).

40. R. Thomas et al., "Women in the Workplace," *McKinsey & Co. & Lean In* (2018), www.mckinsey.com/featured-insights/gender-equality/women-in-the-workplace-2018 (accessed March 10, 2019).

41. S. Thomson, "Here's Why You Didn't Get That Job: Your Name," *World Economic Forum* (May 23, 2017), www.weforum.org/agenda/2017/05/job-applications-resume-cv-name-descrimination/ (accessed March 10, 2019).

42. International Labour Office, "A Quantum Leap for Gender Equality: For a Better Future of Work for All" (2019), www.ilo.org/wcmsp5/groups/public/—dgreports/—dcomm/—publ/documents/publication/wcms_674831.pdf (accessed March 9, 2019); N. Graf et al., "The Narrowing, but Persistent, Gender Gap in Pay," *Pew Research Center* (April 9, 2018), www.pewresearch.org/fact-tank/2018/04/09/gender-pay-gap-facts/ (accessed March 9, 2019).

43. Marianne Cooper, "For Women Leaders, Likability and Success Hardly Go Hand-in-Hand," *Harvard Business Review,* HBR Blog Network (April 30, 2013), http://blogs.hbr.org/2013/04/for-women-leaders-likability-a/ (accessed March 10, 2019).

44. Ken Auletta, "Why Jill Abramson Was Fired," *The New Yorker* (May 14, 2014), www.newyorker.com/business/currency/why-jill-abramson-was-fired (accessed March 10, 2019).

45. C. von Hippel, C. Wiryakusuma, J. Bowden, and M. Shochet, "Stereotype Threat and Female Communication Styles," *Personal Social Psychology Bulletin* 37, no. 10 (2011).

46. J. Bourke, "Diversity and Inclusion: The Reality Gap," *Deloitte Insights* (2017), www2.deloitte.com/insights/us/en/focus/human-capital-trends/2017/diversity-and-inclusion-at-the-workplace.html (accessed March 10, 2019).

47. Ernst & Young, "Point of View: Women on Boards: Global Approaches to Advancing Diversity" (July 2014), www.womenonboards.co.uk/resource-centre/reports/diversity/2014-ey-diversity-global-approach-wob-who-is-doing.pdf (accessed March 10, 2019).

48. European Women on Boards, "Ethics and Boards European Gender Diversity Index" (July 31, 2018), https://europeanwomenonboards.eu/wp-content/uploads/2018/11/ewob_eb_ranking.pdf (accessed March 10, 2019) (countries examined included Belgium, the Czech Republic, Finland, France, Germany, Italy, the Netherlands, Spain, the United Kingdom); A. Ekin, "Quotas Get More Women on Boards and Stir Change from

Within," *Horizon* (September 6, 2018), https://horizon-magazine.eu/article/quotas-get-more-women-boards-and-stir-change-within.html (accessed March 10, 2019); Mission of Norway to the European Union, "Sharing Norway's Experience with Gender Quotas for Boards" (October 17, 2017), www.norway.no/en/missions/eu/about-the-mission/news-events-statements/news2/sharing-norways-experience-with-gender-quotas-for-boards (accessed March 10, 2019); C. Zillman, "The EU Is Taking a Drastic Step to Put More Women on Corporate Boards," *Fortune* (November 20, 2017), http://fortune.com/2017/11/20/women-on-boards-eu-gender-quota/ (accessed March 10, 2019).

49. Deloitte, "Women in the Boardroom: A Global Perspective" (2017), www2.deloitte.com/global/en/pages/risk/articles/women-in-the-boardroom5th-edition.html (accessed March 10, 2019).

50. H. Landy, "Fortune 500 Companies Appointed a Record Percentage of Women to Their Boards Last Year," *Quartz at Work* (July 26, 2018), https://qz.com/work/1340544/the-fortune-500-appointed-a-record-percentage-of-women-to-boards-in-2017/ (accessed March 10, 2019); Judith Warner, "Women's Leadership Gap" (2016), Center for American Progress, www.americanprogress.org/issues/women/report/2015/08/04/118743/the-womens-leadership-gap/ (accessed March 10, 2019).

51. Boston Consulting Group, "Diversity and Inclusion" (2018), www.bcg.com/capabilities/diversity-inclusion/overview.aspx (accessed March 10, 2019).

52. PwC, "2018 Annual Corporate Directors Survey" (October 2018), www.pwc.com/acds2018 (accessed March 10, 2019).

53. M. Tarm, "Brokerage Giant Settles Discrimination Lawsuit," *Boston Globe* (August 29, 2013), www.bostonglobe.com/business/2013/08/28/brokerage-giant-settles-discrimination-lawsuit/X0S7hAbQlYotExOjHZXlQK/story.html (accessed March 10, 2019); C. Suddath, "Hey Merrill Lynch, It's Not a Good Idea to Tell Women to 'Seduce the Boys' Club,'" *Bloomberg Businessweek* (July 29, 2013), www.businessweek.com/articles/2013-07-29/hey-merrill-lynch-its-not-a-good-idea-to-tell-women-to-seduce-the-boys-club (accessed March 10, 2019).

54. M. Rozen, "Merrill Lynch and Wells Fargo Learn Tough Lessons from Discrimination Suits," *Financial Advisor IQ* (June 11, 2018), https://financialadvisoriq.com/c/1998003/229204/merrill_lynch_wells_fargo_learn_tough_lessons_from_discrimination_suits (accessed March 10, 2019); K. Weise, "Meet the Broker Who Made Merrill Pay for Racial Bias," *Bloomberg Businessweek* (December 3, 2013), www.bloomberg.com/news/2013-11-27/merrill-lynch-messed-up-my-career-says-broker-who-won-lawsuit.html (accessed March 10, 2019).

55. Source: Mazzoni Center, "Press Release" (March 29, 2018), https://www.mazzonicenter.org/news/board-directors-mazzoni-center-issues-statement-response-concerns-regarding-ceo-search-process (accessed March 10, 2019).

56. Clarence Thomas, *My Grandfather's Son* (New York: Harper Perennial, 2008), pp. 87–88; quoted in T. Loomis, "The 15-Cent Diploma: Clarence Thomas Says Affirmative Action Cheapened His Yale Law School Degree and Made It Almost Impossible for Him to Find a Law Firm Job," *American Lawyer* 30, no. 6 (2008).

57. Source: General Motors, "Brief of General Motors as Amicus Curiae in Support of Defendants," in *Gratz v. Bollinger*, 539 U.S 244 (2003).

58. Source: United States Court of Appeals.

59. A. Liptak, "Court Backs Michigan on Affirmative Action," *The New York Times* (April 22, 2014), www.nytimes.com/2014/04/23/us/supreme-court-michigan-affirmative-action-ban.html (accessed March 10, 2019).

Chapter 7

Ethical Decision Making: Technology and Privacy in the Workplace

This "telephone" has too many shortcomings to be seriously considered as a means of communication. The device is inherently of no value to us.

Western Union Internal Memo, 1876

Technology is nothing. What's important is that you have a faith in people, that they're basically good and smart, and if you give them tools, they'll do wonderful things with them.

Steve Jobs, Chair, CEO and Co-Founder of Apple, Inc.

Things do not change; we change.

Henry David Thoreau

The right to be let alone is indeed the beginning of all freedom.

William O. Douglas, Supreme Court Justice (1939–1975), in Public Utilities Commission v. Pollak, *343 U.S. 451, 467 (1952) (dissenting)*

Arguing that you don't care about the right to privacy because you have nothing to hide is no different than saying you don't care about free speech because you have nothing to say.

Edward Snowden, former Central Intelligence Agency employee and former contractor for the U.S. government

Opening Decision Point

Being Smart about Smartphones

One afternoon, your team is assembled in a client's conference room, pitching a new database system. This pitch concerns an important sale so, while a colleague presents your team's slides detailing the benefits of your system, you watch the client's team carefully for their reactions and take detailed notes on your smartphone.

The client's chief information officer (CIO) and chief financial officer (CFO) are both present, and you are paying special attention to the CIO, watching her reaction to each feature mentioned during the presentation. By the end of the meeting, you have typed up a brief report that will help your team to prepare for the follow-up visit that is planned for the following week.

When you get back to your own office, your boss—the head of sales—is waiting for you. "This deal is dead in the water," he says. "I just got a call from our client's CFO, and she is furious. She says that you spent the entire meeting fiddling with your phone instead of paying attention. What on earth were you thinking?" While your boss is speaking, you feel your phone vibrating. You are expecting a call from another key client, one who does not like to have to chase you down—ever! Of course, clearly this is not a good time to take a call. But it also is not a good moment to lose a key client either. You know the phone currently is set to ring with a sound after three vibrating alerts.

1. Please list as many ethical issues as you can identify that are raised by the use of smartphones in the workplace.
2. Did you do anything wrong this morning in the meeting?
3. Clearly, this morning's client was offended. Having the benefit of hindsight now, how might you have handled your actions this morning differently in order to have prevented that offense?
4. At what point does behavior some might consider impolite—for instance, actions that might offend others, such as answering emails during a meeting or even playing games because you are bored or tired—cross the line into unethical behavior?
5. What type of policy would you suggest for an organization regarding the use of smartphones in the workplace, if any?
6. Should the rules be different for using smartphones during in-house meetings versus during meetings with clients or suppliers?
7. What will you do next? Will you answer your phone? How will you answer your boss's concerns?

 ## Chapter Objectives

After reading this chapter, you will be able to:

1. Explain and distinguish the two definitions of privacy.
2. Describe the ethical sources of privacy as a fundamental value.
3. Identify the legal sources of privacy protection, including the concept of a "reasonable expectation of privacy."

4. Discuss recent developments in connection with employee monitoring.
5. Identify and explain the risks involved in a failure to understand the implications of technology and its use.
6. Enumerate the reasons why employers choose to monitor employees' work.
7. Discuss the ethics of monitoring as it applies to drug testing.
8. Discuss the ethics of monitoring as it applies to polygraphs, genetic testing, and other forms of surveillance.
9. Explain the interests of an employer in regulating an employee's activities outside of work.
10. Discuss the implications of world events, like recent immigration policy changes, on business decisions about privacy.

Introduction

Law professor Jeffrey Hirsch warns us of the impending onset of the "blended workplace," which he claims is a bit more threatening than its neutral name may sound. Hirsch cautions each of us—as employees or future employees—that our inescapable destiny is dictated by the ease of technology, which is making some jobs and activities easier to perform "while simultaneously providing employers more tools to monitor and control workers—thereby shifting the balance of power further toward business and away from labor."[1] Hirsch admits that this same technology also helps us to seek better working conditions, but he predicts that those benefits will be far outweighed by the threats to worker autonomy and potentially worse infringements.

Are Hirsch's ominous premonitions correct? As an individual, do you sense even now that your personal information is vulnerable, both in your workplace and beyond? Or do you see technology from a different perspective? Do these threats unfortunately intimidate people so that we do not use technology to its fullest capacity and do not get all of its positive value? Scholars Sethi and Stubbings explain that tech could help all of us so much more than it already does. You probably could come up with plenty of other ideas, but they suggest that we could use it far better, such as:

- Tackle burnout by managing productivity more effectively.
- Build social resilience through connecting with people, both on the job and off.
- Encourage adaptability and agility by preparing people for job changes.
- Support "intrapreneurship" (encouraging on-the-job innovations and risk taking).
- Offer much more autonomy.[2]

There can be no doubt that the business world already has gained enormous benefits from the technological revolution. However, we do not have to wait for some far-off future to experience some of the challenges that Hirsch predicts above, as well. We already are grappling with ethical questions, particularly as this

Reality Check   *Privacy in the Future—It Is Now!*

Privacy issues around electronic monitoring are only getting more complicated. Some companies use electronic wristbands and other devices to monitor employee locations, productivity, and even employee communication tendencies.

One company, called Humanyze, specializes in these types of "people analytics." *The Economist* explains:

> Its employees mill around an office full of sunlight and computers, as well as beacons that track their location and interactions. Everyone is wearing an ID badge the size of a credit card and the depth of a book of matches. It contains a microphone that picks up whether they are talking to one another; Bluetooth and infrared sensors to monitor where they are; and an accelerometer to record when they move.

"Every aspect of business is becoming more data-driven. There's no reason the people side of business shouldn't be the same," says Ben Waber, Humanyze's boss. The company's staff are treated much the same way as its clients. Data from their employees' badges are integrated with information from their e-mail and calendars to form a full picture of how they spend their time at work. Clients get to see only team-level statistics, but Humanyze's employees can look at their own data, which include metrics such as time spent with people of the same sex, activity levels and the ratio of time spent speaking versus listening.

Source: "There Will Be Little Privacy in the Workplace of the Future." *The Economist: Special Report* (May 28, 2018), https://www.economist.com/special-report/2018/03/28/there-will-be-little-privacy-in-the-workplace-of-the-future (accessed February 21, 2019).

technology impacts employee and consumer privacy. You may recall in Chapter 1 that information threat, loss, and attack are some of the greatest concerns of executives worldwide.[3] One 2018 study found that, on average, U.S. companies lose $3.6 million annually from data breaches.[4] This chapter will review some of the key ethical issues of technology and privacy, with a particular focus on privacy in the workplace.

privacy
The right to be "let alone" within a personal zone of solitude, and/or the right to control information about oneself.

Privacy issues in the workplace raise ethical issues involving individual rights as well as those involving utilitarian consequences. Workplace privacy issues evoke an inherent conflict (or some might call it a delicate balance) between what some may consider to be a fundamental right of the employer to protect its interests and the similarly grounded right of the employee to be free from wrongful intrusions into her or his personal affairs. This conflict can arise in the workplace environment through the regulation of personal activities or personal choices, or through various forms of monitoring. (See Reality Check "Privacy in the Future—It Is Now!") Some forms of monitoring, such as drug testing, may occur after a job offer has been made but even before the individual begins working. Other forms might also occur once the individual begins to work, such as electronic surveillance of email.

Similarly, contrasting utilitarian arguments can be offered on the ethics of monitoring employees. The employer can argue that the only way to manage the workplace effectively and efficiently is to maintain knowledge about and control over all that takes place within it. The employee can simultaneously contend that she or he will be most productive in a supportive environment based on trust, respect, and autonomy. In any case, the question of balance remains—whose rights should prevail or which consequences take precedent?

This chapter will examine technology and its impact on these issues. We will explore the origins of the right to privacy as well as the legal and ethical limitations on that right. We will also explore the means by which employers monitor performance and the ethical issues that arise in connection with these *potential* technological invasions to privacy. We will then connect these issues of technology and privacy to the balance of rights and responsibilities between employers and employees.

Because of the extraordinary breadth of the technology's reach, this chapter could not possibly address all issues under its umbrella. We have therefore sought to limit our coverage in this chapter to issues of technology and privacy *in the workplace* and related arenas. For instance, the intersection between ethics, intellectual property, the law, and technology opens far too many doors for the survey anticipated by this text and will therefore not be examined within this overview. Similarly, though a phone company's decision whether to comply with the government's request to turn over phone records certainly raises issues of both technology and privacy, it is not necessarily related to issues of employment, so we will not be examining that decision. However, readers should be aware of these issues and seek to apply the lessons of this chapter to wider issues of privacy and technology in business.

The Right to Privacy

privacy rights
The legal and ethical sources of protection for privacy in personal data.

Privacy is a surprisingly vague and disputed value in contemporary society. With the tremendous increase in computer technology in recent decades, calls for greater protection of **privacy rights** have increased. Yet there is widespread confusion concerning the nature, extent, and value of privacy. Some Western countries, for example, do not acknowledge a legal right to privacy as recognized within the United States, while others such as New Zealand and Australia seem far more sophisticated in their centralized and consistent approaches to personal privacy issues. Canada's privacy structure is similar to that in the U.S., where its Privacy Act applies to employee information in federal government institutions and other legislation has somewhat limited application to the private sector.

Even within the United States there is significant disagreement about privacy. The U.S. Constitution makes no mention of a right to privacy, and the major Supreme Court decisions that have relied on a fundamental right to privacy, *Griswold v. Connecticut*[5] and *Roe v. Wade,*[6] remain highly contentious and controversial. As you will read in this section and throughout this chapter, managing issues related to individual privacy is a balancing act between autonomy and access, control and knowledge—and ethical arguments for all sides are awfully persuasive!

Defining Privacy

OBJECTIVE

Two general and connected understandings of privacy can be found in the legal and philosophical literature on this topic: privacy as a *right to be "left alone"* within a personal zone of solitude and privacy as the *right to control information* about oneself. It is worthwhile to consider the connection between these two senses of privacy. Certain decisions that we make about how we live our lives, as well as the control of personal information, play a crucial role in defining our own personal identity. Privacy is important because it establishes the boundary between individuals and thereby defines one's individuality. The right to control certain extremely personal decisions and information helps determine the kind of person we are and the person we become. To the degree that we value the inherent dignity of each individual and the right of each person to be treated with respect, we must recognize that certain personal decisions and information are rightfully the exclusive domain of the individual.

Many people believe that a right to be left alone is much too broad to be recognized as a moral right. It would be difficult for employees, for example, to claim that they should be totally left alone in the workplace. This has led some people to conclude that a better understanding focuses on privacy as involving the *control* of personal information. From this perspective, the clearest case of an invasion of privacy occurs when others come to know personal information about us, as when a stranger reads your email or eavesdrops on a personal conversation. Yet, the claim that a *right* of privacy implies a right to control all personal information might also be too broad. Surely, there are many occasions when others, particularly within an employment context, can legitimately know or need to know even quite personal information about us.

Philosopher George Brenkert has argued that the informational sense of privacy involves a relationship between two parties, A and B, and the nature of the personal information shared about A. Privacy is violated only when B comes to know information about A that B never should have known. For instance, let's say I have a relationship with a mortgage company because I take out a loan to finance my home purchase. My relationship with my mortgage broker justifies my broker having access to my credit rating. On the other hand, my relationship with my students does not justify their access to that same information. My privacy is not violated in the first example, but it would be violated in the second one.

Limiting access to personal information based on one's relationships is an important way to preserve personal integrity and individuality. It is perhaps that *choice* of limitation or control that is the source of one's sense of privacy. As explained by legal scholar Jennifer Moore, "maintaining a zone of privacy gives you a degree of control over your role, relationship, and identity, which you would not have if everyone were aware of all available information about you. The choice is part of what makes it possible to be intimate with your friend and to be professional with your employer."[7]

reciprocal obligation
The concept that, while an employee has an obligation to respect the goals and property of the employer, the employer has a *reciprocal obligation* to respect the rights of the employee as well, including the employee's right to privacy.

OBJECTIVE

Ethical Sources of a Right to Privacy

The right to privacy has its origins in our fundamental, universal right to autonomy, in our right to make decisions about our personal existence without restriction. This right is restricted by a social contract in our culture that prevents us from infringing on someone else's right to her or his personal autonomy. Philosopher and academic Patricia Werhane describes this boundary as a **"reciprocal obligation."** For an individual to expect respect for her or his personal autonomy, that individual has a reciprocal obligation to respect the autonomy of others.[8]

Applied to the workplace, Werhane's concept of reciprocal obligation implies that, while an employee has an obligation to respect the goals and property of the employer, the employer has a reciprocal obligation to respect the rights of the employee as well, including the employee's right to privacy. Werhane has asserted that a bill of rights for the workplace would therefore include both the right of the employee to privacy and confidentiality and the right of employers to privacy in terms of confidentiality of trade secrets and so on. This contention is supported throughout traditional philosophical literature. Kant links the moral worth of individuals to "the supreme value of their rational capacities for normative self-determination" and considers privacy a categorical moral imperative.[9]

hypernorms
Values that are fundamental across culture and theory.

moral free space
That environment where hypernorms or universal rules do not govern or apply to ethical decisions, but instead culture or other influences govern decisions, as long as they are not in conflict with hypernorms. In other words, as long as a decision is not in conflict with a hypernorm, it rests within moral free space, and reasonable minds may differ as to what is ethical.

Ethicists Thomas Donaldson and Thomas Dunfee have developed an approach to ethical analysis that seeks to differentiate between those values that are fundamental across culture and theory, **hypernorms,** and those values that are determined within **moral free space** (which are not hypernorms). In order to identify hypernorms, Donaldson and Dunfee propose that we look to the convergence of religious, cultural, and philosophical beliefs around certain core principles. They offer as examples of hypernorms freedom of speech, the right to personal freedom, the right to physical movement, and informed consent. Individual privacy is at the core of many of these basic minimal rights and is, in fact, a necessary prerequisite to many of them. Indeed, a key finding of one survey of privacy in 50 countries around the world found the following:

> Privacy is a fundamental human right recognized in all major international treaties and agreements on human rights. Nearly every country in the world recognizes privacy as a fundamental human right in their constitution, either explicitly or implicitly. Most recently drafted constitutions include specific rights to access and control one's personal information.[10]

Accordingly, the value of privacy to civilized society is as great as the value of the various hypernorms to civilized existence. Ultimately, the failure to protect privacy may lead to an inability to protect personal freedom and autonomy. It is important to note here, in particular, that this discussion of privacy foundations might be considered by some to be particularly North American–based in its grounding in the protection of liberty and autonomy. These analysts would suggest that a European foundation would be based in a ground of the protection of human dignity.[11] Notwithstanding this claimed distinction in origin (a discussion that is outside of our scope, though not of our interest), there remains little argument of the vital nature of privacy as means by which to ensure other critical and fundamental hypernorms. See the Reality Check "Privacy: Europe Compared to the United States" for more information on the distinctions between Europe and the United States when it comes to privacy protection.

property rights
The boundaries defining actions that individuals can take in relation to other individuals regarding their personal information. If one individual has a *right* to her or his personal information, someone else has a commensurate duty to observe that right.

Finally, legal analysis of privacy using **property rights** perspective yields additional insight. "Property" is an individual's life and all nonprocreative derivatives of her or his life. Derivatives may include thoughts and ideas, as well as personal information. The concept of property *rights* involves a determination of who maintains control over tangibles and intangibles, including, therefore, personal information. Property rights relating to personal information thus define actions that

Reality Check *Privacy: Europe Compared to the United States*

EUROPE

In most European countries, privacy is considered to be a human right and is protected by, among other areas, strong digital privacy protections (see below). Privacy and dignity are often considered as joint principles from a European perspective, and their protection often surprises Americans. For instance, much privacy regulation in Europe emerges from large comprehensive legislation, rather than piecemeal acts applicable only to specific areas of privacy, as is common in the United States.

In Europe:

- The European Union adopted the *General Data Protection Regulation (GDPR)* in 2016 (with implementation deadlines by 2018), replacing earlier data protection law across Europe. The GDPR "strengthens rights of individuals with regard to the protection of their data, imposes more stringent obligations on those processing personal data, and provides for stronger regulatory enforcement powers."

  - The GDPR prohibits personal information from being collected or shared by companies without an individual's express permission. This prohibition prompted a slew of emails literally just days before the GDPR's implementation deadline sent from organizations to their entire mailing lists requesting permission to collect and/or share personal information. Many websites that collect personal data were modified to notify individuals only days—or even hours—before the deadline, for fear of heavy fines if they failed to comply.

  - Information about who is using the data and for what purpose must be provided in a clear, easily understandable manner. Further, individuals have the right to review the data and correct inaccuracies. This even includes data presented by internet search engines.

  - The GDPR levies heavy fines against any company that violates the regulation—up to 20 million euros or 4% of global annual revenue (whichever is greater).

  - GDPR is extraterritorial in its scope, which means that it applies to data collection around the world.

All companies—regardless of their size or location—are required to comply with GDPR if they offer free or paid goods or services to EU residents or monitor their behavior.

- On the other hand, government agencies are mostly exempt from the GDPR (i.e., wiretapping is used 130 times more in the Netherlands than in the United States and citizens still register their addresses with the local police in Germany).

- Companies that process data must register their activities with the government.

- Employers are prohibited from reading their workers' private email. (See additional implications for monitoring later in this chapter.)

- Authorities in some European countries can veto a parent's choice for their baby's name to preserve the child's dignity.

- Only debtors who have defaulted on loans generally receive the European equivalent of a credit report, which places them on a sort of lending "blacklist." Consumers who pay their bills on time do not get a "good" credit score.

- Artists possess inalienable "moral rights" over their creations that supersede copyright and allow them to prevent alterations that they think would show them in a bad light.

UNITED STATES

Europeans reserve a deep distrust for corporations, while Americans seem to be more concerned about government invasions of privacy. (Perhaps this distinction stems from American origins as colonists who chose to leave the British reign?) Nevertheless, privacy laws applicable to nongovernment actors, such as corporations, in the United States is a combination of legislation, regulation, and self-regulation rather than the government.

In the United States:

- The Constitution's Bill of Rights provides a few protections for an individual's right to privacy against government intrusion. For example, the Fourth Amendment bans unreasonable search and seizure. This protection is applicable to an individual's home, car, and person with certain exceptions for probable cause and officer danger, among other things. More recently, it has been applied to an individual's cell phone and other digital items (except when traveling through U.S. Customs and Border Control facilities).

- Employees surrender most of their rights to privacy when they enter and use company property. For instance, an employer usually can review employee emails and internet usage (under certain conditions).

- Courts support broad leeway for press freedom and allow the publication of even intimate details and personal information.

- Most states generally require companies to tell consumers when their personal information has been lost or stolen.

- Search engines and internet providers in the United States generally are protected from liability for passing on data unless they have direct knowledge they are false or violate copyright law.

- Artists can sell their works to the highest bidder with no strings attached and do not maintain a continuing

moral right over the creative product (i.e., when novelists sell the rights for their books to be made into film, they often lose control over how the work is presented on film).

Sources: Privacy International, "General Data Protection Regulation (GDPR)," http://privacyinternational.org/topics/general-data-protection-regulation-gdpr (accessed July 20, 2018); "GDPR Exemptions: Who Is Exempt from GDPR Requirements?" *HIPAA Journal* (May 11, 2018), www.hipaajournal.com/gdpr-exemptions-who-is-exempt-from-gdpr/ (accessed July 20, 2018); U.S. Department of Homeland Security, U.S. Customs and Border Control, "Inspection of Electronic Devices," https://www.cbp.gov/sites/default/files/documents/inspection-electronic-devices-tearsheet.pdf (accessed July 18, 2018); D. Fisher, "Europe's 'Right to Be Forgotten' Clashes with U.S. Right to Know," *Forbes* (May 16, 2014), www.forbes.com/sites/danielfisher/2014/05/16/europes-right-to-be-forgotten-clashes-with-u-s-right-to-know/ (accessed July 20, 2018); HG.org Legal Resources, "Data Protection Law," www.hg.org/data-protection.html (accessed July 20, 2018); Adam Liptak, "When American and European Ideas of Privacy Collide," *The New York Times* (February 27, 2010), www.nytimes.com/2010/02/28/weekinreview/28liptak.html (accessed July 20, 2018).

individuals can take in relation to other individuals regarding their personal information. If one individual has a *right* to her or his personal information, someone else has a commensurate duty to observe that right.

Why do we assume that an individual has the unfettered and exclusive right to her or his personal information? Private property rights depend on the existence and enforcement of a set of rules that define who has a right to undertake which activities on their own initiative and how the returns from those activities will be allocated. In other words, whether an individual has the exclusive right to her or his personal information depends on the existence and enforcement of a set of rules giving the individual that right. Do these rules exist in our society, legal or otherwise? In fact, as we will discuss later, the legal rules remain vague. Many legal theorists contend that additional or clearer rules regarding property rights in personal information would lead to an improved and more predictable market for this information, thus ending the arbitrary and unfair intrusions that may exist today as a result of market failures.

Legal Sources of a Right to Privacy in the United States

Each employee is a human with private thoughts, private communications, and a private life. These remain as dear to the employee the moment after the employee steps into the workplace or switches on an assigned computer as the moment before. Yet, if the employee needs the job, perhaps to pay the rent, feed her children, maintain a living geographically near to her elderly parents, or even maintain her status in the community, or her sense of self, then the American employee must, to a large extent, give up her privacy.[12]

As with others areas of lightning-quick advances, the law has not yet caught up with the technology involved in employee privacy. Many recent advances, thus much recent case law and therefore much of our discussion in this chapter, will focus on employee monitoring, which we will cover in detail shortly. As a result, this is one area where simply obeying the law may fall far short of responsible management practice. While the law might be clear with regard to tapping a worker's telephone, it is less clear in connection with monitoring a worker's email or text messages on a handheld device.

OBJECTIVE

Privacy can be legally protected in the United States in three ways: by the *Constitution* (federal or state), by federal and/or state *statutes,* and by the *common law.* Common law refers to the body of law comprised of the decisions handed down by U.S. courts, rather than specified in any particular statutes or regulations.

Fourth Amendment protection

The U.S. Constitution's Fourth Amendment protection against unreasonable search and seizure extends privacy protections to the public-sector workplace through the Constitution's application to state action.

The U.S. Constitution's **Fourth Amendment protection** against an unreasonable search and seizure governs only the public-sector workplace because the U.S. Constitution applies only to state action. Therefore, unless the employer is the government or other representative of the state (covering approximately 15% of workers in the U.S.[13]), the U.S. Constitution generally will not apply.

U.S. statutes also offer little, if any, protection from workplace intrusions. The **Electronic Communications Privacy Act (ECPA) of 1986** prohibits the "interception" or unauthorized access of stored communications. However, U.S. courts have ruled that "interception" applies only to messages in transit and not to messages that have actually reached company computers. So that is not much help! The result is that the ECPA impacts electronic monitoring only by third parties and not by employers. Further, the ECPA allows interception where consent has been granted. Firms often will have employees consent to monitoring of all communications at the time of hire, so they are immune from ECPA liability. They do not even need consent if the employer provided the service being monitored, such as the email system.

Electronic Communications Privacy Act (ECPA) of 1986

The U.S. statute that establishes the provisions for access, use, disclosure, interception, and privacy protections relating to electronic communications.

Finally, the ECPA only covers electronic, voice, and wire communications, so many of the new ways in which employers might monitor employees were never contemplated by the act (e.g., GPS monitoring). Ultimately, under the act, employers are justified in intercepting email messages as long as they have a valid business reason for doing so (e.g., to ensure that the employee is not using work email to send personal messages or harassing others). The Reality Check "Eyes in the Sky" provides examples of how these issues might arise in the technology environment.

Some states rely on statutory protections rather than common law. Other states provide state constitutional recognition and protection of privacy rights, including Alaska, Arizona, California, Florida, Hawaii, Illinois, Louisiana, Montana, South Carolina, and Washington.[14] However, in all states except California, application of this provision to *private-sector* organizations is limited, uncertain, or not included at all.

intrusion into seclusion

The legal terminology for one of the common-law claims of invasion of privacy. Intrusion into seclusion occurs when someone intentionally intrudes on the private affairs of another when the intrusion would be "highly offensive to a reasonable person."

The "invasion of privacy" claim with which most people are familiar is one that developed through U.S. case law called **intrusion into seclusion.** This legal

Reality Check   *Eyes in the Sky*

Early one morning, a California man told his employer that he was sick and therefore would need to miss an important client meeting that day. At 2 P.M., the employer tracked the employee's smartphone with GPS software installed on the company-provided smartphone and discovered that the employee was lounging poolside at a Las Vegas casino. When the employer confronted the man on his return the following day, the employee explained that he had recovered from his illness and subsequently went to Las Vegas. The employer terminated the man, who sued the employer for wrongful invasion of privacy (based on the cell phone tracking) and the court upheld the employer's actions. The court indicated that the employer's action would have been unlawful if the employer had tracked the employee's phone at midnight, when the employee would not usually have been at work. At that time, the employer would have had no reasonable cause for the intrusion.*

In another case, a construction company used drones to monitor a construction site. At this particular site, two employees were installing electrical wires on the top floors of a building before the walls went up. The drone discovered the employees having sex during their break, and they were subsequently fired. The ex-employees sued, claiming that no one could see them on the top floor from the ground level and the company would not have known that they were having sex if the drone had not been used. The case was settled in the employees' favor.†

*Will Yakowicz, "When Monitoring Your Employees Goes Horribly Wrong," *Inc.* (July 6, 2015), www.inc.com/will-yakowicz/drones-catch-employees-having-sex-and-other-employee-monitoring-gone-wrong.html (accessed July 20, 2018).

†Robert Hackett, "Psst, Your Company Is Watching You Now," *Fortune* (March 13, 2017), http://fortune.com/2017/03/13/company-employee-surveillance-laws-technology/ (accessed February 21, 2019).

violation occurs when someone intentionally intrudes on the private affairs of another when the intrusion would be "highly offensive to a reasonable person." As we begin to live more closely with technology and the intrusions it allows, we begin to accept more and more intrusions in our lives as reasonable; as privacy invasions become more common, they begin to be closer to what is normal and expected. It may no longer be reasonable to be offended by intrusions into one's private life that used to be considered unacceptable. It is important to be aware that, while Georgia was the first jurisdiction whose courts recognized a common law—or court-created—right to privacy, one state, North Dakota, does not recognize any privacy claims generally accepted by the courts.[15]

In *City of Ontario v. Quon* (2010), the U.S. Supreme Court addressed the issue of employer monitoring for the first time. In this case, two California police officers were disciplined after an audit of text messages on city-issued devices found that many of the officers' texts were personal in nature. Though the officers had been assured by their supervisor that an audit would not be performed, the Court determined that the audit was permissible nonetheless because the review of the messages was reasonably "work related."[16]

In a subsequent case, *Riley v. California,* the U.S. Supreme Court unanimously found explicit protection under the Fourth Amendment of cell phones and other similar devices. The Court created a "zone of digital privacy" for the data stored on cell phones, smartphones, and tablets. In *Riley,* the Court found that law enforcement officers may search a device for digital content only after they have secured a search warrant. Though *Riley* is a criminal case, it did not take long for lower courts to apply this precedent to employee privacy considerations. Businesses encounter a number of risks when they monitor and search devices used by employees, whether those devices are owned by the company or by the employee. The acknowledgment by the Supreme Court of the unique nature of today's smart communications devices has heightened the scrutiny with which courts examine access to these devices, whether by other employees or employers. Employers may wish to consider more carefully the nature and extent of searches they may conduct on these devices, but also whether their policies are drafted clearly enough to alert employees of the potential scope of such searches and the level of privacy employees can expect.[17]

Many recent court decisions with regard to monitoring specifically seem to depend on whether the worker had *notice* that the monitoring might occur. Because the basis for finding an invasion of privacy is often the employee's legitimate and reasonable expectation of privacy, if an employee has actual notice, then there truly is no real expectation of privacy. This conclusion was supported in *K-Mart v. Trotti,* where the court held that search of an employee's company-owned locker was unlawful invasion because the employee used his own lock. However, in a later landmark case, *Smyth v. Pillsbury,* Smyth sued after his manager read his email, even though Pillsbury had a policy saying that emails would not be read. The *Trotti* court concluded, "we do not find a **reasonable expectation of privacy** in the contents of email communications voluntarily made by an employee to his supervisor over the company email system notwithstanding any assurances that such communications would not be intercepted by management" (*emphasis added*).[18]

reasonable expectation of privacy
The basis for some common-law claims of invasion of privacy. Where an individual is notified that information will be shared or space will not be private, there is likely no reasonable expectation of privacy.

The end result of *Smyth,* then, is to allow for monitoring even when a firm promises not to monitor! Evidence of the impact of this decision is the fact that only two states, Connecticut and Delaware, require employers to notify workers when they are being monitored. Increasingly, however, states are enacting laws to limit employer monitoring powers. As of 2019, twenty-six states (plus Guam) prohibit employers from obtaining social media passwords from prospective or current employees. Five other states are considering similar legislation.[19] See Table 7.1 for an overview of how the courts have tended to treat the legality of monitoring from a general perspective.

Global Applications

This somewhat unpredictable regime of privacy protection is all the more problematic to maintain when one considers the implications of the European Union's *General Data Protection Regulation (GDPR)* (see the Reality Check "Privacy: Europe Compared to the United States" earlier in the chapter). The GDPR went into effect in 2018, replacing the EU's Directive on Personal Data Protection and strengthening the rights of individuals with regard to the protection of their data by imposing more stringent obligations on those gathering, processing, and maintaining personal data.

The GDPR provides that personal information cannot be collected or shared by companies without individuals' permission. Information about who is using the data and for what purpose it is being collected must be provided in a clear, easily

TABLE 7.1
Legal Status of
Employee Monitoring

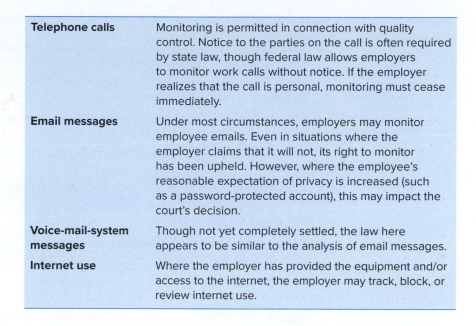

Telephone calls	Monitoring is permitted in connection with quality control. Notice to the parties on the call is often required by state law, though federal law allows employers to monitor work calls without notice. If the employer realizes that the call is personal, monitoring must cease immediately.
Email messages	Under most circumstances, employers may monitor employee emails. Even in situations where the employer claims that it will not, its right to monitor has been upheld. However, where the employee's reasonable expectation of privacy is increased (such as a password-protected account), this may impact the court's decision.
Voice-mail-system messages	Though not yet completely settled, the law here appears to be similar to the analysis of email messages.
Internet use	Where the employer has provided the equipment and/or access to the internet, the employer may track, block, or review internet use.

understandable manner. Further, consumers have the right to review the data and correct inaccuracies. They can also request that their data be erased or "forgotten." All companies—regardless of their size or location—are required to comply with GDPR if they offer free or paid goods or services to EU residents and collect the consumer's personal information. For example, even a small online business based in Ohio that contains a "Contact Us" page on its website to collect name and email information from an interested consumer would be subject to the GDPR if an EU resident stumbled upon the site and submitted her or his information.

The GDPR includes heavy regulatory powers, by imposing heavy fines for those companies that break these regulations—up to 20 million euros or 4% of global annual revenue (whichever is more).[20] In 2019, Google was fined $57 million under the new law, which represented the first significant violation by a U.S corporation. The French data protection oversight agency CNIL claimed that Google did not share with users how their personal information is collected, nor what Google does with it, and that Google did not follow GDPR requirements in gathering consent in connection with personalized ads.[21]

Under both the GDPR and its predecessor, the European Union does not allow the transfer of data on its citizens outside of the country unless the country is deemed to have adequate data privacy laws. Unfortunately, the EU has deemed that the U.S. does not have adequate data privacy laws, but organizations can navigate this by adhering to something called the "Privacy Shield." Under this agreement, U.S. companies must adhere to a detailed set of standards, which surpass what U.S. law typically requires. The Privacy Shield details more than a dozen privacy principles with which companies will have to comply in order to rely on the Privacy Shield as a means to legally transfer data from the EU.[22] (See Table 7.2.)

TABLE 7.2

The European Union Privacy Shield

Source: David Meyer, "Here's What U.S. Firms Will Have to Do under the EU Privacy Shield Deal" (February 29, 2016), http://fortune.com/2016/02/29/privacy-shield-details/ (accessed July 30, 2018).

Under the EU Privacy Shield:

- When using Europeans' data, U.S. intelligence services will have to adhere to the new limits and oversight mechanism.

- The U.S. State Department will have to employ a new watchdog to handle complaints about intelligence-related matters.

- Companies must self-certify compliance with the Privacy Shield and its stated principles. Certifications must be renewed annually.

- Companies must publicly display their privacy policies that show compliance with EU law.

- Companies will have to resolve complaints within 45 days of being filed.

- Companies will have to update their privacy policies to explain how people can access these services.

- Companies will face more restrictions on being able to forward Europeans' personal data to other companies.

Arguably, the GDPR does make the Privacy Shield less relevant given that the GDPR sets higher standards and is more widely applicable, rather than allowing self-selecting companies to opt in.[23] However, as of December 2018, the European Commission reported that "the United States continues to ensure an adequate level of protection for personal data transferred under the Privacy Shield" and that the United States provides an acceptable level of data protection essentially equivalent to that of the European Union.[24]

Given the nature of the legal uncertainty or instability concerning these challenging areas of information gathering, perhaps the only source of an answer is ethics. Yet, "our laws, ethics rules, and codes of professional conduct have never been able to keep up with the pace of technology development. We update them from time to time, but such changes are always reactive, not proactive."[25] Still, as a court put it in regard to the legitimacy of police use of infrared thermal detection devices aimed at an individual's home without a warrant or notification,

> As technology races with ever increasing speed, our subjective expectations of privacy may be unconsciously altered . . . our legal rights to privacy should reflect thoughtful and purposeful choices rather than simply mirror the current state of the commercial technology industry.[26]

Perhaps the more personalized response of Northrup Grumman Corporation's former ethics officer, Frank Daly, sums it up better: "Can this characteristic of speed drive us and have a negative effect upon how we treat other people? You can't rush love or a soufflé."[27]

What are the implications of this definition or understanding of privacy for businesses and for business ethics analysis? In general, one would argue that personal information should remain private unless a relationship exists between the business and the individual that legitimates collecting and using personal information about

The information on the following bulleted list is sometimes required on standard employment applications, though candidates might consider some of it to be private or personal. Which of the following items about an employee might an employer have a legitimate claim to know, and why? What information might lead to unreasonable intrusions or discriminatory practices, and why?

- A job applicant's social security number
- An applicant's arrest record
- An employee's medical records
- An employee's marital status
- Whether a job applicant smokes
- An employee's political affiliation
- An employee's sexual orientation
- An employee's credit rating
- An employee's prior salary

1. What facts are relevant to your decisions?
2. What would the consequences be of refusing to answer any questions on an employment application?
3. Are you basing your decision on particular rights of the employee or the employer?
4. Are there people other than the employer and employee who might have a stake in what information is released to employers?

that individual. For example, to determine the range of employee privacy, we would have to specify the nature of the relationship between employer and employee. The nature of the employment relationship will help determine the appropriate boundary between employers and employees and, therefore, the information that ought to remain rightfully private within the workplace. (See the Decision Point "Inquiring Employers Want to Know" to consider information reasonably related to the job.) If we adopt something like a contractual model of employment, where the conditions and terms of employment are subject to the mutual and informed consent of both parties, then employee consent would become one major condition on what information employers can collect.

We can summarize our preceding examination by saying that employee privacy is violated whenever (1) employers infringe upon personal decisions that are not relevant to the employment contract (whether the contract is implied or explicit) or (2) personal information that is not relevant to that contract is collected, stored, or used without the informed consent of the employee. Further, because consent plays a pivotal role in this understanding, the burden of proof rests with the employer to establish the relevancy of personal decisions and information at issue.

Linking the Value of Privacy to the Ethical Implications of Technology

The advent of new technology challenges privacy in ways that we could never before imagine. For example, consider the implications of new technology on employee and employer expectations regarding the use of time; the distinction between work use and personal use of technology; the protection of proprietary information, performance measurement, and privacy interests; or accessibility issues related to the digital divide. Technology allows for in-home offices, raising extraordinary opportunities and challenges, issues of safety, and privacy concerns (more than 43% of U.S. workers telecommute at least one day a week[28]). Because each of us is capable of much greater production through the use of technology, technology not only provides benefits but also allows employers to ask more of each employee.

Though the following warning from the International Labour Office was issued some time ago, its cautions about the implications of the technology economy are as relevant today as the day they were issued:

> More and more, boundaries are dissolving between leisure and working time, the place of work and place of residence, learning and working. . . . Wherever categories such as working time, working location, performance at work and jobs become blurred, the result is the deterioration of the foundations of our edifice of agreements, norms, rules, laws, organizational forms, structures and institutions, all of which have a stronger influence on our behavioral patterns and systems of values than we are aware.[29]

New technology, however, does not necessarily impact our value judgments but instead simply provides new ways to gather the information on which to base them. Sorting through these issues is challenging nevertheless. Consider the impact of the terrorist attacks on the United States on September 11, 2001, on an employer's decision to share personal employee information or customer information with law enforcement. Private firms throughout the world may be more willing—or less willing—today to share private information than they would have been previously.

Firms often experience, and often find themselves ill prepared for, the unanticipated challenges stemming from new technology. Consider the lesson one firm learned about how problems with Twitter use and abuse might extend beyond the end of the employment relationship. An employee with PhoneDog, a company that provides mobile device news and reviews, created a work-related Twitter account that amassed 17,000 followers.[30] When he left the company, he simply changed the user name of the account and kept it as his own, sending "tweets" that did not link back to or reference PhoneDog. The company sued to recover from the ex-employee the $2.50 per Twitter follower, per month, in revenue that it claims it has lost. The ex-employee claimed that the account belonged to him, not to PhoneDog.

Ultimately, PhoneDog and the ex-employee settled out of court and the former employee kept his Twitter account, along with its followers. We learn from this case that neither individual Twitter users nor a company can own their followers! "No one 'owns' their followers as a matter of property," explains Kevin

Werbach, Wharton professor of legal studies and business ethics. "I don't even know my followers; they can stop following me at any time. It's not that the company is doing something internally with the names to generate more business. It's not like the company's customer list."[31] The lack of legislation or legal precedent means that social media disputes like PhoneDog's become a matter of contract law, says Andrea Matwyshyn, Wharton professor of legal studies and business ethics. "These are questions of contract law between the employee and the company," she notes. "You need to contract very carefully and in advance what social media practices are permissible in the workplace. If a transgression occurs before a written policy or agreement was put into place, the case stands or falls based on the facts around it." Issues addressed by this case did not go unnoticed by businesses; employers with policies governing social media use increased from 55 to 69% in the year following the case.[32]

Do we need "new ethics" for this "new economy"? Perhaps not, because the same values one held under previous circumstances should, if they are true and justified, permeate and relate to later circumstances.[33] However, the perspective one brings to each experience is impacted by the understanding and use of new technology and other advances. As economist Antonio Argandoña cautions, there has been a change in values "that may be caused by the opportunities created by the technology."[34] On the other hand, he points to the possibility that new technology may also do much good, including development of depressed regions, increased citizenship participation, defense of human rights, and other potential gains.

Information and Privacy

A business needs to be able to anticipate the perceptions of its stakeholders in order to be able to make the most effective decisions for its long-term sustainability. New technological advancements are often difficult for the public to understand and therefore ripe for challenge. How do you best manage the entrepreneurial passion for forward momentum with stakeholder comfort and security?

When Google first created its Code of Conduct, it included the deontological imperative "don't be evil" as its motto. Its founders explained that Google sought to "define precisely what it means to be a force for good—always do the right, ethical thing. Ultimately, 'don't do evil' seems the easiest way to summarize it."[35] For instance, Google does not allow gun ads, a decision that upsets the gun lobby. One might expect that Google would be a firm that is especially sensitive to stakeholder concerns as it develops new technology.

Google suggests that it is providing a value to society by offering its free "Gmail" email system. However, in recent years, Google has caused some controversy with its Gmail privacy policies. Originally, Google essentially mined a user's email contents and search engine history to provide that user with targeted marketing and online advertising, specific to the user's interests. Many users were surprised when Google contended in a lawsuit that "Google's 425 million Gmail users have 'no reasonable expectation' that their communications are confidential."[36]

In an about-face in 2017, Google responded to the public backlash to their privacy policies by announcing that Gmail accounts would no longer be scanned or used to personalize advertisements. However, critics pointed out that this announcement did not specify that *other* Google services would refrain from utilizing tracking services (i.e., such as the popular Google search engine).[37] Additionally, third-party data-mining companies often use free apps and services to entice Gmail users into "consenting" to give access to their inboxes without clearly stating what data they collect and what they are doing with it.[38] However, perhaps as one economist wrote, "there is no such thing as a free lunch, and we must look carefully at the business motives behind these firms' generosity." But then how does that square with the same company that has told us in the past, "You should trust whoever is handling your email"?[39]

That trust is truly the crux of the issue with the introduction of new technology, isn't it? When consumers rely on technology provided by a business—from email to internet access and from cell phones to medical labs—they might easily assume that the business will respect their privacy. Most average email users do not understand the technology behind the process. One would like to believe that those responsible for the technology are, themselves, accountable to the user. That would be the ideal.

By failing to fully comprehend and plan for its stakeholders' perceptions of its decisions, Google not only breached ethical boundaries but also suffered public backlash. It did not anticipate concerns over privacy or the controversy its programs would engender. Critics argued that Google should have consulted with stakeholders with regard to each of these and other decisions, determined the best way to balance their interests, and then considered these interests as they introduced new programs, all of which might have precluded the negative impact on its reputation. The lesson learned is that, notwithstanding even reasonable justification, people are simply not comfortable with an involuntary loss of control over these personal decisions. Google failed to consider the perspectives of its stakeholders, the impact of its decisions on those stakeholders, and the fundamental values its decisions implied. Consider the discomfort evidenced in the Decision Point "Technology Dilemmas."

Economist Antonio Argandoña contends that, if new technology is dependent on and has as its substance information and data, significant moral requirements should be imposed on that information. He suggests the following as necessary elements:

- **Truthfulness and accuracy:** The person providing the information must ensure that it is truthful and accurate, at least to a reasonable degree.
- **Respect for privacy:** The person receiving or accumulating information must take into account the ethical limits of individuals' (and organizations') privacy. This would include issues relating to company secrets, espionage, and intelligence gathering.
- **Respect for property and safety rights:** Areas of potential vulnerability, including network security, sabotage, theft of information, and impersonation, are enhanced and must therefore be protected.
- **Accountability:** Technology allows for greater anonymity and distance, requiring a concurrent increased exigency for personal responsibility and accountability.[40]

Questions about using technology for "good" or "evil," from an anonymous web posting:

Management wants me to spy.

Management wants me to spy on a colleague. I'll be using [a spying program] that is 100% hidden, does screen captures, etc. Is there a document out there that I can have management sign to limit my liability? I want signatures from all management stating that they are authorizing me to spy. Thoughts? I have done this before, but this is the first time that they have asked me to compile data against a user for possible use in court. Thanks.

What are some of the questions or concerns you might bring up in an answer and what would you suggest this individual do to respond to them?

1. What are the key facts relevant to your response?
2. What is the ethical issue involved in peer spying in the workplace?
3. Who are the stakeholders?
4. What alternatives would you suggest to this individual, and what alternatives exist for employers who wish to gather information about employees surreptitiously?
5. How do the alternatives compare; how do the alternatives affect the stakeholders?

Imagine how firms may respond to this call for responsibility in the development, manufacturing, marketing, and service related to new production or other corporate activities. What ethical issues does Argandoña's proposal raise, and how will stakeholders be impacted if firms respond positively to this call?

Managing Employees through Monitoring

OBJECTIVE

One of the most prevalent forms of information gathering in the workplace is employer monitoring of employees' work; and technology has offered employers enormous abilities to do this effectively at very low cost. Employers might choose to monitor for a variety of reasons. For example, if an employer has a rule limiting the use of technology, how can it ensure that employees are following that rule? In fact, according to one survey, 88% of employees use social media at least once during every workday and 18% check social media sites *more than ten times* each day![41] But unless your supervisor is looking over your shoulder, it would be difficult to check on your personal use of technology without some advanced form of online monitoring.

email monitoring
The maintenance and either periodic or random review of email communications of employees or others for a variety of business purposes.

In connection with both workplace **email monitoring** and also **internet use monitoring,** a survey conducted by the American Academy of Management found that nearly 80% of large companies monitor their employees' use of email, internet, or phone. That percentage rises to over 90% for firms in particularly information-sensitive industries, such as finance.[42] You will note that these figures are specific to the U.S. For an explanation of how workplace monitoring is different in the EU, see the Reality Check "GDPR Creates Parameters for Monitoring."

Reality Check *GDPR Creates Parameters for Monitoring*

As we discussed earlier in this chapter, the European Union's General Data Protection Regulation (GDPR) includes specific provisions for employers that restrict them in monitoring their employees' activities and processing the information they gather about their workers. While employers may monitor workers who are subject to the GDPR, they are significantly restricted in doing so.

For instance, the employer may monitor and collect information *only* when it is necessary to draft the employment contract or to comply with a legal obligation; necessary to protect the vital interests of an employee or someone else; necessary for some legitimate interest of the employer (unless the fundamental rights of the employee outweigh these interests); or with the employee's consent, among a few other reasons. Continuous monitoring, for instance, is generally not permitted.

Employers also must notify employees who are subject to the GDPR about what information about them can be processed at work, how the information will be processed, why this is necessary, and what rights the employees have to protect their privacy. Note that it is the employee who is protected and covered by the GDPR rather than the employer who is covered, so an employer based outside of the EU might still need to comply with the regulation if it has employees working within the EU.

Source: Legal ICT, "Fact Sheets: Privacy and Monitoring at Work under the GDPR" (n.d.), https://legalict.com/factsheets/privacy-monitoring-work-gdpr/ (accessed March 3, 2019).

---

internet use monitoring
The maintenance and either periodic or random review of the use of the internet by employees or others based on time spent or content accessed for a variety of business purposes.

We have come to expect that our work-related emails are the property of—or at least subject to search by—our employers. For example, after two faculty members at the University of Rochester (NY) filed a sexual harassment claim against a fellow colleague, the emails of both the potential harasser and the complaining faculty were searched. The administration announced that two internal investigations found no credible evidence against the charged harasser. However, the administration uncovered emails from the complaining faculty member that discussed how their department chair handled the colleague charged with sexual harassment, and forwarded these emails to the department chair in question. The chair then confronted the faculty about the emails. The email searches took place without the complaining faculty member's knowledge or consent.[43]

Note that the above discussion refers to work-related emails. If emails are stored or sent using employer-provided devices or platforms, the employer has a strong argument for its business interest in monitoring their contents. However, where the emails are private or stored on or sent from an employee's private device, the employer's argument becomes much weaker.

With the rise of social media and social networking use in recent years, internet use monitoring also is evolving. Employers are concerned about employee productivity and whether their employees may bring too much of their personal lives to the workplace. One CareerBuilder.com survey found that 41% of workers named "the internet" as the largest productivity killer at work, while 37% named "social media."[44]

Employee monitoring has even crossed the threshold from computer use to body autonomy. Biotracking technology, such as Fitbits or Nike+ FuelBands, allow employers to record the number of steps that employees take in a day, their heart rate, what they eat and drink, how much sleep they get, and even their hormone levels. The information gathered from this technology often is incorporated into employee wellness programs.[45] In other applications, Amazon recently has adopted new wristband technology for warehouse workers to monitor and provide feedback about the employee's pace of work.

There even are badges that monitor the tone of your voice, gender of the person you are talking to, and where in the office these conversations are being held.[46] One might imagine how technology such as these could provide helpful information if a claim arose subsequently around a particular inappropriate conversation. But the question of costs versus benefits—intrusion versus valuable data gathering—is arguable.

These applications can become even more intrusive. A Wisconsin-based tech company implants microchips in employees. The company explained that these chips would allow staff seamlessly to be able to log in to their computers, enter locked areas, or access equipment. The program was volunteer based, and the company originally expected only three to four people to participate, but fifty of the company's eighty employees joined the program. Paula Brantner, a senior adviser at Workplace Fairness, a nonprofit public education and advocacy organization that works to promote and protect employee rights, says, "Accepting a certain amount of privacy invasion has increasingly become part of the job. People are just going to accept this as something they have to do to keep their job and, in some ways, we've already lost the battle."[47]

OBJECTIVE

Unfortunately, many of the ethical issues that arise in the area of managing information are not obvious. For instance, when we do not fully understand the technology involved, we might not understand the ethical implications of our decisions. When that occurs, we are not able to protect our own information effectively because we may not understand the impact on our autonomy, the control of our information, our reciprocal obligations, or even what might be best for ourselves! Do you always consider every single person who might see the emails you send? Do you know whether your employer is allowed to read your email? Maybe you think that you are safe because you use a password, but tech experts tell us that any system is penetrable. Employers have been known to read emails randomly to ensure that the employer-provided email system is being used only for business purposes. Is this ethical? Does it matter if there is a company policy that email must be used only for business purposes, or that you were told in advance that your email will be monitored randomly (or not)?

Are the issues raised in connection with workplace email different from those that arise in connection with a traditional written letter? If an act would be wrong or unethical with one form of communication (the letter), does that make it wrong with the other (the email)?

The ethical issues that arise with technology may be enhanced by the knowledge gap that exists between people who *do* understand the technology and others who do not understand it and therefore are unable to protect themselves. You might have thought that deleting that one email was the end of the story, but someone else knew that deleting an email does *not* actually delete it from the company's servers!

Technology allows for access to information that was never before possible. Under previous circumstances, one could usually discover if someone else had steamed open a letter over a teapot (for our younger readers, that was how you surreptitiously opened an envelope without others' knowledge). Today, there are ways to read another's email without the recipient's knowledge. Access might also take place unintentionally. For instance, while doing a routine background check, a supervisor may unintentionally uncover information that is extremely personal and might be completely irrelevant to the individual's work performance.

Moreover, because technology allows us to work from almost anywhere on the planet, we are seldom out of the boundaries of our workplace. For instance, just because you are going to your sister's wedding does not mean that your supervisor cannot reach you. This raises a tough question: *Should* your supervisor try to reach you just because she has the ability to do so? Our total accessibility creates new expectations, and therefore conflicts. One legislator in New York even has proposed legislation that would fine employers for requiring employees to respond to email after work hours or would require a workplace policy for after-hours email correspondence.[48]

Research suggests that our complete accessibility—even if employers do not access us constantly—creates high levels of stress and anxiety on employees and their families. As a result, several countries and companies in the European Union have taken steps to protect employees through "right to disconnect" laws. For instance, as early as 2001, the French Supreme Court held that employees cannot be required to take work home, and later ruled that an employee could not be terminated because she or he is unreachable outside of work hours! More recently, in 2017, France adopted the El Khomri law, which requires employers of fifty or more employees to define the rights of employees to disconnect during after-work hours.

Some companies have gone further in order to make a statement about their work cultures. For instance, Volkswagen's servers simply are not able to send or receive emails to or from individual accounts between 6:15 P.M. and 7 A.M. Daimler offers workers the option to set a holiday message to notify senders not only that the recipient is away, but also that the incoming email will be deleted. The intent is to allow the employee an actual vacation and not to spend the holiday fearing a return to a packed inbox!

Are these realistic solutions to the conflict? How long is reasonable to wait before responding to an email? If someone does not hear from you within 24 hours of sending an email, is it unreasonable for them to resend it? Should a text message be considered more urgent than an email, or do the same answers apply? Continuous accessibility does blur the lines between our personal and professional lives, but an approach that is considered too "relaxed" might open the door to the competition. (See the Reality Check "Is Privacy Perception a Factor of Age?")

Employees might not appreciate that 24/7 accessibility for other reasons, as well. On a number of occasions, employees who have claimed to be ill or otherwise unable to come to work have forgotten that social media posts of their activities are public. David Sharrow claimed that he was wrongfully terminated from his job at the Ziploc Slide-Loc plant in retaliation for taking time off under the Family and

Reality Check   *Is Privacy Perception a Factor of Age?*

There is plenty of evidence that the "Snapchat Generation" does not think of privacy quite the way their parents do.

Several studies have evaluated the differences in perception between the millennial/post-millennial (Generation Z) generations and older generations when it comes to privacy concerns. (Millennials are defined as those born between 1981 and 1996, and post-millennials/Generation Z are defined as those born since 1997.*) Consider the following distinctions and whether you find your own perceptions aligned with those of your age group or older.

- **Definition of Privacy:** Baby Boomers (over 50 years) are 74% more likely to choose a traditional, offline description of privacy ("the right to be free from others watching me") and be less concerned with guarding their privacy in person. For example, Baby Boomers are 42% more likely to walk around naked in locker rooms. Millennials are 177% more likely to choose a modern, datacentric definition ("being able to delete anything about me online").[†]

- **Online Privacy Concerns:** Millennials are more interested in managing their online reputation among their peers and in concealing private or incriminating information from authority figures such as their families, teachers, school administrators, college admissions officers, and potential employers. Millennials are generally more aware of potential data security risks than other generations but are less likely to be concerned about them. In fact, 80% of millennials/post-millennials have invested either "a lot" or "some" trust in their brands when it comes to data, including 67% who have "a lot of trust" in their primary financial institutions. Older adults are more concerned with hiding their personal data from commercial interests, where almost half of millennials in one survey think it is fair for corporations to gather personal information in exchange for a free service.[‡]

- **Government Surveillance:** Even though more Millennials than Boomers trust businesses with their data, they are not as trusting of government surveillance. Nearly 60% of Millennials (in another survey) agreed with a former federal employee's decision to leak information about a U.S. National Security Agency spy program on citizens. Over half of adults aged 50 or older thought the decision was a criminal action. However, what is interesting is that a similar survey in 1971 after the Pentagon Papers were released showed that 75% of adults under 30 thought sharing those documents was the "right thing to do," while only half of those older than 50 agreed. Perhaps when you are born is not as important as how long you have been alive.[§]

*Michael Dimock, "Defining Generations: Where Millennials End and Post Millennials Begin," Pew Research Center (March 1, 2018), www.pewresearch.org/fact-tank/2018/03/01/defining-generations-where-millennials-end-and-post-millennials-begin/ (accessed March 4, 2019).

[†]Abine Report, "From Walking around Naked to Updating Facebook Privacy Settings, Younger Generation's Views on Privacy Are Changing," *PR Newswire* (April 23, 2013), www.prnewswire.com/news-releases/from-walking-around-naked-to-updating-facebook-privacy-settings-younger-generations-views-on-privacy-are-changing-204268481.html (accessed March 4, 2019).

[‡]Sarah Landrum, "Millennials, Trust and Internet Security," *Forbes* (June 28, 2017), https://www.forbes.com/sites/sarahlandrum/2017/06/28/millennials-trust-and-internet-security/#2ae1c0e5555e (accessed March 4, 2019); John Fleming and Amy Adkins, "Data Security: Not a Big Concern for Millennials," *Gallup* (June 9, 2016), https://news.gallup.com/businessjournal/192401/data-security-not-big-concern-millennials.aspx (accessed on March 4, 2019); Amanda Lenhert, "What Americans Think About Privacy, and Why Their Kids Think Differently," Lecture at Chautauqua Institution (July 10, 2014), http://chqdaily.com/2014/07/10/lenhart-adolescents-more-suspicious-of-government-less-suspicious-of-corporate-data-collection-online/ (accessed March 4, 2019).

[§]Lenhert, "What Americans Think About Privacy"; Edward Schwartz, "Millennials Are a Little Confused When It Comes to Privacy," *The Washington Post* (May 13, 2015), www.washingtonpost.com/news/the-fix/wp/2015/05/13/millenials-dont-trust-government-to-respect-their-privacy-but-they-do-trust-businesses-what/?utm_term=.5829d32ebee9 (accessed March 4, 2019); see also Zaid Jilani, "Former CIA Director Michael Hayden Blames Millenials for Government Leaks," *The Intercept* (March 10, 2017), https://theintercept.com/2017/03/10/former-cia-director-michael-hayden-blames-millennials-for-government-leaks/ (accessed March 4, 2019).

Medical Leave Act. Sharrow had given his boss a note saying that he would be off work due to a foot and knee injury. During his time off, Sharrow participated in a charity golf tournament where loads of photos were taken. Sharrow appeared not only in one from the tournament but another captioned "Tubing the Rifle River." As luck would have it, his boss saw the photos. A court upheld his termination. In another case, an employee lied about how he was injured (he was hurt while fishing rather than on the job) and was caught by Facebook photos again![49]

Another challenge posed by the new technology accessible in the workplace is the facelessness that results from its use. If we have to face someone as we make our decisions, we are more likely to care about the impact of that decision on that person. Conversely, when we do not get to know someone because we do not have to see that person in order to do our business, we often do not take into account the impact of our decisions. It is merely a name at the other end of a digital correspondence, rather than another human being.

When people put something in writing (such as a formal letter or contract), we assume that they mean what they say, and we hold them to it as representative of their precise intent. To the contrary, we consider email, texting, and posting on social media sites to be more like a conversation and treat them as such, lobbing notes back and forth, much as we would in a conversation, and permitting the idiosyncrasies that we would allow when speaking. Most of these forms of digital communication arise in a personal context; they are spontaneous, casual, and off-the-cuff. We do not think about them in advance and often write quickly without proofreading them before sending. The bottom line is that we now send messages electronically that we might only have chatted about before! But just think about what that means. . . . People have a record of what we send. They have message archives and screenshots. Your employer (or employee) can hold you to what you wrote in a communication that you intended to be informal. As a result, while we might not think about what we write in advance—or proofread—maybe we should.

Given the ease and informality of electronic communications, we also often "say" (post, text, email, and the like) things to each other that we would never say to someone's face, precisely because we do not have to consider the impact of what we are saying. We are more careless with our communications because they are easier to conduct—just hit a button and they are sent. So whether we should take more care because of legal or ethical implications (or both), the lesson learned is to treat each communication as if it might appear on the front page of the paper (or your boss's desk) tomorrow.

To address some of the ethical issues technology presents, the Computer Ethics Institute has created "The Ten Commandments of Computer Ethics," which include these imperatives (among others):

- Thou shalt not snoop around in other people's computer files.
- Thou shalt think about the social consequences of the program you are writing or the system you are designing.
- Thou shalt always use a computer in ways that ensure consideration and respect for your fellow humans.

TABLE 7.3
Public Access to
Personal Information

Source: InfoCheckUSA,
"Pricing Guide" (2018), www
.infocheckusa.com/background-
check-pricing.htm (accessed
March 4, 2019).

InfoCheck USA provides the following personal information at the listed prices, often instantaneously:

- General all-around background search, $249
- Countywide search for misdemeanors and felonies, $16
- Whether subject has ever spent time in state prison, $10
- Whether subject has ever served time in a federal prison, $20
- National search for outstanding warrants for subject, $20
- Countywide search for any civil filings filed by or against subject, $16
- Subject's driving record for at least three previous years, $15

Of course, such guidelines have no enforcement mechanism and are little more than suggestions. To see the types of additional information available through other web services, see Table 7.3.

Why Do Firms Monitor Technology Usage?

OBJECTIVE

We have just discussed a number of concerns surrounding employee monitoring and the ethical issues it raises. But a firm would not monitor employees unless there were some real benefits to doing so. We will discuss these benefits in a moment, but it is important to mention that the gains are not only for the employers. For instance, by monitoring employee health, workplaces can be made safer for workers and pressure on employees can be reduced. Monitoring communications will allow employees more transparency when striving to demonstrate and prevent sexual harassment or, alternatively, to protect against claims of sexual harassment.

Employers may choose to monitor its employees and collect the information discussed earlier for numerous reasons. Employers collect information about employees in order to place workers into appropriate positions, to ensure their workplaces are in compliance with affirmative action requirements, or to administer workplace benefits.

The employer may also claim that monitoring also allows it to ensure more effective, productive performance because employees are less likely to engage in inappropriate use of technology if they know they will be monitored. However, as you will learn below, monitoring employees can cause a negative impact in terms of higher stress levels.

As discussed above, we all tend to use technology more and more for both personal and professional reasons; of the nearly 7 billion people on our planet, 5 billion have access to a mobile phone.[50] Ninety-five percent of North Americans, 85.2% of Europeans, and a total of just over 55% of the world had internet access in 2018. The United Arab Emirates has the highest penetration rate at 99%, while North Korea has the lowest (.08%), and at 36%, Africa is the continent with the lowest proportion of its population having online access. The fact that almost 2 billion people do not have access to a mobile phone and 45% of the world do not have internet access at all are altogether different and extremely important ethical issues.[51] More than 3.4 billion people around the world now use social media each month (a 9% growth from 2018 to 2019), with nine out of ten of those users accessing their chosen platforms via mobile devices.[52] A 2017 survey found that, during a typical workday, the average office employee spends 56 minutes per day using his or her cell phone *at work* for nonwork activity, 44% are conducting internet searches unrelated to work, and 36% are checking personal social media accounts.[53]

Beyond the management of its human resources, monitoring offers an employer a method by which to protect its other resources. Employers use monitoring to protect proprietary information (intellectual property/data), to guard against theft, to protect their investment in equipment and bandwidth, and to protect against legal liability.[54]

Employees need to take monitoring seriously. Twenty-eight percent of employers report that they have fired workers for using the internet during the workday for non-work-related activity (such as shopping online or checking out social media) and 18% have fired workers because of posts on social media, such as a racist, sexist, or inappropriate posts or comments.[55]

Monitoring Employees through Drug Testing

OBJECTIVE

Employers have had a long history of monitoring employees through testing for the use of substances, such as drugs and alcohol, and there is strong legal support for testing in this area. Because the employer may be held responsible for legal violations committed by its employees during the course of their job, the employer has a vested interest in controlling every aspect of the work environment. Some even argue that there is an *obligation* to test in certain employment contexts. If an employer can demonstrate that testing may prevent harm to other workers or to others outside of the workplace, testing may not only be justified but necessary.[56]

On the other hand, employees may argue that their drug usage is relevant only if it impacts their job performance. Until it does have an impact, some suggest that the employer has no basis for testing and instead it constitutes an invasion of privacy.

Recent legal changes in the U.S., such as the legalization of marijuana in some jurisdictions for medical or recreational purposes, have made for complicated workplace dilemmas. The psychoactive ingredient in marijuana, THC, can remain in one's system for as long as 30 days after use. If you use marijuana legally and on your own time, THC will remain in your system and then appear on any testing that may occur during your work hours. Medical users may medicate more regularly throughout the day and therefore "likely will have a much higher blood-THC content than a casual user, but the casual user likely will be more impaired from a physical and mental standpoint than the chronic one."[57]

Courts in several states—including Connecticut, Maine, and Massachusetts—have ruled that an employee testing positive for marijuana may prevail against an employer under certain circumstances, even where that employer is enforcing drug-free workplace policies. Maine is the only state that has passed legislation explicitly to protect workers from adverse employment action based on their use of marijuana and marijuana products (both recreational and medicinal), provided the use occurs away from the workplace. Determining when the use occurred is still the difficult question to answer. In twelve states—Arkansas, Arizona, Connecticut, Delaware, Illinois, Maine, Massachusetts, Minnesota, Nevada, New York, Pennsylvania, and Rhode Island—medical marijuana users have certain job protections, so preemployment screens or random screens could trigger job protections in those states. However, that does not mean that an employer cannot screen for the substance, retract a job offer, or terminate an employee for a positive marijuana test result, just that some workers may be protected once a positive result occurs.[58]

For workers outside of the U.S., Uruguay was the first country to legalize marijuana use countrywide and Canada was the second (though medical marijuana had been legal there since 2001). Other countries also permit its possession and use, depending on the amount, such as Spain, Peru, and South Africa.[59] As with alcohol in the U.S., while the use of the substance is legal, employers may prohibit its use at work or during working hours, and also may prohibit employees from being at work while impaired. Therefore, employers may test their workers to determine impairment.

Employers might conduct testing on a regular basis, randomly, or for cause. An employer may believe there is "cause" to test if it observes various behaviors such as the ones listed below. These characteristics are offered by the National Council on Alcoholism and Drug Dependence as "warning signs of drug use." However, consider the possibility that someone might present these behaviors but not be using a prohibited substance? What is the cost of an incorrect presumption in connection with drug testing? It does not take a great deal of imagination to come up with other, more innocuous, alternative reasons for these behaviors. Yet, an employer may decide to test based on these "warning signs." Is it ethical to presume someone is guilty based on these signs? Does a person have a fundamental right to be presumed innocent? Or, perhaps, do the risks of that presumption outweigh the individual's right to privacy and protection against intrusion in this situation and justify greater precautions?

Job Performance

- Inconsistent work quality.
- Poor concentration and lack of focus.
- Lowered productivity or erratic work patterns.
- Increased absenteeism or on-the-job "presenteeism."
- Unexplained disappearances from the job site.
- Carelessness, mistakes, or errors in judgment.
- Needless risk taking.
- Disregard for safety for self and others—on-the-job and off-the-job accidents.
- Extended lunch periods and early departures.

Workplace Behavior

- Frequent financial problems.
- Avoidance of friends and colleagues.
- Blaming of others for own problems and shortcomings.
- Complaints about problems at home.
- Deterioration in personal appearance or personal hygiene.
- Complaints, excuses, and time off for vaguely defined illnesses or family problems.[60]

Testing occurs both during employment and also preemployment. A 2018 poll of more than 6,000 human resource professionals found that 63% of companies require job candidates to take a preemployment drug test, and a 2017 study revealed that testing positive for drug use was at its highest rate in 12 years (4.2%).[61] However, there also has been a slow decline in the number of preemployment drug tests due to the growing legality and social acceptance of marijuana, in particular. Drug testing restricts the job pool and, in a tight labor market, testing has a negative impact on productivity and growth. Employers cited an inability by applicants to pass drug tests among reasons for difficulties in hiring, according to surveys conducted by the Federal Reserve in 2017.[62] Do you see a real value in continuing to test? (For a detailed discussion of the intersection of privacy and testing, please see the Reality Check "The Employment Relationship Begins Preemployment" later in this chapter.)

Certainly, for those that do have drug testing requirements, there are legal realities to consider. The Americans with Disabilities Act (ADA) prohibits employers from inquiring about an employee's use of prescription drugs unless the employer has a reasonable basis for believing that the worker poses a safety threat or is unable to do his or her job. "If somebody puts his head down on a desk, do you test him for drugs or not?" asks Dr. Robert DuPont, president of the Institute for Behavior and Health. "The first time you get an employee who says you're harassing them, you're not going to test anyone else even if they're passed out."[63]

Where public safety is at risk, there is arguably a compelling public interest claim from a utilitarian perspective that may be sufficiently persuasive to outweigh any one individual's right to privacy or right to control information about oneself. However, what about jobs in which public safety is not at risk? Is it justifiable to test all employees and job applicants? Is the proposed benefit to the employer sufficiently valuable in your perspective to outweigh the employee's fundamental interest in autonomy and privacy? Should a utilitarian viewpoint govern, or should deontological principles take priority? Should we consider a distributive justice perspective and the fairest result—does distributive justice apply under these circumstances?

Several major retail employers, including Home Depot, IKEA, and Walmart, have comprehensive drug-testing policies for both job applicants and employees. Many stores also promote their "drug-free" workplace policy as a marketing strategy. With just a few exceptions, such policies are legal throughout the United States. The question is, "Are they ethically appropriate?" The Decision Point "Limits on Personal Information in Hiring" explores these issues.

What limits should be placed on the reasons a job applicant can be denied employment? As we discussed earlier, the law prohibits denying someone a job on the basis of race, religion, ethnicity, gender, or disability. The law generally allows denial of a job on the basis of drug use. Like employment at will, the burden of proof lies with the job applicant to demonstrate that the denial was based on the prohibited categories; otherwise, employers need no reason to deny someone a job. Suppose a business wanted to ensure not only a drug-free workplace but also an alcohol-free workplace. Would a business have the ethical right to deny a job, or dismiss an employee, for drinking alcohol? Courts have been asked to decide the legitimacy of dismissals for cigarette smoking, for political beliefs, and for having an abortion. Do you think any of these are legitimate grounds for dismissal? Between 50% and 60% of U.S. employers evaluate applicants' personalities with assessment tools.* Such tests ask many personal questions, including some that concern a person's sexual life. Would a business have an ethical right to deny employment to someone on the basis of the results of a personality test?

What are some of the questions or concerns you might have while trying to answer this challenge? What would you suggest a business do to respond to them?

- What are the key facts relevant to your response?
- What are the ethical issues involved in basing hiring decisions on personal information?
- Who are the stakeholders?
- What alternatives would you suggest to business in considering personal information in hiring, and what alternatives exist for employers?
- How do the alternatives compare for business and for the stakeholders?

Some argue that companies run the risk of bias when conducting personality tests for hiring, particularly with regard to diversity of perspective. One argument is that certain personality traits are not relevant to job performance. But if hiring managers believe that they are relevant, these firms might miss out on individuals who do not fit a particular personality type but whose skills, motivations, and other attributes bring a lot of value to the firm.†

This example is well illustrated in the technology industry. As *Bloomberg* journalist Emily Chang recounts in *Brotopia: Breaking Up the Boy's Club of Silicon Valley,* during the mid-1960s, the tech industry hired two psychologists, William Cannon and Dallis Perry, to determine what type of individuals would make successful programmers. First, they concluded that such individuals needed to enjoy problem solving. Second, they concluded that good programmers "don't like people." Five and a half decades later, this stereotype continues to persist, even though product gaffes have shown, time and time again, of the dangers of not having emotionally intelligent developers who can understand their users' concerns and point of view.‡

Another consideration that is currently being investigated by the Equal Employment Opportunity Commission (EEOC) and in litigation based on the ADA is whether personality tests adversely impact individuals with certain mental illnesses

(continued)

(concluded) such as depression or bipolar disorder. The EEOC is concerned because the tests ask respondents to answer questions honestly, such as "over the course of the day, I can experience many mood changes," and "if something very bad happens, it takes some time before I feel happy again."[§] Employers are watching and waiting for the EEOC's decision because a ruling against personality tests would "set a tremendous precedent," forcing companies and test makers to prove their tests are not discriminatory, says Marc Bendick, an economist and consultant who studies workforce diversity issues.[**]

1. If you were researching this issue for the EEOC, would you conclude that these questions violate the ADA? Do the questions listed inappropriately ask these individuals to reveal a disability?

2. Do you conclude that answering these questions may adversely impact their potential employment?

3. If so, is there an alternative way of protecting against this discrimination while still retaining these assessments?

4. How do the alternatives compare for business and for the stakeholders involved?

*Aon Corporation, "Assessment Barometer 2016" (2016), https://assessment.aon.com/assessment-barometer/ (accessed August 8, 2018); S. Begley, J. Trankiem, and S. Hansel, "Employers Using Personality Tests to Vet Applicants Need Cautious 'Personalities' of Their Own," *Forbes* (October 30, 2014), www.forbes.com/sites/theemploymentbeat/2014/10/30/employers-using-personality-tests-to-vet-applicants-need-cautious-personalities-of-their-own/ (accessed August 8, 2018).

†A. Horton, "The Downsides of Using Personality Tests for Hiring," *Fast Company* (February 23, 2018), www.fastcompany.com/40533339/the-downsides-of-using-personality-tests-for-hiring (accessed March 4, 2019).

‡Ibid.; Emily Chang, *Brotopia: Breaking Up the Boys' Club of Silicon Valley* (Portfolio, 2018).

§L. Weber and E. Dwoskin, "Are Workplace Personality Tests Fair? Growing Use of Tests Sparks Scrutiny amid Questions of Effectiveness and Workplace Discrimination," *The Wall Street Journal* (September 29, 2014), www.wsj.com/articles/are-workplace-personality-tests-fair-1412044257 (accessed March 4, 2019).

**Ibid.

Other Forms of Monitoring

Employers are limited by the courts or regulations in connection with other forms of testing, such as polygraphs or medical tests. They are required to meet certain legal standards such as "business necessity" or "relatedness" or, in the case of polygraphs, by a requirement of "reasonable suspicion." With regard to medical information specifically, employers' decisions in the U.S. are not only governed by the ADA but also restricted by the **Health Insurance Portability and Accountability Act (HIPAA).** HIPAA stipulates that employers cannot use "protected health information" in making employment decisions without the prior consent of the employee. Protected health information includes all medical records or other individually identifiable health information.

In recent years, polygraph and drug testing, physical and electronic surveillance, third-party background checks, and psychological testing have all been used

OBJECTIVE

Health Insurance Portability and Accountability Act (HIPAA) (Pub. L. No. 104-191)
HIPAA stipulates that employers cannot use "protected health information" in making employment decisions without prior consent. Protected health information includes all medical records or other individually identifiable health information.

Genetic Information Nondiscrimination Act of 2008 (GINA)
The Genetic Information Nondiscrimination Act of 2008 (GINA), which took effect on November 21, 2009, makes it illegal to discriminate against employees or applicants because of genetic information. It prohibits the use of genetic information in making employment decisions; restricts employers, employment agencies, labor organizations, and other covered entities from requesting, requiring, or purchasing genetic information; and also limits the disclosure of genetic information.

as means to gain information about employees. As we just discussed above, electronic monitoring and surveillance are increasingly being used in the workplace. But where are we headed in the future? How can our ethical decision-making skills help us to sort through the thorny issues that these new questions pose?

One area that already has raised new questions about privacy is genetic testing. Genetic testing and screening, of both employees and consumers, is a relatively new area of technology development that offers businesses a wealth of information about potential and existing employees and customers—sometimes information beyond what might be related to the job.

Employers might decide to engage in genetic testing of employees based on their perception that testing (and the information they get from it) could encourage behavior change by employees. However, the **Genetic Information Nondiscrimination Act (GINA) of 2008** (which became effective in November 2009) protects employees by prohibiting discriminatory treatment in employment based on genetic information.

GINA defines "genetic information" in a broad sense; your genetic information is not merely information about you, but also your family's medical history (all the way to the fourth degree of kinship), including any disease or disorder or genetic test results of a family member. In addition, GINA restricts employers (and other covered entities) from requesting, requiring, or purchasing any of this genetic information. If they do have access to any of the information, employers are strictly limited in terms of disclosure and subject to conditions similar to the ADA.

GINA does provide for exceptions. For instance, an employer can collect genetic information in order to comply with the Family Medical Leave Act (FMLA) or to monitor the biological effects of toxic substances in the workplace. Also, though GINA contains a strict confidentiality provision, an employer may release genetic information about an employee under certain specific circumstances:

1. To the employee or member upon request;

2. To an occupational or other health researcher;

3. In response to a court order;

4. To a government official investigating compliance with this act if the information is relevant to the investigation;

5. In connection with the employee's compliance with the certification provisions of the FMLA or such requirements under state family and medical leave laws; or

6. To a public health agency.[64]

Finally, the EEOC issued clarifying guidelines in 2010 that include a "safe harbor" liability exception for employers that inadvertently receive genetic information in response to a lawful medical inquiry, so long as the employer has notified the respondent of her or his GINA rights.[65]

While GINA might offer some protections for employees, there are questions as to the effectiveness of genetic testing overall. In one study, researchers asked nine different labs to analyze the same genetic sample and gave nine labs a genetic variant and asked them to analyze it. While the results were relatively similar, agreement on the level of disclosure to the individual was not. In other words, experts do not agree about what is important to disclose to you about your own genetic makeup (up to 22% disagreement in this study). Further, just because you might have a particular genetic variant does not mean that you will develop the underlying disease. So, the value of genetic testing remains somewhat unclear to this day.[66]

Genetic testing is just one of the forms of testing that have evolved from new technology; as technology advances, our ethics and laws need to keep pace, as we have seen. We have mentioned a few others, but employers have used fingerprints, voiceprints, and eye or face scans for all sorts of reasons in the workplace, not only to monitor your work but also to manage access to confidential information. Illinois was one of the first states to enact a Biometric Information Privacy Act in 2008, and, in 2019, its supreme court issued a decision that has implications for employers. Important to employer decisions, that case, *Rosenbach v. Six Flags Entertainment Corp.,*[67] held that it is *not* necessary for an employee to show actual damage but instead merely a violation of the act.

The *Rosenbach* decision is a turning point because it has been difficult to prove harm resulting from the violation of privacy. Therefore, as long as the worker shows that the employer failed to give proper notice, obtain consent, or use a proper standard of care in protecting and managing the information, that worker has a claim. If the employer fails to follow procedures, the court said, "This is no mere 'technicality.' The injury is real and significant." At the time of the decision, there were more than 200 pending cases, so the impact could be significant.[68]

Business Reasons to Limit Monitoring

Notwithstanding any persuasive reasons in favor of workplace monitoring, there may be business reasons to limit monitoring. First, monitoring could create a more suspicious and hostile workplace. By reducing the level of worker autonomy and respect, as well as workers' right to control their environment, employees may sense that the employer has neglected to consider their feelings in this situation; and the employee remains a key stakeholder critical to business success in many ways.

A second concern is that monitoring arguably could reduce effective performance because it can cause increased stress and pressure, which also have the potential to cause physical disorders such as carpal tunnel syndrome.[69] One study found that monitored workers suffered more depression, increased anxiety, severe fatigue and exhaustion, strain injuries, and neck problems than unmonitored workers. Stress might also result from a situation where workers do not have the opportunity to review and correct misinformation in the data collected through monitoring. These factors will lead not only to unhappy, disgruntled workers who perhaps will seek alternative employment but also to lower productivity and performance that will mean higher costs and lower financial returns overall to the employer.

Finally, a third concern is that employees claim that monitoring is an invasion of privacy that violates their fundamental human right to control what others can learn about them.

Balancing Interests

Where should the line be drawn between employer and employee rights? Most of us would agree that installing video cameras in the washrooms of the workplace to prevent theft may be going a bit too far; but knowing where to draw the line before that extreme might be more difficult. As long as technology exists to allow for privacy invasions, should the employer have the right to use it? Does its mere existence make it okay?

Consider whether monitoring could be made (more) ethical or humane. Is it more ethical if an employer gives employees due notice that they will be monitored, plus the opportunity to avoid monitoring in certain situations? For instance, let us assume that an employer wants to monitor random phone calls of its customer service representatives to be sure that these phone representatives are doing a good job. That sounds like a plausible argument from the employer. But it also causes a lot of stress for the people working the call centers because they fear that any minor slips during a call could be their last! The staff and employer might reach a compromise where the employer would notify the workers that certain calls would be monitored, and the reps would be notified that they are being monitored by a "beep" on the line during the monitoring. They would not have advance notice to prepare, but they would be aware during the monitoring process. In addition, if workers needed to make a personal call, they would have access to a phone line that would never be monitored, to avoid any chance of a wrongful invasion of privacy.

Of course, the above approach does not solve *all* of the employer's concerns about good customer service. No solution is perfect. The employer wanted to be sure that its service representatives handled calls in a patient, tolerant, and friendly manner. By notifying workers when they are being monitored, even if they are unable to prepare in advance, the employees are able to ensure that they are on their best behavior during those calls. This effect of employer monitoring is termed the **"Hawthorne effect":** Workers are found to be more productive based on the psychological stimulus of being singled out, which makes them feel more important. In other words, merely knowing one is being studied might make one a better worker. Random, anonymous monitoring may better resolve the employer's concerns (but not those of the worker). Of course, as we just discussed, other research does seem to indicate that random monitoring may lead to lower productivity in some circumstances because of the increased stress it places on the workforce so, as we noted, there is no perfect answer.

Perhaps the most effective means to achieve monitoring objectives while remaining sensitive to the concerns of employees is to strive toward a balance that respects individual dignity while also holding individuals accountable for their particular roles in the organization. A monitoring program developed according

Hawthorne effect
The impact on one's behavior of knowing that one is being studied. In connection with employee monitoring, for instance, merely knowing that one is being monitored may have the effect of enhancing productivity temporarily. However, other research suggests that monitoring may have the opposite effect because it also has been shown to create stress and anxiety (among other consequences), thus reducing productivity.

to the mission of the organization (e.g., with integrity), then implemented in a manner that remains accountable to the impacted employees, approaches that balance. Consider the following parameters for a monitoring policy that endeavors to accomplish the goals described earlier (while remembering the mantra that there is no perfect solution!):

- No monitoring in private areas (e.g., restrooms).
- Monitoring limited to within the workplace.
- Employees should have access to information gathered through monitoring.
- No secret monitoring—advance notice required.
- Monitoring should only result in attaining some business interest.
- Employer may collect only job-related information.
- Agreement regarding disclosure of information gained through monitoring.
- Prohibition of discrimination by employers based on off-work activities.

These parameters allow the employer to effectively and ethically supervise the work employees do, to protect against misuse of resources, and to have an appropriate mechanism by which to evaluate each worker's performance, thus respecting the legitimate business interest of the employer.

Philosopher William Parent looks at this question a little differently and conceives the right to privacy more appropriately as a "right to liberty." He therefore seeks to determine whether the employee's liberty is limited by the employer's actions. He suggests that we consider the following six questions in order to determine whether an employer's actions are justifiable or, alternatively, have the potential for an invasion of privacy:

1. For what purpose is the personal knowledge sought?
2. Is this purpose a legitimate and important one?
3. Is the knowledge sought through the invasion of privacy relevant to its justifying purpose?
4. Is invasion of privacy the only, or the least offensive, means of obtaining the knowledge?
5. What restrictions or procedural restraints have been placed on the privacy-invading techniques?
6. How will the personal knowledge be protected once it has been acquired?[70]

Both of these sets of guidelines may also respect the personal autonomy of the individual worker by providing for personal space within the working environment, by providing notice of where that "personal" space ends, and by allowing access to the information gathered, all designed toward achievement of a personal and professional development objective.

Our discussion to this point has involved the relationship between the employer and the employee within the workplace environment. We have explored the balance between an employer's interest in controlling what happens within that environment, in order to further its business goals, with the employee's right to personal autonomy and privacy. The following section examines whether employers are permitted to tell employees what they can (or cannot) do while they are *not at work*.

Regulation of Off-Work Acts

OBJECTIVE

The regulation of an employee's activities when she or he is away from work is a provocative question, particularly in at-will employment environments. One might say that, if you do not like your employer telling you what to do, just find another job. Whether that is a realistic solution or not, as discussed elsewhere in this chapter, even employers of at-will employees must comply with a variety of statutes that impose certain requirements and limitations on them. For instance, New York's lifestyle discrimination statute prohibits employment decisions or actions based on four categories of off-duty activity: legal recreational activities, consumption of legal products, political activities, and membership in a union.[71]

As you will learn throughout this section, employers do have *some* say over the activities of their employees in *some* areas of their off-work lives. But is it ethical for them to use that power? Are they infringing on their employees' free will and personal choices about how workers live their lives, on their autonomy and right to "self-rule"? What decision will lead to the greatest good for the employer, for the employee, and for society, overall?

Tobacco Use

There is no question that smoking is not good for our health, but, if I make a personal choice to smoke anyway, is it ethical for my employer to restrict that right? Some employers do not necessarily restrict it but instead seek to discourage smoking among their employees in an effort to reduce long-term health care costs, among other reasons. However, a number of states protect workers who choose to use legal substances off the job, including cigarettes.[72] Employers are not allowed to prohibit smoking as a condition of employment in at least twenty-nine states and the District of Columbia (and those states also provide antiretaliation provisions for employers who violate the prohibition). As a result, some companies instead encourage nonsmoking among employees by providing free smoking-cessation programs and other similar wellness services.

Other firms have chosen to use "the stick" rather than "the carrot" to promote nonsmoking. Under the Affordable Care Act (ACA), insurance companies are permitted to charge smokers and other tobacco users up to 50% more than nonsmokers for a health insurance policy. So, while a company cannot prohibit smoking, it can make it costly for the smoker! There are rules under the Health Insurance Portability and Accountability Act (HIPAA) that require firms to offer alternatives to avoid the surcharge, but an employer cannot require an employee actually quit smoking.[73] States can choose to step in and mandate a lower surcharge or none at all, although only seven states/jurisdictions have waived it entirely: California, Connecticut, Massachusetts, New Jersey, New York, Rhode Island, Vermont, and Washington, D.C.[74]

So in the end, we have an unhealthy act that employers would prefer workers avoid, but they cannot prohibit it. At its core, the autonomy of individuals—and their right to do what they choose with their bodies—prevails. While some might argue that the greater good could be served by a smoke-free society or a global ban on tobacco, in this instance, the argument has not succeeded.

Weight Differences

Compared to smoking, employment decisions on the basis of one's size and weight is handled in an entirely different manner by the states. Only one state (Michigan) and six U.S. cities ban discrimination on the basis of weight.[75] In all other U.S. regions, employers are permitted to make employment decisions on the basis of weight, as long as those decisions do not violate the Americans with Disabilities Act (ADA). That question depends on whether the employee's weight results from a disability.

disability
An impairment that substantially limits a major life activity.

Weight beyond the norm, even to a level considered to be obese, is not presumed to be a disability under the ADA. In order to qualify as a **disability,** an impairment must substantially limit a major life activity. The Equal Employment Opportunity Commission (EEOC) has issued guidance explaining that obesity only satisfies these requirements where it is "outside of a 'normal' range" and "results from a physiological disorder."[76]

However, employers should be aware that the ADA also protects workers who are *not* disabled but who still are *perceived as being disabled.* In a 2018 case, a job offer to an individual was rescinded when a post-offer physical revealed that his body mass index (BMI) was higher than the position permitted, for safety reasons. The employer, a railway, argued that workers over a certain BMI were more likely to develop certain medical conditions that could incapacitate them or impact their cognitive ability. The court reiterated that weight is not a protected disability under the ADA. But because the conditions that concerned the railway, such as sleep apnea, diabetes, or heart disease, are actually disabilities, the court expressed concerns that the railway was making decisions based on "the sort of myth, fear, or stereotype which the ADA is meant to guard against." It therefore allowed the case to go forward based on the "regarded as" prong of the ADA.[77] The case was on appeal as of our publication, but it is an important reminder that decisions based on myths, fears, or stereotypes are likely to have significant consequences for all involved.

Marital and Relationship Status

Laws that protect against discrimination based on marital status exist in just under half of the states. However, though workers might be protected based on marital *status* (such as whether someone is single, married, or divorced), they are not necessarily protected against adverse employment actions based on *the identity of the person* they married. For instance, some companies might have an antinepotism policy that says that an employer can refuse to hire or can terminate a worker if her or his spouse works at the same firm, or a conflict-of-interest policy that says that an employer can refuse to hire or can terminate a worker if her or his spouse works at a competing firm.

Because research shows that 36% of workers have dated an office colleague, policies and attitudes on workplace dating have an especially strong potential impact.[78] Forty-five percent of firms have policies addressing workplace dating, and that number may increase as the #MeToo movement raises awareness of relationship dynamics in the workplace.[79] For instance, in 2018, the CEO of tech giant Intel stepped down after an internal investigation discovered that he had a consensual relationship with a subordinate. The relationship was in violation of Intel's strict no-dating policy for all managers.

Davia Temin, chief executive of a reputation and crisis-management firm, explains, "the rise of the #MeToo movement has companies hewing closely to policies on both sexual harassment and consensual relationships, especially for business leaders."[80] Additionally, a New York court decision reaffirmed the employer's right to terminate a worker on the basis of romantic involvement. In *McCavitt v. Swiss Reinsurance America Corp.,*[81] the court held that an employee's dating relationship with a fellow officer of the corporation was not a "recreational activity," within the meaning of a New York statute that prohibited employment discrimination for engaging in such recreational activities. The employee argued that, even though his personal relationship with this fellow officer had no repercussions whatever for the professional responsibilities or accomplishments of either individual involved, and his employer, Swiss Re, had no written antifraternization or antinepotism policy, he was passed over for promotion and then discharged from employment because of his relationship. The court, however, agreed with the employer that termination was permitted because dating was not a recreational activity, and therefore *not* protected from discrimination.

While concerns about workplace dating used to involve predominantly issues of sexual harassment, they are now more likely to involve concerns about claims of retaliation after a relationship is over. However, contrary to the court's holding in *McCavitt,* not everyone agrees that the most effective response to the discovery of an illicit relationship is termination of the individual in power. Consider the questions raised in the Decision Point "To Date or Not to Date."

Sexual Orientation and Gender Identity

What happens if an employer prefers not to hire someone on the basis of her or his sexual orientation? The law offers a different answer to this question based on where the decision is made. Though no federal law expressly bans discrimination on the basis of *sexual orientation* or *gender identity,* some courts (including the Seventh Circuit) and also the EEOC have interpreted Title VII's prohibition of gender discrimination to include these and other areas.[82] However, the Department of Justice does not agree, so the question remains unresolved at the federal level.

Twenty-one states and the District of Columbia prohibit employment discrimination on the basis of sexual orientation. In addition, there are hundreds of local ordinances, and thousands of workplaces, including 91% of *Fortune* 500 companies, that protect LGBT employees against discrimination. In 2019, for instance, New York added "gender identity or expression" as a protected class to its nondiscrimination laws and also banned conversion therapy. The law now protects

What should company leadership do when it learns that the firm's founder is "fraternizing" with an employee who is in a subordinate position? Google co-founder Sergey Brin became romantically involved with a Google employee and subsequently divorced his wife. Complicating things further, Brin's former sister-in-law and former brother-in-law (his ex-wife's family members) both have major positions at Google. Brin insists that nothing about his new—or former—relationship will impact Google from a business perspective. But some suspect that this story is only the beginning of a larger problem for Google.

Google maintains an informal approach to workplace dating, and its code of conduct does not prohibit dating between employees. The code states:

> Romantic relationships between co-workers can, depending on the work roles and respective positions of the co-workers involved, create an actual or apparent conflict of interest. If a romantic relationship does create an actual or apparent conflict, it may require changes to work arrangements or even the termination of employment of either or both individuals involved.*

Brin is an important and, some argue, vital part of the Google company, and also plays a role on its research and development teams. He has a controlling interest of Google stock. According to one article, Larry Page, the CEO and other co-founder, was extremely upset with Brin's relationship, and they did not speak for a time. Further, some Google employees, especially women, were furious that Brin and his girlfriend were not more separated professionally.†

Under a utilitarian analysis, it might appear that the cost of Brin's alleged "errors" compared to the cost of his departure from Google might seem to weigh in favor of keeping Brin employed. Or one could argue that employee morale surrounding this situation is so damaging to the work environment that it outweighs Brin's current and future contributions.

1. Have you considered further challenges in this narrative? Who would be the one to make the decision to fire Brin from the company, given his position and stock holdings? Plus, should his girlfriend be fired? If so, on what basis? Is it possible for them to be professionally separated when one of them is the CEO? Does Google need a clearer policy on workplace romance? If so, how would you suggest Google's policy be modified?

2. Assume you are charged with drafting your organization's policy on workplace dating. In which direction will you tilt with regard to its management of this issue? Utilitarian, or more in line with the 28% of workplaces that simply prohibit workplace dating in order to have a clearer line of demarcation? If you opt for the former, what ethical issues do you anticipate, and how do you plan to respond to them because planning ahead will help you to prepare most effectively and ethically? Who are your stakeholders, and what options do you have in your responses to those stakeholders in order to best meet each of their interests and rights?

3. If you opt for a prohibition, how do you plan to enforce it? Are you willing to hire someone who is dating a current employee? Must they stop dating? What problems might arise as a result of your policy, in either direction?

*Google, Code of Ethics.

†Vanessa Grigoriadis, "O.K., Glass: Make Google Eyes," *Vanity Fair* (April 2014), www.vanityfair.com/society/2014/04/sergey-brin-amanda-rosenberg-affair# (accessed March 5, 2019).

transgender, gender nonconforming, and nonbinary individuals in the workplace, as well as in other environments.

The issue remains a significant one for employers, from both a legal perspective and an ethical one. Approximately 4% of the United States workforce self-identifies as lesbian, gay, bisexual, or transgender (LGBT). Forty percent of these individuals experience harassment and discrimination in their workplaces on the basis of their sexual orientation, in connection with hiring, promotions, and pay (and that number rises to 97% for transgender employees). For this reason, almost half of LGBT employees report that they do not feel that they are safe, comfortable, or protected being open about their identities in the workplace and instead remain in the closet or do not live permanently in their preferred gender role. So their representation in the work place may, indeed, be far higher.[83]

Whether employers *are permitted* to treat LGBT workers differently may be a legal question of jurisdiction, but whether they *should* do so is an ethical question. Let us consider the employer's choice from the perspective of ends-based theories such as utilitarianism. If the employer discriminates on any basis—other than someone's capacity to do a job effectively—that employer will be at a disadvantage compared to its competitors who do not discriminate. It is hard to imagine a job where one's sexual orientation or gender identity reduces her or his ability to perform the essential functions of the position. (See also the Chapter 6 Decision Point "Who Needs Ethics? Can the Market 'Fix' Discrimination?")

One might anticipate objections from one or more stakeholder groups, based on differing underlying belief structures in connection with their religious or other doctrine, for example. They may contend that extending protection to the LBGT community (or prohibiting discrimination and harassment) trespasses on their religious freedom. However, philosophers have clarified that prohibiting discrimination in employment is not equivalent to granting a positive right (such as gay marriage—a topic we are not discussing at this particular moment). The mere act of prohibiting discrimination or harassment does not endorse any individual, trait, characteristic, or lifestyle but instead protects individual dignity. (It also should be noted that Title VII does provide an exemption for religious institutions where the position is specifically connected with the religious activities and mission of a religious organization.)

Similar arguments may be made in connection with means-based ethical theories, such as Kant's principles of autonomy. As discussed in Chapter 3, the Kantian tradition also would consider discrimination against LGBT applicants or employees unethical because it infringes on our free choices about how we live our lives, and our fundamental human right of "self-rule."

Off-Work Use of Technology

The question of monitoring and managing employee online communications while the employee is *off work* is relevant to the issues of technology monitoring discussed earlier in this chapter; this question emerges as an astonishingly challenging area of conflict between employers and employees, and one without much legal guidance, demanding sensitive ethical decision making. For instance, consider the question of the off-duty use of social media sites, like Facebook. As of December 2018, Facebook had 2.32 billion monthly active users worldwide, a usage that encompasses 30% of the world.[84] Though Facebook and other social media sites may initially seem to offer a convenient environment where employees are able to vent about their employment situations, it is not so convenient when one of those vent posts goes viral. Corporate reputations are at stake, and legal consequences can be severe. We discussed a politically charged photo that was posted in our Opening Decision Point in Chapter 6. In another situation, an energy company employee in Detroit was fired after the employee grumbled on Facebook about customers who called the company with complaints when their power went out during storms.[85] A restaurant server in Florida was fired after she shared her frustrations on Facebook about a large group of customers that had ordered $735 in food but did not leave a tip.[86]

In recent cases, though, some employees are fighting back. A Virginia woman posted on Facebook after getting home from work, "Today was the worst!!!!!!!!!!!! Thanks for helping out. Oh wait I am a team of 1 because others have meetings or they to [sic] lazy to get up to help someone." Within a week, she was fired for violating a social media policy that prohibits employees from making online comments that might embarrass the company. She was unable to receive unemployment benefits because she had been fired for misconduct. In response, she filed a lawsuit claiming the policy impeded her right to talk about workplace conditions under the National Labor Relations Act. Her lawsuit cited a 2012 decision by the National Labor Relations Board that struck down a social media policy requiring employees to "communicate with appropriate business decorum" on all electronic media and to refrain from posting statements that damaged the company. She settled with her company three months later.[87]

Of course, our posts stay with us, practically forever. Have you ever thought that what you might post today could get you into trouble years from now? Employers have been known to dig deep into potential employees' past social media posts to learn about them. Younger candidates were not really thinking of their future employers when they were on social media in high school, but perhaps they should have considered how their online persona might look to their future boss. How far back in the past should we consider when evaluating a prospective employee?

In addition, while employers are prevented by law from asking candidates about their religion or prior illegal drug use during a job interview, is it ethical for them to seek out that information through online sources, if the candidate voluntarily discloses it? For instance, in various individuals' profiles on Facebook, there may be posted, "Nothing is more important to me than the values I have learned from being a Seventh Day Adventist." Another person might share her pride at recently getting out of rehab. The prospective employer could never access this information through the interview so is gathering it in this method any more appropriate?

As discussed earlier in the chapter, the laws on this matter vary from country to country and also from state to state. For instance, there are far greater limitations on the collection of personal information in Australia than in the United States.[88] Plus, as of 2018, twenty-six states restrict employers from requiring social media

Uniting and Strengthening America by Providing Appropriate Tools Required to Intercept and Obstruct Terrorism (USA PATRIOT) Act of 2001
A U.S. statute designed to increase the surveillance and investigative powers of law enforcement agencies in the United States in response to the terrorist attacks of September 11, 2001. The act has been lauded as a quick response to terrorism (it was introduced less than a week after the attacks) and for implementing critical amendments to more than 15 important statutes; it also has been criticized for failing to include sufficient safeguards for civil liberties.

passwords from prospective or current employees, and several more state legislatures have bills pending.[89] But, of course, that prohibition is only helpful to individuals if they ensure that their profile settings are not set to share the information publicly.

In signing Illinois's legislation to prohibit employers from requiring job candidates or current employees to submit their social networking passwords, former Illinois governor Pat Quinn compared these passwords to ordinary house keys and said, "members of the workforce should not be punished for information their employers don't legally have the right to have. As use of social media continues to expand, this new law will protect workers and their right to personal privacy."[90]

When comparing these restrictions across cultures, what ethical values should dictate? Should a single, universal value govern an employer's judgment, or should the employer's behavior also vary from country to country, if it is a global operation? Have a look at the "big brother" style of oversight that China already has initiated and how it has impacted and will impact both individuals and employers in the Reality Check "Credit where Due?" Consider what off-works acts you might prohibit if you were an employer—and whether these constraints might vary from one region or country to another.

The Reality Check "The Employment Relationship Begins Preemployment" provides an overview of the intersection of the discussions of the prior two sections in its evaluation of privacy, testing, and off-work acts. While our analysis to this point has addressed the regulation of behavior during employment, perhaps it is important to consider your choices before employment and the impact they will have on an employer's later decisions about hiring you. Alternatively, from the employer's perspective, it is important to understand when it is valuable to test prospective employees or why it might be effective to refrain from testing in the hiring process.

Privacy Rights since September 11, 2001

OBJECTIVE

The terrorist attacks against the United States by al-Qaeda on September 11, 2001, had a major impact on privacy within the U.S., and on the employment environment, in particular. Subsequent to those events, the federal government implemented widespread modifications to its patchwork structure of privacy protections. Specifically, broad-reaching proposals for the expansion of surveillance and information-gathering authority were enacted, over the objections of some civil rights advocates.

The most publicized of these modifications was the adoption and implementation of the **Uniting and Strengthening America by Providing Appropriate Tools Required to Intercept and Obstruct Terrorism (USA PATRIOT) Act of 2001.** The USA PATRIOT Act expands states' rights with regard to Internet surveillance technology, including workplace surveillance, and amended the Electronic Communications Privacy Act. The act also grants access to sensitive data with only a court order rather than a judicial warrant and imposes or enhances civil and criminal penalties for knowingly or intentionally aiding terrorists. In addition,

Reality Check *Credit Where Due?*

You go online to book a flight home for the holidays. The website says that you are blocked from making the booking.

You notice that your internet has been slower than usual in recent weeks.

Your daughter recently was denied admission to the local private school you had hoped would be her ticket to the future.

Bad luck? Perhaps not. Established in 2014 and due for full implementation by 2020, China is the first country to share complete details of its "social credit" system, which measures an individual's social activities, creates a score based on that reputation, and then applies consequences for its citizen's social behaviors.

The program began when the Chinese court system created a list of approximately 32,000 debtors but then expanded when firms such as ride-sharing companies and online dating services sought to access similar information. A point system was established that included values for behaviors such as defaulting on court fines, online gaming activity, shopping habits, or even bad driving or smoking in a nonsmoking area. Certainly, criminal activity would reduce your trustworthiness score. Opportunities exist to raise one's score, as well. The plan is said to be in line with President Xi Jinping's principle of "once untrustworthy, always restricted."

Reports are teeming with people in China being impacted both negatively and positively by their social credit score. Nine million people experienced restrictions on purchases of air and train tickets, and dozens of others who did not complete their military service were barred from continuing their education and refused hotel reservations. One university denied a student entry because of his parent's social credit score. On the other hand, a good score results in better placement on dating sites, better interest rates, and discounts on utilities.

How is the information communicated? In some cases, one's activities are part of an online or public record (such as shopping habits or legal history). In other cases, the public is encouraged to report on each other or activities are otherwise recorded. In a video posted on Twitter by a journalist, train passengers on the Beijing-to-Shanghai journey were informed that "people who travel without a ticket, or behave disorderly, or smoke in public areas will be punished according to regulations and the behavior will be recorded in individual credit information system."*

Employers are subject to similar oversight. Employers also will face restrictions if they are found to have been involved in "financial wrongdoings" or have "failed to pay social insurance or refuse to pay fines." Businesses are strongly encouraged to consult the social credit lists before doing any recruitment or making hiring decisions.

OTHER RELATED ISSUES

Employers should be aware, in connection with any form of lifestyle constraints—whether within or outside of the workplace—that lifestyle discrimination may be unlawful if the imposition of a rule treats one protected group differently than another. For instance, if an employer imposes a rule restricting the use of peyote in Native American rituals that take place during off-work hours, the rule may be suspect and may subject the employer to liability. Similarly, the rule may be unlawful if it has a different impact on a protected group than on other groups.

In 2019, the New York City Commission on Human Rights issued guidelines that directed employers not to discriminate against individuals based on their hair or hairstyle. Specifically, it protects New York employees' right to maintain "natural hair, treated or untreated hairstyles such as locs, cornrows, twists, braids, Bantu knots, fades, Afros, and/or the right to keep hair in an uncut or untrimmed state."† One's decision to express one's identity through this form of expression, therefore, is protected, and a job cannot be denied because an employer believes that someone's hairstyle is not appropriate for a workplace. These guidelines are considered extremely progressive. Historically, the hairstyles mentioned above have not always been deemed by a conservative U.S. society to be appropriate in all workplaces, and, in fact, students have been sent home from school for sporting some of these styles and refusing to change. Yet, from a purely objective perspective, who is to dictate what haircut or style is "proper" for one environment or another? Why is long hair acceptable for women and not (traditionally) as acceptable for men, for instance?

Most U.S. statutes or common-law decisions do allow employers to defend a decision different from these guidelines or rulings, where those decisions or workplace rules:

1. Are reasonably and rationally related to the employment activities of a particular employee;

2. Constitute a "*bona fide* occupational requirement" (BFOQ), meaning a rule that is reasonably related to that particular position; or

3. Are necessary to avoid a conflict of interest or the appearance of a conflict of interest.

*Announcement on Train between Beijing and Shanghai.

†S. Stowe, "New York City to Ban Discrimination Based on Hair," *The New York Times* (February 18, 2019), https://www.nytimes.com/2019/02/18/style/hair-discrimination-new-york-city.html (accessed February 21, 2019).

Sources: A. Ma, "China Ranks Citizens with a Social Credit System," *The Independent* (April 10, 2018), www.independent.co.uk/life-style/gadgets-and-tech/china-social-credit-system-punishments-rewards-explained-a8297486.html (accessed March 5, 2019); Reuters, "Millions in China with Bad 'Social Credit' Barred from Buying Plane, Train Tickets," *Channel News Asia* (March 16, 2018), www.channelnewsasia.com/news/asia/china-bad-social-credit-barred-from-buying-train-plane-tickets-10050390 (accessed March 5, 2019); A. Ma, "China Has Started Ranking Citizens with a Creepy 'Social Credit' System," *Business Insider* (October 29, 2018), www.businessinsider.com/china-social-credit-system-punishments-and-rewards-explained-2018-4 (accessed March 5, 2019); James O'Malley, Tweet from October 29, 2018, https://twitter.com/Psythor/status/1056811593177227264 (accessed March 5, 2019).

the new disclosure regime increases the sharing of personal information between government agencies to ensure the greatest level of protection.

Title II of the act provides for the following enhanced surveillance procedures, all of which have a significant impact on individual privacy and may impact an employer's effort to maintain employee privacy:

- Expands authority to intercept wire, oral, and electronic communications relating to terrorism and to computer fraud and abuse offenses.
- Provides roving surveillance authority under the Foreign Intelligence Surveillance Act (FISA) of 1978 to track individuals. (FISA investigations are not subject to Fourth Amendment standards but are instead governed by the requirement that the search serve "a significant purpose.")
- Allows nationwide seizure of voice-mail messages pursuant to warrants (i.e., without the previously required wiretap order).
- Broadens the types of records that law enforcement may obtain, pursuant to a subpoena, from electronic communications service providers.
- Permits emergency disclosure of customer electronic communications by providers to protect life and limb.
- Provides nationwide service of search warrants for electronic evidence.

These provisions allow the U.S. government to monitor anyone on the internet simply by contending that the information is "relevant" to an ongoing criminal investigation. In addition, the act includes provisions designed to combat money laundering activity or the funding of terrorist or criminal activity through corporate activity or otherwise. All financial institutions must report suspicious activities in financial transactions and keep records of foreign national employees, while also complying with the antidiscrimination laws discussed throughout this text.

The USA PATRIOT Act has been reauthorized three times, and elements have been amended, revised, and extended by several additional bills.[91] In 2015, the main elements of the USA PATRIOT Act were extended through 2019 through the USA Freedom Act, with some modifications as discussed below.

Reality Check *The Employment Relationship Begins Preemployment*

Society has traditionally treated the employment relationship as beginning and ending with the start and end dates of the employment appointment. In fact, the relationship begins prior to hiring and ends, often, only with death.

PREEMPLOYMENT PRACTICES

The importance of the preemployment relationship is commonly overlooked. In spite of this, preemployees (i.e., job candidates) today have few if any legally recognized rights. This is becoming increasingly problematic because of widespread advances in technology and the virtual lack of respect afforded the personal privacy of job-tap seekers.

A number of companies have recently emerged and are taking advantage of new information-gathering technologies by offering these services to employers in the process of hiring new employees. These companies contract with organizations (and individuals) to gather personal information about potential new hires. They gather any information that is requested about job candidates—from credit histories to their driving records.

While collecting data on people prior to their employment is nothing new, the methods used today lack the transparency of the past and skew the balance of power even more toward the employer and away from the employee. Further, employers do not always ask permission or even inform job candidates that they are doing background checks and are often unwilling to reveal to applicants the specific information that has influenced their hiring decisions.

Firms support this sort of information gathering on the basis that it enables them to make better hiring decisions. Even so, the practice is not without serious drawbacks—even from the perspective of the hiring firms. For one reason, the accuracy of third-party information is not always assured. In addition, there are no guarantees that the data collected are complete. Background checks can result in inaccurate or downright erroneous candidate profiles. While employers assume they are finding out relevant information to enhance their hiring decisions, the reality is that the information they are obtaining might be distorted without their knowledge; instead of eliminating certain risky candidates, they might unknowingly be overlooking "diamonds in the rough."

From the perspective of job applicants, the practice of preemployment information gathering is particularly insidious. Job candidates are not always given notice that they are being scrutinized and that the material being collected is highly personal. In addition, job candidates are generally not offered the opportunity to provide any sort of rebuttal to the reports generated by information-gathering agencies. This is especially problematic in situations where candidates are rejected on the basis of background checks.

IMPACT OF PREEMPLOYMENT PRACTICES

To see how this testing can have a negative impact on the hiring process, take the example of Maria, a fictitious job candidate. Maria applies for a job in marketing for a regional department store. She is asked to take a pre-screening drug test and, through this and the personal information she provides as part of a general background check, the potential employer gains access to Maria's credit report. This report reveals that she has a judgment pending against her. Fearing that Maria is an employment risk, the company decides not to hire her.

While the credit report's data might be accurate, it does not tell the complete story about Maria. It does not indicate, for example, that Maria was the victim of identity fraud. In addition, the report might be inaccurate without her knowledge. While Maria should be aware of the credit information in her report, she has not looked at it in some time, and the collecting agency has included some incorrect information. The fact that Maria has an unpaid debt does not provide information inherently relevant to the particular job for which she has applied.

The employer considering Maria's application might rationalize that the background check is necessary to assess her general suitability. Many employers consider this a legitimate purpose and argue that there is a relationship between a candidate's responsibility in handling client affairs and her manner of dealing with personal finances. Although such an argument is not without merit, the result seems somewhat excessive. Consider, for example, the relevance of the driving record of a candidate for a bus driver position: It would seem almost counterintuitive not to inquire into that sort of information.

There are meaningful differences, however, between this situation and that of Maria. Where work is of a particularly sensitive nature or where the level of the open position is high within a company, background checks directly related to performance might be appropriate when linked to a legitimate business purpose. In addition, the type of company or potential liability for the company could also warrant specific checks. In Maria's situation, none of these circumstances are present.

ARGUMENTS AGAINST EXCESSIVE PREEMPLOYMENT TESTING

There are many arguments against preemployment testing, particularly when used indiscriminately. Excessive preemployment testing can be attacked on moral grounds. First, it undermines the dignity of the individual by strengthening the notion of the person as a mere factor of production. It effectively enables employers to treat people as a means to achieving profitable ends without regard for the individual as a person valuable in and of him- or herself. In addition, it creates a climate of suspicion that undermines trust and loyalty and encourages duplicity and insincerity. Finally, it affects the character of the companies and individuals who work there. Companies become secretive and manipulative through such information gathering, and candidates, in turn, do what they can to conceal information they consider potentially unfavorable to their acceptance or advancement. This sort of behavior is to the detriment of the character of both employers and potential employees.

In addition to these sorts of ethical considerations, there are strong business arguments against excessive use of preemployment testing. Unfettered collection of personal information disregards property interests associated with that personal information. Hiring practices involving background checks ignore a person's ownership of information about him- or herself. It also erodes the privacy expectations a person has in his or her personal information. Moreover, it creates a bad first impression for potential employees and detracts from general morale. During bad economic times, this might not matter, but when times are good and employment rates are high, potential job candidates are likely to seek out opportunities with employers who do not utilize such intrusive methods. In addition, current employees—those who stay by necessity or choice—will see themselves in a relationship with an employer who does not trust them or respect individual privacy. In other words, the practice used in hiring spills over and effectively becomes the tenor of the overall employment relationship, and this can prove demoralizing to employees and result in an underlying tone of distrust.

RESPONSIBLE USE OF PERSONAL INFORMATION

The availability of abundant information to employers does not mean that they have to use all of it. Ideally, personal information should remain personal and, at the very least, the individual should have the ability to determine who gains access to his or her personal information and to know when someone obtains that information. It is important here to keep in mind that the availability of access is not the same as the moral right to access information or to use that information in a hiring decision.

As employers consider how to use the information they gather, they should consider "legitimate business purpose" as a guiding principle. Where there is a legitimate business purpose (defined generally to be applied to job function, type of company, and so on) and an identifiable direct correlation between that information and the job candidate, it would then seem appropriate for personal information to be solicited.

At the same time and as Maria's situation illustrates, it now becomes incumbent upon individuals to keep better track of their personal information. Now that individuals are aware that credit checks can be performed and used against them, they need to make sure that the credit bureaus have accurate information. In addition, individuals need to be prepared to respond to anomalies that might exist in their personal information. It is no longer an issue of what is right and what is wrong, but what is going to happen. If we know that employers have access to this information, it is for us to determine what we are going to do about it for ourselves.

Source: Adapted for this publication and used by permission of the authors, Tara J. Radin and Martin Calkins.

The Opening Decision Point asked you to consider the implications of using smartphones in business contexts. It might not have occurred to you previously that smartphones could be a source of ethical problems in the workplace because most people see an iPhone or Android simply as a source of productivity, allowing them to carry a powerful computer combined with a communications device in their pocket or handbag. The convenience of being able to access information, as well as to stay in touch with key clients and co-workers just about anywhere, typically is seen as a benefit rather than a problem. But, as the earlier box illustrated, smartphones—like many new technologies—also raise ethical questions.

Clearly, the Opening Decision Point involved miscommunication from the start. Using the ethical decision-making process, we are confronted with a scenario in which the stakeholders involved perceived the situation from entirely different perspectives. While you were entirely engaged in the meeting and working strenuously to produce the most effective result, your behavior left many involved with the perception that you were instead "checked out" and fiddling with your phone! Certainly, if you had known that was the impression you were likely to create, you would never have made the same decision. Instead, you would have . . . well? What would you have done?

That is the benefit of considering these scenarios at the outset. Not everyone will perceive your behavior from the same vantage point, nor with the same experiential background. You might be the type of person to take notes on your smartphone, while that option might never enter into someone else's mind. By understanding that perspective, you might have started the meeting by letting everyone know that you plan to record some bullet points directly into your phone so that you can upload them electronically the moment you return to your office. In that way, you will be best able to share them with the team in the most efficient manner immediately following the meeting. Everyone would have nodded and appreciated your thoughtfulness. To the contrary, you are left needing to explain the fiasco to your boss.

We should realize, of course, that sometimes it is not at all a matter of misunderstanding; some people actually may be playing games on their phones during meetings, texting with friends, or checking in on Twitter. To the extent that this activity means that they are paying less attention to what others in the meeting are saying, such activities are—at the very least—disrespectful. However, consider far worse implications for the workplace. A one-time offense arguably could be dismissed as simply rude, but ongoing behavior could demonstrate a pattern of rudeness, which implies a lack of overall respect for stakeholders. Respect for the personal dignity of others is a key element of ethical decision making.

Though there would be significant exceptions, of course, some disagreements over the use of smartphones in the workplace might also be generational. Some younger workers who have grown up with mobile phones and who are used to text messaging to keep in near constant contact with friends might see texting during a meeting as normal, and as implying no disrespect at all. Moreover, some of these workers might not even wear a watch anymore and often use their phone as their only method by which to check the time, so checking their phone is no more intrusive to them than someone else glancing at her or his wrist. To the contrary, some (be wary of generalizations here, again) older workers, even many of those who are comfortable using a smartphone, may see such devices more strictly in terms of their usefulness for a narrow range of essential business operations. To these workers, use of a smartphone during a meeting—even to check business-related email—may cross a boundary of propriety.

1. How might you respond if you observed a colleague texting in the middle of a meeting?

2. Would it be different if the meeting involved just the two of you or other people? If the others were work colleagues or colleagues external to your firm?

3. What would you do if you received a text from a colleague in the middle of a meeting (and the colleague is in the same meeting)?

4. Are there new technologies other than smartphones that raise questions such as the ones discussed in this scenario? Does the use of a laptop during a business meeting raise the same or similar issues?

5. Did it occur to you at the end of the Opening Decision Point that perhaps your boss might have given you the benefit of the doubt and asked whether you had been using your phone for note-taking? Does that perspective affect your response at all?

6. When people differ with regard to the proper use of new technologies in the workplace, how should such differences be resolved? Should fans of new technologies be extra cautious? Or should those who resist new technologies be expected to "get with the times"?

Requests from businesses have become a topic of significant concern in recent years. The USA PATRIOT Act allows for and relies on requests from businesses to gather information. In 2013, it was revealed that the National Security Agency (NSA) was harvesting millions of email and instant messaging contact lists, searching email content, and tracking and mapping the location of cell phones, often with the cooperation of telecommunications companies.[92]

Through its PRISM program, the NSA was tapping into the data centers of companies like Yahoo! and Google to collect information from "hundreds of millions" of account holders worldwide on the basis of court-approved explicit access.[93] After this revelation, the large tech companies requested from the U.S. government the ability to be transparent with customers. A deal was brokered, and four of the tech firms that participate in the NSA's PRISM program (Microsoft, Yahoo!, Google, and Facebook) released more information about the volume of data that the government demands they provide. Unfortunately, the government still does not allow these companies to itemize the data collected, so transparency remains relative.[94]

Section 215 of the PATRIOT Act was amended in 2015 by the USA Freedom Act to stop the NSA from continuing its mass phone data collection program. Instead, phone companies will retain the data, and the NSA is permitted only to obtain information about targeted individuals with permission from a federal court.[95] However, the PRISM program (which permits collection of everything besides phone records) was renewed in 2018.[96]

All four of the major companies in the PRISM program, plus many others, have changed their privacy policies to state they will "notify users of requests for their information prior to disclosure unless [they] are prohibited from doing so by statute or court order."[97] This statement does not necessarily protect users under the PRISM program, but it does protect them from other types of searches.

Many organizations previously turned over information requested by law enforcement without telling users. Now, however, most companies like Twitter, Facebook, and Google (plus many more) all notify users of requests for information prior to disclosure unless prohibited by statute or court order.[98]

Of course, the ultimate question is, if it were disclosed that your use could be monitored by the government, and you clicked "agree" to the terms of use when you began using the service, would you care enough to adjust your use?

Questions, Projects, and Exercises

1. Marriott Resorts had a formal company party for more than 200 employees. At one point during the party, the company aired a videotape that compiled employees' and their spouses' comments about a household chore they hated. However, as a spoof, the video was edited to make it seem as if they were describing what it was like to have sex with their partner. One employee's wife was very upset by the video and sued Marriott for invasion of privacy. Evaluate her argument, focusing on the ethical arguments for a violation of her rights.

2. Richard Fraser, an at-will independent insurance agent for Nationwide Mutual Insurance Company, was terminated by Nationwide and the parties disagree on the reason for Fraser's termination. Fraser argues that Nationwide terminated him because he filed complaints regarding Nationwide's allegedly illegal conduct, for criticizing Nationwide to the Nationwide Insurance Independent Contractors Association, and for attempting to obtain the passage of legislation in Pennsylvania to ensure that independent insurance agents could be terminated only for "just cause." Nationwide argues, however, that it terminated Fraser because he was disloyal. Nationwide points out that Fraser drafted a letter to two competitors saying that policyholders were not happy with Nationwide and asking whether the competitors would be interested in acquiring them. (Fraser claims that the letters were drafted only to get Nationwide's attention and were not sent.)

    When Nationwide learned about these letters, it claims that it became concerned that Fraser might also be revealing company secrets to its competitors. It therefore searched its main file server—on which all of Fraser's email was lodged—for any email to or from Fraser that showed similar improper behavior. Nationwide's general counsel testified that the email search confirmed Fraser's disloyalty. Therefore, on the basis of the two letters and the email search, Nationwide terminated Fraser's employment agreement. The search of his email gives rise to Fraser's claim for damages under the Electronic Communications Privacy Act (ECPA) of 1986. Do you believe the employer was justified in monitoring the employee's email and then terminating him? What ethical arguments do you believe either side could use in this case?

3. A customer service representative at an electronics store is surfing the internet using one of the display computers. She accesses a website that shows graphic images of a crime scene. A customer in the store who notices the images is offended. Another customer service representative is behind the counter using the store's computer to access a pornographic site and starts to laugh. A customer asks him why he is laughing. He turns the computer screen around to show her the images that are causing him amusement. Is there anything wrong with these activities?

4. The term *cybersquatting* refers to the practice of registering a large number of website domain names hoping to sell them at huge prices to others who may want the URL or who are prepared to pay to get rid of a potentially confusing domain name. For instance, People for the Ethical Treatment of Animals, which operates www.peta.org, was able to shut down www.peta.com, a pro-hunting website that dubbed itself "People Eating Tasty Animals." Cybersquatters often determine possible misspellings or slightly incorrect websites with the hopes that the intended website will pay them for their new domain. Others might simply hold onto a potentially extremely popular site name based on the expectation that someone will want it. For example, someone paid over $7 million for the address www.business.com. In one case, one day after a partnership was announced that would result in an online bookstore for the Toronto *Globe & Mail* newspaper, with the domain name www.chaptersglobe.com, Richard Morochove, a technology writer, registered the domain chapters-globe.com. When the partnership demanded that he stop using the name, he promptly agreed, as long as he received a percentage of the sales from the Chapters/Globe website. The case went to trial. In situations such as these, do you believe the cybersquatter is doing anything wrong? What options might the "intended website" owner have?

5. Spam, or spamming, refers to the use of mailing lists to blanket usenets or private e-mail boxes with indiscriminate advertising messages. Some people believe that spamming should be protected as the simple exercise of one's First Amendment right to free speech, while others view it as an invasion of privacy or even theft of resources or trespass to property, as Intel argued when a disgruntled ex-employee spammed more than 35,000 Intel employees with his complaints. In that case, the court agreed, considering his email spamming equivalent to trespassing on Intel's property and recognizing that Intel was forced to spend considerable time and resources to delete the email messages from its system.

   It is amusing to note that the source of the term *spam* is generally accepted to be the Monty Python song "Spam spam spam spam, spam spam spam spam, lovely spam, wonderful spam. . . ." Like the song, spam is an endless repetition of worthless text. Others believe that the term came from the computer group lab at the University of Southern California, which gave it the name because it has many of the same characteristics as the lunchmeat Spam:

   • Nobody wants it or ever asks for it.

   • No one ever eats it; it is the first item to be pushed to the side when eating the entree.

   • Sometimes it is actually tasty, like 1% of junk mail that is really useful to some people.[99]

   Using stakeholder analysis, make an argument that spamming is either ethical or unethical.

6. Term papers on practically every subject imaginable are available on the internet. Many of those who post the papers defend their practice in two ways: (1) These papers are

posted to assist in research in the same way any other resource is posted on the web and should simply be cited if used and (2) these papers are posted in order to encourage faculty to modify paper topics and/or exams and not to simply bring back assignments that have been used countless times in the past. Are you persuaded? Is there anything unethical about this service in general? If so, who should be held accountable, the poster, the ultimate user, or someone else?

7. A college provided its security officers with a locker area in which to store personal items. The security officers occasionally used the area as a dressing room. After incidents of theft from the lockers and reports that the employees were bringing weapons to campus, the college installed a video surveillance camera in the locker area. Did the employees have a reasonable expectation of privacy that was violated by the video surveillance? Explain.

8. While some companies block employee access to social networks such as Facebook and Twitter, others have a more permissive attitude. Explain several reasons a company might choose to *permit*—or be indifferent to—employee access to social networks.

9. You work as an accountant at a large accounting firm where your job leaves you with a lot of down time at the office in between assignments. You spend this time on your office computer developing a program that can make your job even more efficient, and it might even be a breakthrough in the industry. This new product could be a huge success and you could make a lot of money. You think of quitting your job and devoting all your time and resources to selling this new product. However, you have developed this product using company equipment and technology, and also used the time you were at work. Do these facts raise any red flags in terms of ethical issues? What should you do?

10. As you learned in this chapter, drug testing in the workplace is a somewhat controversial issue in terms of employer responsibilities and employee rights. Using sources from the web, discuss the pros and cons of these programs.

Key Terms

After reading this chapter, you should have a clear understanding of the following key terms. For a complete definition, please see the Glossary.

disability, *p. 262*
Electronic Communications Privacy Act (ECPA) of 1986, *p. 236*
email monitoring, *p. 245*
European Union's Directive on Personal Fourth Amendment protection, *p. 236*
Genetic Information Nondiscrimination Act (GINA) of 2008, *p. 257*

Hawthorne effect, *p. 259*
Health Insurance Portability and Accountability Act (HIPAA), *p. 256*
hypernorms, *p. 233*
internet use monitoring, *p. 245*
intrusion into seclusion, *p. 236*
moral free space, *p. 233*
privacy, *p. 230*
privacy rights, *p. 231*

property rights, *p. 233*
reciprocal obligation, *p. 232*
Uniting and Strengthening America by Providing Appropriate Tools Required to Intercept and Obstruct Terrorism (USA PATRIOT) Act of 2001, *p. 267*

Endnotes

1. Source: Jeffrey Hirsch, "Future Work" (February 14, 2019), https://ssrn.com/abstract= (accessed February 16, 2019) (crediting University of North Carolina - Chapel Hill Professor Richard Myers with the term, "blended workplace").

2. B. Sethi and C. Stubbings, "Good Work," *Strategy + Business* (February 18, 2019), www.strategy-business.com/feature/Good-Work?gko=a9de1 (accessed February 18, 2019).

3. A. Marshall, "Where Business Is Feeling the Heat," in P. Krielstra, Kroll and Economist Intelligence Unit, *Global Fraud Report* (2007/2008).

4. Poneman Institute, "2018 Cost of Data Breach Study: United States" (June 2018), www03.ibm.com/security/data-breach/ (accessed June 25, 2018).

5. 381 U.S. 479 (1965).

6. 410 U.S. 113 (1973).

7. J. Moore, "Your E-mail Trail: Where Ethics Meets Forensics," *Business and Society Review* 114, no. 2 (2009), pp. 273–93.

8. Patricia Werhane, *Persons, Rights, and Corporations* (Englewood Cliffs, NJ: Prentice Hall, 1985), p. 94.

9. Gerald Doppelt, "Beyond Liberalism and Communitarianism: Towards a Critical Theory of Social Justice," *Philosophy and Social Criticism* 14 (1988), pp. 271, 278.

10. Source: Global Internet Liberty Campaign, "Privacy and Human Rights: An International Survey of Privacy Laws and Practice" (1988), www.gilc.org/privacy/survey/exec-summary.html (accessed July 18, 2018). For an up-to-date listing of international accords relating to privacy, see Electronic Frontier Foundation, "International Privacy Standards," www.eff.org/issues/international-privacy-standards (accessed July 18, 2018).

11. J. Whitman, "The Two Western Cultures of Privacy: Dignity versus Liberty," *Yale Law Journal* 113 (2004), p. 1151; A. Levin, "Dignity in the Workplace: An Enquiry into the Conceptual Foundation of Workplace Privacy Protection Worldwide," *ALSB Journal of Employment and Labor Law* 11, no. 1 (Winter 2009), p. 63; Daniel Fisher, "Europe's 'Right to Be Forgotten' Clashes with U.S. Right to Know," *Forbes* (May 16, 2014), www.forbes.com/sites/danielfisher/2014/05/16/europes-right-to-be-forgotten-clashes-with-u-s-right-to-know/ (accessed July 18, 2018).

12. A. R. Levinson, "Industrial Justice: Privacy Protection for the Employed," *Cornell Journal of Law and Public Policy* 18, no. 3 (2009), http://papers.ssrn.com/sol3/papers.cfm?abstract_id=1269512 (accessed February 21, 2019); P. Kim, "Electronic Privacy and Employee Speech," *Chicago-Kent Law Review* 87, no. 901 (2012), http://ssrn.com/abstract=2049323 (accessed February 21, 2019).

13. M. Sauter, "Public Sector Jobs: States Where the Most People Work for the Government," *USA Today* (June 1, 2018), https://eu.usatoday.com/story/money/economy/2018/06/01/states-where-the-most-people-work-for-government/35302753/ (accessed March 7, 2019). This number is similar to that for Canada, Greece, the U.K., Spain, and Italy. The OECD's report of member countries reports that Norway has the highest representation (30%), while Japan has the lowest (5.9%). OECD, *Government at a Glance* (Paris: OECD Publishing, 2017), p. 91, https://read.oecd-ilibrary.org/governance/government-at-a-glance-2017_gov_glance-2017-en#page1 (accessed March 6, 2019).

14. National Conference of State Legislatures, "Privacy Protections in State Constitutions" (May 5, 2017), www.ncsl.org/research/telecommunications-and-information-technology/privacy-protections-in-state-constitutions.aspx (accessed February 21, 2019).

15. *Lake v. Wal-Mart Stores, Inc.*, 582 N.W.2d 231 (Minn. 1998).

16. *City of Ontario v. Quon*, 560 U.S. 746 (2010).

17. *Riley v. California*, 573 U.S. 373 (2014); *Bakhit v. Safety Marking, Inc.*, 33 F. Supp. 3d 99 (D. Conn. 2014).

18. *K-Mart v. Trotti*, 677 S.W.2d 632 (Tex. Ct. App. 1984); *Smyth v. Pillsbury*, 914 F. Supp. 97, 101 (E.D. Pa. 1996).

19. National Conference of State Legislatures, "State Social Media Laws" (January 2, 2018), www.ncsl.org/research/telecommunications-and-information-technology/state-laws-prohibiting-access-to-social-media-usernames-and-passwords.aspx (accessed February 21, 2019).

20. Privacy International, "General Data Protection Regulation (GDPR), http://privacy-international.org/topics/general-data-protection-regulation-gdpr (accessed February 21, 2019).

21. T. Romm, "France Fines Google Nearly $57 Million for First Major Violation of New European Privacy Regime," *Washington Post* (January 21, 2019), www.washingtonpost.com/world/europe/france-fines-google-nearly-57-million-for-first-major-violation-of-new-european-privacy-regime/2019/01/21/89e7ee08-1d8f-11e9-a759-2b8541bbbe20_story.html?utm_term=.f7147054cc94 (accessed February 18, 2019).

22. International Trade Association, U.S. Department of Commerce, "Privacy Shield Framework—U.S. Businesses," www.privacyshield.gov/US-Businesses (accessed February 21, 2019).

23. N. Nielson, "Privacy Shield Less Relevant Given GDPR, Says Data Chief," *EU Observer* (May 24, 2018), https://euobserver.com/justice/141886 (accessed February 21, 2019).

24. TrustArc., "Privacy Shield Approaching Its 3 Year Anniversary in Operation" (April 25, 2019), www.trustarc.com/blog/2019/04/25/privacy-shield-approaching-its-3-year-anniversary-in-operation/ (accessed May 13, 2019); also see European Commission, "EU-US Data Transfers: Report on the Second Annual Review of the EU-US Privacy Shield" (December 19, 2018), https://ec.europa.eu/info/law/law-topic/data-protection/international-dimension-data-protection/eu-us-data-transfers_en (accessed May 13, 2019).

25. Source: J. Arden, "Techno-Ethics: Anti-Social Networking," *American Bar Association: GPSolo* 29, no. 3 (May/June 2012), www.americanbar.org/publications/gp_solo/2012/may_june/techno_ethics_anti_social_networking.html (accessed February 21, 2019).

26. Source: *State of Washington v. Young*, 123 Wash.2d 173 (1994).

27. Source: Frank Daly, "Reply, Delete. . . or Relate? It's Human Dimension," Lecture as Verizon Professor in Business Ethics and Technology, Bentley College, March 31, 2004.

28. Niraj Chokshi, "Out of the Office: More People Are Working Remotely, Survey Finds," *The New York Times* (February 15, 2017), www.nytimes.com/2017/02/15/us/remote-workers-work-from-home.html (accessed February 21, 2019).

29. Source: U. Klotz, "The Challenges of the New Economy" (October 1999), cited in *World Employment Report 2001: Life at Work in the Information Economy.* (Geneva: International Labour Office, 2001), p. 145.

30. *PhoneDog, LLC v. Kravitz*, Case No. C 11-03474 MEJ, 2011 U.S. Dist. LEXIS 129229 (N.D. Cal. Nov. 8, 2011).

31. Source: Kevin Werbach as cited in Consortium of professors at the University of Pennsylvania Wharton School of Business, "Social Media Followers—Yours, or Your Businesses?" (april 2013). Multihouse Pro.

32. Source: "Whom Do Social Media Followers Belong to—You, or Your Business?" *Knowledge@Wharton, University of Pennsylvania* (March 13, 2013), http://knowledge .wharton.upenn.edu/article/whom-do-social-media-followers-belong-to-you-or-your-business/ (accessed February 21, 2019); A. Fisher, "Who Owns Your Twitter Followers, You or Your Employer?" *Fortune* (December 13, 2012), http://fortune.com/2012/12/13/who-owns-your-twitter-followers-you-or-your-employer/ (accessed February 21, 2019).

33. For a similar interpretation, see B. Kracher and C. Corritore, "Is There a Special E-Commerce Ethics" *Business Ethics Quarterly* 14, no. 1 (2004), pp. 71–94.

34. Antonio Argandoña, "The New Economy: Ethical Issues," *Journal of Business Ethics* 44 (2003), pp. 3–22, 26.

35. Source: Google S-1, Filed with the Securities and Exchange Commission, Appendix B (2004), www.sec.gov/Archives/edgar/data/1288776/000119312504139655/ds1a.htm (accessed July 30, 2018). When Google was reorganized in 2015 as a subsidiary of Alphabet, the motto was moved to the preface of the code of conduct. In 2018, it was removed as an official tenant of the code of conduct, but added in a passing reference of the last sentence in the code: "And remember. . . don't be evil, and if you see something that you think isn't right - speak up." See also Kate Conger, "Google Removes 'Dont Be Evil' Clause from Its Code of Conduct," *Gizmodo* (May 18, 2018), https://gizmodo.com/google-removes-nearly-all-mentions-of-dont-be-evil-from-1826153393 (accessed February 21, 2019).

36. Dominic Rushe, "Google: Don't Expect Privacy When Sending to Gmail," *The Guardian* (August 15, 2013), www.theguardian.com/technology/2013/aug/14/google-gmail-users-privacy-email-lawsuit (accessed February 21, 2019).

37. Joseph Turrow, "Google Still Doesn't Care About Your Privacy," *Fortune* (June 28, 2017), http://fortune.com/2017/06/28/gmail-google-account-ads-privacy-concerns-home-settings-policy/ (accessed February 21, 2019).

38. Douglas MacMillan, "Tech's 'Dirty Secret': The App Developers Sifting through Your Gmail," *The Wall Street Journal* (July 2, 2018), www.wsj.com/articles/techs-dirty-secret-the-app-developers-sifting-through-your-gmail-1530544442 (accessed February 21,2019).

39. Source: Google S-1, filed with the Securities and Exchange Commission. http://www.sec .gov/Archives/edgar/data/1288776/000119312504139655/ds1a.htm (accessed February 21, 2019).

40. Antonio Argandoña, "The New Economy: Ethical Issues," *Journal of Business Ethics* 44 (2003), pp. 3–22, 28.

41. ComPsych, "Digital Distraction at Work: Almost 20 Percent of Workers Check Social Media More Than 10 Times during Workday, According to ComPsych," press release (March 20, 2017), https://www.compsych.com/press-room/press-article?nodeId=d9561871-7e04-4bb7-8d44-6444eb342861 (accessed March 3, 2019).

42. Gina Belli, "How Much Employee Monitoring Is Too Much?" *CNBC.com* (October 13, 2017),www.cnbc.com/2017/10/13/how-much-employee-monitoring-is-too-much.html (accessed March 3, 2019).

43. Lindsay McKenzie, "Who's Reading Your Email?" *Inside Higher Ed* (April 2, 2018), www.insidehighered.com/news/2018/04/02/unauthorized-searches-professors-email-create-rift-rochester (accessed March 3, 2019).

44. Careerbuilder.com, "New CareerBuilder Survey Reveals How Much Smartphones Are Sapping Productivity at Work" (June 9, 2016), www.careerbuilder.com/share/aboutus/pressreleasesdetail.aspx?sd=6%2F9%2F2016&id=pr954&ed=12%2F31%2F2016 (accessed March 3, 2019).

45. Ivan Manokha, "Why the Rise of Wearable Tech to Monitor Employees Is Worrying," *The Conversation* (January 3, 2017), http://theconversation.com/why-the-rise-of-wearable-tech-to-monitor-employees-is-worrying-70719 (accessed March 4, 2019).

46. R. Reice, "Wearables in the Workplace: A New Frontier," *Bloomberg Law* (May 24, 2018), https://news.bloomberglaw.com/daily-labor-report/wearables-in-the-workplace-new-frontier (accessed March 4, 2019); "Smile, You're on Camera: There Will Be Little Privacy in the Workplace of the Future," *The Economist* (March 28, 2018), www.economist.com/special-report/2018/03/28/there-will-be-little-privacy-in-the-workplace-of-the-future (accessed March 4, 2019).

47. Source: Andrea Miller, "More Companies Are Using Technology to Monitor Employees, Sparking Privacy Concerns," *ABC News* (March 10, 2018), https://abcnews.go.com/US/companies-technology-monitor-employees-sparking-privacy-concerns/story?id=53388270 (accessed March 4, 2019). See also, Emine Saner, "Employers Are Monitoring Computers, Toilet Breaks—Even Emotions. Is You Boss Watching You?" *The Guardian* (May 14, 2018), https://www.theguardian.com/world/2018/may/14/is-your-boss-secretly-or-not-so-secretly-watching-you (accessed March 4, 2019).

48. Katie Kindelan, "Proposed Law Giving Workers the 'Right to Disconnect' after Work Draws Mixed Reactions," *ABC News* (March 27, 2018), https://abcnews.go.com/GMA/Living/proposed-law-giving-workers-disconnect-work-draws-mixed/story?id=54035404 (accessed March 4, 2019).

49. *Sharrow v. S.C. Johnson & Son, Inc.*, No. 17-cv-11138, 2018 U.S. Dist. LEXIS 62044 (E.D. Mich. Apr. 12, 2018); *Crowe v. Marquette Transportation Co. Gulf-Inland, LLC*, No. 14-1130, 2015 WL 254633 (E.D. La. Jan. 20, 2015).

50. Rayna Hollander, "Two-thirds of the World's Population Are Now Connected by Mobile Devices," *Business Insider* (September 19, 2017), www.businessinsider.com/world-population-mobile-devices-2017-9 (accessed on March 4, 2019).

51. "Internet Usage Statistics," *Internet World Stats* (2017), www.internet-worldstats.com/stats.htm (accessed March 4, 2019).

52. S. Kemp, "Global Internet Use Accelerates," *We Are Social* (January 31, 2019), https://wearesocial.com/us/blog/2019/01/digital-2019-global-internet-use-accelerates (accessed March 4, 2019).

53. Chris Morris, "Here's How You're Wasting 8 Hours per Work Week," *Fortune* (July 25, 2017), http://fortune.com/2017/07/25/cell-phone-lost-productivity/ (accessed March 4, 2019).

54. Robert Stroymeyer, "How to Monitor Your Employees' PCs without Going Too Far," *PCWorld* (March 22, 2011), www.pcworld.com/businesscenter/article/222169/how_to_monitor_your_employees_pcs_without_going_too_far.html (accessed March 4, 2019).

55. Daree Shannon, "Should What You Say on Social Media Be Grounds for Getting Fired?" *Deliberate Magazine* (May 16, 2018), www.deliberatemagazine.com/should-what-you-say-on-social-media-be-grounds-for-getting-fired/ (accessed August 3, 2018).

56. M. Cranford, "The Ethics of Privacy: Drug Testing, Surveillance, and Competing Interests in the Workplace," University of Southern California, Publication 3291792 (2007), http://wwwlib.umi.com/dissertations/fullcit/3291792 (accessed March 4, 2019).

57. Source: A. Taufen, "How Does Medical Marijuana Use Affect Employment?" *Benefits Pro* (August 12, 2014), www.benefitspro.com/2014/08/12/how-does-medical-marijuanause-affect-employment?t=compliance&page=2&slreturn=1456427268 (accessed March 3, 2019).

58. Allen Smith, "Employers Increasingly Drop Marijuana Testing of Job Applicants," Society for Human Resource Management (April 25, 2018), www.shrm.org/resourcesandtools/legal-and-compliance/employment-law/pages/less-marijuana-testing.aspx (accessed August 8, 2018); Melinda Caterine, "Maine Employers Must Ignore Off-Work Marijuana Use, Cease Testing Applicants," *Littler.com* (January 30, 2018), www.littler.com/publication-press/publication/maine-employers-must-ignore-work-marijuana-use-cease-testing (accessed August 8, 2018).

59. Kindland, "All of the Places in the World Where Pot Is Legal" (January 9, 2018), www.thekindland.com/products/all-of-the-places-in-the-world-where-pot-is-2871 (accessed March 4, 2019).

60. National Council on Alcoholism and Drug Dependence Inc., "Drugs and Alcohol in the Workplace" (n.d.), https://www.ncadd.org/about-addiction/addiction-update/drugs-and-alcohol-in-the-workplace?highlight=WyJkcnVncyIsImRydWdzJyIsInRoZSIsIndvcmtwbGGFjZSJd (accessed August 8, 2018).

61. HireRight.com, "Employment Screening Benchmark Report: 2018 Edition" (2018), http://img.en25.com/Web/HireRightInc/%7B4e41d88e-c1d8-4112-9cfb-431461d4018b%7D_2018_HireRight-Employment-Screening-Benchmark-Report_12-FINAL.pdf (accessed March 4, 2019); Lisa Nagele-Piazza, "Failed Workplace Drug Tests Reach 12 Year High," *Society for Human Resource Management* (May 24, 2017), www.shrm.org/resourcesandtools/legal-and-compliance/employment-law/pages/positive-drug-test-rates-climb.aspx (accessed March 4, 2019).

62. Rebecca Greenfield and Jennifer Kaplan, "The Coming Decline of the Employment Drug Test," *Bloomberg* (March 5, 2018), www.bloomberg.com/news/articles/2018-08-07/gop-pitch-on-robust-economy-a-hard-sell-in-regions-left-behind (accessed March 4, 2019).

63. Source: Katie Zezima and Abby Goodnough, "Drug Testing Poses Quandary for Employers," *The New York Times* (October 4, 2010), https://www.nytimes.com/2010/10/25/us/25drugs.html (accessed March 4, 2019).

64. Genetic Information Nondiscrimination Act of 2008 (Pub. L. No. 110-233), www.govtrack.us/congress/bills/110/hr493 (accessed March 4, 2019).

65. Equal Employment Opportunity Commission, "Genetic Information Discrimination" (n.d.), www.eeoc.gov/laws/types/genetic.cfm (accessed March 4, 2019).

66. R. Green et al., "Exploring Concordance and Discordance for Return of Incidental Findings from Clinical Sequencing," *Genetics in Medicine* 14, no. 4 (April 2012), pp. 405–10, www.ncbi.nlm.nih.gov/pmc/articles/PMC3763716/ (accessed January 22, 2019); E. Schumaker, "Workplace Genetic Testing Isn't Just Unethical, It's Scientifically Unsound," *Huffington Post* (March 14, 2017), www.huffpost.com/entry/workplace-genetic-privacy-bill-gina_n_58c6e4c5e4b081a56dee48cf (accessed January 22, 2019).

67. 2019 IL 123186 (Jan. 25, 2019), www.illinoiscourts.gov/Opinions/SupremeCourt/2019/123186.pdf.

68. Foley & Lardner, "Biometric Privacy: Illinois Supreme Court Decision Allows Claims to Proceed Without Showing of Actual Harm," *Labor & Employment Law Perspectives* (February 4, 2019), www.laboremploymentperspectives.com/2019/02/04/biometric-privacy-illinois-supreme-court-decision-allows-claims-to-proceed-without-showing-of-actual-harm/ (accessed March 29, 2019).

69. W. Herbert and A. K. Tuminaro, "The Impact of Emerging Technologies in the Workplace: Who's Watching the Man (Who's Watching Me)?" *Hofstra Labor and Employment Law Journal* 5 (2009), p. 355; A. Bibby, "You're Being Followed: Electronic Monitoring

and Surveillance in the Workplace" (2006), www.andrewbibby.com/pdf/Surveillance-en.pdf (accessed August 8, 2018).

70. M. Schulman, "Little Brother Is Watching You," *Issues in Ethics* 9, no. 2 (Spring 1998), www.scu.edu/ethics/publications/iie/v9n2/brother.html (accessed August 8, 2018).

71. Scott Horton, "New York Law Protects Employees' Off-Duty Conduct," *Horton Management Law Blog* (September 15, 2017), https://hortonpllc.com/new-york-law-protects-employees-off-duty-conduct/ (accessed March 5, 2019).

72. Off-duty conduct statutes vary based on the levels of protection they provide: (1) use of tobacco only, (2) use of lawful products, and (3) any and all lawful activities. Jurisdictions that have enacted "tobacco only" statutes include CT, DC, IN, KY, LA, ME, MN, MS, MO, MT, NH, NJ, NM, OK, OR, RI, SC, SD, VA, WV, and WY. States that protect the use of "lawful products," "lawful activities," "lawful conduct," or "lawful consumable products" include CA, CO, IL, MT, MN, NV, NC, ND, and WI. For a list of all state statutes, see National Conference of State Legislatures, "State Laws on Employment-Related Discrimination" (2018), www.ncsl.org/issues-research/labor/discrimination-employment.aspx (accessed March 5, 2019); Rishi R. Patel and Harald Schmidt, "Should Employers Be Permitted Not to Hire Smokers? A Review of US Legal Provisions," *International Journal of Health Policy and Management* 6, no. 12 (2017), pp. 701–706, www.ncbi.nlm.nih.gov/pmc/articles/PMC5726320/ (accessed March 5, 2019).

73. For more information, please see N. Keltgan, "Reasonable Alternative Standards: What Are They? Why Should You Care?" *Associate-Benefits and Risk Consulting* (June 23, 2016), www.associatedbrc.com/Resources/Resource-Library/Resource-Library-Article/ArtMID/666/ArticleID/399/Reasonable-alternative-standards-What-are-they-Why-should-you-care (accessed March 5, 2019).

74. Tax Tips, "What Are the Tax Penalties for Smokers?" *Intuit Turbo Tax* (2017), https://turbotax.intuit.com/tax-tips/health-care/what-are-the-tax-penalties-for-smokers/L0Zc0O1Sk (accessed August 8, 2018).

75. The following cities prohibit weight discrimination: Santa Cruz, CA; San Francisco, CA; Washington, DC; Urbana, IL; Binghamton, NY; and Madison, WI. See National Association to Advance Fat Acceptance (NAAFA), "Weight Discrimination Laws" (n.d.), www.naafaonline.com/dev2/education/laws.html (accessed March 5, 2019).

76. Scott Gilbert, "Obesity 'Regarded as' Disability Under ADA," *Polsenelli Labor and Employment Law Blog* (March 9, 2018), www.polsinelliatwork.com/blog/2018/3/9/obesity-regarded-as-disability-under-ada (accessed March 5, 2019); Marjory Robertson, "Is Morbid Obesity a Disability under the ADA? Courts Say No," *Lexology* (February 7, 2017).

77. *Shell v. Burlington Northern Santa Fe Railway Co.*, Case No. 15-cv-11040, 2018 U.S. Dist. LEXIS 35150 (N.D. Ill. Mar. 5, 2018) [Filing 108], *reconsideration denied by and motion granted by* 2018 U.S. Dist. LEXIS 197474(N.D. Ill. Nov. 20, 2018) [Filing 129], *appeal filed,* Case No. 0:19-cv-01030 (7th Cir. Jan. 4, 2019).

78. CareerBuilder.com, "Office Romance Hits 10-Year Low, According to CareerBuilder's Annual Valentine's Day Survey" (February 1, 2018), http://press.careerbuilder.com/2018-02-01-Office-Romance-Hits-10-Year-Low-According-to-CareerBuilders-Annual-Valentines-Day-Survey (accessed March 5, 2019).

79. Vault.com, "The 2018 Vault Office Romance Survey Results" (February 12, 2018), www.vault.com/blog/workplace-issues/2018-vault-office-romance-survey-results/ (accessed March 5, 2019).

80. Source: J. Greene and V. Fuhrmans. "Intel CEO Brian Krzanich Resigns After Violating Company Policy," *The Wall Street Journal* (June 21, 2018), https://www.wsj.com/articles/intel-ceo-brian-krzanich-resigns-after-violating-company-policy-1529586884 (accessed March 5, 2019).

81. 237 F.3d 166 (2d Cir. 2001).

82. Ruling that an employer is prohibited from discriminating on the basis of sexual orientation, holding that "[a]ny discomfort, disapproval, or job decision based on the fact that the complainant—woman or man—dresses differently, speaks differently, or dates or marries a same-sex partner . . . is a reason purely and simply based on sex." *Hively v. Ivy Tech Community College of Indiana*, 853 F.3d 339, 345 (7th Cir. 2017); see also U.S. Equal Employment Opportunity Commission, "Preventing Employment Discrimination Against Lesbian, Gay, Bisexual or Transgender Workers" (n.d.), www.eeoc.gov/eeoc/publications/brochure-gender_stereotyping.cfm.

83. K. Paul, "It's National Coming Out Day—but Nearly 50% of LGBT Americans Are in the Closet at Work," *Marketwatch* (October 11, 2018), www.marketwatch.com/story/half-of-lgbtq-americans-are-not-out-to-co-workers-2018-06-27 (accessed January 26, 2019); K. Baksh, "Workplace Discrimination: The LGBT Workforce," *Huffington Post* (December 6, 2017), www.huffingtonpost.com/kurina-baksh/workplace-discrimination-_b_10606030.html (accessed January 26, 2019).

84. Statista.com, "Number of Monthly Active Facebook Users Worldwide as of 4th Quarter 2018 (in millions)" (2019), www.statista.com/statistics/264810/number-of-monthly-active-facebook-users-worldwide/ (accessed March 4, 2019).

85. Daniel Bean, "11 Brutal Reminders That You Can and Will Get Fired for What You Post on Facebook," *Yahoo.com* (May 6, 2014), www.yahoo.com/tech/11-brutal-reminders-that-you-can-and-will-get-fired-for-84931050659.html (accessed March 5, 2019).

86. Elizabeth Licata, "Outback Server Fired for Facebook Post About Non-tipping Church Group," *Chicago Tribune* (February 11, 2018), www.chicagotribune.com/dining/sns-dailymeal-1870833-outback-steakhouse-server-fired-facebook-post-no-tip-christ-fellowship-church-florida-21118-20180211-story.html (accessed March 5, 2019).

87. Laurence Hammack, "Employee Fired for Facebook Complaints About Her Job Settles Lawsuit in Botetourt," *Roanoke Times* (October 4, 2017), www.roanoke.com/news/local/botetourt_county/employee-fired-for-facebook-complaints-about-her-job-settles-lawsuit/article_745eed20-9945-5946-b14e-56f67d705e8c.html (accessed March 5, 2019).

88. Michael Swinson, "Big Data Is Coming—and It's Getting Personal," *Lexology.com* (May 8, 2014), www.lexology.com/library/detail.aspx?g=5e0236a9-4fbd-4ad3-84cd-d7483a44560f (accessed March 5, 2019).

89. National Conference of State Legislatures, "Employer Access to Social Media Usernames and Passwords," (January 2, 2018), www.ncsl.org/research/telecommunications-and-information-technology/employer-access-to-social-media-passwords-2013.aspx (accessed August 10, 2018).

90. Source: Illinois Government News Network (August 1, 2012), "Governor Quinn Signs Legislation to Protect Workers' Right to Privacy," press release, www3.illinois.gov/PressReleases/ShowPressRelease.cfm?SubjectID=2&RecNum=10442 (accessed March 5, 2019).

91. USA PATRIOT Act of 2001, Pub. L. No. 107-56, www.it.ojp.gov/default.aspx?area=privacy&page=1281.

92. Barton Gellman and Ashkan Soltani, "NSA Collects Millions of E-mail Address Books Globally," *The Washington Post* (November 1, 2013), www.washingtonpost.com/world/

national-security/nsa-collects-millions-of-e-mail-address-books-globally/2013/10/14/8e5 8b5be-34f9-11e3-80c6-7e6dd8d22d8f_story.html (accessed March 5, 2019).

93. Barton Gellman and Ashkan Soltani, "NSA Infiltrates Links to Yahoo, Google Data Centers Worldwide, Snowden Documents Say," *The Washington Post* (October 30, 2013), www.washingtonpost.com/world/national-security/nsa-infiltrates-links-to-yahoo-google-data-centers-worldwide-snowden-documents-say/2013/10/30/e51d661e-4166-11e3-8b74-d89d714ca4dd_story.html (accessed March 5, 2019).

94. Spencer Ackerman and Dominic Rushe, "Microsoft, Facebook, Google and Yahoo Release US Surveillance Requests," *The Guardian* (February 3, 2014), www.theguardian.com/world/2014/feb/03/microsoft-facebook-google-yahoo-fisa-surveillance-requests (accessed March 5, 2019).

95. Erin Kelly, "Senate Approves USA Freedom Act," *USA Today* (June 2, 2015), www.usatoday.com/story/news/politics/2015/06/02/patriot-act-usa-freedom-act-senate-vote/28345747/ (accessed March 5, 2019).

96. Laura Hautala, "NSA Surveillance Programs Live on, in Case You Hadn't Noticed," *CNET.com* (January 18, 2018), www.cnet.com/news/nsa-surveillance-programs-prism-upstream-live-on-snowden/ (accessed March 5, 2019).

97. Source: Electronic Frontier Foundation (2014), "Who Has Your Back? 2014 Report," www.eff.org/who-has-your-back-2014 (accessed March 5, 2019).

98. Electronic Frontier Foundation, "Who Has Your Back? 2014 Report" (2014), www.eff.org/who-has-your-back-2014 (accessed March 5, 2019).

99. "Spam," www.webopedia.com/TERM/s/spam.html (accessed November 2, 2018).

8

Ethics and Marketing

Don't find customers for your products, find products for your customers.
Seth Godin

A magazine is simply a device to induce people to read advertising.
James Collins

If you make customers unhappy in the physical world, they might each tell
6 friends. If you make customers unhappy on the Internet, they can each tell
6,000 friends.
Jeff Bezos, Amazon CEO

I am the world's worst salesman; therefore, I must make it easy for people to buy.
F. W. Woolworth

It is fair to say that marketing has undergone revolutionary changes in recent years as a result of digital technology. In the past, the primary media by which marketers reached their audience were television, radio, newspapers and magazines, direct mail, and billboards. These techniques were identified as indirect marketing because they relied on broad-based media that reached a general audience, a portion of which was thought to include potential customers. Because the audience was general, the ad content itself had to be fairly generic. As the marketing profession became more sophisticated, advertisers were able to rely on more direct marketing techniques to better identify potential customers and thereby direct more targeted and specific ad content to them.

With the explosion of digital technology and the Internet, the nature of the marketing function has changed dramatically. Digital technology has unimaginably increased the amount of information that marketers can compile about consumers; the speed at which that information can be collected, analyzed, and used; and the specificity of both who the consumers are and the details of their behavior and psychology.

Marketing firms have always conducted research on consumers to gather as much information as possible for understanding consumer wants, their dislikes, and their behavior. In just the recent past, market segments would be identified in terms of only a few general demographic variables: male/female, income level (often best estimated only by housing prices in the zip code associated with a consumer), education level, and the like. Today, digital technologies give marketers the ability to segment markets down to the level of individuals and their web browsing or shopping behavior of just the past few minutes.

Cell phone companies, search engines, apps, internet and cable providers, and social networks compile huge amounts of information on consumer behavior. They know what calls are being made, which internet sites are being visited, what products have been viewed, and which programs are being watched. In many cases that information is only aggregated, overall data, but in other cases the data can be individualized and traced to individual mobiles, computers, or social network accounts. Typically, this tracking is done anonymously so that consumers seldom know that it is occurring and have little understanding of what information is being compiled and how it is being used.

Two factors in particular have contributed to this explosion of personal information being available for use by marketers. First is the tremendous increase in mobile devices, smartphones, and tablets. These devices do three things of value to marketers: They are typically associated with one unique individual; they are used by individuals almost constantly throughout the day and night precisely because they are mobile; and they are heavily reliant on apps, small self-contained programs that have proven to be unrivaled in delivering consumers to business, and advertisements to consumers.

The second, and related, factor is the global popularity of social networks such as Facebook, Instagram, Twitter, and LinkedIn. The amount of personal information available about individuals now accessible by others because of social networking would have been inconceivable just a few years ago. Of course, the point of collecting this information is that it is a commodity that can be bought and sold, or "monetized." While it might appear that the product of Google or Bing is a search engine or the product of a Facebook is a social network, in fact searches are free and joining Facebook is free. As a business, search engines such as Google and social networks such as Facebook make their money by selling access to the wealth of information they collect to advertisers and others willing to pay for that access. (Compare to the quote from James Collins that opened this chapter: "A magazine is simply a device to induce people to read advertising.")*

It is worth asking if the ethical principles and guidelines that were appropriate for evaluating traditional marketing techniques are still relevant in the age of digital marketing. Deception, manipulation, unfairness, and loss of privacy are some of the most common concerns raised against traditional advertising and marketing techniques. Consider how these concerns might apply to the following digital marketing activities.

Some modern issues closely parallel previous marketing practices. Deceptive or misleading product endorsements have always been part of marketing, as when actors portraying doctors endorse the alleged health benefits of a diet supplement or support one brand of ibuprofen over another. Today, consumers often research products by consulting user reviews on internet sites such as TripAdvisor or Amazon; "likes" on social media sites such as Facebook; or reviews found in blogs, in tweets, or on message boards. To add credibility, some sites such as Amazon will even identify product reviewers as a "verified purchaser," but consumers have no way of knowing that even these reviewers are truthful. What ethical issues are raised if these digital testimonials were placed by a marketing form hired to promote a particular product or service?

Companies can pay to have consumers' search results enhanced with their own ads that appear as a side banner or to have their website appear first whenever consumers search for a product or a competitor's site. Consumers may believe that the first result to appear in a search is either random or that it simply reveals the most popular result. In fact, browser-based tracking cookies may have resulted in the consumer being instantaneously identified based on browsing and made part of a real-time auction among marketing firms and in milliseconds awarded the top-level banner ad to the auction winner.

Retailer companies use location-based services known as "beacons" to know when particular people enter their store. Beacon technology relies on low-powered Bluetooth signals that can be detected within a few hundred feet. A common use is to install this technology in a company's app, which, like most apps, regularly collects browsing and shopping information about the consumer. When that consumer is near the retail store, ads and enticements specifically targeted to that individual consumer based on past online behavior can be instantly sent to his or her mobile device.

1. Courts sometimes use the "expectation of privacy" as a test for limiting governmental monitoring. Thus, for example, the police can monitor your behavior without a warrant when you are in a public place but not when you are talking on your phone. What expectations of privacy do you have when you are surfing the web? Ordering something from Amazon or Netflix? Spending time on Facebook?

2. Physically stalking someone can be a crime. Are there parallels between physically stalking someone and regularly monitoring his or her activities on the web? How are they similar? How are they different?

3. Most online tracking is done through the use of "cookies," small files stored on a computer or mobile device that provide information about past browsing history. Should consumers have a right to opt out, or should their explicit consent be required before cookies are installed?

4. Information about your online behavior is a commodity that can be bought and sold. Who should own this personal information? Should it be available for sale? By whom?

*Testimony of James Collins to Congress (1907).

Chapter Objectives

After reading this chapter, you will be able to:

1. Apply an ethical framework to marketing issues.
2. Describe the three key concerns of ethical analysis of marketing issues.
3. Describe two interpretations of "responsibility" and apply them to the topic of product safety.
4. Explain contractual standards for establishing business's responsibilities for safe products.
5. Articulate the tort standards for establishing business's responsibilities for safe products.
6. Analyze the ethical arguments for and against strict product liability.
7. Discuss how to evaluate both ethical and unethical means by which to influence people through advertising.
8. Explain the ethical justification for advertising.
9. Trace debates about advertising's influence on consumer autonomy.
10. Distinguish ethical from unethical target marketing, using marketing to vulnerable populations as an example.
11. Discuss business's responsibilities for the activities of its supply chain.

Introduction

Some believe that the very purpose of business is found within the marketing function. The description of business's purpose offered by marketing scholar Theodore Levitt is a case in point. Levitt suggested that:

> The purpose of a business is to create and keep a customer. To do that you have to produce and deliver goods and services that people want and value at prices and under conditions that are reasonably attractive relative to those offered by others. . . . It was not so long ago that a lot of companies assumed something quite different about the purpose of business. They said quite simply that the purpose is to make money. But that is as vacuous as to say that the purpose of life is to eat. Eating is a prerequisite, not a purpose of life. . . . Profits can be made in lots of devious and transient ways. For people of affairs, a statement of purpose should provide guidance to the management of their affairs. To say that they should attract and hold customers forces facing the necessity of figuring out what people really want and value, and then catering to those wants and values. It provides specific guidance, and has moral merit.[1]

marketing
Defined by the American Marketing Association as "an organizational function and a set of processes for creating, communicating, and delivering value to customers and for managing customer relationships in ways that benefit the organization and its stakeholders."

Similarly, the American Marketing Association defines **marketing** in a way that echos the stakeholder model of CSR described in Chapter 5. According to the AMA, marketing is "an organizational function and a set of processes for creating, communicating, and delivering value to customers and for managing customer relationships in ways that benefit the organization and its stakeholders."[2]

The concept of an exchange between a seller and a buyer is central to the market economy and is the core idea behind marketing. Marketing involves all aspects of creating a product or service and bringing it to market, where an exchange can take place. Marketing ethics therefore examines the responsibilities associated with bringing a product to market, promoting it to buyers, and exchanging it with them. But this simple model of a seller bringing a product to the marketplace, and the ethics implicit within it, gets complicated fairly quickly.

Even before a product is created, a producer might first consider who, if anyone, is likely to be interested in purchasing it, or who can be influenced to want to purchase it. The product might then be redesigned or changed in light of what is learned about potential buyers from market research. Once the product is ready for market, the producer must decide on a price that will be mutually acceptable. At first glance, the minimal asking price should be the production cost plus some reasonable profit. But the producer might also consider who the buyers are and what they can afford, how price might influence future purchases, how the price might affect distributors and retailers, and what competitors are charging before settling on a price. The producer might also consider advertising the product to attract new potential purchasers and offer incentives to promote the product among buyers.

The producer must also consider how to bring the product to consumers and therefore consider hiring someone else, a salesperson, or delegating someone, a "retailer," to handle the actual exchange itself. Producers might be more concerned with cash flow than profit and therefore be willing to ask a price that is below production costs. They might consider where and under what conditions the product is sold, and they might decide that the best chance for a sale will occur only among certain people. The producer might also consider issues of volume and price the product in such a way to ensure profit only after certain sales targets are met. The producer might also consider how such factors as price, convenience, reliability, and service might contribute to sustaining an ongoing relationship with the customer. Finally, throughout this entire process, the producer might conduct market research to gather information and use that information in production, pricing, promotion, and placement decisions.

This model gets even more complicated when we recognize the active role that retailers play in these relationships. In many cases, the actual producers are themselves passive participants who respond to decisions made by retailers and other marketing firms. Often the companies actually producing goods are simply hired by the marketing firm to produce a product that has already been fully vetted for the market.

All of these factors are elements of marketing. What, how, why, and under what conditions is something *produced?* What *price* is acceptable, reasonable, fair? How can the product be *promoted* to support, enhance, and maintain sales? Where, when, and under what conditions should the product be *placed* in the marketplace? These four general categories—*product, price, promotion, placement*—are sometimes referred to as the **"Four Ps" of marketing.**

"Four Ps" of marketing
Production, price, promotion, and placement.

Each of these elements raises important ethical questions. What responsibilities do companies have for the quality and safety of the products they produce and sell? Who is responsible for harms caused by a product? Are there some products that should not be produced, or does consumer demand decide all production questions? Is the consumer's willingness to pay the only ethical constraint on fair pricing? Do all customers deserve the same price, or can producers discriminate in favor of, or against, some consumers? Are deceptive or misleading ads ethical? What ethical constraints should be placed on sales promotions? Is the information gathered in market research the property of the business that conducts the research? What privacy protections should be offered for marketing data? Is it ethical to target vulnerable populations such as children or older people? What responsibilities do producers have to retailers? To competitors? To suppliers?

Marketing: An Ethical Framework

OBJECTIVE

We can take the simple model of a single exchange between two individuals as a useful way to introduce an ethical framework for marketing ethics (see Table 8.1). As in previous chapters, this framework will assist the decision maker in arriving at an ethical decision, but it will not definitively prove the "correct" decision as much as it will help reach a rationally responsible decision. In other words, it does not determine the right answer, but instead the framework identifies rights, responsibilities, duties and obligations, causes, and consequences.

This simple situation in which two parties come together and freely agree to an exchange is *prima facie* ethically legitimate. The rights-based ethical tradition described in Chapter 3 would see it as upholding respect for individuals by treating them as autonomous agents capable of pursuing their own ends. This tradition presumes that each individual will abide by fundamental principles. The utilitarian ethical tradition would take the two parties' agreement as evidence that both of them believe they will be better off than they were prior to the exchange and thus conclude that overall happiness is likely to be increased by any exchange freely entered into.

This assessment is only *prima facie* because, like all agreements, certain conditions must be met before we can conclude that autonomy has in fact been respected and mutual benefit has been achieved. Thus, for example, we would need to establish that the agreement resulted from an informed and voluntary consent and that there was no fraud, deception, or coercion involved. When these conditions are violated, autonomy is not respected and mutual benefit is unlikely to be attained. Furthermore, even when such conditions are met, other values may override the freedom of individuals to contract for mutually beneficial purposes. Thus, for example, the freedom of drug dealers to pursue mutually agreeable ends is overridden by society's concern to maintain law and order.

OBJECTIVE

In general, therefore, it will be helpful to keep three concerns in mind as we approach any ethical issue in marketing:

TABLE 8.1
Ethical Issues
in Marketing: A
Framework

Market exchange is *prima facie* ethically legitimate because it involves

- Respect for autonomy
- Mutual benefit

This ethical judgment is conditional because

- The transaction must be truly voluntary
- Informed consent is needed
- Benefits might not occur
- Other values might conflict

These four conditions imply the following four questions, each of which requires considering several factors:

1. Is exchange "voluntary"?
   - Real alternative choices may not be available
   - Anxiety and stress in some purchasing situations
   - Price-fixing, monopolies, price gouging, etc.
   - Targeted and vulnerable consumers

2. Is consent to exchange really "informed"?
   - Lack of information
   - Deception
   - Complicated information

3. Are people truly benefited?
   - Impulse buying, "affluenza," consumerism
   - Injuries, unsafe products
   - "Contrived" wants

4. Competing values
   - Justice—e.g., "redlining" mortgages
   - Market failures (externalities)

- The rights-based ethical tradition would ask to what degree the participants are respected as free and autonomous agents rather than treated simply as means to the end of making a sale.
- The utilitarian tradition would want to know the degree to which the transaction provided actual as opposed to merely apparent benefits.
- Every ethical tradition would also wonder what other values might be at stake in the transaction.

Let us consider these three issues: the degree to which individuals freely participate in an exchange, the benefits and costs of each exchange, and other values that are affected by the exchange.

It is not always easy to determine if someone is being treated with respect in marketing situations. As a first approximation, we might suggest two conditions. First, the person must freely consent to the transaction. But how free is "free"? Surely, transactions completed under the threat of force are not voluntary and therefore are unethical. But there are many degrees of voluntariness. For example, the more a given consumer needs a product, the less free she or he is to choose and therefore the more protection the consumer deserves within the marketplace. Consider the use of the Windows operating system by a large majority of computer users. How voluntary is the decision to use Windows as your computer's operating system? Do most people even make a decision to use Windows? Or consider the anxiety and stress that many consumers experience during a car purchase. When an automobile dealer exploits that anxiety to sell extended warranty insurance or roadside assistance, it is not at all clear that the consumer has made a fully voluntary decision. More dramatic cases of price gouging, price-fixing, and monopolistic pricing clearly raise the issue of freedom in marketing. When a bank or an insurance company is "too big to fail," one must question if its consumers have any real bargaining power in the marketplace. Practices aimed at vulnerable populations such as children and the elderly also raise questions of voluntariness. Thus, an adequate analysis of marketing ethics challenges us to be sensitive to the many ways in which consumer choice can be less than fully voluntary. (To explore what it means to engage in "voluntary" purchasing decisions, see the Reality Check "Impulse Buying.")

A second condition for respect requires that the consent be not only voluntary, but also informed. Informed consent has received a great deal of attention in the medical ethics literature because patients are at a distinct informational disadvantage when dealing with health care professionals. But similar disadvantages can occur in marketing products. Outright deception and fraud clearly violate this condition and are unethical. A consumer's consent to purchase a product is not informed if that consumer is being misled or deceived about the product. But there can also be many more nuanced cases of deception and misleading marketing practices. (To explore what it means for a fully informed decision, see the Reality Check "GMO Labeling: Can Truthful Information Be Misleading?" later in this chapter.)

The complexity of many consumer products and services can mean that consumers may not fully understand what they are purchasing. Consider two famous product safety cases as examples, and consider all that would be involved for a consumer to determine which fuel tank design was safest for subcompact cars, or which tire design is least likely to cause blowouts. Consider also the many people who have very weak mathematical skills. Imagine such a person trying to decide on the economic benefits of whole-life versus term insurance, or a 48-month auto lease versus a five-year purchase loan at 2.9 percent financing. In general, while some businesses claim that an "informed consumer is our best customer," many others recognize that an uninformed consumer can be an easy target for quick profits.[3] Serious ethical questions should be raised whenever marketing practices either deny consumers full information or rely on the fact that they lack relevant information or understanding.

The second ethical concern looks to the alleged benefits obtained through market exchanges. Economics textbooks commonly assume that consumers benefit, almost by definition, whenever they make an exchange in the marketplace.

Reality Check   *Impulse Buying*

Though the cartoon pokes fun at the ability of marketing professionals to "make" us buy certain items, not everyone exercises similar levels of effective judgment necessary to protect him- or herself from poor decisions about credit and debt, good and bad spending choices. Young spenders in particular may not yet be sufficiently experienced—with shopping, spending, or responding to sophisticated marketing campaigns—to adequately protect themselves against strategies designed to encourage impulse buying.

Sales pitches that hype the latest and trendiest items, those that must be purchased today and worn tonight, are difficult to resist for some purchasers who buy in haste and perhaps regret it later. Marketing campaigns are also chastised for creating needs where the purchaser may originally have only sensed a desire. Purchases on impulse are often not reversible, but because they are often so hastily made that the purchaser fails to notice that the product is imperfect or does not match a personal style, they are perhaps most in need of later returns.

In the same way that a hungry person is more likely to buy groceries on impulse than one who has just eaten, we are better off engaging in our purchasing efforts when we are capable of evaluating our options with a clear head (and a full stomach!).

Chris Madden/CartoonStock

But this assumption won't survive close scrutiny. Many purchases do not result in actual benefit.

For example, impulse buying, and the many marketing techniques used to promote such consumer behavior, cannot be justified by appeal to satisfying consumer interests. (See the Reality Check "Impulse Buying.") The ever-increasing number of personal bankruptcies suggests that consumers cannot purchase happiness. Empirical studies provide evidence that suggests that greater consumption can lead to unhappiness, a condition called by some "affluenza."[4] So, if simple consumer satisfaction is not a conclusive measure of the benefits of market exchanges, one must always ask about the goals of marketing. What goods are attained by successfully marketing this product or service? How and in what ways are individuals and society benefited from the product?

Both parties to the marketing exchange are also not benefited in situations in which one party is injured by the product. Unsafe products do not further the utilitarian goal of maximizing overall happiness. It would also be the case that consumers are not benefited if the desires that they seek to satisfy in the market are somehow contrived or manipulated by the seller.

The third set of factors that must be considered in any ethical analysis of marketing includes values other than those served by the exchange itself. Such primary social values as fairness, justice, health, and safety are just some of the values that can be jeopardized by some marketing practices. For example, a bank that offers lower mortgage rates in affluent neighborhoods than it does in poorer neighborhoods might be involved only in deals that are mutually beneficial because they do not, in fact, sell mortgages in the poorer neighborhoods at all. But such contracts would violate important social norms of equal treatment and fairness.

There may be a very strong market for such things as body parts of endangered species. There is also, unfortunately, a market for children. But just because someone wants to buy something and someone else is willing to sell it does not mean that the transaction is ethically legitimate. An adequate ethical analysis of marketing must ask who else might be affected by the transaction. How, if at all, are the interests of these others represented? What social goods are promoted, and which are threatened, by marketing this product?

One must also ask what the true costs of production are. An adequate ethical analysis of marketing must consider externalities, those costs that are not integrated within the exchange between buyer and seller. Externalities show that even if both parties to the exchange receive actual benefits from the exchange, other parties external to the exchange might be adversely affected. One thinks of the environmental or health impact of marketing products such as gas-guzzling SUVs, pesticides, and tobacco as examples in which a simple model of individual consumer exchange would ignore significant social costs. With these general issues in mind, we can now turn to a closer examination of several major aspects of marketing ethics.

Responsibility for Products: Safety and Liability

OBJECTIVE

Few issues have received as much scrutiny in law, politics, and ethics as has the responsibility of business for harms caused by its products. In general, business has an ethical responsibility to design, manufacture, and promote its products in ways that avoid causing harm to consumers.

It will be helpful to review here several different meanings of the word *responsibility* that were introduced in the discussion of corporate social responsibility in Chapter 5. Recall that, in one sense, to be responsible is to be identified as the *cause* of something. Thus, we might say that Hurricane Michael was responsible for millions of dollars in property damages in Florida in 2018. In another sense, responsibility involves accountability. When we ask who will be responsible for the damages caused by Hurricane Michael, we are asking who will pay for the damages. In many cases, someone is held accountable because she or he was at fault, but not in all cases. For example, parents are held accountable for damage caused by their children, even if they were not at fault in causing the damage.

Both law and ethics rely on this framework when evaluating cases in which business products or services cause harm in the marketplace. Contract law, and the ethics implicit in contracts, is one legal approach to product safety. Contracts are a form of a promise, and when a product is sold, there is an implicit promise that it will perform as promised without hurting the user. Tort law provides a second legal approach to product safety. The law of torts recognizes that we all have a general duty not to cause harm to others. A third legal doctrine, strict liability, addresses questions of legal and ethical responsibility for cases in which no one is at fault, but someone has been harmed. Let's look at each of these.

Contractual Standards for Product Safety

OBJECTIVE

caveat emptor approach
Caveat emptor means "buyer beware" in Latin, and this approach suggests that the burden of risk of information shall be placed on the buyer. This perspective assumes that every purchase involves the informed consent of the buyer, and, therefore, it is assumed to be ethically legitimate.

It is fair to say that the standard of *caveat emptor* (let the buyer beware) is in the background to many discussions of product safety. The *caveat emptor* approach adopts a simple model of a contractual exchange between a buyer and seller. This model assumes that every purchase involves the informed consent of the buyer, and, therefore, it is assumed to be ethically legitimate. Buyers have the responsibility to look out for their own interests and protect their own safety when buying a product. From this *caveat emptor* perspective, business's only legal and ethical responsibility is to provide a good or service at an agreed-upon price.

The social contract tradition in ethics holds that this contractual model is the best way to understand ethical responsibilities. From this perspective, the only duties that a person has are those freely taken on within a social contract. Individual contracts and promises are the basis of ethical duties. The implication of this within the business sphere is that unless a seller explicitly warrants a product as safe—unless, in other words, the seller promises otherwise—buyers are liable for any harm they suffer.

But even this simple model of a contractual market exchange would place ethical constraints on the seller. Sellers have a duty not to coerce, defraud, or deceive buyers, for example. Consumers who were injured by a product that was deceptively or fraudulently marketed would have legal recourse to recover damages from the seller. (To explore other ethical restraints on this contractual model, see the Reality Check "*Caveat Emptor* in Buying Drugs.")

implied warranty of merchantability
Implied assurances by a seller that a product is reasonably suitable for its purpose.

Courts have moved away from this *caveat emptor* approach and recognized an implicit promise, or implied warranty, that accompanies any product that is marketed. What the law refers to as the **implied warranty of merchantability** holds that in selling a product, a business implicitly offers assurances that the product is reasonably suitable for its purpose. Even without an explicit verbal or written promise or contract, the law holds that business has a duty to ensure that its products will accomplish their purpose.

The ethics implicit within the contract approach assumes that when consumers adequately understand products well enough, they can reasonably be expected to protect themselves. But consumers don't always understand products fully, and they are not always free to choose not to purchase some things. In effect, the implied warranty standard shifts the burden of proof from consumers to producers by allowing consumers to assume that products were safe for ordinary use. By bringing goods and services to the market, producers were implicitly promising that their products were safe under normal use. The ethical basis for this decision

Reality Check Caveat Emptor *in Buying Drugs?*

Because some drugs are potentially very harmful, governments prevent consumers from purchasing them directly. Instead, physicians and other health care professionals act as gatekeepers and determine who can purchase drugs by issuing prescriptions to their clients. (And note that in most jurisdictions—the U.S. is an exception—pharmaceutical companies are not allowed even to advertise their products, by name, directly to

consumers.) Assume that pharmaceutical companies continue to disclose all the potential side effects of using a drug; would you favor eliminating the gatekeeper function from health care professionals? If consumers were provided with full information about a drug, should they be left free to decide for themselves whether or not to use it? Are there other products that you think should be treated similarly, or are pharmaceuticals in a unique category?

is the assumption that consumers would not give their consent to a purchase if they had reason to believe that they would be harmed by it when used in a normal way.

Of course, if the law will hold business liable for implicit promises, a prudent business will seek to limit its liability by explicitly disowning any promise or warranty. Thus, many businesses will issue a disclaimer of liability (e.g., products are sold "as is") or offer an expressed and limited warranty (e.g., the seller will replace the product but offers no other guarantees). Most courts will not allow a business to completely disclaim the implied warranty of merchantability. If a business is legally liable, simply claiming not to be doesn't make much difference.

Tort Standards for Product Safety

OBJECTIVE

negligence
Unintentional failure to exercise reasonable care not to harm other people. Negligence is considered to be one step below "reckless disregard" for harm to others and two steps below intentional harm.

The use of an implied warranty, and the ethics of contracts that underlies it, answered one set of questions of the responsibility for harms caused by products. But other problems remain. In particular, the ethics of contact law would not apply to the majority of business situations in which consumers do not have a contractual relation with the business that created or manufactured the product. **Negligence,** a concept from the area of law known as torts, provides a second avenue for consumers to hold producers responsible for their products.

The distinction between contract law and tort law calls attention to two different ways to understand ethical duties. Under a contract model, the only duties that a person owes are those that have been explicitly promised to another party. Otherwise, that person owes nothing to anyone. The ethical perspective that underlies tort law holds that we all owe other people certain general duties, *even if we have not explicitly and voluntarily assumed them.* Specifically, I owe other people a general duty not to put them at unnecessary and avoidable risk. Thus, for example, although I have never explicitly promised anyone that I will drive carefully, I have an ethical duty not to drive recklessly down the street.

Negligence is a central component of tort law. As the word suggests, negligence involves a type of ethical neglect, specifically neglecting one's duty to exercise reasonable care not to harm other people. Many of the ethical and legal issues surrounding manufacturers' responsibility for products can be understood as the attempt to specify what constitutes negligence in their design, production, and sale. What duties, exactly, do producers owe to consumers?

strict liability
A legal doctrine that holds an individual or business accountable for damages whether or not it was at fault. In a strict liability case, no matter how careful the business is in its product or service, if harm results from use, the individual or business is liable.

One can think of possible answers to this question as falling along a continuum. On one end of the continuum is the contract-oriented answer: Producers owe only those things promised to consumers in the sales agreement. At the other end is something closer to **strict liability:** Producers owe compensation to consumers for any and all harms caused by their products. In between these extremes is a range of answers that vary with different interpretations of negligence.

Negligence can be characterized as a failure to exercise reasonable care or ordinary vigilance that results in an injury to another. In many ways, negligence simply codifies two fundamental ethical precepts: "ought implies can" (we cannot reasonably oblige someone to do what they cannot do) and "one ought not harm others." People have done an ethical wrong when they cause harm to others in ways that they can reasonably be expected to have avoided. One can be negligent by doing something that one ought not (e.g., speeding in a school zone) or by failing to do something that one ought to have done (e.g., neglecting to inspect a product before sending it to market).

Negligence involves having the ability to foresee the consequences of our acts and failing to take steps to avoid the likely harmful consequences (see the Reality Check "Snapchat: When Is a Company's Product Responsible for Causing Injuries?"). The standards of what can be foreseen, however, raise interesting ethical challenges.

One standard would hold people liable only for those harms they actually foresaw occurring. Thus, for example, as happened in the famous Ford Pinto case, a company would be acting negligently if it brought to market a car that it knew, on the basis of engineering tests, had a fuel tank that would puncture and explode during crashes at speeds below 30 miles per hour.

But this standard of actual foresight is too narrow because it would imply that unthoughtful people cannot be negligent. By applying this standard, a person could escape liability by not actually thinking about the consequences of one's acts. "I never thought about that" would be an adequate defense if we used this standard of negligence. Yet this surely is not an ethically adequate excuse for harming innocent people.

A preferable standard would require people to avoid harms that they *should* have thought about. For example, in the Reality Check on Snapchat, we might judge the company responsible even if we assume that the designers did not actually anticipate that customers would be using the speed filter to record driving at 100 mph. Had they thought about typical users and the fact that they often do unreasonable things, which they would have done had they acted reasonably, they could have foreseen such accidents. Moreover, the fact that Snapchat had received prior complaints about similar accidents suggests that a reasonable person would have concluded that this was a dangerous practice. This "reasonable person" standard is the one most often used in legal cases and seems to better capture the ethical goals of the very concept of negligence. People are expected to act reasonably and are held liable when they are not.

But even the reasonable person standard can be interpreted in various ways. On one hand, we expect people will act in ways that would be normal or average. A "reasonable" person does what we could expect the ordinary, average person to do. But, for example, the average person doesn't always read, or understand,

Reality Check *Snapchat: When Is a Company's Product Responsible for Causing Injuries?*

Snapchat is a photo and video messaging app that sends images that the user can edit with numerous filters to distort or add doodles or commentary to the image before sending. One filter introduced by Snapchat allows the user to record the speed at which she or he was traveling when the image was recorded. Thus, for example, one could send out a selfie taken while flying in an airplane that shows the plane's speed superimposed on the photo. This filter includes a warning against using this filter when one is driving.

In September 2015, an 18-year-old Georgia girl crashed into the back of another car. News reports indicated that she was driving over 100 mph in a 55-mph speed zone and was using the Snapchat speed filter at the time. These news reports indicated that friends in her car had asked her to stop but that she was intent on reaching the 100-mph mark. The driver of the other car was seriously injured, sustaining permanent brain injuries.

Lawyers for the injured driver sued both the girl and Snapchat, claiming that Snapshat should be held responsible for selling a product that it had reason to know would encourage reckless behavior. Months earlier, an online petition was started to request Snapchat to remove the speed filter after reports of other similar accidents.

Snapchat denied responsibility for the accident, pointing out that its terms of service, the small print accompanying the app, advises users against unsafe practices.

The terms of service document included the following: "We also care about your safety while using our Services. So do not use our Services in a way that would distract you from obeying traffic or safety laws. And never put yourself or others in harm's way just to capture a Snap." The Snapchat terms of service statement runs for over 4,500 words, with 22 separate sections, including sections on such topics as arbitration, severability, indemnity, disclaimers, limitation of liability, and venue. In reality, most users seldom read or understand the specifics of the terms of service. While in the ambulance on her way to the hospital, the girl who was driving sent out a Snapchat selfie of her bloody face with the caption "lucky to be alive."

1. What liability, if any, should Snapchat have for the damages caused by this accident? No one denies that the driver bears primary responsibility, but did Snapchat also contribute to the harms caused?

2. What uses could Snapchat have reasonably foreseen for this speed filter? What could Snapchat reasonably be expected to know about the users of its products?

3. Was the advice contained in the terms of service sufficient warning to protect Snapchat from any misuse of its product?

4. Do you think that the speed filter is a dangerous product? Was Snapchat negligent in marketing this product?

warning labels or terms of service. The average person standard when applied to consumers might exempt too many consumers from responsibility for their own acts. Especially when applied to producers, the average person standard sets the bar too low. We can expect more from a person who designs, manufactures, and sells a product than average, especially if the product is intended to be marketed to an adolescent or teen consumer.

These factors lead many to interpret the reasonable person standard as a standard of thoughtful, reflective, and judicious decision making. The problem with this, of course, is that we might be asking more of average consumers than they are capable of giving. Particularly if we think that vulnerable consumers (think of the teenage driver in the Snatchat case) deserve greater protection from harm, we might conclude that this sense of reasonable is too stringent a standard to be applied to consumer behavior. On the other hand, given the fact that producers do have more expertise than the average person, this stronger standard seems more appropriate when applied to producers than to consumers.

Strict Product Liability

OBJECTIVE

The negligence standard of tort law focuses on the sense of responsibility that involves someone being at fault. But there are also cases in which consumers can be injured by a product in which no negligence was involved. In such cases where no one was at fault, the question of accountability remains. Who should pay for damages when consumers are injured by products and no one is at fault? The legal doctrine of strict product liability holds manufacturers accountable in such cases, and it raises unique ethical questions.

Ethical Debates on Product Liability

OBJECTIVE

In the United States and elsewhere, calls to reform product liability laws, and in particular to ease or eliminate the strict product liability standard, have been common. But criticism of strict product liability has not been universal. The European Union, for example, has adopted clear strict liability standards. The EU concluded that "liability without fault [strict products liability] on the part of the producer is the sole means of adequately solving the problem, peculiar to our age of increasing technicality, of a fair apportionment of the risks inherent in modern technological production."[5]

It is fair to say that the business community in the United States and elsewhere has been a strong critic of much of the legal standards of product liability. Liability standards, and the liability insurance costs in which they have resulted, have imposed significant costs on contemporary business. In particular, these critics single out the strict product liability standard as especially unfair to business because it holds business responsible for harms that were not the result of business negligence.

In fact, the rationale often used to justify strict product liability is problematic. Defenders of the strict product liability standard, including juries who decide in favor of injured consumers, often reply with two major claims. First, by holding business strictly liable for any harm their products cause, society creates a strong incentive for business to produce safer goods and services. Second, given that someone has to be accountable for the costs of injuries, holding business liable allocates the costs to the party best able to bear the financial burden. But each rationale is open to serious objections.

The incentive argument seems to misunderstand the nature of strict liability. Holding someone accountable for harm can provide an incentive only if the person could have done otherwise. But this means that the harm was foreseeable and the failure to act was negligent. Surely this is a reasonable justification for the tort standard of negligence. But strict liability is not negligence and the harms caused by such products as asbestos were not foreseeable. Thus, holding business liable for these harms cannot provide an incentive to better protect consumers in the future. See the Reality Check "Should Cities Help Advertise Booze?"

The second rationale also suffers a serious defect. This argument amounts to the claim that business is best able to pay for damages. Yet, many businesses have been bankrupted by product liability claims. And besides, in most instances, *government* is far more capable of bearing the financial burden resulting from injuries than any business is.

Reality Check *Should Cities Help Advertise Booze?*

In April 2019, New York City announced that alcohol ads would no longer be permitted on most city-owned properties, including, for example, bus shelters and recycling bins. The city said the move was a response to well-known problems related to alcohol, including alcohol abuse and various alcohol-related injuries. The loss in advertising revenue to the city, it was thought, was less important than the known public health effects of alcohol.

1. Is such a ban likely to be effective in reducing rates of alcoholism or alcohol-related deaths and injuries?
2. Is the city obligated at least not to contribute—or appear not to contribute—to such problems?
3. Do governments at any level have different obligations than, say, private land owners in this regard?

If it is unfair to hold businesses accountable for harms caused by their products, it is equally (if not more) unfair to hold injured consumers accountable. Neither party is at fault, yet someone must pay for the injuries. A third option would be to have government, and therefore all taxpayers, accountable for paying the costs of injuries caused by defective products. But this, too, seems unfair. Why have everyone share the costs of injuries that result from the decisions of a few?

Another argument for holding business accountable might be more persuasive. Accountability, after all, focuses on those situations where no one is at fault, yet someone has to bear the burdens associated with the harm. But perhaps accountability is best understood as a matter of utilitarian efficiency rather than a matter of ethical principle of desert. When business is held accountable, the costs for injuries will eventually fall on those consumers who buy the product through higher costs, especially higher insurance costs to business. This amounts to the claim that external costs should be internalized and that the full costs of a product should be paid for by those who use the product. Products that impose a cost on society through injuries will end up costing more to those who purchase them. Companies that cannot afford to remain in business when the full costs of their products are taken into account perhaps ought not to remain in business.

Responsibility for Products: Advertising and Sales

OBJECTIVE

Along with product safety, advertising is a second area of marketing that has received significant legal and philosophical attention by those who study business ethics. The goal of all marketing is the sale, the eventual exchange between seller and buyer. A major element of marketing is sales promotion, the attempt to influence the buyer to complete a purchase. (See the Decision Point "Advertising Drugs.") Target marketing and marketing research are two important elements of product placement, seeking to determine which audience is most likely to buy and which audience is mostly likely to be influenced by product promotion.

There are, of course, ethically good and bad ways of influencing others. Among the ethically commendable ways to influence another are persuading, asking, informing, and advising. Unethical means of influence would include threats, coercion, deception, manipulation, and lying. Unfortunately, all too often, sales and advertising practices employ deceptive or manipulative means of influence, or are aimed at audiences that are susceptible to manipulation or deception. The concept of manipulation (and one of the key ways of manipulating people, namely deception) is central to the ethical issues explored in this chapter and can help organize the following sections.

To manipulate something is to guide or direct its behavior. Manipulation need not involve total control, and in fact it more likely suggests a process of subtle direction or management. Manipulating people implies working behind the scenes, guiding their behavior without their explicit consent or conscious understanding. In this way, manipulation is contrasted with persuasion and other forms of rational influence. When I manipulate someone, I explicitly do not rely on that individual's own reasoned judgment to direct her or his behavior. Instead, I seek to bypass the individual's autonomy (although successful manipulation can be reinforced when the person manipulated *believes* she acted of her own accord).

One of the ways in which we can manipulate someone is through deception, one form of which is an outright lie. But I need not deceive you to manipulate you. We can manipulate someone without deception, as when a parent gets her teenager to mow the lawn by making the teen feel guilty about not carrying his share of family responsibilities. Or a professor might manipulate students into studying more diligently by hinting that there may be a quiz during the next class. These examples raise a very crucial point because they suggest that the more one person knows about another person's psychology—his or her motivations, interests, desires, beliefs, dispositions, and so forth—the better able the first person will be to manipulate the other's behavior. Guilt, pity, a desire to please, anxiety, fear, low self-esteem, pride, and conformity can all be powerful motivators. Knowing such things about another person provides effective tools for manipulating her or his behavior.

We can see how this is relevant to marketing ethics. Critics charge that many marketing practices manipulate consumers. Clearly, many advertisements are deceptive, and some are outright lies. We can also see how marketing research plays into this. The more one learns about customer psychology, the better able one will be to satisfy consumers' desires, but the better able one will also be to manipulate their behavior. Consider the cases of digital marketing described in the chapter's opening scenario for examples of how consumer information might be used to manipulate people. Critics also charge that some marketing practices target populations that are particularly susceptible to manipulation and deception.

Ethical Issues in Advertising

OBJECTIVE

The general ethical defense of advertising reflects both utilitarian and Kantian ethical standards. Advertising provides information for market exchanges and therefore contributes to market efficiency and to overall happiness. Advertising information also contributes to the information necessary for autonomous individuals to make

According to Pew Research, pharmaceutical companies spent $27 billion in 2012 promoting their drugs. All but one of the largest 10 firms spent more on marketing than they did on research and development. From 2012 to 2015, direct-to-consumer (DTC) marketing of drugs increased from $3.2 billion to almost $6 billion annually.

Advertisements promoting prescription drugs have increased significantly within the United States since the Food and Drug Administration (FDA) changed regulations in 1997 to allow DTC advertising—most countries still forbid such advertising. Among the most widely marketed drugs have been Lipitor, Zocor, Prilosec, Prevacid, Nexium, Celebrex, Vioxx, Zoloft, Paxil, Prozac, Viagra, Cialis, Levitra, Propecia, and Zyban. These drug names, literally household names today, were unheard of before the turn of the century; yet, together they accounted for over $20 billion in annual sales.

The medications mentioned here treat the following conditions: ulcers and acid reflux (Prilosec, Prevacid, Nexium); high cholesterol (Lipitor, Zocor); arthritic pain (Celebrex, Vioxx); depression, panic attacks, and anxiety (Zoloft, Paxil, Prozac); "erectile dysfunction" (Viagra, Cialis, Levitra); hair loss (Propecia); and cigarette and nicotine withdrawal (Zyban). Ads for these drugs often appeal to such emotional considerations as embarrassment; fear; shame; social, sexual, and romantic inferiority; helplessness; vulnerability; and vanity. Many of these drugs are heavily advertised in women's magazines or during televised sporting events and evening network news shows.

1. Would you favor a ban on direct-to-consumer advertising for prescription drugs?
2. What facts would you want to know before making a judgment about these ads?
3. Which ads, if any, raise ethical questions?
4. Who are the stakeholders in drug advertising? What are the potential benefits and potential harms of such advertising?
5. Are customers for prescription drugs particularly vulnerable to manipulation?
6. What ethical principles have you used in making your judgments?

informed choices. But note that each of these rationales provides an ethical justification only if the information is accurate and relevant.

The principle-based tradition in ethics would have the strongest objections to manipulation. When I manipulate someone, I treat him or her as a means to my own ends, as an object to be used rather than as an autonomous person in his or her own right. Manipulation is a clear example of disrespect for persons because it bypasses their own rational decision making. Because the evil rests with the intention to use another as a means, even unsuccessful manipulations are guilty of this ethical wrong.

As we might expect, the utilitarian tradition would offer a more conditional critique of manipulation—the goodness or badness of manipulation would depend on the consequences. For example, there surely can be cases of well-meaning paternalistic manipulation, in which someone is manipulated for his or her own good. But even in such cases, unforeseen harms can occur. Manipulation tends to erode bonds of trust and respect between persons. It can erode self-confidence and hinder the development of responsible choice among those manipulated. In general, because most manipulation is done to further the manipulator's own ends at the expense of the manipulated, utilitarians would be inclined to think that manipulation lessens overall happiness. A general practice of manipulation, as critics claim often occurs in many sales practices, can undermine the very social practices (e.g., sales) that it is thought to promote as the reputation of sales is lowered.

A particularly egregious form of manipulation occurs when vulnerable people are targeted for abuse. Cigarette advertising aimed at children is one example that has historically received major criticism for years. Marketing practices targeted at older populations for such goods and services as insurance (particularly Medicare supplemental insurance), casinos and gambling, nursing homes, and funerals have been subjected to similar criticisms.

We can suggest the following general guidelines. Marketing practices that seek to discover which consumers might already and independently be predisposed to purchasing a product are ethically legitimate. So, for example, contextual digital ads in which a banner ad for a Montreal hotel appears on your mobile screen immediately after you search for an airline flight to Montreal would seem legitimate. After all, such an ad merely responds to your own expressed interest in visiting Montreal.

Marketing practices that seek to identify populations that can be easily influenced and manipulated, on the other hand, are ethically questionable. Sales and marketing that appeal to fear, anxiety, or other nonrational motivations are ethically improper. For example, an automobile dealer who knows that an elderly woman is anxious about the purchase and who uses this anxiety as a way to sell extended warranty insurance, disability insurance, theft protection products, and the like is unethical. The manner in which this or other information is collected is also subject to ethical concerns. (To explore if consumer privacy might limit how information is collected, see the Reality Check "Does Digital Marketing Raise New Ethical Issues?")

Marketing research seeks to learn something about the psychology of potential customers. But not all psychological categories are alike. Some are more cognitive and rational than others. Targeting the considered and rational desires of consumers is one thing; targeting their fears, anxiety, and whims is another. (To explore another way in which even truthful ads might mislead consumers, see the Reality Check "GMO Labeling: Can Truthful Information Be Misleading?")

Marketing Ethics and Consumer Autonomy

OBJECTIVE

Defenders of advertising argue that despite cases of deceptive practices, overall advertising contributes much to the economy. The majority of advertisements provide information to consumers, information that contributes to an efficient function of economic markets. These defenders argue that over time, market forces will weed out deceptive ads and practices. They point out that the most effective counter to a deceptive ad is a competitor's ad calling attention to the deception. And increasingly, social media gives aggrieved consumers an effective way of voicing their dissatisfaction with their purchases.

Reality Check *Does Digital Marketing Raise New Ethical Issues?*

Deception and manipulation are two ethical concerns that seem as relevant to digital marketing techniques as they do to traditional marketing. But digital marketing has the potential to raise concerns of consumer privacy that did not exist for traditional marketing techniques.

Tracking cookies are one common means by which digital businesses can collect information about consumers. In some cases, the use of cookies is explicitly detailed for consumers, and they are allowed to opt out of their use. In some cases, consumers are warned that by opting out, they risk losing functionality on the site they are visiting. In other cases, known as *stealth tracking*, consumers are unaware that their behavior is being tracked and recorded. Internet service providers (ISPs) and cell phone providers, for example, have the ability to track every online action and phone call. This information uniquely identifies the user and cannot be controlled by the user by deleting cookies or browsing history.

How tracking information is used raises other ethical questions. This information is regularly sold to third parties, most often companies interested in marketing to that user. But others might be interested as well. Already, potential employers have shown an interest in the social network sites of job applicants. Might they be as interested in browsing history?

For example, the dating site OKcupid allowed all registered users to access the personal information provided by users, including not only name, religion, and political sympathies, but also information about personal habits, alcohol and drug use, and sexual interests. All one needed to do to have access to this information was to register on the site and agree to OKcupid's terms of service agreement. This did not prove a deterrent to some Dutch researchers who collected data from the site for a research project and made the data publicly available for others.

Another example involved the legal case *Valentine v. NebuAd, Inc.** This case involved a digital marketing company, NebuAd, that contracted with ISPs to install devices on their networks that monitored ISP subscribers' internet activity and transmitted those data to NebuAd's California headquarters for analysis. The data were used to sell advertising tailored to subscribers' interests, which appeared in place of more generic advertisements on web pages visited by subscribers. In effect, NebuAd stepped into the communication between individuals and the browser they were using to substitute their client's ads for more generic ads that would otherwise have appeared. The advertising profits generated from this activity were split by NebuAd and its ISP partners.

ISP customers filed a class-action lawsuit against both NebuAd and their ISPs alleging that this practice violated their federal and state privacy rights. The case was finally resolved after NebuAd entered bankruptcy and agreed to pay more than $2 million to settle the case.

1. Identify as many ethical issues involved in these cases as you can. Are any of these issues unique to digital marketing?

2. Who are the stakeholders in the OKcupid and NebuAd cases? Who was harmed by NebuAd?

3. Who should own and control personal information collected by cookies? Are there any limits that should be placed on how that information is used and who has access to it?

4. Does an individual relinquish all claims to privacy by posting personal information on a social network site?

*804 F. Supp. 2d 1022 (N.D. Cal. 2011).

Beyond this question of what advertising does *for* people, a second important ethical question asks what advertising specifically and marketing in general do *to* people. People may well benefit from business's marketing of its products. People learn about products they may need or want; they get information that helps them make responsible choices; they even sometimes are entertained. But marketing also helps shape culture and the individuals who are socialized within that culture, some would say dramatically so. Marketing can have direct and indirect influence on the very persons we become. How it does that, and the kind of people we

Reality Check *GMO Labeling: Can Truthful Information Be Misleading?*

Free and informed consent is one of the fundamental ethical conditions on any exchange. Parties to the exchange must understand and give their voluntary consent in order for the exchange to be ethically responsible. By meeting this standard, the exchange will both respect the autonomy of the parties involved and meet utilitarian goals of providing mutual benefit. Product labeling for ingredients and nutritional value are two ways that food labeling serves this ethical goal by providing consumers with the information needed to make a fully informed decision. Should food that contains genetically modified organisms (GMOs) be required to carry a label that identifies them as GMO?

A number of reasons are offered to require GMO labeling. First, and perhaps most importantly, supporters cite a general consumer right to know what they are purchasing. Labels provide consumers with the information they require to make truly informed decisions about food products. This information is particularly important for vegetarians and others who have health or religious reasons to avoid food containing animal products. Thus, labeling serves the ethical goals of mutual benefit and respect for autonomy. Second, label requirements will provide a disincentive for the use of GMO technology and thus reduce the use of herbicides and other chemicals in food production. Third, labeling provides a paper trail of information that can be used to track any potential problems that arise from the use of GMO foods. Finally, GMO labeling is thought to provide a check on the power of large agricultural and chemical corporations that own and control much of the GMO technology and products.

Those who oppose GMO labeling requirements argue that this would mislead and unduly alarm consumers. It is likely that consumers will perceive this as a warning label rather than simply an ingredient label, and this will mislead consumers and discourage them from purchasing the product. Critics argue that there is no evidence that GMO foods are unsafe and that, in fact, they add significantly to agricultural productivity. Thus, anything that discourages GMO foods will reduce the amount of food available for no health or nutritional reason. Critics also point out that they oppose only mandatory labeling, not voluntary labeling. Food producers are always free to label food as GMO-free, as organic food producers already do; thus, consumers who desire GMO-free food already have a way to make informed food choices. Voluntary labeling allows the market to function as the means of meeting this consumer demand. If consumers demand GMO labeling, producers will have a financial incentive to provide it; if they are not demanding GMO labels, then requirements will unnecessarily raise the price of food products.

1. Would you support mandatory labeling for all GMO food products?

2. Besides the sellers and consumers, what other stakeholders should be considered in making this decision?

3. How would you respond to the reasons offered by the side that disagrees with your views?

4. Is it reasonable to expect that some consumers will interpret the label as a warning that GMO foods are unhealthy?

become as a result, is of fundamental ethical importance. Critics of such claims either deny that marketing can have such influence or maintain that marketing is only a mirror of the culture of which it is a part.

The initial proposal in this debate was offered by economist John Kenneth Galbraith in his 1958 book *The Affluent Society.* Galbraith claimed that advertising and marketing were creating the very consumer demand that production then aimed to satisfy. Dubbed the "dependence effect," this assertion held that consumer demand depended on what producers had to sell. This fact had three major and unwelcome implications.

First, by creating wants, advertising was standing the "law" of supply and demand on its head. Rather than supply being a function of demand, demand turns out to be a function of supply. Second, advertising and marketing tend to create irrational and trivial consumer wants, and this distorts the entire economy. The "affluent" society of consumer products and creature comforts is in many ways worse off than so-called undeveloped economies because resources devoted to contrived, private consumer goods are therefore denied to more important public goods and consumer needs. Taxpayers deny school districts small tax increases to provide essential funding while parents drop their children off at school in $70,000 SUVs. A society that cannot guarantee vaccinations and minimal health care to poor children spends millions annually for cosmetic surgery to keep its youthful appearance. Finally, by creating consumer wants, advertising and other marketing practices violate consumer autonomy. Consumers who consider themselves free because they are able to purchase what they want are not in fact free if those wants are created by marketing. In short, consumers are being manipulated by advertising. (To explore another means by which consumer behavior might be influenced, see the Reality Check "New Challenges to Old Problems: From Redlining to E-lining.")

Ethically, the crucial point is the assertion that advertising violates consumer autonomy. The law of supply and demand is reversed and the economy of the affluent society is contrived and distorted, only if consumer autonomy can be violated by advertising's ability to create wants. But can advertising violate consumer autonomy and, if it can, does this occur? Consider the annual investment in this effort (see the Reality Check "Advertising Spending"). Given this investment, what does advertising do *to* people and *to* society?

One point of view within this debate claims that advertising controls consumer *behavior.* Some psychological behaviorists and critics of subliminal advertising, for example, have claimed that advertising can control consumer behavior by controlling their choices. But this is an empirical claim, and the evidence suggests that it is false. For example, some studies show that more than half of all new products introduced in the market fail, a fact that should not be true if consumer behavior really could be controlled by marketing. The claim here is that consumers certainly don't seem controlled by advertising in any obvious sense of that word.

But consumer autonomy might be violated in a subtler way. Rather than controlling behavior, perhaps advertising creates the wants and desires on the basis of which consumers act. The focus here becomes the concept of *autonomous desires* rather than *autonomous behavior.* This is much closer to the original assertion by Galbraith and other critics of advertising. Consumer autonomy is violated by advertising's ability to create nonautonomous desires.

A helpful exercise to understand how desires might be nonautonomous is to think of the many reasons people buy the things they buy and consume the things they do, and why, in general, people go shopping. After certain basic needs are met, there is a real question of why people consume the way they do. People buy things for many reasons, including the desire to appear fashionable, for status, to feel good, because everyone else is buying something, and so forth. The interesting ethical question at this point is where *these* desires originated, and how much marketing has influenced these nonnecessity purchases. These questions and issues are raised in the Reality Check "Advertising for Erectile Dysfunction."

Reality Check *New Challenges to Old Problems: From Redlining to E-lining*

by Tara J. Radin, Martin Calkins, and Carolyn Predmore

Today, more than two decades since the Internet became widely and publicly available, we still lack consensus about the degree of ownership and acceptable limits of data gathering and use. In fact, Richard De George's 1999 remark is arguably more valid now than previously: "The U.S. is schizophrenic about information privacy, wanting it in theory and giving it away in practice."* Such schizophrenia is problematic in itself, but it has been exacerbated by the questionable applications of data collection that have occurred. E-lining (electronic redlining) represents one glaring example of how data gathering crosses moral boundaries.

Redlining is the practice of denying or increasing the cost of services to residents of certain geographic locations. In the United States, it has been deemed illegal when the criteria involve race, religion, or ethnic origin. The term came to prominence with the discussions that led to the Housing Act of 1934, which established the Federal Housing Authority, which later became the Department of Housing and Urban Development. It occurs when financial institutions (banks, brokerages, and insurance companies) literally draw red lines on maps to distinguish between creditworthy and financially risky neighborhoods.

Although illegal, redlining has not died out completely. It reemerged recently when MCI removed international long-distance service via calling cards from pay phones in poorer communities in the suburbs of Los Angeles. It reappeared also in retail sales when Victoria's Secret allegedly tailored its catalog prices along customer demographics (specifically, ethnicity). In this case, two sisters living in different parts of town discovered price differences when discussing items from seemingly identical catalogs. As the two compared prices on the phone, they found that the cost of some items varied by as much as 25 percent. A subsequent and more thorough investigation revealed that Victoria's Secret had been engaging in an extensive practice of price variation according to gender, age, and income. In the end, although Victoria's Secret was vindicated in the court of law, it lost in the court of public opinion.

Finally, it resurfaced when Kozmo.com, an online provider of one-hour delivery services, used zip codes to refuse to deliver merchandise to customers in predominantly black neighborhoods. In all of these cases, companies (to different degrees) "exclude[d] classes of individuals from full participation in the marketplace and the public sphere."

E-lining differs from these more traditional forms of redlining by not drawing a red line on a map, but by using information that Internet users unwittingly leave behind as they surf websites. E-liners use "spyware" programs embedded in web pages to collect information surreptitiously and with little or no outside oversight. They are able to "spy on" surfers in this way without much challenge because, at present, there are few limits on what companies can do with the information they gather.

In recent years companies have used customer information to direct customers to particular products or services. In this way, they have used information in much the same way high-end clothing stores use a list of customer phone numbers to alert customers about newly arrived items that match or complement prior purchases. At other times, businesses have not acted so benevolently. They have used the data they collected in a discriminatory way to direct customers to particular products or services that fit a profile based on demographics. Amazon has received significant criticism for its use of historical purchase information to tailor web offerings to repeat customers. Amazon allegedly used data profiling in order to set prices. In September 2000, Amazon customers determined that they were charged different prices for the same CDs. Although Amazon claimed that the price differentiation was part of a randomized test, the result was price discrimination that appeared to be based on demographics.

This sort of discrimination and deprivation of financial opportunities according to demographics is exactly what the rules against redlining are intended to prevent. The absence of comparable rules against e-lining is not, as some firms might like to argue, an indication that this sort of behavior is acceptable in e-commerce, but, rather, is a reflection of the lag in time it is taking for the legal infrastructure to catch up with e-commerce. Our current legal infrastructure, particularly in the United States, which is aimed almost exclusively toward brick-and-mortar enterprises, does not account for the tremendous amount of information available through e-commerce or for the numerous ways in which e-merchants are able to exploit customers through misuse of that information.

(continued)

The unfortunate reality is that there is not a clear distinction between acceptable and unacceptable forms of information gathering, use, and market segmentation, and e-commerce provides a cloak that insulates from detection many firms engaging in inappropriate behavior.

There are few if any obstacles to firms engaging in questionable e-commerce business practices in the first place. Public outcries are generally short-lived and do not appear to have a significant impact on e-shopping. If anything, e-commerce continues to attract an increasing number of customers. In the meantime, few generally agreed-upon standards exist regarding the acceptable limits of information gathering via the Internet. Instead, businesses are shaping the expectations of web users and society in general as they implicitly set standards to guide future marketers through their irresponsible behavior. They are sending the message "Internet user beware!" to Internet surfers and potential e-customers. As long as the legal infrastructure remains underdeveloped, society remains vulnerable to an increasing number of potential electronic abuses.

*References have been removed but are available from the authors.

Source: Adapted by the authors with permission from work copyrighted (c) by Tara J. Radin, Martin Calkins, and Carolyn Predmore. All rights reserved by the authors.

Reality Check *Advertising Spending*

Between 2015 and 2018, total spending on advertising within the U.S. grew from $183 billion to nearly $224 billion—a jump of nearly 22%. Spending is currently projected to reach $290 billion in 2022. Spending on advertising, in other words, is currently experiencing steady and significant growth.

Not surprisingly, spending on digital advertising is a big contributor to this trend. And it is a global trend, not one specific to the United States. Global spending on digital ads is expected to grow from about $162 billion in 2015 to over $335 billion in 2020. And as a share of total ad spending, spending on digital ads is expected to grow from 32% to 46%.

Sources: "Media Advertising Spending in the United States from 2015 to 2022," Statista (2019), www.statista.com/statistics/272314/advertising-spending-in-the-us/ (accessed May 28, 2019); Cindy Liu, "Worldwide Ad Spending: eMarketer's Updated Estimates and Forecast for 2015–2020," *eMarketer* (October 2016), www.strathcom.com/wp-content/uploads/2016/11/eMarketer_Worldwide_Ad_Spending-eMarketers_Updated_Estimates_and_Forecast_for_20152020.pdf (accessed May 28, 2019).

Marketing to Vulnerable Populations

OBJECTIVE

Consider two examples of target marketing. In one case, based on market research supplied by the manufacturer, an automobile retailer learns that the "typical" customer is a single woman, between 30 and 40 years old; she has an annual income over $50,000; and she enjoys outdoor sports and recreation. Knowing this information, the dealer targets advertising and direct mail to people who fit this rough description. Ads depict attractive and active young people using its product and enjoying outdoor activities. A second targeted campaign is aimed at selling an emergency call device to older widows who live alone. This marketing campaign depicts an elderly woman at the bottom of a stairway crying out, "I've fallen and can't get up!" These ads are placed in media that older women are likely to see or hear. Are these marketing campaigns on an equal ethical footing?

The first marketing strategy appeals to the considered judgments that consumers, presumably, have settled on over the course of their lives. People with similar backgrounds tend to have similar beliefs, desires, and values and often make

Reality Check *Advertising for Erectile Dysfunction*

Perhaps few marketing campaigns have received as much critical attention as the ad campaigns for Viagra, Cialis, and Levitra, drugs intended to counteract erectile dysfunction. Much of the criticism has focused on the ad placements, particularly in places where young children would see them such as during prime-time television and during high-profile sporting events. Other criticisms suggest that although these drugs can be used to treat real medical conditions, they are being marketed as little more than recreational drugs and sex toys. Erectile dysfunction can be a problem for older men, and especially for men recovering from such medical treatments as prostate surgery. But for younger and otherwise healthy men, the primary causes of erectile dysfunction are alcohol consumption, obesity, lack of exercise, smoking, and the use of other prescription drugs. All of these causes are either easily addressed without reliance on pharmaceuticals or, as is the case with alcohol abuse, make erectile dysfunction drugs potentially unsafe.

Arguments in support of direct-to-consumer marketing of prescription drugs are that it provides information to consumers, respects consumer choice, encourages those who are reluctant to seek medical care to do so, gets more people into the health care system, addresses real public health issues, and increases competition and efficiency in the pharmaceutical industry. Opponents claim that these ads increase the unnecessary use of drugs; increase public harms because all drugs have harmful side effects; increase reliance on pharmaceutical health care treatments and discourage alternative therapies and treatments, many of which have fewer side effects; manipulate and exploit vulnerable consumers; often provide misleading and incomplete information; alienate patients from physicians by bypassing the gatekeeper function of medical professionals; and treat social and behavior problems with medical and chemical solutions.

1. What is your judgment about the ethics of advertising Viagra, Cialis, and Levitra? Do the reasons for advertising prescription drugs in general apply equally well to these three drugs?

2. What alternatives exist for marketing prescription drugs?

3. Who are the stakeholders of drug marketing?

4. What are the consequences of alternative marketing strategies?

5. What rights and duties are involved?

similar judgments about consumer purchases. Target marketing in this sense is simply a means for identifying likely customers based on common beliefs and values. On the other hand, there does seem to be something ethically offensive about the second case. This campaign aims to sell the product by exploiting the real fear and anxiety that many older people experience. This marketing strategy tries to manipulate people by appealing to nonrational factors such as fear or anxiety rather than relying on straightforward informative ads. Is there anything to the claim that elderly women living alone are more "vulnerable" than younger women and that this vulnerability creates greater responsibility for marketers? In general, do marketers have special responsibility to individuals who are vulnerable?

Are older people living alone particularly vulnerable? The answer to this depends on what we mean by particularly vulnerable. In one sense, a person is vulnerable as a consumer by being unable in some way to participate as a fully informed and voluntary participant in the market exchange. Valid market exchanges make several assumptions about the participants: They understand what they are doing, they have considered their choice, they are free to decide, and so forth. What we can call *consumer vulnerability* occurs when a person has an impaired ability to make an informed consent to the market exchange. A vulnerable consumer lacks the intellectual capacities, psychological ability, experience, or maturity to make

Reality Check   *Targeting Vulnerable People?*

An important case of marketing drugs to targeted populations involves the drug Strattera, Eli Lilly's prescription medication that controls attention deficit/hyperactivity disorder (ADHD) in children. The ad ran in magazines such as *Family Circle* (September 2003) under the simple title "Welcome to Ordinary." The ad pictured two boys holding up a model airplane that they had finished building, a challenging task for a child with ADHD. The ad reads: "4:30 P.M. Tuesday. He started something you never thought he'd finish. 5:20 P.M. Thursday. He's proved you wrong." The ad suggests that, if a child with ADHD is not "ordinary," it is the parents who are "wrong" because all it would take would be Strattera to solve their problem. The same issue of *Family Circle* contained ads for McNeil Pharmaceutical's Concerta and Shire Pharmaceutical's Adderall, the two major competitors to Strattera.

1. Are these marketing practices ethically responsible?
2. What facts would you want to know before deciding this case?
3. What alternative marketing practices were open to these companies?
4. Who are the stakeholders of your decision? What is the impact of each alternative decision on each stakeholder you have identified?
5. What rights and duties are involved?
6. How would you decide the case? Would you primarily consider consequences, or are important principles involved?

informed and considered consumer judgments. Children would be the paradigmatic example of consumer vulnerability. (See the Reality Check "Targeting Vulnerable People?") The harm to which such people are susceptible is the harm of not satisfying one's consumer desires and/or losing one's money.

There is a second sense of vulnerability in which the harm is other than the financial harm of an unsatisfactory market exchange. Elderly people living alone are susceptible to injuries from falls, from medical emergencies, from expensive health care bills, from loneliness. Alcoholics are susceptible to alcohol abuse, the poor are susceptible to bankruptcy, single women walking alone at night are vulnerable to sexual assault, accident victims are susceptible to high medical expenses and loss of income, and so forth. What we can call *general vulnerability* occurs when someone is susceptible to some specific physical, psychological, or financial harm.

From this we can see that there can be two types of marketing that targets vulnerable populations. Some marketing practices might target those consumers who are likely to be uninformed and vulnerable as consumers. Marketing aimed at children, for example, aims to sell products to customers who are unable to make thoughtful and informed consumer decisions. Other marketing practices might target populations that are vulnerable in the general sense as when, for example, an insurance company markets flood protection insurance to homeowners living in a river's floodplain. Are either, or both, types of targeting ethically legitimate?

As an initial judgment, we might reasonably say that marketing that is targeted at those individuals who are vulnerable as consumers is unethical. This is a case of taking advantage of someone's frailty and manipulating it for one's own advantage. Clearly, a portion of marketing and sales targets people who are vulnerable as consumers. Just as clearly, such practices are wrong.

One way that this issue plays out involves groups who are vulnerable in both senses. Oftentimes people can become vulnerable as a consumer *because* they are vulnerable in some more general sense. The vulnerability that many older adults have with respect to injuries and illness might cause them to make consumer choices based on fear or guilt. A family member grieving over the death of a loved one might make choices in purchasing funeral services based on guilt or sorrow, rather than on a considered judgment. A person with a medical condition or disease is vulnerable, and the anxiety or fear associated with this vulnerability can lead to uninformed consumer choices. A resident of a disadvantaged neighborhood—someone perhaps who is poor, uneducated, and chronically unemployed—is unlikely to weigh the full consequences of the choice of alcoholic beverage.

A number of marketing campaigns seem to fit this model. The most abhorrent (and stereotypical) example is the ambulance-chasing attorney seeking a client for a personal-injury lawsuit. An accident victim is vulnerable to many harms and, while experiencing the stress of this situation, is unlikely to make a fully informed choice about legal representation. Marketing campaigns that target elderly individuals for such products as supplemental medical insurance, life insurance, emergency call devices, funeral services, and insurance often play on the fears, anxiety, and guilt that many older people experience. (See again the Reality Check "Targeting Vulnerable People?" to consider examples of marketing to specific populations.)

But just as people can be made vulnerable as consumers because they are vulnerable to other harms, there can also be cases in which people become vulnerable to other harms because they are vulnerable as consumers. Perhaps this strategy is the most abhorrent case of unethical marketing. Certain products—tobacco and alcohol are the most obvious examples—can make an individual vulnerable to a wide range of health risks. Marketing campaigns for products that target people who are vulnerable as consumers seem ethically repugnant. This explains the particular public outrage directed at tobacco and alcohol companies that target young people. Companies that market alcoholic beverages in poor neighborhoods must take this ethical guideline into account. Marketing malt beverages, fortified wines, and other alcoholic drinks to poor inner-city residents must acknowledge that many people in such situations are not fully autonomous consumers. Many people in such situations drink to get drunk; they drink to escape; they drink because they are alcoholics.

stealth or under-cover marketing
Marketing campaigns that are based on environments or activities where the subject is not aware that she or he is the target of a marketing campaign; those situations where one is subject to directed commercial activity without knowledge or consent.

One final form of marketing to a vulnerable population involves potentially all of us as consumer targets. We are each vulnerable when we are not aware that we are subject to a marketing campaign. This type of campaign is called **stealth or undercover marketing** and refers to those situations where we are subject to directed commercial activity without our knowledge. Certainly we are subjected to numerous communications on a regular basis without paying much attention, such as the billboards at which we might glance sideways as we speed past on a highway. That is not undercover marketing. Instead, undercover marketing is an intentional effort to hide the true marketing element of the interaction. For example, Sony Ericsson Mobile Communications hired 60 actors to pose as tourists in New York City's Empire State Building. The actors were supposed to pretend they were tourists and ask passersby if they would mind taking their pictures. In doing so, the unsuspecting passersby had a chance to see how easy the new Ericsson mobile phone cameras were to operate. The actors praised the phones and said how much they loved them, and the passersby left having had a good experience with the new product, unaware they were just involved in a product test!

With the advent of blogs, Twitter, and Instagram, stealth marketing has hit the internet as well. Internet users reading a product review may find it hard or even impossible to know if the individual posting the review is a user, the product's manufacturer, or even a competitor posting a negative review just to sway consumers away from the product. "Buzz marketing," where people are paid to create a "buzz" around a new product by using it or discussing it in ways that create media or other attention, also creates the potential for unspoken conflicts of interest.

Marketing experts consider stealth marketing extraordinarily effective because the consumer's guard is down; she is not questioning the message as she might challenge a traditional advertising campaign. Consumers tend not to bother to figure out whether the communicator has some sort of financial interest; they see the communication as more personal and often tend to trust the communicator much more than they would trust an advertisement or other marketing material.

These practices would seem unethical on both principle and utilitarian grounds. As a matter of ethical principle, there is a violation of trust in the communication and the intent would appear to be to deceive or manipulate the consumer. The consumer is no longer being treated as an end in itself but instrumentally only as a means to the manufacturer's end. Utilitarian analysis would likely support a critique of these types of practices. Any deceptive practice undermines the mutual benefit that should result from market exchanges. Further, when a consumer cannot trust the company's communication, the consumer may also lose faith in the company as a whole and choose to purchase products and services elsewhere.

Supply Chain Responsibility

OBJECTIVE

In creating a product, promoting it, and bringing it to the market, the marketing function of business involves a wide range of relationships with other commercial entities. Much of the discussion in this chapter has assumed a simple model of a consumer–business relationship. In recent decades, however, the ethical spotlight has focused on the responsibility that a firm has for the activities of these other entities, what we shall refer to as supply chain responsibility. Few businesses have received as much attention in this regard as Nike.

Nike is the world's largest athletic shoe and apparel maker, and has been for many years. In 1999, Nike held over 30% of the world's market share for athletic footwear; together, Nike, Adidas (15%), and Reebok (11%) controlled more than half of the world market. As of 2017, Nike's market share remained in that same range: about 26%. Nike began business in 1964 as Blue Ribbon Sports, an importer and marketer of low-priced Japanese sport shoes. As sales increased, the company began to design its own line of shoes and subcontract the manufacturing of the shoes to Japanese firms, eventually changing its name to Nike. Nike's website described its business philosophy decades later in the following words: "Our business model in 1964 is essentially the same as our model today: We grow by investing our money in design, development, marketing and sales and then contract with other companies to manufacture our products."

In the late 1990s, as discussed in Chapter 6, Nike was subjected to intense international criticism for the working conditions in the factories where its products were manufactured. Critics charged that Nike relied on child labor and sweatshops in producing its shoes. They charged that workers in these factories were paid pennies a day; were subjected to cruel, unhealthy, and inhumane working conditions; were harassed and abused; and were prohibited from any union or collective bargaining activities.

Nike initially seemed to ignore the critics and deflect any criticism by denying responsibility for the behavior of its suppliers. If local manufacturers treated their workers poorly, that was beyond Nike's responsibility. At one point, Nike's vice president for Asia claimed that Nike did not "know the first thing about manufacturing. We are marketers and designers." Nike soon learned that the public was not persuaded by this response. Many other companies have learned this lesson in the years since: The companies whose labels were found in the rubble of the 2013 Rana factory had little success in convincing the public that "it wasn't our factory—they just make clothes for us."

Ordinarily, we do not hold a person responsible for the actions of someone else; we believe that each person is responsible for her or his own actions. But this is not always the case. There is a legal parallel to the idea that a business should be held responsible for the actions of its suppliers. The doctrine of *respondeat superior,* Latin for "let the master answer," holds a principal (e.g., an employer) responsible for the actions of an agent (e.g., an employee) when that agent is acting in the ordinary course of his or her duties to the principal.[6] Thus, in the standard example, an employer can be held liable for damages caused by an accident involving an employee driving the company car on company business.

Normally, holding someone responsible for someone else's actions would be considered unfair. The justification for doing what might otherwise be considered unfair is that the agent is acting on the principal's behalf, at the principal's direction, and that the principal has direct influence over the agent's actions. Thus, if someone is doing something for you, at your direction, and under your influence, then you must take at least some responsibility for that person's actions. Most of the ethical rationale for business's responsibility for the actions of its suppliers stems from two of these conditions: Suppliers often act at the direction of businesses they supply and those businesses often exercise significant influence over the actions of their suppliers.

However, in the multinational apparel and footwear industry, historically the corporate brands accepted responsibility only for their own organizations and specifically did not regard themselves as accountable for the labor abuses of their contractors. This conception changed as multinationals and others became more aware of working conditions in these factories and the lack of legal protections for workers. Today, multinationals customarily accept this responsibility and use their leverage to encourage suppliers to have positive working environments for workers. The new concept of responsibility travels far deeper throughout the entire supply chain system, as is depicted in Figure 8.1.

FIGURE 8.1

A Multinational Corporation's Multiple Lines of Responsibility to Diverse Stakeholders

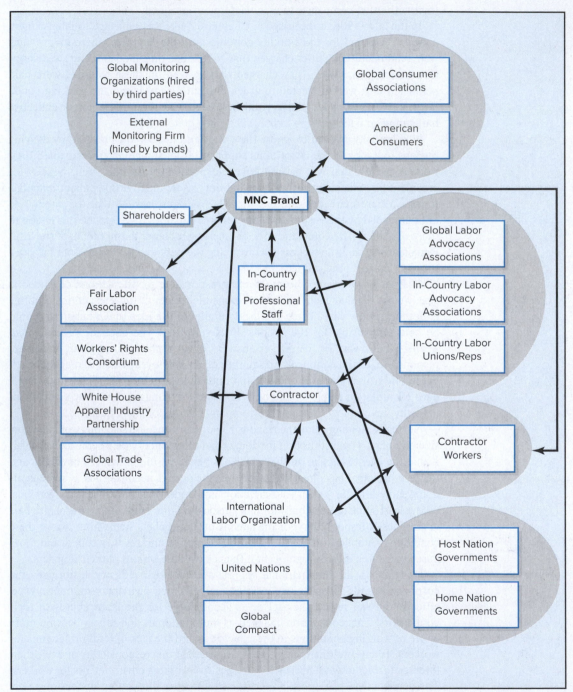

Source: D. Arnold and L. Hartman, "Moral Imagination and the Future of Sweatshops," *Business & Society Review* 108, no. 4 (2003).

In the United States, the Federal Trade Commission (FTC) has the primary responsibility for regulating sales and advertisements. Traditionally, the FTC has relied on two major criteria in establishing standards: deception and unfairness. The two criteria are related in that a marketing technique that deceives a consumer has, at the same time, proven unfair to competitors who now have to compete for that consumer with an undeserved disadvantage. With the advent of digital marketing techniques, the FTC is working, some would say struggling, to establish standards that can keep pace with the rapidly changing environment.

In 2009, the FTC issued a report that cited four basic principles to govern online marketing. Three of the four clearly fit the ethical model traditionally employed. The FTC asserted the importance of "transparency and consumer control" and required "affirmative consent" for any changes in a company's privacy policy and for the use of sensitive personal information (e.g., medical records, financial information) collected about consumers. These standards plainly derive from the ethical standards of autonomy as free and informed consent. The fourth standard recognized the changing role of collecting consumer information and asserted that businesses had a responsibility to "reasonable security" for data collected about consumers.

As if to acknowledge the fast pace of change in digital marketing, only three years later the FTC issued a new report that highlighted five goals for regulating digital marketing. The FTC recommended the development of more effective "Do Not Track" mechanisms to allow consumers to easily opt out of online tracking. It also emphasized the need to include the rapidly expanding mobile technologies under the same regulatory umbrella as computer technologies. Third, it argued for inclusion of third-party "data brokers" in the regulatory scheme and called on these companies to make their operations more transparent to consumers. Fourth, the FTC let it be known that ISPs will face increased government attention in the effort to protect consumer privacy. Fifth, perhaps in recognition that government regulation was lagging behind this rapidly evolving technology, the FTC encouraged all of the relevant stakeholders to "develop industry-specific codes of conduct" and acknowledged that these codes would likely provide the basis for future governmental regulation.

1. How big a role do you think that governmental regulation should play in digital marketing?
2. Are there any laws or regulations that you would like to see applied to digital marketing?
3. Do you think that voluntary self-regulation in the form of industry codes of conduct can effectively protect consumers from unethical practices?
4. Would you favor a "Do Not Track" option that tracks unless a consumer opts out, or an alternative that would require companies to first obtain positive permission before tracking?

Each element of what should strike you as a tremendously complicated set of interrelationships is based on the potential to influence or exercise leverage throughout the system. The question, however, relates back to our earlier discussion of responsibility. How far down—or across—the supply chain should responsibility travel? Should a firm like Nike truly be responsible for the entire footwear and apparel system? If not, where would you draw the line as a consumer, or where would you draw the line if you were the corporate responsibility vice president for Nike? What response will most effectively protect the rights of those involved while creating the most appropriate incentives to achieve profitable, ethical results? In today's increasingly complicated, globalized multinational systems, stakeholders have yet to resolve this challenging dilemma.

Questions, Projects, and Exercises

1. Are some products too dangerous to be marketed directly to the public? What regulations, if any, would you place on the marketing (as opposed to merely the production) of cigarettes? Handguns? Prescription drugs? Lock-pick sets?

2. Conduct a classroom debate on the lawsuit launched against Red Bull in 2014 over its slogan, "Red Bull Gives You Wings!" The complainant in that case argued that the slogan (and the ads that contained it) implied that Red Bull could improve concentration and reaction times. Yet the company provided no scientific evidence for such effects. Search online for further information. Is it enough that "everybody knows" that caffeine-rich drinks give you a "boost," or should the company be obligated to provide evidence of the specific effects it suggests for its product?

3. Research the case *Pelman v. McDonald's Corp.,*[7] in which it was alleged that McDonald's was partially responsible for the health problems associated with the obesity of children who eat McDonald's fast food. Should McDonald's and other fast-food restaurants be judged negligent for selling dangerous products, failing to warn consumers of the dangers of a high-fat diet, and using deceptive advertising?

4. The U.S. Federal Trade Commission regulates advertising on the basis of two criteria: deception and unfairness. How can an ad be unfair? Can you think of examples of an unfair ad? Who gets hurt by deceptive advertising?

5. Take note of several sample prescription drug ads from magazines, newspapers, television, and websites. On the basis of the location of the ad, what do you think is the intended target audience? Are the ads in any way misleading? Are the required side-effect warnings deceptive in any way? Do you believe that health care professionals provide adequate screening to ensure that prescription drugs are not misused?

6. Many salespeople are compensated predominantly on a commission basis. In other words, though the salesperson receives a small base hourly rate, most of her or his compensation derives from a percentage of the price of items sold. Because the salesperson makes money only if you buy something, and he or she makes more money if you spend more money, do you ever trust a salesperson's opinion? What would make you more likely to trust a commission-based salesperson, or less likely? Is there anything a commissioned salesperson could do to get you to trust her or him? Best Buy, the consumer electronics store, communicates to consumers that it does *not* pay its salespeople on the basis of commissions in order to encourage objectivity. Are you more likely to go to Best Buy as a result?

Key Terms

After reading this chapter, you should have a clear understanding of the following key terms. For a complete definition, please see the Glossary.

caveat emptor approach, *p. 295*

"Four Ps" of marketing, *p. 289*

implied warranty of merchantability, *p. 295*

marketing, *p. 288*

negligence, *p. 296*

stealth or undercover marketing, *p. 311*

strict liability, *p. 297*

Endnotes

1. The Levitt quote is taken from Theodore Levitt, "Marketing and the Corporate Purpose: The Purpose Is to Create and Keep a Customer," a speech delivered at New York University, March 2, 1977, available from Vital Speeches of the Day. Similar claims can be found in Theodore Levitt, "Marketing and the Corporate Purpose," *The Marketing Imagination* (New York: Free Press, 1983), chap. 1, pp. 5 and 7.

2. The American Marketing Association definition is taken from its website: www.marketingpower.com/ (accessed April 17, 2010).

3. An informal internet search found more than 100 companies advertising with this slogan. They ranged from real estate companies to antique dealers, and from long-distance phone providers to water filtration systems dealers. Presumably those who disagree do not advertise that fact.

4. See, for example, the PBS video *Affluenza,* produced by KCTS/Seattle and Oregon Public Broadcasting. See also Juliet B. Shor, "Why Do We Consume So Much?" the Clemens Lecture at St. John's University (October 2001), in *Contemporary Issues in Business Ethics,* ed. Joseph DesJardins and John McCall (Belmont, CA: Wadsworth, 2005); Jim Pooler, *Why We Shop: Emotional Rewards and Retail Strategies* (Westport, CT: Praeger, 2003).

5. Council Directive 85/374/EEC of 25 July 1985 on the approximation of the laws, regulations and administrative provisions of the Member States concerning liability for defective products, 1985 O.J. (L 210) 29 (EC).

6. This parallel is explained in Michael Santoro, *Profits and Principles: Global Capitalism and Human Rights in China* (Ithaca, NY: Cornell University Press, 2000), p. 161, and is cited as well by Denis Arnold and Norman Bowie, "Sweatshops and Respects for Persons," *Business Ethics Quarterly* 13, no. 2 (2003), pp. 221–42.

7. 237 F. Supp. 2d 512 (S.D.N.Y. 2003).

Business and Environmental Sustainability

You cannot get through a single day without having an impact on the world around you. What you do makes a difference, and you have to decide what kind of difference you want to make.

Jane Goodall

Growth for the sake of growth is the ideology of the cancer cell.

Edward Abbey

Humankind has not woven the web of life. We are but one thread within it. Whatever we do to the web, we do to ourselves. All things are bound together . . . all things connect.

Chief Seattle

Environmental regulation is a signal of design failure.

William McDonough

Food security can be defined in terms of the availability of adequate nutritious food and the ability of people to have access to that food. Global food security raises a multitude of ethical issues concerning the relationship between individuals, business, government, and the natural environment. Perhaps rivaled only by the decisions we make about energy, our food choices have a profound impact on the environment. And as in the case with energy, the choices we have as consumers are greatly shaped by what happens in business.

At first glance, one might think that food should be treated like any other economic commodity, produced and distributed according to market demand. From this perspective, business in general has no unique ethical responsibilities regarding food. But two factors in particular suggest that there are good ethical reasons for paying close attention to the business of food. First, unlike most other economic goods, food is an essential human need; a case can be made that food is something for which all people have a basic human right. It would be difficult to judge any economic system as ethically adequate if it failed to meet this basic human need for food. Second, food production and distribution can have a profound impact on the earth's biosphere and the long-term productive capacity of the natural environment to provide for human needs. How food is produced—something deeply influenced by business—greatly impacts the ongoing capacity of the earth's biosphere to support life.

These factors are captured in the well-known definition of sustainable development offered by the World Commission on Environment and Development (the "Brundtland Report") in 1987. This definition states that sustainable development "meets the needs of the present without compromising the ability of future generations to meet their own needs." The Brundtland Report concluded that the standard model of economic development, and the role played by business within that model, was failing to meet the needs of large portions of the present human population and was operating in such a way that the ability of future generations to meet their own needs was at risk.

The food business continues to have a deep connection with a wide range of ethical and environmental issues. What we eat, the availability of food, how food is produced, the nutritional quality of food, food safety, who produces food, how food products are processed, and the environmental and social consequences of agriculture all raise important ethical questions.

It seems fair to say that the most important ethical issue concerning food is the fact that hundreds of millions of people do not have enough of it. In 2017, the United Nations Food and Agricultural Organization reported that some 821 million people globally were undernourished. In some areas of sub-Saharan Africa and Southeast Asia, as much as one-third of the population lacks adequate nutritional food. But the same UN report also points out that despite a growing global population, the number of people lacking adequate nutritional food has decreased by 200 million since 1990. Increased agricultural productivity created by modern farming techniques has played a major role in this decrease.

In the past 200 years, observers have often argued that global population growth was outpacing food supply and continued growth was likely to lead to major food shortages and mass starvation. In the early 19th century, Thomas Malthus famously claimed that because population grows exponentially and food growth increases only arithmetically, population size will inevitably outgrow food availability. In the 1960s, Paul Erhlich's book *The Population Bomb* similarly predicted that continued population growth was leading to an imminent global food crisis.

In both cases, food crises were avoided because of improved agricultural productivity that resulted from shifts toward a more centralized and industrial model of agriculture. As a result, both Malthus's and Ehrlich's predictions failed to come true. In the 19th century, the food collapse predicted by Malthus was avoided due to technological advances produced by the Industrial Revolution, advances that greatly increased both the amount of land that could be turned to agriculture and the efficiency and productivity of that land. In the late 20th century and continuing today, technological advances in machinery, irrigation, pesticides, fertilizers, plant and animal breeding, and genetically modified crops have greatly increased food production across the globe.

Critics charge that many of these modern agricultural practices, including the very model of industrial agriculture itself, contribute to a range of health, safety, social, and environmental problems. Intensive farming techniques threaten soil fertility, deplete groundwater supplies, poison soil and water with pesticide residue, disrupt ecosystems, threaten biodiversity, and jeopardize the ongoing productivity of the earth's biosphere. Many critics also claim that the model of contemporary agribusiness has placed significant political, economic, and social power into the hands of a few giant multinational corporations.

Food shortages can also be explained by wider market forces. The type of food that is produced and the uses to which it is put are determined at least as much by market demand as by what people need. Market demand, understood as what someone is willing to pay for, explains why agricultural resources in some of the world's most productive lands are used to produce feed crops for animals rather than food for humans. In 2014, a *National Geographic* story pointed out that almost half of the world's crops are used as animal feed (36%) or for fuel or industrial products (9%).[1]

Modern agriculture accounts for 25% of greenhouse gas emissions and more than 70% of groundwater extraction. In the United States, 75% of corn production is used for animal feed, ethanol production, or sweeteners such as high fructose corn syrup. As societies become more affluent, as happened in Europe and North America and as is happening in China and India, increased demand for beef, dairy products, poultry, and pork diverts an even larger percentage of crops away from fulfilling direct human needs. In terms of pollution, greenhouse gas emissions, and water usage, producing beef, poultry, dairy, and pork products has a much higher environmental toll than grain production.

Of course, agribusiness and food production have an even more direct effect on the natural environment with their treatment of animals. Many critics argue that there are serious ethical issues involved in animal agriculture beyond problematic human health and environmental consequences. Specifically, chickens and turkeys are bred to be overweight flightless animals with little resemblance to the chickens and turkeys of a hundred years ago. Animals are kept in overcrowded facilities, prevented from any form of exercise, fed unnatural diets, dosed with antibiotics and growth hormones, separated from their offspring, mutilated to prevent natural behaviors like flight or pecking, and then slaughtered in brutal, mechanized ways. According to critics, all this is done in the name of market efficiency and profit.

The food industry itself, including agriculture, retail food suppliers, and restaurants, often defends its practices on market demand grounds. From this perspective, the global demand for food could not be met without the industrial

(*continued*)

(concluded)   techniques used in modern agriculture. The type and quality of food available are also dependent on consumer demand. If the market demanded smaller serving sizes, less beef, more fresh fruits and vegetables, and less convenient and inexpensive processed foods, then business would provide it. But, according to the food industry, asking business to do these things without the market demand will result in business failures and food shortages.

1. What food choices have you made so far today? In what ways were your choices shaped or influenced by business decisions and business practices?
2. In what ways and on what grounds does the fast-food restaurant industry compete for customers? What are the environmental and ethical impacts of fast food?
3. In what ways might your food choices shape the way the food industry, including both agriculture and restaurants, interacts with the natural environment?
4. Which individual food choices matter directly, in terms of making a difference in the world? Which choices we make only matter in the aggregate, when many people's choices are added together?

 ## Chapter Objectives

After reading this chapter, you will be able to:

1. Explain how environmental challenges can create business opportunities.
2. Describe a range of values that play a role in environmental decision making.
3. Explain the difference between market-based and regulatory-based environmental policies.
4. Describe business's environmental responsibilities that flow from each approach.
5. Identify the inadequacies of sole reliance on a market-based approach.
6. Identify the inadequacies of regulatory-based environmental policies.
7. Define and describe sustainable development and sustainable business.
8. Highlight the business opportunities associated with a move toward sustainability.
9. Describe the sustainable principles of eco-efficiency, biomimicry, and service.
10. Explain how marketing can be used to both support and detract from the goals of sustainable business.

Introduction

There is a tendency to believe that environmental challenges *always* create a burden on business and that environmental and business interests are *always* in conflict. While environmental regulations can add costs to business operations and restrict business choice, environmental considerations can also provide opportunities for business. Where one automobile manufacturer sees government-mandated fuel efficiency standards as a burden on its ability to sell large sport-utility vehicles (SUVs), another company sees it as an opportunity to market fuel-efficient hybrids. While one agricultural business sees restrictions on pesticide use as a burden, another sees the opportunity to market organic products.

Many observers believe we have entered the sustainability revolution, an age in which the race to create environmentally and economically sustainable products and services is creating unlimited business opportunities. As happened in the Industrial Revolution, there will be winners and losers in this sustainability revolution and, according to supporters, the economic winners will be the firms and industries that do the most environmental good.

As described by geographer Jared Diamond in the best-selling book *Collapse,* human history provides many examples of societies that have run up against the environmental limits of their lifestyles. But the Industrial Revolution of the 18th and 19th centuries brought with it the ability to degrade the natural environment to a greater extent and at a faster rate than ever before. The industrial model of growth and productive efficiency and seemingly unlimited energy supply continued along almost unchecked by environmental regulation until the latter half of the 20th century. As in most other industries, this model reshaped the food and agriculture business (see the Opening Decision Point "The Business of Food").

At the start of the 21st century, the earth is experiencing the greatest period of species extinction since the end of the dinosaurs 65 million years ago. Humans are also threatened by global climate change. These monumental environmental events are largely due to human activity, and specifically to our present arrangements of modern industrial society. Simply put, the way we have done business over the last two centuries has brought us up against the biophysical limits of the earth's capacity to support all human life, and it has already crossed those limits in the case of countless other forms of now-extinct life. Thus, the major ethical question of this chapter is what responsibilities contemporary businesses have regarding the natural environment.

It is fair to say that throughout the history of industrial economies, business most often looked at environmental concerns as unwanted burdens and barriers to economic growth. Nonetheless, the sustainable business and sustainable economic development seek to create new ways of doing business in which business success is measured in terms of economic, ethical, and environmental sustainability, often called the *triple bottom line* approach. The sustainability paradigm sees environmental responsibilities as a fundamental part of basic business practice. Indeed, sustainable business ventures may find that environmental considerations offer creative and entrepreneurial businesses enormous opportunities.

OBJECTIVE

The environmental research and consulting group The Natural Step uses an image of a funnel, with two converging lines, to help business understand the opportunities available in the age of sustainability. The resources necessary to sustain life are on a downward slope. While there is disagreement about the angle of the slope (are we at the start with only a mild slope, or further along with a sharper downward slope?), there is widespread consensus that available resources are in decline. The second

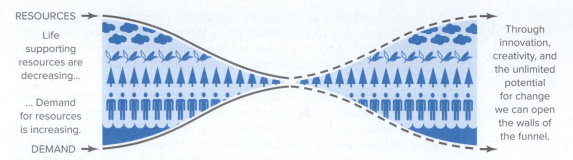

RESOURCES

Life supporting resources are decreasing...

... Demand for resources is increasing.

DEMAND

Through innovation, creativity, and the unlimited potential for change we can open the walls of the funnel.

FIGURE 9.1

The Natural Step's Funnel

Source: Reprinted with permission.

backcasting

The Natural Step challenges businesses to imagine what a sustainable future must hold. From that vision, creative businesses then look backward to the present and determine what must be done to arrive at that future.

line represents aggregate worldwide demand, accounting for both population growth and the increasing demand of consumerist lifestyles. Barring an environmental catastrophe, many but not all industries will emerge through the narrowing funnel into an era of sustainable living. Businesses unable to envision that sustainable future will hit the narrowing wall. Innovative and entrepreneurial business will find their way through. The Natural Step's funnel is illustrated in Figure 9.1.

The Natural Step then challenges business to "backcast" a path toward sustainability. We are all familiar with forecasting, in which we examine present data and predict the future. **Backcasting** examines what the future will be when we emerge through the funnel. Knowing what the future must be, creative businesses then look backward to the present and determine what must be done to arrive at that future. In simple terms, sustainable business must use resources and produce wastes at rates that do not jeopardize human well-being by exceeding the earth's capacity to renew the resources and absorb the wastes. Businesses that do so will succeed in moving through the funnel and emerge as successful in the age of sustainability. The "business case" for sustainability will be examined in more detail in the next section.

This chapter will introduce a range of ethical issues that have set the stage for this transition to an environmentally sustainable future. Environmental issues are no longer at the periphery of business decisions, as burdens to be managed if not avoided altogether; nor are they external regulatory constraints in managerial decision making. (To explore how the insurance industry is thinking about one aspect of environmental sustainability, namely climate change, see the Reality Check "The Insurance Industry and Climate Change.") Environmental sustainability must accompany financial sustainability for business to survive in the 21st century. For reasons of both rights and duties and for promoting the overall social good, sustainable business is the wave of the future.

Business Ethics and Environmental Values

OBJECTIVE

The opening chapters of this text introduced ethics in terms of practical reasoning. Deciding what we should do is the ultimate goal of practical reason, and our values are those standards that encourage us to act one way rather than another. Given this objective, which values and decisions are supported by a concern with the natural environment? Why should we act in ways that protect the natural environment from degradation? Why should business be concerned with, and value, the natural world?

Reality Check *The Insurance Industry and Climate Change*

The insurance industry has a special interest in climate issues: Changes in climate may contribute to the risk of flooding, hurricanes, and wildfires—all things that tend to result in insurance claims that cost the industry money. Thus, when executives in the insurance industry discuss climate change, they are interested in discussing the risks that such changes bring, and they are strongly motivated to get the facts right. What are those executives saying these days about climate change?

According to the Geneva Association, a leading insurance-industry think-tank, "Failure to address climate change has been identified as one of the highest potential socio-economic risks to our society. . . . Increasingly, companies in all sectors are considering climate risk as a core business issue. Traditionally, however, a lack of climate action was linked to reputational risks. Only recently are the financial and economic impacts of climate change being considered. . . ."

Source: Maryam Golnaraghi, *Climate Change and the Insurance Industry: Taking Action as Risk Managers and Investors* (Talstrasse: Geneva Association, 2018).

Human self-interest is the most obvious answer to these questions. Environmental concerns are relevant to business because human beings, both presently living humans and future generations of humans, depend on the natural environment in order to survive. Humans need clean water to drink, healthy air to breathe, fertile soil and oceans to produce food, an ozone layer to screen out solar radiation, and a biosphere that maintains the delicate balance of climate in which human life can exist. Two aspects of contemporary environmental realities underscore the importance of self-interested reasoning.

As documented in Diamond's book *Collapse,* past human societies have often run up against the limits of the local environment's ability to sustain human life. In these historical cases, environmental degradation has been localized to a particular region and has seldom affected more than a generation. In contrast, some contemporary environmental issues have the potential to adversely affect the entire globe and change human life forever. Global climate change, species extinction, soil erosion and desertification, and nuclear wastes will threaten human life into the indefinite future.

Second, the science of ecology and its understanding of the interrelatedness of natural systems have helped us understand the wide range of human dependence on ecosystems. Where once we might have thought that buried wastes were gone forever, we now understand how toxins can seep into groundwater and contaminate drinking water across time and great distances. We now understand how pesticides accumulate throughout the food chain and pose the greatest dangers not only to top predators such as bald eagles, but to human beings as well. Where once we thought that ocean fisheries were inexhaustible and the atmosphere too big to be changed by humans, we now understand that a delicate environmental balance is necessary to maintain life-supporting systems.

By the late 19th century, humans came to recognize the self-interested reasons for protecting the natural environment. The conservation movement, the first phase of modern environmentalism, advocated a more restrained and prudent approach to the natural world. From this perspective, the natural world was still

Reality Check *Will Electric Cars Save the World?*

Given what we know about the environmental impact of the internal combustion engines powering most cars today, many people are pinning their environmental hopes on the growing popularity of electric cars. Electric cars (or, more generally, electric vehicles, or "EVs") are often referred to as producing zero emissions—that is, as producing no pollution at all. But, of course, this is not always strictly accurate. After all, the electricity that powers an EV has to come from somewhere, and some ways of producing electricity are more environmentally friendly than others. If you live in a place where most electricity is generated by coal-fired generating plants, the electricity powering your EV is less environmentally friendly than if you live in a place where electricity is generated by solar panels or by hydroelectric generators.

Some of the factors that might be considered in evaluating the environmental impact of your EV:

- How electricity is generated where you live.
- The mechanical efficiency of your EV (converting stored electricity into motion).

- The environmental impact of the process that manufactured your EV (including smelting the steel and molding the plastic).
- The impact of producing and eventually disposing of the EV's batteries.
- The extent to which the components of the EV itself can be recycled after the EV has reached the end of its useful lifespan.

All things considered, EVs still tend to be better environmentally than old-fashioned gas-burning cars. But a clear assessment of the above factors can help us all understand better the progress that EVs currently represent, and the factors that need to be improved for their full promise to be fulfilled.

---

valued as a resource, providing humans with both direct benefits (air, water, food) and indirect benefits (the goods and services produced by business). Conservationists argued against the exploitation of natural resources as if they could provide an inexhaustible supply of material. They made the case that business had good reasons for conserving natural resources, reasons that paralleled the rationale to conserve financial resources. The natural world, like capital, had the productive capacity to produce long-term income, but only if managed and used prudently.

Besides these self-interested reasons to protect human life and health, the natural environment is essential and valuable for many other reasons. Often, these other values conflict with the more direct instrumental value that comes from treating the natural world as a resource. The beauty and grandeur of the natural world provide great aesthetic, spiritual, and inspirational value. Many people view the natural world as a manifestation of religious and spiritual values. Parts of the natural world can have symbolic value, historical value, and such diverse psychological values as serenity and exhilaration. These values can clearly conflict with the use of the earth itself as a resource to physically, as opposed to spiritually, sustain those who live on it. (The need to balance human interests with more "pure" environmental interests is examined in the Decision Point "Promoting Food Safety or Fighting Food Waste?")

Aesthetic and inspirational values often play out in public debates about economic development. The 1970s song "Big Yellow Taxi" by Canadian folk

Food product date labeling that is intelligible to consumers emerged in the United States in the 1970s amid concerns about food safety and freshness. That history is important because food safety and freshness continue to be the lens through which consumers interpret *any* date printed on food packaging, whether or not its significance is safety or freshness related. One of the fallouts of this is that date labels whose significance is mainly commercial (e.g., "sell by") encourage consumers to throw away and waste food that is edible and poses no inherent safety risk.

In an attempt to reduce food waste, the U.S. Department of Agriculture's Food Safety Inspection Service (FSIS) has issued regulatory guidance encouraging the use of a single date label—"best if used by"—in place of "sell by," "use by," "use before," "best before," and other phrases currently in use on food packaging. FSIS claims that the current array of labels is less clear to consumers and is thus likely treated as if the were really "unsafe after" dates, leading to food waste when consumers throw food out unnecessarily. On the other hand, consumers tend to interpret correctly the meaning of "best if used by" and are less likely to throw away—and waste—perfectly safe food.

1. If consumers have evolved a practice of treating printed "best before" dates as "unsafe after" dates, should the food industry instead be encouraged to print dates that more closely correspond to that evolved expectation?

2. Should the FSIS, whose name suggests consumer safety as its mission, be a mechanism for achieving environmental sustainability-focused goals?

3. Consumer-readable sell-by dating replaced an older system of symbols or numbers whose meaning was understood only by the retailer. It was replaced by consumer-readable date labels in an attempt to achieve increased consumer transparency. How should conflicts between demands for consumer transparency and the policy objective of reducing food waste be decided?

Source: "Should Food Product Date Labeling Promote Consumer Safety or Curb Food Waste?," *Business Ethics Highlights* (December 15, 2016), https://businessethicshighlights .com/2016/12/15/should-food-product-date-labeling-promote-consumer-safety-or-curb-food-waste/ (accessed June 4, 2019).

singer Joni Mitchell captured this sentiment with the well-known lyric "they paved paradise and put up a parking lot." Many critics fault business for destroying natural beauty and replacing it with strip malls, neon signs, fast-food restaurants, and, yes, parking lots.

A final set of values that we will consider involves the moral status of animals and other living beings, an environmental value that has raised some of the most widely publicized ethical challenges to business. Variously referred to as the animal rights, animal liberation, or animal welfare movement, this approach attributes a moral standing to animals. According to many people, animals, and perhaps all other living things, deserve to be respected and treated with dignity. Such a status

As mentioned in the Opening Decision Point "The Business of Food," some animal farming practices, especially within large-scale industrial factory farms, have been criticized as cruel and heartless. Calves are prevented from exercising and intentionally malnourished so that consumers can enjoy tender and pink veal. Chickens are tightly packed in cages with their beaks cut off to prevent them from pecking each other. Cattle are raised in giant feed lots where they spend their time walking in their own manure.

As part of this effort, McDonald's now has a system for auditing suppliers to ensure adherence to the company's animal welfare standards.

Auditing Animal Welfare Practices

McDonald's requires all processing facilities used by our beef suppliers to adhere to our animal welfare

principles, designed to ensure that animals are free from cruelty, abuse and neglect. In addition, abattoirs used by our suppliers are required to be audited by external experts every year. In 2009, 100% of facilities were audited and 100% passed their audits. Facilities that do not pass their audits on the first or second try are given a defined period to make improvements or they will be removed from our supply chain.

Source: McDonald's Corporation, "Worldwide Corporate Responsibility 2010 Report," www.aboutmcdonalds.com/content/dam/AboutMcDonalds/Sustainability/Sustainability%20Library/2010-CSR-Report.pdf.

would create a wide variety of distinctive ethical responsibilities concerning how we treat animals and would have significant implications for many businesses.

To defend this perspective, some argue that many animals, presumably all animals with a central nervous system, have the capacity to feel pain. Reminiscent of the utilitarian tradition described in Chapter 3, this view asserts an ethical responsibility to minimize pain. Inflicting unnecessary pain is taken to be an ethical wrong; therefore, acts that inflict unnecessary pain on animals are ethically wrong. Raising and slaughtering animals for food, particularly in the way industrial farming enterprises raise poultry, hogs, and cattle, would be an obvious case in which business would violate this ethical responsibility, as one side argues in the Reality Check "Treatment of Animals in Agriculture."

A second approach argues that at least some animals have the cognitive capacity to possess a conscious life of their own. Reminiscent of the Kantian ethical tradition described in Chapter 3, this view asserts that we have a duty not to treat these animals as mere objects and means to our own ends. Again, businesses that use animals for food, entertainment, or pets would violate the ethical rights of these animals.

Business's Environmental Responsibility: The Market Approach

While debate continues with regard to some environmental values, an overwhelming consensus exists about the self-interested and prudential reasons for protecting the natural environment: Humans have a right to be protected from undue harm. What controversy remains has more to do with the best means for achieving this goal. Historically, this debate has focused on whether efficient markets or government regulation is the most appropriate means for meeting the environmental responsibilities of business. Each of these two approaches has significant implications for business.

OBJECTIVE

From one perspective, if the best approach to environmental concerns is to trust them to efficient markets, then the responsible business manager simply ought to seek profits and allow the market to allocate resources efficiently. By doing this, business fills its role within a market system, which in turn serves the greater overall (utilitarian) good. On the other hand, if government regulation is a more promising approach, then business ought to develop a compliance structure to ensure that it conforms to those regulatory requirements.

A market-based approach to resolving environmental challenges is reminiscent of the narrow, economic view of CSR described in Chapter 5. Defenders of this market approach contend that environmental problems are economic problems that deserve economic solutions. At heart, environmental problems involve the allocation and distribution of limited resources. Whether we are concerned with the allocation of scarce nonrenewable resources such as gas and oil or with the earth's capacity to absorb industrial by-products such as CO_2 or PCBs, efficient markets can, according to this view, address environmental challenges.

OBJECTIVE

Consider the implications of this model for pollution and resource conservation. In his well-known book *People or Penguins: The Case for Optimal Pollution,* William Baxter argued that there is an optimal level of pollution that would best serve society's interests.[2] This optimal level (and it is likely not zero!) is best attained, according to Baxter, by leaving it to a competitive market.

Denying that there is any "natural" or objective standard for clean air or water (as this view would deny there is an objective state of perfect health), Baxter begins with a goal of "safe" air and water quality, and translates this goal to a matter of balancing risks and benefits. Society *could* strive for perfectly pure air and water, but the costs (lost opportunities) that this would entail would be too high. A more reasonable approach is to aim for air and water quality that is safe enough to breathe and drink without costing too much. This balance, the "optimal level of pollution," can be achieved through competitive markets. Society, through the activities of individuals, will be willing to pay for pollution reduction as long as the perceived benefits outweigh the costs.

The free market also provides an answer for resource conservation. From a strict market economic perspective, resources are "infinite." Julian Simon, for example, has argued that resources should not be viewed as material objects but simply as any means to our ends.[3] History has shown that human ingenuity and incentive have always found substitutes for any shortages. As the supply of any resources decreases, the price increases, thereby providing a strong incentive to supply more or provide a less-costly substitute. Thus, some have argued that we will *never* literally run out of oil, even though oil is technically a nonrenewable source of energy: The more scarce oil gets, the more expensive it will get, which will reduce demand as well as spur innovation in pursuit of substitutes for oil. In economic terms, all resources are "fungible." They can be replaced by substitutes, and in this sense resources are infinite. Resources that are not being used to satisfy consumer demand are being wasted.

⑤
OBJECTIVE

Challenges to this narrow economic view of corporate social responsibility are familiar to both economists and ethicists. Several types of market failures, many of the best known of which involve environmental issues, point to the inadequacy of market solutions. One example is the existence of what economists call externalities, the textbook example of which is environmental pollution. Because the "costs" of such things as air pollution, groundwater contamination and depletion, soil erosion, and nuclear waste disposal are typically borne by parties "external" to the economic exchange (e.g., people downwind, neighbors, future generations), the full costs of these things are not included in the price paid by consumers, and so free-market exchanges cannot guarantee optimal results.

A second type of market failure occurs when no markets exist to create a price for important social goods. Endangered species, scenic vistas, rare plants and animals, and biodiversity are just some environmental goods that typically are not traded on open markets (or, when they are, they are often traded in ways that seriously threaten their viability as when rhinoceros horns, tiger claws, elephant tusks, and mahogany trees are sold on the black market). Public goods such as clean air and ocean fisheries also have no established market price. With no established exchange value, the market approach cannot even pretend to achieve its own goals of efficiently meeting consumer demand. Markets alone fail to guarantee that such important public goods are preserved and protected.

A third way in which market failures can lead to serious environmental harm involves a distinction between individual decisions and group consequences. We can miss important ethical and policy questions if we leave policy decisions solely to the outcome of individual decisions. Consider the calculations that an individual consumer might make regarding the purchase of a large SUV and the consequences of that decision regarding global warming. The additional CO_2 that would be emitted by a single large SUV is miniscule enough that an individual might plausibly conclude that her decision will make no difference. However, if every consumer made exactly the same decision, the aggregate consequences would be huge.

corporate average fuel economy (CAFE) standards
Established by the U.S. Energy Policy Conservation Act of 1975, corporate average fuel economy (CAFE) is the sales-weighted average fuel economy, expressed in miles per gallon (mpg), of a manufacturer's fleet of passenger cars or light trucks. The U.S. federal government establishes CAFE standards as a means of increasing fuel efficiency of automobiles.

This example demonstrates that the overall social result of individual calculations, despite each individual's good actions having a trivial impact, might be significant increases in pollution and such pollution-related diseases as asthma and allergies. A number of alternative policies (e.g., restricting sales of large SUVs, increasing taxes on gasoline, regulating SUVs as cars instead of light trucks in calculating **corporate average fuel economy [CAFE] standards**) that could address pollution and pollution-related disease would never be considered if we relied only on market solutions. Because these are important ethical questions, and because they remain unasked from within market transactions, we must conclude that markets are incomplete (at best) in their approach to the overall social good. In other words, what is good and rational for a collection of individuals is not necessarily what is good and rational for a society.

Such market failures raise serious concerns for the ability of economic markets to achieve a sound environmental policy and to guide business behavior.

Defenders of a narrow economic view of corporate social responsibility do have responses to these challenges, of course. Internalizing external costs and assigning property rights to unowned goods such as wild species are two responses to market failures. But there are good reasons for thinking that such ad hoc attempts to repair market failures are environmentally inadequate. One important reason is what has been called the first-generation problem. Markets can work to prevent harm only through information supplied by the existence of market failures. Only when fish populations in the North Atlantic collapsed, for example, did we learn that free and open competition among the world's fishing industry for unowned public goods failed to prevent the decimation of cod, swordfish, Atlantic salmon, and lobster populations. That is, we learn about market failures and thereby gain the knowledge needed to prevent harms in the future only by sacrificing the "first generation" as a means of gaining this information. When public policy involves irreplaceable public goods such as endangered species, rare wilderness areas, and public health and safety, such a reactionary strategy is ill advised.

Business's Environmental Responsibility: The Regulatory Approach

OBJECTIVE

A broad consensus emerged in the 1970s that unregulated markets are an inadequate approach to environmental challenges. Instead, governmental regulations were seen as the better way to respond to environmental problems. Much of the most significant environmental legislation in the United States, and in other countries, was enacted during the 1970s. In the U.S., the Clean Air Act of 1970 (amended and renewed in 1977), Federal Water Pollution Act of 1972 (amended and renewed as the Clean Water Act of 1977), and the Endangered Species Act of 1973 were part of this national consensus for addressing environmental problems. These moves enjoyed broad political support. Each law was originally enacted by a Democratic Congress and signed into law by a Republican president.

These laws share a common approach to environmental issues. Before this legislation was enacted, the primary legal avenue open for addressing environmental concerns was tort law. Only individuals who could prove that they had been harmed by pollution could raise legal challenges to air and water pollution. That legal approach placed the burden on the person who was harmed and, at best, offered compensation for the harm only after the fact. Except for the incentive provided by the threat of having to pay compensation, U.S. policy did little to prevent the pollution in the first place. Without any proof of negligence, public policy was content to let the market decide environmental policy. Because endangered species themselves had no legal standing, direct harm to plant and animal life was of no legal concern, and previous policies did little to prevent harm to plant and animal life.

The laws enacted during the 1970s established standards that effectively shifted the burden from those threatened with harm to those who would cause the harm. Government established regulatory standards to try to prevent the occurrence of pollution or species extinction rather than to offer compensation after the fact. We can think of these laws as establishing minimum standards to ensure air and water quality and species preservation. Business was free to pursue its own goals as long as it complied with the side constraints these minimum standards established.

The consensus that emerged was that society had two opportunities to establish business's environmental responsibilities. As consumers, individuals could demand environmentally friendly products in the marketplace. As citizens, individuals could support environmental legislation. As long as business responded to the market and obeyed the law, it met its environmental responsibilities. If consumers demand environmentally suspect products, such as large gas-guzzling SUVs, and those products are allowed by law, then we cannot expect business to forgo the financial opportunities of marketing such products.

OBJECTIVE

Several problems suggest that this approach will prove inadequate over the long term. First, it underestimates the influence that business can have in establishing the law. The CAFE standards mentioned previously provide a good example of how this can occur. A reasonable account of this law suggests that the public very clearly expressed a political goal of improving air quality by improving automobile fuel efficiency goals (and thereby reducing automobile emissions). However, the automobile industry was able to use its lobbying influence to exempt light trucks and SUVs from these standards. It should be no surprise that light trucks and SUVs at the time represented the largest-selling, and most profitable, segment of the auto industry.

Second, this approach also underestimates the ability of business to influence consumer choice. To conclude that business fulfills its environmental responsibility when it responds to the environmental demands of consumers is to underestimate the role that business can play in shaping public opinion. Advertising is a $200-billion-a-year industry in the United States alone. It is surely misleading to claim that business passively responds to consumer desires and that consumers are unaffected by the messages that business conveys. Assuming that business is not going to stop advertising its products or lobbying government, this model of corporate environmental responsibility is likely to prove inadequate for protecting the natural environment.

Further, if we rely on the law to protect the environment, environmental protection will extend only as far as the law extends. Yet, most environmental issues, pollution problems especially, do not respect legal jurisdictions. New York State might pass strict regulations on smokestack emissions, but if the power plants are located upwind in Ohio or even further west in the Dakotas or Wyoming, New York State will continue to suffer the effects of acid rain. Similarly, national regulations will be ineffective for international environmental challenges. While hope remains that international agreements might help control global environmental problems, the failure of the international community to reach enforceable carbon emission standards suggests that this might be overly optimistic.

Finally, and perhaps most troubling from an environmental standpoint, this regulatory model assumes that economic growth itself is environmentally and ethically benign. Regulations establish side constraints on business's pursuit of profits and, as long as they remain within those constraints, accept as ethically legitimate

Reality Check *Cap and Trade—a Mixed Approach?*

One strategy that combines elements of both market and regulatory approaches is the so-called cap and trade model that has been proposed in the United States as part of legislation to address carbon emissions. Under the cap and trade model, government sets an overall annual target, or "cap," on the amount of CO_2 emissions nationally. Companies then buy government-issued permits to emit pollution. The permits limit the total overall amount of pollution to the national cap. Individual businesses are free to buy or sell their permits in such a way that an efficient company that emits less pollution than its permits allow can sell its remaining pollution credits to a less-efficient company. By thus creating a market for pollution credits, government regulation creates an incentive for individual businesses to reduce their own pollution. Government can then slowly reduce the overlap pollution target annually to achieve its public policy goal.

Defenders see this approach as a powerful way to use market incentives to reduce pollution. Critics see it as government issuing a "license to pollute," sending the wrong message to businesses and to consumers.

whatever road to profitability management chooses. What can be lost in these discussions is the very important fact that there are many different ways to pursue profits within the side constraints of law. Different roads toward profitability can have very different environmental consequences, as is discussed in the Reality Check "Cap and Trade—a Mixed Approach?"

Business's Environmental Responsibilities: The Sustainability Approach

OBJECTIVE

sustainable development
Development that meets the needs of the present without compromising the ability of future generations to meet their own needs, as defined by the Brundtland Commission in 1987.

sustainable business practice
A model of business practice in which business activities meet the standards of sustainability.

Beginning in the 1980s, a new model for environmentally responsible business began to take shape, one that combines financial opportunities with environmental and ethical responsibilities. The concepts of **sustainable development** and **sustainable business practice** suggest a radically new vision for integrating financial and environmental goals, compared to the growth model that preceded it (as explored in the Reality Check "Why Sustainability?"). These three goals—economic, environmental, and ethical sustainability—are often referred to as the **three pillars of sustainability.** Assessing business activity along these three lines is often referred to as the triple bottom line.

The concept of sustainable development can be traced to a 1987 report from the United Nations' World Commission on Environment and Development (WCED), more commonly known as the Brundtland Commission, named for its chair Gro Harlem Brundtland. The commission was tasked with developing recommendations for paths toward economic and social development that would not achieve short-term economic growth at the expense of long-term environmental and economic sustainability. The Brundtland Commission offered what has become the standard definition of sustainable development. Sustainable development is "development that meets the needs of the present without compromising the ability of future generations to meet their own needs."

Reality Check   *Why Sustainability?*

Three factors are most often cited to explain and justify the need for a model of economic development that stresses sustainability rather than growth.

First, billions of human beings live in severe poverty and face real challenges on a daily basis for meeting their basic needs for food, water, health care, and shelter. Addressing these challenges will require significant economic activity.

Second, world population continues to grow at a disturbing rate, with projections of an increase from 7.7 billion in 2019 to 8.6 billion by 2030. Most of this population growth will occur within the world's poorest regions, thereby only intensifying the first challenge. Even more economic activity will be needed to address the needs of this growing population.

Third, all of this economic activity must rely on the productive capacity of the earth's biosphere. Unfortunately, there is ample evidence that the type and amount of economic activity practiced by the world's economies have already approached, if not overshot, the earth's ability to support human life.

Given these realities, citizens within developed economies have three available paths. First, we can believe that developing economies in places such as China, India, and Indonesia cannot, will not, or should not strive for the type of economic lifestyle and prosperity enjoyed in developed economies. Second, we could believe, optimistically, that present models of business and economic growth can be extended across the globe to an expanding population without degrading the natural environment beyond its limits. Third, we can search for new models of economic and business activity that provide for the needs of the world's population without further degrading the biosphere. Sustainable development and the connected model of sustainable business choose this third path.

---

three pillars of sustainability
Three factors that are often used to judge the adequacy of sustainable practices. Sustainable development must be (1) economically, (2) environmentally, and (3) ethically satisfactory.

Economist Herman Daly has been among the leading thinkers who have advocated an innovative approach to economic theory based on the concept of sustainable development. Daly makes a convincing case for an understanding of economic *development* that transcends the more common standard of economic *growth.* Unless we make significant changes in our understanding of economic activity, unless quite literally we change the way we do business, we will fail to meet some very basic ethical and environmental obligations. According to Daly, we need a major paradigm shift in how we understand economic activity.

We can begin with the standard understanding of economic activity and economic growth found in almost every economics textbook. What is sometimes called the "circular flow model" (Figure 9.2) explains the nature of economic transactions in terms of a flow of resources from businesses to households and back again. Business produces goods and services in response to the market demands of households, then ships the goods and services to households in exchange for payments back to business. These payments in turn are sent back to households in the form of wages, salaries, rents, profits, and interests. Households receive the payments in exchange for the labor, land, capital, and entrepreneurial skills business uses to produce goods and services.

Two aspects of this circular flow model are worth noting. First, it does not differentiate natural resources from the other factors of production. This model does not explain the origin of resources. They are simply owned by households from which they, like labor, capital, and entrepreneurial skill, can be sold to business. Economist Julian Simon has argued, "As economists or consumers, we are interested

FIGURE 9.2

The Circular Flow Model

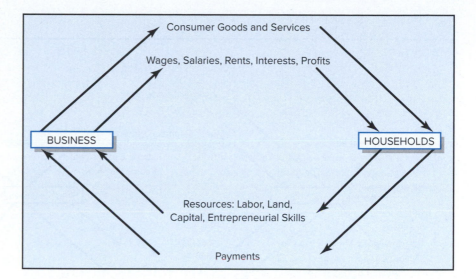

in the particular services that resources yield, not in the resources themselves."[4] Those services can be provided in many ways and by substituting different factors of production. In Simon's terms, resources can therefore be treated as "infinite."

A second observation is that this model treats economic growth both as the solution to all social ills and also as boundless. To keep up with population growth, the economy must grow. To provide for a higher standard of living, the economy must grow. To alleviate poverty, hunger, and disease, the economy must grow. The possibility that the economy cannot grow indefinitely is simply not part of this model.

The three points summarized in the Reality Check "Why Sustainability?" suggest why this growth-based model will be inadequate. According to some estimates, the world's economy would need to grow by a factor of five- to tenfold over the next 50 years to bring the standard of living of present populations in the developing world into line with the standard of living in the industrialized world. Yet, within those 50 years, the world's population will increase by more than 3 billion people, most of them born in the world's poorest economies. Of course, the only source for all this economic activity is productive capacity of the earth itself.

Daly argues that neoclassical economics, with its emphasis on economic growth as the goal of economic policy, will inevitably fail to meet these challenges unless it recognizes that the economy is but a subsystem within earth's biosphere. Economic activity takes place within this biosphere and cannot expand beyond its capacity to sustain life. All the factors that go into production—natural resources, capital, entrepreneurial skill, and labor—ultimately originate in the productive capacity of the earth. In light of this, the entire classical model will prove unstable if resources move through this system at a rate that outpaces the productive capacity of the earth and the earth's capacity to absorb the wastes and by-products of

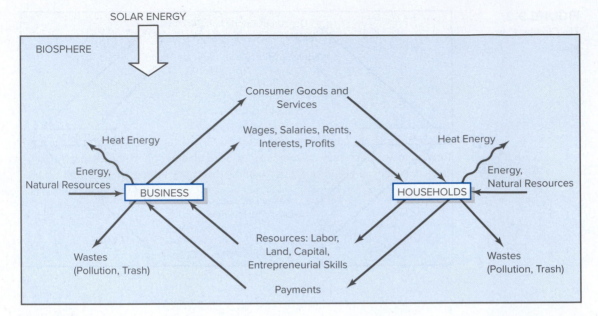

SOLAR ENERGY

BIOSPHERE

Consumer Goods and Services

Heat Energy

Wages, Salaries, Rents, Interests, Profits

Heat Energy

Energy, Natural Resources

BUSINESS

HOUSEHOLDS

Energy, Natural Resources

Wastes (Pollution, Trash)

Resources: Labor, Land, Capital, Entrepreneurial Skills

Wastes (Pollution, Trash)

Payments

FIGURE 9.3

A Model of the Economy (or Economic System) as a Subset of the Biosphere (or Ecosystem)

this production. Thus, we need to develop an economic system that uses resources only at a rate that can be sustained over the long term and that recycles or reuses both the by-products of the production process and the products themselves. A model of such a system, based on Daly's work, is presented in Figure 9.3.

Figure 9.3 differs from Figure 9.2 in several important ways. First, the sustainable model recognizes that the economy exists within a finite biosphere that encompasses a band around the earth that is little more than a few miles wide. From the first law of thermodynamics (the conservation of matter/energy), we recognize that neither matter nor energy can truly be "created"; it can only be transferred from one form to another. Second, energy is lost at every stage of economic activity. Consistent with the second law of thermodynamics (entropy increased within a closed system), the amount of usable energy decreases over time. "Waste energy" is continuously leaving the economic system, and, thus, new low-entropy energy must constantly flow into the system. Ultimately, the only source for low-entropy energy is the sun. Third, this model no longer treats natural resources as an undifferentiated and unexplained factor of production emerging from households. Natural resources come from the biosphere and cannot be created out of nowhere. Finally, it recognizes that wastes are produced at each stage of economic activity, and these wastes are dumped back into the biosphere.

The conclusion that should be drawn from this new model is relatively simple. Over the long term, resources and energy cannot be used, nor waste produced, at rates at which the biosphere cannot replace or absorb them without jeopardizing its ability to sustain (human) life. These are what Daly calls the "biophysical limits to growth."[5] The biosphere can, in theory, produce resources indefinitely, and it can, in theory, absorb wastes indefinitely, but only at a certain rate and with a certain type of economic activity. This is the goal of sustainable development. Finding this rate and the type of economic activity, and thereby creating a sustainable business practice, is the ultimate environmental responsibility of business.

The "Business Case" for a Sustainable Economy

OBJECTIVE

While the regulatory and compliance model tends to interpret environmental responsibilities as constraints upon business, the sustainability model is more forward looking and may present business with greater opportunities than burdens. Indeed, it offers a vision of future business that many entrepreneurial and creative businesses are already pursuing. Many observers argue that a strong economic and financial case can be made for the move toward a sustainable future (but also see the Reality Check "Should Every Business Be Sustainable?").

First, sustainability is a prudent long-term strategy. As the Natural Step's funnel image suggests (see Figure 9.1), business will need to adopt sustainable practices to ensure long-term survival. Firms that fail to adapt to the converging lines of decreasing availability of resources and increasing demand risk their own survival. One can look to the history of the ocean fishing industry as an example.

Second, the huge unmet market potential among the world's developing economies can only be met in sustainable ways. Enormous business opportunities exist in serving the billions of people who need, and are demanding, an expanding range of economic goods and services. The base of the economic pyramid represents the largest and fastest-growing economic market in human history. Yet, the sheer size of these markets alone makes it impossible to meet this demand with the environmentally damaging industrial practices of the 19th and 20th centuries. For example, if China were to consume oil at the same rate as the United States, it alone would consume more than the entire world's daily production and would more than triple the emission of atmospheric carbon dioxide. It is obvious that new sustainable technologies and products will be required to meet the Chinese demand.

Third, significant cost savings can be achieved through sustainable practices. Business stands to save significant costs in moves toward eco-efficiency. Savings on energy use and materials will reduce not only environmental wastes, but spending wastes as well. Minimizing wastes makes sense on financial grounds as well as on environmental grounds.

Fourth, competitive advantages exist for sustainable businesses. Firms that are ahead of the sustainability curve will both have an advantage serving environmentally conscious consumers and enjoy a competitive advantage attracting workers who will take pride and satisfaction in working for progressive firms.

Finally, sustainability is a good risk management strategy. Refusing to move toward sustainability offers many downsides that innovative firms will avoid. Avoiding future government regulation is one obvious benefit. Firms that take the initiative in moving toward sustainability will also likely be the firms that set the standards of best practices in the field. Thus, when regulation does come, these firms will likely play a role in determining what those regulations ought to be.

Reality Check   *Should Every Business Be Sustainable?*

The idea of *sustainability* is everywhere in contemporary business, with virtually all business divisions—including management, marketing, investing, accounting, strategy, and operations—claiming sustainable models and practices. It is difficult to find a major corporation that does not issue an annual sustainability report; by one account 95% of the Global 250 issue annual sustainability reports.* Countless other firms have supplemented, if not replaced, their annual financial report with a broader annual sustainability report.

As originally used by the Brundtland Commission, "sustainable development" was clearly an ethical concept, suggesting an ethical norm to guide practical decision making. Sustainable development was understood as economic activity that met human needs without exploiting the productive capacity of the natural environment. But this demonstrates that the ethical force of sustainable development as envisioned by the Brundtland Report comes from the noun *development,* not from the modifier *sustainable.* That is, the ethical goal is economic development that meets human needs, and because this is an ethically desirable goal, we should seek to achieve this in ways that are environmentally sustainable.

Implicit in this observation is the fact that the words *sustainable* and *sustainability* have no ethical meaning in themselves. To describe something as sustainable is simply to describe it as capable of continuing long term. Not everything that is sustainable is ethically good. We could easily imagine any number of unethical business practices, from deceptive advertising and fraudulent investment schemes to racial discrimination and marketing of dangerous products, as being sustainable.

So we should be wary any time we hear the words *sustainable* or *sustainability* used without specifying what it is that should be sustained. We should always ask: "What is being sustained?" "Should it be sustained?" "How would we contribute to the long-term economic productivity of the global environment by sustaining this organization or this practice?"

*Ernst Ligteringen, keynote speech at the GRI Global Conference on Sustainability and Reporting, May 22, 2013, as reported in *Sustainability Reporting: The Time Is Now,* Ernst & Young (2014), p. 13, www.ey.com/Publication/vwLUAssets/EY-Sustainability-reporting-the-time-is-now/$FILE/EY-Sustainability-reporting-the-time-is-now.pdf (accessed October 14, 2014).

Avoiding legal liability for unsustainable products and environmental damage is another potential benefit. As social consciousness changes, the legal system may soon begin punishing firms that are now negligent in failing to foresee harms caused by their unsustainable practices. Consumer boycotts of unsustainable firms are also a risk to be avoided.

We can summarize these previous sections by reflecting on the ethical decision-making model used throughout this text. The facts suggest that the earth's biosphere is under stress and that much of this comes from the type of global economic growth that has characterized industrial and consumerist societies. The ethical issues that develop from these facts include fairness in allocating scarce resources, justice in meeting the real needs of billions of present and future human beings, and the values and rights associated with environmental conservation and preservation. The stakeholders for these decisions include, quite literally, all life on earth. Relying on our own moral imagination, we can envision a future in which economic activity can meet the real needs of present generations without jeopardizing the ability of future generations to meet their own needs. Sustainability seems to be just this vision. The next section describes directions in which business might develop toward this sustainable model. (To consider how the idea of sustainability might also mislead business, see the Reality Check "Triple Bottom Line: A Trojan Horse?")

Reality Check *Triple Bottom Line: A Trojan Horse?*

The original idea of sustainable development is now often replaced by calls for a more general and vague goal of "social sustainability." When this happens, we should avoid a type of "reverse greenwashing" in which unrelated social concerns are smuggled into the call for sustainable development. John Elkington, the originator of the triple bottom line concept, seems to have done just that. In a 2008 interview with a reporter from the magazine *Mother Jones,* Elkington responded to a question about how he developed the idea of triple bottom line:

> I think quite a number of multinational corporations, in particular U.S. corporations, were quite spooked by the whole social agenda and actively steering away from it. So "triple bottom line" was very

consciously business language, trying to get under the guard of business people. It's almost a Trojan horse trying to give them a sense that this was something that they wanted to play with and subscribe to. Once they started to use the language and commit to it to some degree, we could then define it in ways that could stretch their imaginations a little. That's how it went down.*

In other words, it was justifiable to mislead and manipulate business for the greater good of some unspecified social agenda.

*Jesse Finfrock, "Q&A: John Elkington," *Mother Jones* (November/December 2008).

Principles for a Sustainable Business

OBJECTIVE

Figure 9.3 provides a general model for understanding how firms can evolve toward a sustainable business model. In the simplest terms, resources should not enter into the economic cycle from the biosphere at rates faster than they are replenished. Ideally, waste should be eliminated or, at a minimum, not produced at a rate faster than the biosphere can absorb it. Finally, the energy to power the economic system should be renewable, ultimately relying on the sun or wind, the only energy that is truly renewable.

The precise implications of sustainability will differ for specific firms and industries, but three general principles will guide the move toward sustainability. Firms and industries must become more efficient in using natural resources; they should model their entire production process on biological processes; and they should emphasize the production of services rather than products.

eco-efficiency
Doing more with less. Introduced at the Rio Earth Summit in 1992, the concept of eco-efficiency is a way business can contribute to sustainability by reducing resource usage in its production cycle.

Versions of the first principle, sometimes called **eco-efficiency,** have long been a part of the environmental movement. "Doing more with less" has been an environmental guideline for decades, in addition to being good management practice. On an individual scale, it is environmentally better to ride a bike than to ride in a bus, to ride in a fuel-cell or hybrid-powered bus than in a diesel bus, to ride in a bus than to drive a personal automobile, and to drive a hybrid car than an gas-guzzling SUV. Likewise, business firms can improve energy and materials efficiency in such things as lighting, building design, product design, and distribution channels. Some estimates suggest that with present technologies alone, business could readily achieve at least a fourfold increase in efficiency and perhaps as much as a tenfold increase. Consider that a fourfold increase, called "Factor Four" in the sustainability literature, would make it possible to achieve double the productivity from one-half the resource use.[6] When applied to the additional costs for buildings associated with Leadership in Energy and Environmental Design (LEED) standards, for example, such a return on investment means that companies can quickly recoup this environmental investment.

The second principle of business sustainability can be easily understood by reference to Figure 9.3. Imagine that the waste leaving the economic cycle is being turned back into the cycle as a productive resource. "Closed-loop" production seeks to integrate what is presently waste back into production. In an ideal situation, the waste of one firm becomes the resource of another, and such synergies can create eco-industrial parks. Just as biological processes such as photosynthesis cycle the "waste" of one activity into the resource of another, this principle is a form of biomimicry often referred to as **"closed-loop" production.**

The ultimate goal of this form of biomimicry is to eliminate waste altogether rather than reducing it. If we truly mimic biological processes, the end result of one process (e.g., leaves and oxygen produced by photosynthesis) is ultimately reused as the productive resources (e.g., soil and water) of another process (plant growth) with only solar energy added.

The evolution of business strategy toward biomimicry can be understood along a continuum. The most primitive phase has been described as "take-make-waste." Business takes resources, makes products out of them, and discards whatever is left over. A second phase envisions business taking responsibility for its products from "cradle to grave." Sometimes referred to as "life-cycle" responsibility, this approach has already found its way into both industrial and regulatory thinking. Cradle-to-grave or life-cycle responsibility holds that a business is responsible for the entire life of its products, including the ultimate disposal even after the sale. Thus, for example, a cradle-to-grave model would hold a business liable for groundwater contamination caused by its products even years after they had been buried in a landfill.

Cradle-to-cradle responsibility extends this idea even further and holds that a business should be responsible for incorporating the end results of its products back into the productive cycle. This responsibility, in turn, would create incentives to redesign products so that they could be recycled efficiently and easily.

The environmental design company McDonough and Braungart, founded by architect William McDonough and chemist Michael Braungart, has been a leader in helping businesses reconceptualize and redesign business practice to achieve sustainability. Their book *Cradle to Cradle* traces the life cycle of several products, providing case studies of economic and environmental benefits attainable when business takes responsibility for the entire life cycle of products. Among their projects is the redesign of Ford Motor Company's Rouge River manufacturing plant.

Beyond eco-efficiency and biomimicry, a third sustainable business principle involves a shift in business model from products to services. Traditional economic and managerial models interpret consumer demand as the demand for products—washing machines, carpeting, lights, consumer electronics, air conditioners, cars, computers, and so forth. A **service-based economy** interprets consumer

---

"closed-loop" production
Seeks to integrate what is presently waste back into production in much the way that biological processes turn waste into food.

cradle-to-cradle responsibility
Holds that a business should be responsible for incorporating the end results of its products back into the productive cycle.

service-based economy
Interprets consumer demand as a demand for services, for example, for clothes cleaning, floor covering, cool air, transportation, or word processing, rather than as a demand for products such as washing machines, carpeting, air conditioners, cars, and computers.

demand as a demand for services—for clothes cleaning, floor covering, illumination, entertainment, cool air, transportation, word processing, and so forth.

The book *Natural Capitalism* provides examples of businesses that have made such a shift in each of these industries.[7] This change produces incentives for product redesigns that create more durable and more easily recyclable products.

One well-known innovator in this area is Interface Corporation and its CEO, Ray Anderson. Interface has made a transition from selling carpeting to leasing floor-covering services. On the traditional model, carpet is sold to consumers who, once they become dissatisfied with the color or style or once the carpeting becomes worn, dispose of the carpet in landfills. There is little incentive here to produce long-lasting or easily recyclable carpeting. Once Interface shifted to leasing floor-covering services, it created incentives to produce long-lasting, easily replaceable and recyclable carpets. Interface thereby accepts responsibility for the entire life cycle of the product it markets. Because the company retains ownership and is responsible for maintenance, Interface now produces carpeting that can be easily replaced in sections rather than in its entirety, that is more durable, and that can eventually be remanufactured. Redesigning carpets and shifting to a service lease has also improved production efficiencies and reduced material and energy costs significantly. Consumers benefit by getting what they truly desire at lower costs and fewer burdens.

Sustainable Marketing

OBJECTIVE

sustainable or green marketing
Sustainable or green marketing is the marketing of products on the basis of their environmentally friendly nature.

"Sustainability" was introduced in Chapter 5 as an approach to corporate social responsibility that is gaining influence in all areas of business. **Sustainable or green marketing** is one aspect of this approach that already has changed how many firms do business. The four characteristics (Four Ps) of marketing introduced earlier in Chapter 8—product, price, promotion, and placement—are a helpful way to structure an understanding of sustainable, green marketing.

Product

The most significant progress toward sustainability will depend on the sustainability of products themselves. Discovering what the consumer "really wants" and developing products to meet those wants have always been among the primary marketing challenges. Meeting the real needs of present and future generations within ecological constraints can be understood simply as a refinement of this traditional marketing objective.

Consider, for example, the business differences between marketing the physical pieces of computer hardware and marketing computing services. Should Dell or HP be in the business of selling computer components, or are they selling the service to provide consumers with up-to-date computer hardware, software, and data storage? A later section will examine the distinction between products and service in more depth, but the marketing department should be at the forefront of identifying the real needs of consumers so that a business can develop the long-term relationships with consumers that will ensure both financial and ecological sustainability.

Another aspect of marketing involves the design and creation of products. William McDonough has often described environmental regulation as a design problem; a product or production process that pollutes and wastes resources is a poorly designed product or process. Regulatory mandates usually result when business has a poorly designed product or process. Marketing departments therefore should also be involved in the design of products, finding ways to build sustainability into the very design of each product.

Finally, marketing professionals have an opportunity to influence the packaging of products. Overpackaging and the use of petroleum-based plastics are packaging issues already under environmental scrutiny. Imagine the marketing opportunities if a major soft-drink bottler such as Coke or Pepsi turned to corn-based biodegradable plastics for their bottles. Imagine what the marketing department of a company like Amazon could do if its packing materials were 100% recycled and recyclable. Imagine the marketing opportunities, and responsibilities, of a company such as Walmart if it chose to use its power to persuade its suppliers to reduce unnecessary product packaging.

These three areas come together clearly within the context of extended producer responsibility and take-back legislation in which a firm is held responsible to take back and recycle all the products it introduces into the marketplace. These regulatory developments, now taking hold especially in Europe, will be seen as barriers to profit by some firms. But more creative firms will see opportunities here for generating entire new markets. Take-back legislation provides strong incentives for redesigning products in ways that make it easier to reuse and recycle. Marketing services rather than products, of course, will be the most efficient means for accomplishing this objective.

Price

A second aspect of marketing is price. Sustainability asks us to focus on the environmental costs of resources, the "natural capital" on which most firms rely, and points out that environmental costs are seldom factored into the price of most products. Marketing professionals should play a role in setting prices that reflect a product's true ecological cost.

At first glance, this might seem a peculiar area in which to expect business to move. Internalizing environmental externalities sounds like a polite way of suggesting that business ought to raise its prices. Such a strategy would seem, at best, unrealistic. Government regulation, rather than voluntary action, is more likely to move business in this direction. Without government mandates across the board for an industry, internalizing the costs of natural capitalism into its products will put a company at a comparative disadvantage.

On the other hand, setting prices in such a way that more sustainable products are priced competitively with other products is a more reasonable strategy for sustainable marketing. Ordinarily, we might think that pricing is a straightforward and objective process. One starts with the costs of producing a product, adds a reasonable rate of return, and the result is the asking price. Ultimately, the actual price is whatever buyer and seller agree on. However, this simple model misses some important complexities. To understand some of the complexities of price, and the role of marketing in this, consider the example of hybrid automobiles.

Like any new product, a hybrid automobile required investments in research, design, production, and marketing long before it could be brought to market. For such a complex product as a hybrid automobile, these investments were substantial, well into the hundreds of millions of dollars for each automaker that produces a hybrid. Setting a price for this product involves a complicated process of projecting sales, markets, and a product's life cycle. In one sense, the very first hybrid cost millions of dollars to manufacture, well beyond an affordable and marketable price. Businesses normally take a loss on a new product until such time as economies of scale kick in to lower costs and market share develops sufficiently to produce a revenue stream that can begin to pay down the initial investment and generate profits. Marketing professionals who are aware of sustainability concerns have much to contribute in establishing prices that protect sustainable products from short-term cost–benefit analyses.

Consider also how price functions with such business practices as sales, manufacturer's rebates, cash-back incentives to consumers, bonuses to sales staff, and the use of loss leaders in retailing. Obviously price is often manipulated for many marketing reasons, including promotion to help gain a foothold in a market. Short-term losses are often justified in pricing decisions by appeal to long-term considerations. This seems a perfect fit for sustainable marketing goals.

Perhaps nowhere is price a more crucial element of marketing than it is in marketing to the base of the economic pyramid. Small profit margins and efficient distribution systems within large markets, as demonstrated so clearly by large retailers like Walmart, can prove to be a highly successful business model. An ethically praiseworthy goal would be to export this marketing ingenuity to serve the cause of global sustainability. The Decision Point "Marketing to the Base of the Pyramid" explains the mechanics of this process.

Promotion

A third aspect of marketing, of course, is the promotion and advertising of products. Marketing also has a responsibility to help shape consumer demand, encouraging consumers to demand more sustainable products from business. Without question, marketing has already shown how powerful a force it can be in shaping consumer demand. Marketing has played a major role in creating various social meanings for shopping and buying. Sustainable marketing can help create the social meanings and consumer expectations supportive of sustainable goals. An often-overlooked aspect of advertising is its educational function. Consumers learn from advertising, and so marketers arguably have a responsibility as educators. Helping consumers learn the value of sustainable products, helping them become sustainable consumers, is an important role for sustainable marketing.

In his landmark book, business scholar C. K. Prahalad details the business opportunities that exist for firms that are creative and resourceful enough to develop markets among the world's poorest people.*

Done correctly, marketing to the 4 billion people at the base of the global economic pyramid would employ market forces in addressing some of the greatest ethical and environmental problems of the 21st century.

Obviously, helping meet the needs of the world's poorest people would be a significant ethical contribution. The strategy involves another ethical consideration as well: A market of this size requires environmentally sustainable products and technologies. If everyone in the world used resources and created wastes at the rate Americans do, the global environment would suffer immeasurably. Businesses that understand this fact face a huge marketing opportunity.

Accomplishing such goals will require a significant revision to the standard marketing paradigm. Business must, in Prahalad's phrase, "create the capacity to consume" among the world's poor. Creating this capacity to consume among the world's poor would create a significant win–win opportunity from both a financial and an ethical perspective.

Prahalad points out that the world's poor do have significant purchasing power, albeit in the aggregate rather than on a per capita basis. Creating the capacity to consume among the world's poor will require a transformation in the conceptual framework of global marketing and some creative steps from business. Prahalad mentions three principles as key to marketing to the poor: affordability, access, and availability.

Consider how a firm might market such household products as laundry soap differently in India than in the United States. Marketing in the United States can involve large plastic containers, sold at a low per-unit cost. Trucks transport cases from manufacturing plants to wholesale warehouses to giant big-box retailers where they can sit in inventory until purchase. Consumers wheel the heavy containers out to their cars in shopping carts and store them at home in the laundry room.

The aggregate soap market in India could be greater than the market in the United States, but Indian consumers would require smaller and more affordable containers. Prahalad therefore talks about the need for single-size servings for many consumer products. Given longer and more erratic work hours and a lack of personal transportation, the poor often lack access to markets. Creative marketing would need to find ways to provide easier access to their products. Longer store hours and wider and more convenient distribution channels could reach consumers otherwise left out of the market.

So, too, can imaginative financing, credit, and pricing schemes. Microfinance and microcredit arrangements are developing throughout less-developed economies as creative means to support the capacity of poor people to buy and sell goods and services. Finally, innovative marketing can ensure that products are available where and when the world's poor need them. Base-of-the-pyramid consumers tend to be cash customers with incomes that are unpredictable. A distributional system that ensures product availability at the time and place when customers are ready and able to make the purchase can help create the capacity to consume. Prahalad's approach—tied to moral imagination discussed previously—responds both to the consumers and to the corporate investors and other for-profit multinational stakeholders.

1. Do you think that business firms and industries have an ethical responsibility to address global poverty by creating the capacity to consume among the world's poor? Do you think that this can be done? What responsibilities, ethical and economic, do firms face when marketing in other countries and among different cultures? Imagine that you are in the marketing department of a firm that manufactures a consumer product such as laundry detergent or shampoo. Describe how it might be marketed differently in India.

2. What are the key facts relevant to your judgment?

3. What ethical issues are involved in a firm's decision to market its products among the world's poor by creating the capacity to consume?

4. Who are the stakeholders?

5. What alternatives does a firm have with regard to the way in which it markets its products?

6. How do the alternatives compare; how do the alternatives you have identified affect the stakeholders?

*C. K. Prahalad, *The Fortune at the Bottom of the Pyramid* (Upper Saddle River, NJ: Wharton, 2005).

For example, see the Reality Check "TerraChoice's Seven Sins of Greenwashing" as one effort in consumer education.

Certainly one aspect of product promotion will involve the "green labeling." Just as ingredient labels, nutrition labels, and warning labels have become normal and standardized, environmental pressure may well create a public demand for environmental and sustainable labeling. But history has shown a tendency for some firms to exploit green labeling initiatives and mislead consumers. "Greenwashing" is the practice of promoting a product by misleading consumers about the environmentally beneficial aspects of the product. (The term is a modification of the much older word "whitewashing," which refers to the practice of using cheap white paint to cover up dirt on the walls of a barn.) Labeling products with such terms as *environmentally friendly, natural, eco, energy efficient, biodegradable,* and the like can help promote products that have little or no environmental benefits. Take a look at the Decision Point "Examples of Greenwashing?" to see if you can distinguish the greenwashing claims from the sincere ones.

Placement

The final aspect of marketing involves the channels of distribution that move a product from producer to consumer. Professor Patrick Murphy suggests two directions in which marketing can develop sustainable channels.[8] As typically understood, marketing channels involve such things as transportation, distribution, inventory, and the like. Recent advances in marketing have emphasized just-in-time (JIT) inventory control, large distribution centers, and sophisticated

Reality Check *TerraChoice's Seven Sins of Greenwashing*

SIN OF THE HIDDEN TRADE-OFF

A claim suggesting that a product is "green" based on a narrow set of attributes without attention to other important environmental issues. Paper, for example, is not necessarily environmentally preferable just because it comes from a sustainably harvested forest. Other important environmental issues in the paper-making process, such as greenhouse gas emissions, or chlorine use in bleaching, may be equally important.

SIN OF NO PROOF

An environmental claim that cannot be substantiated by easily accessible supporting information or by a reliable third-party certification. Common examples are facial tissues or toilet tissue products that claim various percentages of post-consumer recycled content without providing evidence.

SIN OF VAGUENESS

A claim that is so poorly defined or broad that its real meaning is likely to be misunderstood by the consumer. "All natural" is an example. Arsenic, uranium, mercury, and formaldehyde are all naturally occurring, and poisonous. "All natural" isn't necessarily "green."

SIN OF WORSHIPING FALSE LABELS

A product that, through either words or images, gives the impression of third-party endorsement where no such endorsement exists; fake labels, in other words.

SIN OF IRRELEVANCE

An environmental claim that may be truthful but is unimportant or unhelpful for consumers seeking environmentally preferable products. "CFC-free" is a common example because it is a frequent claim despite the fact that CFCs are banned by law.

SIN OF LESSER OF TWO EVILS

A claim that may be true within the product category, but that risks distracting the consumer from the greater environmental impacts of the category as a whole. Organic cigarettes could be an example of this sin, as might the fuel-efficient sport-utility vehicle.

SIN OF FIBBING

Environmental claims that are simply false. The most common examples are products falsely claiming to be Energy Star certified or registered.

Source: TerraChoice, *The Sins of Greenwashing: Home and Family Edition* (2010), p. 10, http://sinsofgreenwashing.com/index35c6.pdf (accessed September 5, 2019).

transportation schemes. Murphy foresees new sustainability options being added to this model that emphasize fuel efficiency and alternative fuel technologies used in transportation, more localized and efficient distribution channels, and a greater reliance on electronic rather than physical distribution. More efficient distribution channels can also serve the underserved base of the pyramid consumers.

Consider, as an example, how the publishing industry has evolved its channels of distribution. Originally, books, magazines, catalogs, or newspapers were printed in one location and then distributed via truck, rail, or air across the country. More modern practices piloted by such companies as *USA Today* and *The Wall Street Journal* send electronic versions of the content to localized printers who publish and distribute the final product locally. Textbook publishers do a similar thing when they allow users to select specific content and create a custom-published book for each use. As subscriptions to hard-copy publications decline,

Which of the following corporate marketing initiatives would you describe as an example of greenwashing?

- An ad for the GM Hummer that describes the truck as "thirsty for adventure, not gas." The Hummer was rated at 20 mpg on the highway.
- A major rebranding of the oil company British Petroleum by renaming itself "BP" for "beyond petroleum."
- An "eco-shaped" bottle for the bottled water brand Ice Mountain. For that matter, any bottled water described as "natural," "pure," or "organic."

Which of the following examples, all taken from the Federal Trade Commission, are cases of misleading greenwashing?

- A box of aluminum foil is labeled with the claim "recyclable," without further elaboration. Unless the type of product, surrounding language, or other context of the phrase establishes whether the claim refers to the foil or the box, the claim is deceptive if any part of either the box or the foil, other than minor, incidental components, cannot be recycled.
- A trash bag is labeled "recyclable" without qualification. Because trash bags will ordinarily not be separated out from other trash at the landfill or incinerator for recycling, they are highly unlikely to be used again for any purpose.
- An advertiser notes that its shampoo bottle contains "20 percent more recycled content." The claim in its context is ambiguous. Depending on contextual factors, it could be a comparison either to the advertiser's immediately preceding product or to a competitor's product.
- A product wrapper is printed with the claim "Environmentally Friendly." Textual comments on the wrapper explain that the wrapper is environmentally friendly because it was not chlorine bleached, a process that has been shown to create harmful substances. The wrapper was, in fact, not bleached with chlorine. However, the production of the wrapper now creates and releases to the environment significant quantities of other harmful substances.
- A product label contains an environmental seal, either in the form of a globe icon, or a globe icon with only the text *Earth Smart* around it. Either label is likely to convey to consumers that the product is environmentally superior to other products.
- A nationally marketed bottle bears the unqualified statement that it is "recyclable." Collection sites for recycling the material in question are not available to a substantial majority of consumers or communities, although collection sites are established in a significant percentage of communities or available to a significant percentage of the population.
- The seller of an aerosol product makes an unqualified claim that its product "Contains no CFCs." Although the product does not contain CFCs, it does contain HCFC-22, another ozone-depleting ingredient.

Consumer demand plays a powerful, yet ambiguous, role in the food industry. There clearly is a market demand for super-sized, high-salt, high-fat, sugary, highly processed food. But legitimate questions can be raised about the consumer's understanding of his or her own needs, and his or her ability to influence food production.

In a 2015 report, the U.S. Centers for Disease Control and Prevention found that childhood obesity in the United States nearly tripled between 1980 and 2012, resulting in a wide range of serious health problems including heart disease, high blood pressure, and diabetes. In this sense, millions of people are eating too much of the wrong type of food. Oversized portions of high-calorie, high-fat, and sugary food products directly contribute to significant health problems for children and adults.

In addition to obesity, many other health issues can be traced to what we eat. Artificial food colorings; artificial sweeteners; food additives such as monosodium glutamate, trans fats, nitrates, and high fructose corn syrup; and artificial preservatives such as sodium benzoate have all been linked to human health problems. All of these products are added to food by the food industry.

Defenders of the food industry will point out that business is only responding to consumer demand in providing "super-sized" portions and tasty, inexpensive, and convenient food products. Many additives are included to increase shelf-life of food, to make it more tasty and attractive, or to lower costs.

In 2015, for example, General Mills announced that it would be phasing out the use of synthetic artificial dyes and flavors in its breakfast cereals. In explaining its decision, General Mills claimed that "people eat with their eyes" and want cereals that are "fun" and have "vibrant colors" and "fruity flavor."* Assuming this market demand as a given, General Mills still had the discretion to change how it would meet that demand and chose to reduce the health risks posed by artificial colors and flavors.

But, of course, the consumer demand for colorful, sugary breakfast treats is itself something over which General Mills has at least some influence. Childhood obesity is a major health problem, and marketing high-sugar breakfast treats to children cannot be said to be meeting needs, although it seems to meet consumer preferences. A business also cannot escape responsibility for failing to meet needs for nutritional foods by claiming that it is merely responding to what consumers want if it has spent hundreds of millions of dollars creating and promoting colorful high-sugar treats as "part of a complete breakfast."

Yet, in other ways, consumer demand is changing the nature of the food industry. Organic food sales in the United States have grown by an average of 14 percent annually since the year 2000. Globally, the organic food sales volume almost doubled, from $57 billion to $104 billion between 2010 and 2015. Major retailers such as Whole Foods, Walmart, Kroger, and Costco actively promote organic and sustainably grown food products. Major food producers such as General Mills and Unilever have moved aggressively into the organic and sustainable food market.

1. To what degree should the movement toward organic and sustainably raised food be left to the market? What role, if any, should government regulation play in this regard? What responsibilities does the food industry, including restaurants and grocers, have?

2. Many food products are marketed as "natural." Can you think of any such products that raise ethical problems? Is everything that is natural also good?

3. Sustainable products should be designed to meet the needs of present and future generations. Who decides what people need? Can every product be sustainable?

*James Hamblen, "Lucky Charms, the New Superfood," *The Atlantic* (June 23, 2015).

many newspapers, magazines, and catalogs are taking this a step further by moving toward online publishing.

Murphy also describes a second aspect of the channel variable in marketing that promises significant sustainability rewards. "Reverse channels" refers to the growing marketing practice of taking back one's products after their useful life. The life-cycle responsibility and "take-back" models described previously will likely fall to marketing departments. The same department that is responsible for sending a product out into the marketplace should expect the responsibility for finding ways to take back that product to dispose, recycle, or reuse it.[9]

Questions, Projects, and Exercises

1. As a research project, choose a product with which you are familiar (one with local connections is best) and trace its entire life cycle. From where does this product originate? What resources go into its design and manufacture? How is it transported, sold, used, and disposed of? Along each step in the life cycle of this product, analyze the economic, environmental, and ethical costs and benefits. Consider if a service could be exchanged for this product. Some examples might include your local drinking water, food items such as beef or chicken, any product sold at a local farmer's market, or building materials used in local projects.

2. Search online for a free ecological footprint analysis. You should be able to find a self-administered test to evaluate your own ecological footprint. What comparisons does the test allow? How does your "footprint" compare to that of people in other parts of the world? What share of the world's resources are you using up?

3. Think of a corporate brand that you know and admire. Look online to determine whether the company issues a corporate sustainability report. If it does, look at the report to see whether it impresses you, as a consumer. How do you think this brand compares, in terms of sustainability, to competing brands? If the company doesn't issue a report, can you figure out why?

4. Should businesses be legally required to take back products at the end of their useful life? Are there other, equally effective solutions? Is there a better argument for such a rule with regard to some products rather than others—say, smartphones but not books, or lightbulbs but not sofas?

5. What does the concept "sustainability" really mean when applied to different businesses and industries? What would sustainable agriculture require? What are sustainable energy sources? What would sustainable transportation be? What would be required to turn your hometown into a sustainable community?

6. Investigate what is involved in an environmental audit. Has such an audit been conducted at your own college or university? In what ways has your own school adopted sustainable practices? In what ways would your school need to change to become more sustainable?

7. Do you believe that business has any direct ethical duties to living beings other than humans? Do animals, plants, or ecosystems have rights? What criteria should be used in answering such questions? What is your own standard for determining what objects count, from a moral point of view?

8. Investigate LEED (Leadership in Energy and Environmental Design) building designs. Try typing "LEED" into Google, along with the name of your town or neighborhood, to search for LEED-certified buildings near you. Are there any? Should all new buildings be required by law to adopt LEED design standards and conform to the LEED rating system?

Key Terms

After reading this chapter, you should have a clear understanding of the following key terms. For a complete definition, please see the Glossary.

backcasting, *p. 324*

"closed-loop" production, *p. 340*

corporate average fuel economy (CAFE) standards, *p. 330*

cradle-to-cradle responsibility, *p. 340*

eco-efficiency, *p. 339*

service-based economy, *p. 340*

sustainable business practice, *p. 333*

sustainable development, *p. 333*

sustainable or green marketing, *p. 341*

three pillars of sustainability, *p. 333*

Endnotes

1. Jonathan Foley, "Feed the World," *National Geographic* (May 2014).

2. William Baxter, *People or Penguins: The Case for Optimal Pollution* (New York: Columbia University Press, 1974).

3. Julian Simon, *The Ultimate Resource* (Princeton, NJ: Princeton University Press, 1983).

4. J. Simon, *The Ultimate Resource* (Princeton: Princeton University Press, 1981).

5. Herman Daly, *Beyond Growth* (Boston: Beacon Press, 1996), pp. 33–35.

6. For the Factor Four claim, see Ernst von Weizacker, Amory B. Lovins, L. Hunter Lovins, and Kogan Page, "Factor Four: Doubling Wealth—Halving Resource Use: A Report to the Club of Rome" (Earthscan/James & James, 1997); for Factor 10, see Friedrich Schmidt-Bleek, *Factor 10 Institute Blog,* www.factor10-institute.org/ (accessed April 22, 2010).

7. Paul Hawken, Amory Lovins, and Hunter Lovins, *Natural Capitalism* (Boston: Little Brown, 1999).

8. Patrick E. Murphy, "Sustainable Marketing," Business and Environmental Sustainability Conference, Carlson School of Management, Minneapolis, MN, 2005.

9. Sustainable marketing seems to be a growing field within both business and the academic community. Two of the earliest books in this field, both of which remain very helpful, are Michael J. Polonsky and Alma T. Mintu-Wimsatt, eds., *Environmental Marketing: Strategies, Practice, Theory, and Research* (Binghampton, NY: Haworth Press, 1995); and Donald Fuller, *Sustainable Marketing: Managerial-Ecological Issues* (Thousand Oaks, CA: Sage, 1999). A particularly helpful essay in the Polonsky book is by Jagdish N. Seth and Atul Parvatiyar, "Ecological Imperatives and the Role of Marketing," pp. 3–20. Seth and Parvatiyar are often credited with coining the term *sustainable marketing* in this essay.

10

Ethical Decision Making: Corporate Governance, Accounting, and Finance

It astounds me how little senior management gets a basic truth: If clients don't trust you they will eventually stop doing business with you. It doesn't matter how smart you are.

Greg Smith, "Why I am Leaving Goldman Sachs," *The New York Times,* March 14, 2012

Whenever an institution malfunctions as consistently as boards of directors have in nearly every major fiasco of the last forty or fifty years, it is futile to blame men. It is the institution that malfunctions.

Peter Drucker

It is essential that the activities of corporate executives are under constant, vigorous and public scrutiny, because those activities are crucial to the economic well-being of society.

Ann Crotty

In September 2015, the U.S. Environmental Protection Agency (EPA) announced that it was ordering a recall for more than 500,000 Volkswagens sold in the United States. The EPA reported that VW's diesel engine cars contained software code that manipulated emission tests and allowed the cars to meet required emission standards. The software "defeat devices" activated emission controls only while the car was undergoing testing; however, while driving under normal conditions, the cars emitted nitrous oxide pollution that was more than 30 times higher than what was allowed by law. Investigations followed in other countries and eventually some 11 million vehicles were recalled globally. Within days, Volkswagen's stock price had dropped almost 40%. It is estimated that VW had already paid out more than $30 billion in repairs, fines, and legal settlements as a result of the scandal. This figure does not include lost sales, or the heavy financial losses suffered by thousands of independent VW dealers and suppliers.

For at least one year prior to the EPA announcement, VW and the EPA had discussed apparent discrepancies in the testing data, which VW initially dismissed as the result of testing anomalies. Only after the EPA took steps to withhold approval for all the upcoming 2016 VW diesel cars did VW acknowledge that a real problem existed. Upon the EPA recall announcement in September, VW officials admitted that the problem involved intentional fraud and took responsibility for the scandal.

Volkswagen CEO Martin Winterkorn apologized for "the terrible mistakes of a few people" and, while denying any knowledge of or involvement, resigned within weeks. In a statement accompanying his resignation, Winterkorn said, "I am stunned that misconduct on such a scale was possible in the Volkswagen Group, I am not aware of any wrongdoing on my part." Speaking at a corporate event, VW of America's president Michael Horn admitted that "Our company was dishonest with the EPA and the California Air Resources Board and with all of you."[1] Horn resigned in March 2016.

In March 2019, the U.S. Securities and Exchange Commission charged both Volkswagen and Winterkorn with defrauding American investors and raising money through deceptive claims. In April of the same year, German prosecutors charged Winterkorn and four others with fraud.

But how did it all happen?

Initial reports coming from VW placed responsibility with a small number of engineers, acting under managerial pressure to meet corporate goals for both engine performance and fuel efficiency. But later evidence suggested that as early as 2006, VW management had indications that they were not able to achieve emission standards within established cost targets.

For decades, government regulators across the world have worked with automobile manufacturers to develop environmental and fuel-efficiency standards that would meaningfully improve air quality by reducing pollution, yet still be technologically achievable. Manufacturers chose various strategies to meet these standards. Technological and design advances in engines, body aerodynamics, pollution control devices, and materials all contributed to increasingly fuel-efficient cars. Some manufacturers chose to develop smaller cars, some moved in the direction of hybrids and electric vehicles, and others, like VW, worked to improve diesel technology.

The scandal struck at the heart of the VW brand. Improved diesel engines had become a hallmark of the VW brand of "German engineering." Diesels have always had performance benefits over gas-powered engines. Diesel engines last longer, get better fuel mileage, provide more torque and power, and are more dependable than gasoline engines. Yet, historically they emitted more pollution, especially nitrous oxides and particulate matter (the black soot often seen coming from truck or bus exhaust). VW, a brand long promoted for its engineering skill, marketed its turbocharged direct injection (TDI) engines as a new generation of "smart diesels," able to maintain all the high-performance benefits of diesels while also meeting stringent new environmental standards.

Given the centrality of the new-generation diesels to the VW brand and to its global sales, many observers found it difficult to believe that a widespread fraud involving such a crucial element of its key product could have resulted from "the terrible mistakes of a few people." How could a major scandal involving the fraudulent design and promotion of a core product, especially a product that everyone knew would be subjected to extensive governmental testing and regulation, occur? Even if the decision to insert the defeat device rested with only a few engineers, the scandal could only have occurred if there were widespread failures of oversight and control at every level, from the shop floor to the corporate board room. In the opinion of many, this widespread failure of oversight and control, especially at the management and board levels, was as great a corporate failing as the fraud itself. Where were the oversight and supervision?

A plausible description of the realities leading up to this scandal is that engineers were expected to achieve a balance among three factors that were in tension: They were to develop a diesel engine that met high performance standards while also meeting environmental emission standards. Importantly, they were expected to accomplish this while also meeting cost targets. Later evidence revealed that earlier proposals that would have achieved this balance had been rejected by management because they would have added costs of a few hundred dollars to each vehicle. One option, of course, would have been for management to conclude that this balance could not, therefore, be achieved. However, by most reports the VW corporate culture was such that there was little tolerance for work teams that failed to meet goals and little willingness among management to encourage questions or challenges to their decisions.

Professional codes of ethics can sometimes function to shield engineers from pressures to compromise professional standards in order to meet employer or client goals. Professionals such as lawyers, accountants, and engineers have ethical duties that should override the demands of one's employer. But engineers in Germany do not have the level of professional licensing and training requirements as engineers face in Canada and the United States, for example. In any case, there is little evidence that any VW engineer, the individuals who had direct and firsthand experience of the fraud, stepped forward to take a stand against the fraud. There have been no reported cases of whistle-blowing by anyone within the organization.

VW management would have had many opportunities to prevent the fraud, mitigate its damage, or, at the very minimum, acknowledge and report it sooner. Senior executives failed across the board in their oversight responsibilities. They failed employees by setting unfeasible expectations and being inflexible in the face of evidence that these were unattainable. VW had no internal mechanisms that encouraged or even allowed reporting of malfeasance.

(continued)

(*continued*)

As the scandal unfolded, VW's largest union criticized management for having a "rigid hierarchy" that was authoritarian and unwilling to listen to bad news. Matthias Müller, Volkswagen's new chief executive appointed after the Winterkorn resignation, acknowledged problems with the previous managerial style and promised a more open management style.

One might expect the VW board to have set high expectations and to have held management to them. But, according to press reports, the relationship between the VW board and senior executives had been contentious for a long time. As the scandal became public, board members criticized Winterkorn for failing to keep them informed. Three board members, including government officials and union representatives, revealed that they learned of the scandal only by reading about it in the media. Critics pointed out that either senior executives were unaware of the fraud, in which case they failed in their managerial duties, or they did know and neither fixed the problem nor kept the board informed, in which case they failed other duties.

In a statement released after VW admitted the fraud, Stephan Weil, a board member who is also prime minister of the German state of Lower Saxony, where Volkswagen is based, claimed, "Talks took place for a full year before Volkswagen admitted the deception. This confession should clearly have occurred much earlier." Weil described the failure of senior executives to inform the board "a grave mistake."[2]

Despite these criticisms, the VW board had extended Winterkorn's contract as CEO just two weeks before the public recall announcement from the EPA. Winterkorn certainly knew of the pending EPA action at this point, but most board members claimed that they did not.

But there is evidence that the VW board was in disarray at this time. Winterkorn's contract extension came just four months after a failed attempt to oust him by board chair Ferdinand Piech. Piech, the grandson of VW founder Ferdinand Porsche and often described as the "patriarch" of VW, had held senior leadership positions including CEO or board chair for decades. Peich was well known for his authoritarian management style, which had resulted in similar dismissals of other senior executives. When the attempt to oust Winterkorn failed, Peich resigned as board chair and stepped away from all other roles with VW.

But there were other structural issues with the VW board that might also help explain some of the governance disarray. In the United States and Canada, for example, corporations are governed by a single board of directors, which has the ultimate legal fiduciary responsibility to company shareholders. In Germany, however, corporations are governed by two boards, a supervisory board with general oversight responsibility and a managerial board, which is comprised of senior executives who are responsible for operational oversight. Further, the German workplace democracy model of codetermination legally requires that half the board seats go to representatives of workers.

The VW board is comprised of twenty members. The board chair is former VW corporate finance director. Ten of the remaining nineteen seats are held by representatives of VW's union workers. Four other seats are reserved for members of the Porsche and Piech families, who own 52% of the corporate stock. Prior to the failed attempt to oust Winterkorn, Ferdinand Piech and his wife Ursala held two of the four family board memberships. Two seats are held by representatives of the German state of Lower Saxony, the region in which the VW plant is located and holder of 20% of the corporate stock. Two seats are reserved for representatives of the country of Qatar, which owns 17% of VW stock.

Thus, only 10% of this publicly traded company's stock is freely floating in the marketplace. Of the twenty-person supervisory board, only one member could be classified as independent. Critics suggest that this structure is at the root of VW's dysfunctional governance. Members of the supervisory board have split loyalties that can conflict with the duties for corporate transparency and integrity. For example, the VW facility is reputed to be a highly inefficient production plant. It manufactures slightly more cars than its competitor Toyota but employs almost twice as many workers to do it. It would be difficult, for example, to get approval for job cuts or production transfers from a board with 60% of its membership in the hands of unions and local governments. The split board system can also shield management from oversight from the supervisory board.

In April 2016, in anticipation of its annual stockholders meeting, the VW supervisory board announced that investigations had concluded that VW's executive management was not responsible for the fraud. As a result, the board would recommend that executives receive end-of-year bonuses for 2015. It was also revealed that Martin Winterkorn had received $8 million in compensation for 2015, only half of his 2014 compensation. Union leaders angrily denounced these recommendations, pointing out that employees would be receiving little or no bonuses for 2015 due to the financial losses associated with the scandal.

1. How would you assign responsibility for the VW scandal? What should have been done differently and by whom?

2. Who are the stakeholders in this case? How were the interests of each stakeholder represented?

3. Is it fair to expect any employees, including professionals such as engineers and accountants, to confront management over directives that they believe are unethical?

4. What changes to the VW board would you recommend that might help prevent future scandals?

5. The codetermination principle was created to ensure that employees have a role in managerial decision making, thus creating a more democratic workplace. What are the benefits of this model? What are the disadvantages?

6. What do you understand by "independent" board member? Who or what should an independent board member represent that would be different from other board members?

 ## Chapter Objectives

After reading this chapter, you will be able to:

1. Explain the role of accountants and other professionals as "gatekeepers."

2. Describe how conflicts of interest can arise for business professionals.

3. Outline the requirements of the Sarbanes-Oxley Act.

4. Describe the COSO framework.

5. Define the "control environment" and the means by which ethics and culture can impact that environment.

6. Discuss the legal obligations of a member of a board of directors.

7. Explain the ethical obligations of a member of a board of directors.

8. Highlight conflicts of interest in financial markets and discuss the ways in which they may be alleviated.

9. Describe conflicts of interest in governance created by excessive executive compensation.

10. Define insider trading and evaluate its potential for unethical behavior.

Introduction

As described earlier, the first edition of this textbook was written in 2006, soon after a wave of major corporate scandals had shaken the financial world. Recall those companies involved in the ethical scandals during the early years of this century: Enron, WorldCom, Tyco, Rite Aid, Sunbeam, Waste Management, Health-South, Global Crossing, Arthur Andersen, Ernst & Young, KPMG, J.P. Morgan, Merrill Lynch, Morgan Stanley, Citigroup, Salomon Smith Barney, Marsh & McLennan, Credit Suisse First Boston, and even the New York Stock Exchange itself. At the center of these scandals were fundamental questions of corporate governance and responsibility. Significant cases of financial fraud, mismanagement, criminality, and deceit were not only tolerated, but in some cases were endorsed by those people in the highest levels of corporate governance who should have been standing guard against such unethical and illegal behavior.

Sadly, the very same issues are as much alive today as they were several years ago. Consider the rash of problems associated with the financial meltdown in 2007–2008 and the problems faced by such companies as AIG, Countrywide, Lehman Brothers, Merrill Lynch, and Bear Stearns, and of the financier Bernard Madoff. More recent ethical scandals, many described in this latest edition, have been alleged against such corporations as Volkswagen, Goldman Sachs, Barclays Bank, Walmart, HSBC, Mitsubishi Motors, UBS, SNC Lavalin, and Wells Fargo. Once again, we have witnessed financial and ethical malfeasance of historic proportions and the inability of internal and external governance structures to prevent it.

corporate governance
The structure by which corporations are managed, directed, and controlled toward the objectives of fairness, accountability, and transparency. The structure generally will determine the relationship between the board of directors, the shareholders or owners of the firm, and the firm's executives or management.

At the heart of many of the biggest ethical and business failures of the past decade were aspects of financial and accounting misconduct, ranging from manipulating special-purpose entities to defraud lenders, to cooking the books, to instituting questionable tax dodges, to allowing investment decisions to warp the objectivity of investment research and advice, to Ponzi schemes, to insider trading, to excessive pay for executives, to dicey investments in subprime mortgages and hedge funds, to risky credit default swaps, to fraudulent reporting of loan rates. Ethics in the governance and financial arenas has been perhaps the most visible issue in business ethics during the first decades of the new millennium. Accounting and investment firms that were once looked upon as the guardians of integrity in financial dealings have now been exposed as corrupt violators of the fiduciary responsibilities entrusted to them by their stakeholders.

Many analysts contend that this corruption is evidence of a complete failure in **corporate governance** structures. As we reflect on the ethical corruption and financial failures of the past decade, some fundamental questions should be asked. What happened to the internal governance structures within these firms that should have prevented these disasters? In particular, why did the boards, auditors, accountants, lawyers, and other professionals fail to fulfill their professional, legal, and ethical duties? Could better governance and oversight have prevented these ethical disgraces? Going forward, can we rely on internal governance controls to provide effective oversight, or are more effective external controls and government regulation needed?

Professional Duties and Conflicts of Interest

Enron Corporation
An energy company based in Houston, Texas, that *Fortune* magazine named America's most innovative company for six consecutive years before it was discovered to have been involved in one of the largest instances of accounting fraud in world history. In 2001, with over 21,000 employees, it filed the largest bankruptcy in U.S. history and disclosed a scandal that resulted in the loss of millions of dollars, thousands of jobs, the downfall of Big Five accounting firm Arthur Andersen LLP, at least one suicide, and several trials and convictions, among other consequences. Enron remains in business today as it continues to liquidate its assets.

OBJECTIVE

The watershed event that brought the ethics of finance to prominence at the beginning of the 21st century was the collapse of **Enron Corporation** and of its accounting firm Arthur Andersen, one of the largest accounting firms in the world. The Enron case "has wreaked more havoc on the accounting industry than any other case in U.S. history,"[3] including the demise of Arthur Andersen. Of course, ethical responsibilities of accountants were not unheard of prior to Enron, but the events that led to Enron's demise brought into focus the necessity of the independence of auditors and the responsibilities of accountants like never before.

Accounting is one of several professions that serve very important functions within the economic system itself. Remember that even a staunch defender of free-market economics such as Milton Friedman believes that markets can function effectively and efficiently only when certain rule-based conditions are met. It is universally recognized that markets must function within the law and they must be free from fraud and deception. The LIBOR rate scandal described in the Decision Point "LIBOR Cheating" is a case of how fraud can undermine the integrity of an entire financial system. Some argue that only government regulation can ensure that these rules will be followed. Others argue that enforcement of these rules is the responsibility of important internal controls that exist within market-based economic systems. Several important categories of business professionals—for example, lawyers, auditors, accountants, and financial analysts—function in just this way. Just as the game of baseball requires umpires to act with integrity and fairness, business and economic markets require these professionals to operate in a similar manner by enforcing the rules and attesting to the fundamental fairness of the system.

These professions can be thought of as **gatekeepers** or "watchdogs" in that their role is to ensure that those who enter into the marketplace are playing by the rules and conforming to the very conditions that ensure the market functions as it is supposed to function. Recall from Chapter 3 the importance of role identities in determining ethical duties of professionals. These roles provide a source for rules from which we can determine how professionals ought to act. In entering into a profession, we accept responsibilities based on our roles.

These professions can also be understood as intermediaries, acting between the various parties in the market, and they are bound to ethical duties in this role as well. All the participants in the market, especially investors, boards, management,

On June 27, 2012, as part of a U.S. Department of Justice investigation, Barclays Bank admitted to manipulating and reporting fraudulent interest rates used in international financial markets. Barclays, a multinational financial services and banking firm headquartered in London, was fined more than $450 million (U.S.) by regulators in both the United Kingdom and the United States. Within a week, Marcus Agius, board chair; Bob Diamond, chief executive officer; and Jerry del Missier, chief operating officer, all resigned.

Evidence showed that Barclays had regularly manipulated the LIBOR (London Inter-Bank Offered Rate) interest rate since at least 2005 in order both to profit from large trades and to falsely portray the bank as financially stronger than it was.

The LIBOR is the rate at which major London banks report that they are able to borrow. This rate then serves as the benchmark at which interest rates are set for countless other loans, ranging from credit cards to mortgages and interbank loans. It also acts as a measure of market confidence in the bank; if a bank must pay a higher rate than others to borrow, then markets must have less confidence in the institution's financial strength.

The LIBOR is established in a surprisingly simple manner. Each morning at 11 A.M. London time, members of the British Bankers Association (BBA) report to the financial reporting firm of Thomson Reuters the rates they would expect to pay for loans from other banks. Discarding the highest and lowest quartiles, Thomson Reuters then calculates a daily average, which becomes the daily LIBOR benchmark. Within an hour, Thomson Reuters publicizes this average worldwide, along with all of the individual rates reported to the firm. This benchmark is then used to settle short-term interest rates as well as futures and options contracts. By one estimate, the LIBOR is used to set interest rates for global financial transactions worth more than $500 trillion. The individual rates also provide an indirect measure of the financial health of each reporting institution: the lower their rates, the stronger their financial position.

Evidence shows that as early as 2007, before the major financial collapse of Lehman Brothers and the economic meltdown that followed, regulators in both the United States and the United Kingdom were aware of allegations that Barclays was underreporting its rates. In the early days of the 2008 financial collapse, the *Wall Street Journal* published a series of articles that questioned the integrity of LIBOR reporting and suggested that banks were intentionally misreporting rates to strengthen public perception of their financial health. Timothy Geithner, U.S. secretary of treasury under President Obama, acknowledged that in 2008, when he was chair of the New York Federal Reserve Bank, he recommended that British regulators change the process for setting the LIBOR. In testimony to the U.S. Congress in July 2012, Geithner said, "We were aware [in 2008] of the risks that the way this was designed created not just the incentive to underreport, but also the opportunity to underreport."[*]

Internal documents and emails, acknowledged by Barclays during the investigation, showed that traders, compliance officers, and senior management were aware of and approved the underreporting. An email sent from a Barclays employee to his supervisor in 2007 said: "My worry is that we are being seen to be contributing patently false rates. We are therefore being dishonest by definition and are at risk of damaging our reputation in the market and with the regulators. Can we discuss urgently please?"[†]

1. What ethical issues are involved in this case?
2. Who are the stakeholders in this case? Who was hurt by rate fixing?
3. What responsibilities did senior executives at Barclays have to prevent fraud in circumstances that, in Timothy Geithner's words, created both the incentive and opportunity for fraud?
4. What sort of internal controls might the Barclays board of directors have instituted to prevent such fraud?

*Timothy Geithner, testimony before U.S. Congress, July 2012.
†Brandon Garrett, *Too Big to Jail* (Cambridge, MA: Harvard University Press, 2014).

Sources: Sources for this Decision Point, as well as detailed summaries of the ongoing LIBOR scandal, can be found at the websites for the *Financial Times,* www.ft.com/indepth/libor-scandal (accessed December 27, 2012); and the BBC, www.bbc.co.uk/news/business-18671255 (accessed December 27, 2012).

gatekeepers

Some professions, such as accountant, that act as "watchdogs" in that their role is to ensure that those who participate in the marketplace are playing by the rules and conforming to the conditions that ensure the market functions as it is supposed to function.

conflict of interest

A conflict of interest exists where a person holds a position of trust that requires that she or he exercise judgment on behalf of others, but where her or his personal interests and/or obligations conflict with the proper exercise of that judgment.

OBJECTIVE

and bankers, rely on these gatekeepers. Auditors verify a company's financial statements so that investors' decisions are free from fraud and deception. Analysts evaluate a company's financial prospects or creditworthiness so that banks and investors can make informed decisions. Attorneys ensure that decisions and transactions conform to the law. As suggested by the VW case in the Opening Decision Point, engineers can also have a role to ensure products are safe and legal. Indeed, even boards of directors can be understood in this way. Boards function as intermediaries between a company's stockholders and its executives and should guarantee that executives act on behalf of the stockholders' interests.

The most basic ethical issue facing professional gatekeepers and intermediaries in business contexts involves conflicts of interest. A **conflict of interest** exists where a person holds a position of trust that requires that she or he exercise judgment on behalf of others, but where her or his personal interests and/or obligations conflict with the proper exercise of that judgment. For instance, a friend knows that you are heading to a flea market and asks if you would keep your eyes open for any beautiful quilts you might see. She asks you to purchase one for her if you see a "great buy." You are going to the flea market to buy your mother a birthday present. You happen to see a beautiful quilt at a fabulous price, the only one at the market. In fact, your mother would adore the quilt. You find yourself in a conflict of interest—your friend trusted you to search the flea market on her behalf. Your personal interests are now in conflict with the duty you agreed to accept on behalf of your friend.

Conflicts of interest can also arise when a person's ethical obligations in her or his professional duties clash with personal interests. Thus, for example, in the most egregious case, a financial planner who accepts kickbacks from a brokerage firm to steer clients into certain investments fails in her or his professional responsibility by putting personal financial interests ahead of client interest. Such professionals

According to many observers, there is a deep problem at the heart of modern capitalist economies. Modern economies rely on individuals, legally known as "agents," who work for the best interests of others, the "principals." For the system to work, agents must be loyal representatives of their principal's interests, even in those situations when their own personal interest is at stake. For example, a member of a board of directors may act as an agent for the stockholders, executives act as agents for the boards, and attorneys and accountants act as agents for their clients. This agent–principal model assumes that individuals *can* put their own interests on hold and be sufficiently motivated to act on behalf of another. But this would seem to run counter to a view of human nature that is assumed by much of modern economic theory: Individuals are self-interested—thus, the "agency problem." How can we trust self-interested individuals to act for the well-being of others in cases where to do so their own self-interest must be sacrificed?

Many of the ethical failures described in this chapter can be seen as examples of the agency problem. These are precisely those situations where boards have failed to protect the interests of stockholders; executives have failed to serve their boards; and accountants, lawyers, and financial analysts have failed to act on behalf of their clients.

Economics and management theorists have offered several solutions to the agency problem. Some argue that the best solution is to create incentives that connect the agent's self-interest with the self-interest of the principal. Linking executive compensation to performance by making bonuses contingent on stock price means that an executive gains only when stockholders gain. Placing representatives of major stockholders on corporate boards, as happens at Volkswagen, is another approach to align corporate interests with stockholder interests.

Another approach is to create structures and institutions that restrict an agent's actions. Strict legal constraints would be the most obvious version of this approach. Agents have specific legal duties of loyalty, confidentiality, and obedience and face criminal punishments if they fail to uphold those duties. Professional or corporate codes of conduct and other forms of self-regulation are also versions of this approach.

These two most common answers share a fundamental feature: The agency problem can be solved by connecting motivation to act on the principal's behalf back to the agent's own self-interest. In the first case, motivation is in the form of the "carrot," and the agent benefits by serving the principal; in the second case, motivation is in the form of the "stick," and the agent suffers if she fails to serve her principal.

A third answer to the agency problem denies that there truly is a problem by denying that self-interest dominates human motivation. This third approach points out that, in fact, humans regularly act from loyalty, trust, and altruism. Human relationships are built on trust and reliability; and these motivations are just as basic, just as common, as self-interest. Thus, this approach would encourage corporations to look to moral character and corporate culture to develop policies and practices that reinforce, shape, and condition people to want to do the right thing.

1. Can you think of examples in your own experience where someone is required to work as an agent for another, or when you were involved as an agent? How is the agent motivated in this particular case?
2. If you were asked to design a policy that would provide a solution to the agency problem in the company for which you work, where would you begin?
3. Review the section on virtue ethics in Chapter 3 and explain how the agency problem would be viewed from that perspective.
4. Under what circumstances, or for what kinds of tasks, do you think agency problems are most likely to be a challenge?

fiduciary duties
A legal duty, grounded in trust, to act on behalf of or in the interests of another.

are said to have **fiduciary duties**—a professional and ethical obligation—to their clients, duties rooted in trust that override their own personal interests. (See the Decision Point "How to Solve the 'Agency Problem.'")

Unfortunately, and awkwardly, many of these professional intermediaries are paid by the businesses over which they keep watch, and perhaps are also employed by yet another business. For example, David Duncan was the principal accounting professional employed by Arthur Andersen and assigned to work at Enron. As the Arthur Andersen case so clearly demonstrated, this situation can create real conflicts between a professional's responsibility and his or her financial interests. Certified *public* accountants (CPAs) have a professional responsibility to the public. But they work for clients whose financial interests are not always served by full, accurate, and independent disclosure of financial information. Even more dangerously, they work daily with and are hired by a management team that itself might have interests that conflict with the interests of the firm represented by the board of directors. Thus, real and complex conflicts can exist between professional duties and a professional's self-interest. We will revisit conflicts in the accounting profession later in the chapter. (See Figure 10.1 for an overview of potential conflicts of interest for CPAs.)

In one sense, the ethical issues regarding such professional responsibilities are clear. Because professional gatekeeper duties are necessary conditions for the fair and effective functioning of economic markets, they should trump other responsibilities to one's employer. David Duncan's professional responsibilities as an auditor should have overridden his role as an Andersen employee in large part because he was hired *as* an auditor. But knowing one's duties and fulfilling those duties are two separate issues.

Agency responsibilities generate many ethical challenges. If we recognize that the gatekeeper function is necessary for the very functioning of economic markets, and if we also recognize that self-interest can make it difficult for individuals to fulfill their gatekeeper duties, then society has a responsibility to create institutions and structures that will minimize these conflicts. For example, as long as auditors are paid by the clients on whom they are supposed to report, there will always be a conflict of interest between their duties as auditors and their personal financial

FIGURE 10.1

Conflicts of Interest in Public CPA Activity

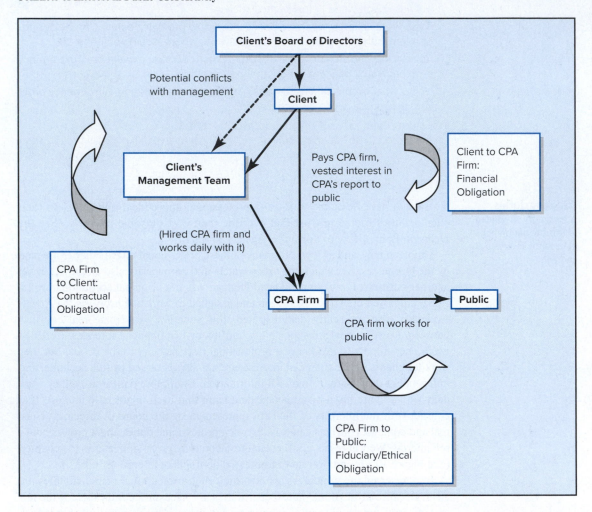

interests. This conflict is a good reason to make structural changes in how public accounting operates. Perhaps boards rather than management ought to hire and work with auditors because the auditors are more likely reporting on the management activities rather than those of the board. Perhaps public accounting somehow ought to be paid by public fees. Perhaps legal protection or sanctions ought to be created to shield professionals from conflicts of interests. These changes would remove both the apparent and the actual conflicts of interest created by the multiple roles—and therefore multiple responsibilities—of these professionals. From the perspective of social ethics, certain structural changes would be an appropriate response to the accounting scandals of recent years. (See Decision Point "What to Do When Faced with Conflict of Interest?")

Conflicts of interest are quite common in modern commerce, and in life more generally, due to the large number of situations in which individuals need to put their trust in the advice or judgment of other people. We trust our doctors to take care of us when we are ill, we trust our lawyers to give us good legal advice, and we trust our investment advisor to give us good advice regarding investments. In each case, we would rightly worry if we found that the professional we are relying on had some interest, such as a financial or personal interest, in the issue at hand. We expect them to focus on our interests, not theirs.

It is important to see that conflict of interest is not an accusation—it is a *situation*. You can easily find yourself in a conflict of interest, through no fault of your own. Sometimes conflicts of interest are impossible to avoid entirely. The real question, from an ethical point of view, is how you *handle* the situation.

One solution that is generally *not* appropriate is simply to "try hard" to act in an unbiased way. That is, individual integrity is not a solution. Many biases are unconscious, and, when in a conflict of interest, even a person of the highest integrity has reason to mistrust his or her own judgment.

Here are the standard steps that most experts recommend, when you find yourself in a conflict of interest:

- Notify the relevant stakeholders. (If you're on a hiring committee, for example, and you notice your sister's CV in the pile, you should speak up immediately to notify the rest of the committee that you are in a conflict of interest.)
- If possible, remove yourself from the decision making. (In the hiring example, you should excuse yourself from the committee entirely, if possible. If that's impossible—perhaps you have special expertise that the committee is relying on—then you should at least leave the room while your sister's CV is being considered and ranked. But that is a distant second best!)

Possibly the most devastating aspect of the banking industry meltdown of the first decade of this century was the resulting deterioration of trust that the public has in the market and in corporate America. Decision makers in large investment banks and other financial institutions ignored their fiduciary duties to shareholders, employees, and the public in favor of personal gain, a direct conflict of interest leading to extraordinary personal ruin and the demise of some of the largest investment banks in the world, and contributing to a major economic crisis that harms millions. The fact is that major federal legislation enacted after Enron to provide regulatory checks on such behavior failed to prevent it from happening.

Critics contend that government regulatory rules alone will not rid society of the problems that led to this crisis. (To explore further how government might have failed in its regulatory role, see the Decision Point "Crony Capitalism: Is Government–Business Partnership the Answer?") Instead, they argue, extraordinary executive compensation and conflicts of interest within the accounting and financial industries have created an environment where the watchdogs have little ability to

Crony capitalism refers to situations in which economic winners and losers are determined by collusion between business and government officials. In contrast, the standard democratic understanding of business and government is that the role of government is to ensure that the public interest is served by an economic system in which participants are motivated by self-interest. On this standard model, the political power of government serves as a counterbalance to the economic power of business and industry. Government acts as a neutral arbitrator and judge to ensure that every economic competitor plays by the rules and conflicts are resolved fairly.

Crony capitalism corrupts this system when government officials conspire with their business partners, or "cronies," to use governmental authority to provide them with illegitimate and unearned benefits. The result is a rigged system in which political power and economic power are combined rather than balanced, and governmental authority serves the private rather than public interests.

Crony capitalism can occur on many levels, ranging from systemic to individual corruption. On a systemic level, entire countries have been characterized by cronyism. For example, a ruling political party or regime might grant government contracts or licenses only to members of their own party, religion, or region, as regularly happens in nondemocratic oligarchies and plutocracies. Cronyism can be less systemic but still widespread as when particular industries or firms gain favored status through campaign donations and intensive lobbying. Cronyism can even exist on the individual level, as when a government official grants a friend a favored status in attaining some governmental benefit.

In contemporary settings critics alleged many causes of crony capitalism. Critics from the left assert that cronyism is an inevitable result of the concentration of power in the hands of a wealthy minority. Some critics claim that the U.S. Supreme Court's 2010 decision in the *Citizens United* case,* which ruled that political spending by corporations was a protected form of free speech under the First Amendment, institutionalized crony capitalism within the political process by allowing undue corporate influence in politics.

Critics from the political right assert that crony capitalism is an inevitable corruption by a growing governmental involvement in the market. From this perspective, it is a mistake to assume that government regulators can escape their own personal interests to make decisions in the public interest. (See again the Decision Point "How to Solve the 'Agency Problem'" for a discussion of a similar issue.) A similar situation occurs in cases of "regulatory capture," alleged to be a common situation in the close working relationship between business and government regulators. By working so closely with the firms that are charged with regulating, and inevitably relying on those firms for much of the information required to do their job, government regulators get co-opted, or "captured," by the regulated. The result is that regulators become more of an advocate for, rather than a check upon, industry.

Both sides agree that a "revolving door" between government work and private enterprise results in too many former government officials entering private industry after leaving office and using their former political influence on behalf of their new employers. Conversely, to fill government positions, administrations recruit candidates from the very industries that they will oversee. Critics on both the left and the right agree that crony capitalism results in unfair market disadvantages for those firms and industries that do business honestly without relying on help from friends in government.

An ethical critique of crony capitalism appeals to some of the most basic values of democratic capitalism. Equal rights are denied when some firms receive unfair advantages. The public interest is corrupted for private gain. The utilitarian and efficiency goals of the market vanish when winners and losers result from manipulated markets. Government authority loses legitimacy and gets replaced by raw power and influence.

The reality of crony capitalism leaves those firms and industries that do play by the rules in a dilemma. On one hand, if they continue to play by the rules as a matter of ethical integrity, they risk losing in the marketplace because of undeserved disadvantages. On the other hand, the cost of succeeding in a corrupt system is to compromise your integrity.

Citizens United v. FEC, 558 U.S. 310 (2010).

Sarbanes-Oxley Act (Public Accounting Reform and Investor Protection Act of 2002)

Implemented on July 30, 2002, and administered by the Securities and Exchange Commission to regulate financial reporting and auditing of publicly traded companies in the United States. SOX or SarbOx (popular shorthands for the act) was enacted very shortly following and directly in response to the Enron scandals of 2001. One of the greatest areas of consternation and debate

prevent harm. Executive compensation packages based on stock options create huge incentives to artificially inflate stock value. Changes within the accounting industry stemming from the consolidation of major firms and avid "cross-selling" of services such as consulting and auditing within single firms have virtually institutionalized conflicts of interest.

Answers to these inherent challenges are not easy to identify. Imagine that an executive is paid based on how much she or he impacts the share price and will be fired by the Board if that impact is not significantly positive. A large boost in share price—even for the short term—serves as an effective defense against hostile takeovers and boosts a firm's ability to access financing for external expansion. In addition, with stock options as a major component of executive compensation structures, a higher share price is an extremely compelling quest to those in leadership roles. That same executive, however, has a fiduciary duty to do what is best for the stakeholders in the long term, an obligation that is often at odds with that executive's personal interests. This is not the best environment for responsible, or even for basically decent, decision making.

The Sarbanes-Oxley Act of 2002

that has emerged surrounding SOX involves the high cost of compliance and the challenging burden therefore placed on smaller firms. Some contend that SOX was the most significant change to the corporate landscape to occur in the second half of the 20th century.

The string of corporate scandals since the beginning of the millennium took its toll on investor confidence. Because reliance on corporate boards to police themselves did not seem to be working, the U.S. Congress passed the Public Accounting Reform and Investor Protection Act of 2002, commonly known as the **Sarbanes-Oxley Act,** which is enforced by the Securities and Exchange Commission (SEC). The act applies to more than 15,000 publicly held companies in the United States and some foreign issuers. (To consider how the European Union addressed similar issues, see the Reality Check "Global Consistencies: The European Union 8th Directive.") In addition, a number of states have enacted

Reality Check   *Global Consistencies: The European Union 8th Directive*

The **European Union 8th Directive,** effective in 2005 (though member states had two years to integrate it into law), covers many of the same issues as Sarbanes-Oxley but applies these requirements and restrictions to companies traded on European Union exchanges. The directive mandates external quality assurances through audit committee requirements and greater auditing transparency.

The directive also provides for cooperation with the regulators in other countries, closing a gap that previously existed. However, contrary to Sarbanes-Oxley, the directive does not contain a whistle-blower protection section, does not require similar reporting to shareholders, and has less detailed requirements compared to Sarbanes-Oxley's section 404.

OBJECTIVE

European Union 8th Directive

Covers many of the same issues as Sarbanes-Oxley but applies these requirements and restrictions to companies traded on European Union exchanges. The updates to the directive in 2005 clarified required duties, independence, and ethics of statutory auditors and called for public oversight of the accounting profession and external quality assurance of both audit and financial reporting processes. In addition, the directive strives to improve cooperation between EU oversight bodies and provides for effective and balanced international regulatory cooperation with oversight bodies outside the EU regulatory infrastructure (e.g., the U.S. Public Company Accounting Oversight Board).

legislation similar to Sarbanes-Oxley that apply to private firms, and some private for-profits and nonprofits have begun to hold themselves to Sarbanes-Oxley standards even though they are not necessarily subject to its requirements.

Sarbanes-Oxley responded to the scandals by regulating safeguards against unethical behavior. Because one cannot necessarily predict each and every lapse of judgment, no regulatory "fix" is perfect. However, the act is intended to provide protection where oversight did not previously exist. Some might argue that protection against poor judgment is not possible in the business environment, but Sarbanes-Oxley seeks instead to provide oversight in terms of direct lines of accountability and responsibility. The following provisions have the most significant impact on corporate governance and boards:

- *Section 201:* Services outside the scope of auditors (prohibits various forms of professional services that are determined to be consulting rather than auditing).
- *Section 301:* Public company audit committees (requires independence), mandating majority of independents on any board (and all on audit committee) and total absence of current or prior business relationships.
- *Section 307:* Rules of professional responsibility for attorneys (requires lawyers to report concerns of wrongdoing if not addressed).
- *Section 404:* Management assessment of *internal controls* (requires that management file an internal control report with its annual report each year in order to delineate how management has established and maintained effective internal controls over financial reporting).
- *Section 406:* Codes of ethics for senior financial officers (required).
- *Section 407:* Disclosure of audit committee financial expert (requires that they actually have an expert).[4]

Sarbanes-Oxley includes requirements for certification of the documents by officers. When a firm's executives and auditors are required to literally *sign off* on these statements, certifying their veracity, fairness, and completeness, they are more likely to personally ensure their truth.

The Internal Control Environment

internal control
A process, effected by an entity's board of directors, management, and other personnel, designed to provide reasonable assurance regarding the achievement of objectives in the following categories: effectiveness and efficiency of operations, reliability of financial reporting, and compliance with applicable laws and regulations.

Committee of Sponsoring Organizations (COSO)
COSO is a voluntary collaboration designed to improve financial reporting through a combination of controls and governance standards called the Internal Control–Integrated Framework. It was established in 1985 by five of the major professional accounting and finance associations originally to study fraudulent financial reporting and later developed standards for publicly held companies. It has become one of the most broadly accepted audit systems for internal controls.

Sarbanes-Oxley and the European Union 8th Directive are external mechanisms that seek to ensure ethical corporate governance by establishing regulations enforced by external bodies and laws. **Internal control** mechanisms are processes established internally, by boards and management, to ensure compliance with financial reporting laws and regulations. One way that many firms ensure appropriate controls within the organization is to utilize a framework advocated by the **Committee of Sponsoring Organizations (COSO).** COSO is a voluntary collaboration of professional audit and accounting organizations that seeks to improve financial reporting through a combination of controls and governance standards called the Internal Control–Integrated Framework. It was established in 1985 by five of the major professional accounting and finance associations, originally to study fraudulent financial reporting and later to develop standards for publicly held companies. COSO describes "control" as encompassing "those elements of an organization that, taken together, support people in the achievement of the organization's objectives."[5] The elements that comprise the control structure will be familiar as they are also the essential elements of culture discussed in Chapter 4. They include:

- *Control environment*–the tone or culture of a firm: "the control environment sets the tone of an organization, influencing the control consciousness of its people."
- *Risk assessment*–risks that may hinder the achievement of corporate objectives.
- *Control activities*–policies and procedures that support the control environment.
- *Information and communications*–directed at supporting the control environment through fair and truthful transmission of information.
- *Ongoing monitoring*–to provide assessment capabilities and to uncover vulnerabilities.

Control environment refers to cultural issues such as integrity, ethical values, competence, philosophy, and operating style. Many of these terms should be reminiscent of issues addressed in Chapter 4 during our discussion of corporate culture. COSO is one of the first efforts to address corporate culture in a quasi-regulatory framework in recognition of its significant impact on the satisfaction of organizational objectives. Control environment can also refer to more concrete elements (that can better be addressed in an audit) such as the division of authority, reporting structures, roles and responsibilities, the presence of a code of conduct, and a reporting structure. It will be helpful to review the Opening Decision Point on VW as you consider the COSO definition.

The COSO standards for internal controls moved audit, compliance, and governance from a *numbers orientation* to concern for the *organizational environment*. The discussion of corporate culture in Chapter 4 reminds us that both internal

control environment
One of the five elements that comprise the control structure, similar to the culture of an organization, and support people in the achievement of the organization's objectives. The control environment "sets the tone of an organization, influencing the control consciousness of its people."

factors such as the COSO controls and external factors such as the Sarbanes-Oxley requirements must be supported by a culture of accountability. In fact, these shifts impact not only executives and boards; internal audit and compliance professionals also are becoming more accountable for financial stewardship, resulting in greater transparency, greater accountability, and a greater emphasis on effort to prevent misconduct. All the controls one could implement have little value if there is no unified corporate culture to support it or mission to guide it. It is reasonable to think that the "rigid hierarchy" of authoritarian management described at VW prevented any internal efforts from preventing the fraud.

In 2004, COSO developed a new system, Enterprise Risk Management–Integrated Framework, to serve as a framework for management to evaluate and improve their firms' prevention, detection, and management of risk. This system expands on the prior framework in that it intentionally includes "objective setting" as one of its interrelated components, recognizing that both the culture and the propensity toward risk are determined by the firm's overarching mission and objectives. Enterprise risk management, therefore, assists an organization or its governing body in resolving ethical dilemmas based on the firm's mission, its culture, and its appetite and tolerance for risk.

Going beyond the Law: Being an Ethical Board Member

duty of care
Involves the exercise of reasonable care by a board member to ensure that the corporate executives with whom she or he works carry out their management responsibilities and comply with the law in the best interests of the corporation.

As suggested previously, the corporate failures of recent years would seem to suggest a failure on the part of corporate boards, as well as a failure of government to impose high expectations of accountability on boards of directors. After all, it is the board's fiduciary duty to guard the best interests of the firm itself. However, in many cases, boards and executives operated well within the law. For instance, it is legal for boards to vote to permit an exception to a firm's conflicts of interest policy, as happened in the Enron case. These actions may not necessarily have been ethical or in the best interests of stakeholders, but they were legal nonetheless. The law offers some guidance on minimum standards for board member behavior, *but is the law enough?*

Legal Duties of Board Members

OBJECTIVE

U.S. law imposes three clear duties on board members: the duties of care, good faith, and loyalty. The **duty of care** involves the exercise of reasonable care by a board member to ensure that the corporate executives with whom she or he works carry out their management responsibilities and comply with the law in the best interests of the corporation. Directors are permitted to rely on information and opinions only if they are prepared or presented by corporate officers, employees, a board committee, or other professionals the director believes to be reliable and competent in the matters presented. Board members are also directed to use their "business judgment as prudent caretakers": The director is expected to be disinterested and reasonably informed, and to rationally believe the decisions made are in the firm's best interest. The bottom line is that a director does not need to be an expert or actually run the company!

duty of good faith
Requires obedience, compelling board members to be faithful to the organization's mission. In other words, they are not permitted to act in a way that is inconsistent with the central goals of the organization.

duty of loyalty
Requires faithfulness; a board member must give undivided allegiance when making decisions affecting the organization. This means that conflicts of interest are always to be resolved in favor of the corporation.

The **duty of good faith** is one of obedience, which requires board members to be faithful to the organization's mission. In other words, they are not permitted to act in a way that is inconsistent with the central goals of the organization. Their decisions must always be in line with organizational purposes and direction, strive toward corporate objectives, and avoid taking the organization in any other direction.

The **duty of loyalty** requires faithfulness; a board member must give undivided allegiance when making decisions affecting the organization. This means that conflicts of interest are always to be resolved in favor of the corporation. A board member may never use information obtained through her or his position as a board member for personal gain, but instead must act in the best interests of the organization.

Board member conflicts of interest present issues of significant challenges, however, precisely because of the alignment of their personal interests with those of the corporation. Don't board members usually have *some* financial interest in the future of the firm, even if it is only through their position and reputation as a board member? Consider whether a board member should own stock. If the board member does own stock, then her or his interests may be closely aligned with other stockholders, removing a possible conflict there. Once again, the VW case shows a board comprised of all major stockholders. However, if the board member does not hold stock, perhaps he or she is actually better positioned to consider the long-term interests of the firm, rather than focusing on the large short-term benefits that could occur as the result of a board decision. In the end, a healthy board balance is usually sought.

The Federal Sentencing Guidelines (FSG), promulgated by the U.S. Sentencing Commission and (since a 2005 Supreme Court decision) discretionary in nature, do offer boards some specifics regarding ways to mitigate eventual fines and sentences in carrying out these duties by paying attention to ethics and compliance. In particular, the board must work with executives to analyze the incentives for ethical behavior by all employees. It must also be truly knowledgeable about the content and operation of the ethics program. The FSG also suggest that the board exercise "reasonable oversight" with respect to the implementation and effectiveness of the ethics/compliance program by ensuring that the program has adequate resources, appropriate level of authority, and direct access to the board. In order to assess their success, boards should evaluate their training and development materials, their governance structure and position descriptions, their individual evaluation processes, their methods for bringing individuals onto the board or removing them, and all board policies, procedures, and processes, including a code of conduct and conflicts policies. It would be an interesting exercise to imagine how the VW scandal might have evolved if Germany had something comparable to the FSG expectations.

OBJECTIVE

Beyond the Law, There Is Ethics

One question we would expect the law to answer, but that instead remains unclear, is whom the board represents. Who are its primary stakeholders, ethically speaking? By U.S. law, the board, of course, has a fiduciary duty to the stockholders.

Reality Check *The Basics*

Bill George, former chair and CEO of medical devices manufacturer Medtronic and a recognized expert on governance, contends that there are 10 basic tenets that boards should follow to ensure appropriate and ethical governance:

1. *Standards:* There should be publicly available principles of governance for the board created by the independent directors.

2. *Independence:* Boards should ensure their independence by requiring that the majority of their members be independent.

3. *Selection:* Board members should be selected based not only on their experience or the role they hold in other firms but also for their value structures.

4. *Selection, number 2:* The board's governance and nominating committees should be staffed by independent directors to ensure the continuity of independence.

5. *Executive sessions:* The independent directors should meet regularly in executive sessions to preserve the authenticity and credibility of their communications.

6. *Committees:* The board must have separate audit and finance committees that are staffed by board members with extensive expertise in these arenas.

7. *Leadership:* If the CEO and the chair of the board are one and the same, it is critical that the board select an alternative lead director as a check and balance.

8. *Compensation committee outside expert:* The board should seek external guidance on executive compensation.

9. *Board culture:* The board should not only have the opportunity but be encouraged to develop a culture including relationships where challenges are welcomed and difference can be embraced.

10. *Responsibility:* Boards should recognize their responsibility to provide oversight and to control management through appropriate governance processes.*

*William W. George, "Restoring Governance to Our Corporations," address given to the Council of Institutional Investors (September 23, 2002), www.bus.wisc.edu/update/fall02/ten_step.htm (accessed April 10, 2010).

However, many scholars, jurists, and commentators are not comfortable with this limited approach to board responsibility and instead contend that the board is the guardian of the firm's social responsibility as well. It is worth noting that the law may be different in other jurisdictions. In Canada, for instance, the Supreme Court of Canada clarified in the 2008 case of *BCE Inc.* that a director's fiduciary obligation is to the corporation itself, rather than to any particular stakeholder (including shareholders).[6] (For one perspective on a board's additional, *ethical* responsibilities, see the Reality Check "The Basics.")

Some executives may ask whether the board even has the legal right to question the ethics of its executives and others. If a board is aware of a practice that it deems to be unethical but that is completely within the realm of the law, on what basis can the board require the executive to cease the practice? The board can prohibit actions to protect the long-term sustainability of the firm. Regardless of the form of the unethical behavior, unethical acts can negatively impact stakeholders such as consumers or employees, who can, in turn, negatively impact the firm, which could eventually lead to a firm's demise. (And good governance can have the opposite effect—see the Reality Check "The Concerns of Corporate Directors.") It is in fact the board's fiduciary duty to protect the firm, and, by prohibiting unethical acts, it is doing just that.

Fortune journalists Ram Charan and Julie Schlosser[7] suggest that board members have additional responsibilities beyond the law to explore and to investigate the organizations that they represent, and they suggest that an open conversation is the best method for understanding, not just what board members know, but also what they

Reality Check *The Concerns of Corporate Directors*

Here are the top five concerns expressed by Canadian corporate directors, as drawn from research conducted by the Clarkson Centre for Business Ethics and Board Effectiveness at the University of Toronto:

Strategic Planning/Risk Management A Board's role in strategic planning is key to the long term success of a corporation. Many Directors believe that their Boards do not allocate enough time to strategy in Board meetings to ensure effective strategic planning. In addition, many Boards do not have the skills and expertise to fully understand the business/industry and drive strategy. . . .

Board Independence In order for shareholders' interests to be optimally represented by the Board of Directors, individual Directors must be able to act independently from the interests of management, and independently from the other Directors on the Board. Material relationships with management increase the potential risk that a Director will put executive interests before those of the shareholder. Optimizing Board independence helps to mitigate the effects of conflicts of interests between management and the Board and better aligns the Board's decisions with shareholder interests.

Top Executive Compensation Boards of Directors are solely responsible for the compensation of the CEO. In order to best align the interests of management and shareholders, compensation must be linked to the company's financial performance. . . . With increased scrutiny by markets and investors since 2008, many Boards are struggling to design pay packages that can attract and retain top management, while ensuring ongoing confidence among the investing public.

Top Executive Succession Planning Many Directors insist that the hiring and firing of the CEO is a Board's most important responsibility. Boards often do not have formal, ongoing plans in place for the succession of the CEO, either in normal or in unexpected circumstances. Sometimes Boards feel a lack of urgency because their current CEO is highly effective. In other cases, Boards find it culturally awkward to broach the subject of a CEO's departure. Regardless of the cause, however, Directors are experiencing increasing internal and external pressures to formalize the CEO succession process.

Board Renewal/Diversity A formal Board renewal process provides Boards with an effective tool for Boards to understand whether and when turnover is needed, as well as whether or not the current balance of skills on the Board is appropriate. . . . The primary goal of Board renewal is to maintain an effective and passionate Board. Formal processes for Board renewal are a powerful tool to enable the achievement of this goal. Boards are facing increased scrutiny from shareholders/stakeholders to increase gender and ethnic diversity. Directors have expressed that increased Board diversity can increase the effectiveness of Board decisions. However, Boards struggle to increase gender and ethnic diversity when seeking the best available candidate to fill the Board seat.

Source: Clarkson Centre for Business Ethics and Board Effectiveness, "Top 5 Director Concerns of Corporate Directors" (August 21, 2012), http://clarksoncentre.wordpress.com/2012/08/21/top-5-concerns-of-corporate-directors/. Used with permission.

do not know. They suggest that board members often ignore even the most basic questions such as how the firm actually makes its money and whether customers and clients truly do pay for products and services. That is rather basic, but the truth is that the financial flow can explain a lot about what moves the firm. Board members should also be critical in their inquiries about corporate vulnerabilities—what could drag the firm down and what could competitors do to help it along that path? Ensuring that information about vulnerabilities is constantly and consistently transmitted to the executives and the board creates effective prevention. Board members need to understand where the company is heading and whether it is realistic that it will get there. This is less likely if it is not living within its means or if it is paying out too much of its sustainable growth dollars to its chief executives in compensation.

Failing in any of these areas creates pressures on the firm and on the board to take up the slack, to manage problems that do not have to exist, to be forced to make decisions that might not have had to be made if only the information systems were working as they should. It is the board members' ultimate duty to provide oversight, which is impossible without knowing the answers to the preceding questions.

Conflicts of Interest in Accounting and the Financial Markets

OBJECTIVE

Conflicts of interest, while common in many situations among both directors and officers as discussed previously, also extend beyond the board room and executive suite throughout the financial arena. In fact, trust and the structures that promote it are integral issues for all involved in the finance industry. After all, what more can an auditor, an accountant, or an analyst offer than her or his integrity and trustworthiness? There is no real, tangible product to sell, nor is there the ability to "try before you buy." Therefore, treating clients fairly and building a reputation for fair dealing may be a finance professional's greatest assets. Conflicts—real or perceived—can erode trust and often exist as a result of varying interests of stakeholders. As discussed earlier in this chapter, public accountants are accountable to their stakeholders—the stockholders and investment communities who rely on their reports—and therefore should always serve in the role of independent contractor to the firms whom they audit. In that regard, companies would love to be able to direct what that outside accountant says because people believe the "independent" nature of the audit. On the other hand, if accountants were merely rubber stamps for the word of the corporation's senior executives, they would no longer be believed or considered "independent."

Although technical definitions vary, accounting is often defined as "the process by which any business keeps track of its financial activities by recording its debits and credits and balancing its accounts." Accounting offers us a system of rules and principles that govern the format and content of financial statements. Accounting, by its very nature, is a system of principles applied to present the financial position of a business and the results of its operations and cash flows. It is hoped that adherence to these principles will result in fair and accurate reporting of this information in a format that can readily be interpreted by others. Now, would you consider an accountant to be a watchdog or a bloodhound? Does an accountant stand guard or instead seek out problematic reporting? The answer to this question may depend on whether the accountant is employed internally by a firm or works as outside counsel.

Linking public accounting activities to the activities of investment banks and securities analysts creates tremendous conflicts between one component's duty to audit and certify information with the other's responsibility to provide guidance on future prospects of an investment. Perhaps the leading example of the unethical effects of conflicts of interest is manifested in the shocking fact that ten of the top investment firms in the country had to pay fines in 2005 for actions that involved mishandling conflicts of interest between research and investment banking.

Companies that engaged in investment banking pressured their research analysts to give high ratings to companies whose stocks they were issuing, whether those ratings were deserved or not.

The ethical issues and potential for conflicts surrounding accounting practices go far beyond merely combining services. They may include underreporting income, falsifying documents, allowing or taking questionable deductions, illegally evading income taxes, and engaging in fraud. In order to prevent accountants from being put in these types of conflicts, the American Institute of Certified Public Accountants (AICPA) publishes professional rules, as do the accounting bodies of other countries. In addition, accounting practices are governed by generally accepted accounting principles (GAAP) established by the Financial Accounting Standards Board that stipulate the methods by which accountants gather and report information. Accountants are also governed by the AICPA's Code of Professional Conduct. The code relies on the judgment of accounting professionals in carrying out their duties rather than stipulating specific rules.

But can these standards keep pace with readily changing accounting and financing activities in newly emerging firms such as what occurred with the evolution of the dot.coms at the turn of the century and as occurred in investment banks in recent years? In complex cases such as these, it can take regulators, legislature, and courts years to catch up with the changing practices in business. In any case, would regulatory standards be enough? The answers to ethical dilemmas are not always so easily found within the rules and regulations governing the industry. Scholar Kevin Bahr identifies a number of causes for conflicts in the financial markets that may or may not be resolved through simple rule-making:

1. *The financial relationship between public accounting firms and their audit clients:* Because audits are paid for by audited clients, there is an inherent conflict found simply in that financial arrangement.

2. *Conflicts between services offered by public accounting firms:* Because many public accounting firms offer consulting services to their clients, there are conflicts in the independence of the firm's opinions and incentives to generate additional consulting fees.

3. *The lack of independence and expertise of audit committees.*

4. *Self-regulation of the accounting profession:* Because the accounting industry has historically self-regulated, oversight has been lax, if any.

5. *Lack of shareholder activism:* Given the diversity of ownership in the market based on individual investors, collective efforts to manage and oversee the board are practically nonexistent.

6. *Short-term executive greed versus long-term shareholder wealth:* Executive compensation packages do not create appropriate incentive systems for ethical executive and board decision making. "Enron paid about $681 million in cash and stock to its 140 senior managers, including at least $67.4 million to former chairman and chief executive Kenneth Lay, in the year prior to December 2, 2001, when the company filed for bankruptcy. Not bad for a company that saw

its stock decline from $80 in January of 2001 to less that $1 when filing for bankruptcy."

7. *Executive compensation schemes:* Stock options and their accounting treatment remain an issue for the accounting profession and the investment community because, though meant to be an incentive to management and certainly a form of compensation, they are not treated as an expense on the income statement. They also tend to place the incentives, again, on short-term growth rather than long-term sustainability.

8. *Compensation schemes for security analysts:* Investment banking analysts have an interest in sales; this is how they generate the commissions or fees that support their salaries. However, the sale is not always the best possible transaction for the client, generating potential conflicts.[8]

Similarly, scholar Eugene White contends that, in part based on the preceding challenges, markets are relatively ineffective and the only possible answer is additional regulation. Though Bahr argues that there may be means by which to resolve the conflicts, such as due notice and separation of research and auditing activities, White instead maintains that these conflicts cannot in fact be eliminated.[9] "Financial firms may hide relevant information and disclosure may reveal too much proprietary information." There remains no perfect solution; instead, the investment community has no choice but to rely in part on the ethical decision making of the agent who acts within the market, constrained to some extent by regulation. Moreover, there is not simply just one solution. Consider how the financial community needed to reply on the honesty of individuals reporting their lending rates for the LIBOR benchmark. It is difficult to imagine an adequate response to this scandal that did not include everything from individual integrity to government regulation, both nationally and internationally.

Executive Compensation

Few areas of corporate governance and finance have received as much public scrutiny in recent years as executive compensation. A *Fortune* cover promised a look "Inside the Great CEO Pay Heist," and the article inside detailed how many top corporate executives now receive "gargantuan pay packages unlike any seen before." In the words of *Fortune*'s headline: "Executive compensation has become highway robbery—we all know that."[10]

In 1965, CEOs at America's largest firms made, on average, about twenty times as much as the typical worker, for an average of $843,000 per year. The ratio peaked in the year 2000, at 376-to-1 (for an average compensation of $20.7 million). By 2016, the ratio was down to a "mere" 271-to-1 ($15.6 million).[11]

Forbes reported that the CEOs of eight hundred major corporations received an average 23% pay raise in 1997 while the average U.S. worker received around 3%. The median total compensation for these eight hundred CEOs was reported as $2.3 million. Half of this amount was in salary and bonuses, and 10% came from

Reality Check *Average CEO to Average Worker Compensation Ratio*

In 2019 the governance data company Equilar provided data on the 2018 salaries, and salary ratios, of the CEOs of the largest companies (by revenue). A few examples:

- Mark Hurd and Safra Catz, the co-CEOs of Oracle, each earned $108 million, which was 1,205 times the earnings of the median Oracle employee.

- Robert Iger, CEO of Disney, earned just $65 million, but that was 1,424 times the pay of the median Disney employee. (Ask yourself: Why was Iger's ratio higher, even though his pay was lower than Hurd's and Catz's?)

- Jonas Prising, the CEO of ManpowerGroup Inc., earned a "mere" $11 million. But that was a whopping 2,508 times as much as the company's median employee!

Source: Equilar, "Equilar 100: CEO Pay at the Largest Companies by Revenue," www.equilar.com/reports/63-table-highest-paid-ceos-2019-equilar-100.html.

such things as life insurance premiums, pension plans and individual retirement accounts, country club memberships, and automobile allowances. Slightly less than half came from stock options. (See Reality Check "Average CEO to Average Worker Compensation Ratio.")

Compensation packages paid to the top executives of ExxonMobil drew harsh public criticism amid rising gas prices and soaring profits. ExxonMobil CEO Lee Raymond received total compensation of $28 million, including $18 million in stock, in 2003 and $38 million, of which $28 million was in ExxonMobil stock, in 2004. In 2005, the year in which he retired, Raymond received $51 million in salary. The interest alone on this three-year salary would, at a modest 5% rate of return, forever produce $5.85 million annually. Apparently this was not sufficient for Raymond's needs because he also received an additional retirement package with a combined worth of $400 million. When he succeeded Raymond, new CEO Rex Tillerson's salary increased 33% to a total of $13 million, including $8.75 million in stock. The combined compensation just for these two executives in 2004 and 2005 was in excess of $500 million. During the same period, ExxonMobil also achieved record profits, earning more than $25 billion in 2004 and $36 billion in 2005.

These gaps continue to increase. For the decade ending in 2000, the U.S. minimum wage increased 36%, from $3.80 per hour to $5.15 per hour. The median household income in the United States increased 43%, from $29,943 to $42,680. The average annual salary for a tenured New York City teacher increased 20%, from $41,000 to $49,030. During this same decade, the total compensation for the Citicorp CEO increased 12,444%, from $1.2 million to $150 million annually. General Electric CEO Jack Welch's salary increased 2,496%, from $4.8 million to $125 million.

Skyrocketing executive compensation packages raise numerous ethical questions. Greed and avarice are the most apt descriptive terms for the moral character of such people from a virtue ethics perspective. Fundamental questions of distributive justice and fairness arise when these salaries are compared to the pay of average workers or to the billions of human beings who live in abject poverty on a global level. Consider Tyco's Dennis Kozlowski's justification of his salary in the Reality Check "How Do Salaries Motivate?"

Reality Check *How Do Salaries Motivate?*

What motivates executives to seek huge compensation packages? Consider this exchange between a *New York Times* reporter and Dennis Kozlowski, former CEO of Tyco International.

> *Reporter:* It's often said that at a certain level it no longer matters how much any of you make, that you would be doing just as good a job for $100 million less, or $20 million less.

> *Kozlowski:* Yeah, all my meals are paid for, as long as I am around. So, I'm not working for that any longer. But it does make a difference in the charities I ultimately leave monies behind to, and it's a way of keeping score.

Source: William Shaw, "Justice, Incentives, and Executive Compensation," in *The Ethics of Executive Compensation*, ed. Robert Kolb (Malden, MA: Blackwell, 2006), p. 93.

OBJECTIVE

But serious ethical challenges are raised against these practices even from within the business perspective. Both *Fortune* and *Forbes* magazines have been vocal critics of excessive compensation while remaining staunch defenders of corporate interests and the free market. Beyond issues of personal morality and economic fairness, however, excessive executive compensation practices also speak to significant ethical issues of corporate governance and finance.

In theory, lofty compensation packages are thought to serve corporate interests in two ways: They provide an incentive for executive performance (a consequentialist justification), and they serve as rewards for accomplishments (a deontological justification). In terms of ethical theory, they have a utilitarian function to the extent that they act as incentives for executives to produce greater overall results, and they are a matter of ethical principle to the extent that they compensate individuals on the basis of what they have earned and deserve.

In practice, reasonable doubts exist about both of these rationales. First, as the *Forbes* story mentioned previously, there is much less correlation between pay and performance than one would expect. At least in terms of stock performance, executives seem to reap large rewards regardless of business success. Of course, it might be argued that in difficult financial times, an executive faces greater challenges and therefore perhaps deserves his salary more than in good times. But the corollary of this is that in good financial times, as when ExxonMobil earns a $30 billion profit, the executives have less to do with the success.

More to the point with regards to governance, there are several reasons why excessive compensation suggests evidence of a failure of corporate boards to fulfill their fiduciary duties. First, as mentioned, is the fact that in many cases there is no correlation between executive compensation and performance. Second, there is also little evidence that the types of compensation packages described earlier are actually needed as incentives for performance. The fiduciary duty of boards ought to involve approving high enough salaries to provide adequate incentive, but not more than what is needed. Surely there is a diminishing rate of return on incentives beyond a certain level. Does an annual salary of $40 million provide twice the incentive of $20 million, four times the incentive of $10 million, and forty times the return of a $1 million salary? That seems unlikely.

FIGURE 10.2
Duties of the Board and Senior Executives That May Give Rise to Conflicts of Interest

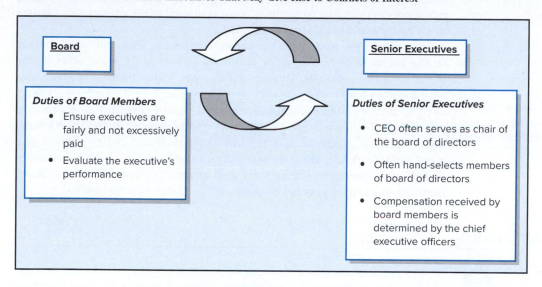

Another crucial governance issue is the disincentives that compensation pack-ages, and in particular the heavy reliance on stock options, provide. When execu-tive compensation is tied to stock price, executives have a strong incentive to focus on short-term stock value rather than long-term corporate interests. One of the fastest ways to increase stock price, for example, is through layoffs of employees. This may not always be in the best interests of the firm, and there is something perverse about basing the salary of an executive on how successful he or she can be in putting people out of work.

Further, a good case can be made that stock options have also been partially to blame for the corruption involving managed earnings. Two academic studies concluded that there is a strong link between high levels of executive compensation and the likelihood of misstating or falsely reporting financial results.[12] When huge amounts of compensation depend on quarterly earnings reports, there is a strong incentive to manipulate those reports in order to achieve the money.

Excessive executive compensation can also involve a variety of conflicts of interests and cronyism. The board's duties should include ensuring that executives are fairly and not excessively paid. They also have a responsibility to evaluate the executive's performance. However, all too often the executive being evaluated and paid also serves as chair of the board of directors. The board is often comprised of members hand-selected by the senior executives. In addition, the compensation board members receive is determined by the chief executive officer, creating yet another conflict of interest. (See Figure 10.2.)

The cronyism does not end at the boardroom door. One of the larger concerns to have arisen in recent years has been the cross-fertilization of boards. At one point, for example, PepsiCo board member Robert Allen sat on the Bristol-Myers

Squibb board alongside Coca-Cola board member James D. Robinson III. Though sitting on a board together obviously does not mean Pepsi's board member will gain access to Coke's secret recipe, it could lend itself to the appearance of impropriety and give rise to a question of conflicts.

In another case involving lesser-known companies, three individuals served on the boards of three companies, with each serving as CEO and chair of one of the companies, Brocade, Verisign, and Juniper. Unfortunately, the companies were found to have backdated stock options, and each firm found itself subject to either Securities and Exchange Commission inquiries or criminal or civil legal proceedings. Cronyism or basic occurrences of overlapping board members might occur, of course, simply because particular individuals are in high demand as a result of their expertise. However, where the overlap results in a failure of oversight and effective governance—the primary legal and ethical responsibilities of board members—the implications can be significant to all stakeholders involved.

Insider Trading

OBJECTIVE

insider trading
Trading of securities by those who hold private inside information that allows them to benefit from buying or selling stock.

No discussion of the ethics of corporate governance and finance would be complete without consideration of the practice of **insider trading** by board members, executives, and other insiders. The issue became front-page news in the 1980s when financier Ivan Boesky was sent to prison for the crime of insider trading. Though it certainly has not left the business pages in the intervening years, it once again gained iconic status when Ken Lay and his colleagues at Enron were accused of insider trading when they allegedly dumped their Enron stock, knowing of the inevitable downturn in the stock's worth, while encouraging others to hold on to it. More recent cases involved financiers and bankers such as Raj Rajaratnam, the billionaire founder of the hedge fund Galleon Group (discussed later), and Fidelity Investments employee David K. Donovan Jr., who was convicted in 2009 for giving his own mother inside information on which she then traded. In 2019, a senior lawyer at Apple, Gene Levoff, was charged with insider trading for selling millions of dollars worth of stock just days before the company announced its quarterly earnings. The earnings announcement, which Levoff had seen before it was made public, resulted in a dip in the company's stock price. The move, according to the charges, saved Levoff more than a third of a million dollars. An additional irony: Levoff's job had previously included watching out for insider trading at Apple.

Insider trading is trading by shareholders who hold private inside information that allows them to benefit from buying or selling stock. Illegal insider trading also occurs when corporate insiders provide "tips" to family members, friends, or others and those parties buy or sell the company's stock based on that information. "Private information" would include privileged information that has not yet been released to the public. That information is deemed material if it could possibly have a financial impact on a company's short- or long-term performance or if it would be important to a prudent investor in making an investment decision.

The Securities and Exchange Commission defines insider information in the following way:

> "Insider trading" refers generally to buying or selling a security, in breach of a fiduciary duty or other relationship of trust and confidence, while in possession of material, nonpublic information about the security. Insider trading violations may also include "tipping" such information, securities trading by the person "tipped" and securities trading by those who misappropriate such information. Examples of insider trading cases that have been brought by the Commission are cases against: corporate officers, directors, and employees who traded the corporation's securities after learning of significant, confidential corporate developments; friends, business associates, family members, and other "tippees" of such officers, directors, and employees, who traded the securities after receiving such information; employees of law, banking, brokerage and printing firms who were given such information in order to provide services to the corporation whose securities they traded; government employees who learned of such information because of their employment by the government; and other persons who misappropriated, and took advantage of, confidential information from their employers.[13]

Because insider trading undermines investor confidence in the fairness and integrity of the securities markets, the commission has treated the detection and prosecution of insider trading violations as one of its enforcement priorities.[14] Accordingly, if an executive gets rid of a stock he knows is going to greatly decrease in worth because of bad news in the company that no one knows except a few insiders, he takes advantage of those who bought the stock from him without full disclosure.

Insider trading may also be based on a claim of unethical misappropriation of proprietary knowledge, that is, knowledge only those in the firm should have, knowledge owned by the firm and not to be used by abusing one's fiduciary responsibilities to the firm. The law surrounding insider trading therefore creates a responsibility to protect confidential information, proprietary information, and intellectual property. That responsibility also exists based on the fiduciary duty of "insiders" such as executives. Misappropriation of this information undermines the trust necessary to the proper functioning of a firm and is unfair to others who buy the stock. Though one might make the argument that, in the long run, insider trading is not so bad because the inside information will be revealed to the public shortly and the market will correct itself, this contention does not take account of the hurt to those who completed the original transactions in a state of ignorance.

Insider trading is considered patently unfair and unethical because it precludes fair pricing based on equal access to public information. If market participants know that one party may have an advantage over another via information that is not available to all players, pure price competition will not be possible and the faith upon which the market is based will be lost.

On the other hand, trading on inside information is not without its ethical defense. If someone has worked very hard to obtain a certain position in a firm and, by virtue of being in that position, the individual is privy to inside information, isn't it just for that person to take advantage of the information because she

Where does a private investor find information relevant to potential stock purchases? Barring issues of insider trading, do all investors actually have roughly equal access to information about companies?

1. What are the ethical issues involved in access to corporate information?

2. Where do private investors go to access information about stock purchases? On whose opinion do they rely? Does everyone have access to these same opinions? If not, what determines access to information in an open market? Instead, is there equal opportunity to have access to information?

3. Who are the stakeholders involved in the issue of access? Who relies on information relevant to stock purchases?

4. Who has an interest in equal access to information?

5. What alternatives are available when considering access to information? How can we perhaps best ensure equal access?

6. How do the alternatives compare, and how do the alternatives affect the stakeholders?

or he has worked so hard to obtain the position? Is it really wrong? Unethical? Consider an issue that might be closer to home. If your brother has always been successful in whatever he does in the business world, is it unethical for you to purchase stock in the company he just acquired? Others don't know quite how successful he has been, so are you trading on inside information? Would you tell others? What about officers in one company investing in the stocks of their client companies? No legal rules exist (in the U.S.) other than traditional SEC rules on insider trading, but is there not something about this that simply feels "wrong"? Consider the ethical issues surrounding access to information in the Decision Point "The Know-It-Alls."

Some people do seem to have access to more information than others, and their access does not always seem to be fair. Consider how Martha Stewart found herself in jail in 2004. Stewart was good friends with Sam Waksal, who was the founder and CEO of a company called ImClone. Waksal had developed a promising new cancer drug and had just sold an interest in the drug to Bristol-Myers Squibb for $2 billion. Unfortunately, though everyone thought the drug would soon be approved, Waksal learned that the Food and Drug Administration had determined that the data were not sufficient to allow the drug to move to the next phase of the process. When this news became public, ImClone's stock price was going to fall significantly.

On learning the news (December 26, 2001), Waksal contacted his daughter and instructed her to sell her shares in ImClone. He then compounded his violations by transferring seventy-nine thousand of his shares (worth almost $5 million) to his daughter and asking her to sell those shares, too. Though the Securities and Exchange Commission would likely uncover these trades, given the decrease in share price, it was not something he seemed to consider. "Do I know that, when I think

Decision Point

Do You Trust Apple? Goldman Sachs? The Two Together?

Early in 2019, tech blogger David Gewirtz wrote a piece about the new "Apple Card"—a sleek, titanium credit card connected to the iPhone. After pointing out several usability challenges, he then moved on to his biggest worry: Financial transactions using the Apple Card would be managed by the financial services company Goldman Sachs.

In launching the Apple Card, Apple is seeking to compete in the credit card market by reducing the friction in retail transactions. It's trying to make transactions simpler, faster, and more convenient because consumers like convenience. The biggest source of friction in commerce, however, is lack of trust: The less we trust our trading partners, the more we (and they) must invest in costly monitoring and enforcement mechanisms in order to do business. As those costs rise, fewer marginal transactions can be executed profitably. That makes trustworthiness perhaps the most significant asset a business firm or a business person can have. The more trustworthy you are, the more marginal business transactions you can make profitable for yourself and your trading partners. Trust is the foundation that a capitalist market is built upon.

Through mechanisms like co-branding and outsourcing, trustworthiness can be gained—or lost—by association. Against this background, Gewirtz's criticism is interesting. He identifies three technical limitations of Apple Card that may limit its acceptance by consumers and merchants, but then turns to a potential source of distrust: Apple's partnership in offering and administering Apple Card with Goldman Sachs. It is up to the reader, of course, to decide whether the author makes a persuasive case against the trustworthiness of Goldman Sachs. (For what it's worth, the legal and ethical failures Gewirtz points to on Goldman's part have to do with things like tax evasion and insider trading, most of which don't directly affect consumers on an individual basis.) The piece illustrates, however, that technical merit is only the beginning of having a good product. Technical merit carries you only so far if people don't trust you—or those you're counting on as agents—to deliver what you promise.

1. Would you trust a financial product backed by Apple, based on Apple's reputation alone?

2. Would you trust a financial product backed by Goldman Sachs, based on Goldman's reputation alone?

3. Are you more, or less, likely to trust an Apple product that is backed by a world-class financial institution—but one with a troubled history?

4. Look online for some of Goldman's history of troubles. Would the type of troubles Goldman has had worry you, as a consumer?

Source: Adapted from "Should Consumers Trust the Goldman Sachs-Connected Apple Card?" *Business Ethics Highlights* (April 4, 2019), https://businessethicshighlights.com/2019/04/04/should-consumers-trust-the-goldman-sachs-connected-apple-card/. Gewirtz's original piece can be found here: David Gewirtz, "Apple Card: Three Fatal Flaws That Hinder Usability (and Then There's Goldman Sachs)," *ZDNet* (April 3, 2019), www.zdnet.com/article/apple-card-three-fatal-flaws-that-hinder-usability-and-then-theres-goldman-sachs/.

Many people and institutions have responsibility for corporate oversight and control. The Opening Decision Point considered most of the key stakeholders: professional employees, management, boards. But government also plays a role, and it is worth considering how government regulators functioned in this case.

It was the responsibility of government regulators to set environmental emission standards. Given the well-established economic problems associated with externalities and the commons, it would be difficult to imagine environmental standards voluntarily emerging from either automobile manufacturers or consumers, especially when these standards add costs to the price of a car. But in establishing these standards, this case shows how governments worked cooperatively with manufacturers, sometimes over decades, to establish meaningful and achievable standards. Government regulators also worked with VW for a year or more to determine the validity of testing results. Despite denials and attempts by VW to mislead regulators, government agencies succeeded in uncovering the fraud and taking strong steps to end the sale of the offending diesel cars. Investigations were extended to include other manufacturers and, while the exact circumstances were different, Mitsubishi Motors admitted in April 2016 that it had manipulated mileage and emission tests on hundreds of thousands of cars for decades.

If anything, critics charged that government regulators were too slow or ineffectual in addressing the problems. In 2012 both Hyundai and Kia were fined for manipulating their fuel economy tests. Critics point out that in the desire to treat manufacturers fairly, and given inadequate funding, government regulators too often leave all testing and reporting responsibility to the manufacturers themselves.

Once the VW fraud was established, other government agencies stepped in to assess the damage, adjudicate disputes, and ensure that consumers and dealers who were deceived received adequate compensation. Thus, government regulated to prevent harms, and enforced compensation for those cases where the harms had occurred. By most measures, government was the only agency that fulfilled its oversight duties.

1. Do you believe that government agencies fulfilled their responsibilities in this case?

2. What else could government do to better create and enforce environmental standards?

3. Are there government policies or actions that could have encouraged better oversight within the VW corporate setting and prevented this from occurring?

about it? Absolutely," says Waksal. "Did I think about it at the time? Obviously not. I just acted irresponsibly."[15] Waksal eventually was sentenced to more than seven years in prison for these actions.

How does Martha Stewart fit into this picture? The public trial revealed that Stewart's broker ordered a former Merrill Lynch & Co. assistant to tell her that Waksal was selling his stock, presumably so that she would also sell her stock.

Stewart subsequently sold almost four thousand shares on December 27, 2001, one day after Waksal sold his shares and one day prior to the public statement about the drug's failed approval.

Stewart successfully avoided prison for several years, and on November 7, 2003, she explained that she was scared of prison but "I don't think I will be going to prison." Nevertheless she was convicted on all counts except securities fraud and sentenced to a five-month prison term, five months of home confinement, and a $30,000 fine, the minimum the court could impose under the Federal Sentencing Guidelines.

During the trial, the public heard the testimony of Stewart's friend, Mariana Pasternak, who reported that Stewart told her several days after the ImClone sale that she knew about Waksal's stock sales and that Stewart said, "Isn't it nice to have brokers who tell you those things?" So, to return to the issue with which we began this tale, it appears that some investors do seem to have access to information not necessarily accessible to all individual investors.

A similar, but more far-ranging situation was revealed in November 2009 when the FBI and U.S. Attorneys announced arrests stemming from a large insider-trading operation at the hedge fund Galleon Group. The Securities and Exchange Commission accused billionaire Raj Rajaratnam and dozens of others associated with the Galleon Group of insider trading that resulted in more than $33 million in profit. They were accused of trading on secret details of corporate takeovers and quarterly earnings leaked to them by company insiders.

Though Stewart, Waksal, Rajaratnam, and others involved in these stories were caught and charged with criminal behavior, many believe they were identified and later charged because they were in the public eye. If others are not in the public eye and also engage in this behavior, can the SEC truly police all inappropriate transactions? Is there a sufficient deterrent effect to discourage insider trading in our markets today? If not, what else can or should be done? Or, to the contrary, is this simply the nature of markets, and those who have found access to information should use it to the best of their abilities? What might be the consequences of this latter, perhaps more Darwinian, approach to insider trading, and whose rights might be violated if we allow it?

Questions, Projects, and Exercises

1. You have been asked by the board of a large corporation to develop a board assessment and effectiveness mechanism, which could be a survey, interviews, an appraisal system, or other technique that will allow you to report back to the board on both individual and group effectiveness. What would you recommend?

2. You have been asked to join the board of a small charitable organization. What are some of the first questions that you should ask, before agreeing to join, and what are the answers that you are seeking?

3. U.S. law imposes duties of care, good faith, and loyalty on corporate boards. Search online to find out: What duties do the laws of other jurisdictions, such as Canada, the UK, and Japan, impose on boards? Are they different in meaningful ways?

4. Scholars have made strong arguments for required representation on boards by stakeholders that go beyond stockholders, such as employees, community members, and others, depending on the industry. What might be some of the benefits and costs of such a process?

5. You are an executive at a large nonprofit organization. Some of your board members suggest that perhaps the company should voluntarily comply with Sarbanes-Oxley. What are some of the reasons the company might consider doing so or not doing so?

6. You are on the compensation committee of your board and have been asked to propose an overall compensation structure to be offered to the next CEO. Explore some of the following websites on executive compensation and then propose a structure or process for determining CEO compensation at your corporation: www.sec.gov/news/speech/spch120304cs.htm; www.investopedia.com/managing-wealth/guide-ceo-compensation/; www.execcomp.org/Basics/Basic/Pay-Packages-Explained.

7. Imagine that a press release has a significant negative impact on your firm's stock price, reducing its value by more than 50% in a single day of trading! You gather from conversations in the hallway that the company's fundamentals remain strong, aside from this one-time event. You see this as a great opportunity to buy stock. Is it appropriate to act on this and to purchase company stock at its (temporary) low price, in hopes of selling it at a profit once the price rebounds? Does it make a difference whether you buy one hundred shares or one thousand shares? Is it OK to discuss the "dilemma" with family members and friends? What should you do if you do mention it to family and friends but then later feel uncomfortable about it?

8. Modify slightly the facts of the previous question. Assume that you are also privy to the annual forecast of earnings, which assures you that the fundamentals remain strong. Stock analysts and investors are also provided this same information. Do your answers to the questions above change at all?

9. In connection with the two previous questions, assume instead that you suspect something significant is about to be made public because senior managers have consistently stayed late, a special board meeting has been called, you and your boss have been advised to be on call throughout the weekend, and various rumors have been floating throughout the company. You are not aware of the specifics, but you can reasonably conclude that it's potentially good or bad news. You decide to call a friend in the accounting department who has been staying late to find out what she knows. In this situation, do your answers about what you might do change? Is it appropriate to partake in the "rumor mill"? Is it appropriate to discuss and confide your observations with family and friends? Is it appropriate to buy or sell company stock based on these observations (you may rationalize that it is only speculation and you do not know the facts)?

10. Have you ever been in, or are you familiar with, a conflict of interest situation? How was it resolved? Can you think of any rules or any practices that could have prevented the situation from occurring? Can you think of any initiatives, structures, or procedures that could make it easy to avoid such conflicts in the future?

Key Terms

After reading this chapter, you should have a clear understanding of the following key terms. For a complete definition, please see the Glossary.

Committee of Sponsoring Organizations (COSO), *p. 367*
conflict of interest, *p. 359*
control environment, *p. 367*
corporate governance, *p. 356*

duty of care, *p. 368*
duty of good faith, *p. 369*
duty of loyalty, *p. 369*
Enron Corporation, *p. 357*
European Union 8th Directive, *p. 366*
fiduciary duties, *p. 361*

gatekeepers, *p. 357*
insider trading, *p. 378*
internal control, *p. 367*
Sarbanes-Oxley Act (Public Accounting Reform and Investor Protection Act of 2002), *p. 365*

Endnotes

1. "VW under Fire Amid EPA Accusations It Cheated on Emissions Tests," *Washington Post* (September 15, 2015),www.washingtonpost.com/business/economy/vw-shares-plunge-as-epa-accuses-automaker-of-cheating/2015/09/21/3c7b2f2e-607b-11e5-8e9e-dce8a2a2a679_story.html (accessed September 10, 2019).

2. Jack Ewing and Jad Mouawad, "Directors Say Volkswagen Delayed Informing Them of Trickery," *The New York Times* (October 23, 2015), https://www.nytimes.com/2015/10/24/business/international/directors-say-volkswagen-delayed-informing-them-of-trickery.html.

3. C. William Thomas, "The Rise and Fall of Enron," *Journal of Accountancy* (April 2002), p. 7.

4. Sarbanes-Oxley Act of 2002, Pub. L. No. 107-204, 116 Stat. 745.

5. Committee of Sponsoring Organizations, "Board Guidance on Control," www.coso.org/guidance.htm (accessed December 27, 2012).

6. *BCE Inc. v. 1976 Debentureholders*, [2008] 3 S.C.R. 560 (Can.).

7. Ram Charan and Julie Schlosser, "Ten Questions Every Board Member Should Ask; And for That Matter, Every Shareholder Too," *Fortune* (November 10, 2003), p. 181.

8. Kevin Bahr, "Conflicts of Interest in the Financial Markets" (Stevens Point, WI: Central Wisconsin Economic Research Bureau, 2002), www.uwsp.edu/busecon/Special%20Reports/2000-2009/2002/Conflicts%20of%20Interest%20in%20the%20Financial%20Markets.pdf (accessed September 10, 2019).

9. Eugene N. White, "Can the Market Control Conflicts of Interest in the Financial Industry?" presentation at the International Monetary Fund (June 4, 2004), www.imf.org/external/np/leg/sem/2004/cdmfl/eng/enw.pdf (accessed April 10, 2010).

10. Geoffrey Colvin, "The Great CEO Pay Heist," *Fortune* (June 25, 2001), p. 64.

11. Lawrence Mishel and Jessica Schieder, "CEO Pay Remains High Relative to the Pay of Typical Workers and High-Wage Earners," Economic Policy Institute (July 20, 2017), www.epi.org/publication/ceo-pay-remains-high-relative-to-the-pay-of-typical-workers-and-high-wage-earners/.

12. J. Harris and P. Bromiley, "Incentives to Cheat: Executive Compensation and Corporate Malfeasance," paper presented at the Strategic Management Society International Conference, Baltimore, MD, 2003; J. Patrick O'Connor Jr., et al., "Do CEO Stock Options Prevent or Promote Corporate Accounting Irregularities?" *Academy of Management Journal* 49, no. 3 (June 2006), as quoted in Jared Harris, "How Much Is Too Much?" in *The Ethics of Executive Compensation,* ed. Robert Kolb (Malden, MA: Blackwell, 2006), pp. 67–86.

13. U.S. Securities and Exchange Commission, "Key Topics: Insider Trading," www.sec.gov/answers/insider.htm (accessed April 24, 2010).

14. U.S. Securities and Exchange Commission, "Insider Trading," www.sec.gov/divisions/enforce/insider.htm (accessed April 10, 2010).

15. "Sam Waksal: I Was Arrogant," *CBS News* (June 27, 2004), www.cbsnews.com/stories/2003/10/02/60minutes/main576328.shtml (accessed April 10, 2010).

Glossary

A

affirmative action   A policy or a program that strives to redress past discrimination through the implementation of proactive measures to ensure equal opportunity. In other words, affirmative action is the intentional inclusion of previously excluded groups. Affirmative action efforts can take place in employment environments, education, or other arenas.

autonomy   From the Greek for "self-ruled," autonomy is the capacity to make free and deliberate choices. The capacity for autonomous action is what explains the inherent dignity and intrinsic value of individual human beings.

B

backcasting   The Natural Step challenges businesses to imagine what a sustainable future must hold. From that vision, creative businesses then look backward to the present and determine what must be done to arrive at that future.

C

categorical imperative   An imperative is a command or duty; "categorical" means that it is without exception. Thus, a categorical imperative is an overriding principle of ethics. Philosopher Immanual Kant offered several formulations of the categorical imperative: act so as the maxim implicit in your acts could be willed to be a universal law; treat persons as ends and never as means only; treat others as subjects, not objects.

***caveat emptor* approach**   *Caveat emptor* means "buyer beware" in Latin, and this approach suggests that the burden of risk of information shall be placed on the buyer. This perspective assumes that every purchase involves the informed consent of the buyer, and, therefore, it is assumed to be ethically legitimate.

change blindness   A decision-making omission that occurs when decision makers fail to notice gradual changes over time.

character   The sum of relatively set traits, dispositions, and habits of an individual. Along with rational deliberation and choice, a person's character accounts for how she or he makes decisions and acts. Training and developing character so that it is disposed to act ethically is the goal of virtue ethics.

child labor   Though the term literally signifies children who work, it has taken on the meaning of exploitative work that involves some harm to a child who is not of an age to justify his or her presence in the workplace. The elements of that definition—harm, age of the child, justification to be in the workplace relative to other options—remain open to social and economic debate. UNICEF's 1997 State of the World's Children Report explains, "Children's work needs to be seen as happening along a continuum, with destructive or exploitative work at one end and beneficial work—promoting or enhancing children's development without interfering with their schooling, recreation and rest—at the other. And between these two poles are vast areas of work that need not negatively affect a child's development."

"closed-loop" production   Seeks to integrate what is presently waste back into production in much the way that biological processes turn waste into food.

code of conduct   A set of behavioral guidelines and expectations that govern all members of a business firm.

Committee of Sponsoring Organizations (COSO)   COSO is a voluntary collaboration designed to improve financial reporting through a combination of controls and governance standards called the Internal Control–Integrated Framework. It was established in 1985 by five of the major professional accounting and finance associations originally to study fraudulent financial reporting and later developed standards for publicly held companies. It has become one of the most broadly accepted audit systems for internal controls.

common-law agency test   A persuasive indicator of independent contractor status that provides the employer the ability to control the manner in which the work is performed. Under the common-law agency approach, the employer need not actually control the work, but must merely have the right or ability to control the work for a worker to be classified an employee.

compliance-based culture   A corporate culture in which obedience to laws and regulations is the prevailing model for ethical behavior.

conflict of interest   A conflict of interest exists where a person holds a position of trust that requires that she or he exercise judgment on behalf of others, but where her or his personal interests and/or obligations conflict with the proper exercise of that judgment.

consequentialist theories Ethical theories, such as utilitarianism, that determine right and wrong by calculating the consequences of actions.

control environment One of the five elements that comprise the control structure, similar to the culture of an organization, and support people in the achievement of the organization's objectives. The control environment "sets the tone of an organization, influencing the control consciousness of its people."

corporate average fuel economy (CAFE) standards Established by the U.S. Energy Policy Conservation Act of 1975, corporate average fuel economy (CAFE) is the sales-weighted average fuel economy, expressed in miles per gallon (mpg), of a manufacturer's fleet of passenger cars or light trucks. The U.S. federal government establishes CAFE standards as a means of increasing fuel efficiency of automobiles.

corporate governance The structure by which corporations are managed, directed, and controlled toward the objectives of fairness, accountability, and transparency. The structure generally will determine the relationship between the board of directors, the shareholders or owners of the firm, and the firm's executives or management.

corporate social responsibility (CSR) The responsibilities that businesses have to the societies within which they operate. In various contexts, it may also refer to the voluntary actions that companies undertake to address economic, social, and environmental impacts of their business operations and the concerns of their principal stakeholders. The European Commission defines CSR as "a concept whereby companies decide voluntarily to contribute to a better society and a cleaner environment." Specifically, CSR suggests that a business identify its stakeholder groups and incorporate its needs and values within its strategic and operational decision-making process.

corporate sustainability report Provides all stakeholders with financial and other information regarding a firm's economic, environmental, and social performance.

cradle-to-cradle responsibility Holds that a business should be responsible for incorporating the end results of its products back into the productive cycle.

culture A shared pattern of beliefs, expectations, and meanings that influences and guides the thinking and behaviors of the members of a particular group.

D

descriptive ethics As practiced by many social scientists, provides a descriptive and empirical account of those standards that actually guide behavior, as opposed to those standards that should guide behavior. Contrast with *normative ethics.*

disability An impairment that substantially limits a major life activity.

diversity Diversity refers to the presence of differing cultures, languages, ethnicities, races, affinity orientations, genders, religious sects, abilities, social classes, ages, and national origins of the individuals in a firm. When used in connection with the corporate environment, it often encompasses the values of respect, tolerance, inclusion, and acceptance.

downsize The reduction of human resources at an organization through terminations, retirements, corporate divestments, or other means.

due process The right to be protected against the arbitrary use of authority. In legal contexts, due process refers to the procedures that police and courts must follow in exercising their authority over citizens. In the employment context, due process specifies the conditions for basic fairness within the scope of the employer's authority over its employees.

duties Those obligations that one is bound to perform, regardless of consequences. Duties might be derived from basic ethical principles, from the law, or from one's institutional or professional role.

duty of care Involves the exercise of reasonable care by a board member to ensure that the corporate executives with whom she or he works carry out their management responsibilities and comply with the law in the best interests of the corporation.

duty of good faith Requires obedience, compelling board members to be faithful to the organization's mission. In other words, they are not permitted to act in a way that is inconsistent with the central goals of the organization.

duty of loyalty Requires faithfulness; a board member must give undivided allegiance when making decisions affecting the organization. This means that conflicts of interest are always to be resolved in favor of the corporation.

E

eco-efficiency Doing more with less. Introduced at the Rio Earth Summit in 1992, the concept of eco-efficiency is a way business can contribute to sustainability by reducing resource usage in its production cycle.

economic model of CSR   Limits a firm's social responsibility to the minimal economic responsibility of producing goods and services and maximizing profits within the law.

economic realities test   A test by which courts consider whether the worker is economically dependent on the business or, as a matter of economic fact, is in business for himself or herself.

egoism   As a psychological theory, egoism holds that all people act only from self-interest. Empirical evidence strongly suggests that this is a mistaken account of human motivation. As an ethical theory, egoism holds that humans ought to act for their own self-interest. Ethical egoists typically distinguish between one's perceived best interests and one's true best interests.

Electronic Communications Privacy Act (ECPA) of 1986   The U.S. statute that establishes the provisions for access, use, disclosure, interception, and privacy protections relating to electronic communications.

email monitoring   The maintenance and either periodic or random review of email communications of employees or others for a variety of business purposes.

employment at will (EAW)   The legal doctrine that holds that, absent a particular contractual or other legal obligation that specifies the length or conditions of employment, all employees are employed "at will." Unless an agreement specifies otherwise, employers are free to fire an employee at any time and for any reason. In the same manner, an EAW worker may opt to leave a job at any time for any reason, without offering any notice at all; so the freedom is *theoretically* mutual.

Enron Corporation   An energy company based in Houston, Texas, that *Fortune* magazine named America's most innovative company for six consecutive years before it was discovered to have been involved in one of the largest instances of accounting fraud in world history. In 2001, with over 21,000 employees, it filed the largest bankruptcy in U.S. history and disclosed a scandal that resulted in the loss of millions of dollars, thousands of jobs, the downfall of Big Five accounting firm Arthur Andersen LLP, at least one suicide, and several trials and convictions, among other consequences. Enron remains in business today as it continues to liquidate its assets.

ethical decision-making process   Requires a persuasive and rational justification for a decision. Rational justifications are developed through a logical process of decision making that gives proper attention to such things as facts, alternative perspectives, consequences to all stakeholders, and ethical principles.

ethical relativism   An important perspective within the philosophical study of ethics that holds that ethical values and judgments are ultimately dependent on, or relative to, one's culture, society, or personal feelings. Relativism denies that we can make rational or objective ethical judgments.

ethical values   Those properties of life that contribute to human well-being and a life well lived. Ethical values would include such things as happiness, respect, dignity, integrity, freedom, companionship, and health.

ethics   Derived from the Greek word *ethos,* which refers to those values, norms, beliefs, and expectations that determine how people within a culture live and act. Ethics steps back from such standards for how people *do* act, and reflects on the standards by which people *should* live and act. At its most basic level, ethics is concerned with how we act and how we live our lives. Ethics involves what is perhaps the most monumental question any human being can ask: How *should* we live? Following from this original Greek usage, ethics can refer to both the standards by which an individual chooses to live her or his own personal life and the standards by which individuals live in community with others (see also *morality*). As a branch of philosophy, ethics is the discipline that systematically studies questions of how we ought to live our lives.

ethics officers   Individuals within an organization charged with managerial oversight of ethical compliance and enforcement within the organization.

European Union 8th Directive   Covers many of the same issues as Sarbanes-Oxley but applies these requirements and restrictions to companies traded on European Union exchanges. The updates to the directive in 2005 clarified required duties, independence, and ethics of statutory auditors and called for public oversight of the accounting profession and external quality assurance of both audit and financial reporting processes. In addition, the directive strives to improve cooperation between EU oversight bodies and provides for effective and balanced international regulatory cooperation with oversight bodies outside the EU regulatory infrastructure (e.g., the U.S. Public Company Accounting Oversight Board).

F

Federal Sentencing Guidelines for Organizations (FSGO) Developed by the United States Sentencing Commission and implemented in 1991, originally as mandatory parameters for judges to use during organizational sentencing cases. By connecting punishment to prior business practices, the guidelines establish legal norms for ethical business behavior. However, since a 2005 Supreme Court decision, the FSG are now considered to be discretionary in nature and offer some specifics for organizations about ways to mitigate eventual fines and sentences by integrating bona fide ethics and compliance programs throughout their organizations.

fiduciary duties A legal duty, grounded in trust, to act on behalf of or in the interests of another.

"Four Ps" of marketing Production, price, promotion, and placement.

Fourth Amendment protection The U.S. Constitution's Fourth Amendment protection against unreasonable search and seizure extends privacy protections to the public-sector workplace through the Constitution's application to state action.

G

gatekeepers Some professions, such as accountant, that act as "watchdogs" in that their role is to ensure that those who participate in the marketplace are playing by the rules and conforming to the conditions that ensure the market functions as it is supposed to function.

Genetic Information Nondiscrimination Act of 2008 (GINA) The Genetic Information Nondiscrimination Act of 2008 (GINA), which took effect on November 21, 2009, makes it illegal to discriminate against employees or applicants because of genetic information. It prohibits the use of genetic information in making employment decisions; restricts employers, employment agencies, labor organizations, and other covered entities from requesting, requiring, or purchasing genetic information; and also limits the disclosure of genetic information.

H

Hawthorne effect The impact on one's behavior of knowing that one is being studied. In connection with employee monitoring, for instance, merely knowing that one is being monitored may have the effect of enhancing productivity temporarily. However, other research suggests that monitoring may have the opposite effect because it also has been shown to create stress and anxiety (among other consequences), thus reducing productivity.

Health Insurance Portability and Accountability Act (HIPAA) (Pub. L. No. 104-191) HIPAA stipulates that employers cannot use "protected health information" in making employment decisions without prior consent. Protected health information includes all medical records or other individually identifiable health information.

human rights Those moral rights that individuals have simply in virtue of being a human being. Also called *natural rights* or *moral rights.*

hypernorms Values that are fundamental across culture and theory.

I

implied warranty of merchantability Implied assurances by a seller that a product is reasonably suitable for its purpose.

inattentional blindness If we happen to focus on or are told specifically to pay attention to a particular element of a decision or event, we are likely to miss all of the surrounding details, no matter how obvious.

insider trading Trading of securities by those who hold private inside information that allows them to benefit from buying or selling stock.

integrative model of CSR For some business firms, social responsibility is fully integrated with the firm's mission or strategic plan.

internal control A process, effected by an entity's board of directors, management, and other personnel, designed to provide reasonable assurance regarding the achievement of objectives in the following categories: effectiveness and efficiency of operations, reliability of financial reporting, and compliance with applicable laws and regulations.

internet use monitoring The maintenance and either periodic or random review of the use of the internet by employees or others based on time spent or content accessed for a variety of business purposes.

intrusion into seclusion The legal terminology for one of the common-law claims of invasion of privacy. Intrusion into seclusion occurs when someone intentionally intrudes on the private affairs of another when the intrusion would be "highly offensive to a reasonable person."

IRS 20-factor analysis   A list of 20 factors to which the IRS looks to determine whether someone is an employee or an independent contractor.

J

just cause   A standard for terminations or discipline that requires the employer to have sufficient and fair cause before reaching a decision against an employee.

M

managerial capitalism   The theory that the primary obligation of business managers is to serve the interests of stockholders by maximizing profits.

marketing   Defined by the American Marketing Association as "an organizational function and a set of processes for creating, communicating, and delivering value to customers and for managing customer relationships in ways that benefit the organization and its stakeholders."

mission statement   A formal summary statement that describes the goals, values, and institutional aim of an organization.

moral free space   That environment where hypernorms or universal rules do not govern or apply to ethical decisions, but instead culture or other influences govern decisions, as long as they are not in conflict with hypernorms. In other words, as long as a decision is not in conflict with a hypernorm, it rests within moral free space, and reasonable minds may differ as to what is ethical.

moral imagination   When one is facing an ethical decision, the ability to envision various alternative choices, consequences, resolutions, benefits, and harms.

morality   Sometimes used to denote the phenomena studied by the field of ethics. This text uses *morality* to refer to those aspects of ethics involving personal, individual decision making. "How should I live my life?" or "What type of person ought I be?" are taken to be the basic questions of morality. Morality can be distinguished from questions of *social justice,* which address issues of how communities and social organizations ought to be structured.

multiculturalism   Similar to diversity, refers to the principle of tolerance and inclusion that supports the co-existence of multiple cultures, while encouraging each to retain that which is unique or individual about that particular culture.

N

negligence   Unintentional failure to exercise reasonable care not to harm other people. Negligence is considered to be one step below "reckless disregard" for harm to others and two steps below intentional harm.

normative ethics   As a *normative* discipline, ethics deals with norms and standards of appropriate and proper (normal) behavior. Norms establish the guidelines or standards for determining what we should do, how we should act, what type of person we should be. Contrast with *descriptive ethics.*

normative myopia   The tendency to ignore, or the lack of the ability to recognize, ethical issues in decision making.

norms   Those standards or guidelines that establish appropriate and proper behavior. Norms can be established by such diverse perspectives as economics, etiquette, or ethics.

O

Occupational Safety and Health Administration (OSHA)   An agency of the federal government that publishes and enforces safety and health regulations for U.S. businesses.

P

perceptual differences   Psychologists and philosophers have long recognized that individuals cannot perceive the world independently of their own conceptual framework. Experiences are mediated by and interpreted through our own understanding and concepts. Thus, ethical disagreements can depend as much on a person's conceptual framework as on the facts of the situation. Unpacking our own and others' conceptual schema plays an important role in making ethically responsible decisions.

personal and professional decision making   Individuals within a business setting are often in situations in which they must make decisions both from their own personal point of view and from the perspective of the specific role they fill within an institution. Ethically responsible decisions require an individual to recognize that these perspectives can conflict and that a life of moral integrity must balance the personal values with the professional role-based values and responsibilities.

personal integrity   The term *integrity* connotes completeness of a being or thing. Personal integrity, therefore, refers to individuals' completeness within themselves, often derived from the consistency or alignment of actions with deeply held beliefs.

practical reasoning   Involves reasoning about what one ought to do, contrasted with *theoretical reasoning,* which is concerned with what one ought to believe. Ethics is a part of practical reason.

principle-based framework   A framework for ethics that grounds decision making in fundamental principles such as justice, liberty, autonomy, and fairness. Principle-based ethics typically assert that individual rights and duties are fundamental and thus can also be referred to as a rights-based or duty-based (deontological) approach to ethics. Often distinguished from consequentialist frameworks, which determine ethical decisions based on the consequences of our acts.

principles   Ethical rules that put values into action.

privacy   The right to be "let alone" within a personal zone of solitude, and/or the right to control information about oneself.

privacy rights   The legal and ethical sources of protection for privacy in personal data.

property rights   The boundaries defining actions that individuals can take in relation to other individuals regarding their personal information. If one individual has a *right* to her or his personal information, someone else has a commensurate duty to observe that right.

psychological egoism   An alleged theory of human motivation that claims that all human actions are selfish and motivated by self-interest.

R

reasonable expectation of privacy   The basis for some common-law claims of invasion of privacy. Where an individual is notified that information will be shared or space will not be private, there is likely no reasonable expectation of privacy.

reciprocal obligation   The concept that, while an employee has an obligation to respect the goals and property of the employer, the employer has a *reciprocal obligation* to respect the rights of the employee as well, including the employee's right to privacy.

reputation management   The practice of caring for the "image" of a firm.

reverse discrimination   Decisions made or actions taken against those individuals who are traditionally considered to be in power or the majority, such as white men, or in favor of a historically nondominant group.

risk assessment   A process to identify potential events that may affect the entity, and manage risk to be within its risk appetite, to provide reasonable assurance regarding the achievement of entity objectives.

S

Sarbanes-Oxley Act (Public Accounting Reform and Investor Protection Act of 2002)   Implemented on July 30, 2002, and administered by the Securities and Exchange Commission to regulate financial reporting and auditing of publicly traded companies in the United States. SOX or SarbOx (popular shorthands for the act) was enacted very shortly following and directly in response to the Enron scandals of 2001. One of the greatest areas of consternation and debate that has emerged surrounding SOX involves the high cost of compliance and the challenging burden therefore placed on smaller firms. Some contend that SOX was the most significant change to the corporate landscape to occur in the second half of the 20th century.

separation thesis   The separation thesis asserts that ordinary ethical standards should be kept separate from, and not be used to judge, business decisions because business has its own standards of good and bad.

service-based economy   Interprets consumer demand as a demand for services, for example, for clothes cleaning, floor covering, cool air, transportation, or word processing, rather than as a demand for products such as washing machines, carpeting, air conditioners, cars, and computers.

social ethics   The area of ethics that is concerned with how we should live together with others and how social organizations ought to be structured. Social ethics involves questions of political, economic, civic, and cultural norms aimed at promoting human well-being.

stakeholder   In a general sense, a stakeholder is anyone who can be affected by decisions made within a business. More specifically, stakeholders are considered to be those people who are necessary for the functioning of a business.

stakeholder model of CSR   The view that business exists within a web of social relationships. The stakeholder model views business as a citizen of the society in which it operates and, like all members of a society, business must conform to the normal range of ethical duties and obligations that all citizens face.

stakeholder theory   A model of corporate social responsibility that holds that business managers have ethical responsibilities to a range of stakeholders that go beyond a narrow view that the primary or only responsibility of managers is to stockholders.

stealth or undercover marketing   Marketing campaigns that are based on environments or activities where the subject is not aware that she or he is the target of a marketing campaign; those situations where one is subject to directed commercial activity without knowledge or consent.

strict liability   A legal doctrine that holds an individual or business accountable for damages whether or not it was at fault. In a strict liability case, no matter how careful the business is in its product or service, if harm results from use, the individual or business is liable.

sustainable business practice   A model of business practice in which business activities meet the standards of sustainability.

sustainable development   Development that meets the needs of the present without compromising the ability of future generations to meet their own needs, as defined by the Brundtland Commission in 1987.

sustainable or green marketing   Sustainable or green marketing is the marketing of products on the basis of their environmentally friendly nature.

sweatshops   A term that remains subject to debate. Some might suggest that all workplaces with conditions that are below standards in more developed countries are sweatshops because all humans have a right to equally decent working conditions. (See the discussion in Chapter 6 and D. Arnold and L. Hartman, "Beyond Sweatshops: Positive Deviancy and Global Labor Practices," *Business Ethics: A European Review* 14, no. 3 [July 2005].) In this text we use the following definition: Any workplace in which workers are typically subject to two or more of the following conditions: systematic forced overtime, systematic health and safety risks that stem from negligence or the willful disregard of employee welfare, coercion, systematic deception that places workers at risk, underpayment of earnings, and income for a 48-hour workweek less than the overall poverty rate for that country (one who suffers from overall poverty lacks the income necessary to satisfy one's basic nonfood needs such as shelter and basic health care).

T

theoretical reasoning   Involves reasoning that is aimed at establishing truth and therefore at what we ought to believe. Contrast with *practical reasoning,* which aims at determining what is reasonable for us to do.

three pillars of sustainability   Three factors that are often used to judge the adequacy of sustainable practices. Sustainable development must be (1) economically, (2) environmentally, and (3) ethically satisfactory.

U

United States Sentencing Commission (USSC)   An independent agency in the United States judiciary created in 1984 to regulate sentencing policy in the federal court system.

Uniting and Strengthening America by Providing Appropriate Tools Required to Intercept and Obstruct Terrorism (USA PATRIOT) Act of 2001   A U.S. statute designed to increase the surveillance and investigative powers of law enforcement agencies in the United States in response to the terrorist attacks of September 11, 2001. The act has been lauded as a quick response to terrorism (it was introduced less than a week after the attacks) and for implementing critical amendments to more than 15 important statutes; it also has been criticized for failing to include sufficient safeguards for civil liberties.

utilitarianism   An ethical theory that tells us that we can determine the ethical significance of any action by looking to the consequences of that act. Utilitarianism is typically identified with the policy of "maximizing the overall good" or, in a slightly different version, of producing "the greatest good for the greatest number."

V

values   Those beliefs that incline us to act or to choose in one way rather than another. We can recognize many different types of values: financial, religious, legal, historical, nutritional, political, scientific, and aesthetic. Ethical values serve the ends of human well-being in impartial, rather than personal or selfish, ways.

values-based culture   A corporate culture in which conformity to a statement of values and principles rather than simple obedience to laws and regulations is the prevailing model for ethical behavior.

virtue ethics   An approach to ethics that studies the character traits or habits that constitute a good human life, a life worth living. The virtues provide answers to the basic ethical question "What kind of person should I be?"

W

whistle-blowing   A practice in which an individual within an organization reports organizational wrongdoing to the public or to others in position of authority.

Index

Page numbers followed by n indicate information in notes.